PREMARITAL AGREEMENTS

Drafting and Negotiation

THIRD EDITION

LINDA J. RAVDIN

AMERICAN BAR ASSOCIATION
Family Law Section

Cover design by Jill Tedhams/ABA Design

Printed in the United States of America.

27 26 25 24 23 5 4 3 2 1

ISBN 978-1-63905-342-1

A catalog record for this book is available from the Library of Congress.

In loving memory of Alex
and Lillian Ravdin.

Contents

Select PDF and Word documents are available for download at
http://ambar.org/Premarital3e

Acknowledgments

My thanks to Gail Baker, former Chair, and my fellow members of the ABA Family Law Section Publications Development Board, for encouraging me to write the first edition of this book, and then for encouraging me to write the second edition. A big thank you to Joe Booth and Sara Busche, current Co-Chairs, for their support of my efforts to write this new edition. A big hand to Allen Bailey for his thorough review of the manuscript of this edition. Special thanks to the late Professor Lew Becker for his thorough review of the manuscript for the first edition and his excellent suggestions about how to make it better. Having served on the Publications Board for a number of years, I know how important the staff of ABA Publishing is to the success of the Family Law Section's publishing program. I am profoundly grateful to Amelia Stone and Jeff Salyards for all they have done to get this book into print and out to the lawyers who may find it useful. The lawyers and staff of my law firm deserve my thanks for making Pasternak & Fidis a place where I look forward to coming to work every day and where contributions to the legal profession are valued and celebrated. Finally, I thank my family, especially my husband, for putting up with my writing projects.

About the Author

Linda J. Ravdin practices family law exclusively as a shareholder in the Bethesda, Maryland, law firm Pasternak & Fidis, P.C. Her practice covers the range of family law issues for families of all kinds, including divorce and separation, dissolution of nonmarital relationships, division of property, divorce taxation, disposition of retirement benefits, resolution of issues involving children, and child and spousal support. She is trained in collaborative law and serves as a mediator. A significant part of her practice involves drafting and negotiation of premarital and postmarital agreements, giving advice to clients and to fellow lawyers regarding construction and validity of existing agreements, and representing divorcing parties who have such an agreement. She is admitted to practice in Maryland, Virginia, and the District of Columbia.

Linda is the author of two other treatises on the subject of premarital agreements, *849-2d Marital Agreements* (Tax Management Inc. 2012) and with Pasternak & Fidis partner Marcia Fidis, *Premarital and Domestic Partnership Agreements* (Maryland State Bar Association 2009). In 2010–2012 she was the ABA Family Law Section Advisor to the Uniform Law Commission Drafting Committee on the Uniform Premarital and Marital Agreements Act. Washingtonian magazine has called her "one of the nation's leading specialists" in premarital agreements. She is also a co-author of Domestic Relations Manual for the District of Columbia (LexisNexis 2002, supplemented annually) and she co-authored the annual supplements for 20 years.

Linda is a member of the American Bar Association Family Law Section and served on its Publications Development Board. She is a Fellow of the American Academy of Matrimonial Lawyers.

Linda J. Ravdin
Pasternak & Fidis, P.C.
Suite 1025
7101 Wisconsin Ave.
Bethesda, MD 20814-6183
301 656-8850
301 656-3053 fax
lravdin@pasternakfidis.com
www.pasternakfidis.com

PART

I

THE LAW OF PREMARITAL AND POSTMARITAL AGREEMENTS

INTRODUCTION 1

§1.01 DEFINITIONS AND TERMINOLOGY

A premarital agreement is a contract between prospective spouses made in contemplation of marriage.[1] Older cases generally use the term "antenuptial agreement." Many courts and drafting lawyers use the term "prenuptial agreement." Some statutes refer to them as marriage contracts or marriage settlements.[2] Modern authorities generally use the term "premarital agreement," consistent with the terminology of the Uniform Premarital Agreement Act (UPAA) and the Uniform Premarital and Marital Agreements Act (UPMAA).[3]

A key requirement for a premarital agreement is that it be executed before the parties get married; calling an agreement signed after the date of marriage a premarital agreement does not make it one.[4] Moreover, the agreement must be executed in contemplation of marriage; thus, a property agreement between cohabitants, or an agreement made in contemplation of registering as domestic partners, but not made in contemplation of marriage, is not a premarital agreement.[5] Cohabitants may want to enter into a comprehensive contract to address the same kinds of issues as parties planning to get married, especially if they live in a jurisdiction that recognizes cohabitant claims.[6] If they want their agreement to survive as a premarital agreement

1. American Law Institute, *Principles of the Law of Family Dissolution: Analysis and Recommendations* (2002) § 7.01(1)(a) (hereafter, *Principles of the Law of Family Dissolution* or *ALI Principles*). Parties contemplating marriage may enter into a religious marriage contract that may be enforceable in a civil court. *See Nouri v. Dadgar*, 245 Md. App. 324, 226 A.3d 797 (2020) (Muslim *mahr*); *Tilsen v. Benson*, 2019 Conn. Super. LEXIS 2475 (unpub.) (Jewish *ketubah*). Contracts of this type are not covered in this book.

2. *See Posner v. Posner*, 233 So. 2d 381, 383 (1970).

3. UPAA §§ 1, *et seq.* (1983); UPMAA §§ 1, *et seq.* (2012).

4. *Steele v. Steele,* 467 N.J. Super. 414, 253 A.3d 1190 (App. Div. 2021).

5. *In re Armour,* 2020 Cal. App. LEXIS 3447 (unpub.).

6. The validity and enforceability of cohabitation agreements is beyond the scope of this book. Such agreements are generally valid and enforceable in the majority of states. See MINN. STAT. ANN § 513.075–.076; TEX. BUS. & COM. CODE ANN. § 26.01; *Zaremba v. Cliburn,* 949 S.W.2d 822 (Tex. App. 1997); *Posik v. Layton,* 695 So. 2d 759 (Fla. Ct. App. 1997); *Salzman v. Bachrach,* 996 P.2d 1263

in the event they marry, the agreement will need to say so expressly,[7] although the better practice is to enter into a new agreement, which could be merely a short agreement that expressly adopts the cohabitation agreement as the parties' premarital agreement.

A postmarital agreement is "an agreement entered into during marriage to define each spouse's property rights in the event of death or divorce."[8] In some states, such an agreement can also fix or waive spousal support.[9] Some authorities call an agreement of this type a "postnuptial agreement." The Uniform Premarital and Marital Agreements Act (UPMAA) uses the term "marital agreement."[10] Unlike a marital settlement agreement executed incident to an existing or planned marital separation, a postmarital agreement is an agreement between spouses who have no present intent to separate or divorce.

This book does not address the validity or enforceability of purported oral premarital agreements. Courts have occasionally treated transactions between spouses, other than a comprehensive written contract identified as such, as constituting a postmarital agreement.[11] This book is concerned only with the drafting and negotiation of express, written premarital and postmarital agreements.

§1.02 OVERVIEW

This book focuses on the following aspects of representation regarding a premarital or postmarital agreement:

- The law of validity and the steps to create a valid agreement;
- The ethical components and the practical techniques of negotiating the terms of the agreement;
- Post-marriage issues; and
- The content of the agreement and drafting techniques to carry out the objectives of the client.

(Colo. 2000); *Donovan v. Scuderi,* 51 Md. App. 217, 443 A.2d 121 (1982); *Tapley v. Tapley,* 122 N.H. 727, 449 A.2d 1218 (1982); *Kozlowski v. Kozlowski,* 80 N.J. 378, 403 A.2d 902 (1979); *Green v. Richmond,* 369 Mass. 47, 337 N.E.2d 691 (1975); *Hay v. Hay,* 100 Nev. 196, 678 P.2d 672, 674 (1984); *Boland v. Catalano,* 202 Conn. 333, 521 A.2d 142 (1987); *Dominguez v. Cruz,* 95 N.M. 1, 617 P.2d 1322 (Ct. App. 1980); *Whorton v. Dillingham,* 202 Cal. App. 3d 447, 248 Cal. Rptr. 405 (1988); *Weekes v. Gay,* 243 Ga. 784, 256 S.E.2d 901 (1979); see also Op. of Va. Atty. Gen. Robert F. McDonnell, 2006 Va. AG Lexis 34 (7/14/06) (unmarried persons can enter into valid contract regarding property rights).

7. It does not appear that the validity and enforceability of such a provision has been tested in any court.

8. *Simmons v. Simmons*, 98 Ark. App. 12, 15, 249 S.W.3d 843, 846 (2007); *see also In re Estate of Wilber*, 165 N.H. 246, 75 A.3d 1096 (2013); *Vaccarello v. Vaccarello*, 757 A.2d 909 (Pa. 2000); *Combs v. Sherry-Combs*, 865 P.2d 50 (Wyo. 1993); *Acre v. Koenig*, 89 Idaho 342, 404 P.2d 621 (1965). An agreement during marriage revoking a prior agreement is itself a postmarital agreement. *Zhou v. Zhang*, 334 Conn. 601, 223 A.3d 775 (2020).

9. See Appendix B(2), State Law Summary: Postmarital Agreements.

10. UPMAA § 2(2).

11. *See, e.g., McGeehan v. McGeehan,* 455 Md. 268, 167 A.3d 579 (2017) (oral agreement coupled with gift deed of real estate to wife took property out of marital estate at divorce and made it wife's separate property); *Austin v. Austin,* 237 Ariz. 201, 348 P.3d 897 (2015) (various instruments executed by parties, including revocable and irrevocable trusts and operating agreement, constituted postmarital agreement).

Part I of this book covers the law relating to the creation of a valid agreement. Chapter 2 summarizes the criteria for validity of premarital agreements, and Chapter 3 summarizes the criteria for validity of postmarital agreements.[12] Chapter 4 provides an extended treatment of the elements of a valid agreement and the legal theories that have been used to attack validity. For example, Chapter 2 identifies voluntariness as a requirement for validity of a premarital agreement in every state, and Chapter 4 discusses, in detail, the case law interpreting voluntariness and the related concepts of duress and undue influence in the formation of premarital and postmarital agreements. Spousal support and lawyers' fees are covered separately in Chapters 5 and 6. Even when a premarital or postmarital agreement is valid, a court may separately consider validity of specific terms addressing these issues.

Parties to a premarital or postmarital agreement sometimes want to include terms that are not enforceable or the enforceability of which is impractical. Chapter 7 briefly addresses some such terms—for example, terms regarding children, including parentage and custody. Chapter 7 also addresses financial terms to benefit children as well as some nonfinancial issues regarding the ongoing marriage.

Chapter 8 discusses a number of issues that can arise after the marriage. For example, a spouse may not comply with an obligation to make cash gifts or a transfer of title during the marriage, make disadvantageous use of his or her assets, or leave employment in the misguided belief that the other party will be more generous than the agreement requires. An understanding of the ways in which postmarriage conduct can affect a party's rights can aid the lawyer at the drafting stage by suggesting terms to better protect the client. Such an understanding can also suggest advice the lawyer should consider giving the client to secure the rights he or she bargained for and to avoid making disadvantageous decisions.

Part II of this book focuses on the process of negotiating and drafting the agreement. Chapter 9 delves into a variety of ethical issues presented in the drafting and negotiation of premarital and postmarital agreements, and Chapter 10 covers the more practical aspects of negotiating the terms. Chapters 11, 12, and 13 are concerned with the text of the agreement. Chapter 12 consists of the text of a model title controls agreement with discussion of each part of the agreement. The discussion is designed to aid the drafter in tailoring the agreement to the needs of the client. Chapter 13 provides alternative model terms for an agreement under which parties share the fruits of their labor.

§1.03 Role of Counsel

This book is written for the lawyer hired to negotiate and draft a premarital or postmarital agreement.[13] The goals of the lawyer for the proponent will generally include the following:

- An agreement that serves the interests of the client by meeting his or her need to protect property rights and income from a spousal claim without creating unnecessary antagonism that may alienate the other party;

12. Appendices B(1) and B(2) are summaries of key statutes and cases on validity of these agreements.

13. *See* Morgan & Turner, Attacking and Defending Marital Agreements 2d ed. (ABA, 2012).

- An agreement that will withstand an attack on validity after death or dissolution;
- An agreement that a putative opponent will be discouraged from attempting to have declared unenforceable; and
- An agreement that clearly and understandably defines the parties' rights and obligations upon death or dissolution.

It is a common misconception that premarital agreements are easy to challenge successfully. There are many reported cases involving challenges to validity. Few were successful at the appellate level. The same is true for postmarital agreements. The threshold for validity in most states is quite low. However, the prevailing proponents were forced to litigate the validity of their agreements through at least one appeal, incurring the cost of litigation and the risk of failure. Unreported are the claims that settled with the proponent making financial concessions and the adverse results in trial courts that were not appealed.

The lawyer hired to draft an agreement has an opportunity. Careful drafting, attention to the procedural steps leading to execution, and appropriate advice can significantly reduce the likelihood of a later challenge to validity as well as the risk that such a challenge will be successful.

The only realistic opportunity the lawyer for an economically weaker party has to achieve a good result is at the negotiation and drafting stage. It generally takes a combination of egregious circumstances and egregious terms to persuade a court to hold a premarital or postmarital agreement invalid.[14] Even when there are egregious circumstances, there can be no assurance a court will invalidate an agreement.[15] The presence of counsel for a weaker party before execution dramatically reduces the likelihood a court will declare an agreement invalid.[16] Assuming a court will someday relieve an unhappy party of the consequences of a foolish bargain or a badly drafted agreement is folly.

§1.04 HISTORY OF THE LAW OF PREMARITAL AGREEMENTS

(a) Premarital Agreements Before *Posner v. Posner*

Historically, public policy favored premarital agreements when fairly made because they were thought to be conducive to marital harmony by enabling future spouses to settle,

---

14. *See, e.g., Parr v. Parr*, 635 N.E.2d 1124 (Ind. Ct. App. 1994) (husband's almost complete nondisclosure, his misrepresentation of his assets, his dominance, and his attorney's failure to provide copy of draft agreement to wife's attorney in advance, although such had been requested, rendered premarital agreement invalid); *Norris v. Norris*, 419 A.2d 982 (D.C. 1980) (premarital agreement sprung on wife one hour before wedding with no disclosure was invalid).

15. *See, e.g., Pajak v. Pajak*, 385 S.E.2d 384 (W. Va. 1989) (premarital agreement valid where signed one day before wedding, wife not advised to retain counsel for independent review, husband made no disclosure of assets, and wife testified she did not understand many terms of agreement); *Howell v. Landry*, 96 N.C. App. 516, 386 S.E.2d 610 (1989) (premarital agreement seen by wife for first time and signed night before Dec. 31 departure for Las Vegas to get married was not product of duress).

16. *See Spiegel v. Spiegel*, 553 N.W.2d 309 (Iowa 1996) (premarital agreement upheld where wife had attorney who negotiated changes); *Kilborn v. Kilborn*, 628 So. 2d 884 (Ala. Civ. App. 1993) (premarital agreement was voluntary where wife signed after two different attorneys advised her against signing); *Hamilton v. Hamilton*, 404 Pa. Super. 533, 591 A.2d 720 (1991) (premarital agreement not product of duress where wife was 18, unemployed, and pregnant but was represented by counsel who advised not to sign).

prospectively, property rights arising upon the death of a spouse. Courts upheld premarital agreements as long as the provisions were fair and reasonable, but they limited enforcement to those agreements made in contemplation of the death of a spouse.[17] Courts generally refused to enforce agreements that determined property and support rights upon divorce. These agreements were thought to destabilize the institution of marriage by making divorce too easy, and thus were contrary to public policy.[18] Moreover, because the state is a third party in actions relating to the marital relationship, courts held that a prospective wife, who was considered to be in an unequal bargaining position, should not be bound by a premarital waiver of support that could leave her a ward of the state.[19]

(b) *Posner v. Posner* and Premarital Agreements at Divorce

In 1970 the Florida Supreme Court, in *Posner v. Posner*,[20] held that premarital agreements determining disposition of assets upon divorce were no longer void ab initio as contrary to public policy. The contemporary view is that premarital agreements that settle questions of property and support rights upon divorce promote and facilitate marriage rather than encourage divorce. As one court observed:

> This society's staggering divorce rate can only place any reasonable person on notice that divorce is as likely an outcome of any given marriage as a permanent relationship. Modern laws that allow alimony to be awarded in no-fault divorces, and that provide for the equitable distribution of all property acquired by joint efforts during the course of a marriage fulfill a useful function in today's society. . . . Nonetheless, it should be obvious that a person like our appellant, . . . who enjoys a financial position that places him in the top one percent of all income-earning Americans, will be reluctant to marry when modern divorce law (including some parameter for judicial caprice) places both his property and his future income at jeopardy. Furthermore, as the facts of this case amply demonstrate, he need not marry. He can conceivably live with a woman for years without any social or financial pressure to formalize his relationship.[21]

Because couples need not marry, and may choose not to do so if marrying puts all their assets and income-earning potential at risk, courts and legislatures have recognized that allowing such persons to enter into a contractual arrangement that reduces their exposure to spousal claims, and predetermines their rights and obligations at the end of the marriage, encourages parties, especially those who have been married previously, to take a chance on love.[22] Since *Posner* was decided, every state and the District of Columbia, either legislatively or through case law, has permitted parties who plan to marry to enter into a premarital

17. *Posner v. Posner*, 233 So. 2d 381 (Fla. 1970); *Bonds v. Bonds*, 24 Cal. 4th 1, 5 P.3d 815 (2000).
18. *Gross v. Gross*, 11 Ohio St. 3d 99, 464 N.E.2d 500 (1984); *Osborne v. Osborne*, 384 Mass. 591, 595–96, 428 N.E.2d 810, 814 (1981).
19. *Posner*, 233 So. 2d at 383.
20. *Id.* at 381.
21. *Gant v. Gant*, 329 S.E.2d 106, 113–14 (W. Va. 1985).
22. "Taking a Chance on Love," Vernon Duke, John La Touche, Ted Fetter.

agreement providing for the disposition of property claims upon divorce or death.[23] Indeed, with limited exceptions, a trial court is obliged to enforce a properly executed premarital agreement; it is not free to ignore it and dispose of property other than according to its terms.[24] In addition to permitting a premarital agreement to determine disposition of property at divorce, the majority of state courts enforce provisions fixing or waiving spousal support upon divorce as well as waivers of lawyers' fees at divorce.[25]

(c) The Uniform Premarital Agreement Act (UPAA)

The modern view of premarital agreements is codified in the UPAA, promulgated in 1983 by the National Conference of Commissioners on Uniform State Laws (also known as the Uniform Law Commission). As of 2022, 26 states (including the District of Columbia) had adopted the UPAA in whole or in part to govern property rights at both death and divorce.[26] West Virginia adopted the validity criteria of the UPAA for premarital agreements that take effect at death while retaining judge-made law to govern disposition of property and spousal support at divorce.[27] The UPAA generally allows parties to contract about any subject not in violation of public policy or a criminal statute, including disposition of property at death or divorce, spousal support, and the control of property during the ongoing marriage.[28]

(d) Evolution of the Law of Validity of Premarital Agreements

As courts and legislatures began to accept premarital agreements for purposes other than disposition of property at death, they began to grapple with the criteria by which the validity of such agreements should be judged in the modern world. The threshold requirement for validity of all agreements is voluntariness. Put another way, the agreement must not have been the product of fraud, duress, or undue influence. This is the standard set by the UPAA and is followed by many other non-UPAA states.[29] The drafters of the UPAA opted for an emphasis on procedural over substantive fairness in the determination of the general validity of a premarital agreement. In doing so, they chose certainty of enforceability as the more important goal, overriding the views of a minority of Commissioners who thought premarital agreement law should favor substantive fairness.[30] Under the UPAA and the law of most states, only in limited circumstances may a divorce court override the terms of an agreement on substantive fairness grounds.[31]

(e) Evolution of the Law of Validity of Postmarital Agreements

Postmarital agreements not executed incident to separation or divorce are of more recent vintage than premarital agreements. The common law disabilities of married women precluded

23. See Appendix B(I), State Law Summary: Premarital Agreements.
24. *Lund v. Lund*, 849 P.2d 731, 740 (Wyo. 1993). See the discussion of the second look in Section 4.08.
25. See Chapter 5 for discussion of spousal support and Chapter 6 for discussion of lawyers' fees.
26. See Appendix B(1), State Law Summary: Premarital Agreements.
27. See Appendix B(1).
28. UPAA § 3.
29. *See In re Estate of Martin*, 938 A.2d 812 (Me. 2008).
30. *Bonds*, 5 P.3d at 823–24.
31. See Section 4.09 for discussion of substantive fairness.

this type of agreement. Currently, in the majority of states, spouses can enter into a postmarital agreement to determine disposition of property at death or divorce. Some states also permit such an agreement to fix or waive spousal support.

(f) Trend Toward Enforceability of Virtually All Premarital and Postmarital Agreements Under Virtually All Circumstances

The trend is quite clear. Challenges to validity of premarital and postmarital agreements are rarely successful. Appellate judges enforce these agreements even when the process leading to execution left little opportunity for meaningful negotiation or legal advice. The UPAA has been criticized by many academic commentators and practitioners.[32] The most compelling critique focuses on the general enforceability of a premarital agreement that was substantively unconscionable at execution but was executed voluntarily with financial disclosure or an effective waiver.[33] By contrast, a commercial contract that was unconscionable at execution is unenforceable.[34] Moreover, the minimal procedural safeguards of the UPAA allow a proponent to present a premarital agreement close to the wedding date with little risk that a court will hold the agreement to be unenforceable on the ground of duress.[35] For the most part, courts have been similarly willing to uphold agreements executed during marriage even when the substantive terms are highly disadvantageous to one party and where the process leading to execution was barely fair.[36] In the majority of states, legislatures and judges have clearly opted for freedom to contract about the financial incidents of marriage and for predictability of enforcement over substantive fairness. In a minority of states, courts review the agreement for substantive fairness at the time of enforcement at divorce.[37]

(g) The Uniform Premarital and Marital Agreements Act

The Uniform Law Commission (ULC) approved the Uniform Premarital and Marital Agreements Act (UPMAA) in 2012. The ULC intended for the UPMAA to replace the UPAA. However, as of December 2022, the UPMAA had been enacted only in North Dakota[38] and Colorado.[39] The UPMAA has more demanding standards for validity of premarital agreements and provides for postmarital agreements to be governed by the same rules regarding

32. *See* Ronald S. Ladden, *Why the Uniform Premarital Agreement Act Should Be Repealed or Modified*, Family Advocate (Winter 2011); Judith Younger, *Lovers' Contracts in the Courts: Forsaking the Minimum Decencies*, 13 WM & MARY J. WOMEN & L. 349 (Winter 2007); Karen Servidea, *Note: Reviewing Premarital Agreements to Protect the State's Interest in Marriage*, 91 VA. L. REV. 535 (2005); *Marriage as Contract and Marriage as Partnership: The Future of Antenuptial Agreement Law*, 116 HARV. L. REV. 2075 (2002–03).

33. *See* J. Thomas Oldham, *With All My Worldly Goods I Thee Endow, or Maybe Not; A Reevaluation of the Uniform Premarital Agreement Act After Three Decades*, 19 DUKE J. GENDER L. & POL'Y 83 (Fall 2011); Judith T. Younger, *Lovers' Contracts in the Courts: Forsaking the Minimum Decencies*, 13 WM. & MARY J. WOMEN & L. 349 (2007).

34. UCC § 2-302(1); RESTATEMENT (SECOND) OF CONTRACTS § 208 (1981).

35. J. Thomas Oldham, *Would Enactment of the Uniform Premarital and Marital Agreement Act in All Fifty States Change US Law Regarding Premarital Agreements?* 46 FAM. L. Q. 367, 370 (Fall 2012).

36. See Chapters 3 and 4.

37. See discussion of states that require substantive fairness for premarital agreements in Section 2.08 and an extended discussion of how states have interpreted the requirement for substantive fairness in Section 4.09.

38. N.D. CENT. CODE §§ 14-03.2-01, *et seq.*

39. COLO. REV. STAT. §§ 14-2-301, *et seq.*

validity and permissible scope.[40] Although it has not accomplished what the ULC hoped, the UPMAA does lay out a set of best practices in the conduct of premarital and postmarital agreement negotiations that lawyers can adhere to.

§1.05 Scope of Premarital and Postmarital Agreements

A premarital agreement allows parties who intend to marry to contract regarding their property and financial rights and obligations at the end of the marriage by death or divorce. By fixing their rights and obligations by contract, parties may largely divest a court of discretion in these areas and may decide for themselves how to allocate the financial and property rights they would otherwise acquire by virtue of the marriage. As one court has observed in adjudicating the validity of a premarital agreement at divorce:

> A primary purpose of an agreement is to modify or shrink the general discretion of the dissolution of marriage judge in doing equity between the parties. The agreement itself is intended to define the mutual equities, and the trial judge is not free to ignore its provisions or to render them ineffective. As a general matter [statutes providing for spousal rights at divorce] do not exist to displace nuptial agreements; rather the statutes exist to set the principles when there is no agreement. Dissolution of marriage courts should attempt to give effect to nuptial agreements that are, as here, properly made and fully enforceable.[41]

In all states, in the absence of an agreement altering spousal rights, spouses acquire legal or equitable rights in property not dependent solely on which spouse holds legal title. A premarital or postmarital agreement generally alters these spousal rights in some fashion. A premarital or postmarital agreement generally addresses four major bodies of spousal property and financial rights and claims:

- Property rights at the death of a spouse;
- Property rights at divorce;
- Spousal support rights after a marital separation and upon divorce; and
- The right to control separate property, however defined, during the marriage and to transfer and otherwise deal in such property without spousal consent.

Some parties may also wish to address other issues, including:

- Lawyers' fees for the negotiations and for the implementation of the terms;
- Lawyers' fees that may be incurred at dissolution or after a party's death as a result of a breach or a failed challenge to validity;
- Allocation of financial responsibility for expenses during the marriage, such as household and common expenses and a party's personal debts and expenses;

40. The UPMAA uses the term "marital agreement." UPMAA § (2)(2).

41. *Hannon v. Hannon*, 740 So. 2d 1181, 1187 (Fla. Dist. Ct. App. 1999); *see also Law v. Law*, 2022 Tenn. App. LEXIS 166 (unpub.) (trial court erred in classifying and dividing property at divorce other than as provided in valid premarital agreement).

- Provisions for transfers during the marriage for the benefit of an economically disadvantaged spouse;
- Financial provisions for children; and
- Personal, nonfinancial rights and obligations.[42]

§1.06 SUBJECTS ON WHICH PARTIES' RIGHTS TO CONTRACT ARE LIMITED

There are some subjects on which the parties' ability to enter into a binding contract is limited:

- An agreement cannot divest a court of jurisdiction to determine custody of a minor child or to set basic support for a minor child.[43]
- In the majority of states, parties may fix or waive spousal support in the event of divorce. Even in these states, however, under some circumstances, a court may refuse to enforce a contractual support waiver. In a minority of states, an agreement may not divest a court of jurisdiction to award spousal support.[44]
- In some states, the rights of third parties may not be adversely affected by a premarital or postmarital agreement. For example, in some community property states, a premarital or postmarital agreement cannot affect the rights of third parties insofar as a spouse has the right to contract debt or alienate, encumber, or lease property.[45] The doctrine of necessaries, under which a spouse may be liable for debts incurred by the other spouse during the marriage, may preclude a spouse from enforcing a premarital or postmarital agreement against a claim of a third-party creditor.[46]
- Some authorities suggest that a premarital agreement that facilitates or promotes divorce will be unenforceable on public policy grounds.[47] For the most part, cases taking this view predate enactment of the UPAA in more than half the states and cases such as *Posner v. Posner*.[48] Nevertheless, some remnants of this prohibition remain and appear in cases from time to time.
- One state, Louisiana, does not permit spouses to completely waive all rights to inheritance in a premarital agreement.[49] Iowa law does not permit a postmarital agreement to waive the spousal elective share.[50]

42. Such terms may be unenforceable or of limited enforceability. See Chapter 7 for further discussion.
43. See UPAA § 3(b), UPMAA § 10, and Chapter 7 of this book.
44. See Appendices B(1) and (2), State Law Summaries, and Chapter 5.
45. *See* LA. CIV. CODE § 2330 (parties to marital contract may not limit rights of third parties in respect to community debt incurred by one party alone).
46. *See, e.g.*, D.C. CODE ANN. § 46-601 (both spouses liable for debt for necessaries for spouse or dependent children); and see Chapter 5 of this book.
47. *See* RESTATEMENT SECOND OF CONTRACTS § 190 (1981); LORD, WILLISTON ON CONTRACTS § 11.7 (4th ed. 1990 & Supp. 2001).
48. *Posner*, 233 So. 2d at 381; see also discussion in Section 4.08(d).
49. LA. CIV. CODE § 2330 (spouses may not renounce or alter order of succession through premarital agreement); *Norsworthy v. Succession of Norsworthy*, 704 So. 2d 953 (La. Ct. App. 1997).
50. *Husseman v. Husseman*, 847 N.W.2d 219 (Iowa 2014).

§1.07 Burden of Proof of Existence and Terms of Premarital or Postmarital Agreement

The party relying on a premarital or postmarital agreement has the burden of proving the existence and terms of the agreement.[51] Because many years may pass after execution of an agreement during which time memories may fade, it is a good idea to have the signing witnessed and/or notarized, whether or not such formalities are required by applicable law, and for parties to execute multiple originals.[52] The client should be advised to keep a signed original or a scanned copy of a signed original of the agreement in a safe place. It is also a good idea for counsel to retain a signed original or a scanned or paper copy of the signed original. When the agreement refers to an asset disclosure schedule as an attachment, counsel should advise the client to retain the schedule and keep it attached to the agreement at all times.[53]

51. *In the Matter of Serodio and Perkins*, 166 N.H. 606 101 A.3d 1069 (2014); *Coxwell v. Coxwell,* 296 Ga. 311, 765 S.E.2d 320 (2014); *In re Marriage of Mueller*, 140 Wn. App. 498, 167 P.3d 568 (2007); *Boetsma v. Boetsma*, 768 N.E.2d 1016 (Ind. Ct. App. 2002); *Wiley v. Iverson*, 295 Mont. 511, 985 P.2d 1176 (1999); *Randolph v. Randolph*, 937 S.W.2d 815 (Tenn. 1996).

52. *See Mays v. Mullins,* 547 S.W.3d 474 (Ark. Ct. App., Div. One, 2018) (resolving dispute over authentication of premarital agreement).

53. *See, e.g., In re Estate of Mary Davis*, 213 S.W.3d 288 (Tenn. App. 2006) (premarital agreement invalid after death of wife after 30 years of marriage where wife's written financial disclosure was not attached to agreement and could not be found).

Criteria for an Enforceable Premarital Agreement

2

§2.01 Scope of This Chapter

This chapter addresses the general validity of premarital agreements and the basic criteria for a valid agreement. The issue of validity of the agreement as a whole must be distinguished from the question of enforceability of a particular provision. For example, in a few states a provision fixing or waiving spousal support is always unenforceable, and in all states, such a provision could become unenforceable as a result of circumstances at divorce.[1] An unenforceable spousal support provision will generally be severable from an otherwise valid agreement.[2]

§2.02 Essential Contractual Elements

A premarital agreement is a contract, albeit of a special type. Thus, to be enforceable, it must adhere to basic requirements for formation of any other contract. The contract must be entered into voluntarily by persons with legal capacity to contract, and there must be consideration.[3]

(a) Consideration

Both the Uniform Premarital Agreement Act (UPAA) and the Uniform Premarital and Marital Agreements Act (UPMAA) provide that a premarital agreement is valid without consideration.[4] However, these acts merely codify the common law principle

1. See Section 5.02(a).
2. See Chapter 12, Paragraph 51.
3. Restatement Second of Contracts §§ 12, 174–77 (1981); *but see* UPAA § 2, cmt. (1983).
4. UPAA § 2; UPMAA § 6 (2012).

that the marriage itself is the consideration for a premarital agreement.[5] Thus, nothing more than marriage is required.

(b) Formalities

Almost uniformly, state law requires that a premarital agreement be in writing and signed by both parties.[6] Before modern enactments, such as the Uniform Premarital Agreement Act, an agreement on consideration of marriage was among those which Statutes of Frauds rendered unenforceable unless there was a written agreement or other writing memorializing the terms. These statutes still exist in many states. The UPAA requires that a premarital agreement be in writing and signed by the parties, as does the UPMAA.[7]

The UPMAA updates the requirement for a writing. A "record" is defined as "information that is inscribed on a tangible medium or that is stored in an electronic medium and is retrievable in perceivable form."[8] The conventional concept of "signed" is also expanded to include the use of an "electronic symbol, sound or process"[9] to "authenticate or adopt a record . . . ."[10] Thus, under the UPMAA parties could enter into an agreement that exists in an electronic format without signing an actual paper document in ink. Nevertheless, many lawyers will continue to prefer creating a paper document and having parties execute multiple originals with inked signatures and initials on every page, including the financial disclosures.

Some states require additional execution formalities such as acknowledgment,[11] recordation in the land records where real estate affected by the contract is located,[12] or witnesses.[13] These requirements are strictly enforced.[14]

(c) Legal Capacity

At common law, legal capacity to contract is an essential element of all contracts.[15] Thus, a premarital contract executed by one who lacked capacity at execution will generally be voidable.[16]

---

5. *Cannon v. Cannon*, 384 Md. 537, 865 A.2d 563 (2005); *Harllee v. Harllee*, 565 S.E.2d 678 (N.C. Ct. App. 2002); *Gross v. Gross*, 11 Ohio St. 3d 99, 464 N.E.2d 500 (1984); *Volid v. Volid*, 6 Ill. App. 3d 386, 286 N.E.2d 42 (1972).

6. *See* ALA. CODE § 8-9-2; GA. CODE ANN. § 13-5-30; IDAHO CODE § 32-917; *Hankins v. Hankins*, 866 So. 2d 508 (Miss. App. 2004). Oral premarital agreements are beyond the scope of this book.

7. UPAA § 2; UPMAA § 6.

8. UPMAA § 2(7).

9. UPMAA § 2(8).

10. *Id.*

11. ARK. CODE ANN. § 9-11-402; N.Y. DOMESTIC RELS. LAW § 236(B)(3).

12. IDAHO CODE § 32-918; ARK. CODE ANN. § 9-11-303.

13. Georgia law defines a premarital agreement made to settle property rights during the marriage or upon death as a marriage contract that must be attested by two witnesses. But, a premarital agreement made in contemplation of divorce does not require witnesses. GA. CODE ANN. § 19-3-63; *Dove v. Dove*, 285 Ga. 647, 680 S.E.2d 839 (2009).

14. *See Galetta v. Galetta*, 2 N.Y.3d 166, 991 N.E.2d 684 (2013).

15. RESTATEMENT SECOND OF CONTRACTS § 12 (1981).

16. *Id.* § 15; UPAA § 2 cmt.; UPMAA § 5 cmt. See further discussion of legal capacity in Section 4.02. There is some suggestion in some cases that statutes such as the UPAA limit defenses to enforcement to those set out in the statute so that common law defenses are no longer viable. *See Sanders v. Sanders*, 2010 Tex. App. LEXIS 8308 (unpub.), where the court observed that, technically, a Texas statute permitting spouses to enter into postmarital agreements limits defenses to enforcement to involuntariness and unconscionablility, but upheld a trial court finding that the wife's lack of capacity rendered the agreement involuntary.

§2.03 APPROACHES TO DETERMINING VALIDITY: PROCESS VERSUS SUBSTANCE

Two schools of thought provide the framework for determining the validity of a premarital agreement. One school of thought considers a premarital agreement to be a contract no different than any other contract and therefore governed by strict contract principles.[17] Parties are assumed to be equally capable of protecting themselves and are thus held to their bargain if the process leading to the execution of the agreement was fair. Adherence to a standard of procedural fairness exclusively will generally permit enforcement of an agreement that was substantively unfair or even unconscionable at execution and remains so at death or divorce. The procedural fairness standard incorporates consideration of substantive terms only to a limited extent. This is the approach taken by the UPAA and many non-UPAA states. Moreover, in the majority of states, the standards for judging procedural fairness allow for a process that is highly disadvantageous to the recipient of a proposed premarital agreement.

In the other school of thought, courts have a greater role to play in insuring a fair result.[18] A substantive fairness analysis is concerned with the adequacy of the terms of the agreement and whether it makes fair and reasonable provision for the economically weaker spouse. Substantive fairness may be judged as of execution, as of enforcement, or both. A substantive fairness review necessarily allows a degree of judicial subjectivity in deciding whether to uphold an agreement.[19] Moreover, a standard of review that allows a judge to determine fairness as of the date of enforcement permits consideration of events occurring during the marriage even though it is precisely to avoid the risk of the uncertainties ahead that motivates many parties to want a premarital agreement in the first place.

Even in states where there is a role for the court to judge substantive fairness at enforcement, courts rarely invalidate on that ground alone.[20] The dominant trend is to permit parties to accept any terms they can agree upon so long as the process by which they got there comports with applicable standards of procedural fairness.

§2.04 FIDUCIARY OR CONFIDENTIAL RELATIONSHIP

Historically, the status of prospective spouse created a fiduciary or a confidential relationship that imposed an obligation of fair dealing and utmost honesty. Because of this relationship of mutual trust and confidence, courts believed that parties to an impending marriage were not dealing at arm's length.[21] Currently, some states retain the principle that prospective

---

17. *Simeone v. Simeone*, 380 Pa. Super. 37, 551 A.2d 219 (1988), *aff'd*, 525 Pa. 392, 581 A.2d 162 (1990).

18. *Button v. Button*, 131 Wis. 2d 84, 94, 388 N.W.2d 546, 550 (1986) (parties "contract in the shadow of the court's obligation to review the agreement").

19. *See Greenwald v. Greenwald*, 154 Wis. 2d 767, 780, 454 N.W.2d 34, 38 (1990) ("An equitableness determination requires an exercise of the trial court's discretion.").

20. See Section 4.09.

21. *Fletcher v. Fletcher*, 628 N.E.2d 1343, 1346 (Ohio 1994); *Rinvelt v. Rinvelt*, 190 Mich. App. 372, 475 N.W.2d 478 (1991); *Frey v. Frey*, 298 Md. 552, 564, 471 A.2d 705, 711 (1984); *Whitney v. Seattle-First Nat'l Bank*, 90 Wash. 2d 105, 108, 579 P.2d 937, 938 (1978); *Del Vecchio v. Del Vecchio*, 143 So. 2d 17, 21 (Fla. 1962).

spouses are in either a confidential or a fiduciary relationship, although modified to impose the obligation on both parties without regard to gender,[22] rejecting the "archaic presumption of dominance by the husband. . . ."[23] Other courts have rejected application of principles of fiduciary or confidential relationships in favor of treating premarital agreements like any other contract.[24] As the California Supreme Court observed in *Bonds v. Bonds*,[25] the UPAA does not contemplate "that the voluntariness of a premarital agreement would be examined in light of . . . strict fiduciary duties. . . ."[26] There is no presumption of undue influence arising from the agreement to marry under the UPAA.[27]

Even when there is no presumption of a fiduciary or a confidential relationship between prospective spouses as a matter of law, such a relationship may exist in a given case as a matter of fact:

> A fiduciary relationship is "something approximating business agency, professional relationship, or family tie impelling or inducing the trusting party to relax the care and vigilance . . . ordinarily exercised." *Asleson v. West Branch Land Co.*, 311 N.W.2d 533, 539 (N.D. 1981). . . . A fiduciary relationship develops when someone is under a duty to act for, or to give advice to, another person upon matters within the scope of the relationship. . . . A fiduciary relationship generally arises from an unequal relationship between the parties. . . . For a fiduciary relationship, the superior party must have a duty to act in the dependent party's best interest. . . . [W]hether a fiduciary relationship exists is generally a question of fact.[28]

The existence of a fiduciary or a confidential relationship as a matter of law, or as a result of the parties' particular circumstances, operates to impose a mutual obligation for full financial disclosure. Further, it requires closer scrutiny of the procedural fairness and substantive terms of the agreement than would be required for an ordinary commercial contract. It also shifts the burden of proof of the elements of validity—most importantly, that the agreement was not secured through undue influence—from the opponent to the proponent of the agreement.[29]

---

22. *Cannon v. Cannon*, 384 Md. 537, 865 A.2d 563 (2005); *In re Estate of J. D. Davis*, 184 S.W.3d 231 (Tenn. App. 2004); *In re Estate of Hollett*, 150 N.H. 39, 834 A.2d 348 (2003); *In re Marriage of Matson*, 107 Wn. 2d 479, 730 P.2d 668 (1986); *Rosenberg v. Lipnick*, 377 Mass. 666, 389 N.E.2d 385 (1979).

23. *Del Vecchio*, 143 So. 2d 17, 21.

24. *Mallen v. Mallen*, 280 Ga. 43, 622 S.E.2d 812 (2005); *Parr v. Parr*, 635 N.E.2d 1124, 1127 (Ind. Ct. App. 1994); *Panossian v. Panossian*, 172 A.D.2d 811, 569 N.Y.S.2d 182 (1991); *Brassey v. Brassey*, 154 A.D.2d 293, 546 N.Y.S.2d 370 (1989); *Laird v. Laird*, 597 P.2d 463 (Wyo. 1979); *Fernandez v. Fernandez*, 194 Cal. App. 2d 782, 15 Cal. Rptr. 374 (1961).

25. 24 Cal. 4th 1, 5 P.3d 815 (2000).

26. *Id.*; 24 Cal. 4th at 29, 5 P.3d at 833.

27. *Marsh v. Marsh*, 949 S.W.2d 734 (Tex. App. 1997); *Parr*, 635 N.E.2d at 1124.

28. *In re Estate of Lutz*, 563 N.W.2d 90, 98 (N.D. 1997) (citations omitted).

29. *See Cannon*, 384 Md. at 563; *Fletcher*, 628 N.E.2d at 1343; *Rinvelt v. Rinvelt*, 190 Mich. App. 372, 475 N.W.2d 478 (1991); *In re Marriage of Matson*, 107 Wn. 479, 730 P.2d 668 (1986).

§2.05 BURDEN OF PROOF OF ENFORCEABLE PREMARITAL AGREEMENT

States take various approaches to placement of the burden of proof required to uphold, or establish the invalidity of, a premarital agreement. The goal of the attorney for the proponent should be an agreement that a court will uphold under any burden of proof that may be applicable, preferably on a motion for summary judgment.

- *Burden on the Opponent at All Times.* Both the UPAA and the UPMAA place the burden of proving invalidity on the opponent of the agreement. That burden never shifts.[30] Some non-UPAA states similarly place the burden of proof on the party opposing enforcement.[31]
- *Burden of Proof on the Proponent at All Times.* A few states put the burden of proof on the party relying on the premarital agreement to prove the existence of a valid contract.[32]
- *Burden on the Opponent, Shifts to the Proponent Once the Opponent Makes a Prima Facie Case.* In a few non-UPAA states, the opponent of the premarital agreement generally has the burden of proving invalidity. However, the burden shifts to the proponent when the opponent makes a prima facie case.[33] Even where the burden is generally placed on the opponent, when the specific facts of the case show the existence of a fiduciary relationship at the time of execution, the burden of proof will shift to the dominant party to disprove fraud or overreaching.[34]
- *Burden on the Proponent, Shifts to the Opponent Once the Proponent Makes a Prima Facie Case.* In Pennsylvania, the proponent bears the burden of proof of financial disclosure, after which the burden shifts to the opponent.[35] Similarly, in Maryland and Oklahoma the proponent bears the burden of proving the agreement was executed voluntarily with full disclosure.[36] If the proponent can show there was an actual give-and-take negotiation, the burden shifts to the opponent to establish another contract defense, such as fraud, duress, coercion, mistake, undue influence, incompetence, or unconscionability.[37]

---

30. UPAA § 6(a); UPMAA § 9(a); *In re Estate of Martin*, 938 A.2d 812 (Me. 2008); *Bonds v. Bonds*, 24 Cal. 4th 1, 5 P.3d 815 (2000); *Marsh v. Marsh*, 949 S.W.2d 734 (Tex. App. 1997); *Lebeck v. Lebeck*, 118 N.M. 367, 881 P.2d 727 (Ct. App. 1994); *Penhallow v. Penhallow*, 649 A.2d 1016 (R.I. 1994).

31. *Reed v. Reed*, 265 Mich. App. 131, 693 N.W.2d 825 (2005); *Couvillion v. Couvillion*, 886 So. 2d 474 (La. App. 2004); *Forsberg v. Forsberg*, 219 A.D.2d 615, 631 N.Y.S.2d 709 (1995); *Pajak v. Pajak*, 385 S.E.2d 384 (W. Va. 1989); *In re Lopata's Estate*, 641 P.2d 952 (Colo. 1982).

32. *See In re Estate of Cassidy*, 356 S.W.3d 339 (Mo. Ct. App. 2011); *Randolph*, 937 S.W.2d 815; *Ex parte Williams*, 617 So. 2d 1032 (Ala. 1992); *In re Est. of Kinney*, 733 N.W.2d 118 (Minn. 2007).

33. *Fletcher*, 628 N.E.2d at 1343; *In re Marriage of Foran*, 67 Wash. App. 242, 834 P.2d 1081 (1992).

34. *In re Estate of Greiff*, 92 N.Y.2d 341, 703 N.E.2d 752, 680 N.Y.S.2d 894 (1998).

35. *Cooper v. Oakes*, 427 Pa. Super. 430, 629 A.2d 944 (1993).

36. *Cannon*, 384 Md. at 563; *Griffin v. Griffin*, 94 P.3d 96 (Okla. App. 2004).

37. *Cannon*, 384 Md. at 572–75, 865 A.2d at 583–85; *see also Griffin*, 94 P.3d 96.

- *Burden on the Opponent, Except if Unrepresented.* One state, West Virginia, in a 2009 opinion, created a new principle regarding allocation of the burden of proof. In *Ware v. Ware*,[38] the West Virginia Supreme Court reaffirmed the presumption of validity announced in *Gant v. Gant*,[39] but limited the presumption to cases where both parties had independent counsel. When only one party had counsel, that party has the burden of establishing validity.

§2.06 LEGAL ADVICE AS A PREREQUISITE TO VALIDITY

(a) Actual Legal Advice

Actual advice of independent counsel is not a prerequisite to validity of a premarital agreement in any state. However, in a few states, in the absence of actual advice there must be either an express, written waiver of the right to such advice,[40] or the opportunity for independent advice,[41] to establish general validity of an agreement. In California, a premarital agreement is not voluntary unless the party against whom enforcement is sought was represented by a lawyer or expressly waived representation in a separate signed writing. An alimony waiver in a California premarital agreement is unenforceable unless the claimant had actual advice of counsel.[42] A premarital agreement governed by Alabama law must either be fair or be entered into voluntarily with competent, independent advice.[43] In Arkansas, a party to a premarital agreement cannot effectively waive financial disclosure without actual legal advice.[44] In South Carolina, parties may, by premarital agreement, exclude property from the marital estate at divorce; such an agreement is presumptively fair if both parties had counsel and executed it voluntarily and with full financial disclosure.[45] West Virginia's high court has ruled that a premarital agreement is entitled to a presumption of validity only when both parties had independent counsel.[46]

(b) Access to Legal Advice

The UPMAA requires that a party receiving a proposed premarital agreement have access to independent legal representation before execution.[47] The UPMAA does not mandate actual legal representation, only a meaningful opportunity for legal advice. This is a significant

38. 687 S.E.2d 382 (W.Va. 2009).
39. 329 S.E.2d 106 (W.Va. 1985).
40. N.J. STAT. ANN. § 37:2-38(c)(4) (premarital agreement unenforceable if executed without independent counsel, or waiver of counsel).
41. *See* MINN. STAT. ANN. § 519.11, subdiv. 1.
42. CAL. FAM. CODE §§ 1612, 1615(c).
43. Brown v. Brown, 26 So. 3d 1222 (Ala. Civ. App. 2009).
44. ARK. CODE ANN. § 9-11-406(a)(2)(ii).
45. S.C. CODE ANN. § 20-3-630(A)(4).
46. *Ware v. Ware*, 687 S.E.2d 382 (W.Va. 2009).
47. UPMAA § 9(a)(2).

departure from prevailing law. Statutes in Connecticut, New Jersey, and Minnesota require access to counsel for general validity,[48] as does case law from Ohio's highest court.[49]

As one court observed: "[I]nequality of [bargaining positions] may be cured by access to legal counsel by the party in the less advantageous bargaining position."[50] Access to legal representation necessarily means both the money to hire a lawyer and a reasonable time to find one, get advice, and consider that advice.[51]

§2.07 REQUIREMENTS FOR VALIDITY: PROCEDURAL FAIRNESS STATES

(a) UPAA and Procedural Fairness States

In the majority of states, a premarital agreement is valid if the process leading to execution was fair. As of 2022, 26 states (including the District of Columbia) have the UPAA, and a number of other states follow criteria similar to those of the UPAA.[52] The key provision of the UPAA regarding general validity is set forth below:

> § 6. Enforcement.
>
> (a) A premarital agreement is not enforceable if the party against whom enforcement is sought proves that:
>
> (1) that party did not execute the agreement voluntarily; or
>
> (2) the agreement was unconscionable when it was executed and, before execution of the agreement, that party:
>
> (i) was not provided a fair and reasonable disclosure of the property or financial obligations of the other party;
>
> (ii) did not voluntarily and expressly waive, in writing, any right to disclosure of the property or financial obligations of the other party beyond the disclosure provided; and
>
> (iii) did not have, or reasonably could not have had, an adequate knowledge of the property or financial obligations of the other party.[53]

---

48. CONN. GEN. STAT. § 46b-36g(a)(4) (premarital agreement not enforceable if party not afforded reasonable opportunity to consult with independent counsel); N.J. STAT. ANN. § 37:2-38(c)(4) (premarital agreement unenforceable as unconscionable if executed without disclosures, or waiver of disclosures, or without independent counsel, or waiver of counsel); MINN. STAT. ANN. § 519.11, subdiv. 1 (premarital agreement is valid with full disclosure and opportunity of each party to consult with legal counsel).

49. *Fletcher v. Fletcher,* 68 Ohio. St. 3d 464, 628 N.E. 2d 1343 (1994).

50. *Harbom v. Harbom,* 134 Md. App. 430, 441, 760 A.2d 272, 277 (2000).

51. UPMAA § 9(b).

52. Nineteen states adopted the UPAA without changing the validity criteria: Arizona, Delaware, District of Columbia, Florida, Hawaii, Idaho, Illinois, Kansas, Maine, Montana, Nebraska, New Mexico, North Carolina, Oregon, Rhode Island, South Dakota, Texas, Utah, and Virginia. See Appendix B(1), State Law Summary: Premarital Agreements. As discussed in the following section, Arkansas, California, Connecticut, and New Jersey added to the process requirements of the UPAA. Four UPAA states, Connecticut, Indiana, Iowa, and Nevada, made changes to the substantive fairness requirements. See Section 2.08.

53. UPAA § 6(a).

Voluntariness is the essential element of a valid premarital agreement under the UPAA. Nothing more is required. Financial disclosure is optional; parties may waive financial disclosure as long as the waiver is voluntary. Even an agreement that was unconscionable at execution is enforceable as long as the parties executed it voluntarily and the party seeking to enforce made actual disclosure, or the other party had pre-existing knowledge or expressly and voluntarily waived disclosure.[54] The premarital agreement will fail, however, even if voluntary, if it was unconscionable at execution *and* there was no actual disclosure, no pre-existing knowledge, and no express voluntary waiver of disclosure.[55] Independent counsel is not a requirement for validity under the UPAA, although the presence or absence of independent counsel is one factor a court may consider in determining voluntariness.

Importantly, the UPAA permits no modification of the disposition of property provisions of a valid premarital agreement in the event circumstances change after execution even if the result at death or divorce will be unconscionable.[56] Under the UPAA, the sole opportunity for modification of the agreement is when a support waiver will cause a spouse to become eligible for public assistance. In that event, the court may award spousal support in the amount necessary to avoid that eligibility. A court award of spousal support terminates upon the death of either party.[57] The UPAA provides no relief for a surviving spouse who may be destitute upon the death of the other spouse.

A number of non-UPAA states take an approach to determining validity of a premarital agreement similar to that of the UPAA.[58] In these states a premarital agreement must be executed voluntarily. In addition, either the agreement must have been fair at execution or there must have been fair and adequate disclosure of the proponent's financial affairs. Like agreements governed by the UPAA, parties may voluntarily enter into an agreement that is unfair (in some states, even unconscionable) so long as there was fair and adequate financial disclosure. Alternatively, parties may opt not to make disclosure so long as the agreement makes fair and adequate provisions for the economically weaker spouse.[59]

Several states have statutes that mandate only that a premarital agreement meet requirements for procedural fairness. Tennessee law requires simply that a premarital agreement be executed "freely, knowledgeably and in good faith without exertion of duress or undue

---

54. *Chaplain v. Chaplain*, 2011 Va. App. LEXIS 15 (unpub.); *Davis v. Miller*, 269 Kan. 732, 7 P.3d 1223 (2000); *Penhallow v. Penhallow*, 649 A.2d 1016 (R.I. 1994); *see also Laube v. Reints* (In re Est. of Laube), 974 N.W.2d 538 (Iowa Ct. App. 2022) (party challenging validity of premarital agreement governed by UPAA based on inadequate financial disclosure must prove both lack of disclosure and lack of knowledge, actual or constructive; party has constructive knowledge if on inquiry notice and fails to inquire).

55. *Silverman v. Silverman*, 206 A.3d 825 (Del. 2022); *Chaplain*, 2011 Va. App. LEXIS 15; *Parr v. Parr*, 635 N.E.2d 1124; *see also In re Marriage of Sarancic*, 2020 Ill. App. Unpub. 870. Fairness and unconscionability are discussed in Section 4.09.

56. *Gonzalez v. Konig*, 561 N.W.2d 94 (Iowa Ct. App. 1997).

57. CLARK, THE LAW OF DOMESTIC RELATIONS IN THE UNITED STATES § 17.6 (2d ed. 1987).

58. Alabama, Maryland, Pennsylvania, Ohio, Oklahoma, Washington, and Wyoming fall into this category. *See* Appendix B(1), State Law Summary: Premarital Agreements.

59. *Cannon v. Cannon*, 384 Md. 587, 865 A.2d 563 (2005); *Lemaster v. Dutton*, 694 So. 2d 1360 (Ala. Civ. App. 1996); *Fletcher*, 628 N.E.2d at 1343; *Taylor v. Taylor*, 832 P.2d 429 (Okla. Ct. App. 1991); *Simeone v. Simeone*, 380 Pa. Super. 37, 551 A.2d 219 (1988), *aff'd*, 525 Pa. 392, 581 A.2d 162 (1990); *In re Marriage of Matson*, 107 Wn. 2d 479, 730 P.2d 668 (1986); *Laird v. Laird*, 597 P.2d 463 (Wyo. 1979).

influence on either spouse."[60] "Knowledgeably" has been held to incorporate the requirement for full financial disclosure.[61] There appears to be no requirement for substantive fairness or conscionability. Indeed, substantive fairness will not save an agreement executed without financial disclosure.[62] Tennessee case law has elevated financial disclosure to the level of public policy.[63]

New York premarital agreements are authorized by a statute that imposes no substantive fairness or conscionability requirement for general validity.[64] Rather, "a duly executed antenuptial agreement is given the same presumption of legality as any other contract, commercial or otherwise. It is presumed to be valid in the absence of fraud. . . ."[65] Financial disclosure is not a prerequisite to validity of an agreement governed by New York law.[66]

(b) UPAA Plus

Four states that adopted the UPAA enhanced the procedural requirements for validity. In Connecticut, the agreement must be executed voluntarily and with full disclosure, and each party must have had an opportunity to consult with independent counsel.[67] Similarly, a premarital agreement governed by New Jersey law must be voluntary, with full disclosure, or an express waiver of disclosure, or each party must have independent counsel, or must waive that right.[68] Arkansas's version of the UPAA requires actual advice of independent counsel for an effective waiver of the right to financial disclosure.[69]

California's version of the UPAA establishes specific procedural prerequisites for a finding of voluntariness:

- A party must either be represented by independent counsel or be advised of that right and must expressly waive the right in a separate signed writing;
- The party must have not less than seven days between the receipt of the agreement coupled with advice to obtain independent counsel and the execution of the agreement;[70] and

60. TENN. CODE ANN. § 36-3-501; *Wilson v. Moore*, 929 S.W.2d 367 (Tenn. Ct. App. 1996).

61. *Kahn v. Kahn*, 756 S.W.2d 685 (Tenn. 1988).

62. *Randolph*, 937 S.W.2d at 815, 821.

63. See *In re Estate of J.D. Davis*, 184 S.W.3d 231 (Tenn. App. 2004), refusing on public policy grounds to enforce a premarital agreement executed in Florida because there was no financial disclosure, even though Florida law did not require financial disclosure.

64. N.Y. DOM. REL. LAW § 236(B)(3); *see Brassey*, 154 A.D.2d 293, 546 N.Y.S.2d 370 (1989).

65. *Elgar v. Elgar*, 238 Conn. 839, 679 A.2d 937 (1996) (applying New York law).

66. *Panossian v. Panossian*, 172 A.D.2d 811, 569 N.Y.S.2d 182 (1991). In New York, unconscionability can be considered only with respect to spousal support.

67. CONN. GEN. STAT. § 46b-36g.

68. N.J. STAT. ANN. § 37:2-38.

69. ARK. CODE ANN. § 9-11-406(a)(2)(ii).

70. The seven-day rule applies only to unrepresented parties; when a party has representation at the time he or she receives a proposed agreement, the waiting period is inapplicable. In *In re Marriage of Caldwell-Faso and Faso*, 191 Cal. App. 4th 945 (Ct. App. 2011), the court acknowledged a separate issue under the statute, whether the seven-day waiting period starts upon presentation of the first proposal or the final version. It did not need to decide this question, however.

- An unrepresented party must be fully informed in writing of the terms of the agreement and the rights being waived. That party must be proficient in the language in which the agreement and the explanation of rights are written, and he or she must sign an acknowledgment of receipt of the advice and explanation along with the identity of the person who provided the advice.[71]

In considering voluntariness, the court may consider other relevant factors.[72]

(c) The Uniform Premarital and Marital Agreements Act (UPMAA)

The Uniform Law Commission (ULC), approved the Uniform Premarital and Marital Agreements Act (UPMAA) in 2012 as a replacement for the UPAA. The UPMAA provides "more robust procedural fairness protections than does the UPAA,"[73] but does not require a fair result. The criteria for validity of a premarital agreement under the UPMAA are in Section 9, Enforcement, which provides:

> (a) A premarital agreement or marital agreement is unenforceable if a party against whom enforcement is sought proves:
>
> (1) the party's consent to the agreement was involuntary or the result of duress;
>
> (2) the party did not have access to independent legal representation under subsection (b);
>
> (3) unless the party had independent legal representation at the time the agreement was signed, the agreement did not include a notice of waiver of rights under subsection (c) or an explanation in plain language of the marital rights or obligations being modified or waived by the agreement; or
>
> (4) before signing the agreement, the party did not receive adequate financial disclosure under subsection (d).
>
> . . . .
>
> (f) A court may refuse to enforce a term of a premarital agreement or marital agreement if, in the context of the agreement taken as a whole[:]
>
> [(1)] the term was unconscionable at the time of signing[; or
>
> (2) enforcement of the term would result in substantial hardship for a party because of a material change in circumstances arising after the agreement was signed].

---

71. CAL. FAM. CODE § 1615(c).

72. CAL. FAM. CODE § 1615(c)(5). California's version of the UPAA also requires that the agreement not be the product of duress, fraud, or undue influence and that each party have legal capacity. CAL. FAM. CODE § 1615(c)(4).

73. Barbara A. Atwood & Brian H. Bix, *A New Uniform Law for Premarital and Marital Agreements*, 46 FAM L.Q. 313, 317–18 (Fall 2012) (hereafter, Atwood & Bix). The authors were, respectively, Chair of the Drafting Committee and Reporter for the Act.

Importantly, the UPMAA de-couples unconscionability from financial disclosure.[74] Thus, unconscionability and failure of financial disclosure are separate grounds that permit a court to refuse enforcement of an agreement. Although the text of Section 9(f) only expressly authorizes a court to refuse enforcement of an unconscionable term, the Comment tells us that Section9(f) is not meant to preclude a court from striking down the entire agreement as unconscionable.[75] In addition, the challenging party's lack of access to counsel is an independent ground on which a court may refuse enforcement.

The UPMAA thus expands from two to five the grounds on which a court may invalidate a premarital agreement.[76] A challenging party can prevail by proving that he or she:

(1) executed the agreement involuntarily or under duress; or

(2) did not receive financial disclosure (actual or constructive) and did not effectively waive disclosure; or

(3) did not have access to independent counsel; or

(4) if unrepresented, did not receive a plain language explanation of rights; or

(5) the agreement was unconscionable when executed.

In addition, Section 5 provides that "principles of law and equity supplement" the UPMAA unless displaced by it. Thus, common law defenses to enforcement, such as lack of legal capacity, misrepresentation, undue influence, and unconscionability, as developed in each state's law, can also provide a basis for a court to invalidate an agreement.[77]

§2.08 REQUIREMENTS FOR VALIDITY: SUBSTANTIVE FAIRNESS STATES

(a) Overview

In a significant minority of states, a court may consider the adequacy of the terms of the agreement—that is, whether the substantive terms meet a minimum threshold of fairness, in addition to basic standards of procedural fairness. The states requiring some degree of substantive fairness are (1) UPAA states: Connecticut, Indiana, Iowa; (2) UPMAA states: Colorado, North Dakota; (3) non-Uniform Act states: Alaska, Georgia, Kentucky, Maryland, Massachusetts, Michigan, Minnesota, Mississippi, Missouri, New Hampshire, South Carolina, Vermont, West Virginia, and Wisconsin.[78] At a minimum, the substantive terms must have been adequate (either fair or conscionable) at execution.

---

74. *Hutchins v. Hutchins*, 393 Mont. 283, 430 P.3d 502 (2018).

75. UPMAA § 9, cmt.

76. Under the UPAA the only grounds on which a court may strike down a premarital agreement are involuntariness and unconscionability coupled with a lack of adequate financial disclosure or an effective waiver of disclosure.

77. UPMAA § 5, cmt.

78. See Appendix B(1), State Law Summary: Premarital Agreements. Maryland is included here, although the law of Maryland is somewhat unclear about what role substantive unconscionability at execution may play in determining validity. *See Cannon v. Cannon*, 384 Md. 537, 865 A.2d 563 (2005). Maryland case law generally provides that a substantively unfair premarital agreement is enforceable if executed voluntarily, without fraud, duress, or overreaching, and with financial disclosure. *Id.* However, in *Cannon*, the court, in *dicta*, said a party could seek to

(b) Fairness as of Execution

Five states, Maryland and Missouri, non-Uniform Act states, and Iowa, Indiana, and Nevada, UPAA states, only consider fairness of the agreement as of execution.[79]

(c) The Second Look at Divorce

The remaining states, known as the "second-look" states, require substantive fairness at the time of enforcement at divorce. In these states, a trial judge may take a second look at the agreement at divorce and evaluate whether the agreement remains fair. Because events subsequent to marriage may affect the validity of an agreement governed by the law of a second-look state, if challenged at divorce, greater care is required in all aspects of the process leading to execution. The stronger party and counsel must consider the fairness of the terms of the agreement at the outset and whether the agreement may become unfair over time. Driving too hard a bargain may prove to be the stronger party's undoing.[80]

The question of the adequacy of substantive terms is judged by one of two standards. Courts in some states invalidate a premarital agreement if it is merely unfair at divorce.[81] More commonly, for a court to invalidate a premarital agreement at divorce, the terms must be unconscionable.[82] An unconscionability standard puts a greater burden on the party challenging enforcement. In a few states, courts have not clearly determined whether the higher fairness standard or the lower unconscionability standard applies.[83]

(d) The Second Look at Death

There is little authority permitting a court to take a second look at a premarital agreement after the death of a spouse and to consider whether it has become unfair or unconscionable.[84] North Dakota appears to be the only state with a specific statute that permits a court to refuse to enforce a provision of a premarital (or postmarital) agreement after the death of a spouse on fairness grounds, but only to avoid substantial hardship because of a material change in circumstances since execution of the agreement.[85] North Dakota is one of only two states that adopted the UPMAA. The UPMAA provides alternative text for adopting

---

invalidate an agreement that was unconscionable at execution, but there is no Maryland case in which an agreement was invalidated on this ground.

79. *In re Marriage of Thomas*, 199 S.W.3d 847 (Mo. Ct. App. 2006). *Cannon*, 384 Md. at 570, 865 A.2d at 582 n.18; IND. CODE § 31-11-3-8; IOWA CODE § 596.8(i).

80. *See Hardee v. Hardee*, 355 S.C. 382, 585 S.E.2d 501 (2003); *MacFarlane v. Rich*, 132 N.H. 608, 567 A.2d 585 (1989); *Button v. Button*, 131 Wis. 2d 84, 95, 388 N.W.2d 546, 550 (1986).

81. WIS. STAT. ANN. § 767.61(2)(L); *In re Estate of Benker*, 416 Mich. 681, 689, 331 N.W.2d 193, 196 (1982).

82. *DeMatteo v. DeMatteo*, 436 Mass. 18, 762 N.E.2d 797 (2002); *Hardee*, 585 S.E.2d at 558; *Edwardson v. Edwardson*, 798 S.W.2d 941 (Ky. 1990); *MacFarlane*, 132 N.H. 608; *Gant v. Gant*, 329 S.E.2d 106 (W. Va. 1985); *Scherer v. Scherer*, 249 Ga. 635, 292 S.E.2d 662 (1982); CONN. GEN. STAT. § 46b-36g(a)(2); IND. CODE § 31-11-3-8; IOWA CODE § 596.8.

83. *Bassler v. Bassler*, 156 Vt. 353, 593 A.2d 82 (1991).

84. *See Bickford v. Bickford*, 12 Mass. L. Rep. 378 (1999) ("The concerns about flexibility and continuing fairness expressed in the divorce context are not applicable when a party seeks to enforce an antenuptial agreement after one spouse's death; rather, finality and certainty in the distribution of the decedent spouse's property are of paramount importance.").

85. N.D. CENT. CODE § 14-03.2-08.6 (2014).

states that wish to permit consideration of parties' circumstances at enforcement,[86] and North Dakota chose that option. How courts in North Dakota apply the second look after death remains to be seen. As the Comment to the UPMAA indicates:

> However, it should be noted that even in such "second-look" states, case law invalidating premarital agreements and marital agreements at the time of enforcement almost universally concerns rights at divorce. There is little case law invalidating waivers of rights arising at the time of death of the other spouse grounded on the unfairness at the time of enforcement.

In a few second-look states, a statute precludes a second look after death. For example, in both Alaska and West Virginia, where the standards for validity of a premarital agreement at divorce are not codified, case law permits a second look at divorce; but a statute provides that an agreement waiving rights at death is valid if voluntary, even if it was unconscionable at execution, so long as there was financial disclosure or an effective waiver.[87] These statutes do not allow for consideration of changed circumstances.

In a Georgia case, *Hiers v. Estate of Hiers*,[88] the court observed that there were no cases where the court applied the second-look analysis after a spouse's death. It went on to evaluate the claim of changed circumstances, and reject it, without deciding whether that factor was generally applicable to a determination of validity after a death. In a case about validity of a postmarital agreement, *Estate of Wilber*,[89] the New Hampshire court said it looked to principles governing premarital agreements for guidance. One factor is whether the facts and circumstances have changed such that the agreement has become unconscionable. However, it did not evaluate this factor in its opinion and upheld the parties' postmarital agreement after the death of the husband. In other second-look states, there are no statutory provisions addressing this question and no case law on point, nor have courts in these states even acknowledged that there is an open question.

§2.09 CONCLUSION

The threshold for creation of a valid premarital agreement is very low in most states. From the standpoint of the weaker party, the result at death or divorce can be very harsh. The UPAA has been criticized by many commentators as failing to adequately protect economically weaker spouses. Counsel representing a stronger party should consider the possibility that applicable law will swing back to an approach that demands more procedural fairness at execution or substantive fairness at enforcement or that a move to a state with more demanding criteria for validity will put validity at risk. Whether it does or not, it is risky for

86. UPMAA § 9(f) provides: "A court may refuse to enforce a term of a premarital agreement or marital agreement if, in the context of the agreement taken as a whole[:] [(1)] the term was unconscionable at the time of signing[; or (2) enforcement of the term would result in substantial hardship for a party because of a material change in circumstances arising after the agreement was signed]."

87. ALASKA STAT. § 13-12-213(b); W. VA. CODE § 42-2-3a (2014).

88. 278 Ga. App. 242, 628 S.E.2d 653, *cert. denied*, 2006 Ga. LEXIS 526 (2000).

89. 165 N.H. 246, 75 A.3d 1096 (2013).

the proponent to rely solely on one element for validity. Moreover, the consequences to the stronger party from a failure of proof can be quite significant. A court will not simply revise the agreement to provide a fairer disposition of property; it will invalidate the agreement in its entirety, thus exposing all of the stronger party's assets and earning capacity to a spousal claim.

The only meaningful opportunity for the weaker party to achieve some degree of financial security is at the drafting and negotiation stage. The reality is applicable law is not likely to swing back and a move will not necessarily improve the weaker party's chances of getting an agreement invalidated. Moreover, the weaker party may be forced to incur substantial legal fees to attempt an attack on validity and cannot count on an award of fees even if the attack is successful.

General Validity and Criteria for an Enforceable Postmarital (or Marital) Agreement

3

§3.01 Scope of This Chapter; Terminology

A postmarital agreement is "an agreement entered into during marriage to define each spouse's property rights in the event of death or divorce."[1] In some states, such an agreement may fix or waive spousal support. As used here, the term refers to an agreement that is not made incident to an imminent separation or divorce.

Agreements of this type are sometimes called marital agreements or postnuptial agreements. When the primary purpose of the agreement is to predetermine spousal rights when a couple is estranged, but is willing to make an attempt at reconciliation, the agreement may be called a reconciliation agreement. In the Uniform Premarital and Marital Agreements Act, the Uniform Law Commission opted to use the term "marital agreement." However, as the case law and statutes in the majority of states generally use the term postmarital agreement or postnuptial agreement, these agreements will be referred to herein as postmarital agreements.

§3.02 Uses of Postmarital Agreements

A postmarital agreement can be useful under a variety of circumstances:

1. *Simmons v. Simmons*, 98 Ark. App. 12, 15, 249 S.W.3d 843, 846 (2007); *see also In re Estate of Wilber*, 165 N.H. 246, 75 A.3d 1096 (2013); *Vaccarello v. Vaccarello*, 757 A.2d 909 (Pa. 2000); *Combs v. Sherry-Combs*, 865 P.2d 50 (Wyo. 1993); *Acre v. Koenig*, 89 Idaho 342, 404 P.2d 621 (1965).

- Parties intended to enter into a premarital agreement but were not able to complete negotiations and drafting before the wedding.[2]
- Parties entered into a premarital agreement, but the process or terms were flawed and can be fixed with a postmarital agreement.[3]
- Parties signed a premarital agreement very close in time to the wedding and may want to sign a simple ratification after the wedding;[4]
- Parties have separated or filed for divorce, or a party has engaged in marital misconduct, and they wish to predetermine disposition of property and, to the extent permitted under state law, support, as a condition of reconciliation.[5]
- A party who operates a business or engages in a professional practice with significant financial exposure, or potential for a professional liability claim, may wish to document a division or transfer of property to protect the other spouse before any creditor claims are made.[6]
- A spouse who may be exposed to a personal injury claim,[7] or a claim for medical care not covered by insurance,[8] may seek an agreement to segregate assets to protect the nondebtor spouse before a claim is made, or a nondebtor spouse may seek an agreement to avoid the liabilities of an impecunious debtor-spouse, particularly in a community property state.[9]
- An agreement may be a necessary component in an estate plan, *e.g.*, where the estate plan calls for segregating property into separate revocable trusts.
- Parties with a premarital or postmarital agreement may wish to make significant revisions to the terms with a superseding instrument.
- Parties want to revoke a premarital or postmarital agreement in its entirety.[10]

---

2. *See Steele v. Steele,* 467 N.J. Super. 414, 253 A.3d 1190 (App. Div. 2021).

3. But this works only if the proponent does not repeat the same mistakes. *See Weidel v. Weidel,* 2021 N.J. Super. Unpub. LEXIS 2829 (unsigned PMA did not provide fair disclosure of husband's property and wife was unrepresented; postmarital amendment invalid where husband's disclosure inadequate and wife did not have independent counsel).

4. See Appendix E, Additional and Optional Terms, for an example.

5. *See Lloyd v. Niceta,* 255 Md. App. 663, 284 A.3d 808 (2022) cert. granted 482 Md. 473, 290 A.3d. 602 (2023); *Hodge v. Parks*, 303 Mich. App. 552, 844 N.W.2d 189 (2008); *Dawbarn v. Dawbarn*, 175 N.C. App. 712, 625 S.E.2d 186 (2006); *Flansburg v. Flansburg*, 581 N.E.2d 430 (Ind. Ct. App. 1991); *Nicholson v. Nicholson*, 199 N.J. Super. 525, 489 A.2d 1247 (App. Div. 1985); *Hoyt v. Hoyt*, 213 Tenn. 117, 372 S.W.2d 300 (1963).

6. *See Elia v. Pifer*, 194 Ariz. 74, 977 P.2d 796 (1998); *see also State v. Wright*, 43 P.3d 203 (Ariz. Ct. App. 2002) (postmarital amendment to premarital agreement was fraudulent conveyance); *Schultz v. Sykes*, 638 N.W.2d 76 (Wis. Ct. App. 2001) (husband's wages subject to garnishment to satisfy tort judgment against wife where marital agreement reclassifying parties' property as separate executed after cause of action arose); *D'Aston v. D'Aston*, 808 P.2d 111 (Utah Ct. App. 1990) (postmarital agreement enforced at divorce over husband's claim executed only to protect marital assets from creditors in pending business litigation).

7. *See Dritselis v. Dritselis*, 2005 Va. App. LEXIS 451 (unpub.) (postmarital agreement proposed by husband to protect assets from potential civil assault claim).

8. *See Friedman v. Friedman*, 100 Cal. App. 4th 65, 122 Cal. Rptr. 2d 412 (2002) (husband sought postmarital agreement to protect wife from medical creditors if bone marrow transplant failed to save his life).

9. *See Bell v. Bell*, 122 Idaho 520, 835 P.2d 1331 (1992) (postmarital agreement to allocate to husband all community debt incurred by him was valid); *see also Seidel v. United States of America*, 2008 U.S. Dist. LEXIS 45826 (D.N.D. Cal. 2008) (postmarital agreement ineffective to protect wife's community assets from husband's community tax liabilities where executed after debt incurred).

10. *Hansen v. Hansen*, 924 N.W.2d 873 (Iowa Ct. App. 2018) (postmarital agreement revoking premarital agreement); *Zhou v. Zhang*, 334 Conn. 601, 223 A.3d 775 (2020) (revocation of postmarital agreement is itself a postmarital agreement).

§3.03 GENERAL VALIDITY OF POSTMARITAL AGREEMENTS

(a) Overview

At common law, spouses generally could not contract with each other.[11] Two legal developments have promoted court and legislative acceptance of postmarital agreements. As courts and legislatures abrogated the common law disabilities of married women, they acquired the right to contract with their husbands for many purposes, including comprehensive postmarital agreements in contemplation of death and dissolution.[12] In *Estate of Harber*,[13] a case of first impression, the Supreme Court of Arizona held a postmarital agreement executed in 1938 by a couple who had no plans to divorce was enforceable when the husband died 24 years later. The court made clear that its holding permitted such an agreement to govern disposition of property at divorce as well as death. The Court of Appeals of Utah came to a similar conclusion in a 1990 case, *D'Aston v. D'Aston*,[14] citing *Harber* and a number of cases from other jurisdictions.

Further, premarital agreements have gained universal acceptance; public policy favors such agreements if fairly made.[15] As postmarital agreements serve similar purposes, public policy supports a consistent approach.[16] As one court observed: "Postnuptial agreements are consistent with public policy; they realistically acknowledge the high incidence of divorce."[17] Put another way: "The modern view is that spouses may freely enter contractual relationships, and courts will uphold them if they satisfy the criteria of contract formation and are otherwise fair."[18] Currently, every state permits spouses to contract with each other for some purposes, although in a small minority, the permissible scope of such an agreement is quite restrictive.[19]

(b) Authority for Comprehensive Postmarital Agreements with Same Validity Criteria as Premarital Agreements

In only a few states is there statutory authority for comprehensive postmarital agreements with criteria for validity that is the same as for premarital agreements. New York, Wisconsin, and Virginia have such statutes, permitting parties to contract about the same subjects, including property rights at both death and divorce as well as spousal support.[20] Virginia's version of the Uniform Premarital Agreement Act (UPAA) includes a provision that applies the Act to all spousal agreements, expressly permitting postmarital agreements that cover

11. 41 AM. JUR. 2D Husband and Wife § 107; *Graham v. Graham*, 33 F. Supp. 936 (E.D. Mich. 1940); *Adams v. Adams*, 113 A. 279 (N.H. 1921).
12. *Adams*, 113 A. 279; *Hallam v. Hallam*, 298 Ill. App. 445, 19 N.E.2d 101 (1939).
13. 104 Ariz. 79, 449 P.2d 7 (1969).
14. 808 P.2d 111 (Utah Ct. App. 1990).
15. See Chapter 2.
16. *Bedrick v. Bedrick*, 300 Conn. 691, 698–99, 17 A.3d 17, 24–25 (2011).
17. *Id.* at 698, 24.
18. *In re Estate of Wilber*, 165 N.H. 246, 249, 75 A.3d 1096, 1099 (2013) (citations omitted).
19. See Section 3.03(d), (e).
20. N.Y. DOMESTIC REL. LAW § 236(B)(3); *Rupert v. Rupert*, 245 A.D.2d 1139, 667 N.Y.S.2d 537 (1997); *Zipes v. Zipes*, 158 Misc. 2d 368, 599 N.Y.S.2d 941 (Sup. Ct. 1993); *Arizin v. Covello*, 175 Misc. 2d 453, 669 N.Y.S.2d 189 (Sup. Ct. 1998); WIS. STAT. ANN. §§ 766.58, 767.255; *Button v. Button*, 131 Wis. 2d 84, 388 N.W.2d 546 (1986); VA. CODE § 20-155.

the same subjects and have the same prerequisites for validity as premarital agreements.[21] Minnesota, by statute, permits a married couple to contract about anything after marriage that they could contract about before.[22] The Uniform Premarital and Marital Agreements Act (UPMAA) creates uniform standards for recognition, validity, and scope of postmarital agreements that are identical to the standards for validity of premarital agreements. Colorado and North Dakota are the only states to have enacted the UPMAA.[23] The UPMAA, which uses the term "marital agreement," defines a marital agreement as an agreement executed by spouses who intend to stay married and which "affirms, modifies, or waives a marital right or obligation during the marriage or at separation, marital dissolution, [or] death of one of the spouses. . . ."[24]

Acting without statutory authority that expressly authorizes postmarital agreements governing property rights at divorce, courts in Alabama, Connecticut, Florida, Georgia, and Massachusetts, have held such agreements generally enforceable at divorce.[25] Case law in these states supports enforceability of provisions fixing or waiving spousal support under the same circumstances that apply to a premarital agreement. Coupled with statutes permitting spouses to waive spousal rights at death, married persons in these states can enter into comprehensive postmarital agreements.

(c) Statutory Authority for Postmarital Agreements Regarding Property Rights at Death or Divorce

The majority of states do not have a single statute or case expressly authorizing comprehensive postmarital agreements governing property rights at death or divorce as well as waiver of spousal support. However, in many states there is a patchwork of statutes and appellate decisions which, taken together, permit spouses to enter into a postmarital agreement conclusively defining their rights to property at death or divorce.

Statutes Permitting Spouses to Contract with Each Other

Statutes in many states expressly permit spouses to contract with each other. Historically, such statutes were referred to as Married Women's Property Acts. These acts ended the historic disabilities of married women, permit married women to contract with their husbands, in some states subject to the rules governing persons standing in a confidential relationship.[26] Statutes permitting spouses to contract with each other without specifying

---

21. VA. CODE ANN. § 20-155; *Galloway v. Galloway*, 47 Va. App. 83, 622 S.E.2d 267 (2005); *Flanary v. Milton*, 556 S.E.2d 767 (Va. 2002).

22. MINN. STAT. ANN. § 519.11.

23. Appendix B(2), State Law Summary: Postmarital Agreements.

24. UPMAA § 2(2).

25. *McGeehan v. McGeehan*, 455 Md. 268, 167 A.3d 579 (2017); *Bedrick v. Bedrick*, 300 Conn. 691, 17 A.3d 17 (2011); *Ansin v. Craven-Ansin*, 457 Mass. 283, 929 N.E.2d 955, (2010); *Vaccarello v. Vaccarello*, 757 A.2d 909 (Pa. 2000); *Tibbs v. Anderson*, 580 So. 2d 1337 (Ala. 1991); *Casto v. Casto*, 508 So. 2d 330 (Fla. 1987); *Sanders v. Colwell*, 283 S.E.2d 461 (Ga. 1981); *Hoyt v. Hoyt*, 213 Tenn. 117, 372 S.W.2d 300 (1963).

26. *See* ALA. CODE § 30-4-9; CAL. FAM. CODE § 721; CONN. GEN. STAT. 46b-36; D.C. CODE § 46-601; FLA. STAT. ANN. § 708.09; HAW. REV. STAT. § 572-22; KY. REV. STAT. ANN. § 404.020; LA. CIV. CODE ANN. art. 2328; MONT. CODE ANN. § 40-2-301; NEV. REV. STAT. ANN. § 123.070; N.M. STAT. ANN. § 40-2-2; N.C. GEN. STAT. § 52-10(a); N.D. CENT. CODE § 14-07-06; OKLA. STAT. tit. 43, § 204; R.I. GEN. LAWS §§ 15-4-3, 15-4-4; S.D. CODIFIED LAWS § 25-2-10; WASH. REV. CODE ANN. § 26.16.150; *see also* Appendix B(2), State Law Summary: Postmarital Agreements.

or limiting the subjects of such a contract appear to permit spouses to enter into a postmarital agreement determining their rights at death or excluding property from the marital estate at divorce.[27]

Statutes Expressly Permitting Postmarital Agreements Excluding Property from the Marital Estate at Divorce

Many states' equitable distribution statutes permit spouses to enter into a valid contract during marriage to exclude property from the marital estate at divorce.[28] Unless such statutes limit their application to an agreement made incident to a separation or divorce, or require court approval for validity, they appear to permit parties not contemplating an immediate separation to execute an agreement regarding disposition of property in the event of a future separation.[29]

Community Property Agreements

Spouses in community property states may execute an agreement to alter the status of property.[30] In Washington, Texas, Idaho, New Mexico, and Louisiana, spouses may by agreement reclassify existing community property as separate property or may opt out of the community property regime as to property to be acquired in the future.[31] Texas and Washington statutes permit spouses to convert what would otherwise be separate property into community property by postmarital agreement.[32]

Statutes Permitting Spouses to Contract Regarding Wills or Rights at Death

Some states have a statute similar to or based on §2-213 of the Uniform Probate Code that permits parties to contract before or after marriage to waive or limit their rights to property at death and with the validity criteria of the UPAA.[33] These statutes do not by their terms authorize enforcement of a postmarital agreement at divorce. Another group of states have a statute permitting a postmarital waiver of rights upon death that requires observance

27. *See Kreytak v. Kreytak*, 82 Haw. 543, 923 P.2d 960 (Ct. App. 1996); *Boyer v. Boyer*, 925 P.2d 82 (Okla. Ct. App. 1996); *Tibbs v. Anderson*, 580 So. 2d 1337 (Ala. 1991); *Estate of Gab*, 364 N.W.2d 924 (S.D. 1985); *Marriage of Myers*, 210 Mont. 173, 682 P.2d 718 (1984); *Estate of Loughmiller*, 229 Kan. 584, 629 P.2d 156 (1981); *Getty v. Damson*, 63 Wash. 2d 526, 387 P.2d 964 (1964); *Smith v. Smith*, 295 Ky. 50, 173 S.W.2d 813 (1943); *Cohn v. Cohn*, 4 Wash. 2d 322, 103 P.2d 366 (1940); *Comstock v. Comstock*, 146 Ark. 266, 225 S.W. 621 (1920).

28. *See, e.g.*, D.C. CODE ANN. § 16-910; 750 ILL. COMP. STAT. § 5/503(a)(4); KY. REV. STAT. ANN. § 403.190; MO. REV. STAT. § 452.330(2); MONT. CODE ANN. § 40-2-304-311; N.C. GEN. STAT. § 52-20; S.C. CODE ANN. § 20-73-630.

29. *In re Marriage of Vella*, 237 Ill. App. 3d 194, 603 N.E.2d 109 (1992); *Bailey v. Bailey*, 330 S.C. 326, 498 S.E.2d 891 (Ct. App. 1998).

30. *See, e.g.*, CAL. FAM. CODE § 721.

31. TEX. FAM. CODE ANN. § 4.102; *Daniel v. Daniel*, 779 S.W.2d 110 (Tex. App. 1989); IDAHO CODE §§ 32-916, 32-917, 32-918; *Stevens v. Stevens*, 16 P.3d 900 (Idaho 2000); WASH. REV. CODE ANN. § 26.16.120; *Marriage of Dewberry & George*, 115 Wash. App. 351, 62 P.3d 525 (2003); NSMA 1978, § 40-2-2 (1907); *Gabriele v. Gabriele*, 421 P.3d 828 (N.M. Ct. App. 2018); LA. CIV. CODE ANN. art. 2328, 2329, 2331, 2336. Termination of the matrimonial regime in Louisiana requires court approval. LA. CIV. CODE ANN. art. 2329.

32. WASH. REV. CODE ANN. § 26.16.120; *Marriage of Schweitzer*, 132 Wash. 2d 318, 937 P.2d 1062 (1997); TEX. FAM. CODE ANN. §§ 4.201, *et seq.*

33. *See, e.g.*, ALASKA STAT. § 13.12.213; KAN. STAT. ANN. § 59-6a-213; MONT. CODE. ANN. § 72-2-224; NEB. REV. STAT. § 30-2316; *Blanchard v. White*, 217 Neb. 877, 351 N.W.2d 707 (1984); *but see Devney v. Devney*, 295 Neb. 15, 886 N.W.2d 61 (2016) (§ 30-2016 does not permit enforcement at divorce of a postmarital agreement not executed incident to separation or divorce).

of rules regarding confidential relations or that there be full disclosure of assets and fair consideration.[34]

Statutes That Permit Postmarital Agreements Not Incident to Separation, but Prohibit Waiver of Support

Several states have a statute similar or identical to the following:

> A husband and wife cannot by any contract with each other alter their legal relation, except as to property and except that they may agree, in writing, to an immediate separation and may make provision for the support of either of them and of their children during such separation.[35]

These statutes appear to permit a spousal contract during marriage that determines property rights at death or divorce, but preclude determination of spousal support unless the agreement is incident to marital separation.

(d) Minority Position: Iowa

Iowa is alone in its lack of authority permitting postmarital agreements not incident to an immediate separation.[36] It has no statute expressly authorizing spouses to enter into such an agreement. Iowa courts have interpreted the lack of statutory authority as prohibiting them.[37] The Iowa version of the UPAA omitted the text that permits parties to amend their premarital agreements, leaving only the power to revoke.[38] Thus, spouses in Iowa cannot amend a premarital agreement, as an amendment is itself a prohibited postmarital agreement. They can only revoke a premarital agreement or enter into a reconciliation agreement, where they agree to continue the marriage and structure their financial relationship in the event of a future divorce.[39]

(e) Permissible Scope Undetermined

In the states that lack some combination of statutory and case authority clearly authorizing spouses to enter into an agreement governing property rights at death or divorce, the

---

34. *See, e.g.*, ALA. CODE § 43-8-72 (spousal contracts subject to rules *re* confidential relations; must be in writing and made after fair disclosure); CAL. FAM. CODE § 721 (same); IND. CODE § 29-1-2-13 (contract waiving spousal rights at death must be in writing with full disclosure and fair consideration); MO. REV. STAT. § 474.220 (same).

35. MONT. CODE. ANN. § 4-2-303; *see also* CAL. FAM. CODE § 1620; N.M. § 40-2-8; NEV. REV. STAT. ANN. § 123.080.

36. Ohio law also prohibited most postmarital agreements. Amendments to the Ohio Code, effective in 2023, now permit such agreements, aligning Ohio with the majority of states and overruling cases interpreting prior law. *See Gomer v. Gomer,* 86 N.E.3d 920 (Ohio Ct. App., 6th Dist. 2018) (agreement in year one of 28-year marriage to define as separate property what would have been marital property was prohibited); *DuBois v. Coen*, 100 Ohio St. 17, 125 N.E. 121 (1919) (property settlement between spouses not incident to marital separation is prohibited and unenforceable at death); *Thompson v. Thompson*, 196 Ohio App. 3d 764, 965 N.E.2d 377 (Ct. App. 10th Dist. 2011) (spouses cannot by agreement convert marital assets and debts to separate assets and debts unless pursuant to an immediate separation).

37. *Hansen v. Hansen*, 924 N.W.2d 873 (Iowa Ct. App. 2018); *In Estate of Shaffer*, 2009 Iowa App. LEXIS 184 (unpub.); *see also Husseman v. Husseman*, 847 N.W.2d 219 (Iowa 2014) (Iowa does not enforce postmarital agreement to waive elective share) (*dicta*); *Estate of Kennedy*, 154 Iowa 460, 135 N.W. 53 (1912) (purported oral postmarital agreement to waive dower was void as prohibited by statute).

38. *Hansen,* 924 N. W.2d at 873.

39. *See Marriage of Cooper*, 769 N.E.2d 582 (Iowa 2009).

permissible scope of such agreements is undetermined at this time. In Oklahoma, for example, there are several code provisions that appear to permit a postmarital agreement for disposition of property.[40] However, the cases are in conflict.[41]

Michigan case law clearly authorizes spouses not contemplating divorce to enter into an enforceable agreement regarding property rights at death.[42] Michigan case law also supports enforcement of a postmarital agreement executed by spouses who have separated and who intend to reconcile.[43] An agreement executed by a couple who were not separated was void as against public policy in *Wright v. Wright*,[44] where it created an economic incentive to abandon the marriage. In *Skaates v. Kayser*,[45] the terms were balanced enough that the agreement did not give either party an economic incentive to divorce; that was the key to a finding of validity. Whether Michigan courts would enforce an agreement at divorce that was less equitable than the agreement in *Skaates* is an open question.

§3.04 CRITERIA FOR VALIDITY OF POSTMARITAL AGREEMENTS

(a) Overview

To be valid, a postmarital agreement must be executed voluntarily by parties with capacity to contract and must be free of fraud, coercion, duress, or undue influence.[46] In some states, the criteria for validity of a postmarital agreement are identical to those that determine validity of a premarital agreement. Thus, questions of voluntariness, duress, coercion, unconscionability, and adequacy of financial disclosure are governed by the same body of law.[47] In other states these agreements are judged by a higher standard.[48] In those states that apply a higher standard to the evaluation of a postmarital agreement than to a premarital agreement, the most significant factors are the application of principles of confidential or fiduciary relationships and the basic contract principle that there must be consideration for the contract beyond the marriage itself. In some states, the criteria for validity are not well-developed.[49]

---

40. OKLA. STAT. tit. 43, § 204 (spouses can contract regarding property, subject to general rules regarding confidential relations).

41. *See Manhart v. Manhart*, 725 P.2d 1234 (Okla. 1986) (postmarital agreement enforceable at divorce); *Boyer v. Boyer*, 925 P.2d 82 (Okla. Ct. App. 1996) (postmarital amendment to premarital agreement valid); *Hendrick v. Hendrick*, 976 P.2d 1071 (Okla. Ct. App. 1998) (amendment to premarital agreement is invalid as postmarital agreement not authorized by Oklahoma law).

42. *Ransford v. Yens*, 132 N.W.2d 150 (Mich. 1965); *Rockwell v. Rockwell*, 24 Mich. App. 593, 180 N.W.2d 498 (1970).

43. *See Hodge v. Parks*, 303 Mich. App. 552, 844 N.W.2d 189 (2014).

44. 279 Mich. App. 291, 761 N.W.2d 443 (2008); *see also Cheff v. Cheff*, 2012 Mich. App. LEXIS 753 (unpub.) (postmarital agreement signed six months after wedding and providing for property division and alimony at divorce, where couple living together at execution, was void as against public policy).

45. 333 Mich. App. 61, 959 N.W.2d 33 (2020).

46. *Stewart v. Combs*, 368 Ark. 121, 243 S.W.3d 294 (2006).

47. See Chapter 4 for discussion of these issues.

48. *See Grossman v. Grossman*, 191 Ore. App. 294, 82 P.3d 1039 (2003); *Pacelli v. Pacelli*, 319 N.J. Super. 185, 725 A.2d 56 (1999).

49. *See, e.g., In re Estate of Wilber*, 165 N.H. 246, 75 A.3d 1096 (2013) (court need not decide whether to apply lower standard governing premarital agreements, where parties are free to reject the terms and not marry, or the higher standard governing contracts between persons in confidential relationship, as challenging party's proof failed under either standard).

(b) Same Validity Criteria as Premarital Agreements

Those states with statutes expressly authorizing comprehensive postmarital agreements provide that the same criteria apply to determine validity of both types of agreement.[50] Courts in a number of states without express statutory authority have analogized postmarital agreements to premarital agreements and have held that the same standards apply to both.[51] Some states have enacted provisions of the Uniform Probate Code that provide the same criteria for validity of a postmarital agreement waiving spousal rights as death as the UPAA.[52] The UPMAA applies the same criteria to validity of both types of agreement.[53]

(c) Close Scrutiny; Confidential or Fiduciary Relationship

Many states recognize, by statute or common law, a presumed confidential or a fiduciary relationship between spouses in an ongoing marriage.[54] Even where there is no legal presumption, such a relationship may have developed as a matter of fact. The safest course of action for the proponent of a postmarital agreement is to conduct the process based on the higher standard required of persons in a confidential or fiduciary relationship.

> The law recognizes that a relationship, known as "confidential relations," may exist between the parties to a transaction where by reason of kinship or professional, business, social, or family relations, "confidence is naturally inspired or, in fact reasonably exists."[55]

A party to a confidential relationship has a right to assume the other party will act in a manner consistent with his or her welfare.[56] The confidential relationship imposes a duty of good faith and fair dealing.[57] Because parties to an ongoing marriage occupy a position of trust, they must exercise a high degree of candor about the facts relevant to the transaction and must fully disclose the existence of assets and other pertinent financial information.[58] A spouse who

---

50. See Appendix B(2), State Law Summary: Postmarital Agreements.

51. *Lipic v. Lipic*, 103 S.W.3d 144 (Mo. App. 2003); *Stoner v. Stoner*, 572 Pa. 665, 819 A.2d 529 (2003); *Allen v. Allen*, 161 Vt. 526, 641 A.2d 1332 (1994); *Estate of Wiseman*, 889 S.W.2d 215 (Tenn. Ct. App. 1994); *Tibbs v. Anderson*, 580 So. 2d 1337 (Ala. 1991); *Gentry v. Gentry*, 798 S.W.2d 928 (Ky. 1990); *Curry v. Curry*, 260 Ga. 302, 392 S.E.2d 879 (1990); *Casto v. Casto*, 508 So. 2d 330 (Fla. 1987); *Stack v. Venzke*, 485 N.E.2d 907 (Ind. Ct. App. 1985).

52. UPC § 2-213; Appendix B(2), State Law Summary: Postmarital Agreements.

53. UPMAA § 9 (2012).

54. Alaska Stat. § 34.77.010; Ala. Code § 30-4-9; Cal. Fam. Code § 721; N.M. Stat. Ann. § 40-2-2; Mont. Code Ann. §§ 40-2-301–40-2-311; *Izzo v. Izzo*, 2010 Tex. App. LEXIS 3623; *Grover v. Grover*, 101 Ark. App. 346, 276 S.W.3d 740 (2008) (applying Fla. law); *Barchella v. Barchella*, 844 N.Y.S.2d 78 (2007); *Dospil v. Dospil*, 2007 Tenn. App. LEXIS 684; *Stoner v. Stoner*, 572 Pa. 665, 819 A.2d 529 (2003); *Grossman*, 82 P.3d 1039; *Marriage of Myers*, 210 Mont. 173, 682 P.2d 718 (1984); *Robert O. v. Ecmel A.*, 460 A.2d 1321 (Del. 1983); *Crawford v. Crawford*, 524 N.W.2d 833 (N.D. 1994); *Manhart v. Manhart*, 725 P.2d 1234 (Okla. 1986); *Marshall v. Marshall*, 166 W. Va. 304, 273 S.E.2d 360 (1980); *Williams v. Waldman*, 108 Nev. 466, 836 P.2d 614 (1992); *Ray v. Ray*, 189 So. 895 (Ala. 1939).

55. *Barker v. Barker*, 75 N.D. 253, 260, 27 N.W.2d 576, 581 (1947), citing 15 C.J.S. 821, 822.

56. *Beesley v. Harris*, 883 P.2d 1343 (Utah 1994); *Bell v. Bell*, 38 Md. App. 10, 379 A.2d 419 (1977); *Miethe v. Miethe*, 410 Ill. 226, 101 N.E.2d 571 (1951).

57. *Grossman*, 82 P.3d 1039; *Beesley*, 883 P.2d 1343; *Daniel v. Daniel*, 779 S.W.2d 110, 115 (Tex. App. 1989); *Estate of Gab*, 364 N.W.2d 924, 925–26 (S.D. 1985).

58. *Stoner*, 572 Pa. 665; *Gabaig v. Gabaig*, 717 P.2d 835 (Alaska 1986); *Daniel*, 779 S.W.2d at 115; *Bodine v. Bodine*, 754 P.2d 1200 (Idaho Ct. App. 1988); *Williams*, 108 Nev. 466; *Pacelli v. Pacelli*, 319 N.J. Super. 185, 725 A.2d 56 (1999). By contrast, when parties have separated and have assumed adversarial positions, any right to rely

received a decided advantage may be required to overcome a presumption of fraud by showing adequate terms for the other spouse, disclosure of rights and financial affairs and actual advice of independent counsel.[59]

In a case of first impression, the highest court of Massachusetts gave judicial recognition to postmarital agreements, laying out criteria for validity and providing for close scrutiny at divorce. In *Ansin v. Craven-Ansin*,[60] the agreement readily passed judicial review; there was full financial disclosure, both parties had independent counsel, and the parties negotiated the terms over a period of months with the wife demanding and getting more favorable terms. The court identified the requirements for validity as requiring court review of:

1. whether each party had an opportunity for independent counsel;
2. whether there was fraud or coercion;
3. whether the parties made full financial disclosure;
4. whether each spouse knowingly, expressly, and in writing agreed to waive the right to have a judge equitably divide property; and
5. whether the terms were fair at execution and remain so at divorce.[61]

The court did not address the question of what judicial review regarding substantive fairness, if any, would be required after the death of a party.

In another case of first impression, *Bedrick v. Bedrick*,[62] Connecticut's highest court held that postmarital agreements are generally enforceable but are subject to special scrutiny because the circumstances "are pregnant with the opportunity for one party to use the threat of dissolution to bargain themselves into positions of advantage."[63] As a consequence, the agreement must be fair and equitable at execution and not unconscionable at divorce. The agreement in *Bedrick* failed the unconscionability test. As in *Ansin*, the court in *Bedrick* had no occasion to address the standards to be used after the death of a party.

(d) Financial Disclosure

As with other questions relating to standards for validity of postmarital agreements, in many states the law relating to financial disclosure is not well-developed. The Connecticut Supreme Court has ruled that spouses must give each other full financial disclosure, including values of joint and separate property, debts, and income.[64] A postmarital agreement receives heightened scrutiny in Connecticut in contrast to premarital agreements governed by Connecticut's version of the UPAA.[65]

---

on trust is vitiated and each party is separately responsible for protecting his or her interests. *Drewry v. Drewry*, 8 Va. App. 460, 383 S.E.2d 12 (1989); *Marschall v. Marschall*, 195 N.J. Super. 16, 477 A.2d 833 (1984); *but see Sanford v. Sanford*, 355 Ark. 274, 137 S.W.3d 391 (2003) (lawyer-husband occupied fiduciary relationship vis à vis estranged wife when he discouraged her from getting separate counsel and reassured her he would protect her interests).

59. *Gabriele v. Gabriele*, 421 P.3d 828 (N.M. Ct. App. 2018).

60. 457 Mass. 283, 929 N.E.2d 955 (2010).

61. *Id.* at 291, 963; *see also Stewart v. Stewart*, 41 A.3d 401 (De. 2012) (higher degree of scrutiny required, triggered by confidential relationship).

62. 300 Conn. 691, 17 A.3d 17 (2011).

63. *Id.* at 701, 26.

64. *Bedrick v. Bedrick*, 300 Conn. 691, 704, 17 A.3d 17, 27 (2011).

65. *Bedrick*, 300 Conn. at 691; see Appendix B(1), State Law Summary: Premarital Agreements.

The UPMAA provides for the same obligation of financial disclosure for both types of agreement,[66] as does the law in those states with comprehensive statutes governing both types of agreement.[67] In some states, a statute permitting a postmarital agreement to determine disposition of property at death specifically requires financial disclosure or an effective waiver.[68] Parties to a postmarital agreement should be able to waive financial disclosure to the same extent as they could for a premarital agreement.[69]

(e) Consideration

The consideration for a premarital agreement is universally deemed to be the marriage itself.[70] This is not necessarily the case with a postmarital agreement. Some states permit a postmarital agreement without additional consideration; most require consideration beyond the marriage itself so that each party must get something in return for what he or she gives up by entering into the agreement.

- *No Consideration Required for Comprehensive Postmarital Agreement.* Consistent with their identical treatment of premarital and postmarital agreements, states that have expressly authorized comprehensive postmarital agreements have generally provided that no consideration is required to form a valid postmarital agreement.[71] Similarly, the UPMAA, adopted in Colorado and North Dakota, provides the same criteria for validity of both types of agreement; in neither case is consideration a requirement.[72]
- *No Consideration Required for Agreement Waiving Spousal Rights at Death.* Several states have statutes providing for postmarital agreements or other instruments waiving spousal rights at death and that expressly provide that no consideration is required for such a waiver.[73]
- *Consideration Required for Waiver of Spousal Rights at Death.* Some states have a statute permitting waiver of spousal rights at death and that expressly requires fair consideration for such a waiver.[74] Absent a statute or other authority expressly permitting a postmarital agreement waiving spousal rights at death without consideration, some consideration is required.[75] Mutual waivers will generally suffice.[76] It appears that a one-way waiver will not. The value of the consideration need not be equal or identical on each side.[77]

---

66. UPMAA § 9 (2012).
67. See Section 3.03(b).
68. See Appendix B(2), State Law Summary, Postmarital Agreements.
69. *Lugg v. Lugg*, 64 A.3d 1109 (Pa. Super. Ct. 2013).
70. *See* UPAA §§ 1, *et seq.* (1983).
71. *See* ALASKA STAT. § 34.77.090; COLO. REV. STAT. § 14-2-303; MONT. CODE ANN. § 40-2-304; VA. CODE ANN. § 20-155; WIS. STAT. ANN. § 766.58; *Laudig v. Laudig*, 425 Pa. Super. 228, 624 A.2d 651 (1993).
72. UPMAA § 6 (2012).
73. CAL. PROB. CODE § 142; FLA. STAT. ANN. § 732.702; 18-C ME. REV. STAT. ANN. § 2-213; N.C. GEN. STAT. § 52-10.
74. *See* IND. CODE § 29-1-2-13; § 2-204; MO. REV. STAT. § 474.220.
75. *Rockwell v. Estate of Rockwell*, 180 N.W.2d 498 (Mich. Ct. App. 1970).
76. *Id.*
77. *Blanchard v. White*, 217 Neb. 877, 351 N.W.2d 707 (1984); *Campbell v. Campbell*, 377 S.W.2d 93 (Ky. Ct. App. 1964).

- *Consideration Required for Comprehensive Postmarital Agreement.* In the absence of express authority for a postmarital agreement without consideration, general principles of contract law apply and there must therefore be some consideration beyond the marriage itself.[78]
- *Consideration for Reconciliation Agreement.* In some states, case law appears to limit postmarital agreements to those executed when spouses are estranged, or when a suit for divorce is pending, and where the purpose is to effect a reconciliation. However, in these states, a spouse's willingness to attempt reconciliation is sufficient consideration.[79]

(f) Fairness of Terms

Some courts have analyzed the substance of a postmarital agreement as a question of whether there was consideration, some as a question of fairness or substantive conscionability.[80] Under either analysis, in states where fairness or conscionability at execution is a requirement for a valid premarital agreement, it will also be a requirement for a postmarital agreement.[81] Similarly, courts in second-look states can be expected to apply the second look at divorce to both types of agreements.[82] The UPMAA requires that a postmarital agreement be not unconscionable as of execution.[83] This is consistent with existing statutory and case law in many states.[84] The law governing questions of fairness as of divorce, whether the court can consider changed circumstances, and whether changed circumstances must have been unanticipated, is not well-developed. Similarly, there is little guidance about whether courts in the second-look states will consider fairness as of the death of a spouse.[85]

Minnesota has its own unique statute governing postmarital agreements determining disposition of property at divorce. It permits such an agreement provided it is procedurally and substantively fair and equitable at execution and enforcement at divorce and otherwise complies with the requirements of a valid premarital agreement. Each spouse must be represented

---

78. *Lloyd v. Niceta,* 255 Md. App. 663, 284 A.3d 808 (Ct. Spec. App. 2022); *Gabriele v. Gabriele,* 421 P.3d 828 (N.M. Ct. App. 2018); *Combs v. Sherry-Combs*, 865 P.2d 50 (Wyo. 1993), citing 3 *Lindey and Parley on Separation Agreements and Antenuptial Contracts* § 91.04(E) at 91–20 (2d ed. 1991); *see also In re Burkle*, 139 Cal. App. 4th 712, 43 Cal. Rptr. 3d 181 (2016) (consideration for a postmarital agreement can consist of resolution of a dispute about property rights); *In re Marriage of Bell*, 360, S.W.3d 270 (Mo. Ct. App., So. Dist. 2011); *In re Marriage of Tabassum and Younis*, 377 Ill. App. 3d 761, 881 N.E.2d 396, reh. den. (2007); *Simmons v. Simmons*, 98 Ark. App. 12, 249 S.W.3d 843 (2007); *Whitmore v. Whitmore*, 8 A.D.3d 371, 778 N.Y.S.2d 73 (2004); *Beesley v. Harris*, 883 P.2d 1343 (Utah 1994); *Conigliaro v. Conigliaro*, 1992 Del. Fam. Ct. LEXIS 41.

79. *See In re Marriage of Hall*, 27 N.E.3d 281 (Ind. Ct. App. 2015).

80. In *Ansin v. Craven-Ansin*, 457 Mass. 283, 929 N.E.2d 955 (2010), the court declined to decide whether consideration should be required for validity of a postmarital agreement because the agreement at issue was supported by consideration. However, it did require substantive fairness at both execution and enforcement at divorce. *See also In re Marriage of Bell*, 360, S.W.3d 270 (Mo. Ct. App., So. Dist. 2011) (postmarital agreement under which wife got no consideration for waiver of rights was invalid as unconscionable).

81. *See Beaman v. Beaman*, 844 N.E.2d 525 (Ind. Ct. App. 2006) (court may only reject postmarital agreement on finding of fraud, duress, other imperfections of consent, or manifest inequity, particularly if resulting from great disparity in bargaining power); *Lipic v. Lipic*, 103 S.W.3d 144 (Mo. App. 2003) (postmarital agreement is binding if process was fair and agreement not unconscionable).

82. See Sections 2.08(c) and 4.09(c). There is little authority for a second look after death. *See* Section 2.08(d).

83. UPMAA § 9(f) (2012). The UPMAA has been adopted only in Colorado and North Dakota.

84. *See, e.g., Lloyd v. Niceta,* 255 Md. App. at 663 (unconscionability of postmarital agreement determined as of execution); *Chen v. Hoeflinger*, 127 Haw. 346, 279 P.3d 11 (Haw. Int. Ct. App. 2012) (same).

85. See Section 2.08(d).

by independent counsel. The agreement is presumed unenforceable if either party files for divorce within two years of execution unless the proponent can prove the agreement is fair and equitable.[86]

(g) Public Policy

Historically, premarital agreements providing for divorce were void as against public policy because they were thought to make divorce too easy for the economically dominant spouse, usually the husband. This notion has given way to virtually universal acceptance of premarital agreements even when the result at divorce is quite harsh for the weaker party. Similarly, there is no longer any generalized public policy against postmarital agreements.[87] Nevertheless, in some states, statutes or case law retain a role for public policy in favor of preserving marriage and against postmarital agreements that encourage divorce. Public policy may occasionally play a role in other types of circumstances. For example, in *Stutz v. Stutz*,[88] the court held such an agreement was invalid as contrary to public policy. The wife had proposed the agreement, which predetermined a disposition of property and support that heavily favored the husband, in return for which the husband would agree to adopt a child.

(h) Independent Advice as a Prerequisite to Validity

Independent advice is not generally a prerequisite to creation of a valid postmarital agreement.[89] However, a few states do require actual advice of independent counsel in some circumstances. California requires independent advice for an effective postmarital waiver of spousal rights at death.[90] In Minnesota, independent counsel is required for a valid postmarital agreement determining property rights at divorce.[91] Moreover, in those states where an express waiver of counsel, or an opportunity for legal advice, is required for an enforceable premarital agreement,[92] courts may impose the same requirement for a valid postmarital agreement.

86. MINN. STAT. ANN. § 519.11.

87. *See Traster v. Traster*, 339 P.3d 778 (Kan. 2014) (public policy inquiry into whether agreement tends to encourage divorce abrogated by statute; just and equitable standard applies equally to both postmarital and separation agreements), op. after remand, 2018 Kan. App. Unpub. LEXIS 321, *rev. denied*, 2019 Kan. LEXIS 221; *Bratton v. Bratton*, 136 S.W.3d 595 (Tenn. 2004) (postmarital agreements not contrary to public policy provided there is consideration and entered into knowledgeably, without fraud or coercion); *Lipic*, 103 S.W.3d 144 (public policy does not oppose premarital agreements contemplating possible marital dissolution; therefore, no public policy reason against postmarital agreement made in contemplation of marriage continuing).

88. 2005 Tenn. App. LEXIS 517 (unpub.).

89. *See Nelson v. Nelson*, 2010 Ala. Civ. App. LEXIS 34 (unpub.); *Stoner v. Stoner*, 572 Pa. 665, 819 A.2d 529 (2003).

90. *See* CAL. PROB. CODE § 143 (postmarital waiver of spousal rights at death not enforceable if surviving spouse not represented by independent counsel at time of signing).

91. MINN. STAT. ANN. § 519.11, subd. 1a(c) (postmarital agreement ineffective unless both parties had independent counsel).

92. *See* Section 2.06.

(i) Court Approval

With few exceptions, court approval is not a prerequisite to create an enforceable postmarital agreement.[93] Louisiana is the rare case where a statute mandates court approval for a postmarital agreement to terminate the matrimonial regime.[94] In some states, a trial court at divorce has some discretion about whether to approve a separation agreement on substantive fairness grounds even when the agreement meets all procedural criteria in that state for an enforceable contract.[95] In those states where a trial judge may review a separation agreement that is otherwise valid for substantive fairness, some courts may analogize a postmarital agreement, insofar as it is intended to take effect at divorce, to a separation agreement, rather than to a premarital agreement. Postmarital agreements in these states may therefore be vulnerable to revision by a judge in future divorce proceedings under some circumstances.[96]

(j) Execution Formalities

Statutes in some states prescribe execution formalities beyond party signatures. For example, Minnesota's statute requires two witnesses and notarization.[97] This requirement has been strictly enforced.[98] New York law similarly requires that a postmarital agreement be in writing, subscribed by the parties and acknowledged or proven in the manner of a deed to be recorded.[99]

(k) Recordation

In some community property states a marital agreement may not be effective to protect a spouse from a claim of a creditor for debt incurred by the other spouse unless the agreement or a memorandum thereof is recorded in the land records.[100]

---

93. *See In re Goldin*, 923 P.2d 376 (Colo. Ct. App. 1996) (court is not free to ignore provisions of a postmarital agreement where statute does not require court approval for validity); *In re Marriage of Vella*, 237 Ill. App. 3d 194, 603 N.W.2d 109 (1992) (postmarital agreement executed during pending divorce proceeding was enforceable where parties reconciled but carried out terms; validity not dependent upon entry of divorce decree approving).

94. La. Civ. Code Ann. art. 2329; *Martello v. Martello*, 960 So. 2d 186 (La. App. 2007); *Williams v. Williams*, 760 So. 2d 469 (La. Ct. App. 2000).

95. 24A Am. Jur. 2d *Divorce and Separation* § 1049. It is important to distinguish between the authority of a court to accept, reject, or modify provisions of a marital agreement regarding custody of or support for a minor child, and its authority to approve or disapprove provisions of a marital settlement agreement regarding disposition of property at divorce and spousal support. The discussion here is concerned only with the question of whether court approval is a necessary prerequisite to an enforceable postmarital agreement insofar as it deals with property and spousal support.

96. *See Traster*, 339 A.3d at 778 (postmarital agreement providing for spousal rights at divorce to be treated the same as separation agreements; therefore, subject to court review at divorce as to whether just and equitable); *In re Marriage of Cooper*, 769 N.W.2d 528 (Iowa 2009) (court may consider marital agreement made by parties in deciding division of property at divorce).

97. Minn. Stat. Ann. § 519.11.

98. *Estate of Francis*, 1998 Minn. App. LEXIS 1379 (12/22/98).

99. N.Y. Dom. Rel. Law § 236(B)(3); *Ballesteros v. Ballesteros*, 137 A.D.3d 722, 26 N.Y.S.3d 571 (App. Div. 2d Dep't 2016); *Galetta v. Galetta*, 2021 NY 3d 186, 969 N.Y.S.2d 826, 991 N.E.2d 684 (2013).

100. *See Seidel v. United States of America*, 2008 U.S. Dist. LEXIS 45826 (D.N.D. Cal. 6/11/08), citing Cal. Fam. Code § 852(b) (transmutation of real property not effective as to third parties without notice unless recorded).

§3.05 CONCLUSION

There is a clearly discernable trend toward greater spousal freedom to contract.[101] This trend affects the general recognition of postmarital agreements, the criteria for their enforceability, and the subjects on which parties are able to contract. At present, in most states, parties have the freedom to make highly disadvantageous premarital agreements and they may do so with a minimal degree of procedural fairness. The dominant trend seems to be to treat postmarital agreements in a similar manner, although in some states, by statute or case law, some additional requirements for validity are present and there are some limitations on the subjects for contract that do not exist with respect to premarital agreements. In some states, the authority for such agreements is not well-developed, and in some it is virtually nonexistent. Therefore, a lawyer preparing a postmarital agreement should take the cautious approach. The agreement should be substantively fair to each party, parties should make financial disclosure, and each party should have independent counsel or a meaningful opportunity for legal advice.

---

101. *See* Sean Hannon Williams, *Postnuptial Agreements*, 2007 WIS. L. REV. 827 (2007).

Creating a Valid Premarital or Postmarital Agreement 4

§4.01 Overview

This chapter addresses the substance of the elements of a valid premarital or postmarital agreement. The prerequisites for a valid premarital agreement range from the most minimal requirements for procedural fairness, which some states equate almost exclusively to voluntariness or financial disclosure, to more substantial requirements, which may include opportunity for advice of counsel and substantive fairness. In many states the standards for validity of a postmarital agreement are somewhat more demanding than for a premarital agreement. Nevertheless, in disputes about both types of agreement, courts are willing to tolerate a process and substance highly favorable to the proponent of the agreement. This chapter discusses the meaning and interpretation courts have given to the elements of validity without regard to which elements are required by which states. Both the lawyer for the proponent and the lawyer for a disadvantaged party should be mindful of the benefits of an agreement that is fair to the latter. This chapter considers process and terms to further that goal.

§4.02 Legal Capacity

A party who lacks capacity to understand the nature and consequences of a transaction, or to make a rational judgment about it, is incompetent to enter into a valid contract.[1] Legal capacity to contract means that a person "possesses sufficient mind to understand, in a reasonable manner, the nature, extent, character, and the effect

1. *Bailey v. Bailey*, 54 Va. Ct. App. 209, 677 S.E.2d 56 (2009); *Wilkes v. Estate of Wilkes*, 305 Mont. 335, 27 P.3d 433 (2001).

of the act or transaction. . . ."[2] Lack of capacity sufficient to void a contract must stem from a mental illness or defect, including congenital deficiencies in intelligence, deterioration caused by old age, and brain damage.[3] Mental illness alone is not sufficient to establish lack of legal capacity.[4] There must be some evidence of irrational or unintelligent behavior to warrant such a finding.[5] A decision that is merely unwise or eccentric does not, without more, establish incapacity.[6] Courts have held the following not to constitute incapacity: immaturity, lack of experience regarding the subject matter, poor judgment, dependence on prescription drugs or alcohol, developmental disability, and emotional distress.[7] The question of legal capacity goes to the ability of the party to understand the transaction, not whether he or she actually did so.[8]

"Capacity to contract may be partial and its existence in respect of a particular transaction may depend upon the nature of the transaction or upon other circumstances."[9] Where one party is incapacitated to some degree at the time of execution of a premarital agreement, a postmarital agreement, or an amendment to either type of agreement, and where the incapacity provides an opportunity for the other party to take advantage of the situation, the instrument will be vulnerable to attack.[10] A party with diminished capacity may be more vulnerable to duress, undue influence, or fraud.[11] Moreover, he or she may have come to rely on the other party to the transaction to such a degree that a fiduciary or confidential relationship has come into being. These facts, if known to counsel, call for extra caution.[12]

Contractual legal capacity requires a higher level of functioning than testamentary capacity, or as a Massachusetts court put it, "something more than a transient surge of lucidity."[13] It involves not merely comprehension of what is going on, but an ability to comprehend the nature and quality of the transaction, together with an understanding of its significance and

---

2. *Knowlton v. Mudd*, 116 Idaho 262, 264, 775 P.2d 154, 156 (Ct. App. 1989); *see also Butler v. Harrison*, 578 A.2d 1098, 1100 (D.C. 1990).

3. Restatement Second of Contracts §§ 12, 15 cmt. b. (1981); *Wilkes*, 305 Mont. 335, 27 P.3d 433.

4. *See In re Estate of Menahem*, 16 Misc. 3d 1125A, 847 N.Y.S.2d 903 (S. Ct. 2007); *but see Harris v. Harris*, 2022 Mich. App. LEXIS 6337 (unpub.) (postmarital agreement void where wife suffered from emotional problems and depression).

5. Restatement Second of Contracts § 15 cmt. c (1981).

6. *Proceedings of the Conference on Ethical Issues in Representing Older Clients; Report of the Working Group on Client Capacity*, 62 Fordham L. Rev. 1003, 1005 (Mar. 1994).

7. *In re Marriage of Sheynkman*, 2005 Wash. App. LEXIS 2428 (unpub.); *Adams v. Adams*, 414 Pa. Super. 634, 607 A.2d 1116 (1992); *Drewry v. Drewry*, 8 Va. App. 460, 467, 383 S.E.2d 12, 15 (1989); *Nasifoglu v. Nasifoglu*, 224 A.D.2d 504, 637 N.Y.S.2d 792 (1996); *Nigro v. Nigro*, 371 Pa. Super. 625, 538 A.2d 910 (1988); *Hughes v. Hughes*, 96 N.M. 719, 634 P.2d 1271 (1981).

8. *Wilkes*, 305 Mont. 335, 27 P.3d 433.

9. Restatement Second of Contracts § 12(1) (1981).

10. *See Bailey v. Bailey*, 54 Va. Ct. App. 209, 677 S.E.2d 56 (2009) (postmarital agreement was invalid due to husband's lack of capacity where he had long-standing psychosis and signed during weekend furlough from psychiatric hospital).

11. Restatement Second of Contracts § 12 cmt. a.

12. *See Goodwin v. Webb*, 568 S.E.2d 311 (N.C. Ct. App. 2002) (wife may have lacked mental capacity to ratify marital settlement signed under duress where she had been subjected to years of physical abuse and had somewhat low IQ).

13. *Farnum v. Silvano*, 27 Mass. App. Ct. 536, 538, 540 N.E.2d 202, 204 (1989); *see also In re Estate of Goldberg*, 153 Misc. 2d 560, 582 N.Y.S.2d 617 (S. Ct. 1992) (rejecting lower standard of testamentary capacity and opting for higher contractual capacity standard for execution of postmarital contract to cancel premarital agreement).

consequences.[14] The Massachusetts Court of Appeals discussed the significance of a party's ability to understand a contract in the context of his or her own particular circumstances. A woman in failing mental and physical health contracted to sell her home to a trusted friend for half its value at a time when she needed cash for nursing home care. The court pointed out the distinction between the seller's awareness that she was selling her house—that is, her "awareness of the surface of [the] transaction,"[15]—and her failure, due to mental impairment, to appreciate the unreasonableness of selling it for far less than fair value given her needs.

Physical illness, infirmity, old age, or forgetfulness do not necessarily mean a person is incapable of entering into a premarital or postmarital contract.[16] But they do suggest that additional caution may be warranted to clearly establish capacity at a point when evidence is readily available. A party's capacity may be established through the testimony of lay witnesses, including those who observed the execution of the agreement, as well as through medical professionals.[17] If there is any question about a client's capacity, it may be appropriate for his or her lawyer to obtain an opinion from the client's physician, and in appropriate cases, from a psychiatrist, before execution. Further, if possible, the agreement should be notarized and witnessed by disinterested persons, even if these formalities are not required by state law, so as to provide a body of testimony, if needed, as to the party's capacity at execution. In some cases, it may be appropriate to tape-record or videotape the execution of the agreement and the interchanges that precede it and to ask each party to explain on the record his or her understanding of the document about to be executed.[18]

The question of legal capacity is closely related to other components of the process. As the court pointed out in *In re Estate of Goldberg*,[19] a significant factor in assessing the capacity of a party to a transaction who may have some deficit is whether that person had the advice and guidance of independent counsel.[20] As discussed further below,[21] independent counsel for the weaker party is the single most important factor in creating an enforceable premarital or postmarital agreement. Where there is any doubt about the legal capacity of an unrepresented party, counsel should do everything within reason to cause that party to obtain independent advice.

§4.03 CONSIDERATION FOR POSTMARITAL AGREEMENT

The law among the states varies as to whether consideration is a requirement for a postmarital agreement.[22] Insofar as consideration is required by governing law, consideration can con-

---

14. *Farnum*, 27 Mass. App. Ct. at 538, 540 N.E.2d at 204.
15. *Id.* at 539, 204.
16. *Logsdon v. Logsdon*, 412 Ill. 19, 104 N.E.2d 622 (1952).
17. *Drewry v. Drewry*, 8 Va. App. at 467–68, 383 S.E.2d at 15.
18. *See DeMatteo v. DeMatteo*, 436 Mass. 18, 762 N.E.2d 797 (2002).
19. 153 Misc. 2d 560, 582 N.Y.S.2d 617 (S. Ct. 1992).
20. See Miller v. Miller, 2022 Md. App. LEXIS 813 (unpub.) (rejecting claim of incapacity based on wife's self-diagnosed postpartum depression, pain due to three root canals, and unbalanced hormones, where wife had independent counsel).
21. See Section 4.06.
22. See Appendix B(2), State Law Summary: Postmarital Agreements.

sist of mutual waivers of rights at death or divorce.[23] This is especially the case when the members of the couple are mature, have independent resources, or have children they wish to provide for. When parties are estranged as a result of one spouse's marital misconduct, the other spouse's willingness to attempt reconciliation, or to forbear from filing suit for divorce, can constitute adequate consideration.[24] When there is a big wealth disparity and the agreement provides little or nothing for the disadvantaged party, it may fail for lack of consideration. The adequacy of consideration for a postmarital agreement and the question of substantive fairness are closely related and overlapping questions.[25]

§4.04 VOLUNTARINESS

(a) Criteria to Determine Voluntariness

Voluntariness is the essential requirement for validity of all premarital and postmarital agreements, consistent with general contract law principles. A voluntary act is one that results from "the free and unrestrained will of the person."[26] A voluntary act is one that is done "intentionally; without coercion."[27] At a minimum, voluntariness in connection with a contract means that the party acted out of his or her own volition, that he or she had a meaningful choice whether to execute it.[28] A contract is not voluntarily executed if it is the product of fraud, duress, or undue influence.[29] A court may consider a number of factors in determining whether a challenging party executed an agreement voluntarily,[30] including:

- Whether the disadvantaged party got independent legal advice or had the opportunity to do so;
- Whether the economically dominant party made adequate financial disclosure;
- The opportunity of the disadvantaged party to negotiate better terms than initially proposed;
- Whether the parties, directly or through counsel, actually engaged in any negotiations and whether the stronger party made changes to the agreement as a result;

23. *Kornegay v. Robinson*, 360 N.C. 640, 637 S.E.2d 516 (2006).
24. *Lloyd v. Niceta*, 255 Md. App. 663, 284 A.3d 808 (Ct. Spec. App. 2022); *Labuz v. Labuz*, 54 N.E.3d 886 (Ill. App. 2016).
25. See Section 4.09.
26. *Bonds v. Bonds*, 24 Cal. 4th 1, 16, 5 P.3d 815, 823 (2000); *see also Sheshunoff v. Sheshunoff*, 172 S.W.3d 686 (Tex. Ct. App. 2005); *Panossian v. Panossian*, 172 A.D.2d 811, 569 N.Y.S.2d 182 (1991).
27. *In re Marriage of Shanks*, 758 N.W.2d 506, 512 (Iowa 2008).
28. *Dornemann v. Dornemann*, 48 Conn. App. 502, 850 A.2d 273 (2004); *Button v. Button*, 131 Wis. 2d 84, 91, 388 N.W.2d 546, 551 (1986).
29. *Moore v. Moore*, 383 S.W.3d 190 (Tex. Ct. App., 5th Dist. 2012); *DeLorean v. DeLorean*, 211 N.J. Super. 432, 511 A.2d 1257 (1986).
30. *L.R.O. v. N.D.O.*, 148 Haw. 336, 475 P.3d 1167 (2020); *Skaates v. Kayser*, 333 Mich. App. 61, 959 N.W.2d 33 (2020); *Francavilla v. Francavilla*, 969 So. 2d 522 (Fla. App. 2007); *In re Estate of Kinney*, 733 N.W.2d 118 (Minn. 2007); *Kornegay v. Robinson*, 360 N.C. 640, 637 S.E.2d 516 (2006); *Cannon v. Cannon*, 384 Md. 537, 865 A.2d 563 (2005); *In re Estate of Hollett*, 150 N.H. 39, 834 A.2d 348 (2003); *Bonds v. Bonds*, 24 Cal. 4th 1, 5 P.3d 815 (2000); *Miles v. Werle*, 977 S.W.2d 297 (Mo. Ct. App. 1998); *In re Marriage of Yager*, 155 Or. App. 407, 963 P.2d 137 (1998); *In re Estate of Lutz*, 563 N.W.2d 90 (N.D. 1997); *Parr v. Parr*, 635 N.E.2d 1124 (Ind. Ct. App. 1994); *Lebeck*, 188 N.M. 367, 881 P.2d 727; *Button*, 131 Wis. 2d 84, 91, 388 N.W.2d 546, 551; *DeLorean*, 211 N.J. Super. 432, 511 A.2d 1257; *Laird v. Laird*, 597 P.2d 463 (Wyo. 1979).

- The timing of presentation of a premarital agreement in relation to the wedding;
- Whether the agreement was presented without any prior warning;
- The parties' intelligence and education levels;
- The parties' prior experience, especially in a prior divorce, the probate of an estate, or a business or profession;
- The parties' relative bargaining power in terms of their economic resources, age, sophistication, education, employment, and experience;
- Whether the disadvantaged party actually had independent advice of any kind from any source;
- Whether each party had adequate time to review the agreement;
- Whether each party understood the terms of the agreement;
- Whether each party understood the marital rights he or she would have if the parties married without an agreement or, in the case of a postmarital agreement, stayed married without an agreement.[31]

Rarely will a single factor cause a court to invalidate an agreement for lack of voluntariness. Indeed, when a court refuses to enforce an agreement, there is usually a combination of egregious factors.[32] The lawyer for the proponent can reduce the risk for his or her client by working to create a combination of factors supportive of voluntariness, such as adequate time, a good financial disclosure, access to counsel, and opportunity to negotiate.

(b) Actual Negotiation or Opportunity to Negotiate Terms

An actual give-and-take negotiation indicates an agreement is a contract between equals.[33] Thus, a challenging party's active role in shaping the terms of an agreement—for example, by proposing the original terms, by negotiating for substantive changes in the proponent's draft agreement, or merely by marking up a draft—virtually negates a claim of duress, undue influence, or lack of voluntariness.[34] This is so even when the proponent does not accept

31. See discussion of knowledge of marital rights in Section 4.07.

32. *See, e.g.*, *In re Estate of Eichstadt*, 983 N.W.2d 572 (S.D. 2022) (wife signed premarital agreement involuntarily where husband drove her to lawyer's office without telling her reason, lied to his lawyer that he had told her in advance of plan for premarital agreement, paced in lawyer's office while wife attempted to read it, wife had 8th grade education and was dependent on husband, and his lawyer did not explain terms); *Moore v. Moore*, 383 S.W.3d 151 (Tex. Ct. App., 5th Dist. 2012) (husband's misrepresentation about purpose of agreement, his financial circumstances, and that wife's lawyer had seen and approved changes, his hiding agreement until hours before wedding and hand-picking her lawyer rendered premarital agreement involuntary).

33. *Cannon v. Cannon*, 384 Md. 537, 865 A.2d 563 (2005); *Dornemann v. Dornemann*, 48 Conn. App. 5102, 850 A.3d. 273 (2004).

34. *See Labuz v. Labuz*, 54 N.E.3d 886 (Ill. Ct. App., 3d Dist. 2016) (postmarital agreement that was extremely unfavorable to husband was valid where the product of a negotiation); *McLeod v. McLeod*, 145 So. 3d 1246 (Miss. Ct. App. 2014) (premarital agreement was not product of duress where parties negotiated terms over several weeks); *Edwards v. Edwards*, 16 Neb. App. 297, 744 N.W.2d 243 (2008) (premarital agreement not product of duress where both parties had counsel and negotiated changes); *Francavilla*, 969 So. 2d 522 (Fla. App. 2007) (premarital agreement valid where negotiated over several months, both parties had counsel, challenging party got favorable changes); *Winchester v. McCue*, 91 Conn. App. 721, 882 A.2d 143 (2005) (premarital agreement valid where parties negotiated through seven drafts); *see also Gottlieb v. Gottlieb*, 138 A.D.3d 30, 25 N.Y.S.3d 90 (2016); *In re Marriage of Murphy*, 359 Ill. App. 3d 289, 834 N.E.2d 56 (2005); *Reed v. Reed*, 265 Mich. App. 131, 693 N.W.2d 825 (2005); *Mallen v. Mallen*, 280 Ga. 43, 622 S.E.2d 812 (2005); *DeMatteo v. DeMatteo*, 436 Mass. 18, 762 N.E.2d 797 (2002); *In re Marriage of Yager*, 155 Or. App. 407, 963 P.2d 137 (1998); *Lemaster v. Dutton*, 694 So. 2d 1360 (Ala. Civ. App. 1996); *In re Marriage of Gardner*, 190 Wis. 2d 217, 234, 527 N.W.2d 701, 706

every change proposed. For example, in *Spiegel v. Spiegel*,[35] the wife's lawyer was able to negotiate three changes to the husband's proposed premarital agreement, but the husband rejected other changes requested by the wife. The court upheld the premarital agreement over the wife's claims of duress and undue influence. Changes made as part of a negotiation need not be significant. That a party obtained any changes before signing tends to show the party was acting out of his or her unrestrained volition and not as a result of undue influence or duress. For example, in *Howell v. Landry*,[36] the court upheld a premarital agreement over an involuntariness claim where the husband presented it to the wife the night before the parties were scheduled to leave for Las Vegas to get married. The wife was initially reluctant to sign, but she made two changes to the agreement and signed.[37]

An invitation to the recipient to propose changes tends to show a premarital agreement was voluntarily executed even if no changes were in fact made. For example, in *Lebeck v. Lebeck*,[38] the husband, a lawyer, drafted the agreement, gave it to the wife, and asked her to have it reviewed by a lawyer of her choice and to either sign it or let him know which part of the agreement was unacceptable to her. She signed without proposing any changes. The court rejected her claim of duress and undue influence.

Even when the agreement is presented as a take-it-or-leave-it proposal, a party's unsuccessful attempt to negotiate changes negates a claim of duress or involuntariness. For example, in *In re Estate of Arbeitman*,[39] the husband gave the wife the premarital agreement, told her to take it to a lawyer, and said that she must sign it before they married. The husband rejected her lawyer's proposed changes, and her lawyer advised her not to sign. She signed several hours before the wedding. Her actions belied her claim of duress.

It stands to reason that the more time the economically weaker party has to consider the proposed terms, which necessarily expands that party's opportunity to negotiate better terms and to consult independent counsel, the more likely a court will uphold the agreement if challenged.[40] It will generally be in the interest of the economically stronger party to accept some proposed changes to favor the other party. As the cited cases illustrate, when a party proposes changes and gets some of them, and then agrees to sign, that is powerful evidence of voluntariness.

(1994); *Simeone v. Simeone*, 380 Pa. Super. 37, 551 A.2d 219 (1988), *aff'd*, 525 Pa. 392, 581 A.2d 162 (1990); *Liebelt v. Liebelt*, 801 P.2d 52 (Idaho Ct. App. 1990).

35. *Spiegel v. Spiegel*, 553 N.W.2d 522 (Iowa 1996).

36. *Howell v. Landry*, 96 N.C. App. 516, 386 S.E.2d 610 (1989).

37. *See also Kellar v. Estate of Kellar*, 172 Wash. App. 562, 291 P.3d 906 (2012); *Friezo v. Friezo*, 281 Conn. 166, 914 A.2d 533 (2007); *Marsh v. Marsh*, 949 S.W.2d 734 (Tex. App. 1997).

38. *Lebeck v. Lebeck*, 118 N.M. 367, 881 P.2d 727 (Ct. App. 1994).

39. *In re Estate of Arbeitman*, 886 S.W.2d 644 (Mo. Ct. App. 1994).

40. *See Simeone v. Simeone*, 380 Pa. Super. 37, 551 A.2d 219 (1988); *Warren v. Warren*, 169 Ill. App. 3d 226, 523 N.E.2d 680 (1988); *In re Marriage of Knoll*, 65 Or. App. 484, 671 P.2d 718 (1983).

§4.05 DURESS, COERCION, UNDUE INFLUENCE, AND OVERREACHING

(a) What Constitutes Duress, Coercion, Undue Influence, or Overreaching, and What Does Not: Overview

A premarital agreement that is the product of duress, coercion, undue influence, or overreaching is not voluntary.[41] Often challengers assert one or more, or all, of these as a basis for voiding an agreement.

Duress is "a 'condition where one is induced by a wrongful act or threat of another to make a contract under circumstances which deprive him [or her] of the exercise of free will.'"[42] A finding of duress requires there to have been affirmative misconduct on the part of the proponent.[43] Pressure or stress from outside forces does not constitute duress.[44] For example, in *Marriage of Hall*,[45] the mere fact that the husband was in jail did not constitute duress so as to require the court to void a postmarital reconciliation agreement. A claim of duress in the execution of a contract requires both a wrongful or unlawful threat and that the challenging party had no reasonable alternative.[46] A threat to do something the proponent had a legal right to do, such as cancel the wedding, is not duress.[47]

When parties are already married, one party's undue pressure that forces a spouse to choose between the family and a disadvantageous postmarital agreement can constitute duress.[48] Other bad conduct, if sufficiently oppressive and threatening, can also constitute duress.[49]

Duress and coercion are closely related but not identical concepts, although often used interchangeably. As one court noted:

> [W]hile "duress" generally occurs by means of actual physical force or threatened physical force to one's person or threats to one's property or reputation, "coercion" is "generally defined more broadly to include undue influence and other lesser forms of compulsion."
>
> "Coercion" occurs where the defending spouse, through undue influence or moral or economic force, compels the challenging spouse to sign a prenuptial agreement

41. *Blonstein v. Blonstein*, 831 S.W.2d 468 (Tex. App.), *writ denied*, 848 S.W.2d 82 (Tex. 1992); *Howell*, 96 N.C. App. at 527, 386 S.E.2d at 617.
42. *In re Estate of Arbeitman*, 886 S.W.2d at 647.
43. *Vanheusden v. Vanheusden*, 2005 Mich. App. LEXIS 643 (unpub.).
44. *Balogh v. Balogh*, 134 Haw. 29, 332 P.3d 631 (2014); *Hood v. Hood*, 72 So. 3d 666 (Ala. Ct. Civ. App. 2011).
45. 27 N.E.3d 281 (Ind. Ct. App. 2015).
46. *In re Marriage of Shanks*, 758 N.W.2d 506 (Iowa 2008).
47. *See Dornemann v. Dornemann*, 48 Conn. App. 502, 850 A.2d. 273 (2004).
48. *See Petracca v. Petracca*, 101 A.D.3d 695, 956 N.Y.S.2d 77 (2012); *Martin v. Martin*, 287 S.W.3d 260 (Tex. Ct. Civ. App., 5th Dist. 2009); *Pacelli v. Pacelli*, 319 N.J. Super. 185, 725 A.2d 56 (1999); *but see Balogh v. Balogh*, 134 Haw. 29. 332 P.3d 631 (2014) (threat to divorce is not an improper threat amounting to duress, as spouse has legal right to seek divorce).
49. *See Casto v. Casto*, 508 So. 2d 330 (Fla. 1987) (husband's threat to blow up house and pour bleach on wife's clothes if she did not sign constituted duress in execution of postmarital agreement).

> under circumstances which, from a subjective viewpoint, evidence that the challenging spouse did not act of his or her own free will.[50]

Another court defines duress as: "Coercion by means of threats or other circumstances that destroy the victim's free will."[51]

Like duress and coercion, undue influence and overreaching are related concepts and are often used together. "Undue influence is influence that deprives one person of his or her freedom of choice and substitutes the will of another in its place."[52] When one party's dominance has so overreached the other party as to enable him or her to obtain an unfair or an unconscionable advantage, a court may find undue influence and refuse enforcement.[53] Undue influence in the making of an agreement, or an amendment to an agreement, can exist where one party's mental capacity is diminished by age or poor health and the other party obtains an advantage for grossly inadequate consideration,[54] or where a party deliberately misrepresents key facts.[55]

A party's decision to enter into a bad bargain does not constitute undue influence on the part of the other party to the agreement.[56] Similarly, a party's pursuit of his or her own objectives in obtaining a premarital agreement does not constitute undue influence on the part of the other party.[57]

An agreement may be the product of overreaching when the result is unfair or when it was brought about by unfair conduct.[58] A New York Court described overreaching as "concealment of facts, misrepresentation, cunning, cheating, sharp practice, or some other form of deception. . . ."[59] However, to warrant voiding the agreement, the challenging party must also prove the overreaching resulted in manifestly unfair terms. When a spouse exploits the other spouse's psychiatric condition that leaves him or her susceptible to undue influence or overreaching, and extracts a postmarital agreement highly unfavorable to the weaker spouse, the combination of procedural irregularity and gross disparity of terms can be enough for a court to void an agreement.[60] Similarly, when one spouse in a marriage has come to rely on

---

50. *Bates v. Bates*, 345 So. 3d 328, 335 (Fla. Ct. App. 3d Dist. 2022) (internal citations omitted).

51. *Kremer v. Kremer*, 912 N.E.2d 617, 628 (Minn. 2018); see also *Lebeck v. Lebeck*, 118 N.M. 367, 881 P.2d 727 (Ct. App. 1994); *Howell v. Landry*, 96 N.C. App. 516, 386 S.E.2d 610 (1989).

52. *Spiegel v. Spiegel*, 553 N.W. 522 (Iowa 1996); *Howell*, 96 N.C. App. at 516.

53. *Carnell v. Carnell*, 398 So. 2d 503, 506 (Fla. Dist. Ct. App. 1981).

54. *Ayers v. Shaffer*, 748 S.E.2d. 83 (Va. 2013).

55. See, e.g., *In re Marriage of Sarancic*, 2020 Il. App. LEXIS 870 (unpub.) (premarital agreement invalid where wife's first language was Bosnian, process and terms were unconscionable, husband told wife that everyone in America has one).

56. *Carnell v. Carnell*, 398 So. 2d 503 (Fla. Dist. Ct. App. 1981).

57. *See Carnell*, 398 So. 2d at 506 (husband insisted on premarital agreement to overcome wife's resistance to remarriage; generous provision for her did not evidence undue influence); *Matuga*, 600 N.E.2d at 141 (wife initiated premarital agreement to protect her property for daughter and agreement achieved her goal; no undue influence); *Hoffman v. Hoffman*, 100 A.D.2d 704, 474 N.Y.S.2d 621 (1984) (claim of fraud, duress, and overreaching negated by evidence opponent originally suggested premarital agreement); *Babb v. Babb*, 270 Ark. 289, 604 S.W.2d 574 (Ct. App. 1980) (wife sought agreement to protect her separate property; agreement valid).

58. *Stewart v. Stewart*, 214 Md. App. 458, 76 A.3d 1221 (2013).

59. *Gottlieb v. Gottlieb*, 138 A.D.3d 30, 37, 25 N.Y.S.3d 90, 97 (2016); *see also Spiegel v. Spiegel*, 206 A.D.3d 1178, 170 N.Y.S.3d 295 (2022).

60. *See Pramagioulis v. Pramagioulis*, 2011 Va. App. LEXIS 20.

and trust the other in the management of marital financial affairs, a postmarital agreement highly disadvantageous to him or her may not hold up if the managing spouse does not handle the process in a fair manner.[61]

A misrepresentation as to the party's objective in seeking a postmarital agreement may constitute overreaching or undue influence such as to undermine its validity.[62] As one court observed, a married person not contemplating divorce may be less likely to investigate the bona fides of the other spouse's actions than would a spouse who is separated or about to be separated:[63]

> [L]ess evidence is required in such cases to establish fraud, oppression, or deception than if the parties had been dealing at arm's length. . . .[64]

(b) Timing of Presentation of Premarital Agreement

It appears to be fairly common for parties to wait until the last minute to execute a premarital agreement. When the agreement was executed is of little consequence, as negotiations that begin well before the wedding can easily last until the day before. More important is when the challenging party saw the agreement for the first time. Yet, even the close proximity of first presentation of a proposed agreement to the scheduled wedding ceremony, standing alone, does not constitute duress.[65] When a premarital agreement was presented close to the wedding with no prior warning, courts have sometimes made a finding of involuntariness based significantly on timing. Even in those cases, however, there were other factors. For example, in *Bauer v. Bauer*,[66] the wife first learned the husband expected her to sign a premarital agreement when he stopped at his lawyer's office as they were leaving town to get married. The wife had no opportunity to consult with independent counsel, and the husband failed to make

---

61. *See Austin v. Austin*, 237 Ariz. 201, 348 P.3d 897 (2015); *Izzo v. Izzo*, 2010 Tex. App. LEXIS 3623 (unpub.).

62. *In re Marriage of Richardson*, 237 Ill. App. 3d 1067, 606 N.E.2d 56 (1992) (husband's misrepresentation of intent to reconcile to induce wife to sign postmarital agreement one factor rendering agreement invalid); *Fogg v. Fogg*, 409 Mass. 531, 536, 567 N.E.2d 921, 923 (1991) (wife misrepresented intent to stay married to induce husband to make property settlement favorable to her; postmarital agreement invalid); *see also Crawford v. Crawford*, 524 N.W.2d 833 (N.D. 1994) (husband's misrepresentation that house would be foreclosed, inducing wife to agree to husband receiving house and custody of four children, rendered separation agreement unconscionable); *In re Marriage of Frederick*, 218 Ill. App. 3d 533, 578 N.E.2d 612 (1991) (wife's execution of letter agreeing to husband's transfer of assets to revocable trust was a sham to defraud her of marital rights where husband did not disclose consultation with divorce lawyer); *Church v. Church*, 96 N.M. 388, 630 P.2d 1243 (Ct. App. 1982) (wife's claim husband obtained financial support from her for medical education by false statements re: future together stated cause of action); *Blaising v. Mills*, 176 Ind. App. 141, 374 N.E.2d 1166 (1978) (former husband's false representations to wife that they would reconcile to induce her to reconvey property awarded to her in divorce rendered transaction voidable as product of undue influence).

63. *Estate of Harber*, 104 Ariz. 79, 88, 449 P.2d 7, 16 (1969).

64. *Estate of Gab*, 364 N.W.2d 924 (S.D. 1985).

65. L.R.O. v. N.D.O., 148 Haw. 336, 475 P.3d 1167 (2020); *Biliouris v. Biliouris*, 67 Mass. App. Ct. 149, 852 N.E.2d 687 (2006); *Yannalfo v. Yannalfo*, 147 N.H. 597, 794 A.2d 795 (2002); *Marsh v. Marsh*, 949 S.W.2d 734 (Tex. App. 1997); *In re Estate of Arbeitman*, 886 S.W.2d 644 (Mo. Ct. App. 1994).

66. 1 Or. App. 504, 464 P.2d 710 (1970).

complete disclosure of his assets.[67] In *Lutgert v. Lutgert*,[68] the husband sprang the premarital agreement on the wife and demanded she sign it hours before the wedding after elaborate plans had been finalized. The only lawyer the wife had the opportunity to consult was the husband's lawyer.[69]

When the proponent discusses the premarital agreement with the other party, even in general terms, well in advance of the wedding so that it does not come as a complete surprise, the close proximity of execution to wedding may not render the agreement unenforceable. For example, in *In re Marriage of Adams*,[70] the court held a premarital agreement signed one hour before the wedding was not the product of duress where the husband told the wife months before he would not remarry without a premarital agreement and the draft agreement was sent to her lawyer during the week before the wedding. In *Osborne v. Osborne*,[71] the court upheld a premarital agreement seen by the husband for the first time just hours before the wedding. The wife had told the husband several times before the marriage that she intended to have her money pass to her children, and they had had a general discussion about a premarital agreement. The court concluded the husband executed the agreement voluntarily and that it was not the product of duress.[72]

When the proponent merely said he or she would not marry without a premarital agreement, that has often been sufficient warning an agreement is coming to negate a claim that the proximity of execution to the wedding rendered it the product of duress.[73] Even where

67. *See also C.S. v. L.S.*, 41 Misc. 3d 1209(A), 980 N.Y.S.2d 274 (Sup. Ct. Nassau Cnty., 2013) (husband presented premarital agreement several days before wedding, after wife had given up apartment, refused to negotiate with hand-picked lawyer, and terms extremely harsh; agreement invalid); *Mamot v. Mamot*, 283 Neb. 659, 813 N.W.2d 440 (2012) (premarital agreement was product of coercion where husband presented agreement five days before wedding, insisted wife sign it that day, wife had no opportunity for legal advice, and there was significant disparity in bargaining power); *Pember v. Shapiro*, 794 N.W.2d 435 (N.D. 2011) (premarital agreement invalid where first seen by husband five hours before wedding and he had no access to legal advice); *Cassidy v. Cassidy*, 356 S.W.3d 339 (Mo. Ct. App. 2011) (agreement invalid where presented six hours before wedding and wife had no time to get legal advice); *In re Estate of Hollett*, 150 N.H. 39, 834 A.2d 348 (2003) (husband's delay in presenting agreement until two days before large wedding, after guests had arrived, coupled with disparity of age, experience, education and bargaining power, and other factors, rendered agreement involuntary); *Hoag v. Dick*, 799 A.2d 391 (Me. 2002) (agreement presented on day of wedding and signed in church parking lot, with no opportunity for independent counsel, and where wife waived all property and support rights was invalid); *but see Hood v. Hood*, 72 So. 3d 666 (Ala. Ct. Civ. App. 2011) (husband presented premarital agreement in his lawyer's office on the way to the courthouse; agreement valid).

68. *Lutgert v. Lutgert*, 338 So. 2d 1111 (Fla. Dist. Ct. App. 1976).

69. *See also Kremer v. Kremer*, 912 N.W.2d 617 (Minn. 2018) (premarital agreement was product of overreaching where husband intentionally created situation, due to timing of presentation, where wife was unable to get legal advice from lawyer of her choice as required by Minnesota common law): *Zawahiri v. Alwattar*, 2008 Ohio App. LEXIS 2928 (unpub.) (Muslim marriage contract presented on day of wedding was product of overreaching); *In re Marriage of Maifield*, 2004 Iowa App. LEXIS 17 (unpub.) (premarital agreement presented for first time on night before wedding during dinner party, no meaningful opportunity for legal advice, and written in legalistic terms, was procured in unfair process and therefore invalid).

70. *In re Marriage of Adams*, 240 Kan. 315, 729 P.2d 1151 (1986).

71. 384 Mass. 591, 428 N.E.2d 810 (1981).

72. *See also In re Marriage of Leathers*, 309 Or. 625, 789 P.2d 263 (1990) (premarital agreement valid where discussed in general terms over extended period although presented to wife for first time evening before departure for Reno to be married); *Simeone v. Simeone*, 380 Pa. Super. 37, 551 A.3d. 219 (1988) (premarital agreement presented for first time on day of wedding was not product of duress where wife and husband negotiated terms over months, changes made at wife's request).

73. *See Elgar v. Elgar*, 238 Conn. 839, 679 A.2d 937 (1996); *In re Marriage of Adams*, 240 Kan. 315, 729 P.2d 1151 (1986).

the opposing party rejected the proponent's initial overture for a premarital agreement, a late presentation will not necessarily be deemed to create duress so long as the party had sufficient opportunity to obtain advice.[74] Even a late presentation with no prior warning will not necessarily render an agreement invalid if the party had the opportunity to protect his or her interests and chose not to.[75]

A late presentation will not cause the agreement to be deemed involuntary if the wedding can be postponed. For example, in *Friezo v. Friezo*,[76] the parties postponed the wedding at least once and could have postponed it further if necessary to allow the wife more time to consider the proposed premarital agreement. The court held the agreement was executed voluntarily. Similarly, when parties have not set a date for the wedding as of when the agreement is executed, the fact that they get married soon after signing is not evidence of duress.[77]

(c) Threat Not to Marry

A threat not to go through with the wedding, standing alone, does not constitute duress in the execution of a premarital agreement.[78] Indeed, such a rule would effectively invalidate most premarital agreements.[79] To constitute duress, a threat must be wrongful though it need not be unlawful.[80] Because neither party is required to marry, a statement that a party will marry only with a premarital agreement is not wrongful.[81] A premarital agreement is often an implicit prerequisite for marriage.[82] Thus, when a party merely states the obvious, this cannot constitute duress.[83] "A party's statement requiring [a premarital agreement] as a condition of marriage is not coercion. The other party is free to leave the relationship if an agreement is objectionable."[84] The social embarrassment of having to cancel a wedding is not sufficiently bad as to render that choice unreasonable under most circumstances. Only where the threat not to marry, implicit in every proposal for a premarital agreement, is coupled with other factors have courts found duress.[85]

---

74. *See Elgar*, 238 Conn. 839 (premarital agreement presented two days before wedding not product of duress, although wife refused to consider premarital agreement when first suggested by husband two months earlier, and nothing said about it in interim); *Spiegel v. Spiegel*, 553 N.W.2d 309 (Iowa 1996) (wife rejected premarital agreement five months before wedding, next mentioned 10 days before, and presented five days before; premarital agreement not signed under duress).

75. *See Kornegay v. Robinson*, 360 N.C. 640, 637 S.E.2d 516 (2006) (agreement was voluntary where wife signed without reading and parties married the same day); *Wiley v. Iverson*, 295 Mont. 511, 985 P.2d 1176 (1999) (agreement voluntary where wife saw agreement and signed a day before wedding without reading).

76. 281 Conn. 166, 914 A.2d 533 (2007).

77. *See In the Matter of Nizhnikov & Nikhnikov*, 168 N.H. 525, 132 A.3d 412 (2016).

78. *Id.*; *Weinstein v. Weinstein*, 36 A.D.3d 797, 830 N.Y.S.2d 179 (2007); *Taylor v. Taylor*, 832 P.2d 429, 431 (Okla. Ct. App. 1991).

79. *Eager v. Eager*, 696 So. 2d 1235, 1236 (Fla. Dist. Ct. App. 1997).

80. *Spiegel v. Spiegel*, 553 N.W.2d 309 (Iowa 1996).

81. *Id.*; *see also In re Marriage of Adams*, 240 Kan. 315, 729 P.3d 1151 (1986); *Howell v. Landry*, 96 N.C. App. 516, 386 S.E.2d 610 (1989).

82. *Spiegel v. Spiegel*, 553 N.W.2d 309; *Howell v. Landry*, 96 N.C. App. at 529, 386 S.E.2d at 617–18.

83. *Osorno v. Osorno*, 76 S.W.3d 509 (Tex. App. 2002); *In re Marriage of Barnes*, 324 Ill. App. 3d 514, 755 N.E.2d 522 (2001); *Lebeck v. Lebeck*, 118 N.M. 367, 881 P.2d 727 (Ct. App. 1994); *Liebelt v. Liebelt*, 8010 2d 42 (Idaho Ct. App. 1990).

84. *In re Marriage of Gardner*, 190 Wis. 2d 217, 527 N.W.2d 701 (1994).

85. *See Hjortaas v. McCabe*, 656 So. 2d 168 (Fla. Dist. Ct. App. 1995) (premarital agreement presented to wife two days before wedding; husband made no asset disclosure and provisions for wife grossly inadequate).

(d) Pregnant Bride

Pregnancy, in and of itself, is insufficient to render a premarital agreement the product of duress or coercion. Claims of duress based on pregnancy have rarely succeeded.[86] For example, in *Hamilton v. Hamilton*,[87] the wife was 18, unemployed, pregnant, and "probably frightened."[88] However, she had a lawyer who advised her not to sign the premarital agreement and whose advice she rejected. The presence of counsel negated any claim of duress arising out of her circumstances. Similarly, in *Kilborn v. Kilborn*,[89] an Alabama case, the pregnant wife consulted a lawyer and the husband made full disclosure. The agreement was upheld. The Alabama court made clear that pregnancy alone did not constitute duress.[90] By contrast, in *Rowland v. Rowland*,[91] a premarital agreement signed by a pregnant 18-year-old was invalid, but only because the husband's lawyer met with both parties without advising the wife she had the right to independent counsel.

(e) Foreign-Born Fiancé(e); Language Barrier; Immigration Visa Set to Expire

A claim of limited English skills will not necessarily cause a court to invalidate a premarital agreement.[92] But, extra caution is in order. For example, in *In re Marriage of Gonzalez*,[93] the wife was born and lived most of her life in Guatemala, and the husband was Austrian. The husband explained the terms of the premarital agreement to her in Spanish, but his explanation was somewhat misleading. The court held she did not knowingly and intelligently waive

86. Courts rejected challenges in the following cases: *Gottlieb v. Gottlieb*, 138 A.D.3d 30, 25 N.Y.S.3d 90 (2016); *Teed v. Teed*, 2013 W. Va. LEXIS 491; *Reizfeld v. Reizfeld*, 125 Conn. App. 782, 40 A.3d 320 (2011); *Francavilla v. Francavilla*, 969 So. 2d 522 (Fla. App. 2007); *Bilouris v. Bilouris*, 67 Mass. App. Ct. 149, 852 N.E.2d 687 (2006); *Marsocci v. Marsocci*, 911 A.2d 690 (R.I. 2006); *Mallen v. Mallen*, 280 Ga. 43, 622 S.E.2d 812 (2005); *Dornemann v. Dornemann*, 48 Conn. App. 502, 850 A.3d 273 (2004); *Osorno*, 765 W.3d 509; *Hosea v. Hosea*, 1997 Mich. App. LEXIS 3829; *Lebeck v. Lebeck*, 118 N.M. 367, 881 P.2d 727 (Ct. App. 1994).

87. 404 Pa. Super. 533, 591 A.2d 720 (1991).

88. *Id.* at 537, 722.

89. 628 So. 2d 884 (Ala. Civ. App. 1993); *see also Reizfeld v. Reizfeld*, 125 Conn. App. 782, 40 A.3d 320 (2011).

90. A year earlier, in *Ex parte Williams*, 617 So. 2d 1032 (Ala. 1992), the Alabama Supreme Court reversed a summary judgment for a husband where he had refused to discuss marriage after learning the wife was pregnant until he presented her with a premarital agreement, and the only attorney who reviewed the agreement for the wife was a friend of the husband. There was a genuine issue of material fact as to whether the husband made full financial disclosure.

91. 74 Ohio App. 3d 415, 599 N.E.2d 315 (1991); *see also In re McCabe*, 975 N.W.2d 35 (Iowa Ct. App. 2022) (premarital agreement invalid where husband presented on day of wedding and wife eight months pregnant); *Dobre v. Dobre*, 2018 N.J. Super. LEXIS 931 (unpub.) (premarital agreement invalid where wife misrepresented purpose of agreement to foreign-born husband, failed to make adequate financial disclosure, and no evidence he had access to counsel); *McKoy v. McKoy*, 95 Va. Cir. 55, 2017 Va. Cir. LEXIS 1 (unpub.) (premarital agreement invalid where wife pregnant, process and substance were unconscionable).

92. L.R.O. v. N.D.O., 148 Haw. 336, 475 P.3d 1167 (2020); *In re Sunshine*, 51 A.D.2d 326, 381 N.Y.S.2d 260, *aff'd*, 40 N.Y.2d 875, 389 N.Y.S.2d 344 (1976); *Bonds v. Bonds*, 24 P.3d 815 (2000); *Panossian v. Panossian*, 172 A.D.2d 811, 569 N.Y.S.2d 182 (1991).

93. 561 N.W.2d 94 (Iowa Ct. App. 1997).

her right to share property acquired during the marriage.[94] In *Chaplain v. Chaplain*,[95] the appeals court reversed a summary judgment for the husband where the wife was a recent immigrant who claimed to have limited English fluency. At trial, the husband was able to prove her English was good enough to understand the premarital agreement and that she had plenty of time to read it. Thus, he ultimately prevailed, but only after two appeals.

California is the only state that mandates that a premarital agreement be written in a language in which the disadvantaged party is proficient.[96] Even without such a mandate, when a weaker party's first language is not English, the proponent's lawyer should inquire into his or her education, experience among English speakers, and English proficiency. Counsel may need to recommend the proponent have a proposed agreement translated unless it is clear that the weaker party is proficient in English.[97] The translation should be appended to the official English version. If possible, the proponent's lawyer could also help the fiancé(e) find a lawyer fluent in his/her language.[98]

A related problem is presented when the weaker party is in the United States on a fiancé(e) visa that will expire soon, putting pressure on the immigrant-fiancé(é) to accept proposed terms or leave the country. When the proponent waits until late to present the agreement, the fiancé(e) lacks resources to hire counsel, or the fiancée becomes pregnant, the agreement may be deemed the product of duress. For example, in *Holler v. Holler*,[99] a South Carolina court threw out a premarital agreement where the Ukrainian wife came into the United States on a fiancée visa. She did not have counsel, and the husband did not have

94. *See also In re Marriage of Sarancic*, 2020 Il. App. LEXIS 870 (unpub.) (premarital agreement invalid where wife's first language was Bosnian with little ability in English, process and terms were unconscionable); *Rabinovich v. Shevchenko*, 93 A.D.3d 774, 941 N.Y.S.2d 173 (2012) (agreement invalid as product of coercion where presented on day of wedding in English with no time to have it translated into wife's native language); *In re Marriage of Bays*, 2004 Cal. App. LEXIS 926 (unpub.) (premarital agreement invalid where wife's first language was Chinese, she did not have counsel, did not know of her community property rights, and husband gave her misleading explanation of purpose of agreement); *In re Estate of Halmaghi*, 184 Mich. App. 263, 457 N.W.2d 356 (1990) (premarital agreement executed in Germany between German husband and Romanian-born refugee with limited command of German was invalid where no evidence interpreter accurately explained wife's marital rights); *but see Barnett v. Barnett*, 2022 Ariz. App. LEXIS 661 (unpub.) (premarital agreement was not involuntary where wife, recent immigrant with limited command of English, signed in office of attorney husband hired for her, and despite fact husband told her it was standard procedure in U.S.).

95. *Chaplain v. Chaplain*, 54 Va. App. 762, 682 S.E.2d 108 (2009), *appeal after remand*, 2011 Va. App. LEXIS 15.

96. CAL. FAM. CODE § 1615(c)(3).

97. *See Reyes v. Reyes*, 2020 Conn. LEXIS 345 (unpub.) (premarital agreement unenforceable where husband did not have it translated, coupled with other process deficiencies, and was substantively unfair at divorce).

98. *See Ostapowicz v. Wisniewski*, 210 Conn. App. 401, 270 A.3d 145 (2022) (premarital agreement valid where Polish fiancée met with Polish-speaking lawyer who explained agreement and answered her questions).

99. 612 S.E.2d 469 (S.C. App. 2005); *see also Ziegler v. Natera*, 229 So. 3d 1240 (Fla. Ct. App. 2019).

the agreement translated.[100] By contrast, in *Wang v. Crumpacker*,[101] the premarital agreement, under which the wife waived spousal support, was signed two weeks before her visa expired and one week before the wedding. The wife had a lawyer who explained the terms, and the wife was actively involved in the negotiations and proposed changes. The Court upheld the agreement as voluntary and not unconscionable.[102]

(f) Emotional Distress (Didn't Want to Do It)

A bare claim that a party did not want to sign a premarital agreement will not support a finding of duress.[103] Indeed, a decision to sign an agreement that a party does not like evidences that the party understood the agreement and had a meaningful choice.[104] For example, five months before the wedding in *Spiegel v. Spiegel*,[105] the wife told the husband she would not sign a premarital agreement. The subject did not come up again until 10 days before the wedding, when the wife again rejected the idea. Five days later, she received a proposed draft. She continued to resist the idea and attempted to talk the husband out of it. But when he insisted, she signed the agreement with certain changes negotiated by her lawyer. The agreement was upheld over her claim of duress.[106]

That a party accepted terms of a premarital agreement while suffering from emotional distress, in and of itself, does not constitute duress or undue influence. Receipt of a proposed premarital agreement, especially when it comes within a few weeks of the wedding, as is often the case, is often distressing to the recipient. That a party signed while feeling such distress has not been sufficient, standing alone, to void a premarital agreement as the product of overreaching.[107] Similarly, distress over marital discord does not make a postmarital agreement the product of duress.[108] This is so even when a spouse threatens to reveal adultery or other misconduct to achieve the agreement. Duress requires a wrongful or unlawful threat. A threat to reveal misconduct is not duress.[109]

---

100. *See also Bates v. Bates*, 345 So. 3d 328 (Fla. App. 2022) (premarital agreement invalid where husband presented it to 18-year-old Colombian fiancée as if it were part of her immigration paperwork, coupled with other deficiencies in process); *Hollar v. Hollar*, 2015 Tenn. App. LEXIS 944 (unpub.) (premarital agreement was signed under duress where husband presented to wife one day before wedding in Columbia, agreement in English, wife only knew Spanish, husband did not provide translator, and wife had no access to counsel). *In re Marriage of Shirilla*, 319 Mont. 385, 89 P.3d 1 (2004) (premarital agreement involuntary where wife and her son would have been forced to return to Russia if parties did not marry; interpreter provided by husband was unable to explain agreement to wife, and lawyer hired for wife did not speak Russian).

101. 2012 Va. App. LEXIS 91; *see also E.K. v. C.K.*, 76. Misc. 3d 1204(A), 172 N.Y.S.3d 873 (Sup. Ct. 2022) (unpub.) (premarital agreement was valid where educated Russian wife, who had two weeks to get agreement translated, opted to rely instead on husband's explanation of terms).

102. When the proponent sponsors the fiancé(e) for permanent resident status, he or she may have a nonwaivable support obligation. See Section 5.05.

103. *DeMatteo v. DeMatteo*, 436 Mass. 18, 762 N.E.2d 797 (2002).

104. *See Weissgerber v. Weissgerber*, 276 Wis. 2d 308, 686 N.W.2d 455 (2004).

105. *Spiegel v. Spiegel*, 553 N.W.2d 309 (Iowa 1996).

106. *See also Elgar v. Elgar*, 238 Conn. 839, 679 A.2d 937 (1996); *DeLorean v. DeLorean*, 211 N.J. Super. 432, 511A.2d 1257 (1986).

107. *See Gottlieb v. Gottlieb*, 138 A.D.3d 30, 25 N.Y.S.3d 90 (2016); *Biliouris v. Biliouris*, 67 Mass. App. Ct. 149, 852 N.E.2d 687 (2006); *Mabus v. Mabus*, 890 So. 2d 806 (Miss. 2003).

108. Campbell v. Campbell, 208 A.D.3d 1050, 173 N.Y.S.3d 372 (App. Div. 4th Dep't 2022); Labuz v. Labuz, 54 N.E.3d 886 (Ill. Ct. App. 2016).

109. Labuz, 54 N.E.3d at 886.

(g) Unequal Bargaining Power

Although facially appealing, in fact, unequal bargaining power will not, standing alone, render an agreement invalid on duress or undue influence grounds,[110] although it is a factor a court can consider in determining voluntariness.[111] Indeed, premarital agreements are often executed by parties whose financial circumstances are disparate.[112] That fact alone will not prevent them from entering into an enforceable agreement.[113] Inequality of bargaining power may be offset by other factors, including, importantly, that the disadvantaged party received financial disclosure, understood the terms of agreement, and had an opportunity to obtain independent legal advice.[114]

(h) Pre-Execution Oral Promise or Unexpressed Intent

There is generally no room for an attack on validity based on an alleged pre-execution oral promise or an intent at variance with the text of the agreement. A party's vague oral promises, often disputed, to tear up an agreement, to take care of the other party, to amend a premarital agreement after the marriage, or to make provisions different from the requirements of the agreement, will not support a finding of fraud or duress.[115] Similarly, a vague understanding that an agreement means something other than what it says will not support such a conclusion. For example, in *Cannon v. Cannon*,[116] the husband sought a premarital agreement to protect himself from the wife's creditors. Because the risk had abated within two years of marriage, the trial court held the agreement lost its viability. The agreement was silent as to its duration. The appellate court reversed and held the agreement was valid.

In a second-look state,[117] a premarital agreement is not rendered unfair at enforcement solely because a party did not live up to a pre-execution oral promise. For example, in *Richard v. Richard*,[118] the wife claimed the husband did not keep his oral promise to pay all living

---

110. *In re Marriage of Shanks*, 758 N.W.2d 506 (Iowa 2008); *Greenwald v. Greenwald*, 154 Wis. 2d 767, 454 N.W.2d 34 (1990).

111. *Mamot v. Mamot*, 283 Neb. 659, 813 N.W.2d 440 (2012).

112. *Gant v. Gant*, 329 S.E.2d 106 (W. Va. 1985).

113. *Greenwald*, 154 Wis. 2d at 786, 454 N.W.2d at 41.

114. *Bonds v. Bonds*, 24 Cal. 4th 1, 5 P.3d 815 (2000), 24 Cal. 4th 1 at 35–36, 5 P.3d 815 at 836–37; *Lemaster v. Dutton*, 694 So. 2d 1360 (Ala. Civ. App. 1986); *Gant*, 329 S.E.3d 106.

115. *Ayers v. Ayers*, 2022 Ala. Civ. App. LEXIS 106, __ So. 3d __ (Ala. Civ. App. 2022); *Hiers v. Estate of Hiers*, 278 Ga. App. 242, 628 S.E.2d 653 (2006); *Boote v. Shivers*, 198 S.W.3d 732 (Tenn. Ct. App. 2005); *Mabus v. Mabus*, 890 So. 2d 806 (Miss. 2003); *but see Stancil v. Stancil*, 2012 Tenn. App. LEXIS 29 (husband's misrepresentations to wife, including purpose of agreement and his intent that it be invalid, rendered agreement unenforceable); *E.C.-P. v. P.P.*, 33 Misc. 3d 1233(A), 946 N.Y.S.2d 66 (Sup. Ct. 2011) (husband's promise that all assets acquired during marriage would be "theirs" and to destroy premarital agreement upon birth of first child was fraudulent; agreement void); *Cassidy v. Cassidy*, 356 S.W.3d 339 (Mo. Ct. App., S.D. 2011) (premarital agreement was result of fraud and overreaching where husband told wife she did not need own attorney, forbid her to tell adult children of marriage plans, lied about value of his farmland, and misrepresented significance of agreement).

116. *Cannon v. Cannon*, 384 Md. 537, 865 A.2d 563 (2005); *see also Marriage of Facter*, 212 Cal. App. 4th 967, 152 Cal. Rptr. 3d 79 (2013) (wife's understanding husband would deposit all earnings into joint account, at variance with text, did not warrant voiding premarital agreement); *Kornegay v. Robinson*, 360 N.C. 640, 637 S.E.2d 516 (2006) (wife's belief premarital agreement applied only in event of divorce where she did not read agreement before signing, did not warrant voiding agreement after husband's death); *Sykes v. Sykes*, 2006 Cal. App. LEXIS 766 (where wife represented by counsel in premarital agreement she had no right to rely on purported oral representations of husband at variance with text).

117. See Section 4.09(c) for discussion of the second look at divorce.

118. *Richard v. Richard*, 2004 Minn. App. LEXIS 1475.

expenses and that her assumption of more than her fair share was a changed circumstance that rendered the agreement unfair at enforcement. The court noted that it was foreseeable that the husband would fail to live up to a promise he did not put in writing.

(i) Threat to Divorce, or False Promise to Reconcile, to Get Postmarital Agreement

A threat to divorce if a spouse refuses a postmarital agreement may constitute duress, undue influence, or overreaching. For example, in *Pacelli v. Pacelli*,[119] the husband presented the postmarital agreement, which was highly advantageous to him, as nonnegotiable. His demand for an agreement forced the wife to choose between her own future financial security and keeping the family together. The court characterized the circumstances surrounding the execution as "inherently coercive."[120] Similarly, in *Gabaig v. Gabaig*,[121] the husband threatened divorce, actively discouraged the wife from consulting counsel and made no disclosure of assets. The court deemed the agreement the product of undue influence. In *Fanning v. Fanning*,[122] the court invalidated a postmarital agreement because the husband threatened to divorce the wife and take their three children. The husband was a lawyer who had won a series of custody cases for fathers; therefore, the wife had reason to think he could make good on his threat.[123] A more subtle form of misconduct, such as the creation of a misleading impression that execution of a postmarital agreement will lead to a reconciliation, may constitute undue influence. Such behavior resulted in the court voiding an agreement in *Derby v. Derby*.[124]

The cases discussed here point to the significant difference between a premarital agreement, where a party generally has a choice between accepting the agreement and cancelling the wedding, and a postmarital agreement, where that choice is no longer available. Forcing a spouse to accept unfair terms as a condition of remaining married is a violation of trust that courts generally do not countenance.[125]

There is also an important distinction between a spouse's demand for a postmarital agreement when the parties are living together in an ongoing marriage and where the parties are estranged as a result of a *bona fide* marital separation or where a spouse is guilty of marital fault. When the parties are estranged, an innocent party's willingness to reconcile, conditional on execution of a postmarital agreement, is not wrongful and therefore not duress.[126] On the

119. 319 N.J. Super. 185, 725 A.2d 56 (1999).

120. *Id.* at 191, 59.

121. 717 P.2d 835 (Alaska 1986).

122. 828 S.W.2d 135 (Tex. App. 1992), *rev'd in part on other grounds*, 847 S.W.2d 225 (Tex. 1993).

123. *See also In re Marriage of Osborne*, 2003 Wash. App. 3077 (2003) (postmarital agreement unenforceable where husband directed wife to lawyer who was not independent, terms of agreement not fair to wife, and husband threatened divorce); *Chait v. Chait*, 256 A.D.2d 121, 681 N.Y.S.2d 269 (1998) (posmarital agreement to extend premarital agreement invalid where wife threatened to take parties' child away and had means to carry out her threat).

124. 8 Va. App. 19, 378 S.E.2d 74 (1989) *see also* Gerwe v. Gerwe, 424 P.3d 1113 (Utah App. 2018); Murray v. Murray, 299 Ga. 703, 791 S.E.2d 816 (2016).

125. *See Marriage of Myers*, 210 Mont. 173, 682 P.2d 718 (1984) (husband took advantage of wife by demanding postmarital agreement transferring half of her separate property to him as a condition of staying married).

126. *See Marriage of Tabassum and Younis*, 377 Ill.App.3d 761, 881 N.E.2d 396, reh den. (2007) (postmarital agreement favorable to wife that parties negotiated while wife was in Canada with parties' child was not product

other hand, a postmarital agreement that is unfair to an innocent spouse and is extracted by a guilty spouse may be voided as the product of duress.[127]

Feelings of fear, panic, or uncertainty do not constitute duress in the execution of a postmarital agreement.[128] Moreover, sometimes the stress is the result of a party's own actions. Self-induced stress does not support a finding that an agreement was signed under duress,[129] nor does a self-inflicted wound.[130] A spouse's pressure on the other spouse to sign a postmarital agreement does not constitute undue influence in the absence of other factors, such as concealment of material facts.[131] Mere pressure caused by outside circumstances does not constitute duress. For example, in *Martello v. Martello*,[132] the wife refused to permit the husband to refinance their residence unless he agreed to cancel their premarital agreement. The cancellation agreement was valid.

However, when a spouse exploits the other spouse's emotional condition to obtain an unfair postmarital agreement, that conduct may well cause the agreement to be unenforceable. For example, in *Blaising v. Mills*,[133] the husband exploited the former wife's emotional distress, her psychological dependence on him, and her desire for reconciliation to pressure her to reconvey to him property she was awarded in their divorce. And in *Pacelli v. Pacelli*,[134] the husband took advantage of the wife's distress at the prospect of a divorce and her strong desire to keep the family together to obtain a patently unfair postmarital agreement, which the court voided.

(j) Confidential or Fiduciary Relationship and Undue Influence

A confidential relationship is one "wherein trust and confidence are reposed on one side and influence and control are exercised on the other. . . ."[135] A confidential relationship may exist as a matter of fact or as a matter of law.[136] In most states, the existence of a confidential relationship does not create a presumption that a premarital agreement was the result of

---

of duress where adulterous husband agreed to terms in order to reconcile); *Gilley v. Gilley*, 778 S.W.2d 862 (Tenn. Ct. App. 1989) (postmarital agreement not signed under duress where husband agreed to wife's terms to preserve marriage after she discovered his adultery).

127. *Grover v. Grover*, 101 Ark. App. 346, 276 S.W.3d 740 (2008) (postmarital agreement was product of duress where parties had reconciled and husband threatened divorce to extract unfair terms); *Marshall v. Marshall*, 166 W. Va. 304, 273 S.E.2d 360 (1980) (postmarital agreement invalid where husband insisted wife convey all marital property to him as condition of reconciliation); *Campbell v. Prater*, 64 Wyo. 293, 191 P.2d 160 (1948) (marriage settlement agreement was product of duress where wife left home without justification and demanded settlement as condition for reconciliation).

128. *See In re Marriage of Tabassum and Younis*, 377 Ill. App. 2d 761 (husband's fear of international custody battle did not render postmarital agreement the product of duress).

129. *Tremont v. Tremont*, 35 A.D.3d 1046, 827 N.Y.S.2d 309 (2006) (postmarital agreement not the result of wife's overreaching where pressure on husband was of his own making).

130. *In re Marriage of Tabassum*, 377 Ill. App. 2d 761 (postmarital agreement in return for reconciliation after husband's adultery, where husband felt fear and panic, was not product of duress).

131. *Reese v. Reese*, 984 P.2d 987 (Utah 1999).

132. 960 So. 2d 186 (La. App. 2007).

133. 176 Ind. App. 141, 374 N.E.2d 1166 (1978).

134. 319 N.J. Super. 185, 725 A.2d 56 (1999).

135. *Manos v. Papachrist*, 199 Md. 257, 261, 86 A.2d 474, 476 (1952).

136. Authorities often discuss the confidential relationship and the fiduciary relationship together. See authorities cited in Sections 2.04 and 3.04(c). No attempt is made here to distinguish them, as the difference should have no effect on how the lawyer conducts the negotiations.

undue influence.[137] The lack of a presumption means the burden is on the party challenging enforcement to present evidence that the other party was in a position of substantial domination that vitiated his or her will and that the other party gained an unconscionable advantage as a result.[138] Such a showing merely shifts the burden of proof to the proponent; he or she can readily meet the applicable burden of proof by showing the transaction was the product of a negotiation.[139]

There is no presumption that either party is the dominant party in a marriage;[140] however, in a dispute about validity of a postmarital agreement the court may need to make findings about whether the parties had a confidential relationship in order to assign the burden of proof.[141] As one court observed, in a marriage one party often assumes a more dominant role so that even the mere fact of dominance cannot be enough to allow a court to conclude an interspousal transaction was the result of undue influence or coercion.[142] Something more than a spouse urging the other spouse to sign a postmarital agreement is required to establish undue influence. Rather, the challenging party must show the other party had "such a superior position of dominance or advantage as would imply a dominating influence sufficient to amount to duress, coercion, or undue influence. . . ."[143] In some states, when a spouse gains an advantage as a result of a postmarital agreement, the transaction is presumed the result of undue influence.[144] In either event, the burden shifts to the advantaged party to prove voluntariness.[145]

When one party has been solely or primarily in charge of family financial affairs, that party's superior position and the other party's trust and confidence require the dominant party to take care to deal fairly in regards to their property interests.[146] Similarly, when one party

---

137. *Womack v. Womack*, 622 N.E.2d 481 (Ind. 1993); *Eckstein v. Eckstein*, 38 Md. App. 506, 379 A.2d 757 (1978); *Polsky v. Polsky*, 467 S.W.2d 860 (Mo. 1971); *Miethe v. Miethe*, 410 Ill. 226, 101 N.E.2d 571 (1951).

138. *Myrick v. Myrick*, 339 Ark. 1, 2 S.W.3d 60 (1999); *Womack v. Womack*, 622 N.E.2d 481 (Ind. 1993); *Matuga v. Matuga*, 600 N.E.2d 138 (Ind. Ct. App. 1992); *Punelli v. Punelli*, 364 N.W.2d 259 (Iowa. Ct. App. 1984); *Bell v. Bell*, 38 Md. App. 10, 379 A.2d 419 (1977); *Polsky v. Polsky*, 467 S.W.2d 860 (Mo. 1971).

139. *See Gottlieb v. Gottlieb*, 138 A.D.3d 30, 25 N.Y.S.3d 90 (2016); *Friedman v. Friedman*, 100 Cal. App. 4th 65, 122 Cal. Rpt. 2d 412 (Cal. App. 2002).

140. *Blum v. Blum*, 59 Md. App. 584, 477 A.2d 289 (1984); *Miethe v. Miethe*, 410 Ill. 226, 101 N.E.2d 571 (1951).

141. *See Espenkotter v. Espenkotter*, 2022 Md. App. LEXIS 841 (unpub.) (summary judgment for estate of husband reversed and remanded for findings on confidential relationship, notwithstanding surviving wife initiated postmarital agreement and had her lawyer draft).

142. *Myrick v. Myrick*, 339 Ark. 1, 8, 2 S.W.3d 60, 64 (1999).

143. *Id.* at 8, 64; *see also Lugg v. Lugg*, 64 A.3d 1109 (Pa. Super. Ct. 2013) (pressure to sign does not rise to level of duress).

144. *Meadows v. Meadows*, 2008 Cal. App. LEXIS 330 (unpub.); *Gabaig v. Gabaig*, 717 P.2d 835, 841 (Alaska 1986) (interpreting California law); *Estate of Gab*, 364 N.W.2d 924 (S.D. 1985); N.M. STAT. ANN. §40-2-2; *Gabriele v. Gabriele*, 421 P.3d 828 (N.M. Ct. App. 2018) (spouses may contract with each other subject to rules governing persons in confidential relationship; spouse who received decided advantage must show adequate consideration, full financial disclosure, disclosure of marital rights, and that other party had competent and independent legal advice).

145. *Myrick*, 339 Ark. at 8, 64–65.

146. *See Miethe v. Miethe*, 410 Ill. 226, 101 N.E.2d 571 (1951) (wife held half of family real estate in constructive trust for husband where she used his wages throughout marriage to buy, renovate, and manage real estate and where wife was solely responsible for all family financial affairs).

has become ill and as a result is unable to handle his or her own financial affairs, a spouse who assumes control must take care not to take advantage of the other party's weakness.[147] A spouse who possesses special knowledge, for example, a lawyer who practices in the area of family law or estates and trusts,[148] or who is a real estate professional,[149] should not take advantage of a less sophisticated spouse.[150] When a lawyer-spouse purports to act as the attorney for the other spouse, he or she will be held to all the legal and ethical obligations of an attorney.

When a postmarital agreement is to be executed as a result of marital discord, to effect a reconciliation or to resolve a financial disagreement, each party must act independently to protect his or her own interests and may not rely on a special confidence placed in the other. For example, in *Punelli v. Punelli*,[151] the parties had marital difficulties for years due to disagreements about business affairs. Their postmarital agreement, executed to effect a reconciliation and with both parties represented by separate counsel, was valid.[152] Such an agreement will be valid even when one party was overly generous in a moment of weakness. For example, in *Jennings v. Jennings*,[153] the husband agreed in writing to transfer half of all his book royalties to the wife after she caught him committing adultery:

> That the husband may have possessed some human frailty or compelling personal agenda will not alone relieve him of his obligations arising under a contract in which he was perfectly capable of negotiating and entering.[154]

Neither the husband's alcoholism nor his desire for reconciliation rendered the agreement unenforceable.[155]

---

147. *See Barchella v. Barchella*, 844 N.Y.S.2d 78 (App. Div. 2007) (postmarital agreement invalid for overreaching where wife signed agreement while suffering complications of surgery); *In re Lundvall's Estate*, 242 Iowa 430, 46 N.W.2d 535 (1951) (wife failed to prove transfers of husband's property to her were voluntary where wife became dominant party after husband suffered head injury and wife took over business affairs); *see also Manos v. Papachrist*, 199 Md. 257, 86 A.2d 474 (1952) (deathbed transfers from wife to husband were product of undue influence).

148. *See Sanford v. Sanford*, 355 Ark. 274, 137 S.W.3d 391 (2003).

149. *See Simon v. Smith*, 273 A.3d 321 (D.C. App. 2022) (postmarital property agreement highly disadvantageous to wife was unconscionable where husband, a real estate investor, exploited her naïveté and trust in his expertise).

150. *See In re Marriage of Osborne*, 2003 Wash. App. 3077 (unpub.) (husband was divorce lawyer and appreciated importance of independent legal advice, but did not explain that to wife and directed her to lawyer with whom he shared office space; postmarital agreement invalid).

151. 364 N.W.2d 259 (Iowa Ct. App. 1984).

152. *See also Dawbarn v. Dawbarn*, 175 N.C. App. 712, 625 S.E.2d 186 (2006) (no fiduciary duty when neither spouse has counsel); *but see Grossman v. Grossman*, 191 Ore. App. 294, 82 P.3d 1039 (2003) (spouses negotiating postmarital agreement have higher fiduciary duty than unmarried persons negotiating premarital agreement).

153. 12 Va. App. 1187, 409 S.E.2d 8 (1991).

154. *Id.* at 1196, 14.

155. *See also Hughes v. Hughes*, 96 N.M. 719, 634 P.2d 1271 (1981) (wife's pressuring husband to transfer certain property into joint names during time he was dependent on prescription drugs and alcohol did not constitute undue influence); *but see Stewart v. Stewart*, 41 A.3d 401 (De. 2012) (alimony provision of postmarital agreement could not withstand higher degree of scrutiny resulting from confidential relationship).

(k) Deliberate Ignorance (Didn't Read Before Signing)

A party's voluntary decision not to read an agreement negates a claim he or she executed the agreement involuntarily.[156] Generally, courts impute knowledge of the terms of an agreement to a party who refuses to read it before signing.[157] Therefore, a party's refusal to read effectively vitiates a claim that he or she did not understand the rights he or she waived by signing the agreement.[158]

(l) Passion

A party's willingness to make overly generous provisions for the other party to a premarital agreement does not constitute undue influence or overreaching after the relationship sours. For example, in *Carnell v. Carnell*,[159] the husband claimed undue influence because he was head over heels in love while, according to him, the wife remained cool throughout the courtship. But he was the one who insisted on a premarital agreement that provided generously for her to overcome her reluctance to marry him. His claim failed.[160] A party who intends to make generous provisions for a spouse-to-be needs to understand that he or she will be held to the agreement.

(m) Domestic Violence

An act of physical violence, threat of bodily harm, or other action constituting domestic violence could be the predicate for a duress claim in connection with either type of agreement.[161]

156. *Teed v. Teed*, 2013 W.Va. LEXIS 491; *Vanderbilt v. Vanderbilt*, 2013 Ohio App. LEXIS 1121 (unpub.); *Cooper v. Guido* (*In re Will and Estate of Cooper*), 75 So. 3d 1104, *cert. denied* 76 So. 3d 169 (2011); *Marriage of Hill and Dittmer*, 202 Cal. App. 4th 1046, 136 Cal. Rptr. 3d 700 (2011); *Kornegay v. Robinson*, 176 N.C. App. 19, 625 S.E.2d 805 (2006); *Cannon v. Cannon*, 384 Md. 537, 865 A.2d 563 (2005); *Pajak v. Pajak*, 385 S.E.2d 384 (W.Va. 1989).

157. *Brown v. Brown*, 26 So. 3d 1210 (Ala. Civ. App. 2007); *Kornegay v. Robinson*, 176 N.C. App. 19; *Vogt v. Vogt*, 831 So. 2d 428 (La. App. 2002); *Hale v. Robertson*, 60 S.W.3d 686 (Mo. App. 2001); *Pownall v. Pownall*, 197 Ariz. 577, 5 P.3d 911 (2000); *Lizzio v. Lizzio*, 1999 Mich. App. LEXIS 2188; *Busch v. Busch*, 732 A.2d 1274 (Pa. Super. Ct. 1999); *Wiley v. Iverson*, 295 Mont. 511, 985 P.2d 1176 (1999); *In re Estate of Garbade*, 221 A.D.2d 844, 633 N.Y.S.2d 878 (1995); *Lee v. Lee*, 35 Ark. App. 192, 816 S.W.2d 625 (1991); *Pajak*, 385 S.E.2d 384; *In re Marriage of Knoll*, 65 Or. App. 484; *Hook v. Hook*, 69 Ohio St. 2d 234, 431 N.E.2d 667 (1982).

158. *In re Estate of Kloster*, 965 N.W.2d 637 (Iowa Ct. App. 2021); *In re Estate of Smid*, 756 N.W.2d 1 (S.D. 2008); *Hiers v. Estate of Hiers*, 278 Ga. App. 242, 628 S.E.2d 653 (2006); *Mallen v. Mallen*, 283 Ga. 43, 622 S.E.2d 812 (2005); *Vogt*, 831 So. 2d 428; *Banks v. Evans*, 347 Ark. 383, 64 S.W.3d 746 (2002); *Liebelt v. Liebelt*, 801 P.2d 52 (Idaho Ct. App. 1990); *Pajak*, 385 S.E.2d 384; *see also Est. of Eskra*, 78 Cal. App. 5th 209, 293 Cal. Rptr. 3d 370 (2022) (wife not entitled to rescind premarital agreement that included death provisions she wanted removed where she declined to read before signing); *Corwell v. Corwell*, 2013 Ill. App. Unpub. LEXIS 1118 (admitted refusal to read negates claim that document offered into evidence is not genuine); *Scott v. Scott*, 19 A.3d 302 (De. 2011) (husband's refusal to read revocation of premarital agreement weighed against his claim of lawyer misconduct in representing both parties); *but see Carter v. Fairchild-Carter*, 187 A.D.3d 1360, 133 N.Y.S.3d 316 (2020) (premarital agreement set aside for fraud where husband presented final version one day before wedding, wife did not read, but husband falsely represented that agreed changes had been made); *Austin v. Austin*, 237 Ariz. 201, 348 P.3d 897 (Ct. App. 2015) (wife's failure to read postmarital agreement does not vitiate her claims where husband breached fiduciary duty).

159. 398 So. 2d 503 (Fla. Dist. Ct. App. 1981).

160. *See also Sanders v. Sanders*, 288 S.W.2d 473 (Tenn. Ct. App. 1955) (provision of premarital agreement for all property to be jointly titled, surviving spouse to take all, and party filing for divorce to forfeit all, was not violation of public policy where husband agreed to terms to get wife to marry him for the third time).

161. *See Lewis v. Lewis*, 234 A.3d 706 (Pa. Super. Ct. 2020) (postmarital agreement); *Treadway v. Treadway*, 324 So. 3d 842 (Ala. Civ. App. 2020), reh'g denied, 2020 Ala. Civ. App. LEXIS 392 (postmarital agreement); *Rosberg v. Rosberg*, 2019 Neb. App. LEXIS 120 (unpub.) (premarital agreement).

However, cases where domestic violence was evident in connection with such an agreement are rare, as are cases where domestic violence seemed to matter to the outcome. For example, in *Schechter v. Schechter*,[162] the court observed that the husband was emotionally and economically abusive during the entire relationship, including, apparently, before the parties executed the premarital agreement. However, it voided the agreement because the husband's financial disclosure was misleading and because the agreement was substantively unfair to the wife. It did so without drawing a connection between the unfair terms and the abusive conduct.[163] *Marriage of Iqbal v. Khan*[164] involved a postmarital agreement where there were hints of domestic violence—the wife and children stayed in a women's shelter at some point before execution of the agreement—that appeared not to figure into the court's decision to void the agreement on other grounds. The grounds for decision included substantive unconscionability but did not include that the contract prohibited a party from calling the police unless for a life-or-death emergency.[165]

§4.06 INDEPENDENT COUNSEL

Advice of independent counsel is the single most important factor in establishing voluntariness and, hence, the validity of a premarital or postmarital agreement.[166] The presence of independent counsel can make the difference between a summary judgment in favor of the proponent and a trial at which the proponent risks an adverse result.[167] When the weaker party had actual advice of counsel, or had a meaningful opportunity to consult with counsel and elected not to do so, any claim of undue influence in the execution of a premarital agreement is effectively vitiated.[168] A proponent is better protected from the risk and expense of litigation when a weaker party has counsel or a meaningful opportunity to get legal advice.

---

162. 88 Mass. App. Ct. 239, 37 N.E.3d 632 (2015).

163. However, the husband's abusive conduct was important to the court's custody decision.

164. 11 N.E.3d 1 (Ill. Ct. App 2014).

165. *See also Andrew B. v. Abbie B.*, 494 P.3d 522 (Alaska 2021) (*dicta*) (domestic violence in relationship may affect voluntariness even if threats of violence were not used directly in connection with premarital agreement); *Rosberg v. Rosberg*, 2019 Neb. App. LEXIS 120 (premarital agreement invalid for duress, no opportunity for independent legal advice; husband threatened wife with death); *Goodwin v. Webb*, 568 S.E.2d 311 (N.C. Ct. App. 2002) (wife may have lacked mental capacity to ratify marital settlement signed under duress where she had been subjected to years of physical abuse and had somewhat low IQ).

166. *Edwards v. Edwards*, 16 Neb. App. 297, 744 N.W.2d 243 (2008); *Reece v. Elliott*, 208 S.W.3d 419 (Tenn. App. 2006); *In re Estate of Lutz*, 563 N.W.2d 90 (N.D. 1997).

167. *In re Marriage of Barnes*, 324 Ill. App. 3d 514, 755 N.E.2d 522 (2001) (summary judgment as to validity of premarital agreement properly granted where both parties had counsel); *Gould v. Rafaeli*, 822 S.W.2d 494 (Mo. Ct. App. 1991) (premarital agreement upheld on summary judgment despite significant disparity in assets where both parties had counsel and husband's lawyer got draft agreement and wife's financial disclosure two weeks before wedding); *Nanini v. Nanini*, 166 Ariz. 287, 802 P.2d 438 (Ct. App. 1990) (summary judgment proper where wife had independent counsel, agreement recited detailed disclosure was attached, and a reading of text of premarital agreement was sufficient for wife to understand its effect on her legal rights).

168. *See DeMatteo v. DeMatteo*, 436 Mass. 18, 762 N.E.2d 797 (2002); *Spiegel v. Spiegel*, 553 N.W.2d 309 (Iowa 1996); *Matuga v. Matuga*, 600 N.E.2d 138, 141 (Ind. Ct. App. 1992).

(a) Actual Advice of Independent Counsel

When the party opposing enforcement received actual independent legal advice before execution, that fact alone can conclusively establish voluntariness. For example, in *In re Marriage of Yager*,[169] the wife took the draft premarital agreement to independent counsel who asked her if she had any questions and in whose presence she signed the agreement. The court upheld the agreement. In *Harbom v. Harbom*,[170] the wife was represented by her father, who was a lawyer and who negotiated the premarital agreement with the groom's father, obtaining changes favorable to the wife. The agreement was upheld.[171] The presence of an actively involved lawyer may render other deficiencies in the process, the substantive terms, or the text of the agreement of no consequence. For example, in *Head v. Head*,[172] the husband sold his major asset, his interest in the company that produced the Prince tennis racket, for 17 times its disclosed net book value six months after execution of a marital agreement settling the wife's challenge to the validity of their premarital agreement. The court rejected her claim the settlement agreement was invalid; she and her counsel were well aware that net book value understated actual value, and they had rejected a prior settlement offer as inadequate.[173]

The proponent of the agreement is not obliged to inquire into the professional competence of the other party's lawyer, nor is the purported ineffectiveness of a party's lawyer a basis on which a court may invalidate an agreement.[174]

(b) Signing Against Legal Advice

Some proponents may resist advice to encourage the weaker party to get counsel out of fear he or she will advise against signing. However, when a disadvantaged party gets legal advice not to sign, that will usually negate a claim of involuntariness. Indeed, the very act of signing against legal advice evidences a conscious, willful decision that is inconsistent with a later claim of duress, undue influence, or lack of knowledge of marital rights.[175] The proponent

---

169. *In re Marriage of Yager*, 155 Or. App. 407, 963 P.2d 137 (1998).

170. *Harbom v. Harbom*, 134 Md. App. 430, 760 A.2d 272 (2000); *see also Edwards v. Edwards*, 16 Neb. App. 297, 744 N.W.2d 243 (2008); *Francavilla v. Francavilla*, 969 So. 2d 522 (Fla. App. 2007); *Reece*, 208 S.W.3d 419; *Winchester v. McCue*, 91 Conn. App. 721, 882 A.2d 143 (2005).

171. *See also Murphy v. Murphy*, 359 Ill. App. 3d 289, 834 N.E.2d 56 (2005); *Boote v. Shivers*, 198 S.W.3d 732 (Tenn. Ct. App. 2005).

172. *Head v. Head*, 59 Md. App. 570, 477 A.2d 282 (1983).

173. *See also Reece v. Elliott*, 208 S.W.3d 419 (Tenn. Ct. App. 2006) (premarital agreement valid although husband provided incomplete valuation data where wife had attorney with whom she reviewed asset disclosure and did not ask questions); *DeMatteo v. DeMatteo*, 436 Mass. 18, 762 N.E.2d 797 (2002) (premarital agreement valid where husband retained $100 million in premarital assets, wife got home and $35,000 per year in support, and wife had attorney who actively negotiated terms); *In re Marriage of Ross*, 670 P.2d 26 (Colo. Ct. App. 1983) (premarital agreement valid despite lack of disclosure of asset values where both parties had independent counsel).

174. *Gottlieb v. Gottlieb*, 138 A.D.3d 30, 25 N.Y.S.3d 90 (2016); *Teed v. Teed*, 2013 W.Va. LEXIS 491; *Kellar v. Kellar*, 172 Wash. App. 562, 291 P.3d 906 (2012).

175. *See Fordeley v. Fordeley*, 2020 Ohio App. LEXIS 4229 (unpub.); *Silverman v. Silverman*, 206 A.3d 825 (Del. 2018); Vanderbilt *v. Vanderbilt*, 2013 Ohio App. LEXIS 1121 (unpub.); *Barocas v. Barocas*, 94 A.D.3d 551, 942 N.Y.S.2d 491 (2012); *Tyler v. Tyler*, 990 So. 2d 423 (Ala. Civ. App. 2008); *Webb v. Webb*, 18 Misc. 3d 822, 851 N.Y.S.2d 828 (Sup.Ct. 2007); *Biliouris v. Bilouris*, 67 Mass. App. Ct. 149, 852 N.E.2d 687 (2006); *Hiers v. Estate of Hiers*, 278 Ga. App. 242, 628 S.E.2d 653 (2006); *Dornemann v. Dornemann*, 48 Conn. App. 502, 850 A.2d 273 (2004); *Hardee v. Hardee*, 355 S.C. 382, 585 S.E.2d 501 (2003); *Lipic v. Lipic*, 103 S.W.3d 144 (Mo. App. 2003); *Marriage of Drag*, 326 Ill. App. 3d 1051, 762 N.E.2d 1111 (2001); *In re Marriage of Gardner*, 190 Wis. 2d 217, 527 N.W.2d 701 (1994); *In re Estate of Arbeitman*, 886 S.W.2d 644 (Mo. Ct. App. 1994); *Flansburg*

will be better protected if the other party gets advice not to sign and either rejects the advice or insists on changes to the terms, than if he or she enters into an agreement with an unrepresented party.

(c) Access to Independent Counsel—Time and Money

Only a few states' laws require access to counsel prior to execution as a condition for validity of a premarital or postmarital agreement.[176] Though access to counsel is not a mandate for general validity in any other states, it is nevertheless in the best interests of both parties that the recipient of an agreement have such access.[177] The UPMAA describes the concept of access to include both the money to hire a lawyer and a reasonable amount of time to find a lawyer, get advice, and consider the advice.[178]

The UPMAA recognizes that the right to access to counsel will not be meaningful if the recipient of the proposed agreement does not have the financial means to hire a lawyer. Section 9(b)(2) requires a proponent who is represented by counsel to pay "the reasonable fees and expenses" of the other party if he or she is unable to pay his or her own. The comments suggest that the obligation is to make funds available for a lawyer competent in this area of the law. In cases where there is a significant wealth disparity, proponents wishing to reduce future litigation risk will offer to pay for a lawyer with experience and skill and will not attempt to impose an arbitrary limit on his or her total fee.[179]

When the weaker party opts not to obtain independent counsel, it will be in the proponent's best interest to be able to prove he or she was clearly advised to get legal advice.[180] Such proof can demonstrate voluntariness. For example, in *In re Marriage of Knoll*,[181] the husband's lawyer advised the wife many times over a seven-month period to obtain independent counsel. She declined to do so. The premarital agreement was voluntary.[182] By contrast, lack of such proof may put enforceability at risk. For example, in *In re Estate of Lutz*,[183] the late husband's lawyer testified he advised the wife to retain separate counsel, but the wife denied his claim. Moreover, the lawyer blurred his own role by preparing wills for both parties prior to the marriage. The appeals court reversed a summary judgment for the husband's

---

v. Flansburg, 581 N.E.2d 430 (Ind. Ct. App. 1991); *Hamilton v. Hamilton*, 404 Pa. Super. 533, 591 A.2d 720 (1991); *DeLorean v. DeLorean*, 211 N.J. Super. 432, 511 A.2d 1257 (1986); *but see Kearney v. Kearney*, 129 So. 3d 381 (Fla. Ct. App. 2013) (advice of two lawyers not to sign postmarital agreement did not save agreement from finding it was product of overreaching where husband provided inadequate financial disclosure and misrepresented purpose of agreement); *see also Penrod v. Penrod*, 624 S.W.3d 905 (Mo. Ct. App. 2021) (claim lawyer was incompetent as basis for finding premarital agreement invalid rejected where wife refused to waive attorney-client privilege to permit her lawyer to testify).

176. See Sections 2.06, 3.04(h) and Appendices B(1) and B(2) of this book.

177. *See Stewart v. Stewart*, 214 Md. App. 458, 76 A.3d 1221 (2013); *Smith v. Smith*, 66 A.D.3d 534, 887 N.Y.S.2d 565 (2009).

178. UPMAA § 9(b).

179. *Smith*, 66 A.D.3d 534.

180. See Appendix G for model letters to an unrepresented party advising him or her to retain counsel.

181. *In re Marriage of Knoll*, 65 Or. App. 484, 671 P.2d 718 (1983).

182. *See also In re Marriage of Shanks*, 758 P.2d 506 (Iowa 2008); *Pownall v. Pownall*, 197 Ariz. 577, 5 P.3d 911 (2000); *Greenwald v. Greenwald*, 154 Wis. 2d 767, 454 N.W.2d 34 (1990); *Hosea v. Hosea*, 1997 Mich. App. LEXIS 3829; *Warren v. Warren*, 169 Ill. App. 3d 226, 523 N.E.2d 680 (1988).

183. *In re Estate of Lutz*, 563 N.W.2d 90 (N.E. 1997).

estate. Clear, unequivocal, and incontrovertible proof of advice to the wife might have obviated the need for a trial.[184]

Unadorned advice to retain counsel may be insufficient in some circumstances. For example, in *In re Marriage of Foran*,[185] the husband's lawyer advised the wife to retain counsel but failed to advise her why it was so important to do so. The wife did not understand that the premarital agreement allowed the husband to build up his separate estate at the expense of the marital community, a provision the court deemed unfair to her. The insufficiency of the advice caused the court to invalidate the agreement. Worse than unadorned advice to obtain counsel is advice to obtain counsel coupled with communications having the effect of discouraging the party from taking that advice. For example, in *Button v. Button*,[186] the husband's lawyer, after advising the wife she could take the agreement to a lawyer of her choice, said that doing so would show she did not trust the husband and his lawyer. Predictably, she did not retain separate counsel. The agreement was invalid.[187]

Counsel for a represented party should strongly urge the other party to obtain counsel. And, every agreement executed by an unrepresented party should contain an acknowledgment that the party received such advice.[188] A court is unlikely to find that a party who had sufficient time to seek counsel, and chose not to do so, was the victim of duress or overreaching.[189] The more disadvantageous an agreement is to one party, the more important it is that the party be urged as strongly as possible to obtain independent advice.

It may be that the weaker party will accept the advice to get independent counsel and that independent counsel will recommend changes to favor that party. Thus, the stronger party may need to make concessions to get an agreement acceptable to both parties. It will generally be far better for the stronger party to make concessions to achieve an agreement that will hold up if challenged than to strike a hard bargain with a party who lacked representation, only to have to defend the agreement at a later date with the accompanying risk of an adverse ruling and the transactional costs of mounting a defense.

(d) Role of Proponent or Proponent's Counsel in Selection of Lawyer for Other Party

It is appropriate for counsel for the proponent to recommend a lawyer to the weaker party when he or she does not know a qualified lawyer. Making a recommendation furthers the interest of the proponent in validity as long as it is done in an appropriate manner. Whenever

---

184. *See also Mamot v. Mamot*, 283 Neb. 659, 813 N.W.2d 440 (2012) (wife did not have access to counsel where husband presented agreement and insisted she sign that day; agreement invalid); *Pember v. Shapiro*, 794 N.W.2d 435 (N.D. 2011) (premarital agreement invalid where prepared by wife's lawyer five hours before wedding, husband not advised to get legal advice and had no time to do so); *Matson v. Matson*, 107 Wash. 2d 479, 730 P.2d 668 (1986) (wife received no specific verbal encouragement to retain counsel; agreement invalid).

185. *In re Marriage of Foran*, 67 Wn. App. 242, 834 P.2d 1081 (1992).

186. *Button v. Button*, 131 Wis. 2d 84, 388 N.W.2d 546 (1986).

187. See Chapter 9 for a more extended discussion of ethical considerations in dealing with an unrepresented party.

188. *See Marsh v. Marsh*, 949 S.W.2d 734 (Tex. App. 1997).

189. *See McLeod v. McLeod*, 145 So. 3d 1246 (Miss. Ct. App. 2014); *Ex parte Walters*, 580 So. 2d 1352 (Ala. 1991).

possible, the proponent's lawyer should offer several names. The lawyer should make it clear to the other party that he or she is free to hire someone else. The lawyer may need to disclose a personal or professional relationship with the recommended lawyer—for example, a family connection or a prior affiliation in the same law firm. Ideally, the recommended lawyer will have experience and skill in drafting and negotiating marital agreements.

The lawyer must strike the appropriate balance. The over-involvement of a party or counsel in the selection of counsel for the other party may undermine the independence of that party's counsel such that the very purpose of urging that party to obtain counsel is defeated.[190] In *Sogg v. Nevada State Bank*,[191] the husband's lawyer, who had represented the wife in her prior divorce, selected a lawyer for the wife who had an office down the hall and made an appointment for her. He never told her she could select her own lawyer, and she had reason to trust him because of their prior lawyer-client relationship. These circumstances contributed to the court's decision to void the premarital agreement.[192]

In other cases, courts have been considerably more tolerant of the proponent's over-involvement in the sélection of counsel for the other party.[193] Nevertheless, it should be obvious that both parties are better served when the disadvantaged party's lawyer is both competent and truly independent.[194]

---

190. *See C.S. v. L.S.*, 41 Misc. 3d 1209(A), 980 N.Y.S.2d 274 (Sup. Ct. Nassau Cnty., 2013) (husband presented premarital agreement to wife several days before wedding, in shared office suite of his lawyer and hand-picked lawyer for wife; agreement invalid); *Ex parte Williams*, 617 So. 2d 1032 (Ala. 1992) (summary judgment for husband reversed where only lawyer pregnant wife consulted was friend of husband); *Orgler v. Orgler*, 237 N.J. Super. 342, 568 A.2d 67 (App. Div. 1989) (husband's selection of wife's attorney coupled with inadequate disclosure rendered agreement invalid even though lawyer advised wife not to sign).

191. 832 P.2d 781 (Nev. 1992).

192. *See also Spiegel v. Spiegel*, 206 A.D.3d 1178, 170 N.Y.S.3d 295 (2022) (husband not entitled to summary judgment as to validity of premarital agreement where his lawyer chose lawyer for wife without telling her, sent the draft agreement to wife's lawyer without her knowledge, and husband directed his lawyer to convey husband's intent that wife's lawyer's role was limited to explaining terms and did not include negotiating better terms for her); *Bates v. Bates*, 345 So.3d 328 (Fla. Ct. App. 2022) (premarital agreement invalid as product of coercion where 41-year-old husband hired Colombian lawyer for 18-year-old fiancée and directed her lawyer to backdate agreement); *Moore v. Moore*, 383 S.W.3d 190 (2012), *reh'g overruled*, 2012 Tex. App. LEXIS 10194, *rev. denied*, 2013 Tex. LEXIS 294 (premarital agreement unenforceable where husband insisted wife select lawyer of his choice); *Marriage of Osborne*, 2003 Wash. App. LEXIS 3077, 119 Wn. App. 1065 (2003) (unpub.) (postmarital agreement invalid where husband, who was a lawyer, steered wife to lawyer with whom husband shared office space); *In re Marriage of Richardson*, 237 Ill. App. 3d 1067, 606 N.E.2d 56 (1992) (estranged couple engaged in extended negotiations for postmarital agreement for reconciliation; wife's first lawyer, an experienced domestic relations practitioner, recommended she not sign the husband's draft; husband's lawyer brought in inexperienced former associate, made the initial contact purportedly on the wife's behalf, shut the prior lawyer out of further communications, and told new lawyer his fee would be paid by husband; postmarital agreement invalid).

193. *See, e.g.*, *Hudson v. Hudson*, 408 S.C. 76, 757 S.E.2d 727 (S.C. Ct. App. 2014), *cert. denied* 2014 S.C. LEXIS 565 (premarital agreement was valid although husband insisted wife get legal advice from a friend of his); *Friezo v. Friezo*, 281 Conn. 166, 914 A.2d 533 (2007) (upholding premarital agreement where husband arranged for his sister-in-law to handpick wife's lawyer, an inexperienced associate in sister-in-law's law firm, who did not charge for services), *see also Kambitsis v. Kambitsis*, 2020 N.J. Super. LEXIS 690 (unpub.); *Cooper v. Guido* (*In re Will of Cooper*), 75 So. 3d 1104 (Miss. Ct. App. 2011); *Tyler v. Tyler*, 990 So. 2d 423 (Ala. Ct. Civ. App. 2008).

194. *See Barocas v. Barocas*, 94 A.D.3d 551, 942 N.Y.S.2d 491 (2012) (premarital agreement was not product of duress or overreaching, nor was it unconscionable, where wife's lawyer told her it was unfair and advised against signing).

§4.07 KNOWLEDGE OF MARITAL RIGHTS

Knowledge of marital rights and the effect of a premarital or postmarital agreement on those rights can be seen as one factor in determining voluntariness or as a distinct requirement for validity.[195] In the majority of states, knowledge of marital rights is not a distinct requirement; it is merely a factor in evaluating voluntariness.[196] Indeed, a requirement for a separate explanation of marital rights would almost mandate legal advice.[197] Even in those states where there is no requirement for a separate explanation of marital rights, it is in the interest of both parties that each receives such an explanation.

> In order for a waiver of interest to be valid, the waiver must have been made knowingly, voluntarily and intelligently. Essential to a knowing, voluntary and intelligent decision to waive rights and property in exchange for marriage is knowledge of the extent of the rights and property being waived. In other words, there must be full disclosure and understanding of the nature and consequences of the agreement prior to its execution.[198]

Knowingly, or knowingly and intelligently, means that the party had knowledge of the financial affairs of the other party as well as some understanding of his or her marital rights in the absence of agreement and the effect of the agreement on those rights.[199] It is not necessary that the party have an in-depth understanding of every paragraph of the agreement; a general understanding of the key features of the agreement and how they alter marital rights is sufficient. For example, in *Bonds v. Bonds*,[200] the California Supreme Court held the wife's understanding that the premarital agreement altered community property law to permit each party to retain all earnings as separate property was adequate. Similarly, in *Boetsma v. Boetsma*,[201] the wife's understanding that she would receive nothing from the husband's estate except what he left her in his will was sufficient knowledge even though her lawyer did not explain each of the statutory spousal rights she waived.

The more disadvantageous a proposed premarital agreement is to one party, the more important it is that he or she understands the effect of the agreement on the rights he or she would have upon marriage in the absence of agreement. For example, in *In re Marriage of*

---

195. *See In re Marriage of Lewis*, 808 S.W.2d 919 (Mo. Ct. App. 1991) (requirement for disclosure includes both spousal legal rights and property interests); *In re Estate of Halmaghi*, 184 Mich. App. 263, 457 N.W.2d 356 (1990) (without disclosure of marital rights, there can be no knowing waiver).

196. *See In re Estate of Smid*, 756 N.W.2d 1 (S.D. 2008); *Stoner v. Stoner*, 572 Pa. 665, 819 A.2d 529 (2003); see also Section 4.04(a).

197. In some cases, such as where parties intend to enter into a postmarital agreement governed by New Mexico law, the proponent of such an agreement must show that the other party was knowledgeable <u>and</u> got legal advice. *Gabriele v. Gabriele*, 421 P.3d 828 (N.M. Ct. App. 2018).

198. *Parr v. Parr*, 635 N.E.2d 1124, 1129 (Ind. Ct. App. 1994).

199. *In re Estate of Murphy*, 661 S.W.2d 657 (Mo. Ct. App. 1983); *see also Eyster v. Pechenik*, 887 N.E.2d 272 (Mass. Ct. App. 2008) (not enough that party knows marriage confers some undefined rights; meaningful understanding means party understands disposition of property and support claims could be very different from outcome if parties divorced without agreement).

200. *Bonds v. Bonds*, 24 Cal. 4th 1, 5 P.3d 815 (2000); *see also Friezo v. Friezo*, 281 Conn. 166, 914 A.2d 533 (2007) (detailed understanding of law of divorce is not necessary; wife's understanding purpose of agreement to protect husband's assets in event of divorce was sufficient).

201. 768 N.E.2d 1016 (Ind. Ct. App. 2002).

Foran,[202] the wife gave up virtually all marital rights and effectively foreclosed herself from ever acquiring any property rights resulting from the husband's work efforts during the marriage. In voiding the agreement, the court said: "[A]lthough Peggy's execution of the contract was in one sense 'voluntary,' it was in no sense 'intelligent,' that is, there is not sufficient evidence from which we can conclude that Peggy fully understood the legal consequences of the contract."[203] The court went on to say that it would not enforce a patently unfair premarital contract without evidence the disadvantaged party had a full understanding of the legal consequences of the contract.

An agreement should not be drafted in such a way as to make it overly difficult to understand. For example, in *Sanford v. Sanford*,[204] the husband, a lawyer, drafted a postmarital property settlement agreement and a trust agreement that allowed him to control and sell the wife's half of the marital estate. He deliberately made the documents confusing and difficult to understand. The wife prevailed on a claim of breach of fiduciary duty where the husband interpreted his rights vis-à-vis the wife too favorably to himself.[205]

At a minimum, each party should be given a copy of the agreement to read ahead of time.[206] If the terms of the agreement can be understood by a reasonably intelligent adult with no legal training, a reading of the document will be enough to convey adequate knowledge.[207] For example, in *Nanini v. Nanini*,[208] the wife correctly understood the premarital agreement to provide that what was his was his and what was hers was hers. This showed she had an adequate understanding.[209]

The more experience and education the recipient of the agreement has before execution, the more likely that party will have sufficient knowledge of his or her marital rights to effectively waive them. Relevant experience can include a prior divorce, administration of a deceased spouse's estate, management of rental property or other investments, and working as an owner, manager, or employee of a business or professional services firm.[210] A spouse with a professional degree or license, such as a lawyer or a CPA, can be presumed to have sufficient knowledge to protect his or her own rights.[211] A party who has been divorced can be assumed to understand the rights of spouses at divorce.[212]

---

202. *In re Marriage of Foran*, 67 Wn. App. 242, 834 P.2d 1081 (1992).

203. *Id.* at 257, 1090.

204. 355 Ark. 274, 137 S.W.3d 391 (2003).

205. Among other things, the husband took the position that a clause stating he was responsible for all taxes did not mean he was actually responsible to pay them. *Id.* at 288, 399.

206. *See Sogg v. Nevada State Bank*, 832 P.2d 781 (Nev. 1992) (premarital agreement invalid where wife was not given copy of agreement to take with her to read and did not have opportunity for independent advice).

207. *Friezo v. Friezo*, 281 Conn. 166, 914 A.2d 533 (2007); *Wiley v. Iverson*, 295 Mont. 511, 985 P.2d 1176 (1999); *Pajak v. Pajak*, 385 S.E.2d 384 (W. Va. 1989).

208. *Nanini v. Nanini*, 166 Ariz. 287, 802 P.2d 438 (Ct. App. 1990).

209. *See also Panossian v. Panossian*, 172 A.D.2d 811, 569 N.Y.S.2d 182 (1991) (premarital agreement valid where wife understood that neither party would have right to receive anything from the other in event of divorce).

210. *See Griffin v. Griffin*, 94 P.3d 96 (Okla. Civ. App. 2004); *Wiley v. Iverson*, 295 Mont. 511, 985 P.2d 1176 (1999); *Hoffman v. Hoffman*, 100 A.D.2d 704, 474 N.Y.S.2d 621 (1984); *Hartz v. Hartz*, 248 Md. 47, 234 A.2d 865 (1967).

211. *See Hale v. Robertson*, 60 S.W.3d 686 (Mo. App. 2001); *Daniel v. Daniel*, 779 S.W.2d 110 (Tex. App. 1989); *Head v. Head*, 59 Md. App. 570, 477 A.2d 282 (1983); *Babb v. Babb*, 270 Ark. 289, 604 S.W.2d 574 (Ct. App. 1980).

212. *See Edwards v. Edwards*, 16 Neb. App. 297, 744 N.W.2d 243 (2008) (wife's prior divorce gave her experience with process and knowledge of spousal support awards); *Werther v. Werther*, 9 Misc. 3d 1114(A), 808

The presence of independent counsel is the best insurance the proponent of the agreement can get that the other party has sufficient knowledge and understanding of his or her marital rights and the effect of the agreement on those rights.[213] As one court observed, "knowledge of one's legal rights is a conclusion that flows from the opportunity to obtain counsel."[214] A claim that a party did not understand the legal effect of an agreement will fail when the party had sufficient time to obtain legal advice and decided to forgo that opportunity.[215] A party who has counsel has a responsibility to ask questions and is charged with any lack of knowledge of marital rights.[216]

§4.08 FINANCIAL DISCLOSURE

(a) Overview

This section addresses what constitutes adequate financial disclosure and the mechanics of such disclosure.[217] The purpose of financial disclosure is to allow a party to make an informed decision about whether to sign an agreement waiving marital rights that would otherwise accrue or to negotiate for better terms.[218] The responsibility for imparting adequate knowledge is on the party who relies on the agreement.[219] The other party is not required to conduct a financial investigation.[220]

As is evident from the discussion below, in many reported cases something less than complete, detailed written disclosure of the identity of all assets with current and accurate values, and all sources and amounts of income, was sufficient for a court to uphold an agreement. However, in all cases, a proponent was forced to defend the agreement with all the expense and risk entailed in litigation. Memories fade, files are destroyed or lost, and witnesses die or become incompetent.[221] Due to age or ill health, parties themselves may not be

---

N.Y.S.2d 921 (Sup. Ct. 2005) (wife's four prior divorces undermined claim she did not understand premarital agreement).

213. *Griffin*, 94 P.3d 96; *Bonds v. Bonds*, 24 Cal. 4th 1, 5 P.3d 815 (2000), 24 Cal. 4th 1 at 5, P.3d 815; *In re Estate of Lutz*, 563 N.W.2d 90 (N.D. 1997); *Daniel*, 779 S.W.2d 110; *Gant v. Gant*, 329 S.E.2d 106 (W. Va. 1985).

214. *Kellar v. Kellar*, 172 Wn. App. 562, 589, 291 P.3d 906, 920 (2012).

215. *See Simeone v. Simeone*, 380 Pa. Super. 37, 551 A.2d 219 (1988), *aff'd*, 525 Pa. 392, 581 A.2d 162 (1990); *see also Wiley*, 295 Mont. 511; *In re Marriage of Knoll*, 65 Ore. App. 484, 671 P.2d 718 (1983).

216. *DeMatteo v. DeMatteo*, 436 Mass. 18, 762 N.E.2d 797 (2002).

217. The discussion here is about financial disclosure. There is no general support in the case law of premarital and postmarital agreements for the notion that parties must disclose their character flaws or a health condition that may negatively affect the other party. *See Farris v. Farris,* 202 So. 3d 223 (Miss. Ct. App. 2016) (premarital agreement was not invalid due to husband's failure to disclose herpes); *but see Walker v. Walker,* 2020 Tenn. App. LEXIS 47 (unpub.) (premarital agreement invalid where husband deliberately hid ownership of condominium with former girlfriend even though value apparently was small relative to his other assets).

218. *Darr*, 950 S.W.2d 867; *Greenwald v. Greenwald*, 154 Wis. 2d 767, 454 N.W.2d 34 (1990).

219. King v. King, 638 S.W.3d 464 (Ky. Ct. App. 2021).

220. *Parrett v. Wright*, 2017 Ohio App. LEXIS 5494; *Blige v. Blige*, 283 Ga. 65, 656 S.E.2d 822 (2008); *Winchester v. McCue*, 91 Conn. App. 721, 882 A.2d 143 (2005); *Ryken v. Ryken*, 461 N.W.2d 122 (S.D. 1990).

221. *See Williams v. Williams*, 868 S.W.2d 616 (Tenn. Ct. App. 1992) (premarital agreement invalid where only evidence regarding disclosure came from surviving wife who denied knowledge of decedent's assets); *Button v. Button*, 131 Wis. 2d 84, 388 N.W.2d 546 (1986) (attorney and husband had no recollection or record of financial disclosure or explanation of wife's rights; premarital agreement invalid).

able to provide testimony.[222] Cases that go to trial over the adequacy of financial disclosure often involve competing factual narratives.[223] When resolution turns on credibility, the decision is virtually irreversible on appeal.[224] The proponent who fails to adequately disclose, and document that disclosure, runs the risk that his or her story will be disbelieved even if true. At the drafting stage, counsel has an opportunity to reduce this risk for the proponent.[225]

(b) Mechanics of Financial Disclosure

Parties may make financial disclosure through a variety of methods.

Written, Itemized Statement

A written, itemized list of major assets and liabilities and their values, as well as amounts and sources of income, is the best evidence of adequate disclosure. One court has called this the gold standard.[226] Asset schedules are usually attached to and made a part of the agreement by reference, but this is not a precondition to validity in a majority of states.[227] They could be exchanged between the parties or counsel but not attached to the agreement.[228] It is the better practice to attach them unless there is a good reason not to do so. It is appropriate for the agreement to recite that disclosures are attached; the lawyer for the proponent should confirm that they are.[229] When the parties execute the agreement, they should initial all the pages, including the asset disclosure.

Written Statement of Net Worth and Income without Itemization

A general disclosure of net worth without details will suffice as fair disclosure in many cases.[230]

---

222. *See In re Estate of Benker*, 416 Mich. 681, 331 N.W.2d 193 (1982) (premarital agreement containing no recitation of disclosure invalid where surviving wife incompetent and drafting attorney could only testify to normal procedure in eliciting oral disclosure).

223. *See Chaplain v. Chaplain*, 54 Va. App. 762, 682 S.E.2d 108 (2009), *opinion after remand*, 2011 Va. App. LEXIS 15, where the husband made no written financial disclosure and he had a net worth of $20 million. The appellate court reversed a summary judgment for the husband where he claimed the wife knew he was very wealthy and she claimed he said he was poor. On remand, the husband prevailed because he established that the agreement was voluntary and not unconscionable, making the adequacy of financial disclosure moot.

224. *See, e.g.*, *Mamot v. Mamot*, 283 Neb. 659, 813 N.W.2d 440 (2012) (conflicting testimony of parties as to whether husband made financial disclosure; wife failed to meet her burden).

225. *See Crowder v. Crowder*, 28 Phila. 225 (Ct. Com. Pl. 1994) (husband's detailed and accurate list of assets and values was full disclosure; agreement valid); *In re Estate of Thies*, 273 Mont. 272, 903 P.2d 186 (1995) (litigation could have been avoided with written list of assets and values).

226. *Cannon v. Cannon*, 384 Md. 537, 573, 865 A.2d 563, 584 (2005); *see also Pollock-Halvarson*, 576 N.W.2d 451; *Randolph v. Randolph*, 937 S.W.2d 815, 821 (Tenn. 1996); *In re Estate of Thies*, 273 Mont. 272 at 279, 903 P.2d 186 at 190; *Simeone v. Simeone*, 380 Pa. Super. 37, 551 A.2d 219 (1988), *aff'd*, 525 Pa. 392, 581 A.2d 162 (1990).

227. New Jersey's version of the UPAA requires the financial disclosure to be in writing and annexed to the agreement, although the same statute permits parties to waive disclosure.

228. *See Dornemann v. Dornemann*, 48 Conn. App. 502, 850 A.2d 273 (2004).

229. *See Remillard v. Remillard*, 2022 Va. App. LEXIS 417 (unpub.); *Dobre v. Dobre*, 2018 N.J. Super. LEXIS 931 (unpub.).

230. *In re Lopata's Estate*, 641 P.2d 952 (Colo. 1982); *see also Branch v. Branch*, 508 S.W.3d 911 (Ark. Ct. App. 2016) (list of accounts without balances coupled with statement of net worth was adequate for premarital agreement); *Marriage of Hill and Dittmer*, 202 Cal. App. 4th 1046, 136 Cal. Rptr. 3d 700 (2011) (statement of net worth in premarital agreement was adequate); *Warren v. Warren*, 169 Ill. App. 3d 226, 523 N.E.2d 680 (1988) (husband's general recital of source of wealth and that he was multimillionaire was adequate disclosure); *Kahn v. Kahn*, 756 S.W.2d 685 (Tenn. 1988) (husband's accurate statement of net worth and annual income without detail

Financial Records and Other Raw Data

In lieu of, or in addition to, a written asset list or more informal methods of disclosure, a party may provide actual financial records reflecting the existence and value of assets and amounts and sources of income.[231] These can include account statements, a loan application, tax returns, and retirement plan account statements. Even where the relevant information is not obvious, but may require some effort at understanding, provision of financial records may be enough in some cases. Particularly is this true with income tax returns, which can provide a wealth of information but may require some effort to interpret.[232]

Oral Exchange of Information

Parties may provide financial information through oral disclosures.[233] An oral disclosure may be sufficient but can be more difficult to prove if there is a dispute.[234]

Preexisting Knowledge; Informal Disclosure

Preexisting actual, not merely constructive, knowledge of a party's assets can satisfy the requirement that a party have knowledge of the other's financial affairs.[235] A general understanding of the nature and extent of the other party's property will often suffice.[236] When the opposing party worked for the proponent and gained firsthand knowledge of his or her finances, courts have generally deemed that sufficient knowledge.[237] This is especially the case when the disadvantaged party worked as a bookkeeper for the other party and thus gained knowledge of business or personal financial transactions.[238] Similarly, where the proponent can prove that the other party gained substantial information as a result of living with the other party, knowing the party for a period of time, living in the same neighborhood,

---

was adequate); *In re Estate of Hill*, 214 Neb. 702, 335 N.W.2d 750 (1983) (husband's accurate oral statement in lawyer's office of approximate net worth was fair disclosure); *but see In re Marriage of Sarancic*, 2020 Fla. App. LEXIS 870 (unpub.) (statement of net worth without detail was inadequate).

231. *See Gould v. Rafaeli*, 822 S.W.2d 494 (Mo. Ct. App. 1991).

232. *See Daniel v. Daniel*, 779 S.W.2d 110 (Tex. App. 1989) (husband, who was lawyer and CPA, could have discovered marital estate earned $1 million in trust controlled by wife by examining their joint tax returns; postmarital agreement upheld); *but see Oldani v. Oldani*, 132 Conn. App. 609, 34 A.3d 407 (2011) (financial disclosure was inadequate as to income where provided gross rental income, mortgage payments, operating expenses, and husband's percentage interest in each property, but did not state husband's net income).

233. *See Pulley v. Short*, 261 S.W.3d 701 (Mo. Ct. App. 2008); *Wilson v. Moore*, 929 S.W.2d 367 (Tenn. Ct. App. 1996); *In re Marriage of Rahn*, 914 P.2d 463 (Colo. Ct. App. 1995); *Hunsberger v. Hunsberger*, 653 N.E.2d 118 (Ind. Ct. App. 1995); *In re Estate of Hartman*, 399 Pa. Super. 386, 582 A.2d 648 (1990).

234. *See Parr v. Parr*, 635 N.E.2d 1124 (Ind. Ct. App. 1994) (oral disclosure in presence of husband's attorney just before premarital agreement executed insufficient where no one remembered specifics of disclosure).

235. *In re Marriage of Delaney*, 298 Wis. 2d 247, 726 N.W.2d 356 (2006); *see also In re Marriage of Bliss*, 382 Mont. 370, 367 P.3d 395 (2016) (omission of wife's pet grooming businesses did not render premarital agreement invalid where husband knew about them and wife operated them from shared home); *Estate of Wilber*, 165 N.H. 246, 75 A.3d 1096 (2013) (lack of financial disclosure statement did not show postmarital agreement obtained through nondisclosure where parties were married for 50 years).

236. *In re Lopata's Estate*, 641 P.2d 952 (Colo. 1982); *Schutterle v. Schutterle*, 260 N.W.2d 341 (S.D. 1977); *In re Broadie's Estate*, 493 P.2d 289 (Kan. 1972).

237. *See In the Matter of Nizhnikov & Nikhnikov*, 168 N.H. 525, 132 A.3d 412; (2016); *McLeod v. McLeod*, 145 So. 3d 1246 (Miss. Ct. App. 2014); *Friezo v. Friezo*, 281 Conn. 166, 914 A.2d 533 (2007); *Mabus v. Mabus*, 890 So. 2d 806 (Miss. 2003); *Banks v. Evans*, 347 Ark. 383, 64 S.W.3d 746 (2002); *Wiley v. Iverson*, 295 Mont. 511, 985 P.2d 1176 (1999).

238. *See McLeod*, 145 So. 3d 1246; *Mabus v. Mabus*, 890 So. 2d 806 (Miss. 2003); *Lawson v. Loid*, 896 S.W.2d 1 (Ky. 1995); *Greenwald v. Greenwald*, 154 Wis. 2d 767, 454 N.W.2d 34 (1990); *D'Onofrio v. D'Onofrio*, 200 N.J. Super. 361, 491 A.2d 752 (1985); *In re Marriage of Knoll*, 65 Ore. App. 484, 671 P.2d 718 (1983).

moving in the same social circles, or otherwise being in a position to observe the party's assets, sources of income, or standard of living, that knowledge may suffice.[239]

Reliance solely on preexisting knowledge is risky for the proponent. A court will not infer that a party gained adequate knowledge merely because the parties lived in the same community before marriage.[240] The proponent will need to prove actual knowledge. Some circumstances create greater risk for the proponent. These include where the proponent lives modestly relative to his or her means,[241] a short courtship,[242] and where the proponent is extremely wealthy.[243]

Recital in Agreement

A formal recital that the parties are familiar with each other's property, or that the parties made disclosures to each other before execution, is prima facie evidence of full disclosure or preexisting knowledge even though the substance of the disclosure is not made part of the agreement.[244] But, a recital that the parties made full disclosure will not support validity if the statement is untrue.[245] Similarly, a recital that parties provided schedules that are attached to the agreement is insufficient if the purported schedules are not attached or are blank.[246] Repeating the same untrue statement several times in the body of the agreement will not save it.[247]

(c) Content of Financial Disclosure

Generally, the cases describe the content of the required disclosure for a premarital agreement as full and fair disclosure, or fair and adequate disclosure, of relevant financial information.[248] The Uniform Premarital Agreement Act (UPAA) describes the content of the

239. *See In re Marriage of Snyder*, 977 N.W.2d 115 (Iowa Ct. App. 2022); *In re Estate of Martin*, 938 A.2d 812 (Me. 2008); *Darr v. Darr*, 950 S.W.2d 867 (Mo. Ct. App. 1997); *Strait v. Strait*, 686 So. 2d 1230 (Ala. Civ. App. 1996); *In re Estate of Thies*, 273 Mont. 272, 903 P.2d 186 (1995); *Nanini v. Nanini*, 166 Ariz. 287, 290, 802 P.2d 438, 441 (Ct. App. 1990); *Pajak v. Pajak*, 385 S.E.2d 384 (W. Va. 1989); *In re Marriage of Adams*, 240 Kan. 315, 729 P.2d 1151 (1986); *Schutterle*, 260 N.W.2d 341; *Lutgert v. Lutgert*, 338 So. 2d 1111 (Fla. Dist. Ct. App. 1976); *Laird v. Laird*, 597 P.2d 463 (Wyo. 1979); *Hartz v. Hartz*, 248 Md. 47, 234 A.2d 865 (1967).

240. *Shinn v. Schaal*, 394 N.J. Super. 55, 925 A.2d 88 (2007); *Williams v. Williams*, 868 S.W.2d 616 (Tenn. Ct. App. 1992).

241. *See Blige v. Blige*, 283 Ga. 65, 656 S.E.2d 822 (2008) (premarital agreement failed for lack of disclosure where husband was truck driver and failed to disclose substantial cash); *Bauer v. Bauer*, 1 Or. App. 504, 464 P.2d 710 (1970) (premarital agreement invalid where husband made no disclosure and lived modestly relative to his wealth).

242. *See Kosik v. George*, 452 P.2d 560 (Or. 1969) (disclosure inadequate where no actual disclosure and courtship lasted only eight days).

243. *See In re Estate of Benker*, 416 Mich. 681, 331 N.W.2d 193 (1982) (lack of formal, written disclosure coupled with evidence husband was secretive about money and lived modestly supported finding of nondisclosure); *see also Chaplain v. Chaplain*, 54 Va. App. 762, 682 S.E.2d 108 (2009), *opinion after remand*, 2011 Va. App. LEXIS 15 (summary judgment for husband reversed where no written disclosure, husband had $20 million, but lived modestly; on remand, upholding agreement where conflicting testimony showed wife had knowledge of husband's wealth).

244. *Griffin v. Griffin*, 94 P. 3d 96 (Okla. Civ. App. 2004); *Kitchens v. Estate of Kitchens*, 850 So. 2d 215 (Miss. App. 2003); *In re Estate of Thies*, 273 Mont. 272, 903 P.2d 186 (1995); *Cooper v. Oakes*, 427 Pa. Super. 430, 629 A.2d 944 (1993); *Hartz v. Hartz*, 248 Md. 47, 234 A.2d 865 (1967).

245. *Shinn*, 394 N.J. Super. 55; *Alexander v. Alexander*, 279 Ga. 116, 610 S.E.2d 48 (2005); *In re Estate of Geyer*, 533 A.2d 423 (Pa. 1987).

246. *King v. King*, 638 S.W.3d 464 (Ky. Ct. App. 2021).

247. *See McKoy v. McKoy*, 95 Va. Cir. 55, 2017 Va. Cir. LEXIS 1 (unpub.).

248. *Pollock-Halvarson v. McGuire*, 576 N.W.2d 451 (Minn. Ct. App. 1998); *Darr v. Darr*, 950 S.W.2d 867 (Mo. Ct. App. 1997); *In re Estate of Hartman*, 399 Pa. Super. 386, 582 A.2d 648 (1990).

required financial disclosure as "fair and reasonable disclosure of the property [and] financial obligations"[249] of the disclosing party. Relevant financial information generally includes amounts and sources of income as well as assets and liabilities.[250] The UPMAA fills in some gaps in the UPAA, requiring disclosure of property and debt, including a good faith estimate of values, as well as disclosure of income.[251] Some cases have held that a disclosure that identified assets without providing values was sufficient to uphold a premarital agreement.[252] The text of the UPMAA requires more than mere identity of assets.

The content of the disclosure required in a given case depends in part on the scope of the agreement and in part on the alternative provisions, if any, made for the economically weaker party. For example, in *King v. King*,[253] the husband's failure to disclose his income did not render the premarital agreement invalid where it did not waive the wife's right to share in property acquired with income earned during the marriage. Similarly, in *In re Estate of Beesley*,[254] a premarital agreement was valid, although the husband made no disclosure, where the wife received a larger share of his estate than she would have been entitled to receive under Utah's elective share statute. By contrast, in *Corbett v. Corbett*,[255] the husband did not disclose his income and the premarital agreement waived alimony. His omission was material to the wife's decision whether to accept the terms. Therefore, the agreement was invalid.

Courts have generally not required that disclosure be minutely detailed,[256] that every asset be itemized, or that every asset be valued precisely.[257] Indeed, courts have generally rejected the argument that a detailed list of every asset with accurate values is a prerequisite to validity.[258] Most courts have taken a fairly pragmatic approach to evaluating the adequacy of financial disclosures. "Fair and full disclosure" of assets is often held to mean something less than complete disclosure in a strict sense. Of greater significance than precise valuation is that such information as is provided not mislead the other party.[259] "Disclosure may be

---

249. UPAA § 6(a)(2)(ii). No court or legislature has made formal appraisal a requirement for fair disclosure of asset values.

250. *Nitkiewicz v. Nitkiewicz*, 369 Pa. Super. 504, 535 A.2d 664 (1988).

251. UPMAA § 9(d)(1) (2012). The UPMAA has been adopted only in North Dakota and Colorado.

252. *Cannon v. Cannon*, 384 Md. 537, 865 A.2d 563 (2005); *Marriage of Yager*, 155 Or. App. 407, 963 P.2d 137 (1998); *Gooch v. Gooch*, 10 Ark. App. 432, 664 S.W.2d 900 (1984).

253. 66 S.W.3d 28 (Mo. Ct. App. 2001).

254. 883 P.2d 1343 (Utah 1994).

255. 280 Ga. 369, 628 S.E.2d 585 (2006).

256. *Del Vecchio v. Del Vecchio*, 143 So. 2d 17, 21 (Fla. 1962).

257. *See Pollock-Halvarson v. McGuire*, 576 N.W.2d 451, 456 (Minn. Ct. App. 1998); *Miles v. Werle*, 977 S.W.2d 297 (Mo. Ct. App. 1998); *Greenwald v. Greenwald*, 154 Wis. 2d 767, 454 N.W.2d 34 (1990); *In re Estate of Hopkins*, 166 Ill. App. 3d 652, 520 N.E.2d 415 (1988).

258. *See In re Marriage of Yager*, 155 Or. App. 407, 963 P.2d 137 (1998); *but see Jacobitti v. Jacobitti*, 263 N.J. Super. 608, 623 A.2d 794 (App. Div. 1993) (detailed disclosure of financial worth is required; agreement reciting parties' net worth and annual incomes without detail was invalid).

259. *See Peters-Riemers v. Riemers*, 644 N.W.2d 197 (N.D. 2002) (disclosure inadequate where husband stated net worth of $470,000 but recent loan application claimed net worth of $1.3 million plus); *Davis v. Miller*, 269 Kan. 732, 7 P.3d 1223 (2000) (husband's disclosure of interest in closely held corporation, provision of current balance sheet, and book value sufficient, although fair market value was substantially higher, where wife not misled and had opportunity to request more information or independent valuation); *Pollock-Halvarson v. McGuire*, 576 N.W.2d 451 (Minn. Ct. App. 1998) (husband's omission of accidental death and VA insurance policies was insignificant).

imprecise only to the extent that it does not obscure the general financial resources of the parties."[260]

A disclosure that accurately reveals the nature and extent of property holdings will often suffice even if the disclosure does not include valuations. For example, in *In re Marriage of Yager*,[261] the husband took the wife to visit his real estate holdings and gave her a copy of his marital settlement with his previous wife that identified property he would receive but without valuations. The court found that the wife's awareness of the husband's interest in the properties and that his interest had substantial value, was sufficient.[262] Most courts seem to consider it more important that parties disclose the existence of all significant assets than that values be fully disclosed.[263] When value is disclosed, the disclosure must be substantially accurate, but need not disclose 100 percent of the value of all assets based on current valuations. Thus, in *Darr v. Darr*,[264] a five-month-old financial statement that disclosed 88 percent of the husband's monthly income was adequate.

Counsel should generally begin with the presumption that parties should provide an itemized list of assets and liabilities with current good faith statements of value as well as sources and amounts of income.[265] There may be situations where counsel or the client decides that disclosure this detailed or extensive is unnecessary; however, there are no reported cases where an agreement was unenforceable because a party provided too much financial information.[266] A detailed written disclosure provides a record of what was disclosed that survives death, loss of memory, destruction of files, or a change of heart.

---

260. *Simeone v. Simeone*, 380 Pa. Super. 37, 551 A.2d 219, 221; *see also Shinn v. Schaal*, 394 N.J. Super. 55, 925 A.2d 88 (2007) (disclosure of assets valued at $850,000 inadequate where life insurance application stated $6 million net worth); *In re Estate of Geyer*, 533 A.2d 423 (husband's understatement of value of his estate by more than 50 percent was substantial nondisclosure; premarital agreement invalid); *Posner v. Posner*, 257 So. 2d 530 (Fla. 1972) (husband's failure to reveal right to income from trust and right to invade principal was material nondisclosure that rendered premarital agreement invalid); *but see Hill v. Hill*, 356 N.W.2d 49 (Minn. Ct. App. 1984) (husband's 50 percent understatement of net worth was good faith error resulting from recent real estate appreciation; disclosure sufficient).

261. *In re Marriage of Yager*, 155 Or. App. 407, 963 P.2d 137 (1998).

262. *See also Hutchins v. Hutchins*, 393 Mont. 283, 430 P.3d 502 (2018) (disclosure of assets without values was adequate); *Cannon v. Cannon*, 384 Md. 537, 865 A.2d 563 (2005) (same); *In re Marriage of Gardner*, 190 Wis. 2d 217, 234, 527 N.W.2d 701, 706 (1994) (disclosure of book value rather than fair market value of closely held corporation was sufficient); *but see McMullin v. McMullin*, 926 S.W.2d 108 (Mo. Ct. App. 1996) (husband's disclosure of nature of assets without values insufficient where wife lacked other information about his assets); *but see Dodson v. Dodson*, 779 So. 2d 638 (Ga. 2015) (husband's disclosure of assets, including business interests, without values was insufficient; premarital agreement is void).

263. *See Marsocci v. Marsocci*, 911 A.2d 690 (R.I. 2006); *Cannon v. Cannon*, 384 Md. 537; *but see In re Marriage of Delaney*, 298 Wis. 2d 247, 726 N.W.2d 356 (2006) (list of assets without values provided insufficient financial disclosure notwithstanding waiver and wife's testimony as to lack of interest in this information; premarital agreement invalid).

264. *Darr v. Darr*, 950 S.W.2d 867 (Mo. Ct. App. 1997).

265. See Appendix C, Personal Information Worksheet, which incorporates an asset worksheet that can be used to create a detailed disclosure.

266. However, there is rarely a reason for a party to provide a detailed inventory of all of his or her ordinary household effects. He or she may reasonably group such items with a description such as "furniture and household effects" and a gross good faith estimate of value.

(d) Disclosure Regarding Closely Held Business

Disclosure of the value of an interest in a closely held business presents a special challenge. The value of a closely held business may not be readily ascertainable, the owner may be reluctant to disclose information that could be of interest to competitors, a prior spouse, or the other party's prior spouse. The owner's partners may not wish to have such information shared.[267]

It is a mistake for the owner to assume that the other party's knowledge of the existence of the business is tantamount to an understanding of its value.[268] *Restatement Third of Property* takes the position that the owner must provide an appraisal,[269] but there is no support in the case law for such a requirement.[270] However, an owner who fails to provide meaningful disclosure of known data does so at his or her own peril.[271] The owner could provide the gross revenues of a business, his or her percentage interest, salary, or other compensation received from the business, and the like.[272] He or she could also provide documents, such as tax returns, an application for key-person insurance, a balance sheet, or a profit and loss statement. The owner's statement of value should be appropriately qualified so as not to be misleading.[273] When the value is stated as book value, it is especially important that the disclosure include an acknowledgment that actual value may be higher.[274]

Counsel for the business owner should inquire whether there have been any appraisals of the business or of any major assets, such as a building, and for what purpose. For example, has an appraisal been done in connection with a transfer from a member of the older

---

267. See Section 4.08(l) for discussion of privacy concerns.

268. *See In re Estate of Davis*, 213 S.W.3d 288, 297 (Tenn. App. 2006) (premarital agreement invalid after death of wife where husband knew wife owned music company but wife provided no value and asset was "of a type that a person cannot simply look at and get a reasonable understanding of its value"); *In re Estate of Baker v. King*, 207 S.W.3d 254 (Tenn. Ct. App. 2006) (wife's knowledge husband owned gas station insufficient where she had no information about value of business); *In re Estate of Hansen*, 77 Wash. App. 526, 892 P.2d 764 (1995) (husband's knowledge wife owned oil business insufficient where he did not know value).

269. RESTATEMENT THIRD OF PROPERTY § 9.4, cmt. H ("In circumstances in which the decedent's property consists importantly of assets for which an immediately ascertainable market price is not available, such as close-corporation shares or interests in real estate, the duty to disclose asset values requires the decedent to supply suitable appraisals.").

270. *See Stewart v. Stewart*, 214 Md. App. 458, 76 A.3d 1221 (2013) (rejecting wife's claim financial disclosure was inadequate because it did not include accountant's statement or information from which she could calculate future earnings).

271. *Shinn v. Schaal*, 394 N.J. Super. 55, 925 A.2d 88 (2007) (business-owner husband's disclosure was inadequate where he omitted values for certain major assets while disclosing others valued at $850,000 and where recent life insurance application claimed net worth of $6 million); *see also In re Marriage of Van Ert*, 54 N.E. 3d 928 (Ill. App. 2016) (marital agreements void for fraud where husband did not disclose offer to buy business for $26 million, claimed valued at $1.2 million).

272. *See, e.g., Waton v. Waton*, 887 So. 2d 419 (Fla. Dist. Ct. App. 2004).

273. *See Steele v. Steele*, 467 N.J. Super. 414, 253 A.3d 1190 (2021) (husband's use of different methods to value different business interests was misleading and undervalued by millions).

274. *See Head v. Head*, 59 Md. App. 570, 477 A.2d 282 (1983); (marital settlement resolving dispute over premarital agreement was valid where husband sold company for 17 times book value soon after settlement, but where he disclosed book value with statement that actual value could be much higher); *DeLong v. DeLong*, 1998 Mo. App. LEXIS 69 (husband's disclosure was adequate where he provided book value and stated actual value could be two to three times book); *Orgler v. Orgler*, 237 N.J. Super. 342, 568 A.2d 67 (App. Div. 1989) (husband's use of book rather than fair market value, which husband knew was less than true value, rendered premarital agreement invalid); *Dion v. Dion*, 1984 Pa. Dist. & Cnty. Dec. LEXIS 52 (husband's use of book value of company when he knew company worth several times that was material misrepresentation; premarital agreement invalid).

generation of owners, for estate tax purposes upon the death of an owner, or in connection with an owner's divorce? Has the owner received an offer to purchase the business?[275] Or, has the owner personally, or the business entity itself, submitted a loan application with a statement of value or stated a value on a personal or business net worth statement or on an application for key-person insurance? These documents will be discoverable in future litigation over validity. The disclosure for the agreement should not contradict other statements of value made close in time to the agreement, or the disclosure should include an acknowledgement of and an explanation for the disparity.[276]

(e) Disclosure of Future Inheritance, Bonus, or Other Expectancies

A party is under no obligation to disclose his or her family's wealth,[277] and, in some cases, may not be able to do so. However, when a party has a reasonable expectation of a substantial future inheritance, it will often be in that party's interest to make some disclosure to reduce the incentive to challenge validity. The content will depend upon the party's circumstances. When the value of a party's current assets is modest, but he or she can expect to come into a large fortune, whether outright or in trust, the lawyer for that party should consider whether to disclose the approximate value thereof, to the extent known. Counsel may need to seek this information, as well as permission to disclose it, from the client's family or the family estate planning lawyer. As the client's parents and other family members are not parties to the agreement, they are under no obligation to disclose the nature and value of the assets they own outright or through a revocable trust. However, especially when a parent has encouraged a young adult child to get a premarital agreement, he or she will likely understand why it is in the best interest of the child, as well as the family, to make a reasonable disclosure.

Where a party reasonably anticipates a substantial change in his or her financial circumstances in the foreseeable future, he or she should generally provide that information. For example, in *Dardick v. Dardick*,[278] the court upheld a premarital agreement where the husband had failed to disclose an agreement with his employer that he would receive $500,000 if his company was sold. Two years after the marriage, the company was sold, and the husband received stock valued at $500,000. The court held the husband's right to this payment was speculative at the time of the premarital agreement because it depended on certain contingencies. Had the future payment been less speculative, or closer in time, it may well have been in the husband's interest to disclose it (assuming disclosure would not violate a confidentiality obligation to his employer), along with a statement that the payment is uncertain.

(f) Disclosure of Interest in a Trust

A party who is a beneficiary or a settler of a trust will need to make adequate disclosure of his or her interest. In general, the party will need to disclose vested rights, such as an interest as a beneficiary in an irrevocable trust or a revocable trust of which the party is the settlor.[279]

275. *See In re Marriage of Van Ert*, 54 N.E. 3d at 928.

276. *See Peters-Riemers v. Riemers*, 644 N.W.2d 197 (N.D. 2002); *Shinn v. Schaal*, 394 N.J. Super. 55, 925 A.2d 88 (2007).

277. *See Jundt v. Jundt*, 2006 Minn. App. LEXIS 369 (unpub.).

278. 948 S.W.2d 268 (Mo. Ct. App. 1997).

279. *See In re Marriage of Wanger*, 2016 Ill. App. Unpub. LEXIS 416.

The kinds of information the party as beneficiary or settlor should disclose (and the other party should request) includes:

- the name of the trust;
- the identity of the settlor;
- the value of trust assets;
- the nature of trust assets;
- the number and identity of trust beneficiaries (is the party to the agreement the sole beneficiary or only one of several?);
- the identity of the trustee;
- the current rights of the party, if any, to income and principal, and whether the trustee has discretion to withhold distributions from the party;
- the history of income and principal distributions, if any, to the party;
- what future rights the party has and when these rights come into being, such as upon a parent's death or upon reaching a certain age;
- whether the party has a power of appointment and whether it permits the party to exercise it in favor of a spouse;
- whether the trust is revocable or irrevocable; and
- whether trust assets will be includible in the gross estate of the party (or anyone else) for federal estate tax purposes.[280]

(g) Disclosure of Hard-to-Value Assets

As discussed in regard to a closely held business, a party who owns valuable assets whose value is not readily ascertainable should provide whatever relevant information he or she does have. For example, he or she could state the amount of insurance coverage for jewelry, artwork, antiques, or other collectibles. He or she could provide an inventory with the dates of purchase and purchase price of such items. When the asset is a nonmarketable security or an interest in a limited partnership, he or she could state the amount paid and date of purchase. In all cases, the statement of value should be qualified with a statement as to the basis for the valuation, the source of valuation information, and that the stated value is an estimate.

(h) Disclosure of Debt

Disclosure of debt is usually less important than disclosure of assets. Courts have generally observed that omission of debt is an error that favors the weaker party since it means that the marital rights he or she waived were actually worth less.[281] However, counsel should generally opt to have the client include debt and request that the other party do so. This can be especially important when parties intend to share the fruits of their labor since one party's premarital or marital debt can drain marital resources.[282] Other circumstances can cause one

280. Anne W. Coventry & Linda J. Ravdin, *Premarital Agreements & Trusts*, 38(2) FAM. ADVOC. (Fall 2015).

281. *See Rostanzo v. Rostanzo*, 73 Mass. App. Ct. 588, 900 N.E.2d 101 (2009); *Azarova v. Schmitt*, 2007 Ohio App. LEXIS 586 (unpub.).

282. *See Keith v. Keith*, 37 S.D. 132, 156 N.W. 910 (1916) (premarital agreement void where wife agreed to pool assets with husband based on his fraudulent concealment of his insolvency).

party's debt to be detrimental to the other party. For example, in *Haigh v. Comm'r, I.R.S.*,[283] the wife made a premature withdrawal from her IRA before marriage and did not pay the penalty. The premarital agreement required joint income tax returns. Had the husband known of the wife's income tax liability, he could have proposed the agreement not include such a provision.[284]

(i) Waiver of Financial Disclosure

Waiver of financial disclosure can take several forms, including a blanket waiver of all disclosure and a limited disclosure coupled with a waiver of all disclosure beyond that provided by each party. Some courts recognize an implied waiver under some circumstances. The UPAA expressly permits parties to waive all financial disclosure.[285] The waiver must be in writing and voluntary, and it must be express.[286] Moreover, if the agreement is unconscionable at execution, the waiver must be executed before the execution of the agreement.[287] Similarly, the UPMAA permits parties to waive financial disclosure and does not require actual advice of counsel for an effective waiver, consistent with the UPAA and the law in the majority of the non-UPAA states. The UPAA implies that a waiver must be in a separate writing.[288] The UPMAA states expressly that a waiver must in a separate signed writing.[289] Both the UPMAA and the UPAA require the waiver to be executed before the agreement, though there is nothing in the text or comments that suggests the waiver must be signed on a different day.

A party may elect to condition a waiver on his or her receipt of some financial disclosure. Nothing in the UPAA or the UPMAA precludes such a partial disclosure coupled with waiver.[290] There is little authority in the non-UPAA states that addresses specifically the viability of an express waiver of financial disclosure in a premarital agreement. However, general contract law principles permitting contracting parties to waive known rights should permit such a waiver.[291] In states where an implied waiver, as discussed below, has served

283. 2009 Tax Ct. Memo LEXIS 140 (6/15/09).

284. Mandatory joint income tax returns is not a good idea in any event. See Chapter 12, Paragraph 15, and Comment.

285. *In re Marriage of Solano*, 124 N.E.3d 1097 (Ill. App. 2019).

286. UPAA § 6(a) (1983). The Arkansas version of the UPAA requires that such a waiver be done after actual, not merely opportunity for, consultation with counsel. *See* ARK. CODE ANN. § 9-11-406(a)(2)(ii). The Connecticut version of the UPAA deleted the option for parties to expressly waive disclosure. One Connecticut court in an unreported opinion stated that the Connecticut Premarital Agreement Act, CONN. GEN. STAT. §§ 46b-36a *et seq.*, did not permit parties to waive disclosure without addressing whether general contract law principles permit such a waiver. *Intravia v. Intravia*, 2003 Conn. Super. LEXIS 2805 (unpub.). However, in *Intravia*, where there was no formal asset disclosure, the agreement recited that the parties, both represented by counsel, were satisfied with the financial information they had, and did not need more. Such a recitation is tantamount to a waiver.

287. See Section 2.07(a) for full text of Section 6 of the UPAA. See Appendix E, Additional and Optional Terms, for a form for a pre-execution waiver.

288. A premarital agreement is unenforceable if unconscionable at execution "and, *before execution*, . . . [the challenging] party . . . did not . . . expressly waive in writing. . . ." UPAA § 6(a)(2)(ii) (emphasis added).

289. However, in Colorado, one of the two states that have adopted the UPMAA, the legislature omitted the provision permitting waiver. See Appendix B(1), State Law Summary: Premarital Agreements.

290. *In re Marriage of Solano*, 124 N.E.3d at 1097.

291. *See, e.g., Harbom v. Harbom*, 134 Md. App. 430, 450, 760 A.2d 272, 283 n.2 (2000) ("an intended spouse may assent . . . to forego disclosure of the other spouse's assets so long as the assenting party entered into the agreement voluntarily, freely and with full knowledge of its meaning and effect"); *but see In re Estate of J.D. Davis*, 184

to render a disclosure adequate, an express, written voluntary waiver should be at least as enforceable. Similarly, in states where preexisting knowledge of financial affairs, informal disclosure, or a bare recital that parties made financial disclosure is sufficient, an express, voluntary waiver should also suffice.

In a variety of circumstances, courts have held a party's conduct to constitute an implied waiver of all disclosure or of any disclosure beyond that which the other party elected to make. These include:

- A party is given some disclosure and forgoes an opportunity to make further inquiry after being on notice of facts that may call for it;[292]
- A party is given access to financial records and declines to review them;[293]
- Refusal of an offer to provide full disclosure, or other conduct showing disclosure would have had no effect on the decision to sign the agreement;[294]
- A party's stated lack of interest in the other party's assets or their value;[295]
- A party's failure to request a more accurate or current valuation of assets;[296]
- A refusal to read the agreement;[297]
- A party's failure to correct the other party's misstatement that disclosure was made;[298]
- A party's material failure to disclose assets may render deficiencies in the other party's disclosure of no consequence;[299]
- Where neither party made any disclosure;[300] and
- Where the party challenging validity initiated the agreement to protect his or her more substantial estate from an economically weaker party.[301]

Waiver has an important role to play in virtually every agreement. Even where each party has provided a detailed list of assets with values, the agreement should include an express waiver of any further disclosure. A waiver coupled with disclosure signals that each party is

S.W.3d 231 (Tenn. App. 2004) (Tennessee's strong public policy favors disclosure; agreement signed in Florida while parties were residents, and where financial disclosure not required, was invalid).

292. *See Northington v. Northington*, 257 So. 3d 326 (Ala. Civ. App. 2017); *Reece v. Elliott*, 208 S.W.3d 419 (Tenn. App. 2006); *Griffin v. Griffin*, 94 P.3d 96 (Okla. Civ. App. 2004); *Davis v. Miller*, 269 Kan. 732, 7 P.3d 1223 (2000); *Gardner v. Gardner*, 190 Wis. 2d 217, 527 N.W.2d 701 (1994); *In re Estate of Stephenson*, 243 Neb. 890, 503 N.W.2d 540 (1993); *Daniel v. Daniel*, 779 S.W.2d 110 (Tex. App. 1989).

293. *In re Marriage of Burkle*, 139 Cal. App. 4th 712, 43 Cal. Rptr. 3d 181 (2006).

294. *See Marriage of Hill and Dittmer*, 202 Cal. App. 4th 1046, 136 Cal. Rptr. 3d 700 (2011); *Greenwald v. Greenwald*, 154 Wis. 2d 767, 454 N.W.2d 34 (1990).

295. *See Reece*, 208 S.W.3d 419; *Schutterle v. Schutterle*, 260 N.W.2d 341 (S.D. 1977).

296. *See In re Marriage of Spiegel*, 553 N.W.2d 522 (Iowa 1996).

297. *In re Estate of Smid*, 756 N.W.2d 1 (S.D. 2008); *Brown v. Brown*, 26 So. 3d 1210 (Ala. Civ. App. 2007); *Hiers v. Estate of Hiers*, 278 Ga. App. 242, 628 S.E.2d 653 (2006); *Cannon v. Cannon*, 384 Md. 537, 865 A.2d 563 (2005); *Hale v. Robertson*, 60 S.W.3d 686 (Mo. App. 2001); *Busch v. Busch*, 732 A.2d 1274 (Pa. Super. Ct. 1999); *Wiley v. Iverson*, 295 Mont. 511, 985 P.2d 1176 (1999); *Cantrell v. Estate of Cantrell*, 19 S.W.3d 842 (Tenn. App. 1999); *In re Estate of Peterson*, 221 Neb. 792, 381 N.W.2d 109 (1986).

298. *See In re Estate of Thies*, 273 Mont. 272, 903 P.2d 186 (1995); *In re Neis' Estate*, 225 P.2d 110 (Kan. 1950).

299. *See In re Cohen's Will*, 13 Misc. 2d 384, 176 N.Y.S.2d 67 (Sup. Ct. 1958) (surviving wife's concealment of her substantial assets rendered her claim of lack of knowledge suspect).

300. *See In re Marriage of Ross*, 670 P.2d 26 (Colo. Ct. App. 1983).

301. *See In re Estate of White*, 718 S.W.2d 185 (Mo. Ct. App. 1986).

satisfied with the other's disclosure and has enough information to decide whether to sign the proposed agreement or negotiate for revisions to the terms. A waiver can insulate the agreement from attack based on trivial or inadvertent omissions. A waiver may save an agreement where the nondisclosure is more substantial. For example, in *Marsocci v. Marsocci*,[302] the husband identified his main assets, including six pieces of real estate, without providing values. The agreement did not include a waiver of further disclosure. Inclusion of a waiver could have eliminated the disclosure issue as a viable ground of attack. A waiver may not save an agreement where a party makes a deliberate, material omission.[303]

A lawyer for an economically disadvantaged party should start with a presumption that a blanket waiver of disclosure is inappropriate. Counsel will need adequate financial disclosure to advise the client about the rights he or she is waiving, to develop possible negotiating options, and to formulate a reasonable approach to improving the terms for his or her client.

(j) Misrepresentation or Fraud in Disclosure

There are few reported examples of outright fraud or misrepresentation in the financial disclosure associated with a premarital or postmarital agreement as distinguished from mere insufficiency of data. In *Griffin v. Griffin*,[304] the husband's financial disclosure for the premarital agreement identified his closely held business assets with values that the written asset statement described as on an income tax basis. But his lawyer made oral statements to the wife and her lawyer that the stated values were at fair market value. The wife argued those statements constituted a fraudulent misrepresentation. The court rejected her claim. It identified the elements of fraud:

> (1) that the representations must have been material to the contract or transaction at the time they were made; (2) the misrepresented facts must be facts of which the victim is ignorant, and which a person of ordinary sagacity and diligence would have acquired no knowledge; (3) *the misrepresentations must be well calculated to deceive, and to induce the victim to make the contract*; *and* (4) *they must have induced him to do so*.[305]

The court concluded that the lawyer's comments were not intended to deceive, and that the wife did not rely on them, as she arrived at the meeting having already decided to sign the agreement based on the written disclosure provided to her counsel three weeks earlier. Importantly, the agreement included appropriate qualifiers, including an acknowledgment that the values were only estimates and that it was possible there were assets the husband overlooked.

302. 911 A.2d 690 (R.I. 2006).

303. *See In re Marriage of Wanger*, 2016 Ill. App. Unpub. LEXIS 416 (waiver did not save agreement where husband deliberately withheld information about trusts and other assets); *Kwon v. Kwon*, 333 Ga. App. 130, 775 S.E.2d 611 (2015) (waiver did not save premarital agreement where husband's disclosure omitted two LLCs); *see also McKoy v. McKoy*, 95 Va. Cir. 55, 2017 Va. Cir. LEXIS 1 (unpub.) (premarital agreement providing parties waived all disclosure beyond that provided in attached disclosure statement did not save agreement where disclosure was not attached).

304. 94 P.3d 96 (Okla. Civ. App. 2004).

305. *Id.* at 102 (italics in original).

By contrast, in *Shinn v. Schaal*,[306] the husband disclosed assets valued at $850,000 and identified other assets without assigning values. His total estate was actually worth about $6,000,000, according to his life insurance application. The trial judge deemed the financial disclosure inadequate but could easily have characterized it as deliberately misleading or fraudulent.[307] The premarital agreement was invalid.

A misleading financial disclosure may, especially when combined with other misleading statements, render a postmarital agreement the product of overreaching. In *Kearney v. Kearney*,[308] the husband provided inadequate, ambiguous, and misleading information about a key asset, his business. Moreover, he led the wife to believe the postmarital agreement was a routine transaction to permit him to recapitalize the business, when he intended it to predetermine parties' rights at divorce. It was invalid.[309]

A disclosure that overvalues, rather than undervalues, a party's worth may be adequate under some circumstances and misleading or fraudulent in others. The purpose of requiring financial disclosure is to permit each party to know the extent of marital rights he or she is waiving. That purpose is not undermined when a party inflates his or her net worth.[310] On the other hand, when a party's rights under the agreement depend on accurate information, as, for example, when the agreement provides a surviving spouse will receive a stated percentage of a deceased spouse's estate, misleadingly high asset values may constitute fraud sufficient to void the agreement. In *Keith v. Keith*,[311] a premarital agreement was void for fraud where the husband induced the wife to agree to pool her property with his based on his misrepresentation that he had assets when he was in fact insolvent.

---

306. *Shinn v. Schaal*, 394 N.J. Super. 55, 925 A.2d 88 (2007).

307. *See also In re Est. of Stokes*, 2022 Tenn. App. LEXIS 64 (unpub.) (premarital agreement unenforceable where decedent omitted substantial assets); *Gomer v. Gomer*, 86 N.E.3d 920 (Ohio Ct. App. 2017) (husband omitted substantial cash on deposit; premarital agreement invalid); *Petracca v. Petracca*, 101 A.D.3d 695, 956 N.Y.S.2d 77 (App. Div. 2d Dep't, 2012) (disclosure of assets valued at $22 million was inadequate where understated by $11 million; postmarital agreement invalid); *In re Estate of Cassidy*, 356 S.W.3d 339 (Mo. Ct. App. So. Dist. 2011) (gross undervaluation of farmland was fraudulent; premarital agreement invalid); *Blige v. Blige*, 283 Ga. 65, 656 S.E.2d 822 (2008) (omission of substantial cash savings was material and rendered agreement invalid); *In re Marriage of Delaney*, 298 Wis. 2d 247, 726 N.W.2d 356 (2006) (list of assets without values insufficient and not cured by boiler-plate waiver); *Peters-Riemers*, 644 N.W.2d 197 (N.D. 2002) (disclosure inadequate where husband stated net worth of $470,000 but recent loan application showed net worth of $1.3 million); *and see In re Marriage of Van Ert*, 54 N.E.3d 928 (Ill. App. 2016) (trial court erroneously dismissed wife's petition alleging fraud in connection with marital settlement agreement where husband did not disclose offer to purchase business for $16 million, claimed assets he would have after divorce only valued at $1.2 million, and sale of business consummated two hours after divorce); *Chaplain v. Chaplain*, 54 Va. App. 762, 682 S.E.3d 108 (2009) (summary judgment for husband reversed where did not provide written financial disclosure, wife testified he said he was poor, but had $20 million), *opinion after remand*, 2011 Va. App. LEXIS 15 (unpub.) (credibility contest resolved in husband's favor where he testified wife knew of his substantial wealth).

308. 129 So. 3d 381 (Fla. Ct. App., 1st Dist. 2013).

309. *See also Schechter v. Schechter*, 88 Mass. App. Ct. 239, 37 N.E. 3d 632 (2015) (husband's misleading statement about ownership of business rendered premarital agreement invalid); *Morris v. Morris*, 2014 W.Va. LEXIS 276 (husband's understatement of income and misrepresentations about character and value of property, coupled with unfairness of terms, rendered postmarital agreement invalid).

310. *See Azarova v. Schmitt*, 2007 Ohio App. LEXIS 586 (unpub.); *Salame v. Salame*, 1996 Conn. Super. LEXIS 936; *In re Estate of Arbeitman*, 886 S.W.2d 644 (Mo. Ct. App. 1994).

311. 37 S.D. 132, 156 N.W. 910 (1916); *see also Whicker*, 1994 Tenn. App. LEXIS 713 (unpub.) (premarital agreement was void where wife induced to share her assets with husband based on his false financial disclosure overvaluing his assets).

(k) The Lawyer's Role in Financial Disclosure for a Premarital or Postmarital Agreement

A common feature of many appellate cases involving a challenge to validity of a premarital or postmarital agreement is a last-minute exchange of financial disclosures with little or no lawyer involvement.[312] There is an important role for the lawyer to play in assisting the client to make adequate disclosure and that role should begin well before the day of execution. The lawyer can reduce the risk for the proponent of the agreement by taking a proactive role in conducting the financial disclosure. If, for example, the client is a business owner, his or her lawyer may need to learn enough about the business to assist the owner to make a fair and accurate statement about value. Information about the size of the business, what type of goods or services the business sells, how long the business has existed, whether the client is a founding member or inherited his or her interest, and how the business is organized will help to develop a plan for the statement of value. The client's CPA or financial advisor may be able to help formulate an accurate statement of value or determine what documents of the business should be provided.

A wealthy client who has an estate planning lawyer or a financial advisor may be able to enlist him or her to provide an accurate statement of all or many assets.[313] The advisor may be able to provide a statement regarding securities, for example, with the client preparing a list of real estate properties and high-value tangible personal property.

From the perspective of the weaker party, it will generally be in his or her interest for the lawyer to evaluate the adequacy of a proposed agreement, and to begin a negotiation, only after the proponent has provided financial disclosure. The weaker party's lawyer may need to insist on receiving the disclosure before evaluating the proposed terms.

There is an important link between financial disclosure and the presence of independent counsel for the weaker party.[314] When the challenging party had counsel, and his or her counsel received financial disclosure, counsel's knowledge is imputed to the client.[315] Counsel is charged with protecting the interests of his or her client.[316] That includes understanding valuation issues, such as the difference between book value and market value, asking for additional financial information and documents, and making a judgment about whether he or she has enough information to advise the client. Moreover, independent counsel is responsible for deciding whether to waive all disclosure or agree on partial disclosure coupled with a waiver. It is his or her job to explain the right to disclosure and the consequences of a waiver. The presence of independent counsel can render deficiencies in financial disclosure of no importance.[317]

---

312. *See, e.g., Walker v. Walker*, 2020 Tenn. App. LEXIS 47 (unpub.).

313. Appendix C includes a worksheet that the client can use as a starting point to prepare a financial disclosure if that information is not readily available in another format.

314. *See In re Marriage of Delaney*, 298 Wis. 2d 247, 726 N.W. 2d 356 (2006) (husband's financial disclosure inadequate and his chosen lawyer purported to represent both parties; premarital agreement invalid; contrasting with case where disclosure arguably deficient but challenger had independent counsel and agreement upheld).

315. *Friezo v. Friezo*, 281 Conn. 166, 914 A.2d 533 (2007); *Boote v. Shivers*, 198 S.W.3d 732 (Tenn. App. 2005).

316. *See Head v. Head*, 59 Md. App. 570, 477 A.2d 282 (1983).

317. *Beyor v. Beyor*, 158 Conn. App. 752, 121 A.3d 734 (2015) (husband's omission of $394,000 of Schedule E income not fatal to validity where both parties had counsel); *Reece v. Elliott*, 208 S.W.3d 419 (Tenn. App.

(l) Addressing Privacy Concerns in the Disclosure of Financial Data

Financial disclosure will often include personal information many parties would prefer be kept confidential. Particular information, such as business information or the value of a parent's estate, may be especially sensitive. A party may have concerns about the disclosure of financial information to a new spouse's adult children or other family members. Moreover, the existence or terms of a premarital or postmarital agreement may be discoverable in litigation between a party and his or her former spouse.[318] There are several steps that counsel may take, as well as agreement provisions, to address these concerns:

- Parties could sign a pre-execution confidentiality agreement prior to making any disclosures. This should protect a wealthy party's sensitive financial information during the time the parties are negotiating, and before they sign an agreement with a superseding confidentiality provision, or in the event negotiations break down and the parties either break off the engagement or decide to marry without a premarital agreement.
- Financial documents may be provided for examination by a party and counsel, but they will not be entitled to retain copies, or only the party's lawyer will be entitled to retain copies. The agreement should identify each document provided. Counsel should maintain a file with copies, and counsel for the party receiving disclosure in this manner should sign an attached certification acknowledging having examined the documents with his or her client. The agreement should include a waiver of further financial disclosure.
- The agreement may include a provision requiring each party to maintain the confidentiality of financial information received from the other party.
- The agreement may include a separate short-form acknowledgment of the existence of the agreement, permitting parties to deal freely with their own property without having to show the entire agreement, with attached disclosure schedules, to a third party.
- The parties may provide written, detailed financial disclosure schedules to each other, but not physically attach them to the agreement, and the agreement acknowledges that each party received the schedule and is satisfied.[319]
- The agreement may disclose each party's net worth in the aggregate, without an itemized list of assets, and gross income without itemizing sources. This could be combined with providing a less detailed list of assets or some financial documents.

2006) (wife had counsel, husband disclosed assets, but not values for all, asset list revealed husband was man of wealth; financial disclosure was adequate); *In re Marriage of Gardner*, 190 Wis. 2d 217, 527 N.W.2d 701 (1994) (wife's decision not to request fair market value of husband's business where husband disclosed book value, but acknowledged fair market value could be much higher, after consult with her lawyer-CPA, and with understanding of different valuation methods, was waiver of disclosure of fair market value); *see also Griffin v. Griffin*, 94 P. 3d 96 (Okla. Civ. App. 2004).

318. *See In the Interest of Knott*, 118 S.W.3d 899 (Tex. Ct. App. 2003); *Shinkle v. Shinkle*, 255 Mich. App. 221, 663 N.W.2d 481 (2002); *In re Marriage of Puterbaugh*, 327 Ill. App. 3d 792, 764 N.E.2d 582 (2002).

319. This option may not be available in New Jersey. The New Jersey version of the UPAA requires that a statement of assets be annexed to the agreement, N.J. Stat. § 37-2-33 (2014), although another provision allows parties to waive financial disclosure. N.J. Stat. § 37-2-38.c (2014)

- A business owner may provide a detailed list of nonbusiness assets and their values, and use a different method to disclose information about the business. For example, he or she may provide for examination of business documents as described above, but without leaving a copy in the possession of the other party.

§4.09 SUBSTANTIVE FAIRNESS OR CONSCIONABILITY OF TERMS

(a) Overview

In the majority of states, a court may consider the adequacy, or fairness, of the substantive terms of a premarital or postmarital agreement to some degree and under some circumstances in determining enforceability. The discussion below focuses on the question of fairness, or conscionability, in the determination of validity of the agreement as a whole.[320] There are two distinct questions in the substantive fairness analysis:

- What fairness standard applies? States differ as to how extreme the unfairness must be to warrant denying enforcement of an agreement. In some states, the agreement must satisfy the higher fairness standard.[321] Most states apply a standard of unconscionability.[322] The unconscionability standard creates a heavy burden for a party seeking to invalidate an agreement.[323] A standard of mere unfairness is somewhat easier for a challenger to meet.[324]
- When is fairness judged? The substantive fairness of the terms may be judged as of the execution of the agreement or as of enforcement. Where adequacy of the substantive terms is judged as of execution, there is no role for consideration of subsequent events.[325] This is the majority position. In a significant minority of states, the court can consider the effect of the agreement on the weaker party as of enforcement; this is known as the second look.[326]

There are few reported cases where an agreement was invalidated solely on the ground of substantive unfairness or unconscionability. Procedural and substantive fairness are closely linked; one tends to prove the other.[327] When a court invalidates an agreement, there is often

320. Fairness of a spousal support waiver in an otherwise valid agreement is a separate question. See Chapter 5.

321. *Skaates v. Kayser*, 333 Mich. App. 61, 959 N.W.2d 33 (2020) (terms of postmarital agreement must not give one spouse economic incentive to divorce); *Stewart v. Stewart*, 214 Md. App. 458, 76 A.3d 1221 (2013) (premarital agreement must be fair and equitable at execution).

322. *Upham v. Upham*, 36 Mass. App. Ct. 295, 301, 630 N.E.2d 307, 311 (1994) (conscionability and fairness are different, but overlapping, standards).

323. *See* David Cotter, *Substantive Sufficiency of Marital Agreements: Unconscionability and Unfairness*, 17 DIVORCE LITIG. 173 (Nov. 2005).

324. *Id.*; *Stewart*, 76 A.3d 1221; *In re Marriage of Shanks*, 758 N.W.2d 506, 512 (Iowa 2008).

325. *Mabus v. Mabus*, 890 So. 2d 806 (Miss. 2003); *Friedman v. Friedman*, 100 Cal. App. 4th 65, 122 Cal. Rptr. 2d 412 (2002).

326. The states that require substantive fairness at divorce are Alaska, Connecticut, Georgia, Kentucky, Massachusetts, Michigan, Minnesota, Mississippi, New Hampshire, North Dakota, South Carolina, Vermont, West Virginia, and Wisconsin. See Appendix B(1), State Law Summary: Premarital Agreements.

327. *See Tyler v. Tyler*, 990 So. 2d 423 (Ala. Civ. App. 2008) (proof of procedural fairness tends to prove substantive fairness).

a combination of factors that includes both procedural irregularities and extreme substantive unfairness.[328]

(b) Unconscionability or Unfairness at Execution

The UPAA permits a premarital agreement to be voided for unconscionability under certain circumstances but does not define the term.[329] The comment provides the following explanation:

> The standard of unconscionability is used in commercial law, where its meaning includes protection against one-sidedness, oppression, or unfair surprise. . . . [330]
>
> Unconscionability can be procedural or substantive.
>
> Procedural unconscionability involves bargaining naughtiness in the formation of the contract, *i.e.*, fraud, coercion, undue influence, misrepresentation, inadequate disclosure. . . . Substantive unconscionability . . . involves the harsh, oppressive, and one-sided terms of a contract, *i.e.*, inequality of the bargain. . . . The inequality of the bargain, however, must be so manifest as to shock the judgment of a person of common sense.[331]

Most courts deem an agreement unenforceable for unconscionability at execution only when it is the result of both a grossly unfair process ***and*** grossly unfair terms.[332] These courts hold that "unconscionability is the absence of meaningful choice . . . together with terms that are so oppressive that no reasonable person would make them and no fair and honest person would accept them."[333] However, some courts consider procedural and substantive unconscionability separately so that a premarital or postmarital agreement that was executed fairly may nevertheless be unenforceable if the substantive terms were extremely harsh at execution.[334]

---

328. *See, e.g.*, *Schechter v. Schechter*, 88 Mass. App. Ct. 239, 37 N.E.3d 632 (2015) (inadequate and misleading financial disclosure combined with harsh terms as of execution; agreement invalid).

329. Under the UPAA, a premarital agreement is unenforceable if it was executed involuntarily, *or* it was unconscionable at execution *and* the challenging party did not receive adequate financial disclosure, did not have adequate preexisting knowledge of the other's financial affairs, and did expressly waive such disclosure in writing. UPAA § 6.

330. UPAA § 6 cmt.

331. *King v. King*, 442 S.E.2d 154, 157 (N.C. App. 1994).

332. *Sanderson v. Sanderson*, 295 So. 3d 421 (Miss. 2018); *Stewart v. Stewart*, 214 Md. App. 458, 76 A.3d 1221 (2013); *Reizfeld v. Reizfeld*, 125 Conn. App. 782, 40 A.3d 320 (2010) (same); *In re Estate of Dito*, 2008 Cal. App. LEXIS 2683; *see also Baker v. Baker*, 622 So. 2d 541 (Fla. Dist. Ct. App. 1993) (premarital agreement that would leave wife a pauper was enforceable where executed freely with full disclosure and where wife represented by counsel who negotiated a change to terms); *DeLorean v. DeLorean*, 211 N.J. Super. 432, 511 A.2d 1257 (1986) (premarital agreement that provided little for spouse not unconscionable where executed voluntarily with full disclosure).

333. *Remillard v. Remillard*, 2022 Va. App. LEXIS 417 (unpub.); *Hardee v. Hardee*, 355 S.C. 382, 389, 585 S.E.2d 501, 505 (2003); *see also Beyor v. Beyor*, 158 Conn. App. 752, 121 A.3d 734 (2015); *Allard v. Allard*, 308 Mich. App. 536, 867 N.W.2d 866 (2014); *Barocas v. Barocas*, 94 A.D.3d 551, 942 N.Y.S.2d 451 (2012); *In re Marriage of Shanks*, 758 N.W.2d 506, 512 (Iowa 2008); *Kornegay v. Robinson*, 360 N.C. 640, 637 S.E.2d 516 (2006); *Waton v. Waton*, 887 So. 2d 419 (Fla. Dist. Ct. App. 2004).

334. *See Potts v. Potts*, 303 S.W.3d 177 (Mo. Ct. App. 2010) (substantive unconscionability is sufficient to deny enforcement of premarital agreement); *see also Marriage of Callahan*, 984 N.E.2d 531 (Ill. Ct. App. 2015) (gross disparity may be enough in some cases to invalidate marital settlement for unconscionability); *Marriage of Iqbal*

An unconscionability standard requires a showing of a more extreme form of unfairness than a standard that permits an agreement to be voided because it is merely unfair or unreasonable.[335] Courts have described an unconscionable agreement as one that is "blatantly one-sided and . . . rankly unfair,"[336] one in which the "inequality [is] . . . strong, gross and manifest. . . ."[337] An unconscionable agreement is one that no nondelusional person would make and no honest and fair person would accept, one that shocks the conscience.[338] The unconscionability standard is intended to provide predictability of enforcement to contracting parties by precluding courts from rewriting their contract except under the most extreme circumstances.[339] Thus, it requires a showing of extreme or gross unfairness.[340]

A South Carolina case provides a good example of how a combination of extreme procedural and substantive unfairness in a premarital agreement can produce a finding of invalidity. In *Holler v. Holler*,[341] the wife was an uneducated Ukrainian national. Shortly after arriving in the United States, she became pregnant with the husband's child. Her visa was due to expire on December 4, 1997, unless she married. The wife attempted to translate the agreement into Russian but was unable to complete the translation. Moreover, there were terms she did not understand even after translation into Russian. She was completely dependent on the husband and had no money to hire counsel. The wife signed the agreement on November 25, and the parties married on December 1, 1997. The court first found that the wife signed the agreement under duress. Further, because she had no meaningful choice, and because the terms of the agreement were so weighted in the husband's favor, the agreement was unconscionable at execution.[342]

---

and Khan, 11 N.E.3d (Ill. Ct. App. 2014) (postmarital agreement was unenforceable where wife got nothing of value).

335. *Upham v. Upham*, 36 Mass. App. Ct. 295, 630 N.E.2d 307 (1994).

336. *Weber v. Weber*, 589 N.W.2d 358, 361 (N.D. 1999), *quoting Crawford v. Crawford*, 524 N.W.2d 833, 836 (N.D. 1994).

337. *Darr v. Darr*, 950 S.W.2d 867, 871 (Mo. Ct. App. 1997), *quoting McMullin v. McMullin*, 926 S.W.2d 108, 110 (Mo. Ct. App. 1996).

338. *Skotnicki v. Skotnicki*, 237 A.D.2d 974, 975, 654 N.Y.S.2d 904, 905 (1997).

339. *DeMatteo v. DeMatteo*, 436 Mass. 18, 762 N.E.2d 797 (2002); *Hawxhurst v. Hawxhurst*, 318 N.J. Super. 72, 723 A.2d 58 (1998); *Ryan v. Ryan*, 659 N.E.2d 1088, 1093 (Ind. Ct. App. 1995); *MacFarlane v. Rich*, 132 N.H. 608, 567 A.2d 585 (1989); *Warren v. Warren*, 169 Ill. App. 3d 226, 523 N.E.2d 680 (1988); *Jackson v. Seder*, 467 So. 2d 422 (Fla. Dist. Ct. App.), *review denied*, 479 So. 2d 118 (Fla. 1985); *but see In re Marriage of Bernard*, 137 Wn. App. 827, 155 P.3d 171 (2007) (premarital agreement unenforceable where terms unfair to wife even though she had independent counsel who advised her not to sign).

340. *DeLorean v. DeLorean*, 211 N.J. Super. 432, 511 A.2d 1257 (1986).

341. 612 S.E.2d 469 (S.C. App. 2005).

342. For other extreme cases, *see In re Marriage of Sarancic*, 2020 Il. App. LEXIS 870 (unpub.) (premarital agreement was procedurally and substantively unconscionable where provided nothing for wife who was impoverished at the outset, no financial disclosure, wife's first language was Bosnian, husband made misrepresentations to wife about terms); *Sanderson*, 295 So. 3d at 421 (premarital agreement was unenforceable where terms were extremely harsh and where husband presented agreement close to wedding with no time for legal advice from lawyer of wife's choice); *Petracca v. Petracca*, 101 A.D.3d 695, 956 N.Y.S.2d 77 (2012) (postmarital agreement invalid where wife waived almost all property rights in estate of over $30 million, and husband threatened divorce and undervalued assets by $11 million); *Fetters v. Fetters*, 26 N.E.3d 1016 (Ind. Ct. App. 2015) (wife was 16-year-old who left school to marry husband twice her age, did not have a lawyer, agreement extremely disadvantageous to her; premarital agreement unconscionable as a matter of law).

It is not the role of the court to relieve a party of a bad bargain.[343] Thus, the mere fact that the result is harsh will not mean a premarital or postmarital agreement will be unenforceable as unconscionable.[344] Rather, there must be a "gross disparity in the value exchanged."[345] Mere unfairness of result is not tantamount to unconscionability.[346] An agreement is not unconscionable because it perpetuates an existing economic disparity,[347] nor because the disposition of property varies from what the disadvantaged spouse could expect in the absence of agreement.[348] Mere unfairness in a postmarital agreement is not tantamount to unconscionability, nor is regret over a bad bargain.[349] As one court observed:

> The term "fair," without some further elaboration, gives no guidance whatsoever concerning which agreements will be binding and which agreements will be struck down. Furthermore, candor compels us to raise to a conscious level the fact that, as in this case, prenuptial agreements will almost always be entered into between people with property or an income potential to protect on one side and people who are impecunious on the other. Measuring an agreement by an undefined judicial standard

---

343. *Reizfeld v. Reizfeld*, 125 Conn. App. 782, 40 A.3d 320 (2014); *Barocas v. Barocas*, 94 A.D.3d 551, 942 N.Y.S.2d 491 (2012); *In re Marriage of Shanks*, 758 N.W.2d 506, 512 (Iowa 2008); *Galloway v. Galloway*, 47 Va. App. 83, 622 S.E.2d 267 (2005); *Pollock-Halvarson v. McGuire*, 576 N.W.2d 451 (Minn. Ct. App. 1998).

344. *See Lloyd v. Niceta*, 255 Md. App. 663, 284 A.3d 808 (Ct. Spec. App. 2022) (postmarital agreement not unconscionable where husband agreed to pay wife $7 million if he committed adultery or other sexual misconduct where husband alone controlled whether penalty clause was triggered); *Baker*, 622 So. 2d 541 (where wife chose own lawyer and both parties freely agreed to enter into premarital agreement before engagement, there was full financial disclosure and no fraud or overreaching; premarital agreement leaving 71-year-old wife who gave up alimony from prior husband with little income was not unconscionable).

345. *Drewry v. Drewry*, 8 Va. App. at 473, 383 S.E.2d at 18, *quoting Derby v. Derby*, 8 Va. App. 19, 28, 378 S.E.2d 74, 79 (1989).

346. *See Chiles v. Chiles*, 779 S.W.2d 127 (Tex. App. 1989) (wife did not sustain burden of proof of unconscionability by showing of mere unfairness); *see also Balogh v. Balogh*, 134 Haw. 29, 332 P.3d 631 (2014) (mere fact agreement allocated property differently from expected allocation in absence of agreement does not render it unconscionable); *In re Marriage of Dewberry*, 115 Wash. App. 351, 365, 62 P.3d 525, 531 (2003) ("There is nothing unfair about two well-educated working professionals agreeing to preserve the fruits of their labor for their individual benefit.").

347. *Reizfeld v. Reizfeld,* 125 Conn. App. 782, 40 A.3d 320 (2011); *Mallen v. Mallen*, 280 Ga. 43, 622 S.E.2d 812 (2005); *Warren v. Warren*, 169 Ill. App. 3d 226, 523 N.E.2d 680 (1988).

348. *Sanderson,* 295 So. 3d at 421 (substantive unconscionability of premarital agreement is not judged by comparison with what challenging party would have received in absence of agreement); *Dawbarn v. Dawbarn*, 175 N.C. App. 712, 625 S.E.2d 186 (2006) (postmarital reconciliation agreement under which the husband transferred three pieces of real estate to the wife as her separate property, proposed after wife caught husband in extramarital affair, did not violate public policy by giving wife economic incentive to leave the marriage, as real estate would be her separate property whether parties divorced or stayed together); *Griffin v. Griffin*, 94 P.3d 96 (Okla. Civ. App. 2004) (no public policy prevents parties from entering into premarital agreement waiving right to equitable distribution of property); *Wilkes v. Estate of Wilkes*, 305 Mont. 335, 27 P.3d 433 (2001) (premarital agreement providing nothing for wife at husband's death was not unconscionable where she was 21 and developmentally disabled at marriage and husband was a 62-year-old sophisticated businessman and had assets he wished to preserve for children of prior marriage; concurring opinion described the agreement as not passing the laugh test but nevertheless enforceable); *but see Marsocci v. Marsocci*, 911 A.2d 690 (R.I. 2006) (premarital agreement unconscionable where precluded wife from acquiring any interest in husband's marital income but agreement enforceable as voluntary under Rhode Island UPAA); *In re Marriage of Foran*, 67 Wash. App. 242, 834 P.2d 1081 (1992) (premarital agreement that effectively precluded wife from acquiring any community property was invalid); *Ryan v. Ryan*, 659 N.E.2d 1088, 1093 (Ind. Ct. App. 1995) (agreement that "divides property . . . so as to leave one spouse . . . with insufficient property to provide for his or her reasonable needs" may be unconscionable).

349. *Bedrick v. Bedrick*, 300 Conn. 691, 17 A.3d 17 (2011).

> of fairness is an invitation to the very wealth distribution that these agreements are designed to prevent.[350]

Similarly, the Alabama Court of Appeals has stated:

> The fairness of an antenuptial agreement is not to be judged based upon a comparison of what the spouse takes under the agreement with what he or she would have taken without the agreement. Likewise, a court should not concern itself with the disparity in income between the parties to an antenuptial agreement in the absence of fraud, duress, or other culpable conduct on the part of one of the parties. . . . Typically, the reason parties enter into antenuptial agreements is because they have vastly different incomes and assets that they wish to protect in the case of divorce or death. The very impetus behind the creation of such agreements should not be a reason to set them aside as inequitable.[351]

That an agreement applies equally to both parties is evidence of conscionability even if their financial circumstances are greatly disparate at execution.[352] Indeed, because the marriage itself is valuable consideration for a premarital agreement, disparity in disposition of property does not render a premarital agreement lacking in consideration.[353] In many cases, mutual waivers will be sufficient to pass the test of conscionability. This is especially true when parties have children from prior marriages they wish to protect,[354] when both parties have adequate resources even if unequal,[355] and when the agreement makes some provision, even a very modest one, for the disadvantaged party.[356]

(c) The Second Look: Unfairness or Unconscionability at Divorce

In states where governing law permits consideration of substantive fairness or conscionability of a premarital or postmarital agreement at divorce,[357] the authority for a second look means the court may consider whether the agreement was fair or conscionable at execution and, if it was, whether it remains fair or conscionable at divorce.[358] The second look at divorce allows the court to invalidate a premarital or postmarital agreement in its entirety or to invalidate

350. *Gant v. Gant*, 329 S.E.2d 106 (W. Va. 1985); *see also DeMatteo v. DeMatteo*, 436 Mass. 18, 762 N.E.2d 797 (2002).

351. *Lemaster v. Dutton*, 694 So. 2d 1360 (Ala. Civ. App. 1996).

352. *In re Marriage of Haenisch*, 2021 IL App. LEXIS 1277 (unpub.); *Miles v. Werle*, 977 S.W.2d 297 (Mo. Ct. App. 1998); *Ryan*, 659 N.W.2d 1088, 1093; *Gould v. Rafaeli*, 822 S.W.2d 494 (Mo. Ct. App. 1991); *Gentry v. Gentry*, 798 S.W.2d 928 (Ky. 1990); *Gant v. Gant*, 329 S.E.2d 106 (W. Va. 1985); *Barnhill v. Barnhill*, 386 So. 2d 749, 751 (Ala. Civ. App.), *cert. denied*, 386 So. 2d 752 (Ala. 1980); *but see Kremer v. Kremer*, 912 N.W.2d 617 (Minn. 2018) (mirror terms of premarital agreement do not create fairness where there was gross disparity at outset); *McKoy v. McKoy*, 95 Va. Cir. 55, 2017 Va. Cir. LEXIS (unpub.) (same).

353. *See Sanders v. Sanders*, 288 S.W.2d 473 (Tenn. Ct. App. 1955) (husband got what he bargained for when agreed to extremely generous terms to persuade wife to marry him for the third time).

354. *Kornegay v. Robinson*, 360 N.C. 640, 637 S.E.2d 516 (2006).

355. *See Colon v. Colon*, 2006 N.J. Super. LEXIS 1795 (unpub.) (App. Div.).

356. *Laube v. Reints (In re Est. of Laube)*, 974 N.W.2d 538 (Iowa Ct. App. 2022).

357. There is little authority for a second look after a spouse's death. See Section 2.08(d).

358. The 14 second-look states are Alaska, Connecticut, Georgia, Kentucky, Massachusetts, Michigan, Minnesota, Mississippi, New Hampshire, North Dakota, South Carolina, Vermont, West Virginia, and Wisconsin. See Appendix B(1), State Law Summary: Premarital Agreements.

only part.[359] When the agreement is challenged at divorce, the court may therefore consider the property disposition and spousal support provisions as a whole and separately.[360] It could leave the property division as provided in the agreement and invalidate a spousal support waiver.[361] The trial court can also separately consider a fee-shifting provision and invalidate it as unconscionable at divorce while upholding the validity of the agreement as a whole.[362]

On paper it may seem somewhat easier to have a premarital or postmarital agreement declared invalid on substantive fairness grounds in a second-look state. However, there are few reported cases where a challenger was successful solely on the ground of substantive unfairness or unconscionability at divorce.[363] Often, when a challenging party in a second-look state is successful it is because of procedural defects at execution combined with extreme substantive unfairness at divorce.[364]

Even when a challenger in a second-look state is successful, he or she often remains significantly disadvantaged economically. For example, in *Lane v. Lane*,[365] a Kentucky case, when the parties married the husband was a 26-year-old stockbroker making $166,000 a year and the wife was a motel clerk making $19,000. The marriage lasted less than 10 years. The wife had stayed home to raise the parties' two children. At divorce the husband was making $1 million a year. Under the premarital agreement, the husband would receive the vast majority of assets acquired during marriage and the wife was entitled to no spousal support. The trial court invalidated the support waiver and awarded the wife $12,000 a month for three years. However, it left the property provisions in place. As a result, the vast disparity in the parties' economic circumstances, which grew exponentially during the marriage, remained intact.

The most common approach to the determination of fairness at enforcement of a premarital agreement is to evaluate whether circumstances since execution have so changed from the reasonable expectations of the parties as to render enforcement unconscionably unfair.[366] Generally, changed circumstances must have been unforeseeable at execution.[367] Thus, a

359. *See, e.g., Lane v. Lane*, 202 S.W.3d 577 (Ky. 2006) (invalidating alimony waiver in premarital agreement but leaving disposition of property terms intact).

360. In addition to the 14 second-look states, six states permit a second look only as to spousal support. Spousal support is addressed in Chapter 5.

361. *Lane*, 202 S.W.3d 577. An invalid spousal support waiver will generally be severable so that the agreement will remain valid as a whole.

362. *Grabe v. Hokin*, 341 Conn. 360, 267 A.3d 145 (2021).

363. *See, e.g., Wisth v. Wisth*, 754 N.W.2d 254 (Wis. Ct. App. 2008) (husband procured premarital agreement through unfair process; *in dicta*, also unfair in result at divorce).

364. *Id.*

365. *Lane v. Lane*, 202 S.W.3d 577 (Ky. 2006).

366. *See Hudson v. Hudson*, 408 S.C. 76, 757 S.E.2d 727 (Ct. App. 2014), *cert. denied* 2014 S.C. LEXIS 565; *Schoenborn v. Schoenborn*, 144 Conn. App. 846, 74 A.3d 482 (2013); *Richard v. Richard*, No. A04-746 2004 LEXIS 1475 (Minn. App. Dec. 28, 2004); *In re Marriage of Krejci*, 266 Wis. 2d 284, 667 N.W.2d 780 (Ct. App. 2003); *Butcher v. Butcher*, 2003 Mich. App. LEXIS 325; *Gentry v. Gentry*, 798 S.W.2d 928 (Ky. 1990); *MacFarlane v. Rich*, 132 N.H. 608, 567 A.2d 585 (1989); *Scherer v. Scherer*, 249 Ga. 635, 292 S.E.2d 662 (1982).

367. *Gant v. Gant*, 329 S.E.2d 106 (W.Va. 1985); *see also Hutchison v. Hutchison*, 2009 Mich. App. LEXIS 1594 (husband's physical abuse of wife and threats designed to force her to quit work were unforeseeable at execution of premarital agreement; alimony and property awarded despite waiver); *Hardee v. Hardee*, 355 S.C. 382, 585 S.E.2d 501 (2003); (premarital agreement upheld where wife's serious health problems known at execution, deterioration foreseeable, and two attorneys advised her not to sign); *Knutson v. Knutson*, 246 Wis. 2d 988, 632 N.W.2d 123 (Ct. App. 2001) (no changed circumstances after marriage where wife quit work before signing premarital agreement); *Upham v. Upham*, 36 Mass. App. Ct. 295, 630 N.E.2d 307 (1994) (premarital agreement

premarital agreement that perpetuates an existing disparity in resources is not unconscionable at enforcement where it was executed voluntarily and with full disclosure.[368] Similarly, a premarital agreement is not void on unfairness grounds because a party continued to work and grow his or her assets,[369] or because a successful businessperson continued to be successful.[370] Such a circumstance is generally anticipated. When a professional couple enters into a premarital agreement that allows each to retain the fruits of his or her labor, the fact that one party was more successful does not render the agreement unfair at enforcement,[371] especially when the party challenging enforcement was the original proponent of the agreement.[372] There is room for a court to consider a party's own financial mismanagement in rejecting a challenge at the second-look stage.[373] However, when an agreement is drafted with the intent that each party be able to build assets, and one spouse fails to contribute to expenses, so that the other spouse bears a disproportionate share and is unable to acquire property while the other spouse does, the agreement may fail the second-look test.[374]

Foreseeability is an objective standard, determined by what parties reasonably could have anticipated under the circumstances.[375] However, some cases seem to focus on what the parties themselves actually anticipated. For example, in *In re Marriage of Zernia*,[376] the court held a premarital agreement unenforceable because the parties departed from their own expectations about how they would conduct their financial affairs, thus applying a subjective standard, what the parties themselves foresaw, rather than an objective one. In *Gant v. Gant*,[377] the court posited that the parties might have had three children, all under the age of five, at the time of divorce, rendering the wife in need of support for herself so that she could care for them. The wife in *Gant* was only 34 on the date of marriage. In *Warren v. Warren*,[378] where the parties were at retirement age when they married, the court suggested a party's deterioration in health might be an unforeseeable changed circumstance. That a woman of childbearing age might have children, or a retired person might suffer deterioration in health, seem obviously foreseeable.[379] The extent to which courts will hold parties to an objective standard has yet to be fully articulated.

---

did not become unconscionable because wife's assets at divorce greater than husband's although husband started with more; this was what husband bargained for when he sought agreement).

368. *Fercho v. Fercho*, 982 N.W.2d 540 (N.D. 2022); *Reizfeld v. Reizfeld*, 125 Conn. App. 782, 40 A.3d 320 (2014); *Allard v. Allard*, 308 Mich. App. 536, 867 N.W.2d 866 (2014); *Sides v. Sides*, 290 Ga. 68, 717 S.E.2d 472 (2011).

369. *Winchester v. McCue*, 91 Conn. App. 721, 882 A.2d 143 (2005).

370. *See In re Marriage of Holmes*, 2012 Minn. App. Unpub. LEXIS 896.

371. *Borofsky v. Cardill*, 957 A.2d 404 (Vt. 2008); *Reed v. Reed*, 265 Mich. App. 131, 693 N.W.2d 825 (2005).

372. *Schoenborn v. Schoenborn*, 144 Conn. App. 846, 74 A.3d 482 (2013).

373. *See Grabe v. Hokin*, 341 Conn. 360, 267 A.3d 145 (2021) (premarital agreement not unconscionable at divorce where wife grew her assets while husband was unproductive); *Weissgerber v. Weissgerber*, 276 Wis. 2d 308, 686 N.W.2d 455 (2004) (premarital agreement was not unfair at divorce where wife's financial position was a result of her refusal to work at her business and her decision to incur substantial debt to pursue litigation over agreement).

374. *See Shehan v. Shehan*, 2012 S.C. App. Unpub. LEXIS 447.

375. *Warren v. Warren*, 169 Ill. App. 3d 226, 523 N.E.2d 680 (1988).

376. 347 Wis. 2d 549, 830 N.W.2d 723 (2013).

377. *Gant v. Gant*, 329 S.E.2d 106 (W. Va. 1985).

378. 169 Ill. App. 3d 226.

379. *See Grabe*, 341 Conn. at 360 (that parties to premarital agreement who married in their thirties had children was a foreseeable circumstance).

Some cases hold that an agreement may be unconscionable that leaves a spouse destitute, or likely to become a public charge, or with a standard of living far below that enjoyed before the marriage without requiring that the circumstances at enforcement be unforeseeable.[380]

Courts in second-look states seem quite willing to uphold an agreement that preserves a party's exclusive right to premarital and inherited property at divorce.[381] Such an agreement that provides for equal division of assets acquired through marital efforts will generally be upheld as not unfair or unconscionable on a second look.[382] An agreement that strips a party of all rights to property derived from common efforts may fail.[383]

Bedrick v. Bedrick[384] is a rare postmarital agreement case from a second-look state. The court held the agreement to be unenforceable as unconscionable at divorce. The terms were extreme. The agreement provided for the wife to receive only 8 percent of the value of the assets and no spousal support, and for the husband to retain his carwash business. The parties had a child born after the last addendum to the agreement. The dearth of postmarital agreement cases in second-look states means continued uncertainty until courts provide more guidance.

(d) Fairness of Terms and the Business Owner

The same legal standards for validity apply to a premarital or postmarital agreement executed by a business owner as by any other contracting party. However, in many cases, extra caution is called for in the negotiations to formulate the terms. When there is a big wealth disparity between the parties, as well as a disparity in experience, sophistication, and bargaining ability, the owner can be somewhat more vulnerable to a claim of duress or undue influence. Moreover, it will often be in the best interests of the owner to have an agreement under which he or she will retain exclusive rights to the business, including all appreciation and all good will, whether personal or business good will. The agreement could be a title-controls type of agreement or a sharing agreement under which the owner's interest in an existing or future business is defined as separate property. In these circumstances, the owner and his or her counsel should consider terms to mitigate the substantive unfairness, if such exists at execution or can be anticipated as the business grows.[385] For example:

- The agreement could provide for provisions for cash gifts during the marriage; a transfer of an asset, such as a home, into joint names; creation of other joint assets, such as a securities portfolio or a cash savings account; funding an IRA, a cash settlement at divorce or death, or a combination thereof.

380. *See, e.g., Kelcourse v. Kelcourse*, 87 Mass. App. 33 23 N.E.2d 124 (Mass. Ct. App. 2015); *Bassler v. Bassler*, 156 Vt. 353, 593 A.2d 82 (1991).

381. *Austin v. Austin*, 445 Mass. 601, 839 N.E.2d 837 (2005).

382. *See, e.g., In re Marriage of Hoffman*, 2012 Wash. App. LEXIS 1136; *Vanheusden v. Vanheusden*, LEXIS 643 (Mich. Ct. App. Mar. 10, 2005).

383. *See Wisth v. Wisth*, 754 N.W.2d 254 (Wis. Ct. App. 2008) (premarital agreement that permitted husband to pay debt on his separate property with marital funds and retain sole interest in separate assets was substantively inequitable); *In re Marriage of Krejci*, 266 Wis. 2d 284, 667 N.W.2d 780 (Ct. App. 2003) (premarital agreement unfair at divorce where wife worked in husband's business without pay for 18 years).

384. 300 Conn. 691, 17 A.3d 17 (2011).

385. If the other party is wealthy, or is likely to inherit substantial wealth, or can become wealthy through his or her own business or employment, these concerns may not exist.

- The agreement could predetermine an amount and duration of spousal support or reserve the spouse's right to seek an award.
- The agreement could provide for the business owner to retain exclusive rights to the value of the business, but for monies earned from working in the business, and assets acquired with earnings, including retirement benefits, to be marital property.
- The agreement could provide for a surviving spouse through life insurance, surviving spouse rights to a retirement plan, or other specified surviving spouse rights, with the owner free to determine disposition of the business at his or her death.
- The agreement could provide for a waiver of fees at divorce, so that the challenging party will not be able to seek a fee award for the purpose of challenging validity, and for prevailing party fees and costs to deter a challenge to validity.[386]

The agreement need not make unusually generous provisions for the nonowner; when the agreement makes provisions for the nonowner, especially when he or she is able to improve upon the terms through a negotiation, the owner can have a high degree of confidence it will be upheld if challenged.[387]

(e) Protecting the Agreement from a Substantive Unconscionability Challenge

Where a couple is older and each already has sufficient resources to maintain his or her standard of living, an agreement in which each waives claims against the other at death or divorce will usually not raise fairness concerns. Similarly, when the agreement provides for the parties to share the fruits of their labor or reserves a spousal support claim, under most circumstances the agreement will pass any fairness or conscionability test. Even when the couple is young and may have children, if each has substantial earning capacity or has acquired or will inherit substantial wealth, substantive fairness will likely not be a concern.

When there is a significant disparity in wealth at the outset, counsel for both parties should consider substantive fairness of the terms of a premarital agreement as part of the negotiation process. Similarly, when a spouse proposes terms for a postmarital agreement that are extremely favorable to him or her, counsel for both parties should consider terms to mitigate the disparity.

A wealthy party can insulate an agreement to some degree by conducting a process that is fair in every way,[388] and by making reasonable provisions for an economically weaker party to create some financial security for him or her that may include some transfers of separate property, for spousal support, or for some of each.[389] Merely stating in the agreement that no

386. See Chapter 6.

387. *See, e.g., Miller v. Miller*, 2022 Md. App. LEXIS 813 (unpub.) (premarital agreement between very successful business owner and fiancée was valid where provided for substantial transfers of husband's premarital property, support for her child, a lump sum, and spousal support).

388. *See Mallen v. Mallen*, 280 Ga. 43, 622 S.E.2d 812 (2005) (premarital agreement that perpetuated vast disparity of wealth not unconscionable where parties actively negotiated terms); *Beyor v. Beyor*, 158 Conn. App. 752, 121 A.3d 734 (2015) (agreement not unconscionable at divorce where both parties had counsel and husband made adequate financial disclosure despite extreme disparity in income and assets).

389. *See Austin*, 445 Mass. 601 (premarital alimony waiver not unconscionable at divorce where wife to receive real estate, cash, and other assets valued at $1.8 million).

change in circumstances will affect enforceability is insufficient to insulate an agreement in a second-look state.[390]

(f) Too Generous—Too Bad

The principle that courts will not relieve a party of the consequences of a bad bargain applies equally to a wealthy party to a premarital agreement who in retrospect decides he or she was too generous or who suffered a reversal of fortune. For example, in a case of colossal chutzpah,[391] the husband in *Carnell v. Carnell*[392] insisted on a premarital agreement to allay the wife's fears about remarriage. The agreement, which the lawyer-husband drafted, made extremely generous provisions for the wife. When the marriage ended two years later, the husband argued the premarital agreement was the product of overreaching on the theory that he was swept off his feet. In rejecting his claim, the court observed: "The controlling question here is whether there was overreaching and not whether the bargain was good or bad."[393] Similarly, in *Stadther v. Stadther*,[394] the court rejected the husband's gross unfairness claim where he actively participated in formulating the generous terms of the agreement in order to persuade the wife to marry him.

In *Marsh v. Marsh*,[395] the wife would agree to marry again only if the husband promised to provide for her financially. The premarital agreement, drafted by the wife's lawyer, required the husband to transfer half his assets into a trust of which the wife was trustee and sole principal beneficiary. The parties were equal income beneficiaries. The husband foolishly refused advice to get separate counsel. There was no fraud, overreaching, misrepresentation, threat, or duress. Only after the marriage did the husband get legal advice to discover the agreement was flawed. The court rejected his claim of unconscionability. In so holding, the court in essence said that when the process was fair, whatever substantive terms the parties agreed to were conscionable. That the result disproportionately benefited one party was not a basis to find unconscionability.[396]

A change in the parties' fortunes with the result that the party who was weaker at execution is stronger financially at the end of the marriage does not render an agreement

---

390. *Grabe v. Hokin*, 341 Conn. 360, 267 A.3d 145 (2021).

391. "Gall, brazen nerve, effrontery, incredible gall, presumption plus arrogance. . . ." LEO ROSTEN, THE JOYS OF YIDDISH (1970).

392. *Carnell v. Carnell*, 398 So. 2d 503 (Fla. Dist. Ct. App. 1981).

393. *Id.* at 506.

394. 526 So. 2d 598 (Ala. Civ. App. 1988).

395. *Marsh v. Marsh*, 949 S.W.2d 734 (Tex. App. 1997).

396. For other cases where a court rejected a party's attempt to void a generous premarital agreement he or she lived to regret, *see In re Feneis*, 2022 Minn. App. LEXIS 358 (unpub.); *Pariser v. Shriar*, 487 P.3d 387 (Mont. 2021); *Labuz v. Labuz*, 54 N.E. 3d 886 (Ill. Ct. App. 2016); *Kuchera v. Kuchera*, 983 So. 2d 776 (Fla. Ct. App. 2008); *In re Marriage of Sheynkman*, 2005 Wash. App. LEXIS 2428 (unpub.); *Hawxhurst v. Hawxhurst*, 318 N.J. Super. 72, 723 A.2d 58 (1998); *Penhallow v. Penhallow*, 649 A.2d 1016 (R.I. 1994); *Rinvelt v. Rinvelt*, 190 Mich. App. 372, 475 N.W.2d 478 (1991); *see also Lloyd v. Niceta*, 255 Md. App. 663, 284 A.3d 808 (2022) (postmarital agreement not unconscionable where husband agreed to pay wife $7 million if he committed adultery or other sexual misconduct); *Nilles v. Nilles*, 955 N.E.2d 611 (Ill. Ct. App. 2011) (marital settlement agreement became unconscionable where nonmodifiable support obligation became unduly burdensome due to change in husband's fortunes).

unconscionable in result if it will not leave the other party destitute.[397] For example, in *Schoenborn v. Schoenborn*,[398] the husband, who had $1.5 million in assets at execution, proposed the agreement. The wife was just starting her career as a dentist and had nothing. At divorce his assets had grown to $2 million and hers to $1.5 million. The court rejected his challenge to validity on the grounds of unconscionability.

California appears to be the only state where courts give serious consideration to a claim that a premarital agreement was too generous to the economically weaker party. In the guise of a public policy that discourages divorce, a court may invalidate a premarital agreement that creates an economic incentive for the weaker spouse to leave the marriage.[399] Thus, in California a wealthy party who has a change of heart may have a chance to get an overly generous premarital agreement thrown out. The courts in these few cases do not acknowledge that an agreement that heavily favors a wealthy party can give that party an economically inexpensive exit from marriage. By contrast, a North Carolina case rejected a challenge on public policy grounds to a postmarital agreement that the husband argued was overly generous to the wife.[400] The agreement provided for the adulterous husband to make transfers of property to her during the marriage that became her separate property immediately, regardless of how the marriage ended.

§4.10 SUMMARY—BEST PRACTICES; MAKING A RECORD

Most challenges to validity of premarital and postmarital agreements fail. However, when an agreement is challenged the proponent incurs the risk and expense of litigation. A demonstrably fair process can reduce risk for the proponent. The lawyer for the proponent needs to assume the proponent, or his or her estate, will have the burden of proof of validity, if the agreement is challenged at dissolution or after his or her death, and should conduct the process so as to be able to meet that burden.[401] Moreover, as a challenge to validity may come after the death of the proponent, who will therefore not be able to provide testimony about the parties' interactions relating to validity, a record of the process, such as correspondence evidencing that the weaker party had sufficient time and an opportunity to get legal advice, can be critical.

A party to a civil lawsuit may be entitled to summary judgment when (1) there is no genuine issue as to any material fact, and (2) the moving party is entitled to judgment as a matter of law.[402] Summary judgment means the proponent is not forced to go to trial and rely

397. *Reed v. Reed*, 265 Mich. App. 131, 693 N.W.2d 825 (2005); *Friedman v. Friedman*, 100 Cal. App. 4th 65, 122 Cal. Rptr. 2d 412 (2002); *Upham v. Upham*, 36 Mass. App. Ct. 295, 630 N.E.2d 307 (1994).

398. 144 Conn. App. 846, 74 A.3d 482 (2013).

399. *See Bellio v. Bellio*, 105 Cal. App. 4th 630, 129 Cal. Rpt. 2d 556 (2003).

400. *Dawbarn v. Dawbarn*, 175 N.C. App. 712, 625 S.E.2d 186 (2006).

401. *See Espenkotter v. Est. of Espenkotter*, 2022 Md. App. LEXIS 841 (unpub.) (summary judgment for late husband's estate as to validity of postmarital agreement reversed and remanded for findings as to whether parties had confidential relationship, shifting burden of proof to husband's estate).

402. *Sheshunoff v. Sheshunoff*, 172 S.W.3d 686 (Tex. Ct. App. 2005); *In re Marriage of Barnes*, 325 Ill. App. 3d. 514, 755 N.E.2d 522 (2001); *Gould v. Rafaeli*, 822 S.W.2d 494 (Mo. Ct. App. 1991); *Nanini v. Nanini*, 166 Ariz. 287, 802 P.2d 438 (Ct. App. 1990).

on winning a credibility contest.[403] The lawyer for the proponent should therefore aim for a written record that will establish all material facts and the right to judgment as a matter of law under the legal principles for validity in the applicable jurisdiction.[404] Ideally, the written record will show at a minimum:

- Voluntariness;
- Fair and adequate financial disclosure; and
- Substantive fairness, which need not equate to provisions comparable to what the weaker party could expect in the absence of agreement.

The standards for validity are very low in most states. The lawyer can serve his or her client best by insisting on a higher standard than the minimum. Even in states where the law does not require substantive fairness at execution or enforcement, when there is a significant disparity in resources, the stronger party will reduce his or her risk by making provisions for the other party that will create some financial security for him or her. The written record should show:

- The disadvantaged party received a proposed draft premarital agreement enough in advance of the wedding that he or she had a meaningful opportunity to consider the terms, get legal advice, and negotiate for better terms; or, in the case of a postmarital agreement, that the recipient had sufficient time and was not placed under any undue time pressure;
- Actual legal representation or a meaningful opportunity for such representation, which, in some cases, needs to include an offer, in writing, from the proponent or his or her lawyer, to pay the legal fees for the disadvantaged party;
- An actual negotiation in which the proponent made changes requested by the weaker party and correspondence evidencing such; and
- When there is a significant disparity in resources that is likely to be perpetuated, the agreement makes some provisions for the weaker party upon death or dissolution to provide some degree of financial security.

---

403. *See, e.g., Quarles v. Quarles*, 285 Ga. 762, 683 S.E.2d 583 (2009) (summary judgment for validity of premarital agreement was inappropriate where husband did not make financial disclosure; premarital standard of living was insufficient as a matter of law to put wife on notice of his income; whether husband disclosed income was material fact in dispute and dispute was genuine); *and see Nelson v. Estate of Nelson*, 53 So. 3d 922 (Ala. Civ. App. 2010) (summary judgment for validity of postmarital agreement upheld where agreement showed disclosure, wife was well-educated and not prevented from getting legal advice).

404. *See Kelly v. Kelly,* 518 P.3d 326 (Idaho 2022) (both parties had counsel; changes made at request of wife; wife got financial disclosure and expressly waived further disclosure; premarital agreement valid on summary judgment).

SPOUSAL SUPPORT 5

§5.01 OVERVIEW

Historically, a premarital agreement determining property and support at divorce was void as against public policy. A premarital agreement that waived or limited spousal support was thought to promote divorce by permitting the husband to abuse the wife knowing his liability for post-divorce support was limited by contract.[1] Currently, in the majority of states, parties may enter into a premarital contract that fixes or completely waives spousal support, subject to the court's power to refuse enforcement of the waiver under certain limited circumstances.

Statutes in some states permit spouses to enter into a postmartial contract regarding their property rights at divorce but prohibit enforcement of a support waiver. In other states courts treat postmarital agreements the same as premarital agreements in regard to enforceability of support waivers.[2] The law regarding general enforceability of postmarital agreement provisions fixing or waiving spousal support is less well-developed than that governing premarital agreements.

There is an important distinction between support for a former spouse and support for an existing spouse. In some states, the right to fix or waive support for a spouse is more limited than for a former spouse. Most frequently, the issue arises after a separation when a spouse seeks temporary support while he or she litigates the validity of the agreement or other issues in the case or while the parties await entry of a judgment of divorce.

Before a court will be required to reach the issue of enforceability of a waiver of post-divorce spousal support, it must first determine validity of the agreement as a whole. If the agreement is valid as a whole, the court may then separately consider whether to enforce or modify the spousal support provisions to the extent state law

---

1. *In re Marriage of Pendleton and Fireman*, 5 P.3d 839, 99 Cal. Rptr. 2d 278 (2000); *Crouch v. Crouch*, 385 S.W.2d 288 (Tenn. Ct. App. 1964).
2. See Appendix B(2), State Law Summary: Postmarital Agreements.

permits. An unenforceable spousal support waiver will generally be severable so that the remainder of the agreement can still be enforced as written.[3]

A party may seek to enforce or void a spousal support provision of a premarital or postmarital agreement in a state other than the state whose law the agreement provides will govern the dispute. The Uniform Premarital Agreement Act (UPAA), the Uniform Premarital and Marital Agreements Act (UPMAA), and general choice-of-law jurisprudence allow parties to select the law that will govern their agreement.[4] However, the law and public policy of the forum state may override the parties' contractual choice of law and permit the court to impose a support obligation different from that to which the parties agreed.

This chapter is concerned with general enforceability of provisions limiting court authority to award support in accordance with applicable law. Options for terms providing support and issues about drafting waivers are discussed in Chapter 12.

§5.02 Enforceability of Premarital Agreement Provisions Fixing or Waiving Post-Divorce Spousal Support

(a) Minority Position: No Premarital Waiver Permitted

In a minority of states, parties may not fix or waive spousal support in a premarital agreement.[5] Among the UPAA states, only Iowa, New Mexico, and South Dakota law preclude enforcement of a premarital agreement support waiver.[6] As a result, in these states parties to a premarital agreement are in the same position with respect to the spousal support claim of a dependent spouse at divorce as in the absence of a premarital agreement. Among the non-UPAA states, only Mississippi law appears to make a premarital support waiver not binding on the court at divorce.[7]

(b) Majority Position: Premarital Agreement Fixing or Waiving Post-Divorce Spousal Support Generally Enforceable

The modern view, adopted by a majority of states, gives parties virtually a free hand to agree to any support obligation they wish, including a complete waiver, subject to court authority to override the waiver only if unconscionable at divorce. This position is represented by the

---

3. *See Lane v. Lane*, 202 S.W.3d 577 (Ky. 2006); *Austin v. Austin*, 445 Mass. 601, 839 N.E.2d 837 (2005); *Cary v. Cary*, 937 S.W.2d 777 (Tenn. 1996); *Howell v. Landry*, 96 N.C. App. 516, 386 S.E.2d 610 (1989); see also Chapter 12, Paragraph 51, regarding severability.

4. UPAA § 3(a)(7) (1983); UPMAA § 4 (2012); see also Chapter 12, Paragraph 56 and accompanying Comment, for discussion of choice-of-law.

5. Included in the category of states where no premarital waiver is permitted are only states that have, by statute or case law, expressly prohibited enforcement of premarital waivers in the 50+ years since *Posner v. Posner*, 237 So. 2d 186 (Fla. Dist. Ct. App. 1970). See discussion of *Posner* in Section 1.04(b).

6. Iowa Code § 596.5(2) (premarital agreement may not adversely affect spouse's right to support); N.M. Stat. Ann. § 40-3A-4(B) (same). South Dakota's version of the UPAA is silent. S.D. Codified Laws §§ 25-2-16 to 25-2-25. Older case law precludes a premarital support waiver, *Connolly v. Connolly*, 270 N.W.2d 44 (S.D. 1978), and the South Dakota Supreme Court rejected taking upon itself the decision to modernize state law by permitting such a waiver. *Sanford v. Sanford*, 694 N.W.2d 283 (S.D. 2005).

7. *Mabus v. Mabus*, 890 So. 2d. 806 (Miss. 2003).

UPAA, the UPMAA, and the majority of non-Uniform Act states.[8] The UPAA permits parties to completely waive spousal support as well as to fix spousal support at a level far below what the dependent spouse could receive from a court in the absence of agreement, leaving only the narrowest opportunity for a court to override the waiver.[9] Twenty-three of the 26 jurisdictions that have enacted the UPAA have included the provisions permitting parties to contract to fix or waive spousal support as well as both of the states (Colorado and North Dakota) that have enacted the UPMAA.

§5.03 ENFORCEABILITY OF POSTMARITAL AGREEMENT TERM FIXING OR WAIVING SPOUSAL SUPPORT

As discussed in Chapter 3, several states have statutes expressly permitting spouses to execute a postmarital agreement as comprehensive as a premarital agreement, including disposition of property at death or divorce as well as fixing or waiving spousal support at divorce.[10] In Colorado and North Dakota, the UPMAA allows for a postmarital agreement to fix or waive spousal support.[11] In these states, spouses may contract regarding spousal support under the same rules that govern spousal support in a premarital agreement. Similarly, in those states where parties to a premarital agreement are not permitted to bind a future divorce court regarding spousal support,[12] a postmarital agreement not incident to separation may not be binding as to spousal support in a future divorce proceeding, but there is little guidance at present.

North Carolina, which permits parties to a premarital agreement to waive spousal support, has a statute that precludes such a waiver in a postmarital agreement not incident to separation.[13]

Case law in Alabama, Florida, Pennsylvania, Tennessee, and Georgia indicates their courts will permit a postmarital agreement not incident to an immediate separation to predetermine spousal support conclusively in the event of a future divorce proceeding.[14] However, the status of a postmarital support waiver in these states is not yet clear. *Adams v. Adams*,[15] a Pennsylvania case, for example, involved a comprehensive separation agreement, not a postmarital agreement, but the Pennsylvania court applied the same validity criteria as it

---

8. See Appendix B(1), State Law Summary: Premarital Agreements.

9. UPAA § 3(a)(4) (1983).

10. New York, Colorado, Wisconsin, Louisiana, and Virginia have such statutes. See Appendix B(2), State Law Summary: Postmarital Agreements.

11. See Appendix B(2), State Law Summary: Postmarital Agreements.

12. See Appendix B(1), State Law Summary: Premarital Agreements.

13. *See* N.C. GEN. STAT. § 50-20 (husband and wife can enter into written agreement before, during, and after marriage regarding property); *Stegall v. Stegall*, 100 N.C. App. 398, 397 S.E.2d 306 (1990), *cert. denied*, 328 N.C. 274, 400 S.E.2d 461 (1991) (separation agreement providing for spousal support void unless parties are separated or planning imminent separation).

14. *Adams v. Adams*, 414 Pa. Super. 634, 607 A.2d 1116 (1992); *Tibbs v. Anderson*, 580 So. 2d 1337 (Ala. 1991); *Casto v. Casto*, 508 So. 2d 330 (Fla. 1987); *Scherer v. Scherer*, 249 Ga. 635, 292 S.E.2d 662 (1982); *Hoyt v. Hoyt*, 213 Tenn. 117, 372 S.W.2d 300 (1963).

15. 414 Pa. Super. 634, 607 A.2d 1116 (1992).

applies to premarital agreements and the language of the opinion was expansive enough to suggest that all three types of agreement would be treated the same way. Similarly, in *Tibbs v. Anderson*,[16] the Alabama court looked to premarital agreement cases for standards by which to judge validity, including cases that expressly permit premarital support waivers. However, the question of a support waiver at divorce was not before the court. In *Hoyt v. Hoyt*,[17] the issue was enforceability of a reconciliation agreement providing for disposition of property and spousal support in the event the reconciliation proved unsuccessful. The Tennessee court upheld the agreement, including the provisions regarding spousal support, but the gap between the execution of the agreement and the filing of the divorce action was less than a year.

In *Casto v. Casto*,[18] the Florida court said: "Postnuptial agreements regarding alimony and marital property are properly enforceable in dissolution proceedings."[19] The *Casto* court described the agreement at issue there variously as a postnuptial agreement and a separation agreement. The agreement was executed a year before suit for divorce was filed but the parties were separated at the time. In subsequent cases,[20] Florida courts have distinguished litigation settlement agreements from what they characterized as the postnuptial agreement in *Casto*. In doing so, they reaffirmed that the validity requirements for premarital and postmarital agreements are the same in Florida without distinguishing between a postmarital agreement executed during an ongoing marriage and one executed incident to separation.[21] The *Casto* line of cases suggests Florida courts would give effect to a postmarital agreement made by parties to an ongoing marriage and not incident to a planned separation. However, none of the reported Florida cases actually involved such an agreement.

In the majority of states, there is not yet a significant body of case law regarding enforceability of a support waiver in a postmarital agreement not executed incident to immediate separation or divorce or the circumstances under which a court may refuse to enforce such a waiver. Guidance may be found in the body of law regarding enforceability of premarital agreement support waivers.[22] Courts may look there when confronted with a postmarital agreement waiving support. Indeed, the most significant feature of both types of agreements, insofar as they incorporate spousal support waivers, is that such a waiver may precede a divorce filing by many years during which circumstances may change in unanticipated ways. By contrast, a separation agreement is generally made at a time when relevant circumstances are known. Thus, premarital agreement case law is the more relevant guide to assess the risk that such a waiver will not hold up in the event of a divorce.

In some states courts have authority to modify spousal support provisions of a separation agreement without a finding of unconscionability. A court in these states may well decide to

16. 580 So. 2d 1337 (Ala. 1991).
17. 213 Tenn. 117, 372 S.W.2d 300 (1963).
18. 508 So. 2d 330 (Fla. 1987).
19. *Id.* at 333.
20. *See Crupi v. Crupi*, 784 So. 2d 611 (Fla. Dist. Ct. App. 2001); *Petracca v. Petracca*, 706 So. 2d 904 (Fla. Dist. Ct. App. 1998).
21. Florida adopted the UPAA effective October 1, 2007; Fla. Stat. Ann. §§ 61.079, *et seq.*
22. *See Bevilaqua v. Bevilacqua*, 201 Conn. App. 261, 242 A.3d 542 (2020) (standards for determining whether premarital or postmarital agreement has become unconscionable at enforcement are analogous).

treat such a provision in a postmarital agreement in a manner similar to the treatment it would receive in a separation agreement in that state. Thus, a postmarital agreement provision waiving or otherwise limiting a spouse's support rights at divorce may be deemed modifiable in the event of changed circumstances or otherwise in accordance with the principles that would govern modifiability of support provisions of a separation agreement.[23] Until clear authority emerges, the viability of postmarital agreement support waivers in these states will be uncertain.

§5.04 CIRCUMSTANCES UNDER WHICH COURT MAY REFUSE ENFORCEMENT OF WAIVER OF POST-DIVORCE SPOUSAL SUPPORT IN OTHERWISE VALID AGREEMENT

Even in the majority of states that permit parties to fix or waive post-divorce in a premarital or postmarital agreement, courts are authorized to refuse enforcement under some circumstances:

- Under the UPAA, a court may refuse enforcement of a waiver in a premarital agreement if the waiver would make the claimant eligible for public assistance.[24] The same standard applies under North Dakota's version of the UPMAA.[25]
- Some UPAA states have changed the criteria for determining when a court may override a premarital agreement waiver from welfare eligibility to avoidance of undue and unforeseeable hardship.
- Colorado's version of the UPMAA permits the court to refuse enforcement of a support waiver that has become unconscionable.[26] Similarly, the terms relating to spousal support of a premarital or postmarital agreement governed by New York law must not be unconscionable at divorce.[27] To be unconscionable, the claimant need not be eligible for public assistance. Something less extreme will suffice.
- In the 14 second-look states,[28] because the court can consider whether a premarital agreement remains substantively fair (or not unconscionable) at divorce, it can separately consider fairness of the spousal support waiver.[29]
- In the remaining states where a spousal support waiver is otherwise permissible, by statute or case law, a court can override a premarital agreement waiver under extreme circumstances.[30]

---

23. *Toni v. Toni*, 636 N.W.2d 396 (N.D. 2001); *Lipps v. Loyd*, 967 P.2d 558, 562 n.1 (Wyo. 1998), citing *Dorr v. Newman*, 785 P.2d 1172, 1178 (Wyo. 1990).

24. UPAA § 6(b) (1983); *see also* Reyes v. Reyes, 2020 Conn. Super. LEXIS 345 (unpub.); *Sims v. Sims*, 55 Va. App. 340, 685 S.E.2d 869 (2009).

25. UPMAA § 9(e) (2012).

26. COLO. REV. STAT. § 14-2-309(5).

27. N.Y. DOMESTIC REL. LAW § 236(B)(3); Maddaloni v. Maddaloni, 36 N.Y.S.3d 695 (App. Div. 2016).

28. See Section 4.09 for discussion of the second look at divorce.

29. *See Sailer v. Sailer*, 764 N.W.2d 445 (N.D. 2009); *Lane v. Lane*, 202 S.W.3d 577 (Ky. 2006); *Hardee v. Hardee*, 355 S.C. 382, 585 S.E.2d 501 (2003); *Osborne v. Osborne*, 384 Mass. 591, 428 N.E.2d 810 (1981).

30. *See, e.g.*, Kambitsis v. Kambitsis, 2020 N.J. Super. LEXIS 690 (unpub.); Maddaloni, 36 N.Y.S.3d at 695; *O'Daniel v. O'Daniel*, 419 S.W.3d 280 (Tenn. Ct. App. 2013).

It seems reasonable to assume that courts will refuse enforcement of postmarital agreement spousal support waivers under legal principles comparable to those applicable to a premarital agreement waiver in that state absent statutes or case law that expressly treat them differently.

Enforceability of a provision fixing or waiving spousal support in an otherwise valid agreement implicates several distinct questions:

- What level of hardship must the claimant experience to warrant an award?
- Must the level of hardship required to warrant an award exist on the date of divorce, or is it sufficient that it is reasonably anticipated to occur in the foreseeable future?[31]
- Must the circumstances have changed since execution of the agreement?
- Must changed circumstances have been unforeseeable?
- When an award is appropriate, what are the criteria for determining the amount and duration?

There is some variation among the states as to the degree of post-divorce hardship required to support a finding of unconscionability. At its most extreme, unconscionability is defined as welfare eligibility as in the UPAA[32] and the UPMAA.[33]

The UPAA provides:

> (b) If a provision of a premarital agreement modifies or eliminates spousal support and that modification or elimination causes one party to the agreement to be eligible for support under a program of public assistance at the time of separation or marital dissolution, a court, notwithstanding the terms of the agreement, may require the other party to provide support to the extent necessary to avoid that eligibility.[34]

Some states have rejected the welfare eligibility standard and opted for a standard of changed circumstances that render the dependent spouse unable to meet his or her basic needs.[35] A spousal support waiver that will require a dependent spouse with a work history to return to the workforce is not likely to be considered unconscionable or unfair at divorce,[36] nor is a waiver where the claimant is employed, is well educated, and has a substantial work history, even if there is a big disparity in the parties' incomes.[37]

Statutes or case law in a number of states require that any changed circumstance be unanticipated or unforeseeable to justify a support award over a waiver.[38] For example, the

31. *See O'Daniel*, 419 S.W.3d at 280 (spousal support waiver in premarital agreement is unenforceable where wife's medical condition and future health-care costs will bankrupt her unless husband is ordered to pay support).

32. UPAA § 6(b) (1983); *Sims*, 55 Va. App. 340; *Osborne*, 384 Mass 591; *Cary v. Cary*, 937 S.W.2d 777 (Tenn. 1996).

33. UPMAA § 9(e) (2012).

34. UPAA § 6(b) (1983).

35. *See* Bevilacqua v. Bevilacqua, 201 Conn. App. 261, 242 A.3d 542 (2020); *Lane v. Lane*, 202 S.W.3d 577; *Gross v. Gross*, 11 Ohio St. 3d 99, 464 N.E.2d 500 (1984); *Newman v. Newman*, 653 P.2d 728 (Colo. 1982).

36. *See In re Marriage of Barnes*, 324 Ill. App. 3d 514, 755 N.E.2d 522 (2001); *Dipasquale v. Dipasquale*, 199 Wis. 2d 123, 545 N.W.2d 519 (1995).

37. *See Menkhaus v. Menkhaus*, 2022 Ohio App. LEXIS 2251 (unpub.).

38. *See Lang v. Lang*, 275 Wis. 2d 878, 685 N.W.2d 172 (2004) (trial court refused enforcement of premarital agreement where parties did not anticipate wife's significant mental health, alcohol, and drug problems and inability to work; alimony properly awarded); *In re Marriage of Barnes*, 324 Ill. App. 3d (reduction in wife's

Indiana and Illinois versions of the UPAA permit a modification of support provisions to the extent necessary to alleviate extreme hardship caused by changed circumstances not reasonably foreseeable at execution.[39] California's version of the UPAA permits a court to deny enforcement of a premarital support waiver on the ground of unconscionability but does not define unconscionability.[40] It appears that in California, to be unconscionable, a spousal support waiver would have to render a spouse without a means of support due to unanticipated and extreme circumstances. In *In re Marriage of Rosendale*,[41] the California Court of Appeals dealt with a claim that a spousal support waiver in a premarital agreement was unconscionable. Eight years after the marriage, the wife suffered a debilitating auto accident that left her seriously injured and unable to work. The appellate court refused enforcement of the support waiver, observing:

> Courts cannot permit one spouse to discard his or her disabled spouse without providing spousal support, even when a spousal support waiver in a premarital agreement would permit the same, if it would be unconscionable to do so at the time enforcement of the waiver is sought.[42]

In the 2013 case *Marriage of Facter*,[43] the California Court of Appeals had no difficulty upholding a ruling that a spousal support waiver was unconscionable at enforcement. There was a vast disparity in the parties' education and earnings and the agreement provided the wife with very little property.

In those states that permit a finding of unconscionability based on hardship less extreme than welfare eligibility, the criteria for the award appears to be that which is required to raise the dependent spouse's circumstances above the unconscionability bar, but not to the level to which the spouse might be entitled in the absence of agreement. The dependent spouse is not entitled to an award that provides a standard of living commensurate with what the payor can afford.[44] The standard of living established during the marriage is pertinent to the determination of reasonable needs, but a spousal support waiver is not unconscionable merely because it would result in a spouse not continuing to enjoy the higher marital standard of living.[45] Courts have been willing to tolerate a fairly extreme disparity in post-divorce incomes. In *Gross v. Gross*,[46] for example, the Ohio Supreme Court deemed a waiver unconscionable

---

standard of living after divorce was foreseeable where there was gross disparity in resources at outset); *Gould v. Rafaeli*, 822 S.W.2d 494 (Mo. Ct. App. 1991) (significant disparity in wealth at outset, husband's economic dependence, and husband's leaving employment as taxi driver in Israel did not warrant award of spousal support).

39. IND. CODE ANN. § 31-11-3-8(b); 740 ILL. COMP. STAT. § 10/7(b); *see Marriage of Goldin*, 2014 Ill. App. LEXIS Unpub. 588 (where husband began marriage with $500,000 in assets, husband elected to be self-employed and dabble in another business, no evidence his waiver of support imposed hardship on him).

40. CAL. FAM. CODE § 1612(c).

41. 119 Cal. App. 4th 1202, 15 Cal. Rptr. 3d 137, *rev. granted*, depublished by 2004 Cal. LEXIS 9655 (2004). Under California's rules, when the Supreme Court granted review, it rendered the court of appeals' opinion unpublished. The ultimate outcome of the litigation is unreported.

42. *Id.* at 1214, 145.

43. 212 Cal. App. 4th 967, 152 Cal. Rptr. 3d 79 (2013).

44. *DeMatteo v. DeMatteo*, 436 Mass. 18, 762 N.E.2d 797 (2002); *Gould v. Rafaeli*, 822 S.W.2d 494 (Mo. Ct. App. 1991).

45. *See Lane v. Lane*, 202 S.W.3d 577 (Ky. 2006); *In re Marriage of Dechant*, 867 P.2d 193 (Colo. Ct. App. 1993); *Vanderbilt v. Vanderbilt*, 2014 Ohio App. LEXIS 3589 (unpub.).

46. 23 Ohio App. 3d 172, 492 N.E.2d 476 (1985).

because it would compel the wife to accept a post-divorce standard of living much lower than the opulent standard of living she enjoyed during the marriage. Yet the actual award after the remand was a small percentage of the husband's income and appears not to have been sufficient to actually permit a continuation of her accustomed lifestyle.[47]

In some cases where a foreseeability standard has been applied, the courts seemed to focus more on what the parties themselves actually contemplated when they fashioned their premarital agreement provisions rather than what they could have foreseen had they given more thought to the future. For example, in *Gant v. Gant*,[48] the court laid down a rule that spousal support provisions of a premarital agreement would be enforced if and to the extent circumstances at the end of the marriage are roughly what the parties foresaw and provided for when they executed the agreement. Where, on the other hand, circumstances change in a way the parties did not anticipate, the court may modify spousal support to take account of such circumstances. "[T]he passage of time, a change of position based upon reasonable reliance on the permanence of the marriage, and the birth of children are relevant factors, among others, for a court to consider."[49]

(a) Enforceability of Premarital Support Waiver Undetermined

In four states, Michigan, Vermont, Washington, and Wyoming, there is not yet clear authority as to whether a premarital agreement support waiver is ever enforceable. The law in these states is still developing. In all four states, case law has permitted a premarital agreement to determine property disposition at divorce, but modern authority for or against enforceability of a premarital support waiver is lacking.[50]

§5.05 ENFORCEABILITY OF SUPPORT WAIVER WITH RESPECT TO RESIDENT ALIEN SPOUSE OR FORMER SPOUSE

Notwithstanding a premarital or postmarital agreement waiving spousal support, when the support claimant is a sponsored immigrant, and the spouse is the sponsor, the claimant may be able to obtain some limited support. A person who petitions for admission of a spouse or fiancé(e) as a family member will sign a United States Citizenship and Immigration Services Affidavit of Support, the Form I-864, as the sponsor.[51] The Form I-864 is a contract between the sponsor and both the sponsored immigrant and the U.S. government under which the sponsor promises to provide support to the immigrant sufficient to maintain him

---

47. *See also Arizin v. Covello*, 175 Misc. 2d 453, 669 N.Y.S.2d 189 (Sup. Ct. 1998) (wife's income over $750,000, husband's $25,000; not sufficient to justify spousal support award); *Newman v. Newman*, 653 P.2d 728 (Colo. 1982) (husband's income of $90,000 and wife's of $18,000 did not warrant support award).

48. 329 S.E.2d 106 (W. Va. 1985).

49. *Id.* at 116.

50. *See In re Marriage of Matson*, 107 Wash. 2d 479, 730 P.2d 668 (1986); *Laird v. Laird*, 597 P.2d 463 (Wyo. 1979); *Lund v. Lund*, 849 P.2d 731 (Wyo. 1993); *Stearns v. Stearns*, 66 Vt. 187, 28 A. 876 (1894), *Woodington v. Shokoohi*, 288 Mich. App. 352, 792 N.W.2d 63 (2010).

51. 8 U.S.C.A. § 1183a(a)(1); *and see* Veronica Tobar Thronson, *Til Death Do Us Part: Affidavits of Support and Obligations to Immigrant Spouses*, 50 FAM. CT. REV. 594 (Oct. 2012) (hereafter, "Thronson").

or her at 125 percent of the federal poverty line.[52] The sponsor's obligation terminates when the immigrant becomes a U.S. citizen or becomes credited with 40 quarters of covered employment in the Social Security system.[53] The sponsored spouse can be credited with quarters worked by the sponsoring spouse during the marriage.[54]

Divorce does not terminate the sponsor's obligation,[55] even when the sponsored spouse makes no request for support at the time of the divorce.[56] The immigrant-spouse is entitled to enforce his or her right to support independent of any state law or contractual waiver that may otherwise apply.[57] In *Naik v. Naik*,[58] the wife had a diploma in mechanical engineering and was fluent in English and Hindi, the marriage was short, the parties had no children, and the wife never left the workforce. Under New Jersey's criteria for determining post-divorce support, she was not eligible for an award of alimony. Nevertheless, the court determined that she was entitled to an adjudication of her rights under the Form I-864. The husband's obligation, however, would be limited to making up the difference between her actual income and 125 percent of the federal poverty level. The obligation under the I-864 is separate and distinct from an obligation that a court may impose upon granting a divorce, exercising discretion, and applying the state's criteria for such an award. The rights under the I-864 are contractual; there is no room for a decision based on fairness or equity.[59] Even domestic violence committed by the sponsored spouse does not excuse the sponsoring spouse from the I-864 obligation.[60]

The contract created by the I-864 provides the sponsored immigrant with a personal cause of action against the sponsoring spouse.[61] The sponsored spouse is entitled to a judgment representing the difference between 125 percent of the federal poverty level for each post-divorce year and the sponsored immigrant's actual income for that year.[62] If state law otherwise permits a complete waiver of spousal support, the trial judge has no authority to award more than 125 percent of the federal poverty level.[63] Some courts have held the sponsored immigrant has no obligation under the I-864 to seek or obtain employment to mitigate

52. 8 U.S.C.A. § 1183a.

53. 8 U.S.C.A. § 1183a(3)(A)–(B); *Thronson*, at 601. The obligation also terminates on the death of either party or the immigrant's permanent departure from the United States. 8 U.S.C.A. § 1183a(a)(2), (3).

54. *Id.*

55. *Erler v. Erler*, 824 F.3d 1173 (9th Cir. 2016); *Chang v. Crabill*, 2011 U.S. Dist. LEXIS 67501 (N.D. Ind. 2011).

56. *Shah v. Shah*, 2014 U.S. Dist. LEXIS 4596 (D.N.J. Jan. 14, 2014); *see also Hrachova v. Cook*, 2009, U.S. Dist. LEXIS 102067 (M.D. Fla. 2009); *Thronson*, at 601.

57. *Liu v. Mund*, 686 F.3d 418 (7th Cir. 2012) (former wife entitled to support under I-864 notwithstanding her violation of state court support award that required her to look for work); *see also Moody v. Sorokina*, 40 A.D.3d 14, 830 N.Y.S.2d 399 (2007); *Cheshire v. Cheshire*, 2006 U.S. Dist. LEXIS 26602 (D.M.D. Fla., May 4, 2006).

58. 399 N.J. Super. 390, 944 A.2d 713 (2008).

59. *Greenleaf v. Greenleaf*, 2011 Mich. App. LEXIS 1718.

60. *Belevich v. Thomas*, 17 F.4th 1048 (11th Cir. 2021) (sponsored husband's alleged sexual abuse of child of one of his sponsors does not terminate sponsor's obligation under I-864).

61. *Shumye v. Felleke*, 555 F. Supp. 2d 1020 (N.D. Cal. 2008). The sponsor may also be required to reimburse an agency that provided the immigrant spouse with means-tested public assistance. 8 U.S.C.A. § 1183a(b)(1)(A); 8 C.F.R. § 213a.2(d); *Stump v. Stump*, 2005 U.S. Dist. LEXIS 45729 (D.N.D. Ind. May 27, 2005).

62. *Younis v. Farooqi*, 597 F. Supp. 2d 552 (D.Md.2009); *Cheshire*, 2006 U.S. Dist. LEXIS 26602; *Shumye*, 555 F. Supp. 2d 1020.

63. *Barnett v. Barnett*, 2022 Ariz. App. LEXIS 661 (unpub.).

the sponsor's obligation,[64] although the law on this point is undeveloped.[65] Income from the sponsored immigrant's assets held in his or her home country will be counted, but only if the property is specifically identified on the I-864.[66] The sponsored immigrant has no obligation under the I-864 to notify the sponsor when one of the termination events has occurred.[67] The termination events do not include remarriage or cohabitation.[68] The sponsored immigrant's income for purposes of determining a shortfall includes benefits, such as a housing subsidy or education grant, but not a student loan, a cash payment to carry out a property settlement, or child support.[69]

With few adjudicated cases, the law about whether a marital agreement can effectively waive a spouse's right to seek support under the I-864 is undeveloped, although it appears likely that courts will generally refuse enforcement of purported contractual waivers that conflict with the obligation under an I-864.[70] The U.S. District Court for Hawaii held that such a waiver is binding on the spouses but not on a public agency providing means-tested public assistance. But, other federal and state courts have held that such a waiver does not preclude the sponsored spouse from seeking support under the I-864.[71]

A party to a premarital agreement who will be sponsoring a spouse for permanent resident status should consult with an immigration lawyer about what steps he or she may be able to take to mitigate the risk of having to support the sponsored spouse despite a waiver, or of having to incur the risk and expense of litigation over a claim. In some cases, the sponsored spouse may have substantial property interests, or the terms of the agreement may provide for the sponsoring spouse to transfer property during the marriage or pay a lump sum in the event of divorce. Neither a transfer of property during marriage nor a lump sum payment at divorce will relieve the sponsoring spouse of the I-864 obligation. In *Golipour v. Moghaddam*,[72] the wife had a substantial dowry (between $150,000 and $300,000) but the husband was nevertheless obligated to pay support. To the extent the lawyer for the sponsoring spouse is able to do so, he or she should draft so that any payout takes account of the obligation under the I-864. For example, the agreement could provide that the sponsoring spouse will pay spousal support after divorce in an amount sufficient to comply with the I-864 obligation; such payments should not be characterized as a property settlement. It could further provide that the payout will be reconfigured as a lump sum in the event the sponsored spouse becomes a

---

64. *Belevich*, 17 F.4th at 1048; *Liu v. Mund*, 686 F.3d 418 (7th Cir. 2012); *Sultana v. Hossain*, 2022 U.S. Dist. LEXIS 162759 (N.D. Tex. Sept. 8, 2022); *Carlborg v. Tompkins*, 2010 U.S. Dist. LEXIS 117252 (W.D. Wis. Nov. 3, 2011); *Cheshire*, 2006 U.S. Dist. LEXIS 26602.

65. *See Motlagh v. Motlagh*, 100 N.E.3d 937 (Ohio Ct. App. 2d Dist., 2017); *Carlborg*, 2010 U.S. Dist. LEXIS 117252; *Barnett v. Barnett*, 238 P.3d 594 (Alas. 2010).

66. *Ainsworth v. Ainsworth*, 2004 U.S. Dist. LEXIS 28961 (D.M.D. La., May 27, 2004) (unpub.).

67. *Shumye*, 555 F. Supp. 2d 1020.

68. 8 U.S.C.A. § 1183a(a)(2), (3).

69. *Motlagh*, 100 N.E.3d at 937; *Younis*, 597 F. Supp. 2d 552; *Shumye*, 555 F. Supp. 2d 1020.

70. *Blain v. Herrell*, 2010 U.S. Dist. LEXIS 76257 (D. Haw. July 21, 2010).

71. *Erler v. Erler*, 824 F.3d 1173 (9th Cir. 2016) (premarital agreement); *Golipour v. Moghaddam*, 438 F. Supp. 3d 1290 (Utah 2020) (postmarital agreement); *Shah v. Shah*, 2014 U.S. Dist. LEXIS 4596 (D.N.J. Jan. 14, 2014); *Backman v. Backman*, 364 Ga. App. 549, 875 S.E.2d 510 (2022) (premarital agreement); *see also Toure-Davis v. Davis*, 2014 U.S. Dist. LEXIS 42522 (D. Md. Mar. 28 2014) (I-864, signed after execution of premarital agreement, waived provision of premarital agreement that waived spousal support).

72. *Golipour*, 438 F. Supp. 3d at 1290.

U.S. citizen or is credited with 40 quarters of covered employment under the Social Security system.

§5.06 Enforceability of Spousal Support Waiver in a Domestic Violence Proceeding

A common feature of some states' domestic violence statutes is a provision for an award of spousal support as part of the spectrum of relief a court may afford the victim.[73] A court may determine on public policy grounds that a law of this type supersedes a contractual waiver of support. There appears to be no reported case where a court ruled on such an award over a premarital or postmarital agreement waiver as part of the relief in a domestic violence proceeding.[74]

The UPMAA, Section 10(b)(2), provides that a term of a premarital or marital agreement is unenforceable insofar as it limits remedies available to a victim of domestic violence. This provision would aid a victim, but only to the limited extent of the remedy otherwise available, such as support during the existence of a civil protection order.

Courts in states where a judge may consider whether an agreement has become unfair or unconscionable in its entirety, or whether a support waiver has become unfair or unconscionable,[75] could consider the effect of domestic violence on the victim's economic circumstances.[76]

§5.07 Enforceability of Provision Fixing Post-Divorce Support When It Is the Support Payor Who Seeks Relief from the Terms of Agreement

In the usual situation, the spousal support claimant seeks to undo a spousal support waiver or an arguably inadequate contractual support provision. The UPAA and the UPMAA provide a way out for the support claimant, albeit only to a limited extent, as discussed earlier.[77] These statutes do not address the less common situation where the payor seeks a way out of what in retrospect seems a too-generous payment obligation. Changed circumstances may affect the ability of the payor to pay the support provided under an agreement. Even where changed circumstances are genuine, and not merely a change of heart, courts have generally been unsympathetic. As an Indiana court observed:

73. *See, e.g.*, Code of Maryland, Family Law § 4-506(d)(9) (protective order may include "emergency family maintenance necessary to support any person eligible for relief . . .").

74. *But see Hutchison v. Hutchison*, 2009 Mich. App. LEXIS 1594 (unpub.), where the husband's physical abuse of the wife caused the court to void a premarital agreement and award alimony. Michigan is a second-look state.

75. *See Shell v. Shell*, 2010 Ohio App. LEXIS 1841 (unpub.) (postmarital agreement is unenforceable insofar as it purports to preclude spouse from seeking civil protection order); *Van Wagner v. Van Wagner*, 868 N.E.2d 924 (Ind. Ct. App. 2007) (support awarded over waiver during pendency of suit where husband assaulted wife); see also Appendices B(1) and B(2).

76. See Sections 4.05(a) and 4.09(c).

77. UPAA § 6(b) (1983); UPMAA § 9(e) (2012).

> By setting out a specific amount of "alimony," Husband accepted the risk that the stated amount might represent a larger share of his net worth at the time for performance than was the case at the time of execution. The drastic financial reversal that Husband suffered was a foreseeable event. Even if it were not foreseeable, Husband would not be relieved from his obligations. . . . [78]

The wealthy party who benefits from an agreement limiting the other spouse's property rights at dissolution, or that predetermines his or her support obligation, must assume the risk of a change in his or her fortunes.

§5.08 ENFORCEABILITY OF PROVISIONS FIXING OR WAIVING SUPPORT DURING MARRIAGE

(a) Overview

A premarital or postmarital agreement in which parties waive spousal support may include a waiver of support that might otherwise be payable while the parties are still married. The issue of support for a current, as opposed to a former, spouse may arise under several circumstances:

- In a suit for separate maintenance brought by a spouse, or by a guardian or conservator for an incompetent spouse, not as part of a proceeding for divorce or legal separation;
- On a spouse's motion for temporary, or *pendente lite*, support ancillary to a suit for divorce; and
- In a suit against a spouse by a third-party creditor who supplied necessaries, such as hospital care, to the other spouse.

(b) Enforceability of Support Waiver in Suit for Separate Maintenance or During Pendency of Divorce Proceeding

A contractual waiver of support for a spouse stands on a different footing than a waiver of support payable to a former spouse after divorce. Public policy may preclude enforcement of the former. Criminal nonsupport statutes, where they still exist, and noncriminal statutes that impose an obligation on spouses to support each other, could serve as the basis for rejection of such a provision in an otherwise valid premarital or postmarital agreement. Some authorities assert that a majority of states' laws preclude enforcement of a waiver of temporary

78. *Justus v. Justus*, 581 N.E.2d 1265, 1275 (Ind. Ct. App. 1991); *see also Soldwedel v. Soldwedel*, 2021 Ariz. App. LEXIS 688 (unpub.) (husband not entitled to modification of alimony to account for change in tax law that eliminated alimony deduction); *Vogt v. Vogt*, 831 So. 2d 428 (La. App. 2002) (premarital agreement for alimony at 20 percent of husband's income for life did not violate Louisiana public policy); *MacFarlane v. Rich*, 132 N.H. 608, 567 A.2d 585 (1989) (husband's early retirement due to poor health not a changed circumstance where parties anticipated possible disability and made specific provisions for support reduction, but only in event husband received disability payments, not if he merely took early retirement); *Buettner v. Buettner*, 89 Nev. 39, 505 P.2d 600 (1973) (husband not entitled to relief from generous support obligation on unconscionability grounds although wife left after four months of marriage).

support.[79] However, some cases cited in support of that position predate enactment of the UPAA or other statutory provisions or more recent court decisions. In the majority of states, including the UPAA states, there is no clear authority concerning enforceability of a waiver of temporary support. The law is still evolving; a majority position has yet to develop.

As of 2022, among the non-UPAA states, Pennsylvania and New York courts have expressly held that a waiver of temporary alimony is fully enforceable to the same extent as a waiver of post-divorce support. Pennsylvania courts have rejected the idea that a court could enforce an agreement selectively. Rather, if the proponent made full and fair financial disclosure, provisions "waiving . . . alimony, alimony *pendente lite*, counsel fees or expenses . . . will be given effect. . . ."[80] Similarly, New York's statute,[81] which permits parties to contract about the amount and duration of alimony, has been deemed broad enough to permit a premarital waiver of temporary support so long as the waiver is express.[82] The New York statute requires the maintenance provisions to have been fair at execution and not unconscionable at divorce. Thus, a waiver of temporary support could, under some circumstances, be voided. However, in *Arizin v. Covello*,[83] the wife had income of over $750,000 per year and the husband had income of $25,000. That disparity did not prevent the court from denying him temporary support.

Courts in Alaska, Maryland, and Missouri have held that a premarital waiver of temporary support is generally enforceable without addressing whether and under what circumstances a court may make an award over a waiver. In Maryland, for example, several cases have held that the validity of an award of temporary alimony turns on the validity of the agreement as a whole.[84] However, these cases did not involve a long marriage or a claimant in desperate circumstances.[85]

Two non-UPAA states, Georgia and Louisiana, that otherwise permit a waiver of post-divorce support, have expressly rejected premarital agreement waivers of temporary support. Thus, in these states, a waiver cannot divest the court of authority to award support for a spouse while the parties remain married.[86] Similarly, in Ohio it appears that a court may award temporary support over a waiver.[87]

---

79. *See* Jonathan E. Fields, *Forbidden Provisions in Prenuptial Agreements: Legal and Practical Considerations for the Matrimonial Lawyer*, 21 J.A.A.M.L. 413, 423 (2008).

80. *Karkaria v. Karkaria*, 405 Pa. Super. 176, 189, 592 A.2d 64, 71 (1991); *see also Gerlach v. Gerlach*, 2000 Pa. Dist. & Cnty. Dec. LEXIS 303.

81. N.Y. DOMESTIC REL. LAW § 236(B)(3).

82. *Vinik v. Lee*, 96 A.D.3d 522, 947 N.Y.S.2d 424 (2012); *Edmonds v. Edmonds*, 184 Misc. 2d 928, 710 N.Y.S.2d 765 (Sup. Ct. 2000); *Arizin v. Covello*, 175 Misc. 2d at 458, 669 N.Y.S.2d at 192.

83. *Arizin*, 669 N.Y.S.2d189.

84. *Cannon v. Cannon*, 384 Md. 537, 865 A.2d 563 (2005); *Frey v. Frey*, 298 Md. 552, 471 A.2d 705 (1984).

85. *See also Beal v. Beal*, 88 P.3d 104 (Alaska 2004) (premarital agreement can preclude interim alimony); *Darr v. Darr*, 950 S.W.2d 867 (Mo. Ct. App. 1997) (denial of award of temporary support upheld where such award depends on validity of agreement and agreement deemed valid); *but see Hawley v. Hawley*, 904 S.W.2d 584, 586 (Mo. Ct. App. 1995) ("It is questionable whether a spouse has the right to contract away the duties and obligations imposed by marriage and Missouri common law by executing an antenuptial agreement . . .").

86. *Langley v. Langley*, 279 Ga. 374, 613 S.E.2d 614 (2005); *Holliday v. Holliday*, 358 So. 2d 618, 620 (La. 1978); *Hall v. Hall*, 4 So. 3d 254 (La. Ct. App. 2009).

87. *See Buzard v. Buzard*, 2012 Ohio App. LEXIS 2339.

The UPAA permits parties to contract regarding "the modification or elimination of spousal support,"[88] as does the UPMAA.[89] Neither uniform act expressly addresses whether an agreement may eliminate the duty to support a spouse before divorce. The UPAA permits parties to contract about any other matter "not in violation of public policy or a statute imposing a criminal penalty."[90] The text appears to leave room for individual UPAA states to decide whether to reject premarital waivers of pre-divorce support on either public policy or criminal liability grounds. A 2008 Nebraska case, *Edwards v. Edwards*,[91] held such a waiver is permitted by the Nebraska UPAA.[92] By contrast, an Idaho court has rejected enforcement of a waiver of the right to support during the marriage. Idaho is a UPAA state.[93] Florida enacted the UPAA effective October 1, 2007.[94] A series of pre-UPAA cases preclude enforcement of a waiver of temporary support.[95] Cases decided after its enactment have reaffirmed on public policy grounds the prohibition on enforcement of provisions in any type of marital agreement waiving such support.[96] A smattering of cases from other UPAA states have rejected premarital agreement support waivers, but these cases predate enactment of the UPAA in those states.[97]

There is little authority regarding enforceability of a waiver of temporary support or separate maintenance in a postmarital agreement. States that permit such a waiver in a premarital agreement may enforce such a waiver to the same extent. In some states, there are specific statutes that appear to preclude enforcement of such a waiver.[98]

---

88. UPAA § 3(a)(4) (1983).
89. UPMAA § 2 (2012).
90. UPAA § 3(a)(8) (1983).
91. 16 Neb. App. 297, 744 N.W.2d 243 (2008); CODE OF NEB. § 42-1004(1)(d).
92. *See also Litt v. Litt*, 2016 Conn. Super. LEXIS 234 (unpub.) (waiver of temporary support in premarital agreement governed by N.Y. law is enforceable).
93. *State of Idaho v. Suiter*, 138 Idaho 662, 67 P.3d 1274 (Ct. App. 2003) (statutory duty of support during marriage required wife to pay for husband's defense to criminal charges to the extent she was able to do so despite premarital agreement).
94. FLA. STAT. § 61.079(7)(b) (court may award spousal support if waiver causes spouse to be eligible for public assistance at time of separation).
95. *See Blanton v. Blanton*, 654 So. 2d 1240 (Fla. Dist. Ct. App. 1995); *Belcher v. Belcher*, 271 So. 2d 7 (Fla. 1972).
96. *See Khan v. Khan*, 79 So. 3d 99 (Fla. Ct. App. 2012).
97. *McHugh v. McHugh*, 181 Conn. 482, 436 A.2d 8 (1980); *Eule v. Eule*, 24 Ill. App. 3d 83, 320 N.E.2d 506 (1974); *Motley v. Motley*, 255 N.C. 190, 120 S.E.2d 422 (1961); *Marschall v. Marschall*, 195 N.J. Super. 16, 477 A.2d 833 (1984); *In re Marriage of Mathiasen and Naughton*, 219 Cal. App. 3d 1428, 268 Cal. Rptr. 895 (1990); *Dimick v. Dimick*, 112 Nev. 402, 915 P.2d 254 (1996).
98. MONT. CODE ANN. § 40-2-303 (husband and wife cannot alter their legal relation except as to property and except they may agree in writing to an immediate separation and to provide for support); NEV. REV. STAT. ANN. § 123.080 (same); OKLA. STAT. tit. 43, § 205 (same); *Towles v. Towles*, 256 S.C. 307, 182 S.E.2d 53 (1971) (postmarital agreement not enforceable on public policy grounds insofar as it precluded wife from ever suing husband so as to permit husband to avoid support obligation during marriage). RESTATEMENT (SECOND) OF CONTRACTS § 190(1) (1981) states, in part: "A promise by a . . . married person, other than as part of an enforceable separation agreement, it is unenforceable on grounds of public policy if it would change some essential incident of the marital relationship in a way detrimental to the public interest in the marriage relationship." Comment a defines support as one of the essential incidents of marriage that parties may not alter by contract.

(c) Premarital Support Waiver as Affecting Spousal Liability to Third Parties: The Necessaries Doctrine

The common law necessaries doctrine, codified in some states, held the husband solely liable to third parties for necessary goods and services, such as medical care, provided to the wife. At common law, a wife had no corresponding liability for necessaries provided to her husband.[99] The majority of states that have considered the issue have made the necessaries doctrine gender neutral.[100] The necessaries doctrine generally provides a remedy for a third-party creditor rather than a cause of action for a spouse against the other spouse.[101] Most of the appellate cases dealing with the issue of necessaries involve a third-party claim for payment of medical bills. However, a third-party claim for provision of other types of necessary goods or services could also be the subject of a suit against a non-debtor spouse.[102]

Few cases have addressed the question of the extent to which a party may, through a premarital or postmarital agreement, avoid liability for necessaries incurred by the other spouse during the marriage. Because the necessaries doctrine is designed to protect third-party creditors, and does not act to establish intraspousal rights, it would appear parties cannot avoid such liability as may exist under governing law by execution of a premarital or postmarital agreement.[103]

A premarital or postmarital agreement may nevertheless offer some protection for a spouse's assets in the event the other spouse incurs sizable medical bills or the cost of nursing home or in-home nursing care. In states where parties may contract before or during marriage regarding support during an ongoing marriage, an agreement requiring each spouse to pay for his or her own necessaries, including medical and health-care expenses, would ordinarily be binding on the parties and require the spouse who incurred the debt to spend his or her resources first.[104]

---

99. *Connor v. Southwest Florida Regional Medical Center, Inc.*, 668 So. 2d 175 (Fla. 1995); *North Carolina Baptist Hospitals, Inc. v. Harris*, 319 N.C. 347, 354 S.E.2d 471 (1987); *Marshfield Clinic v. Discher*, 105 Wis. 2d 506, 314 N.W.2d 326 (1982); *Jersey Shore Medical Center-Fitkin Hospital v. Baum's Estate*, 84 N.J. 137, 417 A.2d 1003 (1980).

100. *See* VA. CODE ANN. § 55-37; CONN. GEN. STAT. § 46b-37; 750 ILL. COMP. STAT. § 65/15; *Cheshire Medical Center v. Holbrook*, 663 A.2d 1344 (N.H. 1995); *Landmark Medical Center v. Gauthier*, 635 A.2d 1145 (R.I. 1994); *Bartrom v. Adjustment Bureau, Inc.*, 618 N.E.2d 1 (Ind. 1993); *St. Francis Regional Medical Center v. Bowles*, 251 Kan. 334, 836 P.2d 1123 (1992); *Medical Business Associates, Inc. v. Steiner*, 588 N.Y.S.2d 890 (App. Div. 1992); *Hulse v. Warren*, 777 S.W.2d 319 (Mo. Ct. App. 1989); *North Carolina Baptist Hospitals, Inc.*, 319 N.C. 347; *Borgess Medical Center v. Smith*, 149 Mich. App. 796, 386 N.W.2d 684 (1986); *Richland Memorial Hospital v. Burton*, 282 S.C. 159, 318 S.E.2d 12 (1984); *Kilbourne v. Hanzelik*, 648 S.W.2d 932 (Tenn. 1983); *Jersey Shore Medical Center-Fitkin Hospital*, 84 N.J. 157.

101. *See Recovery Resources, LLC, v. Cupido*, 818 N.W.2d 787 (N.D. 2012); *Medical Business Associates, Inc.*, 588 N.Y.S.2d 890; *see also In re Estate of Noel*, 965 N.W.2d 192 (Iowa Ct. App. 2021) (where premarital agreement silent on payment of expenses, wife not entitled to reimbursement from husband's estate for his medical expenses paid for by her).

102. *See State of Idaho v. Suiter*, 138 Idaho 662, 67 P.3d 1274 (Ct. App. 2003) (criminal defense costs); *Medical Business Associates, Inc.*, 588 N.Y.S.2d 890 (common law doctrine of necessaries made husband liable to third party for shelter, clothing, and medical care furnished wife).

103. *Hawley v. Hawley*, 904 S.W.2d 584 (Mo. Ct. App. 1995) (doubtful parties can waive right to support during ongoing marriage, but lack of support waiver in premarital agreement here renders wife liable for husband's nursing home expenses on petition of husband's conservator); *Atkins v. Atkins' Administrator*, 203 Ky. 291 (1924) (parties cannot defeat rights of third-party creditors by premarital agreement).

104. *See Schlaefer v. Financial Management Svc., Inc.*, 196 Ariz. 336, 996 P.2d 745 (2000) (parties to premarital agreement can agree to keep property and debts separate during marriage; therefore, wife's debt for medical care

Where the spouse who incurred the debt is a dependent spouse, or has substantially lesser means than the other spouse, in many states courts may apply the same principles that reject waivers of support during an ongoing marriage to preclude such a waiver from being effective regarding third-party creditor rights. In a suit between the parties themselves for support or separate maintenance, the dependent spouse would have a right to seek spousal support to meet his or her basic needs. The result should not be different if it is the creditor who seeks vindication of the spousal support duty.

(d) Premarital Support Waiver as Affecting Liability for Medicaid Recoupment

A spouse who has insufficient resources for medical or nursing home care may become eligible for Medicaid. A premarital or postmarital agreement that makes each party solely responsible for his or her own medical and nursing home expenses may not be binding on a state agency seeking recoupment of Medicaid benefits paid on behalf of an institutionalized spouse.[105]

§5.09 INSULATING A WAIVER OF SPOUSAL SUPPORT FROM SUCCESSFUL ATTACK

When there is a significant disparity in resources at the outset, or a couple may have children and a parent may leave the workforce,[106] or other factors indicate that a weaker party could become impoverished as a result of a support waiver, counsel for the stronger party should consider provisions to reduce risk for that party and counsel for the weaker party should propose terms to better provide for his or her financial security.

When an agreement provides a meaningful amount of spousal support, evidencing that the parties did foresee and provide for the payee's future need, or when it provides alternative means to meet the needs of a dependent spouse, the provisions are more likely to be upheld even when they provide a standard of living after divorce less luxurious than what a wealthy spouse can afford.[107] Spousal support and other issues, such as provisions for disposition of

---

was not community obligation); *Johnson v. Johnson*, 811 S.W.2d 822 (Mo. Ct. App. 1991) (where parties signed premarital agreement, spouse who received service and who has sufficient assets primarily liable as between parties, thus defeating claim of recipient spouse's conservator); *Atkins*, 203 Ky. 291 (premarital agreement requiring parties to provide own support with separate assets binding on parties but not on third-party creditors).

105. *See Poindexter et al. v. State of Illinois*, 372 Ill. App. 3d 1021, 869 N.E.2d 139 (2007); *Commissioner v. Spellman*, 173 Misc. 2d 979, 661 N.Y.S.2d 895 (1997); *see also Morenz v. Wilson-Coker*, 415 F.3d 230 (2d. Cir. 2005).

106. *See, e.g., Barocas v. Barocas*, 94 A.D.3d 551, 942 N.Y.S.2d 491 (2012) (where parties entered marriage with disparity in wealth, husband entitled to all property acquired during marriage, and parties had children, wife entitled to evidentiary hearing on request for spousal support).

107. *See Gottlieb v. Gottlieb*, 138 A.D.3d 30, 25 N.Y.S.3d 90 (2016) (premarital agreement support wavier was not unconscionable where required husband to buy and maintain all expenses of luxury apartment for wife until children reached majority, for health insurance for wife, and for spousal support until youngest child reached age four); *Snedaker v. Snedaker*, 660 So. 2d 1070 (Fla. Dist. Ct. App. 1995) (where wife requested and got $42,000 per year, premarital support provision upheld against wife's attempt to get more from extremely wealthy husband); *see also Fercho v. Fercho*, 982 N.W.2d 540 (N.D. 2022) (premarital agreement was not substantively unconscionable

property and for support of children, are interrelated.[108] When the wealthier spouse agrees to transfer property to the less wealthy spouse, or where the agreement otherwise creates property rights for the disadvantaged party, that can help to insulate a spousal support waiver by providing an alternative means of support.[109] If the property provisions of the agreement allow the economically weaker party to acquire assets from which he or she may derive support, a court at divorce is less likely to override a spousal support waiver or a limitation on spousal support.[110] Where parties expect to have children, terms that provide for the children can also help to insulate a spousal support waiver, as it will relieve the less wealthy party of these expenses and allow him or her to save and create a nest egg. For example, the agreement could require a wealthy spouse to provide a home for the other spouse and future children; to pay for their medical, educational, and enrichment activity expenses; to create and fund Section 529 accounts; to provide life insurance; or to create a trust for their benefit.[111]

There are steps a wealthier party can take during the marriage to better protect the viability of a support waiver. The parties may wish to consider getting a private policy of disability insurance for a spouse, if he or she qualifies, as well as long-term care insurance to meet future nursing home expenses. A stronger party who will agree to a contractual obligation to pay for such insurance should first find out whether insurance is available at a cost that is acceptable to him or her. Even when the agreement does not include a contractual obligation, a wealthier party may opt to pay premiums during the marriage to provide financial security for the spouse and mitigate the harshness of a support waiver. A stronger party could agree to fund an annuity for the weaker party, make cash gifts to be used for savings and investment, or contribute to the weaker party's IRA. The stronger party could also consider some voluntary property transfers, such as retitling a premarital home into joint names, after several years of marriage. This could be accompanied by an amendment to the premarital agreement

---

where reserved claim for spousal support, but provided court could not consider either party's income from nonmarital property in determining amount).

108. *Kambitsis v. Kambitsis*, 2020 N.J. Super. LEXIS 690 (unpub.) (App. Div.).

109. *See Tschider v. Tschider*, 2019 N.D. 112, 926 N.W.2d 126 (provision for term-limited support not unconscionable where wife would leave marriage with $3 million in assets); *Austin v. Austin*, 445 Mass. 601, 839 N.E.2d. 895 (2005) (where wife to receive $1.8 million in assets, alimony waiver upheld); *Belcher v. Belcher*, 307 So. 2d 918 (Fla. Dist. Ct. App. 1975) (wife's alimony waiver upheld where husband transferred valuable property to her after marriage).

110. *See Biliouris v. Biliouris*, 67 Mass. App. Ct. 149, 852 N.E.2d 687 (2006) (alimony waiver not unfair as of execution where agreement permitted wife to accrue interest in assets acquired through employment during marriage); *D'Onofrio v. D'Onofrio*, 200 N.J. Super. 361, 491 A.2d 752 (1985) (lack of equitable distribution at divorce requires court to address wife's needs in context of spousal support award); *Hill v. Hill*, 356 N.W.2d 49 (Minn. Ct. App. 1984) (premarital agreement allocating virtually all marital property to husband upheld, but wife with no assets and serious medical problems entitled to spousal support notwithstanding her waiver); *Warren v. Warren*, 169 Ill. App. 3d 226, 523 N.E.2d 680 (1988) (premarital agreement must provide financial equity through property or support provisions); *Osborne v. Osborne*, 604 So. 2d 858 (Fla. Dist. Ct. App. 1992) (award of support exceeding that provided in premarital agreement upheld where husband titled all property acquired during marriage in his name alone).

111. A premarital or postmarital agreement cannot limit a court's authority to order a parent to pay support for a minor child after a divorce. However, nothing precludes a party from committing to pay expenses that a court has no power to impose, such as, in most states, an obligation to pay for college or to provide for a child through a will or other estate planning documents, or to otherwise provide more generously than the law requires. See Section 7.03.

that ratifies the agreement. The stronger party should also avoid economic decisions that harm the spouse.[112]

Counsel drafting an agreement to be governed by the law of a second-look state needs to be particularly attentive to the possibility of post-marriage events that may affect enforceability of a support waiver or a provision fixing spousal support at a low level.[113] When the agreement provides a meaningful amount of support, so that the trial court at the second-look stage cannot hold the support provision unconscionable, the trial court is not free to rewrite the spousal support provision to suit the court's sense of fairness. Rather, the court must enforce the contract as written.[114]

---

112. *See, e.g.*, *Corwell v. Corwell*, 2013 Ill. App. Unpub. 1118 (alimony award over premarital waiver upheld where husband diverted income from wife, who worked for his company, such that she lost 16 years of social security contributions).

113. The second-look states are Alaska, Connecticut, Georgia, Kentucky, Massachusetts, Michigan, Minnesota, Mississippi, New Hampshire, North Dakota, South Carolina, Vermont, West Virginia, and Wisconsin. See Section 4.09.

114. *See Korff v. Korff*, 64 Mass. App. Ct. 94, 831 N.E.2d 385 (2005) (trial court erred in rewriting percentage alimony formula).

Lawyers' Fees and Costs 6

§6.01 Overview

Lawyers' fees in connection with a premarital or postmarital agreement are incurred at the negotiation and drafting stage and, again, at the litigation stage if there is a dispute about validity at divorce or after a death. Parties may also incur fees at death or divorce to implement the agreement, or to resolve a dispute about their rights under the agreement, even where there is no dispute about validity. Further, parties may incur lawyers' fees and costs to litigate issues not governed by the agreement, such as custody and support for a child, spousal support where there is no waiver, or division of property to the extent not predetermined by contract.

A variety of circumstances may arise during a divorce proceeding that may call for some form of fee shifting:

- One party may seek an initial fee award to enable that party to challenge the validity of the agreement as a whole.
- Parties may disagree over the interpretation of the agreement insofar as it determines disposition of property or relates to spousal support. Because a premarital or postmarital agreement is not necessarily self-executing, and indeed may require a further determination of rights upon divorce, a party may seek a fee award for legal representation even when validity of the agreement is not in dispute.
- The validity of the agreement as a whole may not be in dispute, but a party may challenge the validity of certain provisions, such as a spousal support waiver, and may seek a fee award to pursue the challenge.
- A party may seek a fee award for the part of a divorce matter that is not governed by the agreement, such as custody, child support, or spousal support.

§6.02 FEE SHIFTING IN THE ABSENCE OF CONTRACT

In general, the so-called American Rule holds that each party to a legal dispute or transaction, such as the negotiation of a premarital or postmarital agreement, must bear his or her own legal fees and costs of litigation.[1] However, in the domestic relations arena, statutes and appellate decisions have carved out many exceptions to the American Rule so that, in the absence of a binding agreement waiving fees and costs, a judge may order one party to pay some or all of the costs and lawyers' fees incurred by the other party to resolve a dispute. Most significantly, in domestic relations litigation, in the absence of a valid contractual waiver, a court may be able to order the economically stronger party to advance monies to the weaker party to enable the weaker party to litigate the validity of the agreement, or may be able to award that party his or her fees at the conclusion of the litigation even when the challenge to validity fails.

Unlike in divorce litigation, statutory fee shifting in probate proceedings to permit an impecunious party to litigate an elective share claim against the estate, or to resolve other disputes about his or her rights, is not the norm. Rather, the American Rule requires a surviving spouse who seeks to challenge validity and take an elective share to bear his or her own fees.[2] If the challenger prevails, his or her right to fees will depend on the provisions of state probate law. Generally applicable statutes and rules governing fee shifting for litigation of a frivolous claim may apply when a party seeks unsuccessfully to litigate validity of an agreement after the death of the other party in the absence of a contractual fee-shifting provision.

§6.03 FEES FOR WEAKER PARTY FOR THE NEGOTIATION AND DRAFTING OF A PREMARITAL OR POSTMARITAL AGREEMENT

When there is a substantial wealth disparity, the economically stronger party will often pay the legal fees for the weaker party to enable him or her to retain counsel for the negotiation of a premarital or postmarital agreement. It is in the best interests of both parties that the weaker party have competent representation for the negotiation. When the weaker party has competent representation, he or she may be able to negotiate for better terms than originally proposed. In fact, the only realistic opportunity to improve the terms is at the negotiation stage. The stronger party benefits when the weaker party has competent representation, as this strengthens validity and greatly reduces the likelihood of a successful challenge.[3]

Whether a stronger party should agree to pay the weaker party's fees depends on several factors, including, especially, the weaker party's resources. When a lawyer is contacted by a weaker party and assesses that he or she may not be able to afford the fees the lawyer expects to charge for competent representation, it is appropriate for the lawyer to reach out to counsel for the proponent to discuss arrangements for payment of fees. The payor could be the other

1. CLARK, THE LAW OF DOMESTIC RELATIONS IN THE UNITED STATES § 17.2 (2d ed. 1987).

2. *See Dowling v. Rowan*, 270 Va. 510, 621 S.E.2d 397 (2005) (probate court properly denied husband's claim for attorneys' fees arising from failed elective share claim in violation of premarital agreement, adhering to American Rule, and rejecting argument litigation was necessary to administer estate).

3. See discussion at Section 4.06.

party to the agreement, a trustee of the other party's trust, or a parent or other relative. The third-party payor can advance monies to the weaker party at the outset to enable him or her to have an initial consultation and, as appropriate, to pay a fee advance and periodic invoices for representation in the negotiations. Alternatively, the payor can pay the weaker party's lawyer directly. There is no support in the case law of validity that favors or disfavors either approach. When parties are already married and contemplating a postmarital agreement, it is appropriate for the lawyer to explore with the client and opposing counsel the arrangements for payment of each party's fees for the representation. A spouse who is in control of most or all of the assets should not attempt to use that power to restrict the weaker party's representation.

The lawyer for the weaker party should be mindful of MRPC 1.8(f):

> (f) A lawyer shall not accept compensation for representing a client from one other than the client unless:
>
> (1) the client gives informed consent;
> (2) there is no interference with the lawyer's independence of professional judgment or with the client-lawyer relationship; and
> (3) information relating to representation of a client is protected as required by Rule 1.6.

One facet of avoiding such interference is the lawyer for the weaker party may have to resist an effort to restrict the amount of time he or she devotes to the negotiations and the amount of fees he or she will charge to render competent services. In some representations, the circumstances of retention and communications from opposing counsel make it evident that the stronger party is prepared to pay the fees without interference. In other circumstances, the lawyer will need to be more proactive in establishing the ground rules regarding the time needed to render competent services and payment of his or her fees. He or she may need to insist on an adequate fee advance and timely payment of invoices.

§6.04 ENFORCEABILITY OF CONTRACTUAL WAIVER OF FEES IN DIVORCE

The Uniform Premarital Agreement Act (UPAA) permits parties to contract with respect to a variety of subjects, including disposition of property upon separation, divorce, or death, and determination of spousal support, but does not expressly include lawyers' fees as a subject for agreement.[4] A catchall permits parties to contract on any other subject "not in violation of public policy. . . ."[5] The UPAA appears to permit inclusion of a waiver of the right to a fee award from the other spouse in a future divorce proceeding. An economically stronger party will generally benefit from such a waiver. The Uniform Premarital and Marital Agreements Act (UPMAA) permits a premarital or postmarital agreement to waive legal fees and costs.[6]

4. UPAA § 3(a)(1), (3), and (4) (1983).
5. *Id.* § 3(a)(8).
6. UPMAA § 2(4) (2012) (waivable marital rights include fees and costs). Only two states have adopted the UPMAA, North Dakota and Colorado. Colorado's version of the UPMAA permits a court to make a fee award over a waiver if the waiver has become unconscionable as of enforcement. COLO. REV. STAT. § 14-2-309(5) (2014).

Most courts that have ruled on a fee request made by a spouse during a divorce proceeding to enable him or her to challenge the validity of an agreement have held a contractual fee waiver to control.[7] Courts that have held a fee waiver generally unenforceable have done so on the theory that the party disadvantaged by the premarital agreement should not have to forgo the opportunity to litigate his or her claim due to lack of funds,[8] or that the obligation to pay lawyers' fees springs from the same nonwaivable obligation to pay spousal support during an ongoing marriage.[9] In Florida, where case law predating Florida's enactment of the UPAA (effective October 1, 2007) rejected waivers of temporary spousal support, the courts have also generally held a lawyers' fee waiver unenforceable insofar as it may apply to fees incurred while the parties are still married.[10] However, Florida courts may be moving away from general rejection of comprehensive fee waivers for fees incurred before divorce.[11] In New York, where a fee waiver is generally valid, courts have the authority to determine whether the waiver is unconscionable at divorce and to make an award over a waiver. This authority stems from the same statute that permits a court to evaluate a support waiver for unconscionability.[12]

General invalidity of a fee waiver does not guarantee that a spouse will receive a fee award. The court will not be justified in making a fee award where the claimant is unable to show need.[13] General validity of a lawyers' fee waiver does not mean a court can never make a fee award. Some courts have held that a lawyers' fee waiver is not enforceable if unconscionable at divorce even where the agreement as a whole is upheld.[14] Moreover, where a court deems a support waiver unenforceable, even if the agreement is generally enforceable, it may link it to a lawyers' fee waiver in the same agreement and hold both unenforceable.[15] In a

7. *See Erickson v. Erickson-Mitchell*, 2007 Tenn. App. LEXIS 345 (unpub.); *Kessler v. Kessler*, 33 A.D.3d 42, 818 N.Y.S.2d 571 (2006); *Montoya v. Montoya*, 91 Conn. App. 407, 881 A.2d 319 (2005), *rev'd in part on other grounds*, 280 Conn. 605, 909 A.2d 947 (2006); *Hardee v. Hardee*, 558 S.E.2d 264, 348 S.C. 84 (Ct. App. 2001); *Taylor v. Taylor*, 832 P.2d 429 (Okla. Ct. App. 1991); *Karkaria v. Karkaria*, 405 Pa. Super. 176, 592 A.2d 64 (1991); *Gross v. Gross*, 23 Ohio App. 3d 172, 492 N.E.2d 476 (1985).

8. *See Urbanek v. Urbanek*, 484 So. 2d 597 (Fla. Dist. Ct. App. 1986) (permitting husband to offset fee award against lump sum support due wife under agreement would put wife in untenable position of having to forgo representation); *Hill v. Hill*, 356 N.W.2d 49 (Minn. Ct. App. 1984) (award of fees necessary to do substantial justice where wife could not have pursued appeal of adverse ruling on validity of agreement and premarital support waiver); *see also Lashkajani v. Lashkajani*, 911 So. 2d 1154 (Fla. 2005).

9. *See Blanton v. Blanton*, 654 So. 2d 1240 (Fla. Dist. Ct. App. 1995).

10. *See id.* (husband's duty of support includes duty to pay fees incurred during marriage to challenge validity of premarital agreement when normal criteria for fee award met even when validity of agreement ultimately upheld).

11. *See Lashkajani*, 911 So. 2d at 1154 (upholding loser-pays provision).

12. *Anonymous v. Anonymous*, 123 A.D.3d 581, 999 N.Y.S.2d 386 (2014).

13. *Eule v. Eule*, 24 Ill. App. 3d 83, 320 N.E.2d 506 (1974).

14. *See Rosenbaum-Golden v. Golden*, 381 Ill. App.3d 65, 884 N.E.2d 1272 (2008) (wife entitled to interim fee award as advance against marital estate to litigate property rights under premarital agreement where husband had greater resources and was uncooperative in discovery); *In re Marriage of Ikeler*, 161 P.3d 663 (Colo. 2007) (enforcement of fee waiver in premarital agreement may be unconscionable and therefore unenforceable at divorce); *Ex parte* Walters, 580 So. 2d 1352 (Ala. 1991) (court may not award attorneys' fees if waived unless inequitable and unjust).

15. *See In re Marriage of Purcell*, 99 Or. App. 668, 783 P.2d 1038 (1989) (where trial court found spousal support waiver unenforceable as unconscionable, court had authority to award statutory attorneys' fees); *Warren v. Warren*, 169 Ill. App. 3d 226, 523 N.E.2d 680 (1988) (fee waiver unenforceable where support waiver unfair at divorce); *Gross v. Gross*, 23 Ohio App. 3d 172, 492 N.E.2d 476 (1985) (fees may be awarded for efforts to increase inadequate spousal support under agreement although fees incurred in unsuccessful challenge to general validity subject to contractual fee waiver).

state where a premarital agreement must be fair at enforcement, the judge hearing a divorce may also separately deem a fee waiver unenforceable.

Even when there is no dispute about the validity of a premarital agreement, divorcing parties may incur fees to resolve a dispute about their obligations or rights under the agreement. Courts in some states have interpreted their statutory provisions for fee shifting to permit an award to enable a weaker party to litigate his or her rights, despite a waiver, when there is a significant disparity in resources.[16] Other courts give effect to a waiver if the agreement is valid as a whole.[17]

In states where parties may effectively waive pendente lite spousal support, they may similarly waive the right to seek an award of pendente lite lawyers' fees.[18] However, for such a waiver to be effective, it must be express.[19]

In those states where enforceability of a fee waiver has not yet been ruled on, courts may analogize such a waiver to a waiver of spousal support. For example, a South Carolina court, ruling for the first time that a lawyers' fee waiver in an otherwise valid premarital agreement is enforceable, applied the body of law from other jurisdictions permitting a premarital spousal support waiver.[20]

§6.05 ENFORCEABILITY OF FEE WAIVER FOR CUSTODY AND CHILD SUPPORT

A premarital agreement cannot predetermine custody of and support for a minor child.[21] A premarital agreement may include a provision requiring each party to bear his or her own lawyers' fees in connection with a suit for divorce and waiving each party's claim to seek a fee award from the court. Some courts have interpreted a general fee waiver in a premarital agreement not to apply to litigation of subjects not governed by the agreement, such as custody and child support,[22] or may have a statute that expressly allows for a fee award for custody or child support when necessary to protect the best interests of a child.[23] Other courts have held that a waiver of lawyers' fees for litigation of custody and child support, whether

---

16. *See Rosenbaum-Golden*, 381 Ill. App.3d at 65 (fee award to wife did not violate premarital agreement waiver where award was advance against marital assets and husband had much greater resources); *Kessler v. Kessler*, 33 A.D.3d. 42, 8118 N.Y.S.2d 571 (2006) (court had authority to award attorneys' fees to implement rights under premarital agreement, but not fees incurred in unsuccessful attempt to invalidate agreement, where great disparity in resources).

17. *Nack v. Dickerson*, 2007 Va. App. LEXIS 339 (unpub.); *Hardee v. Hardee*, 355 S.C. 382, 585 S.E.2d 501 (2003).

18. *Trbovich v. Trbovich*, 122 A.D.3d 1381, 997 N.Y.S.2d 855 (2014).

19. *Vinik v. Lee*, 96 A.D.3d 522, 947 N.Y.S.2d 424 (2012) (waiver of fees in premarital agreement did not bar temporary relief, including interim fees).

20. *Hardee*, 355 S.C. 382.

21. See Sections 7.02 and 7.03; *see* UPAA § 3(b); UPMAA § 10 (2012).

22. *In re Marriage of Erpelding*, 917 N.W.2d 235 (Iowa 2018); *Gottlieb v. Gottlieb*, 138A.D.3d 30, 25 N.Y.S.3d 90 (2016); *In re Marriage of Burke*, 96 Wash. App. 474, 980 P.2d 265 (1999); *see also In re Marriage of Ikeler*, 161 P.3d 663 (Colo. 2007) (marital agreement fee waiver was unenforceable as unconscionable where wife was stay-at-home mother of triplets).

23. *See In re D.M.L.*, 2022 Tex. App. LEXIS (unpub.).

express or implied, violates public policy and is therefore unenforceable.[24] By contrast, in a New York case, *Arizin v. Covello*,[25] the court upheld a premarital agreement fee waiver in its entirety although custody of two children was at issue. Virginia courts interpret a general waiver of fees at divorce to encompass all issues in the case, including fees for determining custody and child support, and they uphold such waivers if the agreement is otherwise valid.[26]

When a premarital or postmarital agreement includes a provision that requires each party to bear his or her own fees to implement its terms, it can include the following:

> The waiver of attorney's fees and costs under this Paragraph __shall not apply to fees or costs incurred to determine custody of or support for a minor child of the parties, and each party expressly reserves the right to make an application for such fees in accordance with the law of the state with jurisdiction to resolve such issues.

Such language will make the parties' intent unambiguous and should therefore avoid the necessity for court interpretation. It will often be in the best interests of an economically disadvantaged party for the agreement to include the preceding text. Otherwise, a wealthy party may have an unfair advantage in a future custody or child support dispute. If parties intend that a waiver of fees at divorce include fees for determining custody or child support, the agreement should say so expressly. Whether such a waiver will be enforceable will depend on the law of the forum.

§6.06 Enforceability of Fee Waiver to Determine Spousal Support

Courts have held a contractual fee waiver inapplicable to litigation of spousal support where such a claim was nonwaivable,[27] or had not been waived, and to litigation of a claim for temporary support or separate maintenance where a waiver of these rights was unenforceable.[28]

§6.07 Reservation of Future Fees

The lawyer for a weaker party should consider whether to accept a blanket waiver of future fees for a divorce or propose some specific terms to take account of, for example, that the

24. *Kelly v. Kelly*, 518 P.3d 326 (Idaho 2022); Riemann v. Toland, 269 A.3d 229 (Me. 2022); *J.A.S. v. S.W.S*, 2021 Ala. Civ. App. LEXIS 73 (unpub.); *In re Marriage of Erpelding*, 917 N.W.2d at 235; *In re Marriage of Best*, 387 Ill. App. 3d 948, 901 N.E.2d 967 (2009); *see also In re Marriage of Lane*, 2011 Cal. App. LEXIS 265 (unpub.) (fee waiver did not encompass fees for custody and child support, and had it done so, waiver would have violated public policy).

25. 175 Misc. 2d 453, 669 N.Y.S.2d 189 (1998); *but see Gottlieb*, 25 N.Y.S.3d 90.

26. *See Armstrong v. Armstrong*, 2019 Va. App. LEXIS 258 (unpub.).

27. *In re Marriage of Erpelding*, 917 N.W.2d at 235.

28. *Walker v. Walker*, 765 N.W.2d 747 (S.D. 2009); *Lebeck v. Lebeck*, 118 N.M. 367, 881 P.2d 727 (Ct. App. 1994); *In re Marriage of Purcell*, 99 Or. App. 668, 783 P.3d 1038 (1989); *but see Rutledge v. Rutledge*, 45 Va. App. 56, 608 S.E.2d 504 (2005) (marital agreement providing husband would contribute specified amount to wife's attorneys' fees, and otherwise waived fee claims, prohibited award of fees for proceeding for modification of indefinite alimony).

party may need money for fees (and possibly for costs, such as for a property appraisal) initially to hire counsel and may not have ready access to the necessary funds. Where the agreement reserves spousal support or does not predetermine division of shared property, the disadvantaged spouse will need access to funds to secure these rights. When the agreement will create a pool of shared assets, it could provide expressly for each party to have access to marital/community funds for this purpose. When there is a big wealth disparity, a weaker party may want to reserve a claim, while the wealthy party waives.

§6.08 PREVAILING PARTY (LOSER-PAYS) FEES

Only a few cases arising out of divorce litigation have addressed a prevailing party provision in a premarital agreement. A provision making a losing party liable for the fees of the prevailing party could simply say that the court may award fees against a party who breaches the agreement. Some courts may hold that a challenge to validity is not a breach.[29] Therefore, it is appropriate for the fee-shifting provision to make explicit that a prevailing party in a dispute about validity is entitled to seek a fee award. Nevertheless, when the losing party is the spouse who is disadvantaged by the agreement, some courts have been reluctant to enforce such a provision,[30] or have held that such a provision violates public policy.[31] Other courts have enforced a contractual provision for fee shifting to the losing party.[32]

A 2005 Florida decision articulates the case for enforcement of a prevailing-party fee provision. In *Lashkajani v. Lashkajani*,[33] the trial court found that the husband made a full and frank financial disclosure and that the substantive terms of the premarital agreement were fair, and the premarital agreement was valid. It awarded the husband a modest amount of fees as the prevailing party from which the wife appealed. The court noted that a prevailing-party clause properly protects a party who relied on the agreement and creates a disincentive to a frivolous challenge while also creating a disincentive to a valid challenge. It was not unfair to place the risk on the challenger, who knew the circumstances of execution, could best evaluate the merits, and was aware of the prevailing-party clause when he or she signed

---

29. *See Litt v. Litt*, 2016 Conn. Super. LEXIS 234 (unpub.).

30. *See In re Marriage of Pond*, 676 N.E.2d 401 (Ind. Ct. App. 1997) (loser-pays provision unconscionable as applied to wife where vast disparity in income would permit husband, but not wife, to litigate validity of agreement); *In re Marriage of Bowers*, 143 Or. App. 24, 922 P.2d 722 (1995) (trial court can award fees to prevailing party under loser-pays provision and to losing party under statutory authority based on need; awards could cancel each other out); *In re Marriage of Purcell*, 99 Or. App. 668 (where premarital agreement generally valid, but spousal support waiver invalid, trial court could award wife fees notwithstanding loser-pays provision); *see also Grabe v. Hokin*, 341 Conn. 360, 267 A.3d 145 (2021) (enforcement of fee-shifting to husband who challenged validity of premarital agreement would have been unconscionable as it would financially cripple him; wife did not appeal award); *Steele v. Steele*, 467 N.J. Super. 414, 253 A.3d 1190 (App. Div. 2021).

31. *Soldwedel v. Soldwedel*, 2021 Ariz. App. LEXIS 688 (unpub.) (contractual fee-shifting to loser under premarital agreement violated public policy; but trial court not precluded from making award to prevailing party under statute giving court discretion to award fees); *see also Bobrow v. Bobrow*, 241 Ariz. 592, 391 P.3d 646 (2017) (fee shifting in premarital agreement violated public policy but issue not preserved for appeal).

32. *See Miller v. Miller*, 2022 Md. App. LEXIS 813 (unpub.); *AXA Equitable Life Ins. Co. v. Grissom*, 2012 U.S. Dist. LEXIS 166613 (M.D. Tenn. 2012); *Berg v. Young*, 175 So. 3d 863 (Fla. Ct. App., 4th Dist. 2015); *Kellar v. Estate of Kellar*, 172 Wn. App. 562, 291 P.3d 906 (2012); *Nadolski v. Nadolski*, 2008 LEXIS 363 (unpub.); *Kantor v. Kantor*, 116 Nev. 886, 8 P.3d 825 (2000).

33. 911 So. 2d 1154 (Fla. 2005).

the agreement.[34] Florida case law at that time did not enforce a premarital agreement waiver of pre-divorce spousal support or lawyers' fees incurred before divorce.[35] Here the appellate court made a distinction between nonwaivable temporary support for a spouse, which includes interim lawyers' fees, and fees incurred to protect the contract itself.

When the loser received substantial assets under an agreement, an effort to better his or her position at the expense of the other party may well be punished through a fee award under a contract provision for fee shifting to the loser.[36] When it is the wealthier spouse seeking to void what in retrospect seems a too-generous provision for the less wealthy spouse, courts have had no trouble enforcing a prevailing-party provision.[37]

Although some courts, under some circumstances, may refuse to enforce a fee-shifting provision against a disadvantaged party, it is nevertheless often appropriate to include such a provision. It may discourage some potential litigants from pursuing a meritless claim. It may also result in a court refusing to make a pendente lite award to enable a party to litigate validity, forcing him or her to bear the economic risk of the litigation.

---

34. *See also Nadolski*, 2008 Va. App. LEXIS 363 (trial court should have awarded husband fees under prevailing party provision of postmarital agreement where wife filed for divorce and sought relief contrary to terms of agreement); *Montoya*, 91 Conn. App. 407, 881 A.2d 319 (trial court properly awarded fees to husband under prevailing party provision for defending against failed attempt to have premarital agreement declared invalid).

35. The court in *Lashkajani* did not rule on the quite substantial fee award the trial court made to the wife for the dissolution proceedings. The agreement, in addition to the prevailing-party provision, required each party to bear his or her own legal fees and costs in the event of divorce but the trial judge nevertheless made an award to the wife. Whether it could do so over a contractual waiver was not before the appellate court. See Section 6.04.

36. *See Miller v. Miller,* 2022 Md. App. LEXIS 813 (unpub.) (husband awarded $58,000 in fees to defend validity of premarital agreement where wife had counsel, parties negotiated over five weeks, wife proposed and got better terms; terms included asset transfer wife could not have gotten in absence of agreement); *Davis v. Miller*, 269 Kan. 732, 7 P.3d 1223 (2000) (court awarded husband $300,000 in attorneys' fees incurred to defend validity of postmarital agreement).

37. *See In re Marriage of Christen*, 899 P.2d 339 (Colo. Ct. App. 1995) (wife entitled to fees incurred for enforcement under premarital agreement loser-pays provision where husband sought to void generous spousal support provision).

7 Child Provisions, Nonfinancial Provisions, Provisions Governing the Ongoing Marriage, Marital Misconduct, and Grounds of Divorce

§7.01 Overview

This chapter addresses child provisions and certain nonfinancial agreement provisions, including provisions regarding marital misconduct and grounds of divorce.

Provisions regulating the parties' personal rights during the ongoing marriage are not otherwise addressed in this book. The tension between the state's interest in preserving and protecting marriage and the private right to contract is quite apparent when it comes to provisions of an agreement that purport to govern the parties' personal conduct, living arrangements, or other nonfinancial matters during the marriage. Courts are ill equipped to interfere in matters relating to the ongoing marriage and are generally reluctant to do so.[1] The Uniform Premarital Agreement Act (UPAA) permits parties to a premarital agreement to "contract with respect to any other matter, including their personal rights and obligations, not in violation of public policy or a statute imposing a criminal penalty."[2] Thus, "subject to the public policy limitation, an agreement may provide for such matters as the choice of abode, freedom to pursue career opportunities, upbringing of children and so on."[3]

1. *Kilgrow v. Kilgrow*, 268 Ala. 475, 107 So. 2d 885 (1958) (court has no authority to settle dispute between parents who are not separated about where child should attend school); *see also* Rasmusen & Stake, *Lifting the Veil of Ignorance: Personalizing the Marriage Contract*, 73 Ind. L.J. 453, 462 (Spring 1998).
2. UPAA § 3(a)(8) (1983).
3. *Id.*, cmt.

However, "no special provision is made for enforcement of provisions of a premarital agreement relating to personal rights and obligations."[4] In sum, couples may wish to include such provisions in a premarital or postmarital agreement but, with few exceptions, the parties will be left to themselves to enforce them.

§7.02 PARENTAGE, PARENTAL RIGHTS, AND CHILD REARING DURING MARRIAGE AND AFTER DIVORCE

(a) Custody of Minor Child After Divorce or Dissolution

Statutes and case law uniformly preclude parties to a premarital or postmarital agreement from contracting to divest a court of authority to make or modify custodial arrangements for a minor child upon separation or divorce.[5] Parties may wish to have the agreement state their intentions in this regard. For example, they may wish to acknowledge their intent that they will have joint legal or shared physical custody of an existing or an unborn child. Such a provision will not bind a court in a future custody dispute.[6] However, it will generally be severable from provisions regarding property and spousal support; its unenforceability will not affect the validity of the agreement as a whole.

(b) Religious Upbringing of Children

In the early part of the twentieth century, courts generally upheld marital agreements regarding the religious upbringing of an unborn child. The right of a parent, particularly the father, to raise children in a chosen religion was held to be almost sacrosanct.[7] More recently, as interfaith marriages have increased, courts have become reluctant to choose one parent's religion over the other's. After the Supreme Court decision in *Wisconsin v. Yoder*,[8] state courts were compelled to recognize the rights of both parents to raise their children in their own faiths.

Parties may wish to agree in advance about the religious upbringing of an existing or unborn child. However, absent a showing of substantial risk of harm to a child, a court will not enforce that agreement at divorce so as to exclude a parent from indoctrinating the child

4. *Id.* § 6, cmt.

5. *See* RESTATEMENT SECOND OF CONTRACTS § 191 (1981); MD. CODE ANN., FAM. LAW § 8-103(a) (court may modify provision of marital agreement relating to custody of minor child); *Spurlin v. Spurlin,* 289 Ga. 818, 716 S.E.2d 209 (2011); *In re Marriage of Best*, 387 Ill. App. 3d 948, 901 N.E.2d 967 (2009); *Kessler v. Kessler*, 33 A.D.3d 42, 818 N.Y.S.2d 571 (2006); *R.R. v. M.H.*, 426 Mass. 501, 689 N.E.2d 790 (1998); *In re Marriage of Littlefield*, 133 Wn. 2d 39, 940 P.2d 1362 (1997); *Combs v. Sherry-Combs*, 865 P.2d 50 (Wyo. 1993); *see also In re Marriage of Iqbal and Khan*, 11 N.E.3d. 1 (Ill. Ct. App. 2014) (court is not bound by postmarital agreement providing for third party to determine custody rights); *Kelm v. Kelm*, 92 Ohio St. 3d 223, 749 N.E.2d 299 (2001) (*Kelm II*) (court is not bound by marital settlement agreement provision for binding arbitration of future dispute regarding custody).

6. *Combs v. Sherry-Combs*, 865 P.2d at 54; *Edwardson v. Edwardson*, 798 S.W.2d 941 (Ky. 1990); *Osborne v. Osborne*, 384 Mass. 591, 428 N.E.2d 810 (1981).

7. *Ramon v. Ramon*, 34 N.Y.S.2d 100 (Dom. Rel. Ct. 1942); *Weinberger v. Van Hessen*, 260 N.Y. 294, 183 N.E. 429, 431 (1932).

8. 406 U.S. 205 (1972).

in a different religious faith.[9] As the Pennsylvania court in *Zummo v. Zummo*[10] observed, parents in an intact family make decisions about religious upbringing on an ad hoc basis without state intervention. State intervention is permitted in such decisions only on a showing of harm. State intervention in religious upbringing decisions is no more appropriate after a divorce.[11] In rejecting enforcement of a premarital agreement to raise a child in a particular religion, the court in *Zummo* cited the vagueness of such an agreement, the risk it would excessively entangle the courts in religious matters, and most significantly, the right of all persons to "doubt, and to change their religious convictions, and to expose their children to their changed beliefs."[12] The court went on to say:

> [I]t is also generally acknowledged that it would be difficult, if not impossible, for an interreligious couple engaged to be married to project themselves into the future so as to enable them to know how they will feel about religion, if and when their children are born, and as the children grow; and that it would be still more difficult for such a couple to attempt to project themselves into the scenario of a potential divorce after children were born, in order to accurately anticipate the circumstances under which religious upbringing agreements would be enforced if such agreements were given legal effect. . . . Consequently, while religious upbringing agreements may serve an important and beneficial purpose by promoting careful consideration of potential difficulties prior to marriage, and also may carry moral weight and religious sanction, parties entering into such agreements generally will not be able to anticipate the fundamental changes in circumstances between their prenuptial optimism, their struggles for accommodation, and their ultimate post-divorce disillusionment. . . . [13]

Courts in a number of states have held premarital religious upbringing agreements unenforceable insofar as such an agreement precludes a parent from exposing a child to beliefs contrary to those of the faith in which the parties agreed to raise the child.[14] Only where there is evidence of substantial risk of actual, demonstrable harm to an existing child have courts limited a parent's right to expose a child to that parent's religious beliefs and practices. Typically, such a limitation has been imposed when a child has developed a religious identity that is threatened by a parent's conduct.[15] Courts shrink from interfering in religious upbringing disputes, even when the family unit has fallen apart, as where parties have separated, except

9. *In re Marriage of Nuechterlein*, 225 Ill. App. 3d 1, 587 N.E.2d 21 (1992).

10. 394 Pa. Super. 30, 574 A.2d 1130 (1990).

11. *Id.* at 49, 1140.

12. *Id.* at 62, 1146.

13. *Id.* at 63–64, 1147 (citations omitted; footnote omitted).

14. *In re Marriage of Weiss*, 42 Cal. App. 4th 106, 49 Cal. Rptr. 2d 339 (1996); *Sotnick v. Sotnick*, 650 So. 2d 157 (Fla. Dist. Ct. App. 1995); *Hornung v. Hornung*, 1 Neb. App. 6, 485 N.W.2d 335 (1992); *Wood v. Wood*, 39 Del. Ch. 523, 168 A.2d 102 (1961); *Gottlieb v. Gottlieb*, 31 Ill. App. 2d 120, 175 N.E.2d 619 (1961); *McLaughlin v. McLaughlin*, 20 Conn. Supp. 278, 132 A.2d 420 (1957); *Stanton v. Stanton*, 213 Ga. 545, 100 S.E.2d 289 (1957); *but see Stevenot v. Stevenot*, 133 A.D.2d 820, 520 N.Y.S.2d 197(1987) (oral agreement before or during marriage to raise child in particular religion not enforceable after divorce unless incorporated in divorce judgment); *In re Marriage of Wolfert*, 42 Colo. App. 433, 598 P.2d 524 (1979) (same).

15. *Kendall v. Kendall*, 426 Mass. 238, 687 N.E.2d 1228 (1997); *MacLagan v. Klein*, 123 N.C. App. 557, 473 S.E.2d 778 (1996); *Kirchner v. Caughey*, 326 Md. 567, 606 A.2d 257 (1991).

in extreme circumstances. Not surprisingly, therefore, they are even less likely to interfere in such a dispute while the parties are still living together. *Kilgrow v. Kilgrow*[16] is a rare case where parties to a premarital agreement specifying religious upbringing who were still living together sought court intervention. The court refused to get involved, essentially telling the parties they had to settle the issue themselves.

(c) Parentage, *de Facto* Parenthood, and Parental Rights

Many same-sex couples intend to make children a part of their family, or may already have done so, and they may wish to establish legal parentage in both partners. A single parent who does not have a co-parent may want to establish parentage in a spouse after marriage. The discussion below is concerned with contract terms that may be appropriate to carry out a shared intent to establish parentage, recognizing that a contract alone may not be sufficient to fully protect both parties and their children. This is distinct from the question of a court's authority to resolve a dispute between parents regarding allocation of time and decision-making authority incident to dissolution. The law regarding the rights of *de facto* parents upon dissolution is beyond the scope of this book. Couples who choose to enter into a premarital or postmarital agreement may wish to foreclose litigation of *de facto* parenthood in favor of contractual terms that, to the extent permitted by law, predetermine their parentage rights. Some agreement terms parties and counsel may wish to consider include:

- A provision that a biological or adoptive parent will participate in a second-parent adoption, if permitted by state law, so as to make his or her partner an adoptive parent;
- A provision that a biological or adoptive parent will participate in a court proceeding for entry of a consent joint custody order during the marriage so as to create custodial rights in both parties;[17]
- A provision that both parties will be financially responsible for any child they agree to bring into their family during the marriage and in the event of dissolution;
- A provision for co-parenting of a child previously born to or adopted by either spouse so that the other spouse can be considered the *de facto* parent.[18]

Parties need to understand that once parentage is created, the other parent cannot be divested of his or her parental rights simply because the parties are no longer a couple or a parent decides that the other parent is unsuitable. In considering appropriate terms, counsel should give some thought to whether the agreement should include terms requiring a written consent of both parties before they become joint parents inasmuch as parenthood carries financial obligations.

---

16. *Kilgrow v. Kilgrow*, 268 Ala. 475.

17. *See In re Bonfield*, 97 Ohio St. 3d 387, 780 N.E.2d 241 (2002) (juvenile court has jurisdiction to determine custody of child on joint petition of legal mother and her same-sex partner to establish shared parenting).

18. *See, e.g., Frazier v. Goudschaal*, 296 Kan. 730, 295 P.3d 542 (2013) (co-parenting agreement between two women was enforceable contract that created *de facto* parentage); *In re Mullen*, 129 Ohio St. 3d 417, 953 N.E.2d 302 (2011) (parent may by agreement voluntarily share care, custody, and control of child with nonparent); *A.C. v. C.B.*, 113 N.M. 581, 829 P.2d 660 (1992) (agreement between unmarried partners to co-parent child born to one of them may be enforceable if in best interest of child).

(d) Disposition of Stored Embryos

Parties who have used or intend to use assisted reproductive technology to create a family may wish to include terms in a premarital or postmarital agreement addressing their rights to stored embryos in the event of a separation or divorce or the death of one party. Many of the cases addressing questions of enforcement of a contract regarding disposition of stored embryos have involved a pre-implantation contract with an IVF clinic.[19] The discussion here is concerned with provisions of a premarital or postmarital agreement that may allow a spouse to use an embryo after a separation or divorce or the death of the other spouse or may preclude him or her from doing so. Courts have taken several approaches to resolving disputes over disposition of embryos after a marriage has broken down: "(1) the contractual approach, (2) the contemporaneous consent model, and (3) the balancing test."[20] Courts adhering to the contractual approach hold parties to the contract they signed prior to undergoing IVF as to disposition of embryos.[21] By contrast, a Massachusetts case held that a spouse may withdraw consent to implantation under an IVF clinic contract,[22] and a New Jersey court has employed a balancing test under which the interests of both parties must be considered.[23]

One court, in enforcing a contract with an IVF clinic, which gave the wife the final decision as to disposition of stored embryos, explained that "giving effect to a valid agreement evincing the parties' intent regarding disposition of embryos is consistent with our statutory and case law that give similar effect to prenuptial agreements and agreements made during a marriage."[24] Parties to a premarital or postmarital agreement may wish to include provisions regarding disposition of stored embryos. However, in this dynamic area of the law, the outcome of a future dispute is uncertain.[25]

§7.03 FINANCIAL PROVISIONS FOR CHILDREN

(a) Overview

Under most circumstances, it is neither necessary nor appropriate to spell out in an agreement the parties' financial commitment to a minor child during the ongoing marriage. Every parent has a common law and statutory duty to provide basic support for his or her minor child.

---

19. The adequacy of form contracts provided by IVF clinics to enable parties to choose disposition of embryos is beyond the scope of this book. *See* Deborah Forman, *Émbryo Disposition and Divorce: Why Clinic Consent Forms Are Not the Answer*, 24 J.A.A.M.L. 57 (2011).

20. *Jocelyn P. v. Joshua P.*, 250 Md. App. 435, 250 A.3d 373 (2021); *In re Marriage of Witten*, 672 N.W.2d 768, 774 (Iowa 2003). Some states have enacted statutes directing judges at divorce to determine disposition. *See* ARIZ. CODE, A.R.R. § 25-318.03.

21. *See, e.g., Bilbao v. Goodwin*, 333 Conn. 599, 217 A.3d 977 (2019); *Roman v. Roman*, 193 S.W.3d 40 (Tex. Ct. App., 1st Dist., 2006); *In re Marriage of Litowitz*, 146 Wn. 2d 514, 48 P.3d 261 (2002); *Kass v. Kass*, 91 N.Y.2d 554, 696 N.E.2d 174, 673 N.Y.S.2d 350 (1998); *see also In re Marriage of Nash*, 2009 Wash. App. LEXIS 1272 (parties marital settlement agreement regarding disposition of frozen embryos is enforceable).

22. *A.Z. v. R.Z*, 431 Mass. 150, 725 N.E.2d 1051 (2000) (IVF clinic consent form is not binding between spouses).

23. *J.B. v. M.B.*, 170 N.J. 9, 783 A.2d 707 (2001); *see also Reber v. Reber*, 42 A.3d 1131 (Pa. Super. 2012).

24. *In re Marriage of Dahl*, 222 Ore. App. 572, 19583, 4 P.3d 834, 840 (2008).

25. *See* Mark P. Strasser, *You Take the Embryos but I Get the House (and the Business): Recent Trends in Awards Involving Embryos upon Divorce*, 57 BUFFALO L. REV 1159 (July 2009).

Therefore, an agreement requiring a party to do no more than the law requires will have no effect on the parties' legal obligations, and an agreement that requires less will not preclude the court from ordering a parent to meet his or her threshold obligation.[26] A contract will not divest a court of authority to order a parent to provide appropriate support for a minor child upon separation or divorce.[27]

By contrast, parties may enter into an enforceable agreement that expands the financial obligations of one or both parties to provide for a child during the marriage or in the event of separation or divorce or upon the death of a party. Thus, parties may contract to provide for payment of private school tuition, post-majority periodic support to a parent with whom a child will be living, to pay for college or graduate school, or to provide life insurance for the benefit of a child. To the extent parties choose to contract beyond the scope of the state-mandated duty of minority support, their obligations will be governed exclusively by the law of contracts.

(b) Limits on Courts' Authority Regarding Financial Provisions for Children in the Absence of Contract

There are limits on the authority of courts to require parents to provide material benefits for a child. First, courts generally may intervene only after a marital separation. They have no authority to regulate the extent to which parents in an intact family provide for children beyond the basic necessities of life.[28] Second, there are a variety of material benefits that family courts have no, or limited, power to bestow. For example, under ordinary circumstances a court at divorce may not order a parent to pay for a child to attend private school, go to sleep-away summer camp, or study abroad. Finally, courts' powers generally end at the applicable age of majority or at the death of the parent. Thus, courts may not order a parent to pay support after a child becomes an adult under state law,[29] and generally have no power to require a parent to provide for a child after the death of the parent,[30] although in some states

26. MD. CODE ANN., FAM. LAW §§ 12-202 (court shall determine child support using presumptive child support guideline), 8-103(a) (court may modify agreement regarding support of minor child); *Werther v. Werther*, 9 Misc. 3d 1114A, 808 N.Y.S.2d 921 (2005) (provision in premarital agreement eliminating child support obligation is void as against public policy); *Walsh v. Walsh*, 333 Md. 492, 635 A.2d 1340 (1994) (court must scrutinize child support agreement for compliance with child support guideline and must determine whether downward deviation in child's best interests); *Monmouth Cty. Div. of Soc. Services v. G.D.M.*, 308 N.J. Super. 83, 705 A.2d 408 (1997) (parties to a divorce may not contract away child's right to support); *see also Nkopchieu v. Minlend*, 59 Va. App. 299, 718 S.E. 2d 470 (2011) (former wife entitled to QDRO for child support arrearage notwithstanding premarital agreement waiver of claims to retirement benefits).

27. *See* UPAA § 3(b) (1983) ("The right of a child to support may not be adversely affected by a premarital agreement."); *In re C.G.G.*, 946 P.2d 603 (Colo. Ct. App. 1997); *Walsh v. Walsh*, 333 Md. 492, 635 A.2d 1340 (1994); *Combs v. Sherry-Combs*, 865 P.2d 50 (Wyo. 1993); *Edwardson v. Edwardson*, 798 S.W.2d 941 (Ky. 1990); *Marriage of Fox*, 58 Wash. App. 935, 795 P.2d 1170 (1990); *Huck v. Huck*, 734 P.2d 417 (Utah 1986); *McHugh v. McHugh*, 181 Conn. 482, 436 A.2d 8 (1980); *see also In the Interest of Knott*, 118 S.W.3d 899 (Tex. Ct. App. 2003) (parties' right to enter into premarital agreement taking new wife's income out of community did not violate public policy or state law regarding husband's support obligation to child of previous marriage).

28. *See Kern v. Kern*, 360 So. 2d 482 (Fla. Dist. Ct. App. 1978) (child of intact marriage has no right to compel parents to provide college education).

29. *Stokes v. Maris*, 596 So. 2d 879 (Miss. 1992); *In re Dissolution of Marriage of Lazor*, 59 Ohio St. 3d 201, 572 N.E.2d 66 (1991).

30. *Reinhardt v. Reinhardt*, 131 So. 2d 509 (Fla. Dist. Ct. App. 1961) (absent enforceable contract, parent's duty to support minor child ends on death of parent).

there is authority permitting a court at divorce to order a parent to maintain life insurance for the benefit of a minor child.[31]

(c) Enforceability of Contractual Financial Provisions for Children Generally

The principle that the law does not preclude parties to an agreement from being more generous than the law requires operates in the area of contracts regarding children.[32] Generally, courts uphold agreements for the benefit of children insofar as they provide support at a higher level, or for a longer duration, than would be required by state law, or that provide support for a stepchild for whom the obligor would otherwise have no legal obligation.[33]

To the extent parties choose to contract beyond the scope of the state-imposed duty of support, their obligations will be governed exclusively by the law of contracts.[34] Courts enforce agreements that require a payment of basic support that exceeds the amount otherwise payable under state law as well as agreements that provide benefits that the court has no power to order.[35] For example, courts will enforce a contract for payment of private school expenses even where there is no showing of special need.[36] They will also enforce a contract requiring a parent to provide a home for a custodial parent and child.[37]

State courts will protect a child from a parental agreement that provides too little support. There is virtually no protection for the payor who contracts to pay an amount for the benefit of a child that may in retrospect appear to be too generous, that the party later comes to regret, or that changed circumstances render burdensome.[38] The showing that a party must make to be relieved of a burdensome obligation to a minor child is much greater than merely a change of circumstances. One court described the necessary showing as requiring:

---

31. *See Nichols v. Tedder*, 547 So. 2d 766 (Miss. 1989); VA. CODE §§ 20-103, 107.1:1.

32. *See Pursley v. Pursley*, 144 S.W.3d 820 (Ky. 2004); *Ottino v. Ottino*, 21 P.3d 37 (N.M. Ct. App. 2000); *Goldin v. Goldin*, 34 Va. App. 95, 538 S.E.2d 326 (2000).

33. *Lanahan v. Nevius*, 317 A.2d 521, 525 (D.C. 1974).

34. *Treadaway v. Smith*, 325 S.C. 367, 376, 479 S.E.2d 849, 854 (Ct. App. 1996) ("The court's duty is to enforce the contract made by the parties regardless of its wisdom or folly, apparent unreasonableness, or the parties' failure to guard their rights carefully"); *Blackburn v. Blackburn*, 526 S.W.2d 463 (Tenn. 1975) (agreement outside scope of legal duty of child support during minority is contractual and enforceable as any other contract); *see also Ortiz v. Ortiz*, 2010 N.M. App. Unpub. LEXIS 194; *Rogers v. Rogers*, 662 So. 2d 1111 (Miss. 1995); *Richter v. Richter*, 666 So. 2d 559 (Fla. Dist. Ct. App. 1995); *Hirtle v. Hirtle*, 217 Conn. 394, 586 A.2d 578 (1991); *Tiffany v. Tiffany*, 1 Va. App. 11, 332 S.E.2d 796 (1985).

35. *Goldin v. Goldin*, 34 Va. App. 95; *Matter of L.M.H. v. D.S.H.*, 2005 Del. Fam. Ct. LEXIS 135.

36. *See Solis v. Tea*, 468 A.2d 1276 (Del. 1983) (re-evaluating father's contractual obligation to pay for private school based on stricter showing of unforeseen change in circumstances due to factors beyond payor's control).

37. *See Gumberg v. Gumberg*, 755 So. 2d 710 (Fla. Dist. Ct. App. 1999) (court had power to enforce premarital agreement requiring father to provide home for wife and any future children if court awarded her custody); *In re Marriage of Littlefield*, 133 Wash. 2d 39, 940 P.2d 1362 (1997) (father's promise in premarital agreement to provide home of specified value to wife and any minor children parties might have was enforceable child support obligation).

38. *Goldin v. Goldin*, 34 Va. App. 95, 538 S.E.2d 326 (2000) (marital settlement agreement requiring husband to pay support for each child to age 23 or college graduation required continued support for 20-year-old pregnant daughter who lived with neither parent); *Katz v. Katz*, 258 Ga. 184, 366 S.E.2d 766 (1988) (parties can incur enforceable contractual obligations that go beyond the minimum requirements of the law); *Gaddis v. Gaddis*, 20 Ill. App. 3d 267, 314 N.E.2d 627 (1974) (party not entitled to be relieved of contract to pay both periodic post-majority support and costs of college regardless of ability to pay).

proof of an unforeseen adverse change of financial condition due to factors beyond the obligor's control, coupled with a finding that enforcement of the original commitment would not be in the child's best interest, *i.e.*, would likely curtail a future ability of the parent to contribute to the child's support.[39]

(d) Subjects for Financial Agreements Regarding Children

There are a variety of material benefits for children that parties may wish to contract about in a premarital or postmarital agreement and that are outside the scope of the basic support duty:

- Payment of periodic support after divorce to a parent on behalf of a child, or directly to the child, after a child reaches majority;
- Payment of certain specified expenses for a child after the child reaches majority, such as medical insurance premiums, uninsured medical expenses, automobile expenses, or general living expenses;
- Support or other financial provisions for a disabled child;
- Payment of college or graduate school expenses for a period of time or in an amount that exceeds what could otherwise be awarded by a court, and that may include a host of related expenses, such as computer equipment, study abroad, transportation costs, participation in activities, and the like;
- Minority support that goes beyond that which a court could order or which allocates a disproportionate share of the support to one parent;
- An obligation to make gifts to, or for the benefit of, a child, such as an annual gift into a custodial or college savings account;
- In-kind benefits, such as the purchase or lease of a home for a custodial parent, or the right to remain in a jointly titled home for an extended period of time beyond what a court has the authority to order;
- Material benefits for a child that would otherwise be considered discretionary during an ongoing marriage, such as payment of the cost of private school, college, study abroad, summer camp, enrichment activities, and similar items;
- Support for a stepchild during marriage or after divorce who would otherwise not be entitled to such support;
- Payment of expenses for life cycle events, such as a Bar or Bat Mitzvah, confirmation, graduation, or wedding; and
- Post-death financial support and estate planning obligations, such as life insurance or other beneficiary designations, establishment of a trust, or testamentary dispositions for a child or stepchild.

(e) Support for a Stepchild

At common law, a stepparent has no duty to support a stepchild during a marriage "except where the stepparent voluntarily takes the stepchild into his family and assumes the duty of

39. *Solis v. Tea*, 468 A.2d 1276, 1283 (Del. 1983).

support."[40] In a number of states, such a duty is imposed by statute.[41] Generally, a stepparent's support obligation ends upon separation or divorce.[42] However, courts have enforced contracts under which a stepparent agreed to pay support for a stepchild after divorce.[43] An agreement in which a stepparent agrees to support a child of the other party should address several important issues:

- Whether support will continue after a separation or divorce;
- In the event the support obligation will survive a separation, the amount of support to be provided or a formula or set of well-defined criteria by which the amount will be determined;
- The duration of the obligation and whether it will terminate at the age of majority or be extended to a later point;
- The criteria for modification of the obligation, such as, in the event the payor experiences a change in his/her ability to pay support or provide other economic benefits for a child;
- Enforcement of the obligation; and
- What will be included in the obligation and whether it will be limited to a basic support payment or whether additional obligations, such as direct payment of medical insurance, uninsured medical expenses, college expenses, and the like, will be included.

When the terms of the agreement only require support during the ongoing marriage, it should not be necessary to specify with particularity the extent of the payor's obligation. Ordinarily, a statement that the obligor will provide a home and basic necessities in accordance with the family's general standard of living should be sufficient. Courts do not ordinarily intervene in an intact family and the payor is entitled to exercise the same discretion as any parent to determine how luxurious a lifestyle to provide a child. More care is required when the payor will commit to expenditures that are not included in a parent's legal duty of support, such as payment for private school, summer camp, post-majority support, or college expenses. A nonparent who contractually commits to such extras is in the same position as a parent who does so.

---

40. CLARK, THE LAW OF DOMESTIC RELATIONS IN THE UNITED STATES § 7.2 (2d ed. 1987) (hereafter, "Clark"); Sweet, Annotation, *Stepparent's Postdivorce Duty to Support Stepchild*, 44 A.L.R. 4th 520, 531–39 (1986); AM. JUR. 2D, *Parent and Child* § 88; *Bagwell v. Bagwell*, 698 So. 2d 746 (La. Ct. App. 1997); *see also In the Interest of Knott*, 118 S.W.3d 899 (Tex. Ct. App. 2003) (new wife's income not included in community income for purposes of determining father's support obligation to child of previous marriage where father and new wife had premarital agreement excluding her income).

41. *See* Laura Morgan, *The Rights, Duties and Responsibilities of Stepparents to Their Stepchildren*, 8 DIVORCE LITIG. 185 (Sept. 1996).

42. CLARK § 7.2.

43. *Dewey v. Dewey*, 886 P.2d 623 (Alaska 1994); *Brown v. Brown*, 287 Md. 273, 412 A.2d 396 (1980); *see also T. v. T.*, 216 Va. 867, 224 S.E.2d 148 (1976) (court will enforce express oral contract under which husband promised to treat wife's unborn child as his own and husband therefore required to support child after divorce).

(f) College Expenses and Savings for College

Some parties may want to include an obligation for a wealthy party to pay college expenses, or create savings for these expenses, for an existing child or a future child. An agreement could provide, without elaboration, that the wealthy parent will be responsible for all college expenses. When the agreement requires a parent to fund a Section 529 plan or state tuition contract, it should also specify whether a party's obligation is limited to the funds available as a result of these savings. *Bender v. Bender*[44] illustrates the importance of specifying the relationship between a contractual college obligation and a contractual obligation to set aside money for a child. There, the parties' agreement required the father to pay for college, and in a separate provision required him to establish trusts. He considered the trust obligation to be the vehicle by which he would meet his college obligation, but the court disagreed and ordered him to pay for college out of his personal funds notwithstanding the availability of trust monies.[45]

When parties are already married and have a child, they may want a postmarital agreement to elaborate in more detail about the obligation to pay college expenses. For example, they may want to address: How will funds from other sources be applied, such as savings, trust funds, gifts from family members, custodial accounts, tuition discounts available to faculty members, scholarships, loans and other financial aid, Section 529 accounts, and state tuition contracts?[46] Will student loans and scholarships be applied first to meet expenses for which parties are not contractually obligated so that a child who obtains financial aid can attend a more expensive school than parents are obligated to pay for? Will gifts from one parent's family members be credited to that parent's obligation only or will they be credited *pro rata*? How will custodial funds be treated? In the absence of a contract specifying how such funds will be credited, some authorities indicate a parent may not discharge a contractual obligation to pay college expenses by using a child's funds from a custodial account even when the parent funded the account for that very purpose.[47] However, the obligation to apply funds from other sources may be made a condition precedent to a parent's obligation to pay the remaining expenses.[48] The contract should make it clear if this is the parties' intent.

(g) Estate Planning Obligations or Other Provisions for a Child After Parent's Death

Absent a contract, a parent's obligation to support a minor child terminates on the death of the parent.[49] An agreement can provide for a continuation of child support payments from the

44. *See Bender v. Bender*, 715 A.2d 1199 (Pa. Super. Ct. 1998).

45. *See also Reynolds v. Diamond*, 605 So. 2d 525 (Fla. Dist. Ct. App. 1992) (father's obligation for college not limited to VA benefits where agreement did not so provide).

46. *See Bender*, 715 A.2d at 1199.

47. *See Brodsky v. Brodsky*, 319 Md. 92, 570 A.2d 1235 (1990); *but see Turecki v. Turecki*, 211 A.D.2d 450, 621 N.Y.S.2d 53 (1995) (father did not violate separation agreement requiring him to pay children's college expenses when he directed children to use custodial accounts he funded).

48. *See Troha v. Troha*, 105 Ohio App. 3d 327, 663 N.E.2d 1319 (1995) (contract can be interpreted to require use of custodial funds and savings as condition precedent to father's obligation).

49. *Reinhardt v. Reinhardt*, 131 So. 2d 509 (Fla. Dist. Ct. App. 1961); *Miller v. Miller*, 154 Ohio St. 530, 97 N.E.2d 213 (1951).

decedent's estate,[50] or for life insurance.[51] Similarly, parties may contract to obligate one or both to fund a trust for a child.[52] Life insurance can be a viable option for parties who wish to make provisions for a child by providing for the surviving parent.[53]

Information the Lawyer Will Need to Get From the Client and the Other Party

- Does the party already have life insurance?
  - If so, an individual policy or an employer-sponsored benefit?
  - If the former, who owns the policy? the insured? an irrevocable trust?
  - What type of insurance? whole life, term?
  - What is the amount of the death benefit?
  - If term, when does the term expire?
  - What is the premium amount?
  - If whole life, what is the cash value?
  - Is the insured obligated (by contract or court order) to maintain the policy for a prior spouse or an existing child?
- If the agreement will require an individual policy of life insurance, can he or she acquire it at an acceptable cost?
- If an employer-sponsored policy:
  - Identity of the employer;
  - Amount of the death benefit;
  - Can the employee elect additional coverage?
  - Can the employee convert to an individual policy upon leaving the employer; at an acceptable cost?
  - Does the death benefit reduce at retirement?
  - The lawyer should get the summary plan description.

Provisions for Individual Life Insurance

When a premarital or postmarital agreement provides for a surviving spouse to have a right to death benefits under an individual life insurance policy, there are several possible approaches:

- The spouse will be named beneficiary of an existing individual policy;
- Ownership of an existing individual policy will be transferred to the spouse;
- Each party will acquire a policy of life insurance during the marriage with a specified death benefit and will pay the premiums as a marital obligation.
- The wealthy spouse will acquire a new policy with a specified death benefit and name the other spouse as beneficiary or transfer ownership to the spouse;
- The wealthy spouse will create an irrevocable life insurance trust for the benefit of the spouse to hold an existing policy or a policy to be acquired thereafter.

---

50. *Reinhardt*, 131 So. 2d 509.
51. *Miller*, 154 Ohio St. 530.
52. *See Bender v. Bender*, 715 A.2d 1199 (Pa. Super. Ct. 1998).
53. See Appendix E, Additional and Optional Terms, for one example of such a provision.

The agreement should specifically identify the policy. An agreement that says an insured will maintain his or her "current life insurance policy" is inadequate. Counsel for the beneficiary-spouse should verify that the policy is in force and that the insured can keep it in force solely by payment of premiums for the duration of the obligation. If the death benefit will reduce at some point, the agreement should be clear whether the recipient is entitled to cash to make up the difference.[54] If the agreement will provide for acquisition of a new policy, the parties should first determine that a policy is available at an acceptable cost and whether the prospective insured is insurable.[55] Parties must consider whether to require term insurance or a form of insurance that builds cash value. The agreement should specify whether the insured, the beneficiary, or a trust will pay the premiums. For prospective spouses and spouses in an intact marriage, the agreement should specify whether premiums will be paid from a shared pool of money or from one party's separate property.

The agreement should address whether the beneficiary will retain the right to life insurance after a divorce and whether the right is tied to spousal support or a minor child. The agreement should also say when the obligation of the insured to pay premiums will end—only at death or upon dissolution? When the agreement provides for a term policy, will the obligation end at the end of the term, or will the insured be obligated to provide a replacement policy?

Private Sector Employer-Sponsored Life Insurance

The Employee Retirement Income Security Act (ERISA) governs employee welfare plans, including life insurance.[56] ERISA is implicated when an agreement creates a right to death benefits under an employer-provided life insurance policy. Two key features of ERISA:

- Every employee welfare plan must be administered in accordance with the instruments governing the plan. These include the plan itself and the beneficiary designation.[57]
- ERISA preempts all state law claims or rights regarding welfare plan benefits held in the plan.[58]

A spouse's contractual right to employer-sponsored life insurance will be ineffective against the plan administrator unless the participant files a beneficiary designation with the plan. It is appropriate for the agreement to give the spouse-beneficiary the right to verify compliance. The client should be advised that he or she will need a new beneficiary designation if the participant changes jobs and that the insurance may cease or be reduced upon retirement.

54. *See Estate of Blumenthal*, 812 A.2d 1279 (Pa. Super. 2002) (extrinsic evidence where premarital agreement ambiguous whether wife to receive amount of death benefit in effect at marriage or only the reduced amount payable at husband's death).

55. *See Weber v. Brinaks (In re Estate of Weber)*, 2015 Iowa App. LEXIS 750 (unpub.) (wife not entitled to damages for husband's failure to get life insurance where he was uninsurable).

56. 29 U.S.C. § 1002(1).

57. 29 U.S.C. § 1104(a)(1)(D); *Egelhoff v. Egelhoff*, 532 U.S. 141 (2001).

58. 29 U.S.C. § 1144(a); *Egelhoff*, 532 U.S. at 141.

The use of employer-sponsored insurance to protect a surviving spouse is fraught with risk. The insured spouse may change jobs, perhaps several times, and each time will need to opt into the new employer's life insurance plan, if there is one, and file a new beneficiary designation. Parties who can afford it, and are willing to do so, should consider an individual policy instead. When a premarital or postmarital agreement creates a right for a spouse to be the beneficiary of employer-sponsored life insurance, he or she will need to take steps during the marriage to secure these rights. The agreement, standing alone, is insufficient;[59] rather, the plan administrator must pay benefits in accordance with the plan documents even when the insured breached a contract to make a spouse beneficiary.[60]

ERISA preemption precludes a state law remedy for breach, such as injunction or constructive trust, so long as the benefits are held by the plan.[61] That leaves open the question of enforcement once the benefits are paid to the named beneficiary. Some courts have ruled that ERISA preemption precludes a state law contract or quasi-contract remedy against the named beneficiary.[62] Other courts hold that ERISA preemption ends once the life insurance is paid out, after which a court may utilize a state law remedy to enforce the contract.[63] The Supreme Court to date has left this question unresolved.[64]

A Qualified Domestic Relations Order (QDRO) can be used to enforce a contractual obligation to maintain a spouse as beneficiary by requiring the plan administrator to pay benefits to the spouse-beneficiary; but a QDRO is only available when parties divorce.[65]

Enforcement Issues

Whether the agreement provides for individual life insurance or life insurance under an employer plan, counsel for the beneficiary-spouse should consider terms to secure his or her rights, such as:

- The spouse has the right to require periodic verification that the policy remains in force.
- The waiver of the spousal elective share or other spousal rights is conditional on receipt of the life insurance.
- The spouse has a right to cash as a creditor of the estate in the contractual amount.
- The beneficiary designation is irrevocable except with consent of the beneficiary, if permitted under the plan.
- Ownership of an individual policy is to be transferred to the beneficiary.

---

59. 29 U.S.C. § 1104(a)(1)(D); *Kennedy v. Plan Adm'r for DuPont Sav. & Inv. Plan,* 555 U.S. 285, 299–300 (2009).

60. 29 U.S.C. § 1104(a)(1)(D).

61. *Cent. States v. Howell,* 227 F.3d 672 (6th Cir. 2000).

62. *See Barnett v. Barnett,* 67 S.W.3d 107 (Tex. 2001).

63. *Andochick v. Byrd,* 709 F.3d 296 (4th Cir. 2013); *Cent. States,* 227 F.3d at 672; *Est. of Kensinger v. URL Pharma, Inc.,* 674 F.3d 131 (3d Cir. 2012); *Sweebe v. Sweebe,* 712 N.W.2d 708 (Mich. 2006).

64. *Kennedy,* 555 U.S. 285.

65. *Metropolitan Life Ins. Co. v. Pettit,* 164 F.3d 857 (4th Cir. 1998).

(h) Modification of Contractual Obligations

Before a child reaches the age of majority, courts generally have authority to modify contractual child support if necessary to make adequate support available to the child or in the event changed circumstances affect the ability of the payor to pay.[66] Once the child has reached the applicable age of majority, the court loses whatever statutory authority it had to modify support in either direction.[67] Thus, a change for the better in the ability of the payor to pay will not provide the basis for a court to increase the amount payable after the child reaches majority.[68]

A party who will agree to a contractual obligation for a child that exceeds the statutory duty may place reasonable limits on that obligation, including the right to seek modification if circumstances warrant.[69] A provision for modification may simply take the form of determining a process, such as a motion for modification to the court that has child support jurisdiction,[70] or binding arbitration.[71] The agreement could also provide a formula for modification of support, such as a periodic exchange of income tax returns with a reallocation of financial responsibility *pro rata* as incomes change relative to each other.

(i) Enforcement Issues

Unless and until a contract for financial provisions for a child is incorporated or otherwise made a part of a court order, the obligation is enforceable only as a contract. Thus, the parent who is entitled to payments, or the child, may obtain a money judgment for breach of contract, specific performance, or other contract remedies. However, once such a contract is incorporated in a court order, some states will enforce it as a court order for child support, meaning that the obligor may be held in contempt for a violation of the terms of the contract. Other states will enforce such an obligation only as a contract; contempt will not be an available remedy.[72]

---

66. *Goldin v. Goldin*, 34 Va. App. 95, 538 S.E.2d 326 (2000); *Hirtle v. Hirtle*, 217 Conn. 394, 586 A.2d 578 (1991); *Penland v. Penland*, 521 S.W.2d 222 (Tenn. 1975).

67. *Hirtle*, 217 Conn. at 397, 586 A.2d at 579; *Jones v. Jones*, 244 Ga. 32, 257 S.E.2d 537 (1979); *Penland*, 521 S.W.2d at 224.

68. *Richter v. Richter*, 666 So. 2d 559 (Fla. Dist. Ct. App. 1992); *Tiffany v. Tiffany*, 1 Va. App. 11, 332 S.E.2d 796 (1985). In states where the age of majority for child support purposes is 21 or older, a court may have some authority to modify a college obligation in the event of changed circumstances, just as it would any other child support obligation, until the child reaches majority. However, the safest course for the drafting attorney is to assume the contract will be enforced as written and that neither party will be successful in getting it modified later.

69. *Hirtle*, 217 Conn. at 394, 586 A.2d at 578.

70. *Katz v. Katz*, 258 Ga. 184, 366 S.E.2d 766 (1988) (decree-incorporated agreement for post-majority support provided obligation was modifiable based on changed circumstances, court had jurisdiction to modify); *Dewey v. Dewey*, 886 P.2d 623 (Alaska 1994) (decree-incorporated agreement for basic minority support of stepchild modifiable on showing of changed circumstances).

71. *See Kelm v. Kelm*, 68 Ohio St. 3d 26, 623 N.E.2d 39 (1993).

72. *See Penland v. Penland*, 521 S.W.2d 222 (Tenn. 1975) (obligation to pay college expenses is purely contractual and is therefore not enforceable by contempt); *Brown v. Brown*, 287 Md. 273, 412 A.2d 396 (1980) (same); *McClain v. McClain*, 235 Ga. 659, 221 S.E.2d 561 (1975) (agreement for post-majority support that was incorporated in divorce decree is enforceable by contempt); *Hirtle v. Hirtle*, 217 Conn. 394, 586 A.2d 578 (1991) (same).

§7.04 PROVISIONS REGARDING RELIGIOUS DIVORCE

Parties who for religious reasons may need to obtain an ecclesiastical divorce or annulment in the event the marriage ends in a civil divorce, may wish to include a provision obligating the other party either to provide a religious divorce or to appear before a religious tribunal. Courts have generally held that secular provisions of a religious marriage agreement may be enforced.[73] In *Avitzur v. Avitzur,*[74] the court reasoned that a provision in a Jewish marriage contract, a Ketubah, that required the parties to submit to a rabbinic tribunal on matters relating to the marriage was analogous to an agreement for alternative dispute resolution, such as arbitration.[75] Accordingly, the court granted specific performance. That agreement, however, did not require the husband to grant the wife a Jewish divorce, something only he could do, only that he appear before the tribunal. Other cases have gone a step further and ordered a husband to comply with an agreement to grant the wife a religious divorce.[76]

§7.05 GROUNDS OF DIVORCE

(a) Penalty for Marital Misconduct

Courts in some states have upheld agreements that made more favorable provisions for one spouse if the other spouse initiates the separation, commits marital misconduct, or files for divorce first.[77] For example, in *Sanders v. Sanders,*[78] a premarital agreement under which a spouse who filed for divorce forfeited all marital property was upheld, albeit under rather unusual circumstances; the husband agreed to generous terms and to the forfeiture provision to induce the wife to marry him for the third time. In *Laudig v. Laudig,*[79] the court upheld a postmarital agreement in which the wife would receive only a small part of the marital property if she was again unfaithful.

By contrast, California courts seem to have elevated no-fault divorce to such public policy importance that a contractual penalty for misconduct may be unenforceable. In *In re Marriage of Mehren and Dargan,*[80] the parties had separated because of the husband's cocaine

73. *Akileh v. Elchahal,* 666 So. 2d 246 (Fla. Dist. Ct. App. 1996); *Aziz v. Aziz,* 127 Misc. 2d 1013, 488 N.Y.S.2d 123 (Sup. Ct. 1985).

74. 58 N.Y.2d 108, 446 N.E.2d 136, 459 N.Y.S.2d 572 (1983).

75. *See also Meshel v. Ohev Sholom Talmud Torah,* 869 A.2d 343 (D.C. 2005) (agreement to submit dispute to religious tribunal honored as agreement to arbitrate).

76. *Scholl v. Scholl,* 621 A.2d 808 (Del. Fam. Ct. 1992); *Minkin v. Minkin,* 180 N.J. Super. 260, 434 A.2d 665 (1981).

77. *See Ford v. Blue,* 106 S.W.3d 470 (Ky. App. 2003) (agreement giving wife 50 percent more cash if husband filed first would have been enforceable had wife not filed first).

78. 288 S.W.2d 473 (Tenn. Ct. App. 1955).

79. 425 Pa. Super. 228, 624 A.2d 651 (1993); *see also Lloyd v. Niceta,* 482 Md. 733, 290 A.3d 602, *cert. granted* 482 Md. 473, 290 A.3d. 602 (2023) (postmarital agreement that imposed $7 million penalty on husband for future adultery or other sexual misconduct was enforceable); *Belke v. Belke,* 2022 Pa. Super. LEXIS 2088 (unpub.) (postmarital agreement was enforceable that gave wife 100 percent of assets and 60 percent of husband's income if husband committed illicit acts or sought divorce).

80. 118 Cal. App. 4th 1167, 13 Cal. Rptr. 3d 522 (Ct. App. 2004).

addiction. They attempted a reconciliation accompanied by an agreement that provided the husband would forfeit his interest in certain community property if he resumed using drugs. The court refused to enforce the forfeiture. It reasoned that the legislative decision to eliminate fault made an agreement that seeks to punish spousal misconduct one that has an illegal objective.[81] Similarly, Iowa and Hawaii courts will not enforce an agreement that injects marital fault into the disposition of property.[82]

In states where parties may contract about marital misconduct, such misconduct alone does not vitiate an agreement; rather, if parties intend not to be bound by the agreement if one party commits marital fault, the agreement must say so expressly. An agreement could provide that marital misconduct vitiates the agreement, thus reinstating parties to the marital rights they would have had without an agreement.[83] A vague provision that an agreement will be voided if a party violates the marriage vows will not be sufficient. Something more specific is required.[84] Such a provision, under which the premarital agreement would be void if the husband left the wife for another woman, was upheld in *MacFarlane v. Rich*,[85] against a public policy argument.

The Uniform Premarital and Marital Agreements Act (UPMAA) provides that a term is unenforceable that limits the grounds of divorce, or penalizes a spouse for initiating a divorce.[86] However, that provision does not appear to preclude a penalty clause for misconduct, which is a separate question from whether grounds may be limited. As there are so few reported cases enforcing or rejecting such a provision, parties who elect to include a penalty clause face some uncertainly about whether it will be enforceable.

(b) Terms Limiting Grounds of Divorce

Some parties may wish to include a provision that any separation of the parties will be deemed voluntary for purposes of grounds of divorce, thus waiving in advance any fault ground that a party may have in states that still have fault grounds. In states that have eliminated fault divorce entirely, there should be no problem with such a provision. In some fault states, courts may enforce a provision that waives fault or, as in *Vakil v. Vakil*,[87] that imposes a penalty for contesting the divorce. At least one fault state, Louisiana, treats marital misconduct as a matter of public policy and therefore appears not to enforce such a waiver

81. *See also Diosdado v. Diosdado*, 97 Cal. App. 4th 470, 118 Cal. Rptr. 2d 494 (2002) (postmarital agreement providing financial penalty for infidelity invalid as violation of public policy underlying no-fault divorce law).

82. *Crofford v. Adachi*, 150 Haw. 518, 506 P.3d 182 (2022) (postmarital agreement unenforceable where property disposition favorable to wife triggered by husband's infidelity as violation of public policy favoring no-fault divorce); *In re Marriage of Cooper*, 769 N.W.2d 582 (Iowa 2009) (same), *citing Diosdado*, 97 Cal. App. 4th 470.

83. *Gross v. Gross*, 11 Ohio St. 3d 99, 464 N.E.2d 500 (1984); *Maloy v. Maloy*, 362 So. 2d 484 (Fla. Dist. Ct. App. 1978); *Sims v. Sims*, 186 N.W.2d 491 (Neb. 1971).

84. *Moss v. Moss*, 187 A.D.2d 775, 589 N.Y.S.2d 683 (1992).

85. 132 N.H. 608, 567 A.2d 585 (1989).

86. UPMAA § 10(b)(3), (4).

87. 66 Mass. App. Ct. 526, 849 N.E.2d 233 (2006).

provision.[88] By contrast, courts is Idaho will enforce a term of a premarital agreement that limits the fault grounds on which a party may file for divorce.[89]

Under the UPMAA, a term that purports to modify the grounds for dissolution or penalizes a party for initiating a legal proceeding is unenforceable.[90] A provision that penalizes a party too harshly for seeking a divorce may not be enforceable on public policy grounds.[91]

A fault waiver should be deemed severable from the rest of the agreement. Therefore, its unenforceability will have no effect on the parties' property and support rights under the contract.

---

88. *See Boudreaux v. Boudreaux*, 745 So. 2d 61 (La. Ct. App. 1999) (premarital agreement may not alter marital obligations; therefore, parties may not waive fault). It appears that in Louisiana, parties are also precluded from enforcing a provision fixing spousal support without regard to fault of the payee. Thus, an agreement provision that would require payment of alimony to an adulterous spouse would appear to be unenforceable. *Vogt v. Vogt*, 831 So. 2d 428 (La. App. 2000).

89. *Bettwieser v. Bettwieser*, 2022 Idaho App. LEXIS 342 (unpub).

90. UPMAA § 10(b)(3), (4).

91. *See In re Marriage of Iqbal and Khan*, 11 N.E.3d 1 (Ill. Ct. App., 2d Dist. 2014); *but see Lloyd v. Niceta*, 2022 Md. App. LEXIS 762.

Postmarriage Issues 8

§8.01 Overview

This chapter addresses a number of issues that may arise after a marriage or after execution of a postmarital agreement. The parties may want to amend or revoke their agreement. Parties without a premarital agreement may wish to enter into a postmarital agreement. Conduct of the parties after execution of the agreement may give rise to a claim that the contract has been amended, abandoned, or modified.[1] Common circumstances that may give rise to a claim of abandonment or rescission are discussed in this chapter. Most claims of abandonment or rescission fail.

Parties to a premarital or postmarital agreement may effectively modify or vitiate its terms, without formally amending it or abrogating the agreement as a whole, by commingling, retitling, or gifting property during the marriage that the agreement otherwise permits them to keep separate. This may occur as a natural evolution during the marriage. An agreement does not preclude a party from being more generous than required.[2] Indeed, a standard provision of such agreements acknowledges the parties' rights to make and receive gifts from each other. It is important for parties to understand that such transfers may not constitute fulfillment of a contractual obligation to make transfers upon death or dissolution unless the agreement specifically so provides.[3] Parties must also understand that they will have no right to recoup gifts or voluntary payments if the marriage fails, unless the agreement creates such a right. For example, a party may elect to pay nonmarital debt of the other spouse. Unless the agreement expressly provides for reimbursement, the payor will have no right to recoup.[4]

1. *In re Marriage of Crawford*, 2004 Iowa. App. LEXIS 1306 (unpub.); *In re Estate of Catto*, 88 Wash. App. 522, 944 P.2d 1052 (1997); *In re Marriage of Christensen*, 543 N.W.2d 915, 918 (Iowa Ct. App. 1995); *Rogers v. Yourshaw*, 18 Va. App. 816, 448 S.E.2d 884 (1994); *Gustafson v. Jensen*, 515 So. 2d 1298 (Fla. Dist. Ct. App. 1987).
2. *Spencer v. Estate of Spencer*, 313 S.W.3d 534 (Ky. 2010).
3. *See Skeynkman v. Skeynkman*, 2005 Wash. App. LEXIS 2428 (unpub.).
4. *Rhodes v. Rhodes*, 692 N.W.2d 157 (N.D. 2005).

In a variety of ways, a party's contractual property rights at death or divorce may be adversely affected by unilateral actions of the other spouse. Whether disposition of funds or assets is for a proper purpose, such as to pay debt, or for an improper purpose, such as to support a paramour, the result for the other spouse is the same. Parties may wish to preserve their rights to make gifts to children and other third parties, to spend their own money as they please, including on luxury items, and to otherwise deal freely with their property. Indeed, premarital and postmarital agreements commonly provide that parties are free to dispose of their separate property during marriage as they wish.

When the agreement provides for the less wealthy spouse to receive a percentage share of property at divorce or death, counsel for that party should consider the effect of post-execution activities on the pool of assets from which that spouse's share will be determined. Similarly, when the agreement will provide that the less wealthy spouse will receive a share of a specified asset, such as an interest in real estate titled solely in the name of the other spouse, counsel will need to consider including in the agreement limitations on the other spouse's ability to reduce the value of that asset so as to defeat the rights of the disadvantaged party. "The duty of good faith is an implied condition in every contract. . . ."[5] However, reliance on implied obligations will generally offer less protection to the disadvantaged party than will an express provision designed to limit the other spouse's opportunity to defeat the parties' intent.

The issues in this chapter are of particular concern when the parties opt for an agreement that provides for sharing the fruits of their labor and for each to have exclusive rights to premarital, inherited, and gifted assets. If the agreement predetermines disposition of marital property, there will be little or no opportunity for a court to adjust the division to take account of post-marriage conduct.

§8.02 Formal Amendments, Postmarital Agreements, and Other Formal Acts

(a) Formal Amendment to Premarital Agreement

Every premarital agreement should include a provision requiring any amendment to be in writing and signed by the parties. Counsel for the weaker party should give some thought to the subject of future amendments, especially when there is a large wealth disparity and the terms are inadequate to provide him or her with future financial security. It will usually be better for the weaker party if the agreement does not create an obstacle to amendments that improve his or her position. Even a requirement that an amendment be notarized can be disadvantageous as it can leave that spouse vulnerable to a claim of other family members seeking to undo an unnotarized amendment making more generous provisions for a widow or widower.

---

5. *In re Chayka's Estate*, 47 Wis. 2d 102, 107, 176 N.W.2d 561, 564 (1970) (wife's transfer of substantial assets to new husband violated contract for joint wills by defeating intent of parties that all property was to go to designated person upon death of surviving spouse).

An amendment can also be useful for the economically stronger party. He or she may feel the need to insist on a premarital agreement that provides little or nothing for the other party with a view to renegotiating after several years, or may need to renegotiate to maintain domestic harmony. An amendment that favors the weaker party should be coupled with ratification of the original agreement. A postmarital ratification strengthens validity.[6]

Amendment Under the UPAA

The Uniform Premarital Agreement Act (UPAA) provides that a premarital agreement may be amended or revoked after marriage. The amendment or revocation is effective only if it is in writing and signed by both parties. The amendment or revocation is enforceable without new consideration.[7] The UPAA is consistent with preexisting case law permitting parties to freely amend their premarital agreement.[8]

Amendment Under the UPMAA

The Uniform Premarital and Marital Agreements Act (UPMAA)[9] creates proposed uniform standards for recognition and validity of marital agreements.[10] The UPMAA defines a marital agreement as an agreement executed by spouses who intend to stay married and that "affirms, modifies, or waives a marital right or obligation during the marriage or at separation, marital dissolution, [or] death of one of the spouses. . . ."[11] A marital agreement includes an amendment to a premarital agreement as well as an agreement revoking a premarital agreement or a marital agreement;[12] thus, parties to such must comply with the heightened process requirements of UPMAA § 9, including financial disclosure and access to counsel. Such an agreement is enforceable without consideration.[13]

Other States

Parties should be able to amend or modify a premarital agreement in those states that have not adopted the UPAA, the UPMAA, or another specific statute governing amendments. General principles of contract law, which permit parties to freely amend their own contracts, are applicable to a postmarital amendment to a premarital contract, except as a statute or case expressly limits amendments.[14] Some authority suggests that because a postmarital

---

6. See Section 8.04.

7. UPAA §§ 2, 5 (1983).

8. *Turner v. Black*, 19 Ill. 2d 269, 166 N.E.2d 588 (1960); *see also Turner v. Turner*, 89 S.E.2d 245 (N.C. 1955) (parties to premarital agreement providing for property rights at death or divorce may alter, amend or revoke agreement by mutual consent); *O'Dell v. O'Dell*, 26 N.W.2d 401 (Iowa 1947) (same).

9. The Uniform Law Commission adopted the UPMAA in 2012. To date, only two states have enacted it, North Dakota and Colorado.

10. The Drafting Committee chose to call this type of agreement a marital agreement. However, in the case law they are most frequently referred to as a postmarital agreement or a postnuptial agreement or, in some cases, a reconciliation agreement.

11. UPMAA § 2(2).

12. UPMAA § 2(2); cmt.

13. UPMAA § 6.

14. *Rupert v. Rupert*, 245 A.D.2d 1139, 667 N.Y.S.2d 537 (1997) (premarital agreement prohibiting amendments unless in writing and duly executed was amended by letter signed by party against whom enforcement sought); *Bradley v. Bradley*, 164 P.3d 537 (Wyo. 2007) (Minnesota law governed amendment to premarital agreement with Minnesota choice-of-law provision). It appears that in Iowa parties may not amend their premarital agreement, although they may revoke it in its entirety. *Hansen v. Hansen*, 924 N.W.2d 873 (Iowa Ct. App. 2018).

amendment is a new contract,[15] its validity is governed by the same criteria as a postmarital agreement.[16] In those states that impose heightened scrutiny to the determination of the validity of postmarital agreements, an amendment may therefore receive the same treatment.

(b) Revocation of Premarital or Postmarital Agreement

Parties to a premarital or postmarital agreement may revoke the agreement by an express superseding agreement, thus restoring each to the spousal rights they would have accrued but for the existence of the agreement. The UPAA and UPMAA provide that parties may revoke a premarital agreement without consideration.[17] Courts in nonuniform act states have come to the same conclusion.[18]

(c) Postmarital Agreements

A postmarital agreement "is an agreement entered into during marriage to define each spouse's property rights in the event of death or divorce."[19] Many states' laws also permit parties to fix or waive spousal support in such an agreement. As used herein, the term refers to an agreement made at a time when parties do not intend to separate or divorce, including such an agreement made by parties who are estranged but who intend to reconcile. Parties who married without a premarital agreement, or who encounter circumstances after marrying that warrant a spousal contract, but who have no immediate plan to separate or divorce, may enter into a postmarital agreement.[20]

§8.03 CONDUCT GIVING RISE TO CLAIM AGREEMENT HAS BECOME UNENFORCEABLE

Parties not happy with the terms of a premarital or postmarital agreement face the reality that it is extraordinarily difficult to succeed in a challenge to validity; the standards for a valid premarital or postmarital agreement create a low bar, as discussed at length elsewhere in this book.[21] Nevertheless, parties have attempted a variety of legal theories and factual claims to attack enforceability. The discussion that follows points up opportunities for terms that can be included in an agreement and for legal advice to better protect the client.

---

15. *Hendrick v. Hendrick*, 976 P.2d 1071, 1073 (Okla. Ct. App. 1998). *See also Bradley*, 164 P.3d 537 (amendment to premarital agreement governed by same statutory criteria for validity as postmarital agreement; interpreting Minnesota law).

16. See Chapter 3 and Appendix B(2), State Law Summary: Postmarital Agreements.

17. UPAA § 5; UPMAA § 6; *Scott v. Scott*, 19 A.3d 302 (De. 2011).

18. *Martello v. Martello*, 960 So. 2d 186 (La. App. 2007); *In re Estate of Goldberg*, 153 Misc. 2d 560, 582 N.Y.S.2d 617 (S. Ct. 1992); *Turner v. Turner*, 89 S.E.2d 245 (N.C. Ct. App. 1955); *Turner*, 19 Ill. 2d 269; *O'Dell*, 26 N.W.2d 401 (Iowa 1947) (same).

19. *Simmons v. Simmons*, 98 Ark. App. 12, 15, 249 S.W.3d 843, 846 (2009).

20. See Chapter 3 for extended treatment of this subject and Appendix B(2), State Law Summary: Postmarital Agreements.

21. See Chapter 4.

(a) Termination of Engagement Followed by Reconciliation

A standard provision in premarital agreements says the agreement will take effect upon marriage and will be void if the parties do not marry.[22] When the marriage is called off after execution of a premarital agreement, but the parties later reconcile and marry on another date, the initial calling off of the wedding may give rise to a claim that the parties repudiated the agreement. Some courts have treated the question whether the parties intended to repudiate the agreement, so that it was not revived when the marriage plans were revived, as a question of fact to be determined from all the surrounding circumstances.[23] The UPAA is silent about revocation before marriage. A North Carolina case posits that general contract law principles therefore apply, leaving room for a case-by-case evaluation of the parties' intent.[24] By contrast, Virginia courts treat the question as a matter of law under the UPAA, holding that only a signed writing will revoke the premarital agreement.[25] In non-UPAA states, courts may interpret a local Statute of Frauds to preclude any but a signed writing to effect a revocation.[26]

A premarital agreement need not cite a specific date of the planned marriage; it could merely say that the parties intend to marry after executing the agreement.[27] Citing a specific date, if followed by a temporary termination of the engagement followed by rescheduling, may make a factual dispute about whether parties revoked the agreement more likely. In any event, when the particular circumstances call for it—especially, for example, when parties terminate an engagement and then reschedule the wedding after an extended hiatus—they should execute a new agreement, a ratification of the previous agreement, or a document stating expressly that they revoke the previously executed agreement.

(b) Purported Oral Amendment to Premarital Agreement

Every premarital and postmarital agreement should provide that it may only be amended in a writing that is signed by the parties. The UPAA precludes enforcement of a purported oral amendment,[28] as does the UPMAA.[29] Although general contract law principles permit parties to orally modify or rescind a contract, including that provision of the contract that precludes oral modification,[30] courts have generally rejected claims of oral amendment of a premarital agreement. Many states retain a Statute of Frauds that can serve as the basis to reject such a claim. Statutes of Frauds typically require a contract made on consideration of marriage to be in writing.[31] Further, where a claimed oral modification purports to waive a substantive right,

---

22. See Appx. 17, Model Title-Controls Agreement, para. 40.

23. *Sykes v. Sykes*, 2006 Cal. App. Unpub. 766; *In re Estate of Pate*, 119 N.C. App. 400, 459 S.E.2d 1 (1995); *Schwartz v. Schwartz*, 112 A.D.2d 154, 490 N.Y.S.2d 841 (1985).

24. *Huntley v. Huntley*, 140 N.C. App. 749, 538 S.E.2d 239 (2000).

25. *Smith v. Smith*, 19 Va. App. 155, 449 S.E.2d 506, 507 n.1 (1994).

26. *See Lemaster v. Dutton*, 694 So. 2d 1360 (Ala. Civ. App. 1996) (purported oral modification has no effect on contract that falls within Statute of Frauds requirement for signed writing; premarital agreement is agreement on consideration of marriage and therefore modifiable only by signed writing).

27. See Appx. D, Model Title-Controls Agreement, recital 1.

28. UPAA § 5; *see also Drumheller v. Drumheller*, 2002 Va. App. LEXIS 584 (claimed oral amendment to premarital agreement is ineffective).

29. UPMAA §§ 2(2), 6 (2012).

30. LORD, WILLISTON ON CONTRACTS § 39:26 (4th ed. 1990); RESTATEMENT SECOND, CONTRACTS § 150 (1981).

31. *See Lemaster*, 694 So. 2d 1360 (premarital agreement, as contract made on consideration of marriage, could be modified only in writing).

such as the elective share rights of a surviving spouse, other applicable statutory provisions, such as a provision of a probate code, may mandate a writing.

(c) Purported Oral Revocation; Destruction or Loss of Original

Notwithstanding a provision in an agreement precluding an oral revocation, when a party states an intent that the agreement be rescinded and couples that statement with conduct consistent with that intent, some courts have held that the parties revoked the agreement.[32] The UPAA requires that a revocation be made in a signed writing.[33] Courts in North Carolina, Virginia, Iowa, and Arkansas have strictly construed the UPAA to require a signed writing to revoke a premarital agreement.[34] In these states, mere destruction of an agreement coupled with a stated intent to revoke is insufficient, as is an untrue statement that the agreement has been destroyed.[35] Other states retain common law principles under which destruction may constitute revocation or abandonment.[36] Even in states where case law may appear to leave some room for a claim of oral revocation, such a case will often be difficult to make.[37]

(d) Postmarital Conduct Arguably Inconsistent with Continued Viability of Agreement

A party's conduct after marriage, or after execution of a postmarital agreement, may be at odds with a stated objective for entering into an agreement of protecting his or her exclusive rights to nonmarital assets. Such conduct does not constitute an abandonment of the agreement as a matter of law. It can nevertheless give rise to a claim of abandonment of the agreement as a whole or may result in a party having abandoned some of his or her rights under the agreement. When parties to an agreement pool all their resources, commingle their bank accounts, and purchase assets from pooled accounts, they may effectively abandon the agreement by merging their separate estates.[38] Even when the parties do not completely merge all their property interests, commingling some assets may effectively abrogate the agreement as to those assets.[39] In *Simoni v. Simoni*,[40] the husband transferred assets into joint names during the marriage. He failed to disclose to his estate planning lawyer that he had a

---

32. *See Pitrolo v. Pitrolo*, 2014 W. Va. LEXIS 1092; *Jensen v. Jensen*, 753 P.2d 342 (Nev. 1988); *Gustafson v. Jensen*, 515 So. 2d 1298 (Fla. Dist. Ct. App. 1987); *In re Marriage of Young*, 682 P.2d 1233 (Colo. Ct. App. 1984).

33. UPAA § 5.

34. *In re Estate of Weber*, 871 N.W.2d 520 (Iowa Ct. App. 2015); *Muchmore v. Trask*, 666 S.E.2d 667 (N.C. Ct. App. 2008) (applying California's version of UPAA); *Miller*, 207 Va. App. LEXIS 340; *Banks*, 347 Ark. 383.

35. *Makoui v. Makoui*, 2011 Va. App. LEXIS 360 (unpub.).

36. *Carter v. Carter*, 656 S.W.2d 257 (Ky. Ct. App. 1983).

37. *See In re Marriage of Corwell*, 2013 Ill. App. LEXIS 1118 (unpub.) (evidence insufficient to prove loss of original rendered premarital agreement abandoned); *Elvidge v. Elvidge*, 2007 Wash. App. LEXIS 3205 (unpub.) (husband's unilateral statement of intent to revoke premarital agreement insufficient to revoke); *Felkner v. Felkner*, 652 S.W.2d 174 (Mo. Ct. App. 1983) (husband's destruction of premarital agreement in response to wife's complaints did not show mutual intent to rescind).

38. *See Tweeten v. Tweeten*, 772 N.W.2d 595 (N.D. 2009); *Fredericks v. Fredericks*, 2009 Ky. App. LEXIS 732 (unpub.); *In re Marriage of Fox*, 58 Wn. App. 935, 795 P.2d 1170 (1990); *In re Marriage of Pillard*, 448 N.W.2d 714 (Iowa Ct. App. 1989); *In re Marriage of Young*, 682 P.2d 1233 (Colo. Ct. App. 1984); *Mumm v. Mumm*, 63 Wn. 2d 349, 387 P.2d 547 (1963); *but see In re Estate of Brosseau*, 176 Ill. App. 3d 450, 531 N.E.2d 158 (1988).

39. *Roberts v. Roberts*, 173 N.C. App. 354, 618 S.E.2d 761 (2005); *Black v. Black*, 2005 Mich. App. LEXIS 3220 (unpub.); *In re Marriage of Fox*, 58 Wn. App. 935; *Brandt v. Brandt*, 145 Wis. 2d 394, 427 N.W.2d 126 (Ct. App. 1988).

40. 102 Ohio App. 3d 628, 657 N.E.2d 800 (1995).

premarital agreement, and it was not mentioned in his will or trust. He was unable to produce the document at trial. His conduct during the 18-year marriage caused the court to deem the agreement abandoned. Similarly, in *Gamache v. Smurro*,[41] the husband did not mention the parties' premarital agreement during the 20 years of marriage and offered it into evidence in the divorce only after the trial was underway. Moreover, he took joint title to disputed real estate with a deed reciting it was community property, contrary to his rights under the agreement. The husband's conduct, coupled with the deed language, superseded the agreement.[42]

The mere fact that parties choose to title some property interests jointly does not support a conclusion that they abandoned a premarital agreement.[43] The fact that parties present themselves to third parties as business partners, when one party is the owner, does not necessarily render the agreement abandoned.[44] Some courts strictly construe the UPAA to preclude application of an equitable remedy, such as estoppel, to preclude enforcement.[45] The mere fact that parties used one party's separate property, such as a home, does not support a claim the parties revoked an agreement.[46]

(e) Parties Become Business Partners

Some cases have addressed a claim that parties abandoned a premarital agreement by engaging in a joint business venture.[47] In *In re Marriage of Baxter*,[48] for example, the wife left her job to help the husband in his golf course development business, where she worked without pay. She also cosigned notes and cashed in some retirement benefits to pay debt owed by the husband's pro shop. The parties' combined efforts to preserve the golf course as a going concern effectively rescinded the otherwise valid premarital agreement even though the parties did not have an express oral or written agreement to rescind.[49] By contrast, in *In re Marriage of Bowers*,[50] the wife's work for the husband's corporation for no salary did not constitute modification or abandonment of the premarital agreement where the wife was compensated for her unpaid work through corporate earnings deposited into joint accounts.

These cases point up the importance of a business owner taking appropriate steps to protect his or her exclusive rights to a business the premarital agreement was designed to protect. A spouse who works in the business should receive a salary and the same benefits afforded other employees, or the spouse should be compensated indirectly, as illustrated by *Bowers*.

41. 904 A.2d 91 (Vt. 2006) (interpreting California law).

42. *See also K. v. B.*, 13 A.D.3d 12 (N.Y. App. Div. 2004) (premarital agreement did not determine property rights at divorce where husband did not produce it until his testimony at trial).

43. *Succession of Jenkins*, 87 So. 3d 230 (La. Ct. App. 2012).

44. *See In re Marriage of Corwell*, 2013 Ill. App. Unpub. LEXIS 1118.

45. *See Makoui v. Makoui*, 2011 Va. App. LEXIS 360.

46. *See In re Marriage of Loomis*, 247 Ore. App. 127, 268 P.3d 700 (2011).

47. This question is distinguished from claims that have arisen where the continued validity of the agreement is not in dispute, but the parties' rights are changed because of business activities they engaged in after execution. See discussion in Section 8.06.

48. 139 Or. App. 32, 911 P.2d 343 (1996).

49. *See also In re Marriage of Krejci*, 266 Wis. 2d 284, 667 N.W.2d 780 (Ct. App. 2003) (premarital agreement unfair at divorce, and, therefore, unenforceable, because wife worked in husband's resort business without pay for 18 years); *In re Marriage of Zimmerman*, 714 P.2d 927 (Colo. Ct. App. 1986) (parties abandoned premarital agreement insofar as they invested separate property in joint business).

50. 143 Or. App. 24, 922 P.2d 722 (1996).

Moreover, when the spouse contributes money to the business, the contributions should be documented, for example, by a promissory note.[51]

(f) Separation or Divorce Followed by Reconciliation

Parties to a premarital agreement who marry and separate, and then reconcile without expressly abrogating or affirming their prior agreement, may create uncertainty about the continuing viability of the agreement. The dispute will arise after a party's death or a subsequent separation when one party, or his or her heirs, will want the agreement to be viable and the other party will not. Under the UPAA, a reconciliation following a marital separation is insufficient, standing alone, to constitute revocation of a premarital agreement. The UPAA permits revocation only in a writing signed by both parties.[52] This provision has been strictly construed.[53] Nevertheless, the cautious approach, from the standpoint of the spouse who gains from the viability of the agreement, is for parties to sign a ratification after reconciliation.

When parties to a premarital agreement divorce and remarry, the agreement is not revived unless the parties expressly agree in writing to revive it.[54]

(g) Provision of More Generous Benefits under Will or *Inter Vivos* Transfer

A party's voluntary provision of more generous terms in a will or by *inter vivos* transfer than is required by a premarital or postmarital agreement is not evidence of an intent to abrogate the agreement as a whole. Such conduct is entirely consistent with the rights of the parties under the agreement.[55] In fact, standard provisions of such an agreement acknowledge the parties' rights to give and receive gifts. Similarly, when a wealthier party pays the other party's expenses, that does not waive the payor's contractual rights or render the agreement unenforceable as a whole. Moreover, in many states, spouses have a legal duty to support each other; compliance with that obligation cannot constitute an abandonment of the agreement.[56]

(h) Breach of Agreement

When one party so completely breaches a premarital agreement as to defeat the very purpose of the agreement, a court may deem the agreement abandoned, or, put another way, it may deem the other party's performance excused.[57] By contrast, a simple breach, for example, by a failure to make a new will required by the agreement, or by making a will that does

51. *In re Marriage of Weiss*, 357 Mont. 320, 239 P.3d 123 (2010) (husband entitled to sole interest in business acquired after marriage where premarital agreement so provided and wife's contribution of cash to enable husband to buy interest was documented as loan to husband, which husband repaid).

52. UPAA § 5; *Banks v. Evans*, 347 Ark. 383, 64 S.W.3d 746 (2002).

53. *See Miller v. Miller*, 2007 Va. App. LEXIS 340 (unpub.); *Brewster v. Ferrarese*, 2003 Cal. App. Unpub. LEXIS 6364.

54. *Herpich v. Estate of Herpich*, 994 So. 2d 1195 (Fla. Ct. App. 2008); *In re Estate of Broadhurst*, 737 S.W.2d 504 (Mo. Ct. App. 1987).

55. *Roberts v. Roberts*, 173 N.C. App. 354, 618 S.E.2d 761; *Vaccarello v. Vaccarello*, 757 A.2d 909, 911 (Pa. 2000); *In re Estate of Lutz*, 620 N.W.2d 589 (N.D. 2000); *Walsh v. Young*, 139 N.H. 693, 660 A.2d 1139 (1995); *In re Estate of Barnes*, 41 Colo. App. 246, 586 P.2d 238 (1978); *In re Strickland's Estate*, 181 Neb. 478, 149 N.W.2d 344 (1967); *Peet v. Monger*, 244 Iowa 247, 56 N.W.2d 589 (1953).

56. *Sailer v. Sailer*, 764 N.W.2d 445 (N.D. 2009).

57. *Doster v. Doster*, 853 So. 2d 147 (Miss. Ct. App. 2003); *Prather v. Cox*, 689 S.W.2d 623 (Ky. Ct. App. 1985); *Dutton v. Marshall*, 729 So. 2d 860 (Ala. Civ. App. 1998); *Estate of Lampert v. Estate of Lampert*, 896 P.2d 214 (Alaska 1995).

not conform completely to the testator's obligations under the agreement, does not warrant rescission if the agreement can be enforced through an ordinary contract remedy, such as specific performance.[58] Similarly, when a party agrees to make transfers during the marriage but fails to do so, and when the amount due the other party can be readily quantified, such a simple breach does not entitle the injured party to rescind.[59] Only when the failure to perform is complete and total is the breach a basis for rescission.[60] However, when a party refuses to comply with an agreement and the other party acquiesces, that may constitute a rescission.[61]

(i) Disadvantageous Change of Position

A party's post-marriage actions detrimental to his or her own financial interests is not a sufficient basis for a court to void an otherwise valid agreement,[62] or, in a second-look state, to conclude it is unfair at enforcement. Thus, in *In re Marriage of Stout*,[63] the wife gave up a favorable grazing lease after the marriage. When the marriage failed less than 18 months later, the court rejected her argument that the agreement was unenforceable because the husband failed to disclose his intent to insist that she give up the lease as a condition of staying married. Problems such as this may be avoidable. The husband claimed the wife agreed before marriage to give up the lease. Had this been the case, it would have been appropriate for the wife to insist that the agreement make some financial provisions for her in consideration for the financial security she would be giving up by marrying. The wife claimed it was not until after the marriage that the husband insisted that she give up the lease. In such an event, it would have been appropriate for the wife to insist on an amendment to the premarital agreement to protect her from the loss of her livelihood.

In *Crews v. Crews*,[64] the parties lived in the husband's home, which the agreement defined as his separate property. During the marriage, the husband paid the mortgage and the wife paid day-to-day common living expenses. As a result, his income enhanced his separate asset and the wife's income was consumed. The court observed that the wife knew when she agreed to these arrangements that she had no right to any equity in the home. Her decision to go along with the arrangement was disadvantageous to her; but, as a matter of contract law, she was entitled to no relief. Knowing that paying day-to-day expenses would not create an asset for her, the wife could have insisted on a different arrangement. A spouse who agrees to

58. *Skaates v. Kayser*, 333 Mich. App. 61, 959 N.W.2d 33 (2020); *Teed v. Teed*, 2013 W. Va. LEXIS 491 (unpub.); *In re Estate of Martin*, 938 A.2d 812 (Me. 2008); *Chipman v. Chipman*, 975 So. 2d 603 (Fla. Ct. App. 2008); *Seherr-Thoss v. Seherr-Thoss*, 141 P.3d 705 (Wyo. 2006); *Colello v. Colello*, 9 A.D.3d 855, 780 N.Y.S.2d 450 (2004); *In re Marriage of Smith*, 115 S.W.3d 126 (Tx. Ct. App. 2003); *Sheperd v. Sheperd*, 876 P.2d 429 (Utah Ct. App. 1994); *Brees v. Cramer*, 322 Md. 214, 586 A.2d 1284 (1991); *In re Estate of Parker*, 171 Ill. App. 3d 538, 525 N.E.2d 1149 (1988); *Gillilan's Estate v. Gillilan's Estate*, 406 N.E.2d 981 (Ind. Ct. App. 1980); *In re Johnson's Estate*, 202 Kan. 684, 452 P.2d 286 (1969); *Dehart v. Dehart*, 109 W. Va. 370, 154 S.E. 870 (1930); *see also Laube v. Reints (In re Est. of Laube)*, 974 N.W.3d 538 (Iowa Ct. App. 2022) (husband's or his estate's failure to provide long-term care insurance not a material breach that would make entre premarital agreement unenforceable); *Anonymous v. Anonymous*, 123 A.D.3d 581, 999 N.Y.S.2d 386 (2014) (husband's failure to transfer real estate, as provided in premarital agreement, did not render agreement invalid as fraudulent).

59. *Branch v. Branch*, 2016 Ark. App. 613, 508 S.W.3d 911 (2016).

60. *Harllee v. Harllee*, 565 S.E.2d 678 (N.C. Ct. App. 2002); *Dutton*, 729 So. 2d 860.

61. *Liebelt v. Liebelt*, 801 P.2d 52 (Idaho Ct. App. 1990).

62. *Ayers v. Ayers*, 2022 Ala. Civ. App. LEXIS 106, (unpub.).

63. 261 Mont. 10, 861 P.2d 856 (1993).

64. 107 Conn. App. 279, 945 A.2d 502 (2008).

stay home to raise children, or to make career sacrifices to further the other spouse's career, and who has a premarital agreement that allows the working spouse to retain the fruits of his or her labor, needs to understand that he or she may not be able to recoup.[65]

The same principle applies when the wealthier party uses his or her separate property in a manner that later proves disadvantageous. For example, in *Robbins v. Robbins*,[66] the husband took a margin loan secured by his separate property securities account to purchase a jointly titled apartment. Had the parties gotten a mortgage on the property instead, under the terms of the agreement, the husband would have gotten credit for paying it down with his separate property funds. Because he voluntarily used the proceeds of a loan on his separate property to pay cash for the apartment, he was entitled to no credit and the wife benefitted. The terms of the agreement did not permit the court to relieve him of the consequences of his voluntary act.

(j) Conduct That Renders Agreement Unfair at Enforcement

In states that require that a premarital agreement be substantively fair or not unconscionable at enforcement, postmarital conduct can put the enforceability of an agreement at greater risk than in those states where fairness is judged solely at execution.[67] For example, in *In re Marriage of Krejci*,[68] the husband owned a lakeside resort and the premarital agreement made it his separate property. During the 18-year marriage, both parties worked in the resort and the wife was never paid a salary. Moreover, the parties commingled their assets, including assets the wife inherited during the marriage, and the husband used marital earnings to make improvements at the resort. The court concluded it would be unfair to enforce the agreement and gave the wife an award based on a portion of the appreciation in value of the resort. A provision that stated expressly that the resort would remain the husband's separate property, regardless of any monetary or nonmonetary contributions she made to it, might have better put the wife on notice that she would accrue no interest and she could have insisted on receiving a salary. Alternatively, the husband could have paid her a salary and perhaps insulated

---

65. *See In re Marriage of Corwell*, 2013 Ill. App. Unpub. LEXIS 1118 (premarital agreement was enforceable notwithstanding change in manner of compensating wife for services to husband's business resulted in her receiving 40 percent less in social security benefits); *In re Marriage of Hoffman*, 2012 Wash. App. LEXIS 1136 (unpub.) (wife's decision not to work did not render premarital agreement unfair); *Johnson v. Johnson*, 2011 Ohio App. LEXIS 440 (unpub.) (premarital agreement did not become unenforceable because wife voluntarily left job); *Knise v. Knise*, 2008 Conn. Super. LEXIS 320 (unpub.) (premarital agreement was not unconscionable at divorce because wife spent separate funds during marriage where she did so voluntarily); *Peden v. Peden*, 972 So. 2d 106 (Ala. Civ. App. 2007) (valid premarital agreement controlled disposition of property; husband who placed assets in wife's name to avoid seizure by former wife or other creditors not entitled to constructive trust); *Richard v. Richard*, 2004 Minn. App. LEXIS 1475 (unpub.) (premarital agreement not substantively unfair at divorce because wife paid living expenses that husband had orally agreed to pay although payment created hardship for her); *In re Marriage of Weissgerber*, 276 Wis. 2d 308, 686 N.W.2d 455 (Ct. App. 2004) (wife's refusal to work, irresponsible management of money, including incurring debt in pursuit of meritless litigation over premarital agreement, and lavish spending, did not render premarital agreement unfair at divorce); *In re Estate of Brosseau*, 176 Ill. App. 3d 450, 531 N.E.2d 158 (premarital agreement was not abrogated as result of husband's improvements to wife's real estate).

66. 39 Misc. 3d 1216(A), 975 N.Y.S.2d 369 (Sup. Ct. N.Y. Cnty. 2013).

67. See Section 4.09(c).

68. 266 Wis. 2d 284, 667 N.W.2d 780 (Wis. Ct. App. 2003); *see also In re Marriage of Zernia*, 347 Wis. 2d 549, 830 N.W.2d 723 (2013).

himself from her claim.[69] In a state that does not require substantive fairness at either execution or enforcement, the wife in a situation like that in *Krejci* would have no remedy. Unless the agreement makes provisions for the spouse, for example, where the agreement provides the parties will share the fruits of their labor, it is in the spouse's best interests not to work for free and for the lawyer to advise him or her of that. *Krejci* also points up that event when a court in a second-look state holds an agreement unfair at enforcement, the disadvantaged spouse often remains quite disadvantaged. The husband left the marriage with the resort, then valued at $400,000, and which had more than doubled in value during the 18-year marriage. The wife, who had contributed a $90,000 inheritance to acquisition of joint property and other common purposes, got an $80,000 judgment against the husband plus the right to a piece of real estate with $23,000 in equity. Even in second-look states, a remedy at divorce, which may be inadequate, is a poor substitute for a party taking care to preserve his or her own property interests.

(k) Changes in Applicable Law that Renders Agreement Unfair at Enforcement

A different type of change that may arguably render an agreement unfair at enforcement is a change in the law that disadvantages one party or changes their rights in some fashion. For example, in 2017, in the Tax Cuts and Jobs Act, Congress eliminated the provisions of the Internal Revenue Code that allowed spousal support to be deductible from the income of the payor and includible in the income of the payee.[70] A party who negotiated a premarital or postmarital agreement before the law changed that provides for a predetermined amount of support that was to be deductible will nevertheless be obligated to pay in accordance with the terms of the agreement.

(l) Change of Fortunes

When parties enter into a premarital agreement under which each party retains control of all property titled in his or her name, the fact that one party was very successful in growing his or her assets is not a basis to invalidate the agreement.[71] Similarly, that a financial obligation has become economically burdensome to the party who was stronger at the outset does not warrant a court refusing enforcement.[72] The economically dominant party who obtains an agreement to protect his or her assets and earnings must take the risk of a loss in value and plan accordingly.

---

69. *See, e.g.*, *Butcher v. Butcher*, 2003 Mich. App. LEXIS 325 (unpub.) (premarital agreement was not substantively unfair at divorce due to wife's contributions of labor to husband's rental property where husband paid her hourly wage for her work).

70. Pub. L. No. 115-97, § 11051(b)(1)(B), struck § 71, which permitted the payor to deduct alimony payments from his or her income and § 215, which required the payee to report such payments as income on his or her tax returns.

71. *See Schoenborn v. Schoenborn*, 144 Conn. App. 846, 74 A.3d 482 (2013); *In re Marriage of Weiss*, 42 Cal. App. 4th 106, 49 Cal. Rptr. 2d 339 (1996); *Reed v. Reed*, 265 Mich. App. 131, 693 N.W.2d 825 (2005); *Mabus v. Mabus*, 890 So. 2d 806 (Miss. 2003); *Friedman v. Friedman*, 100 Cal. App. 4th 65, 122 Cal. Rptr. 2d 412 (2002); *Upham v. Upham*, 36 Mass. Ct. App. 295, 630 N.E.2d 307 (1994).

72. *Justus v. Justus*, 581 N.E.2d 1265 (Ind. Ct. App. 1991).

(m) Marital Misconduct, Adultery, Domestic Violence

Marital misconduct, such as adultery or desertion, does not generally render a premarital agreement unenforceable,[73] nor affect a party's rights under it, unless the agreement expressly so provides.[74] The court voided a premarital agreement in *D'Arc v. D'Arc*,[75] although it had to strain to find a contractual basis for doing so, after the husband hired a hit man to kill the wife. *D'Arc* presents an extremely unusual set of facts. An Arizona court came to a different conclusion in a case where the wife attempted to poison the husband, holding the premarital agreement remained enforceable.[76] If the parties wish some or all of their rights under the agreement to be affected by marital misconduct, the agreement should say so expressly. Courts in some states refuse to enforce penalty provisions.[77]

Misconduct could cause a change in circumstances that renders a premarital agreement unenforceable in a second-look state. For example, in *Hutchison v. Hutchison*,[78] a Michigan case, the husband's domestic violence rendered the wife unable to work. As a result, the premarital agreement was unenforceable in its entirety and the court awarded the wife both spousal support and more than half the marital property. Domestic violence is a pervasive problem, but there are few cases involving a premarital or postmarital agreement and a claim of domestic violence. Legal scholars have observed that domestic violence can take the form of economic abuse in which the perpetrator controls the victim's access to resources by withholding needed funds, exploiting the victim's own resources, and interfering with his or her employment or education. [79] However, there is little to guide the practitioner about the circumstances that may cause a court to invalidate an agreement because of such behavior. *Schechter v. Schechter*[80] is a rare case from a second-look state involving a premarital agreement where the court found that the husband subjected the wife to emotional and economic abuse throughout the relationship. However, it voided the agreement because the husband's financial disclosure was misleading and because the agreement was not fair as of execution. In doing so, it did not draw a connection to the history of premarital domestic abuse as a basis

---

73. *See Forgey-Lewis v. Lewis*, 2011 Tenn. App. LEXIS 29 (unpub.) (trial court properly awarded alimony to wife where agreement provides for support to spouse not at fault); *see also Ayers v. Ayers*, 2022 Ala. Civ. App. LEXIS, 106, (unpub.); *Hubbard v. Bentley*, 17 So. 3d 652, 654 (Ala. Civ. App. 2008); *Sanford v. Sanford*, 694 N.W.2d 283 (S.D. 2005); *Korff v. Korff*, 64 Mass. App. 94 831 N.E.2d 385 (2005).

74. *Perkinson v. Perkinson*, 802 S.W.2d 600 (Tenn. 1990); *Maloy v. Maloy*, 362 So. 2d 484 (Fla. Dist. Ct. App. 1978); *Sims v. Sims*, 186 N.W.2d 491 (Neb. 1971); *Sparrow v. Sparrow*, 172 Minn. 91, 214 N.W. 791 (1927); *Crise v. Smith*, 150 Md. 322, 133 A. 110 (1926). In some states courts refuse to enforce a penalty for adultery as against the public policy favoring no-fault divorce. *See Crofford v. Adachi*, 506 P.3d 182 (Haw. 2022).

75. 164 N.J. Super. 226, 395 A.2d 1270 (Ch. Div. 1978), *rev'd in part, aff'd in part*, 175 N.J. Super. 598, 421 A.2d 602 (App. Div. 1980).

76. *In re Soldwedel*, 2021 Ariz. App. Unpub. LEXIS 688.

77. California and Iowa have rejected enforcement of a penalty clause for marital misconduct on public policy grounds. *Mehren v. Dargan*, 118 Cal. App. 4th 1167, 13 Cal. Rpt. 3d 522 (Ct. App. 2004); *In re Marriage of Cooper*, 769 N.W.2d 582 (Iowa 2009). However, neither of these cases involved a claim of domestic violence.

78. 2009 Mich. App. LEXIS 1594 (unpub.).

79. *See* Christine Kim, *Credit Cards: Weapons for Domestic Violence*, 22 DUKE J. GENDER L. & POL'Y 281 (Spring 2015); Donna Harrington Conner, *Financial Freedom: Women, Money, and Domestic Abuse*, 20 WM. & MARY J. WOMEN & L. 339 (Winter 2014); Margaret E. Johnson, *Redefining Harm, Reimagining Remedies, and Reclaiming Domestic Violence Law*, 42 U.C. DAVIS L. REV. 1107 (Apr. 2009).

80. 88 Mass. App. Ct. 239, 37 N.E.3d 632 (2015).

to void the agreement.[81] In *VanWagner v. VanWagner*,[82] the wife's testimony that during the marriage the husband did not allow her to work, coupled with his physical abuse, could have supported a conclusion she was the victim of economic abuse. However, the court held it was bound by the terms of the premarital agreement regarding disposition of property.[83]

It does not appear that a court in a UPAA state has discretion to void a premarital agreement because of domestic violence. For example, Nebraska is a UPAA state, and its case law does not recognize domestic abuse as a basis to void a premarital agreement.[84] However, an agreement cannot effectively preclude a spouse from seeking a civil protection order.[85]

A general character flaw that makes continuation of marriage unacceptable is not the sort of unforeseeable circumstance that may render an agreement unenforceable.[86]

§8.04 CONDUCT THAT ENHANCES ENFORCEABILITY—RATIFICATION AND ESTOPPEL

Parties' conduct during the marriage may ratify, and therefore strengthen the enforceability of, a premarital or postmarital agreement. When a party accepts the benefits of an agreement, a court may conclude that he or she ratified it.[87] When parties behave with respect to their property consistent with the terms of a premarital or postmarital agreement, such conduct can be powerful evidence of their understanding of their property rights as defined in their agreement.[88]

Ratification during the marriage can be a powerful tool to protect a party's interest in enforceability. For example, in *Nanini v. Nanini*,[89] the premarital agreement provided that each party would retain all separately titled property and all earnings from personal services. During the marriage, the husband paid all living expenses, funded a joint stock account, and gave the wife a generous allowance. During the same period, the wife amassed a considerable separate estate that she took pains to keep secret from the husband. Her conduct, consistent with her rights under the agreement, negated her claim she lacked understanding of the terms or was the victim of fraud or duress.[90]

---

81. The domestic abuse during the marriage did, however, loom large in the court's decision about custody.

82. 868 N.E.2d 924 (Ind. Ct. App. 2007) (unpub.).

83. *See also Allard v. Allard*, 308 Mich. App. 536, 867 N.W.2d 866 (2014) (domestic violence is not sufficient to void premarital agreement); *Hollar v. Hollar*, 2015 Tenn. App. LEXIS 944 (unpub.) (wife left husband to reside in domestic violence shelter; premarital agreement invalid due to late presentation, failure to translate into wife's language).

84. *Cenovic v. Cenovic*, 2010 Neb. App. LEXIS 5 (unpub.).

85. *Snell v. Snell*, 2010 Ohio App. LEXIS 1841 (unpub.).

86. *See In re Marriage of Barnes*, 324 Ill. App. 3d 514, 755 N.E.2d 522 (2001) (that husband had character flaws was foreseeable as he had been married four times before; his bad behavior did not affect parties' rights under premarital agreement).

87. *Tremont v. Tremont*, 35 A.D.3d 1046, 827 N.Y.S.2d 309 (2006); *Schutterle v. Schutterle*, 260 N.W.2d 341 (S.D. 1977); *Stawski v. Stawski*, 43 A.D.3d 776, 843 N.Y.S.2d 544 (2007).

88. *See Moquin v. Bergeron*, 338 So. 3d 918 (Fla. App. 2022) (parties titling of property during marriage evidenced their understanding agreement made title determinative of rights at divorce): *Cook v. Cook*, 26 Neb. App. 137, 918 N.W. 2d 1 (2018) (same); *In re Marriage of Irons*, 2016 Kan. App. Unpub. LEXIS 574 (same).

89. 166 Ariz. 287, 802 P.2d 438 (Ct. App. 1990).

90. *See also Penrod v. Penrod*, 624 S.W.3d 905 (Mo. Ct. App. 2021) (premarital agreement was valid where challenger kept premarital assets separate per terms of agreement); *Rio v. Rio*, 110 A.D.3d 1051, 974 N.W.S.2d 491

A party's dealings with property during the marriage consistent with his or her rights under an agreement may constitute ratification of the agreement. For example, in *Hartz v. Hartz*,[91] the wife ratified the premarital agreement when she executed deeds of trust on her sole signature, something she could not have done without a premarital agreement. When parties transfer title to property in accordance with the terms of an agreement, that may also constitute ratification.[92] Similarly, a party's handling of his or her own property after a spouse's death as provided in a premarital agreement may ratify the agreement.[93]

A contract requiring wills with mirror provisions becomes irrevocable upon the death of one party to the contract.[94] When parties enter into a premarital agreement requiring one or both parties to make a will for the benefit of the other spouse, children, or third parties, and when the surviving party accepts the benefits of the contract by taking property in accordance with the estate planning provisions made by the other spouse, that party will be estopped from making a disposition of his or her property other than in accordance with the contract.[95]

Under some circumstances, a party's silence during marriage may be treated as a ratification where the party fails to speak up until after a death. For example, in *Hartz*,[96] the wife saw a will in which the husband referred to the premarital agreement as not requiring any bequest to her. Her failure to disabuse the husband of his belief in the validity of the agreement contradicted her later claim of invalidity.[97] A surviving spouse's silence for an extended period after the other spouse's death may also constitute ratification.[98] But, mere silence during the marriage may not always constitute an estoppel such that a party is precluded from challenging validity at divorce. As the court observed in *Fetters v. Fetters*:[99] "As a practical matter, is it unclear how Julie could have unilaterally disavowed the premarital agreement

---

(2013) (where husband relied on postmarital agreement as to order setting his maintenance obligation, he ratified agreement and cannot challenge validity); *Head v. Head*, 59 Md. App. 570, 477 A.2d 282 (1984) (wife's retention of cash and property received under marital settlement agreement resolving disputed premarital agreement ratified settlement and precluded rescission on fraud grounds); *Comstock v. Comstock*, 146 Ark. 266, 225 S.W. 621 (1920) (wife's acceptance of cash in settlement of her rights under premarital agreement estopped her to deny validity).

91. 248 Md. 47, 234 A.2d 865 (1967); *see also Colon v. Colon*, 2006 N.J. Super. Unpub. LEXIS 1795 (premarital agreement not unconscionable because it permitted husband to retain all appreciation of his assets where during marriage wife devoted her time to managing her inherited assets into multimillion-dollar enterprise). *Curry v. Curry*, 260 Ga. 302, 392 S.E.2d 879 (1990) (wife's acceptance of benefits of postmarital agreement for five years estopped her to claim lack of consideration).

92. *In re Marriage of Vella*, 237 Ill. App. 3d 194, 603 N.W.2d 109 (1992).

93. *See In re Stever's Estate*, 392 P.2d 286 (Colo. 1964) (surviving wife's removal of all household effects and lease of marital home, consistent with rights under will executed in conformity with premarital agreement, negates claim agreement was invalid).

94. *Keats v. Cates*, 100 Ill. App. 2d 177, 241 N.E.2d 645 (1968).

95. *Sonnicksen v. Sonnicksen*, 45 Cal. App. 2d 46, 113 P.2d 495 (1941).

96. *Hartz*, 248 Md. 47.

97. *See also Kornegay v. Robinson*, 360 N.C. 640, 637 S.E.2d 516 (2006) (trial court properly granted summary judgment to estate of decedent over wife's challenge to premarital agreement where wife waited until after death to claim invalidity and where she had received more than $300,000 from husband); *Serbus' Estate v. Serbus*, 324 N.W.2d 381 (Minn. 1982) (wife's silence for 16 years, after having signed premarital agreement and postmarital consent to will, negated her claim premarital agreement was invalid); *In re Strickland's Estate*, 181 Neb. 478, 149 N.W.2d 344 (1967) (wife's silence during 11 years of marriage and her claim of fraud only after husband's death, when her goal of protecting her own estate for her daughter was accomplished, defeats her claim of invalidity).

98. *See In re Estate of Smid*, 756 N.W.2d 1 (S.D. 2008).

99. 26 N.E.3d 1016 (Ind. Ct. App. 2015); *see also Walker v. Walker*, 2020 Tenn. App. LEXIS 47 (unpub.).

while still remaining married to Jay."[100] Postexecution silence may not constitute ratification of an unconscionable agreement.[101] Some courts have held that the equitable doctrines of ratification, laches, and estoppel cannot be applied to premarital agreements, reasoning that an agreement "that is substantively and procedurally unfair is void from the inception and is incapable of ratification."[102] However, when a postmarital agreement provides substantial economic benefits for a spouse during the marriage, his or her acceptance of those benefits may well constitute ratification. In *In re Marriage of Burkle,*[103] the postmarital agreement was negotiated incident to a reconciliation. Under it, the husband was to pay the wife $1 million a year while the parties remained married, and $30 million if they divorced. Her acceptance of the annual payment for over five years, coupled with her silence after learning about the husband's business ventures that called into question his financial disclosure, ratified the agreement.

Where the agreement requires the proponent of the agreement to take certain actions, such as to retitle or transfer property, establish a joint bank account, make a beneficiary designation, make cash transfers, write a will, or establish a trust, the party should be advised of the importance of carrying out these obligations. Doing so, and the other party's acceptance of the benefits of the agreement, can significantly insulate the agreement from a successful challenge.[104]

Parties to a premarital agreement may choose to enter into a formal, written amendment. Any such amendment should include an express ratification of the original agreement except as expressly modified. Where a party accepts the benefits of such an amendment, he or she will have an overwhelmingly difficult burden to meet to successfully challenge validity of the agreement.[105]

There are a variety of terms the lawyer for a wealthy party can consider that would support an argument that a weaker party ratified a premarital or postmarital agreement. The key to ratification is that the agreement provide for transfers or other actions during the marriage, before the marriage ends by death or dissolution, and that the wealthy party actually carry out the obligations. For example:

- An obligation to make cash gifts, to fund an IRA, to transfer sole title to marketable securities, or to otherwise make transfers that will create a nest egg for the weaker party, regardless of how the marriage ends;

100. 26 N.E.3d at 1022 n.4; *see also Flaherty v. Flaherty*, 128 So. 3d 920 (Fla. Ct. App. 2d Dist. 2013) (mere silence during marriage does not constitute ratification; mere passage of time during marriage is not laches).

101. *See McMullin v. McMullin*, 926 S.W.2d 108 (Mo. Ct. App. 1996) (wife not estopped to deny validity of premarital agreement, although husband fully performed by adopting and educating her children, where agreement was unconscionable); *see also In re Estate of Hollett*, 150 N.H. 39, 834 A.2d 348 (2003) (wife's silence during marriage did not ratify premarital agreement obtained in procedurally unfair manner as not reasonable to expect disadvantaged party to challenge validity at the risk of disrupting the marriage).

102. *Knapp v. Ginsberg*, 67 Cal. App. 5th, 282 Cal. Rptr. 3d 403 (2021); *Kellar v. Estate of Kellar*, 172 Wn. App. 562, 585, 291 P.3d 906, 918 (2012), *rev. den.* 2013 Wash. LEXIS 865 (unpub.) (citation omitted).

103. 139 Cal. App. 4th 712, 43 Cal. Rptr. 3d 181 (2d Dist. 2006).

104. *See Rogers v. Gordon*, 404 N.J. Super. 213, 961 A.2d 11 (2008); *see also In re Estate of Wilber*, 165 N.H. 246, 75 A.3d 1096 (2013).

105. *See Webb v. Webb*, 18 Misc. 3d 822, 851 N.Y.S.2d 828 (Sup. Ct. 2007).

- An obligation to transfer title to a marital home into survivorship, or to acquire a new home in survivorship and to pay the costs of acquisition;
- An obligation to create and fund a joint cash or securities account upon marriage or after execution of a postmarital agreement;
- An obligation to make estate planning provisions for the spouse through a will or revocable trust that exceeds the rights he or she would have without a premarital or postmarital agreement.

As discussed elsewhere in this book, ERISA provides that a premarital waiver of surviving spouse rights in a qualified retirement plan is not effective. The plan participant will, therefore, need to have the spouse sign a consent to waive his or her spousal rights after the date of marriage, enabling the plan participant to name a beneficiary other than the spouse.[106] That waiver can include an acknowledgment that the parties entered into a premarital agreement and that the parties, by executing the waiver, ratify the agreement. When both parties have a retirement plan that is to remain the separate property of the plan participant, each may be entitled to require the other to execute a waiver; when they both do so, a court should hold that those acts constitute ratification.

§8.05 CONDUCT THAT MAY ALTER RIGHTS, OBLIGATIONS, OR EXPECTATIONS UNDER THE AGREEMENT, OR CREATE OPPORTUNITY FOR DISPUTE

(a) Commingling

Commingling occurs when marital/community and separate money or other assets are intermingled in such a way that separate property loses its character and becomes indistinguishable from that with which it was mixed.[107] Commingling includes depositing separate property funds and marital/community funds in a joint financial institution account.[108] It also includes depositing marital/community funds into a separately titled account with funds defined as separate property. Commingling can result in an asset that a premarital or postmarital agreement defines as a party's separate property becoming transformed, or transmuted, into marital/community property.[109] For example, in *Compton v. Compton*,[110] the parties, each of whom had sizable estates at marriage, were entitled under their premarital agreement to preserve their separate property. Ignoring his lawyer's advice, the husband contributed substantial separate monies into a joint account that was used, among other things, to improve the

106. See Chapter 12, Model Paragraphs 23–27 and accompanying Comment.

107. *Long v. Long*, 129 Md. App. 554, 743 A.2d 281 (2000); *Anderson v. Anderson*, 29 Va. App. 673, 514 S.E.2d 369 (1999). The commingling discussed here is commingling that results in the transformation to marital or community property of a particular asset that would otherwise be separate under the agreement. Under such circumstances, the agreement as a whole remains viable. This is to be distinguished from the situation where parties commingle their estates so completely that everything becomes a marital asset and the agreement is essentially vitiated. See Section 8.03(d).

108. In re Marriage of Nash, 644 S.W.3d 683 (Tex. Ct. App. 2022).

109. *In re Marriage of Thomas*, 199 S.W.3d 847 (Mo. Ct. App. 2006).

110. 902 P.2d 805 (Alaska 1995).

wife's separate property. In rejecting the husband's claim for reimbursement of his separate property contributions, the court observed that the agreement did not preclude the parties from transmuting separate property to marital property during the marriage.[111]

The models in this book define all jointly titled financial institution accounts as marital property without regard to the source of funds. Joint title is determinative; the spouse who benefits from joint titling is not required to prove the transferor-spouse intended to make a gift, and the text does not allow a party to trace out separate property (with a limited exception).[112] This model text is intended to foreclose litigation over intent. A party can protect his or her exclusive right to separate property by segregating separate fungible assets from marital or community assets. Indeed, a party who wishes to maintain sole rights to separate property should avoid depositing separate funds and marital or community funds into the same bank account and using the account to acquire assets, even if separately titled, or using a combination of marital and separate funds to purchase jointly titled assets.[113] From the perspective of an economically weaker party, it will generally not be in his or her interest to be forced to prove the other spouse intended a gift when he or she funded a jointly titled financial institution account; therefore, a provision that makes it clear that joint title means the asset is marital/community property can better protect a weaker party.

Commingling involves the actual commingling of assets themselves. Combining information about assets—for example, on a loan application, net worth statement, or tax return—does not cause separate assets to become marital or community property.[114] The model agreement provides expressly that combining information in this manner does not cause separate property to become marital or community property.[115]

(b) Effect of Creation of Jointly Titled Property or of Transfer to Sole Title on Parties' Rights at Divorce

When a party transfers separate property to the sole name of the other party or titles property jointly that would otherwise be separate property under the terms of a premarital agreement, in the event of a dispute at divorce a court may treat such a transfer as a gift.[116] When the

---

111. *Id.* at 810; *see also Nack v. Dickerson*, 2007 Va. App. LEXIS 339 (unpub.) (transfer of husband's separate securities account into joint names, purportedly solely for convenience, coupled with multiple transactions in account, caused account to become marital asset notwithstanding premarital agreement permitting each party to retain sole interest in separate assets); *Bilouris v. Bilouris*, 67 Mass. App. 149, 852 N.E.2d 687 (2006) (evidence did not support trial court finding that building was husband's separate property under premarital agreement where parties mortgaged joint property and used proceeds to acquire building); *Sharpe v. Sharpe*, 536 So. 2d 434 (La. Ct. App. 1988) (husband made substantial deposits of his separate cash into wife's account; court rejected his claim for reimbursement based on the terms of premarital agreement).

112. See Chapter 12, Paragraph 7(H) of the model agreement.

113. *See Richard v. Richard*, 2004 Minn. App. LEXIS 1475 (unpub.) (parties to premarital agreement segregated separate and marital funds; assets acquired with separate funds were therefore nonmarital and not divisible at divorce); *see also Rich v. Rich*, 337 So. 3d 138 (Fla. Ct. App. 2d Dist. 2022).

114. *See Holston v. Holston*, 2013 Ala. Civ. App. LEXIS 121 (May 17, 2013) (filing of joint tax returns did not convert earnings to marital property where premarital agreement clearly defined as separate).

115. Est. of Eagle v. Eagle, 2022 Va. App. LEXIS 474 (unpub.); see Appx. D, Model Title-Controls Agreement, Paragraph 7(C).

116. *Est. of Eagle*, 2022 Va. App. LEXIS 474; *In re Marriage of Berger*, 357 Ill. App. 3d 651, 829 N.E.2d 879 (2005); *Barton v. Barton*, 996 P.2d 1 (Wyo. 2000); *Harbom v. Harbom*, 134 Md. App. 430, 760 A.2d 272 (2000); *Hrudka v. Hrudka*, 186 Ariz. 84, 93, 919 P.2d 179, 188 (Ct. App. 1995); *Coffman v. Adkins*, 338 N.W.2d 540 (Iowa Ct. App. 1983).

agreement provides that property rights are determined by title, a party's decision to title newly acquired property in joint names, or in the sole name of the other spouse, or to transfer existing property to sole or joint title, alters the character of the property, but that has not always stopped a party who regretted his or her generosity from attempting to reclaim it as his or her separate property. In *Bowen v. Bowen*,[117] the husband provided all the funds to acquire four pieces of real estate and took title with the wife. He claimed his intent was not to make a gift to the wife in the event of divorce and that joint title was merely an estate planning device. The court rejected application of equitable theories, such as resulting trust, as well as presumptions, such as the rebuttable presumption of gift. Rather, the contract dictated that joint title meant equal ownership rights. Similarly, in *Barton v. Barton*,[118] a premarital agreement provided for the parties to retain premarital and inherited property. The husband used inherited money to buy a house that he titled in the wife's name. At divorce he argued he did not intend a gift but rather made the transfer only to protect the property from claims in litigation with children of his prior marriage. He also argued that the source of funds for acquisition determined his rights notwithstanding title. The court held he had not rebutted the presumption of gift.[119] In both *Bowen* and *Barton*, the husband could have preserved his right to the disputed property in the event of divorce by titling the property in his name alone. Alternatively, he could have insisted on a postmarital agreement to preserve a right to have the property transferred back to him in the event of divorce. Such a provision will be disadvantageous to a weaker party if the marriage ends in separation or divorce.

In fact, courts have sometimes ruled for a spouse who transferred assets even where a premarital agreement did not appear to permit such a claim. In *Osborne v. Osborne*,[120] for example, the wife took title to several pieces of real estate in joint names, although she provided all the funds for purchase from her separate property. The husband argued the wife intended to make a gift of the properties, and the wife argued no such intent; the court sided with the wife. Similarly, in *Dardick v. Dardick*,[121] the agreement provided that jointly titled property the parties acquired together would be equally the separate property of each party. The husband opened joint bank accounts into which he made the only deposits and used the account to purchase a home and investments titled in his name. At divorce, the wife argued the home and investments were marital property because they were purchased with jointly titled funds. The court rejected her argument, finding that the creation of a joint account to enable the husband to pay household expenses did not convert all purchases from the account into marital property "in view of the express provisions of the agreement."[122] However, the

---

117. 352 S.C. 494, 575 S.E.2d 553 (2003).

118. *Barton*, 996 P.2d 1.

119. *See also In re Marriage of Bliss*, 382 Mont. 370, 367 P.3d 395 (2016); *Heaton v. Heaton*, 2014 Tenn. App. LEXIS 536 (unpub.); *Boyd v. Boyd*, 2010 Ky. App. LEXIS Unpub. 160, *rev. denied*, 2011 Ky. LEXIS 410 (unpub.); *In re Marriage of Cullman*, 185 Ill. App. 3d 1029, 541 N.E.2d 1274 (1989).

120. 384 Mass. 591, 428 N.E.2d 810 (1981).

121. 948 S.W.2d 268 (Mo. Ct. App. 1997).

122. *Id.* at 270; *see also Reed v. Reed*, 2004 Tenn. App. LEXIS 889 (unpub.) (premarital agreement provision for rights to after-acquired property to be determined by title inapplicable to preexisting bank account retitled in joint names; retitling was solely for convenience, and accounts remained sole property of original owner); *Bilouris v. Bilouris*, 67 Mass. App. 149, 852 N.E. 2d 687 (2006) (trial court properly gave husband monetary credit for land he contributed from separate property on which jointly titled home was built where husband testified no intent to make gift notwithstanding terms of premarital agreement that acknowledged parties could give and receive gifts);

agreement appeared to have contradictory provisions: one made jointly titled property, the joint bank account, arguably one-half each party's separate property; another made property acquired by one party, the solely titled home and investments, arguably that party's separate property, although purchased from the joint account.

When an agreement gives a party the right to an instrument documenting his or her entitlement to a return of separate property funds he or she contributes to a jointly titled asset, the burden is on that party to request the other party to sign the necessary document. A failure to ask may be tantamount to a forfeiture of his or her rights. For example, in *Haas v. Hatz*,[123] the premarital agreement gave each party the right to a mortgage lien for separate money contributed to a marital home. The husband never asked the wife to sign a mortgage. As a result, the default provision for equal division of a jointly titled home applied despite his much greater contribution of separate funds ($2.1 million versus $80,000 from the wife). The husband could have asserted his right to a mortgage before putting $2.1 million of his separate money into the joint home. Alternatively, the premarital agreement could have included a formula giving each party a *pro rata* share of the equity in the event of a divorce. In that case, he would not have needed to obtain an additional instrument to protect his separate property interest.

These cases illustrate the importance of the lawyer at the drafting stage addressing the joint title problem and advising the client about the effect of postagreement transfers on his or her property rights in the event of death or divorce. In *Osborne* and *Dardick*, the spouse who retitled ultimately prevailed, but only after having to incur the cost and risk of litigation. By contrast, in *Barton v. Barton*,[124] the court entertained a husband's claim that he did not intend a gift but ultimately rejected his claim on the evidence.

The model agreements in this book provide expressly that a jointly titled financial institution account is marital property, and that any asset acquired with funds from such an account is also marital property. Similarly, real estate titled in a survivorship form is defined as marital property.[125] When an agreement provides that jointly titled property will be divided equally at divorce, that leaves no room for a court to take into account who paid the expenses of the property and to order reimbursement.[126] Similarly, the model agreements provide that a party's transfer of title to property into the sole name of the other party results in the property becoming the recipient's separate property. The purpose of such provisions is to clearly define the parties' rights and preclude the type of litigation over intent that occurred in the cases cited above. A party who wants to make transfers, but wants the right to take them back if the marriage fails, will need to get the other party to agree in writing.

In re Marriage of Gardner, 190 Wis. 2d 216, 234, 527 N.W.2d 701, 706 (1994) (husband's deposit of substantial monies from his separate estate into jointly titled bank account did not transmute his separate property into marital property).

123. 2008 Mich. App. LEXIS 2252 (unpub.).

124. *Barton v. Barton*, 996 P.2d 1; *also see Gamache v. Smurro*, 904 A.2d 91 (Vt. 2006) (interpreting California law) (deed conveying 100 percent interest in real estate to parties as community property superseded premarital agreement under which wife waived all interest in husband's 10 percent share then owned with other family members); *Lung v. Lung*, 655 N.E.2d 607 (Ind. Ct. App. 1995) (husband changed status of his separate real estate to marital when he transferred title to joint names; property divisible at divorce despite claim he meant only to provide for wife in event of his death).

125. However, this would not preclude terms to allow a contributing party to receive his or her separate contribution back upon separation or divorce. See Chapter 12, Paragraphs 28–32, of the model agreement.

126. *In re Marriage of Chez*, 1 N.E.3d 1224 (Ill. Ct. App. 2013).

(c) Effect of Joint Title with Right of Survivorship at Death

A valid agreement waiving marital rights does not defeat a party's rights under an instrument providing for rights of survivorship. Thus, unless the premarital or postmarital agreement provides otherwise, real estate or other property that is held in a form of survivorship title will pass to the survivor.[127] In most cases, this is the result parties intend; saying so expressly in the agreement may eliminate a claim that might be made by other beneficiaries of a deceased spouse. Similarly, when a spouse transfers ownership of a separate asset into tenants in common ownership, by virtue of title, the surviving spouse will retain his or her share. This is consistent with the right of parties to a premarital or postmarital agreement to transfer assets during life, including to each other.[128]

(d) Use of Funds from Joint Bank Account

Parties' rights during marriage to a jointly titled financial institution account is a separate question from what rights each may have upon death or dissolution. When parties establish a joint bank account, they authorize each other to withdraw and use funds on deposit regardless of their relative contributions or who would have the right to the funds at divorce or death. For example, in *Smith v. Smith*,[129] the husband deposited an inheritance into a joint account so that the wife could write checks. She withdrew a substantial sum from the account. Because the trial court denied a divorce, it was without jurisdiction to determine the parties' marital property rights; thus, the husband was not entitled to an order compelling the wife to return the funds. In titling jointly, the husband took the risk that the funds in the account would be consumed, commingled with marital funds, or dissipated during the marriage.

(e) Lack of Adequate Financial Records

When the agreement provides for determination of parties' rights to an asset based on the parties' relative financial contributions, each party must keep adequate financial records to be able to establish his or her claim. When a party fails to maintain records, the claim may fail even though the agreement as a whole remains valid.[130] When a party engages in multiple transactions, moves money around, and commingles marital and separate funds, he or she may not be able to retain assets the agreement was designed to protect unless he or she has adequate records that enable him or her, or a CPA or other expert witness, to identify and trace (insofar as the agreement permits).[131] A party who wants to preserve nonmarital assets must also secure his or her records from loss, destruction, or misconduct of the spouse.[132]

---

127. *Miller v. Miller*, 117 N.C. App. 71, 450 S.E.2d 15 (1994).

128. *See Spencer v. Estate of Spencer*, 313 S.W.3d 534.

129. 656 So. 2d 1143 (Miss. 1995).

130. *In re Marriage of Vinson*, 2015 Tex. App. LEXIS 8123 (unpub.); *Short v. Short*, 356 S.W.3d 235 (Mo. Ct. App., E.D. 2011); *Steinke v. Steinke*, 2006, Ohio App. LEXIS 4106 (unpub.); *In re Marriage of Johnston*, 255 Mont. 421, 843 P.2d 760 (1992).

131. *See In re Marriage of Nash*, 644 S.W.3d 683, (Tex. App. 6th Dist. 2022); *Rahnema v. Rahnema*, 2006 Va. App. LEXIS 92 (unpub.).

132. *See Ostapowicz v. Wisniewski*, 210 Conn. App. 401, 270 A.3d 145 (2022) (wife removed boxes of husband's documents showing nonmarital source of husband's business).

(f) One Party Controls Finances to the Detriment of the Other Party

Where an agreement determines parties' rights at death or divorce according to title, a party's control over family financial affairs may work to the disadvantage of the other party. For example, in *Martin v. Farber*,[133] the husband turned all his paychecks over to the wife, who made investments in her name alone. The parties' premarital agreement, executed in 1939, gave the husband no rights to the wife's estate at death. The court held a constructive trust could be imposed, premised on the wife's dominant position in financial matters, but it limited the scope of the trust to those assets the husband was able to trace to his paychecks.[134] Because the wife came to the 44-year marriage with inherited assets, the husband may well have had a difficult time establishing his claim. The constructive trust remedy after the damage has been done is a poor substitute for prevention of the problem in the first place. A client who is entering into a marriage with little or no property and no rights except by title should be advised to retain title to his or her own assets and income to the fullest extent possible.

(g) Provisions for Surviving Spouse at Variance with Provisions Required by Agreement

When an agreement provides that a party will have the right to a specified percentage of, or a cash bequest from, the decedent's estate, a different form of benefit for the survivor will not satisfy the contractual obligation. For example, in *Ayoob v. Ayoob*,[135] the premarital agreement provided the wife would receive $5,000 in cash upon the husband's death. During the marriage he made her beneficiary of a $5,000 life insurance policy. This did not satisfy his obligation under the contract. The premarital agreement could have given the husband more than one option to satisfy his obligation. Alternatively, a postmarital amendment could have permitted him to substitute the life insurance for the cash bequest.

Parties may sign various estate planning documents over the course of a marriage and may engage in various property transactions that can affect the rights of the surviving spouse as well as the assets that will go to the heirs of the decedent. For example, in *Walker v. Walker*,[136] the premarital agreement provided that the marital home would be titled as tenants by the entirety and that the husband's estate would pay off the mortgage. Over a period of years, the parties (using the husband's lawyer, the same lawyer who drafted the premarital agreement) executed various estate planning documents, including trusts that purported to each hold a 50 percent tenants-in-common interest in the home and that gave the wife only a life estate in the husband's half interest. None of the instruments referred to the premarital agreement, nor did they expressly or implicitly modify the premarital agreement. After the husband's death, and over the objection of his heirs, the court held that the wife was entitled to sole ownership of the home and to have the husband's estate pay off the mortgage. The parties could have expressly amended the premarital agreement to provide for the estate

133. 68 Md. App. 137, 510 A.2d 608 (1986).

134. *See also Simons v. Simons*, 312 Neb. 136, 978 N.W.2d 121 (2022) (constructive trust imposed where husband controlled financial affairs to wife's detriment under terms of premarital agreement).

135. 74 Cal. App. 2d 236, 168 P.2d 462 (1946).

136. 2022 Md. App. LEXIS 92 (unpub.).

planning arrangements they later came to decide upon. That would have made their intent, if they had such a mutual intent, clear.

(h) Claim That Parties Became Business Partners

When parties with a premarital or postmarital agreement defining their property rights engage in a business venture, such as real estate investing, their activities will not necessarily alter their rights under a premarital agreement unless they enter into a separate agreement governing their rights.[137] For example, in *Barton v. Barton*,[138] the parties contributed to acquisition of several pieces of rental real estate with the husband contributing more. The parties had no written partnership agreement to give him rights at divorce proportionate to his contribution. The court rejected his claim to more than half. Similarly, in *Estate of Kilbourn v. McIntyre*,[139] the husband made what he characterized as "business claims" against the wife's estate despite a premarital agreement waiving all claims at death as spouse "or otherwise."[140] The parties each owned investment real estate and the husband owned a construction company. During the marriage they allocated tasks between them with the wife handling all the money, taxes, and accounting and the husband providing labor and materials for repair and maintenance. The court rejected his claim for compensation for labor and reimbursement for materials; rather, it held him to the waiver.[141] When one spouse takes title to a business but leads the other spouse to believe he or she is a joint owner, and the nonowner works in the business without compensation, a court may treat the business as a marital/community asset notwithstanding the terms of a premarital agreement that purports to make the business nonmarital property.[142]

A general waiver does not necessarily preclude a claim arising out of a business transaction. For example, in *Liptrap v. Coyne*,[143] the surviving wife was statutorily entitled to sue the husband's estate for reimbursement of payments she made after his death, pursuant to a guaranty agreement on debt he incurred to acquire a motel. The husband was the sole promisor on the note, although the parties took title to the motel as tenants by the entirety.[144]

These cases point out that parties with a premarital or postmarital agreement who decide to engage in joint investing or other business activities should get legal advice about how to structure their arrangements to be consistent with their intentions and to enter into appropriate additional agreements.

---

137. For cases that have dealt with a claim that a joint business venture effectively abrogated a premarital agreement, see Section 9.10 of this book.

138. *Barton v. Barton*, 996 P.2d 1 (Wyo. 2000).

139. 898 S.W.2d 583 (Mo. Ct. App. 1995).

140. *Id.* at 587.

141. *See also In re Marriage of Weiss*, 357 Mont. 320, 239 P.3d 123 (2010) (wife's transfer of cash to husband did not constitute investment such as to create joint venture where premarital agreement expressly negated intent, unless in express, signed writing, and evidence supported finding transfer was loan).

142. *See Simons v. Simons,* 312 Neb. 136, 978 N.W. 2d 121 (2022).

143. 675 S.E.2d 693 (N.C. App. 2009).

144. Interestingly, in *Liptrap* the wife also sought to have the husband's estate pay the entire $450,000 balance on the note as the sole promisor even though she would apparently receive the entire interest in the motel. The opinion does not address the outcome of this claim. The premarital agreement could have anticipated this problem and provided expressly that the survivor would take encumbered property subject to all liens.

(i) Use of Separate Assets to Benefit Other Spouse's Separate Property; Nonconforming Payments

When a premarital or postmarital agreement clearly provides that one spouse's separately titled real estate is his or her separate property, the other spouse's voluntary decision to pay the mortgage does not convert it to marital/community property under the agreement;[145] nor does a spouse's contribution to improvements on separate property entitle him or her to reimbursement unless the agreement expressly provides for such.[146] When an agreement requires a spouse to make cash payments to the other spouse during the marriage, purchase of an asset for him or her does not satisfy the obligation unless the agreement expressly allows for more than one way of complying.[147] Similarly, voluntary payments of support not required by an agreement do not fulfill a contractual support obligation; nor does a voluntary transfer of an asset during marriage fulfill an obligation to make a cash payment at dissolution.[148]

(j) Bona Fide Sale; Transfer to Third Party or to Trust

When a premarital agreement identifies and gives a party rights with respect to a particular asset, such as a shared home, a sale, or other disposition of that property may create a dispute at dissolution or death unless the agreement is carefully drafted or the parties agree to amend to take the change into account. For example, when a premarital agreement provides for a surviving spouse to receive a solely owned home of the other spouse at death, counsel should consider the possibility that the owner will mortgage the property, sell the home and not replace it, or sell and replace it with a home that will not meet the needs of the survivor. The agreement can address these contingencies,[149] including the possibility the owner will transfer the home to a revocable trust.[150] A party's action or inaction during the marriage with respect to his or her property interests described in the agreement may amount to a waiver or estoppel, unless the agreement, or an amendment or other instrument, specifically addresses how that interest is to be treated.[151]

(k) Gifts to and Support for Children, Former Spouses, and Other Family Members

Parties entering into a premarital or postmarital agreement often have preexisting legal or moral obligations to children, prior spouses, elderly parents, or others. Such parties will want

145. *See Bennett v. Bennett*, 103 A.D.3d 825, 960 N.Y.S.2d 179 (2013).

146. *Tsoucalas v. Tsoucalas*, 2013 Va. App. LEXIS 144 (unpub.).

147. *See Marinakos v. Cutlip*, 2011 Ariz. App. Unpub. LEXIS 1033.

148. *In re Marriage of Cutler*, 251 P.3d 112 (Kan. Ct. App. 2011).

149. *See Lund v. Lund*, 849 P.2d 731 (Wyo. 1993) (trial court's refusal to enforce premarital agreement giving wife rights in certain real estate sold during marriage was abuse of discretion where parties amended to provide for cash payment; sale of property did not render premarital agreement unenforceable); *see also Loewinger v. Loewinger*, 64 Va. App. 1, 763 S.E.2d 826 (2014) (husband sold home in which wife was entitled under premarital agreement to half of marital appreciation and used it to buy other assets; trial court made no award; appeal dismissed on other grounds).

150. *See In re Estate of Loftis*, 2015 Tex. App. LEXIS 10940 (unpub.) (surviving spouse entitled to home under terms of premarital agreement where husband had transferred it to his revocable trust).

151. *See Bickel v. Haley*, 2015 Ky. App. LEXIS 8 (unpub.) (husband waived claim to garage built on wife's land, and specifically identified as his in premarital agreement, when he joined in conveyance of land to wife's children and said nothing about his rights for 11 years).

to preserve their right to continue to meet these obligations without being penalized. The very reason many people seek a premarital agreement before entering into a subsequent marriage is to protect their estate for a child or other family members. When parties will maintain entirely separate estates, this should not be a concern. However, when parties will share some property interests, or a survivor will have the right to a percentage of the estate of the first to die, counsel should consider the potential effect of transfers.

Two cases in which the issue of transfers during life arose after the death of a party illustrate contrasting results. In *Stichter v. Zuidema*,[152] the premarital agreement gave the wife, but not the husband, the right to deal freely with her property as though she was unmarried. She had the right to one-fifth of his estate upon his death. During the marriage, he gave away $500,000 to one of his children.[153] The court held the agreement did not prohibit the husband from transferring property during his life. By contrast, in *Pierce v. Pierce*,[154] the parties' postmarital agreement provided for the husband to leave his entire estate to the wife and for the wife to give all her paychecks, save a small amount for her personal use, to the husband. During the marriage, the husband made substantial gratuitous transfers to third parties. In the trial court, the wife unsuccessfully sought to impose a constructive trust on the transferred property, arguing the agreement impliedly precluded such transfers. Ultimately, she prevailed on appeal. When a party contracts to leave a specified percentage of his or her estate to a spouse, that party impliedly promises not to make disproportionate *inter vivos* transfers.[155] But reliance on implied promises to preserve an estate intact is risky. In *Pierce*, the wife prevailed, but only after an appeal. Moreover, the husband's conduct was extreme. As seen in *Stichter*, a party disadvantaged by *inter vivos* transfers does not always prevail.[156]

(l) Remarriage After Death of Other Spouse

A surviving spouse with a premarital agreement may remarry. Unless he or she obtains a premarital agreement with the new spouse, the new spouse may acquire an elective share claim. If the premarital agreement requires the survivor to leave property to children or others upon his or her death, the new spouse's elective share claim may interfere with the rights of the intended beneficiaries of the original agreement. Or, a surviving spouse may make a will favoring a new spouse contrary to a premarital contract, make *inter vivos* gifts to the new spouse, or give away assets the parties agreed would go to others. The rights of a third-party beneficiary under a contract are generally held to trump the rights of a new spouse.[157] A court may impose a constructive trust to enforce the property rights of beneficiaries under a

---

152. 269 Ill. App. 3d 455, 646 N.E.2d 296 (1995).

153. The complainants in this case were other children and grandchildren, not the wife. The problem illustrated by the case would be the same, however, if it were the wife who complained.

154. 994 P.2d 193 (Utah 2000).

155. *Cohen v. Estate of Cohen*, 23 Ohio St. 3d 90, 491 N.E.2d 698 (1986); *Dubin v. Wise*, 41 Ill. App. 3d 132, 354 N.E.2d 403 (1976).

156. *See also Gianakos v. Magiros*, 234 Md. 14, 197 A.2d 897 (1964) (transfers by husband to children two and a half months before marriage, where husband retained control over transferred property, was not in fraud of wife's rights as widow).

157. *Gregory v. Estate of Gregory*, 315 Ark. 187, 866 S.W.2d 379 (1993); *Keats v. Cates*, 100 Ill. App. 2d 177, 241 N.E.2d 645 (1968); *Rubenstein v. Mueller*, 19 N.Y.2d 228, 225 N.E.2d 540, 278 N.Y.S.2d 845 (1967); *Sonnicksen v. Sonnicksen*, 45 Cal. App. 2d 46, 113 P.2d 495 (1941).

premarital contract when a will departs from the parties' agreement.[158] A better way to avert this problem is to provide in the premarital or postmarital agreement for the use of a trust for the benefit of the surviving spouse during his or her life. A trust can preserve assets for the ultimate beneficiaries while meeting the surviving spouse's needs during his or her life.

(m) Post-Death Transfer in Derogation of Contractual Obligations

Some agreements are created to provide for a surviving spouse and then to benefit third parties, such as a child or other family member, upon the survivor's death. When the survivor will control the entire estate until his or her death, his or her handling of property, or the acquisition of property rights of a new spouse or partner, may adversely affect the rights of the ultimate beneficiaries.[159] For example, in *Cline v. Graves*,[160] the premarital agreement provided each spouse would transfer property into joint ownership with right of survivorship, that they would execute reciprocal wills, and that upon the survivor's death the property would go to the husband's children and grandchildren. After the husband's death, the wife transferred substantially all of the inherited property to her family members through pay-on-death instruments so that when she died there was very little in her probate estate. The premarital agreement did not expressly commit the wife not to deplete the estate through *inter vivos* transfers, but the court had no trouble concluding that such a promise was implicit. The court observed:

> [T]he surviving spouse has a right to use and convey property covered by the agreement for all appropriate living expenses and maintenance, which could include even modest gifts. However, the surviving spouse cannot defeat the agreement by giving away all of the property without consideration by way of a disguised testamentary disposition.[161]

When the agreement allows a surviving spouse to control assets that are to go to third parties at his or her death, it is appropriate to include express restrictions on *inter vivos* gifts.

(n) Financial Mismanagement, Bad Investments, Frivolous Expenditures, Dissipation, and Other Financial Misconduct

When a premarital or postmarital agreement allows each party to retain all assets and income acquired by him or her before or after marriage, with mutual waivers of all rights at death or divorce, one party's financial misconduct may have little or no impact on the other party's contractual rights. However, when the agreement provides for sharing of assets acquired during the marriage, financial misconduct is a matter of concern. A variety of activities may

---

158. *Keats*, 100 Ill. App. 2d 177.

159. *See In re Chayka's Estate*, 47 Wis. 2d 102, 107, 176 N.W.2d 561, 564 (1970) (contract for joint will providing for all property to go to a designated person on death of survivor was violated when surviving wife gave away substantial portion of estate to new husband); *but see Patecky v. Friend*, 220 Or. 612, 350 P.2d 170 (1960) (contract to make joint will enforceable, but not necessarily against a new spouse without knowledge).

160. 641 S.W.2d 151 (Mo. Ct. App. 1982).

161. *Id.* at 154; *see also Estate of Draper v. Bank of America*, 205 P.3d 698 (Kan. 2009) (deceased wife violated duty of good faith implied in premarital agreement when she transferred almost all assets into irrevocable trusts that did not benefit husband's sons contrary to agreement providing husband would leave estate to her, and she would leave estate to his sons; constructive trust was appropriate remedy).

fall under the rubric of financial misconduct: conduct that may cause a party to lose money or property, sometimes because of culpable misconduct, sometimes because of ineptitude, sometimes a bit of each.

A divorce court may find dissipation when one spouse "uses marital property for his [or her] own benefit and for a purpose unrelated to the marriage at a time when the marriage is undergoing an irreconcilable breakdown."[162] Generalized financial misconduct over the course of the marriage is ordinarily insufficient to support a finding of dissipation. Generally, a party's expenditure of money, including using a line of credit secured by marital property, such as a home equity loan, to meet routine living expenses during marriage or after separation is not dissipation.[163] Further, parties have the right to use marital funds for extraordinary expenses, such as school tuition.[164] Expenditures that may ultimately benefit only one party, and monies spent on luxury items, do not constitute dissipation even though the result may be to diminish the marital/community estate.[165] Generally, parties in a marriage have the right to spend marital funds for their own enjoyment.[166]

Generally, a decision made in good faith that leads to a bad result, such as a decision to invest in a business that later fails, will not be deemed dissipation of assets.[167] A court may find that a highly speculative investment made during a marital breakdown was done in bad faith.[168] Activities, such as criminal conduct, that may cause loss of assets through forfeitures or expenditures on lawyers' fees, or gambling, may be deemed dissipation.[169] But crime and gambling will not always be found to be dissipation.[170] A transfer of assets to an irrevocable trust, to an offshore entity, or to a third party, for inadequate consideration, when done in anticipation of a divorce suit, or after suit has been filed, may constitute dissipation.[171] So may transfers to a paramour or monies spent in pursuit of an adulterous relationship.[172]

---

162. *Herron v. Johnson*, 714 A.2d 783, 786 (D.C. 1998) (citations omitted); *see also Gershman v. Gershman*, 286 Conn. 341, 943 A.2d 1091 (2008); *Jeffcoat v. Jeffcoat*, 102 Md. App. 301, 649 A.2d 1137 (1994); *In re Marriage of O'Neill*, 138 Ill. 2d 487, 563 N.E.2d 494 (1990).

163. *Amburn v. Amburn*, 13 Va. App. 661, 414 S.E.2d 847 (1992); *but see Robertson v. Loy*, 2022 Va. App. LEXIS 21 (unpub.) (wife's borrowing against equity in solely owned real estate that husband was entitled to receive under premarital agreement after separation notice was in breach of his rights).

164. *In re Marriage of Coyle*, 671 N.E.2d 938 (Ind. Ct. App. 1996).

165. *See Roberts v. Roberts*, 670 N.E.2d 72 (Ind. Ct. App. 1996) ("Each party to a marriage typically spends some part of marital funds for his or her own purposes."); *In re Marriage of Coyle*, 671 N.E.2d at 943.

166. *Kothari v. Kothari*, 255 N.J. Super. 500, 605 A.2d 750 (1992).

167. *McDavid v. McDavid*, 333 S.C. 490, 511 S.E.2d 365 (1999); *but see In re Marriage of DeVine*, 869 S.W.2d 415 (Tex. App. 1993) (investment losses chargeable to wife where she encouraged husband to invest in various development projects over many years without disclosing her romantic involvement with general partner).

168. *Gadomski v. Gadomski*, 245 A.D.2d 579, 664 N.Y.S.2d 886 (1997); *Booth v. Booth*, 7 Va. App. 22, 371 S.E.2d 569 (1988).

169. *Carrick v. Carrick*, 560 N.W.2d 407 (Minn. Ct. App. 1997); *DeLorenzo v. DeLorenzo*, 736 So. 2d 805 (Fla. Dist. Ct. App. 1999); *In re Marriage of Rodriguez*, 266 Kan. 347, 969 P.2d 880 (1998).

170. *See In re Marriage of Williams*, 84 Wn. App. 263, 927 P.2d 679 (1996) (wife's recreational gambling was not dissipation where she worked three jobs); *In re Marriage of O'Neill*, 138 Ill. 2d 487, 563 N.E.2d 494 (loss of assets resulting from rape charge that did not lead to marital separation until four years later was not dissipation).

171. *Riechers v. Riechers*, 178 Misc. 2d 170, 679 N.Y.S.2d 233 (Sup. Ct. 1998); *Maharam v. Maharam*, 245 A.D.2d 94, 666 N.Y.S.2d 129 (1997); *In re Marriage of Frederick*, 218 Ill. App. 3d 533, 578 N.E.2d 612 (1991); *Gaudio v. Gaudio*, 23 Conn. App. 287, 580 A.2d 1212 (1990).

172. *Osuna v. Quintana*, 993 S.W.2d 201 (Tex. App. 1999); *Beers v. Beers*, 724 So. 2d 109 (Fla. Dist. Ct. App. 1998); *Maharam*, 245 A.D.2d at 95, 666 N.Y.S.2d at 130.

At divorce, in the absence of agreement, when a court has determined a party has dissipated a marital asset, the court may treat the asset as though it is still extant and in the actual possession of the dissipating spouse. It may fashion a property award to compensate the innocent spouse by giving him or her a greater share of what remains or by entering a money judgment against the spouse who dissipated.[173] The cited cases arose at divorce where there was no premarital agreement. There is little guidance in the case law about what courts will do when a party with a premarital agreement raises a financial misconduct claim.

(o) Disproportionate Payment of Common Expenses; Payment of Other Spouse's Obligations

A premarital agreement does not preclude a spouse from paying all or a disproportionate share of common living expenses or paying expenses that are otherwise the responsibility of the other spouse. Parties may wish to include a provision in their agreement allocating some or all living expenses; or they may agree from time to time to an allocation, and evidence their agreement in a writing, which may be less formal than an amendment to the agreement. If they do not, a party's voluntary payment of such expenses does not generally create an enforceable claim against the spouse who benefited.[174]

(p) Bankruptcy

A party who agrees in a premarital or postmarital agreement to make transfers of cash or property to the spouse in the event of a marital separation or divorce may seek to discharge these obligations in a bankruptcy proceeding.[175] Such a debt may be dischargeable or not. The Bankruptcy Code defines a Domestic Support Obligation (DSO) as a debt to spouse or former spouse "in the nature of alimony, maintenance, or support . . . of such spouse [or] former spouse . . . without regard to whether such debt is expressly so designated;" and that is "established or subject to establishment . . . by reason of applicable provisions of—(i) a separation agreement, divorce decree, or property settlement agreement; (ii) an order of a court of record. . . ."[176] A DSO is an exception to the right to a discharge under Chapters 7, 11, 12, and 13 of the Bankruptcy Code, so that a debt found to be a DSO is not dischargeable.[177] Whether the parties intended a contractual obligation to make one or more cash payments to be support or a property settlement is not always obvious. The court must determine if the payment obligation is in the nature of alimony as a matter of federal law, although it looks to state law concepts of alimony and property division to make this determination.[178] The court must look to a number of factors to determine parties' intent, including whether it terminates upon death or remarriage, and whether the obligation is essential to enable the payee to meet

173. *Beers*, 724 So. 2d 109; *Herron*, 714 A.2d 783, 786; *Maharam*, 245 A.D.2d at 95, 666 N.Y.S.2d at 130; *Nedblake v. Nedblake*, 682 S.W.2d 852 (Mo. Ct. App. 1984).

174. See In re Est. of Noel, 965 N.W.2d 192 (Iowa Ct. App. 2021).

175. *See* SHAYNA & BRUCE STEINFELD, THE FAMILY LAWYER'S GUIDE TO BANKRUPTCY (4th ed., ABA 2018).

176. 11 U.S.C. § 101(14A). The Code definition of DSO also includes child support, which is beyond the scope of the discussion here.

177. 11 U.S.C. § 523(d); *see also* STEINFELD, *supra* note 175, at 9.

178. STEINFELD, *supra* note 175, at 148; *see also DeStefano v. DeStefano* (*In re Stefano*), 2013 Bankr. LEXIS 4764 (D.N.J.).

his or her basic needs.[179] The distinction is important because DSOs are automatically non-dischargeable.[180] By contrast, a property settlement obligation is non-dischargeable under Chapters 7, 11, and 12; however, a debtor who is able to carry out a Chapter 13 plan can discharge a non-DSO property settlement.[181] The lawyer for an economically weaker party should consider the potential for financial reverses that may affect his or her client's ability to enforce the bargained-for rights under the agreement.

Parties are bound by the terms of their premarital or postmarital agreement when a spouse files for bankruptcy. For example, when an agreement provides that a joint account is marital or community property, the parties are bound by that provision, regardless of their intent in creating joint accounts, for purposes of determining the property rights of the debtor-spouse and the nondebtor-spouse.[182]

The Bankruptcy Code does not expressly include the term "premarital agreement" in describing the types of instruments giving rise to a claim of nondischargeability. However, courts have held that the text of the statutes includes this type of agreement.[183]

179. STEINFELD, *supra* note 175, at 14.

180. *See Sparks v. Sparks* (*In re Sparks*), 206 B.R. 481, 1997 Bankr. LEXIS 334, Bankr. Ct. N.D. Ill, E.D. (Mar. 24, 1997) (debtor not entitled to summary judgment that wife's right under premarital agreement to cash payment tied to length of marriage was property settlement and not support; court must determine based on all relevant facts); *Vaudreuil v. Busconi*, 182 B.R. 618, 1995 U.S. Dist. LEXIS 8023 (D. Mass. 1995) (debtor not entitled to summary judgment that his support obligation under premarital agreement was dischargeable as a property settlement where there was genuine issue whether parties intended payments as support or property settlement).

181. 11 U.S.C. § 523(a)(15); STEINFELD, *supra* note 175, at 11–12.

182. *See In re David Folsom*, 2011 U.S. Dist. LEXIS 88181 (S.D. Cal.).

183. *Davis v. Saulsbury* (*In re Saulsbury*), 2012 Bankr. LEXIS 5251 (N.D.N.Y.).

PART

II

Role of Counsel, Ethics, Negotiation, and Drafting the Agreement

9 Ethical Issues in the Representation of Clients in Premarital and Postmarital Agreements

§9.01 Overview

This chapter addresses ethics issues that may arise in the representation of a party to a premarital or postmarital agreement, including

- Dealing with a client whose capacity may be diminished;
- Dealing with an unrepresented party;
- Lawyer competence, particularly in the representation of the weaker party;
- Representation of both parties to an agreement (*i.e.*, joint representation);
- Avoiding participation in client fraud or other inappropriate conduct in the negotiation of an agreement; and
- The lawyer as mediator.

Unethical behavior on the part of a lawyer for one of the parties is not an independent basis for attacking the validity of an agreement, nor does it create an independent cause of action for legal malpractice.[1] However, lawyer misconduct may cause a court to deem an agreement the product of undue influence,[2] or may require the court to invalidate the agreement for failing to adhere to statutory requirements,

1. *See Wiebel v. Morris*, 2009 U.S. Dist. LEXIS 46088 (D.N.J. 2009).

2. *See Parr v. Parr*, 635 N.E.2d 1124, 1127 (Ind. Ct. App. 1994); *Faiman v. Faiman*, 2008 Conn. Super. LEXIS 3078 (unpub.) (handpicked lawyer for wife negotiated changes to agreement drafted by husband's lawyer without ever communicating with wife until day of signing; agreement invalid); *see also Rhoualmi v. Shelton*, 963 So. 2d 232 (Fla. Ct. App. 2007), denying review of a trial court judgment against a woman who claimed to have entered into a premarital agreement with the decedent and then married him. The trial court opinion (unpublished) described a series of events in which the wife, with the participation of a lawyer, took advantage of an elderly incapacitated man to obtain the premarital agreement, enter into a sham marriage, and gain control over his assets. The trial court voided the marriage, the premarital agreement, and the property transfers.

such as witness signatures.[3] The combination of improper joint representation and other factors, such as inadequate disclosure, can cause a court to invalidate an agreement.[4] Incompetent lawyering may expose the lawyer to a claim of malpractice or a violation of the Rules of Professional Conduct even when the validity of the agreement is upheld.[5] It goes without saying that it is never in the lawyer's best interest to put his or her livelihood and reputation at risk for a client looking to cut corners in the negotiation of a premarital or postmarital agreement.

Estate of Campbell v. Chaney[6] was a malpractice action against a drafting lawyer filed after the deceased husband's estate settled the widow's challenge to the validity of a premarital agreement. The lawyer's experts testified the widow's claim would have failed had it been tried. The court rejected the lawyer's summary judgment motion, holding that the alleged deficiencies in the process leading to execution provided a basis on which a trier of fact could find that the estate suffered a loss when it settled a case whose outcome was not certain. The estate did not have to prove the widow's claim of invalidity would have succeeded in order to prevail against the lawyer. Rather, the court held:

> *The negligence of an attorney does not depend on whether the agreement can be enforced.* If an attorney drafts a prenuptial agreement without attaching a financial statement, the fact-finder could conclude that the attorney failed to use reasonable care, that is, that the attorney was negligent. It is immaterial that the agreement might later be enforced after a finding that the widow already knew the financial information. The fact-finder could still find that the attorney failed to exercise reasonable care in drafting the agreement. If that failure caused the estate to settle a claim that a proper agreement would have made meritless, then the attorney may be held liable.[7]

The discussion that follows is concerned with ethics issues of particular interest in the drafting and negotiation of premarital and postmarital agreements. A variety of other ethical obligations come into play, as they do in any representation, including the duty to maintain client confidences,[8] to protect attorney-client privilege in the event of future litigation,[9] to provide

---

3. *See Frederick v. Wallerich*, 907 N.W.2d 167 (Minn. 2018) (malpractice suit against lawyer who drafted premarital agreement without statutorily required witness signatures).

4. *See In re Estate of Benker*, 416 Mich. 681, 331 N.W.2d 193 (1982); *see also Weidel v. Weidel*, 2021 N.J. Super. Unpub. LEXIS 2829 (lawyer conflict of interest plus other deficiencies; premarital agreement invalid).

5. *Friezo v. Friezo*, 281 Conn. 166, 914 A.2d 533 (2007); *DeMatteo v. DeMatteo*, 436 Mass. 18, 762 N.E.2d 797 (2002); *Price v. Price*, 289 A.D.2d 11, 733 N.Y.S.2d 420 (2001); *see also Sherman v. Ellis*, 246 A.3d 1126 (Del. 2021); *Watts v.* Goetz, 311 So. 3d 253 (Fla. Dist. Ct. App. 2020); *Natan v. Law Offices of Karol & Velen*, 2018 Cal. App. Unpub. LEXIS 870.

6. 169 Wis. 2d 399, 485 N.W.2d 421 (Ct. App. 1992).

7. *Id.* at 410, 425 (emphasis added); *see also Pope v. Zanetis*, 2002 U.S. Dist. LEXIS 4551 (S.D. Ind. Feb. 22, 2002) (statute of limitations on legal malpractice arising out of premarital agreement did not accrue until divorce); *Greene v. Morgan, Theeler, Cogley & Petersen*, 575 N.W.2d 457 (S.D. 1998) (summary judgment should not have been granted lawyer in former client's suit over validity where lawyer failed to advise client that otherwise valid agreement was not enforceable as to wife's alimony waiver); *Brust v. Newton*, 70 Wash. App. 286, 852 P.2d 1092 (1993) (lack of disclosure and other factors caused husband to settle wife's suit over validity of agreement resulting in jury verdict against husband's lawyer).

8. MRPC 1.6 (Confidentiality of Information).

9. *See Pagliara v. Pagliara*, 2020 Tenn. App. LEXIS 299 (unpub.) (unreported) (wife not entitled to shield attorney-client communications from discovery where she insisted third party attend meetings with lawyer).

competent and diligent representation,[10] to charge a reasonable fee,[11] and to refuse to assist a client to perpetrate a fraud.[12]

§9.02 DEALING WITH A CLIENT WHOSE CAPACITY TO CONTRACT MAY BE DIMINISHED

The proper conduct of a representation when the client's mental capacity may be diminished is a problem with no easy solution. The question of client capacity may present itself under a variety of circumstances, including:

- A potential client with whom the lawyer has no prior relationship may seek representation in connection with a premarital or postmarital agreement, or the other party to the proposed agreement, or a third party, such as an adult child, seeks such representation on behalf of the client. After undertaking the representation, the lawyer may come to suspect the client is impaired.
- An existing client who evidences some diminution in mental capacity seeks representation in connection with a premarital or postmarital agreement, an amendment to an agreement, or an agreement to revoke an existing agreement.
- A couple with whom the lawyer has an existing lawyer-client relationship seeks representation in connection with a postmarital agreement (or an amendment or revocation of an existing premarital agreement) where it appears one member of the couple may have diminished capacity.

The question is not simply whether the client is entirely lacking in legal capacity to contract. A client's capacity may be diminished but not entirely lacking. Such a person may be vulnerable to fraud or undue influence as well as physical harm. Indeed, the ABA Model Rules recognize that a client's capacity to make decisions may be diminished as a result of being at risk of physical harm. The issues that a lawyer for a client whose capacity may be diminished must consider include these:

- Does a new client with whom the lawyer has no prior relationship have sufficient capacity to form a lawyer-client relationship?[13]
- Can the lawyer continue an attorney-client relationship with an existing client whose capacity may be diminished?
- Can the lawyer engage in, or continue, a joint representation?
- What steps can the lawyer take to assess client capacity?
- What information can the lawyer reveal, and to whom, to assess client capacity?

---

10. MRPC 1.1 (Competence), 1.3 (Diligence).
11. MRPC 1.5 (Fees).
12. *See Idaho State Bar v. Smith*, 513 P.3d 1154 (Idaho 2022).
13. *Proceedings of the Conference on Ethical Issues in Representing Older Clients; Report of the Working Group on Client Capacity*, 62 FORDHAM L. REV. 1003, 1004 (Mar. 1994) (hereafter, *Report of the Working Group on Client Capacity*); ABA Formal Op. 96-404 (1996); MODEL RULES OF PRO. CONDUCT r. 1.14 (Client Under a Disability) cmt. [1] (AM. BAR ASS'N 2013); *see also* Charles P. Sabatino, *Representing a Client with Diminished Capacity: How Do You Know It* and *What Do You Do about It?* 16 J.A.A.M.L. 481 (2000).

- What steps can the lawyer take to protect the client if the lawyer determines that protective steps are necessary, and what information can the lawyer reveal to take protective action?

In some circumstances the client may be so incapacitated that he or she cannot form or continue a lawyer-client relationship.[14] Where the client does not wholly lack capacity, or where the lawyer already has a relationship with the client when diminution in capacity comes to light, most authorities advocate staying with the representation rather than withdrawing.[15] This necessarily means the lawyer must "accept responsibility for determining when to question capacity and how to respond appropriately to the situation."[16] In questioning capacity, the lawyer is advised to consider the following:

- The client's ability to articulate reasoning behind a decision;
- The variability of the client's state of mind;
- The client's ability to appreciate consequences of the decision;
- The irreversibility of the decision;
- The substantive fairness of the decision; and
- The consistency of the decision with lifetime commitments of the client.[17]

The lawyer is further advised to speak with the client alone.[18] This is particularly important when there are any indicators that the client may be under pressure or at risk of physical harm from a spouse, paramour, family member, or someone else in a position of trust. The factors identified above recognize that "when the consequences of a decision are greater in terms of irreversibility, fairness to interested parties, and deviance from lifetime commitments of the client, then it is clinically and ethically appropriate to expect a higher level of functioning on the first three variables."[19]

ABA Model Rule 1.14 addresses the lawyer's role in dealing with client incapacity in several important respects.[20] First, the rule allows the lawyer to act to protect a client's interests when the client's capacity is diminished; the client need not be wholly lacking in legal capacity. Second, the lawyer's options for protecting the client include seeking appointment of a guardian as well as actions short of seeking such an appointment, which may be far more intrusive than necessary. This can include "consulting with individuals or entities that have the ability to take action to protect the client. . . ."[21] Appropriate indi-

14. *Report of the Working Group on Client Capacity*, at 1004; *see also Donnelly v. Parker*, 158 U.S. App. D.C. 335, 486 F.2d 402, 407 n.20 (D.C. Cir. 1973) (client's insanity or severe mental difficulty may operate to suspend or terminate preexisting attorney-client relationship); *In re Houts*, 7 Wash. App. 476, 499 P.2d 1276 (1972) (client's incompetency terminates lawyer's authority to act).

15. Model Rules of Pro. Conduct r. 1.14 (2013); ABA Formal Op. 96-404 (1996) (Client Under a Disability); *Report of the Working Group on Client Capacity*, at 1009.

16. *Report of the Working Group on Client Capacity*, at 1005.

17. *Id.* at 1007; *see also* MRPC 1.14 cmt. [6] (2013).

18. *Report of the Working Group on Client Capacity*, at 1007.

19. *Id.*

20. MRPC 1.14 (Client with Diminished Capacity) (a) (2013): "When a client's capacity to make adequately considered decisions in connection with a representation is diminished, whether because of minority, mental impairment or for some other reason, the lawyer shall, as far as reasonably possible, maintain a normal client-lawyer relationship with the client."

21. MRPC 1.14(b) (2013).

viduals may include family members and medical providers. In cases where the lawyer has reason to believe the client or potential client has been the victim of domestic violence, an adult protective services agency may be an appropriate entity from which to seek protection on behalf of the client. Third, the lawyer may reveal client confidences to the extent necessary to protect the client's interests.[22]

In deciding whether to take protective action, and what action to take, the lawyer should be guided by the goals of respecting the wishes and values of the client, to the extent known, otherwise, according to the client's best interest; intruding into the client's decision-making autonomy to the least extent possible; maximizing client capacities; and maximizing family and social connections and community resources.[23]

In sum, a lawyer faced with a client who may be impaired and who seeks to execute a premarital or postmarital agreement, or to amend or cancel an agreement,[24] must weigh the extent of the client's functioning, with the assistance of a diagnostician in appropriate cases,[25] as it relates to the particular terms sought, and other relevant factors. When a client who may be impaired has been asked to execute an agreement, including a revocation of an agreement, that appears highly unfavorable to the client, or to his or her children, the situation calls for caution.[26] In some instances, the lawyer may need to seek appointment of a guardian to obtain court approval of the agreement.[27]

§9.03 ROLE OF COUNSEL FOR THE PROPONENT IN DEALING WITH AN UNREPRESENTED PARTY

(a) Advice to Unrepresented Party to Get Independent Counsel

When the economically weaker party is represented by counsel, it is that lawyer's responsibility to protect his or her client's interests.[28] However, when the weaker party does not have counsel, counsel for the proponent must take a more active role in dealing with the other party in order to further the interest of the proponent in securing the agreement from a successful attack on validity. This is particularly important when there is a substantial disparity in economic power and the proposed terms will perpetuate the disparity.

22. *Id.* at 1.14.

23. *Report of the Working Group on Client Capacity*, at 1009; MRPC 1.14 cmt. [5].

24. *See In re Estate of Goldberg*, 153 Misc. 2d 560, 582 N.Y.S.2d 617 (Sur. Ct. 1992) (higher contractual capacity, rather than lower testamentary capacity, required to execute postmarital agreement cancelling premarital agreement).

25. *See* ABA Informal Op. 89-1530, 5 *ABA/BNA Lawyers' Manual of Professional Conduct* 360 (Oct. 8, 2009) (lawyer may consult client's physician to determine whether client is able to make informed decision about representation; disclosure to physician of otherwise confidential information impliedly authorized by Model Rule 1.6 to carry out representation).

26. *See Farnum v. Silvano*, 27 Mass. App. Ct. 536, 540 N.E.2d 202 (1989); *Knowlton v. Mudd*, 116 Idaho 262, 775 P.2d 154 (Ct. App. 1989).

27. *See In re Estate of Soper*, 598 S.W.2d 528 (Mo. Ct. App. 1980) (guardian appointed for purpose of obtaining court approval of estate planning for incompetent spouse).

28. *Head v. Head*, 59 Md. App. 570, 477 A.2d 282 (1984).

In *Bonds v. Bonds*,[29] the California Supreme Court upheld a premarital agreement, finding it was voluntary notwithstanding the wife's lack of independent counsel. There was a substantial factual basis for the trial court's finding of voluntariness. The intermediate appeals court was critical of the conduct of the husband's lawyers for failing to explain to the wife that her interests conflicted with the husband's, for failing to urge her to retain independent counsel, and for explaining the agreement to the wife paragraph by paragraph, which may have misled her to think they represented both parties.[30] Similarly, in *Serbus' Estate v. Serbus*,[31] the drafting lawyer did not advise the wife to obtain separate counsel, nor did he discuss with the wife the nature or value of the husband's property, and the husband did not make a written disclosure. In both cases, the agreement was vulnerable; the proponent prevailed but was forced to litigate validity through appeal. These cases point out how precautions in dealing with an unrepresented party may reduce litigation risk.

Counsel should explain—preferably in writing—his or her role as lawyer solely for the proponent and should encourage the other party to obtain independent advice concerning the agreement.[32] The advice to retain counsel should be forceful and unequivocal. It should not be coupled with contradictory messages that may discourage the unrepresented party from getting independent advice. For example, in *In re Marriage of Matson*,[33] the parties met with the husband's lawyer twice. Only at the second meeting the day before the wedding, scheduled for the purpose of executing the agreement, did the lawyer suggest that either party could have "someone else"[34] look at it. The lawyer never explained to the wife, and she did not understand, how much she was disadvantaged by the agreement. The court held the agreement was involuntary. Here the lawyer's equivocal, eleventh-hour suggestion to the wife that she get independent advice fell far short of what the situation called for to protect the interests of the husband. Had the lawyer urged the wife to get independent counsel at the first meeting, the result could have been different.[35]

In *In re Marriage of Foran*,[36] the court discussed the dilemma faced by a lawyer for the economically stronger party. It noted the primary purpose of independent counsel for the weaker party is to negotiate a fair contract, not merely to explain how unfair the proposed agreement is. Thus, if the stronger party's lawyer is successful in convincing the weaker party to obtain counsel, the stronger party may have to make economic concessions. However, the

29. 24 Cal. 4th 1, 5 P.3d 815 (2000).

30. *Bonds* has been legislatively overruled. California Family Code § 1615(c) requires independent counsel, or an express, written waiver. California Family Code § 1612 requires independent counsel for an effective alimony waiver.

31. 324 N.W.2d 381 (Minn. 1982).

32. *See McKee-Johnson v. Johnson*, 444 N.W.2d 259 (Minn. 1989); *see also Owen v. Owen*, 759 S.E.2d 468 (W. Va. 2014) (wife did not have opportunity for independent legal advice where agreement presented the day of signing in office of husband's lawyer, despite lawyer's testimony he advised her he represented only husband and where agreement contained untrue recital that wife had assistance of counsel); *In re Estate of Lutz*, 563 N.W.2d 90, 98 (N.D. 1997) ("[l]ack of adequate legal advice to a prospective spouse to obtain independent counsel is a significant factor in weighing the voluntariness of a premarital agreement"); see Appendix G for model letters to an unrepresented party.

33. 107 Wn. 2d 479, 730 P.2d 668 (1986).

34. *Id.* at 481, 669.

35. *See also Button v. Button*, 131 Wis. 2d 84, 388 N.W.2d 546 (1986) (husband's lawyer told wife she could have independent counsel, but that doing so would show she did not trust husband or his lawyer; agreement invalid).

36. 67 Wash. App. 242, 834 P.2d 1081 (1992).

alternative, not advising the party forcefully enough to get counsel, may undermine the validity of the entire agreement. Counsel for the stronger party should explain the benefits to that party of the lawyer urging the weaker party to get a lawyer. The benefits for the proponent far outweigh the disadvantages.[37]

(b) Assistance to Unrepresented Party in Selection of Counsel

There are a variety of ways by which counsel for the proponent may assist the other party to find a lawyer for the representation. He or she could provide information about local referral networks, such as a bar association service, or about online resources. If the weaker party has a will, the lawyer could recommend returning to the estate planning lawyer for representation or a referral. There is no ethical prohibition on counsel for a proponent providing the other party with the names of lawyers whom he or she may consider hiring for the representation. The mere fact that the proponent's lawyer recommended a lawyer to the other party does not demonstrate duress or overreaching.[38]

ABA Model Rule 8.4(c) (2013) prohibits a lawyer from making a statement that is deceptive or misleading. A number of cases where validity of an agreement was in dispute involved a party, or his or her lawyer, handpicking a lawyer for the weaker party without telling the party that he or she had a choice.[39] This fact alone has not resulted in an agreement being held the product of duress or undue influence, but it could when combined with other bad facts.[40] Whether a disciplinary authority might decide that a recommendation is deceptive or misleading when the lawyer fails to make express that other party is not obliged to choose the recommended lawyer is a separate issue. The better practice is for the lawyer providing a referral to clearly communicate that the other party is free to choose his or her lawyer and is not limited to the recommended lawyers. Ideally, the proponent's lawyer would provide a referral only if requested to do so. The proponent's lawyer can advise his or her client to pass along to the fiancé(e) that his or her lawyer will provide referrals if asked.[41]

The reporters are full of cases where a court upheld the validity of an agreement despite the overinvolvement of the lawyer for the proponent in the selection of a lawyer for the opposing party and the apparent willingness of that lawyer to participate in a process that restricted his or her ability to provide meaningful legal advice.[42] These cases illustrate the point made in Section 9.01 that a deficiency in the quality of the services of the weaker party's lawyer will not necessarily cause a court to hold an agreement to be invalid. However, it may expose the lawyer to a complaint of ethical misconduct or malpractice.[43]

---

37. See Section 4.06 for further discussion.
38. *Barocas v. Barocas*, 94 A.D.3d 551, 942 N.Y.S.2d 491 (2012).
39. *See, e.g., Spiegel v. Spiegel*, 206 A.D.3d 1178, 170 N.Y.S.3d 295 (2022); *Fordeley v. Fordeley*, 2020 Ohio 5380 (Ct. App.) (unpub.); *see also Miller v. Miller*, 2022 Md. App. LEXIS 813 (unpub.) (husband's lawyer provided names of five lawyers).
40. *Spiegel*, 206 A.D.3d 1178, 170 N.Y.S.3d 295.
41. See Appendix G, Letters to Unrepresented Party.
42. See also Section 4.06(d).
43. *See Zimmie v. Calfee, Halter & Griswold*, 43 Ohio St. 3d 54, 538 N.E.2d 398 (1989) (statute of limitations on legal malpractice claim arising out of lawyer's arguably deficient handling of financial disclosure for premarital agreement began to run when trial judge in parties' suit for divorce held premarital agreement invalid).

(c) Payment of Fees of Unrepresented Party

When there is a significant disparity in the parties' resources, counsel for the stronger party should discuss with his or her client paying the fees for the weaker party to retain counsel. For some weaker parties, hiring counsel may not be viable unless the other party pays the fees. There is no prohibition on the proponent paying the other party's legal fees.[44] Indeed, some authorities come close to requiring that he or she do so; even where there is no mandate, it will often be in the best interests of both parties that the stronger party pay the weaker party's fees. The lawyer for the weaker party under these circumstances must abide by the obligation of MRPC 1.8:

> (f) A lawyer shall not accept compensation for representing a client from one other than the client unless:
>
> (1) the client gives informed consent;
>
> (2) there is no interference with the lawyer's independence of professional judgment or with the client-lawyer relationship; and
>
> (3) information relating to representation of a client is protected as required by Rule 1.6 [Confidentiality of Information].[45]

The Uniform Premarital and Marital Agreements Act (UPMAA) makes access to counsel a requirement for validity of a premarital or marital agreement.[46] Access to counsel includes sufficient funds to hire a lawyer.[47] In some cases, this may require that the proponent of the agreement pay the fees of the other party in order to make his or her right to access to counsel meaningful. The UPMAA approach, though only adopted in two states to date, Colorado and North Dakota, reflects best practices.

(d) Meeting with Unrepresented Party; Providing Explanation of Rights

If the other party to a premarital or postmarital agreement opts not to retain counsel, despite being urged to do so, counsel for the proponent must consider whether to meet with the unrepresented party, and whether to meet with that party alone or together with the proponent, for the purpose of explaining the agreement and answering questions. Meeting with the unrepresented party alone poses risks for both counsel and the proponent. For example, in *Sumpter v. Kosinski*,[48] the lawyer met with the wife alone. The wife later claimed the lawyer told her she would be well provided for through a new will, a claim the lawyer denied. Had the court credited the wife's claim, it might well have invalidated the agreement.

Some courts have approved of the proponent's lawyer meeting with an unrepresented party to explain the agreement,[49] or have considered the failure of the proponent's lawyer to

---

44. *Id.*

45. *See also* MRPC 5.4(c) (lawyer shall not permit person who pays the lawyer for services for another to direct or regulate the lawyer's professional judgment).

46. UPMAA § 9(a)(2) (2012).

47. *Id.*, § 9(b).

48. 165 Mich. App. 784, 419 N.W.2d 463 (1988).

49. *Bonds v. Bonds*, 24 Cal. 4th 1, 5 P.3d 815 (2000); *Randolph v. Randolph*, 937 S.W.2d 815 (Tenn. 1996); *Penhallow v. Penhallow*, 649 A.2d 1016 (R.I. 1994); *Martin v. Martin*, 612 So. 2d 1230 (Ala. Civ. App. 1992); *In*

review the terms of the agreement with an unrepresented party as a factor in determining that the agreement is invalid.[50] As one court observed:

> It is consistent with an attorney's duty to further the interest of his or her client for the attorney to take steps to ensure that the premarital agreement will be enforceable. After discussing the matter with his or her client, an attorney may convey such information to the other party as will assist in having the agreement upheld, as long as he or she does not violate the duty of loyalty to the client or undertake to represent both parties without an appropriate waiver of the conflict of interest.[51]

The proponent's lawyer may explain the terms of the proposed agreement to an unrepresented party without giving advice to him or her; at least some courts take that approach.[52] A translation of the agreement from conventional legal contract language into plain English may be all that is called for under the circumstances. An explanation that includes a discussion about spousal rights at death or divorce in the absence of an enforceable agreement and how the agreement alters those rights may well be a step too fair. The complexity of the law of property rights at death and divorce makes any explanation risky because it will almost never be adequate. For example, in *Azarova v. Schmitt*,[53] the wife was Ukrainian and did not have separate counsel. There were several deficiencies in the process. Among them, the court faulted the husband's lawyer for explaining that the wife would have no right to the appreciation of the husband's premarital property but failing to explain the difference between active and passive appreciation.

The better practice is not to meet with the unrepresented party in person other than to oversee execution and preferably with a notary present. Counsel may provide a written, limited explanation of rights.[54] A written explanation can eliminate the risk of differing recollections but will not solve the problem of the adequacy of the explanation. If the proponent's lawyer does choose to provide an in-person explanation of the terms of a premarital or postmarital agreement and their effect on the unrepresented party, he or she must strike a delicate balance between saying too much and not saying enough. ABA Model Rule 4.3 provides some guidance:

> In dealing on behalf of a client with a person who is not represented by counsel, a lawyer shall not state or imply that the lawyer is disinterested. When the lawyer knows or reasonably should know that the unrepresented person misunderstands the lawyer's role in the matter, the lawyer shall make reasonable efforts to correct the misunderstanding. The lawyer shall not give legal advice to an unrepresented person, other than the advice to secure counsel, if the lawyer knows or reasonably should

---

re Marriage of Leathers, 309 Or. 625, 789 P.2d 263 (1990); *In re Estate of Hartman*, 399 Pa. Super. 386, 582 A.2d 648 (1990); *McKee-Johnson v. Johnson*, 144 N.W.2d 259 (Minn. 1989); *Warren v. Warren*, 169 Ill. App. 3d 226, 523 N.E.2d 680 (1988); *Serbus' Estate v. Serbus*, 324 N.W.2d 381 (Minn. 1982).

50. *See In re Estate of Eichstadt*, 983 N.W.2d 572 (S.D. 2022).

51. *Bonds v. Bonds*, 24 Cal. 4th 1, 31, 5 P.3d 815, 833 (2000).

52. *In re Estate of Eichstadt*, 983 N.W.2d 572 (S.D. 2022) (had proponent's lawyer explained terms of proposed premarital agreement to wife, as distinguished from giving advice, that would not have been a joint representation prohibited by Rule 1.7)

53. 2007 Ohio App. LEXIS 586 (unpub.).

54. See Appendix G.

> know that the interests of such a person are or have a reasonable possibility of being in conflict with the interests of the client.[55]

The comment adds the following:

> Whether a lawyer is giving impermissible advice may depend on the experience and sophistication of the unrepresented person, as well as the setting in which the behavior and comments occur. This Rule does not prohibit a lawyer from negotiating the terms of a transaction . . . with an unrepresented person. So long as the lawyer has explained that the lawyer represents an adverse party and is not representing the person, the lawyer may inform the person of the terms on which the lawyer's client will enter into an agreement . . . , prepare documents that require the person's signature and explain the lawyer's own view of the meaning of the document or the lawyer's view of the underlying legal obligations.[56]

Counsel for the proponent should not advise the other party whether the agreement is fair or reasonable, whether it is in the best interests of that party to sign it, whether disclosure is adequate, or whether the agreement will be enforceable. The giving of advice creates an attorney-client relationship.[57] Discussing the subject of the transaction with an unrepresented party does not create such a relationship.[58]

In communicating with the unrepresented party, counsel must take care not to leave the impression that he or she is acting for both parties or is acting as a neutral. For example, in *Rowland v. Rowland*,[59] the premarital agreement probably would have been upheld if the lawyer had not met with the wife and had merely handed her the agreement to sign. It was his blurring of his own role by inviting questions without delineating the limits on his role that caused the court to void the agreement.

(e) Dealing with an Unrepresented Party with Whom the Lawyer Has a Prior Relationship

When the lawyer for the proponent and the unrepresented party have a prior lawyer-client relationship, it is particularly important that the lawyer who meets, or otherwise communicates, with that party clearly delineate the limits on his or her role. In such a situation, that party may misunderstand the lawyer's obligation of loyalty to the lawyer's client and may mistakenly believe the lawyer will act to protect the interests of both. In *Fletcher v. Fletcher*,[60] for example, the parties had been represented in their divorces from their previous spouses by members of the same law firm, one of whom then represented the husband in connection with the premarital agreement. The wife was advised she could have separate counsel, but she declined. The husband's lawyer met with the wife and gave her some explanation of the terms of the agreement, but he did not fully explain her marital rights and how those rights would be

55. MRPC 4.3.
56. MRPC 4.3 cmt. [2].
57. *Bohn v. Cody*, 119 Wn. 2d 357, 363, 832 P.2d 71, 75 (1992).
58. *Id.* at 364, 75.
59. 74 Ohio App. 3d 415, 599 N.E.2d 315 (1991).
60. 628 N.E.2d 1343 (Ohio 1994).

affected by the agreement. The wife claimed the husband's lawyer gave her misleading information about her right to equitable distribution upon divorce. The agreement was upheld, but the appellate court observed that there was sufficient evidence to support a decision voiding the agreement had the trial court so ruled. By contrast, in *Simon v. Smith,*[61] a longtime lawyer for a party for business matters represented the other party for a postmarital agreement. Such a clear conflict of interest caused the court to void the agreement.[62]

The lawyer's ethical obligations are implicated when the other party is a former client for whom the lawyer provided domestic relations representation or estate planning services,[63] or advice regarding a family business.

Rule 1.9 Duties to Former Clients

(a) A lawyer who has formerly represented a client in a matter shall not thereafter represent another person in the same or a substantially related matter in which that person's interests are materially adverse to the interests of the former client unless the former client gives informed consent, confirmed in writing.

. . . .

(c) A lawyer who has formerly represented a client in a matter or whose present or former firm has formerly represented a client in a matter shall not thereafter:

(1) use information relating to the representation to the disadvantage of the former client except as these Rules would permit or require with respect to a client, or when the information has become generally known; or

(2) reveal information relating to the representation except as these Rules would permit or require with respect to a client.[64]

Under some circumstances, a representation like that which occurred in *Fletcher* might well be deemed substantially related under R. 1.9(a), or to involve the use of client confidences under R. 1.9(c).[65] Such a conflict is waivable but only with informed consent.[66] In the *Fletcher* opinion, for example, there was a discussion about whether the wife knew her rights incident to divorce. Had that been a determinative issue in the case, her prior divorce counsel's knowledge of the extent of her understanding of marital rights at divorce—knowledge

61. 273 A.3d 321 (D.C. 2022).

62. See also *Sogg v. Nevada State Bank*, 832 P.2d 781 (Nev. 1992) (husband's lawyer represented wife in her divorce, selected a lawyer for her and made appointment, never told her she could select her own lawyer; prior lawyer-client relationship contributed to the court's decision to void premarital agreement).

63. *See Pope v. Zanetis,* 2002 U.S. Dist. LEXIS 4551 (S.D. Ind. 2022) (determining accrual of cause of action for legal malpractice where lawyer represented both unmarried parties for estate planning, then only husband for premarital agreement).

64. MRPC 1.9.

65. *See Mathias v. Mathias*, 188 Wis. 2d 280, 525 N.W.2d 81 (Ct. App. 1994); *Demis v. Demis*, 168 A.D.2d 840, 564 N.Y.S.2d 515 (1990); *Cleland v. Cleland*, 404 A.2d 905 (Conn. Super. Ct. 1979); *Gardine v. Cottey*, 230 S.W.2d 731 (Mo. 1950); *see also In re Wilder*, 764 N.E.2d 617 (Ind. 2002).

66. MRPC 1.9(a); *see also id.* 1.7(a)(2), defining concurrent conflict of interest to include "a significant risk that the representation . . . will be materially limited by the lawyer's responsibility to . . . a former client. . . ."

he would have gained in the professional relationship—could have been relevant in the future dispute over the premarital agreement in which his firm represented the husband.

The lawyer should not undertake a representation like that which occurred in *Fletcher* without taking precautions, including advising the now-adverse former client clearly and in writing:

- That the lawyer only represents one party;
- That the former client should retain independent counsel;
- Of the reasons why independent counsel is necessary; and
- Of the lawyer's role as advocate solely for his or her client.

Further, the lawyer should obtain, expressly and in writing, consent to the representation from both the current client and the former client.[67]

(f) Lawyer for the Proponent Does Estate Planning for Both Parties

An estate planning lawyer who represents a proponent of a premarital or postmarital agreement may be or become the estate planning lawyer for both parties. The Rules of Professional Conduct permit such joint representation so long as the lawyer complies with the applicable rules.[68] When that lawyer drafts estate planning documents at variance with the terms of the agreement, without expressly advising a party who may be disadvantaged to get separate representation, he or she creates an opportunity for litigation after a party's death. For example, in *Walker v. Walker*,[69] the premarital agreement entitled the surviving wife to the marital home and required the husband's estate to pay off the mortgage. During the marriage, the parties executed numerous estate-planning documents, including trusts, prepared by the husband's longtime lawyer (who had represented the husband for the premarital agreement), which were less favorable to the wife. After the husband's death, his estate argued that these instruments impliedly amended the premarital agreement. The court ruled against the husband's estate. In doing so, it said:

> . . . [T]he subsequent trusts were created by her husband's longtime lawyer, Mr. Holdman. Mr. Holdman was not called to testify about what, if any, advice or explanation he may have provided [the wife] about the trusts or their impact on the Prenuptial Agreement—an agreement that was signed at a time when [the wife] had the advice of independent counsel. [The wife] never had separate legal representation during the marriage.[70]

Here, the lawyer's conflict of interest and his failure to either get the proper waiver from the wife, or advise her to get independent counsel, disserved his own client, the husband. The parties could have entered into an express amendment to the premarital agreement, or the estate-planning documents could have been written to acknowledge the parties' intent to

67. *Id.* 1.9; *see also id.* 1.7(a)(2).
68. MRPC 1.7 (Conflict of Interest; Current Clients), 1.8 (Conflicts of Interest; Current Clients: Specific Rules), and 1.9 (Duties to Former Clients).
69. 2022 Md. App. LEXIS 92 (unpub.).
70. *Id.* (italics in original).

modify the agreement; in either case, had the lawyer prepared these documents, he would have needed to recognize the conflict of interest and act accordingly.

§9.04 ETHICAL ISSUES AND COUNSEL FOR THE ECONOMICALLY WEAKER CLIENT

The first question a lawyer must confront when asked to represent a weaker party in connection with a premarital agreement is whether to agree to take the representation. It appears to be quite common for proponents to present a proposed premarital agreement close to the wedding date. ABA Model Rule 1.1 mandates that a lawyer act competently and not accept a representation unless he or she has the skill and knowledge to provide competent representation. Even a lawyer who has the necessary expertise may not be able to make adequate use of it when the agreement is presented at the eleventh hour. Many experienced lawyers simply refuse to accept a representation that is too close to the wedding date unless the parties can agree to postpone the ceremony or are willing to turn the intended premarital agreement into a postmarital agreement.

In *Friezo v. Friezo*,[71] the wife first received a copy of the proposed agreement on November 5. There was significant time pressure, as the marriage had to take place by November 30 due to her immigration status. Her lawyer was able to negotiate some changes to the agreement, but it remained quite disadvantageous to her. The trial court invalidated the agreement and was highly critical of the wife's lawyer. The appellate court reversed. The trial court may well have been unfair to the lawyer. However, his agreeing to take the matter at such a late date made him vulnerable to criticism.[72]

Friezo illustrates another common situation that implicates the lawyer's ethical obligations. The husband, after giving the wife the proposed agreement, directed her to contact his sister-in-law, who was a lawyer. The sister-in-law then brought the wife to the inexperienced associate in her law firm who handled the negotiations. The associate got a signed conflict-of-interest waiver, but not a signed engagement agreement, and did not charge a fee. The trial court thought the lawyer's representation was either incompetent or not truly independent. The appellate court, however, concluded that there was no evidence to support his lack of independence. This may well have been the right decision under the circumstances, but it points out how the lawyer left himself vulnerable to attack. It was apparent the husband used a member of his family to handpick a lawyer for the wife. The lawyer's willingness to participate, however decent his motives (and he may not have had a choice), put him at risk for a claim of ethical misconduct or malpractice.

The weaker party's right to independent counsel will not be meaningful if that party does not have adequate funds to pay counsel to do a fully competent job. Therefore, in some cases it will be appropriate for counsel for a weaker party to ask the proponent's counsel to have the

71. *Friezo v. Friezo*, 281 Conn. 166, 914 A.2d 533 (2007).

72. *See also Hudson v. Hudson*, 408 S.C. 76, 757 S.E.2d 727 (2014) (premarital agreement was not unconscionable where lawyer-husband referred wife to close friend of his who did not explain terms, but where wife was aware of inadequacy of advice when she decided to sign).

proponent advance sufficient monies to the weaker party at the beginning of the negotiation to pay the reasonably anticipated fees.[73] In doing so, counsel should bear in mind that the client must consent to third-party payment and that the lawyer may not permit the stronger party's payment to interfere with counsel's independence.[74]

§9.05 JOINT REPRESENTATION

(a) Overview

Best practices dictate that each party to a premarital or postmarital agreement have independent counsel. Even where the rules of ethics permit a joint representation, it is almost never in the interest of either party, or the lawyer, that the lawyer undertake such a representation. Some parties will want to use one lawyer for the agreement for financial reasons, because they do not see the need for separate counsel, because they perceive the use of separate counsel as creating animosity where none existed previously, or because they have developed a professional relationship with one lawyer they both trust.[75] However, the arguments against joint representation in a given matter, even when the parties say they want it, almost always outweigh the arguments in favor.[76] There is also a body of cases where the lawyer seemingly acted as counsel for both parties, gave the impression that he or she was doing so, or failed to appreciate that the other party may not have understood the lawyer's role, often to the detriment of a weaker party who may not have understood the lawyer's role as counsel solely for the other party.

In some situations joint representation is not possible, including those where state law mandates actual advice of independent counsel or the opportunity for such advice, or where there is a nonwaivable conflict of interest.[77] In other situations, Rule 1.7 appears to permit joint representation with adequate safeguards.[78] Whether joint representation is permissible under the conflict-of-interest rules depends on a number of factors, including the age and health of the parties; their relative financial circumstances; whether one party is in a dominant role, or, on the other hand, whether one party is susceptible to undue influence due to

73. *See* ALI, PRINCIPLES OF THE LAW OF FAMILY DISSOLUTION § 7.04 cmt. e.

74. MRPC 1.8(f), 5.4(c).

75. *See Report of the Special Study Committee on Professional Responsibility; Comments and Recommendations on the Lawyer's Duties in Representing Husband and Wife*, 28 REAL PROP. PROB. & TR. J. 765, 770 (Winter 1994) ("family needs, tax incentives, and the very nature of marriage often make separate counseling unnecessary, and indeed, inappropriate").

76. Some academic commentators advocate for joint representation as the norm based on a belief that separate representation creates unnecessary antagonism and that the requirement for separate representation is premised on outmoded ideas about the need to protect women. *See* Elizabeth R. Carter, *Rethinking Premarital Agreements: A Collaborative Approach*, 46 N.M. L. REV. 354 (Summer 2016). However, a substantial body of case law demonstrates that a weaker party of either gender will be better served by having independent counsel who can evaluate the proposed terms, suggest ideas to improve the terms for him or her and engage in a negotiation with the proponent's lawyer, or advise about alternative modes, such as mediation, that will assist to arrive at terms that are acceptable to both parties.

77. *See* ARK. CODE ANN. § 9-11-406(a)(2)(ii); CAL. FAM. CODE § 1615(c); CONN. GEN. STAT. § 46b-36g; MINN. STAT. ANN. § 519.11; S.C. CODE ANN. § 20-7-473; *Ware v. Ware*, 687 S.E.2d 382 (W. Va. 2009).

78. MPRC 1.7.

diminished capacity or other reasons; the parties' objectives and whether they agree on the objectives; and whether the proposed terms are fair to both parties given their circumstances.

Joint representation can make the lawyer vulnerable to an accusation of unethical conduct or professional malpractice.[79] Moreover, the wrong decision about joint representation can frustrate the objectives of one or both parties by rendering the agreement unenforceable or by forcing a party, or his or her heirs, to litigate validity. For example, in *Sumpter v. Kosinski*,[80] the husband's longtime lawyer, who had also represented the wife in a prior divorce, offered to represent both parties without explaining the wife's right to independent counsel or disclosing the potential conflict in the dual representation. He advised the wife it was in her interest to sign the agreement. The trial court voided the agreement because of what it deemed the lawyer's constructive fraud in engaging in a joint representation without informed consent. The ruling voiding the agreement was reversed on appeal over a strong dissent. A drafting lawyer can take no comfort from a case like *Sumpter*; a change of one vote would have voided the agreement.[81]

The decision about joint representation requires a balancing act. On the one hand, the clients assert their desire for joint representation to reduce the cost of the agreement and the potential for acrimony. The lawyer wishes to accommodate their desires; indeed, he or she risks losing both clients for refusing to bow to their wishes. On the other hand, the lawyer will be held responsible for a wrong decision that leaves a client, or his or her heirs, exposed to the risk and the cost of litigation. The lawyer considering a request for joint representation should begin with a strong presumption against it.

(b) Directly Adverse Joint Representation and Waiver

The ABA Model Rules preclude a representation of one client that is directly adverse to the interests of another but permit the clients to waive the conflict with certain safeguards:

> 1.7 Conflict of Interest: Current Clients
>
> (a) Except as provided in paragraph (b), a lawyer shall not represent a client if the representation involves a concurrent conflict of interest. A concurrent conflict of interest exists if:
>
> > (1) the representation of one client will be directly adverse to another client; or
> >
> > (2) there is a significant risk that the representation of one or more clients will be materially limited by the lawyer's responsibilities to another client. . . .

79. *See Klemm v. Superior Court*, 75 Cal. App. 3d 893, 901, 142 Cal. Rptr. 509, 514 (1977) (agreement negotiated without independent representation vulnerable to easy attack as having been procured by misrepresentation, fraud, and overreaching); *see also Friedman v. Friedman*, 100 Cal. App. 4th 65, 122 Cal. Rptr. 2d 412 (2002); *Crest Investment Trust, Inc. v. Comstock*, 23 Md. App. 280, 327 A.2d 891 (1974).

80. *Sumpter v. Kosinski*, 165 Mich. App. 784, 419 N.W.2d 463 (1988).

81. *See also Parr v. Parr*, 635 N.E.2d 1124 (Ind. Ct. App. 1994) (husband's lawyer met with both parties, failed to send draft agreement to wife's lawyer, and supervised inadequate oral financial disclosure; agreement invalid); *In re Estate of Benker*, 416 Mich. 681, 331 N.W.2d 193 (1982) (lawyer's representation of both parties without informed consent and in absence of evidence of asset disclosure rendered premarital agreement invalid).

(b) Notwithstanding the existence of a concurrent conflict of interest under paragraph (a), a lawyer may represent a client if:

(1) the lawyer reasonably believes that the lawyer will be able to provide competent and diligent representation to each affected client;

. . .

(4) each affected client gives informed consent, confirmed in writing.[82]

Where the parties' interests are in direct conflict, as they are in a premarital agreement negotiation, as well as, in many cases, a postmarital agreement negotiation, consent to joint representation is insufficient. "The lawyer must also objectively determine that . . . joint representation of one [party] will not adversely affect the relationship with, or representation of the other."[83] The West Virginia Supreme Court has held that joint representation for a premarital agreement is not possible; the interests of the parties are fundamentally antagonistic, and the conflict is not waivable.[84] Notwithstanding the general permissibility of a joint representation (except in West Virginia), counsel should begin with a strong presumption against it.

The parties themselves may not be the best judges of the risks to their interests in a joint representation. As one authority has observed, engaged parties may "have expectations about their future partner that may disarm their capacity for self-protective judgment, or their inclination to exercise it. . . ."[85] It is the lawyer's responsibility, in the first instance, to evaluate whether he or she can adequately serve the interests of both clients in a joint representation.[86] There are some circumstances in which the lawyer should rule out directly adverse joint representation even with client consent:

- When the parties have substantially disparate assets and or incomes;[87]
- When the proposed terms of the agreement are disadvantageous to one party, which includes the more common situation where the economically weaker party is asked to accept very little upon death or dissolution and the less common one where the economically stronger party proposes to make overly generous provisions for the weaker party;
- When the lawyer has a preexisting significant personal or lawyer-client relationship with one of the parties such that the lawyer has a greater stake in maintaining the existing relationship with that party than with the other party;

82. MRPC 1.7.

83. Pearce, *Family Values and Legal Ethics: Competing Approaches to Conflicts in Representing Spouses*, 62 FORDHAM L. REV. 1253, 1259 (Mar. 1994) (hereafter, *Family Values and Legal Ethics*); *see also* MRPC 1.7 cmt.

84. *Ware v. Ware*, 687 S.E.2d 382 (W. Va. 2009).

85. PRINCIPLES OF THE LAW OF FAMILY DISSOLUTION § 7.02, cmt. c.

86. *See* MRPC 1.7 cmt. [15] ("representation is prohibited if in the circumstances the lawyer cannot reasonably conclude that the lawyer will be able to provide competent and diligent representation").

87. By contrast, a lawyer might well be able to represent both parties to a premarital agreement in a situation such as the following: The parties are both older; there is no possibility of their having children together; they each have substantial assets; they will each be able to live comfortably upon termination of the marriage by death or divorce; and they each advise the lawyer before the lawyer agrees to take on the representation that they want an agreement in which each waives all spousal claims either might have. In such a case, the lawyer's role could be characterized as mere scrivener. See discussion in Section 8.05(c).

- When before agreeing to meet with both parties the lawyer has received confidences from one party which that party does not want disclosed to the other party and which are material to the representation; and
- When there is reason to believe that one party may be unable to adequately protect his or her own interests due to diminished capacity or for other reasons, such as youth, naiveté, lack of education or experience, dominance by the other party, or domestic violence.[88]

Joint representation implicates two important values in the lawyer-client relationship: the client's right to confidentiality[89] and the client's right to the lawyer's loyalty.[90] The duty of loyalty requires the lawyer to exercise independent judgment on behalf of, and to give independent advice to, the client free of any conflicting claims on the lawyer's loyalty from any other source. As the comments to ABA Model Rule 1.7 point out:

> Even where there is no direct adverseness, a conflict of interests exists if there is a significant risk that a lawyer's ability to consider, recommend or carry out an appropriate course of action for the client will be materially limited as a result of the lawyer's other responsibilities or interests. . . . The conflict in effect forecloses alternatives that would otherwise be available to the client.[91]

In most states, a premarital or postmarital agreement that is substantively unfair at execution will nevertheless be upheld if the proponent provided fair disclosure of assets and the challenging party executed the agreement voluntarily. When there is a significant disparity in resources and when the agreement is highly disadvantageous to one party, or may become so over time, a lawyer representing both parties is in a poor position to recommend to the weaker party that he or she not sign the agreement or negotiate modifications that require the stronger party to make concessions. Yet a creative approach to improving the terms of agreement for the weaker party may be exactly what the situation calls for. On the other hand, if the wealthier party is elderly or ill, a plan to be overly generous to a newly acquired spouse may suggest diminished capacity or undue influence that the lawyer should be free to consider without divided loyalty. As one authority has observed, the lawyer-client relationship for estate planning purposes may begin with representation of one party in a variety of other matters, such as in connection with business interests. Often the preexisting relationship "reflects the relative economic power of the spouses."[92] The spouse with the greater need for continuing legal services is the more valuable client.[93] The conflict-of-interest rules preclude a joint representation in these circumstances if the lawyer's interest in maintaining the existing relationship precludes "undivided loyalty to the new client-spouse."[94]

88. *See, e.g., Drewry v. Drewry*, 8 Va. App. 460, 383 S.E.2d 12 (1989).
89. MRPC 1.6.
90. *Id.* 1.7.
91. *Id.* 1.7 cmt. [8].
92. Collett, *Disclosure, Discretion, or Deception: The Estate Planner's Ethical Dilemma from a Unilateral Confidence*, 28 REAL PROP. PROB. & TR. J. 683, 709 (Winter 1994).
93. *Id.* at 709–10.
94. *Id.* at 709.

In the examples discussed above, the lawyer's ability to be loyal to both clients is likely to be tested to the breaking point.[95] In the language of ABA Model Rule 1.7(b)(1), the lawyer will not be able to form a reasonable belief that he or she will be "able to provide competent and diligent representation to each affected client[.]" Moreover, there is little benefit to either party in joint representation in these scenarios. The greater the disparity in assets and/or bargaining power at the execution stage, the more vulnerable is the agreement to a challenge to validity. The stronger party is likely to be better off if the lawyer agrees to represent only that party and takes the steps appropriate to dealing with an unrepresented party than to take on a joint representation. Similarly, the weaker party is likely to be better off if the lawyer rejects joint representation, urges the weaker party to retain independent counsel, explains why, and in appropriate cases recommends that the stronger party agree to pay the weaker party's legal fees.

(c) Joint Representation: Lawyer as Mere Scrivener

Some authorities describe a possible role for the lawyer in the preparation of an agreement as that of mere scrivener or scribe, suggesting that where the lawyer does no more than take what the parties say they want and create a document with the usual legal terminology, the scribe need not necessarily give any advice or counsel or inquire into the underlying facts.[96] The outcomes in the cited cases notwithstanding, it is risky for the lawyer to assume a court will agree that his or her decision to act as mere scrivener was appropriate.

One of the problems with such a joint representation is that the lawyer in the mere scrivener role may need to remain consciously ignorant of facts that an independent lawyer would want to know.[97] For example, in *Drewry v. Drewry*,[98] a dispute about validity of a marital settlement agreement, the lawyer knew the wife had been hospitalized for psychological problems but apparently did not obtain a detailed mental health history, and he had only limited knowledge of the parties' property interests. From that limited knowledge, he thought an agreement in which the wife got a total of $25,000 for her property and support rights after a 25-year marriage was fair. Clearly an independent lawyer, knowing of the wife's recent treatment for depression and the facts relevant to her marital rights, might have come to a

---

95. *See In re Wilder*, 764 N.W.2d 617 (In. 2002) (lawyer sanctioned for representation of former member of domestic partnership in connection with dissolution after having represented both parties in partnership matters).

96. *See Hutchins v. Hutchins*, 393 Mont. 283, 430 P.3d 502 (2018) (premarital agreement initiated by husband, drafted by lawyer chosen by him, that recited drafting lawyer did not represent either party, was valid); *Estate of Schaefer*, 281 A.3d 1044 (Pa. Super. Ct. 2022) (premarital agreement valid after death of husband where parties, both in their 80s, used one lawyer with no prior relationship with either party, parties sought agreement with mutual waivers at death); *Mabus v. Mabus*, 890 So. 2d 806 (Miss. 2003) (premarital agreement was valid where lawyer clearly limited role to drafting and told parties to get separate counsel if they disagreed with terms); *Hill v. Hill*, 356 N.W.2d 49 (Minn. Ct. App. 1984) (lawyer considered himself as representing both parties, drafted agreement as instructed without providing advice to either; premarital agreement valid); *Newman v. Newman*, 653 P.2d 728 (Colo. 1982) (premarital agreement valid where wife met with husband and husband's lawyer, but lawyer merely acted as scrivener and did not advise wife regarding her interests); *see also Scott v. Scott*, 19 A.3d 302 (Del. 2011).

97. "[M]ultiple party representation is necessarily superficial. . . . [T]he means for protecting the superficiality . . . is ignorance of any facts known to one of the individuals but not to the other." *Family Values and Legal Ethics* at 1281.

98. 8 Va. App. 460, 383 S.E.2d 12 (1989). The Virginia version of the UPAA also governs validity of marital settlement agreements.

different conclusion and advised her not to sign the agreement.[99] An independent lawyer might also have negotiated a better deal for the wife. Had she signed the agreement as presented, rejecting informed legal advice, or had counsel negotiated improved terms, the later litigation might have been foreclosed.

However appealing joint representation may be, it can often be disadvantageous to the stronger party. In *Dion v. Dion*,[100] for example, the husband's lawyer met with both parties and thought he represented both parties to the premarital agreement. The husband disclosed his business at book value when the actual value was much higher. The court voided the premarital agreement. Had the wife had independent representation, the outcome might well have been different.[101] In *In re Marriage of Delaney*,[102] the husband hired a lawyer to draft a premarital agreement, but the lawyer met with both parties and the agreement recited that he represented both. The husband's financial disclosure was inadequate, and the lawyer did not advise the wife she had a right to ask for more information. The trial court rejected the husband's argument that the wife waived further disclosure, even though the agreement had an express waiver; the court was dismissive of the waiver as mere boilerplate. Like *Dion*, the outcome might have been different had the wife had independent counsel.

(d) Avoiding Unintentional Joint Representation

Whether a lawyer-client relationship is formed turns on the subjective belief of the client if that belief is reasonable under the surrounding circumstances.[103] Thus, under some circumstances, a court may deem a lawyer's conduct to constitute joint representation even when the lawyer did not intend such. Where this occurs, and where the lawyer does not give adequate explanation and obtain informed consent to the joint representation, the agreement is vulnerable. For example, in *Rowland v. Rowland*,[104] the husband's lawyer met with both parties, did not advise the 18-year-old woman of her right to independent counsel, offered to answer questions, but did not volunteer any explanation of the terms of the premarital agreement. The court treated the lawyer's conduct as if he had engaged in a joint representation; and because he failed to get informed consent, the court held the agreement was the product of overreaching. Highly significant to the court's decision was the fact that the lawyer met with the parties together but failed to make his role clear. The court observed: "This pro forma exercise cannot be proof of [the wife's] knowing, intelligent and voluntary consent to the agreement. . . ."[105] The husband would have been better off, according to the court, if the lawyer had merely handed the wife the agreement and told

99. *See also In re Marriage of Egedi*, 88 Cal. App. 4th 17, 24, 105 Cal. Rptr. 2d 518, 524 n.5 (2001) (recognizing exception to general rule that scrivener should not give advice where agreement terms are grossly unfair to one party, in which case lawyer should decline joint representation).

100. 1984 Pa. Dist. Cnty. Dec. LEXIS 52.

101. *See, e.g.*, *Head v. Head*, 59 Md. App. 570, 477 A.2d 282 (1984), where the parties settled a dispute over their premarital agreement. The wife then attacked the settlement, claiming the husband's disclosure of the book value of his business was fraudulent. She had counsel who understood the difference between book and fair market value and who had rejected earlier settlement offers as inadequate. The court upheld the agreement.

102. 298 Wis. 2d 247, 726 N.W.2d 356 (2006).

103. *Bohn v. Cody*, 119 Wn. 2d 357, 832 P.2d 71 (1992).

104. *Rowland v. Rowland*, 74 Ohio App. 3d 415, 599 N.E.2d 315 (1991).

105. *Id.* at 424, 321.

her to sign it. If she had signed, she would have been bound by the agreement, whether or not she read or understood it.[106]

Another circumstance in which the lawyer's blurring of his or her role can have unintended consequences occurs when the lawyer prepares wills for both parties but purports to represent only one of them in the preparation of a premarital or postmarital agreement without making the distinction clear. In *In re Estate of Lutz*,[107] the court reversed a summary judgment for the deceased husband's estate where the wife alleged she was not adequately advised of her right to independent counsel in connection with the parties' premarital agreement. The husband's lawyer had prepared wills for both of them. She believed the lawyer represented both of them for all purposes. The lawyer's representation of both of them for one purpose, but only the husband for a related purpose, put the validity of the premarital agreement at risk.[108]

Another twist on the unintended joint representation scenario can occur where one of the parties is a lawyer and purports to give legal advice to the other party or discourages the other party from retaining separate counsel. For example, in *Cook v. Cook*,[109] the husband drafted a property settlement agreement for the parties in which he retained all of the community interest in his law practice. In voiding the agreement, the court observed that a lawyer-client relationship may be formed even if the parties are related, that when a lawyer-party prepares an agreement and represents that it is fair, the agreement is the product of a lawyer-client relationship.[110] As such, it is subject to close scrutiny, the lawyer has a duty of full disclosure, and the transaction must be "fundamentally fair and free of professional overreaching."[111] The agreement in *Cook v. Cook* did not meet this standard.[112] Not every agreement drafted by a

106. *Id.*; *see also Fletcher v. Fletcher*, 628 N.E.2d 1343 (Ohio 1994) (wife's prior client relationship with law firm that prepared premarital agreement for husband may have led wife to place undue trust in them and could have led to finding of overreaching had wife's version of events been credited); *Hale v. Hale*, 74 Md. App. 555, 539 A.2d 247 (1988) (separation agreement was void where husband's lawyer knew wife believed he represented both parties and did not advise her forcefully enough to retain independent counsel).

107. 563 N.W.2d 90 (N.D. 1997).

108. Ultimately, the premarital agreement was upheld, but only after two more appeals. *In re Estate of Lutz*, 595 N.W.2d 590 (N.D. 1999) (*Lutz II*); *In re Estate of Lutz*, 620 N.W.2d 589 (N.D. 2000) (*Lutz III*).

109. 112 Nev. 179, 912 P.2d 264 (1996).

110. *Id.* at 184, 267; *see also Sanford v. Sanford*, 355 Ark. 274, 137 S.W.3d 391 (2003) (husband breached fiduciary duty to wife when he acted as her lawyer in preparation of property settlement agreement, and as trustee of the trust created to manage joint assets, discouraged her from hiring separate counsel, and did not explain his conflict of interest).

111. *Cook*, 112 Nev. at 184, 912 P.2d at 267.

112. *See also Izzo v. Izzo*, 2010 Tex. App. LEXIS 3623 (unpub.) (postmarital agreement invalid where lawyer-husband breached fiduciary duty as wife's lawyer); *In re Marriage of Tamraz*, 2005 Cal. App. Unpub. LEXIS 5686 (premarital agreement was not enforceable where lawyer-husband drafted it, provided inadequate and misleading explanations of terms, and did not advise wife to get independent counsel); *In re Marriage of Osborne*, 2003 Wash. App. LEXIS 3077 (unpub.) (postmarital agreement was not executed with advice of independent counsel where husband, a lawyer, directed wife to colleague who was not independent and husband did not explain purpose or need for independent advice); *Webb v. Webb*, 16 Va. App. 486, 431 S.E.2d 55 (1993) (property settlement agreement was invalid where lawyer-husband drafted, discouraged wife from getting independent advice, and withheld information about his retirement benefits); *Williams v. Waldman*, 108 Nev. 466, 836 P.2d 614 (1992) (when husband gave legal advice to wife, he became her lawyer and transaction therefore judged by standards applicable to attorney-client business transaction).

lawyer who is also a party will be held the product of an attorney-client relationship.[113] It is only when the lawyer goes beyond the role of party to the agreement and assumes the role of advisor to the other party that a lawyer-client relationship is formed.

§9.06 LAWYER AS MEDIATOR

A lawyer may serve as a neutral to assist parties to negotiate the terms of an agreement. Mediator is one such role. Mediation is defined as "a process in which a mediator facilitates communication and negotiation between parties to assist them in reaching a voluntary agreement regarding their dispute."[114] Parties who agree to participate in a mediation governed by the Uniform Mediation Act (UMA), or a similar act or court rule in their jurisdiction, may do so in a writing that provides for communications made during the mediation process to be privileged against disclosure, affording the parties a forum in which to communicate confidentially with the mediator and the other party to extend offers and discuss ideas for resolution, personal information, and concerns relating to the terms of agreement.[115] The mediator should be impartial.[116] Under the UMA, he or she must make sufficient inquiry to determine whether there is a financial or personal interest in the outcome or a present or past relationship with a party that may affect impartiality.[117]

Parties who choose mediation may elect a mediation model in which only the parties attend mediation sessions with the mediator, or they may elect to have lawyers present.[118] When lawyers do not attend and participate, parties will likely benefit from having legal advice before the mediation and between sessions if there will be more than one.

Whether the mediator can draft an agreement for the parties resulting from a successful mediation, or is limited to drafting a memorandum of understanding or term sheet, will depend on state law and local ethics rules and opinions, as to whether a lawyer functioning as a neutral may take on the drafting role, whether the drafting role creates a conflict of interest, and whether the conflict is waivable.[119] Whether or not the mediator prepares a draft agreement, he or she should advise each party that before signing an agreement, he or she should get independent legal advice and have his or her lawyer review the agreement, explain the terms, and advise about the legal rights he or she will be waiving.

---

113. *See, e.g.*, *Lebeck v. Lebeck*, 118 N.M. 367, 881 P.2d 727 (Ct. App. 1994) (agreement drafted by lawyer-husband was valid where he gave it to wife, asked her to propose changes, and advised her to get independent counsel).

114. Uniform Mediation Act § 2(2) (2003) (hereafter, UMA).

115. *Id.* §§ 4, 8.

116. ABA Model Standards of Conduct for Mediators, Standard II (Impartiality) (hereafter, Model Standards for Mediators) (2005).

117. UMA § 9(a).

118. *Id.* § 10; *see also* Model Standards for Mediators, Standard III (Conflicts of Interest).

119. *See* FORREST S. MOSTEN ET AL., THE COMPLETE GUIDE TO MEDIATION 150–51 (2d ed. ABA 2015).

§9.07 SUMMARY: BEST PRACTICES

When called upon to represent a party to a premarital or postmarital agreement, a lawyer who wishes to adhere to the highest standards of practice should consider the following:

- It is almost never appropriate for one lawyer to represent both parties.
- The lawyer for the proponent should urge an unrepresented party to get legal advice, explain why he or she should do so, and refrain from any communication or conduct that may send a contrary message.
- The proponent's lawyer may assist the weaker party to identify a competent lawyer—for example, by recommending a lawyer or several lawyers—but should not state or imply that the party has no choice in the selection.
- When the situation calls for it, the lawyer for the stronger party should recommend that he or she agree to pay the legal fees of the weaker party to enable him or her to hire a lawyer.
- The lawyer for the proponent should act promptly to prepare a draft premarital agreement that can go to the other party as far in advance of the wedding as circumstances permit.
- It is appropriate for the lawyer for a stronger party to counsel his or her client about the benefits for both parties of making provisions for the financial security of an economically weaker party when he or she does not have adequate resources.
- If the weaker party elects not to get legal advice, the text of the agreement should clearly state that he or she had an opportunity to do so and chose not to, and that the lawyer for the proponent represented only the proponent.

10 Information Gathering, Preparation for, and Negotiating the Terms

§10.01 Overview

This chapter addresses some of the practical problems in the representation of a client seeking a premarital or a postmarital agreement or who has been presented with such an agreement. The lawyer's conduct of the representation will differ according to whether he or she is representing the party who seeks to initiate a premarital agreement—the proponent—or the other party and whether there is a significant disparity in resources or the parties are in comparable bargaining positions. When the couple is older and each person has sufficient resources to provide for his or her own needs, often they both want an agreement, their bargaining positions are more or less equal, and they share the objective of keeping their assets separate. By contrast, where there is a significant financial disparity or a big age difference, or when the parties are young, entering into a first marriage, and may have children, the matter can be more challenging to resolve. The negotiations may require a significant amount of lawyer time, often compressed into an uncomfortably short span of time.

Other considerations come into play when the parties are already married and are considering entering into a postmarital agreement or an amendment to a premarital agreement. One such consideration is the reasons for seeking an agreement—for example, the parties intended to enter into a premarital agreement but ran out of time and were unable to complete the negotiations before the wedding, they are estranged and want to enter into a postmarital agreement that will govern their rights if an attempt to reconcile fails, or they have been married for a number of years and want a postmarital agreement as part of their estate planning. Another consideration is the parties' current circumstances, including age and health, and whether a spouse's capacity may be diminished.

Parties often wait to initiate the process of getting a premarital agreement until later than is ideal. Thus, one of the primary challenges for counsel for the proponent of a premarital agreement is to gather sufficient information, draft an agreement and make revisions requested by the client, provide the proposed agreement to the other party, and then conduct negotiations, all while the wedding date is quickly approaching.

§10.02 New Client Intake

When a new potential client calls to make an appointment for a premarital agreement, the lawyer, or the staff person who handles such matters, will need to obtain certain information immediately to determine whether he or she can consider taking the matter. In addition to the name of the fiancé(e) to do a conflict check, the lawyer will need to find out whether he or she will be drafting the agreement, or reviewing an agreement prepared, or to be prepared, by the other party's lawyer. The lawyer will also need to know the planned wedding date. If the date is close, the lawyer should explore with the potential client whether postponing the wedding is an option or whether the parties would consider a postmarital agreement.[1] The closer the wedding date, the more cautious the lawyer should be about accepting a representation.

The lawyer needs to be particularly wary about agreeing to represent a weaker party for a premarital agreement when the wedding date is close, especially if the agreement has not yet been drafted. Without seeing the proposed terms, the lawyer may not be able to assess adequately whether he or she will have sufficient time to do a competent job until the representation is underway. The lawyer's decision to withdraw later, due to inability to carry out a competent representation, will likely mean leaving the client without a lawyer. Moreover, when a stronger party deliberately waits to present an agreement until close to a wedding date that cannot be postponed, it is often because he or she intends it to be a take-it-or-leave-it agreement. There is little the lawyer for a weaker party can contribute in this circumstance, except to advise the client not to sign.

Assuming the lawyer decides to see the potential client, he or she will need to begin immediately to gather the facts relevant to the representation. A questionnaire that the client can fill out ahead of time and bring to the first meeting can be quite useful.

1. Before offering the client the option of postponing the agreement until after the wedding, the lawyer will need to be familiar with applicable law regarding enforceability of a postmarital agreement not incident to a marital separation, whether the criteria for validity of a postmarital agreement are different than for a premarital agreement, and the permissible scope of such an agreement. In some states, parties may be able to waive spousal support in a premarital agreement, but not in a postmarital agreement. See Chapter 3 of this book for further discussion of postmarital agreements.

§10.03 THE INITIAL CONSULTATION

(a) Information Gathering

The lawyer for a proponent will need to gather a substantial amount of information about the client and his or her fiancé(e) at the initial consultation.[2] Information counsel will need to gather includes:

- Prior marital history, whether a prior marriage ended in death or divorce, including whether a party has children he or she wants to provide for, and whether he or she has financial obligations to a former spouse or a child;
- When a party has a defined benefit pension plan and has been married before, counsel will need to find out if a prior spouse has a right to a share of the benefit and whether he or she is entitled to a survivor benefit;
- If the parties are already married, and have been for some time, the history of the current marriage; what prompted the decision to seek a postmarital agreement; any history of marital misconduct; any history of domestic violence, threats, exercise of unreasonable control, or economic pressure; and any history of financial misconduct;
- Education, current employment, and, in some cases, employment history. Among other things, this information can help counsel evaluate a party's level of sophistication and experience in legal matters, contracts, financial and investment issues, and other related areas. It may also help identify retirement benefits that will need to be considered and disclosed;
- Citizenship and, if not a U.S. citizen, visa status (especially whether a party is in the United States on a fiancé(e) visa);
- If a party's first language is not English, the extent of his or her study of English and the length of time he or she has lived, worked, or studied among English speakers;
- Ages of the parties;
- Parties' health;
- Amounts and sources of income of each party;
- Assets and liabilities of each party;
- Whether a party expects an inheritance or has an interest in a trust or estate;
- Whether the parties are likely to have children together and their expectations about whether one of them will leave the workforce to care for them;
- Whether each party has sufficient resources to provide for his or her own future needs independently of the other party;
- Whether there is a significant disparity in the parties' assets and resources;
- Whether a party has a business or professional services practice that he or she wishes to preserve from spousal claims;
- The likelihood of a party needing nursing home care; the expectations of the parties regarding their care at the end of their lives; provisions previously made for meeting

2. See Appendix C, Personal Information Worksheet, for a form that counsel can use to collect information from a potential client seeking a premarital or postmarital agreement or who is or expects to be the recipient of a proposed agreement.

long-term care needs, such as long-term care insurance; whether a party may need Medicaid to pay for nursing home care; and the effect this may have on the other spouse and his or her financial security;

- Whether parties have plans to move to another state and, if known, where;
- To the extent known, the parties' plans for the near future, such as a plan to retire;
- The ability of each party, especially the less wealthy party, to acquire assets in the future through savings from employment, future inheritances, family gifts, and other means;
- In addition, counsel will need to explore the client's goals and objectives in seeking an agreement, and, to the extent known, the fiancé(e)'s or spouse's objectives.

(b) Client Questions About Premarital and Postmarital Agreements

At the initial consultation, the lawyer will need to give advice about the law relating to premarital agreements and answer client questions. Below are some frequently asked questions about premarital agreements and suggested answers. These can be adapted for a client considering a postmarital agreement.

What is a premarital agreement?

A premarital agreement is a contract entered into by a couple who plan to marry. It determines their rights regarding property and support when the marriage ends, whether by death or divorce. Some premarital agreements provide that each party will keep all money earned and property acquired before or after marriage; in other words, what is his is his, and what is hers is hers. Other agreements provide for each party to keep premarital and inherited property and for property acquired through employment during the marriage to be shared. Some agreements provide for one spouse to make transfers of cash or property to the other spouse or provide for spousal support for a dependent spouse in the event of divorce.

Do I really need a premarital agreement?

Every married couple has a premarital agreement. State laws provide certain property rights for a surviving spouse after the first spouse dies. State laws also provide for division of property if the parties divorce and for support for a spouse who is unable to support him or herself. In that sense, state law is the parties' agreement. Some couples choose to write their own agreement to meet their own objectives and reflect their own values rather than leave it to state law to determine their rights at death or divorce.

My fiancé(e) asked me to sign a premarital agreement. Doesn't that mean he/she does not trust me?

Not really. There are many reasons a person considering marriage may want a premarital agreement. A party may wish to provide for children of a prior marriage in his/her will. The state law rights of surviving spouses make that difficult without a premarital agreement. In fact, a premarital agreement can improve family relationships when a stepparent enters the picture by giving children the peace of mind of knowing that their inheritance expectations remain intact. In some cases, both parties have children and assets from a prior marriage. A premarital agreement can allow each to provide for his or her own children regardless of which of them dies first. Even when a party has no children, he or she may want an agreement to have the right to direct assets to his or her family rather than have them go to a surviving spouse's nieces and nephews. When there is a family business, the party, and his or her family members, may feel a premarital agreement is necessary to protect the business in the event of a death or divorce. With the high rate of divorce, even hopeless romantics must recognize the risk of failure. When a party has been married and divorced, he or she may be reluctant to marry again without a premarital agreement. For many couples it is better to acknowledge the possibility of divorce and agree on a fair division of property in advance, if things do not work out for them, rather than to take their chances with the courts.

Are premarital agreements only for the very rich?

Not at all. Moreover, many people who consider themselves middle class have substantial assets they may wish to protect. One reason even a person of modest means may want an agreement is to decide in advance how assets accumulated during the marriage will be handled in the event of divorce. Deciding such matters in advance, before a breakdown in the relationship, can significantly reduce legal fees for divorce and can give both parties peace of mind. Similarly, a premarital agreement can provide for a surviving spouse and for children in a way that can reduce conflict after a death, especially in a blended family.

My fiancé(e) and I plan to have children. Can my premarital agreement say that if we get divorced, we will have joint custody and we will share the children's expenses equally?

Yes. But a premarital agreement cannot prevent a court from deciding custody and determining the parties' obligations for support of their minor children despite what the agreement says. Some couples want to state their intent in the agreement. The court will not be bound by it.

I want a premarital agreement. When should I broach the subject with my fiancé(e)?

As soon as possible after deciding to get married, before booking the caterer or putting down a large deposit for a honeymoon cruise. Unfortunately, many people procrastinate because they are uncomfortable bringing up the subject. The longer you wait, the more difficult the conversation becomes. It is also unfair to the other party to delay; delay may make it difficult for him or her to obtain competent counsel and to negotiate the terms. Unfairness breeds unhappiness, and that is not a good way to begin a marriage. Ideally, the parties will have at least three or four months to consider and negotiate the terms of agreement; when they are planning a large wedding, they would allow six months, if possible. Ideally, they would complete the negotiations and sign *before* the wedding invitations go out.

What are the requirements for a valid premarital agreement?

First, both parties must enter into the agreement voluntarily. Second, both parties should make a fair disclosure of their assets and income.

In some states, a premarital agreement must be fair to the economically weaker party at the time it is signed. In some states, a judge has the power to consider whether a premarital agreement is fair at the time of divorce.[3] In these states, this means that events that occur after marriage could cause a judge to throw out the agreement. The law in this state is that a premarital

3. See Appendix B(1), State Law Summary: Premarital Agreements.

agreement does not need to be fair at the time it is signed. However, if you move to one of the states where the agreement must be fair at divorce, and the marriage does not work out, a judge in that state might apply its law and invalidate the agreement if it is unfair at that time. [***Alternative*:** This state is one of the states where a judge may consider fairness as of divorce.] It is usually better for both parties if they can agree on terms that are fair to both of them.

Does my fiancé(e) have to have a lawyer for the agreement to be valid?

No. There is no requirement that both parties have lawyers in order to create a valid premarital agreement. However, it is a very good idea for both parties to have independent legal advice. Independent counsel for your fiancé(e) can help negotiate the terms and can make sure he or she understands how the agreement will affect his or her rights. You should encourage your fiancé(e) to get a lawyer.

We both agree that we want a premarital agreement, and we know what we want in it. Can you represent both of us?

No. Even when a couple sees eye to eye on what should go in their premarital agreement, each of them should get independent legal advice. A premarital agreement alters the rights a spouse will have if the marriage ends in divorce or when the first of them dies. Sometimes an agreement that seems fair at the outset may have unexpected consequences. Each of you should receive independent advice about the rights you would have if you married without an agreement and how the agreement might affect you later. Each should get advice about any additional terms that you should consider.

Aren't premarital agreements easy to break?

No. This is a myth. If parties enter into an agreement voluntarily and with adequate disclosure of assets, the court will uphold it and enforce it according to its terms. The court will enforce the agreement even if it is quite unfair to one party. This is one reason it is so important that both parties have independent counsel; independent counsel can make sure your fiancé(e) understands that he or she cannot change the terms of the agreement later unless you both agree.

What things should I do to make sure my agreement is valid?

First, provide an accurate statement of your assets and debts and your amounts and sources of income. Second, encourage your fiancé(e) to get a lawyer. You may need to consider paying the legal fees for your fiancé(e)'s lawyer. Third, be open to considering proposals from your fiancé(e)'s lawyer to revise the proposed terms, and be willing to accept some revisions that improve the terms for your fiancé(e). It is not in your interest to have an agreement that will result in your fiancé(e) becoming impoverished after your death or a divorce. This will only give him or her an incentive to try to have the agreement invalidated. You will get more protection for your interests if you and your fiancé(e) can agree on terms that will allow each of you to have enough economic resources to live after the marriage ends by death or divorce.

Can I get a premarital agreement that says I do not have to pay spousal support if the marriage breaks down?

In most states parties are free to enter into a premarital agreement that provides that neither party will be obligated to pay spousal support to the other. Most of the time a waiver of support is enforced at divorce. However, in some states, a judge can award support at divorce, even though the agreement waived spousal support, when the person seeking support will suffer extreme hardship. There are a few states where courts do not enforce spousal support waivers. The law in this state is that a support waiver is enforceable unless the spouse seeking support will go on welfare. However, if you move to another state, a court in that state might apply its own law. As we get into a more specific discussion about the terms of the agreement, we should consider how to best formulate the terms to reduce the risk for you.

(c) Discussion of Applicable Law in the Absence of Agreement

The lawyer should give the client a brief explanation of the law that would apply at death or divorce if the parties married without a premarital agreement or did not enter into a postmarital agreement, as the case may be. A premarital or postmarital agreement operates on these rights. The client will need to understand what he or she may be waiving or asking the other party to waive. Each party's marital rights in the absence of an agreement are the framework for the decisions to be made about the terms of the contract.

(d) Determining Proponent's Objectives

In developing provisions for disposition of property and other spousal rights in a premarital or postmarital agreement, it is important to determine what the client who is seeking an agreement wants to accomplish. Thus, a key question for the client is: "What is your objective in seeking a premarital [or postmarital] agreement?" An open-ended discussion in which the client talks and the lawyer listens will often help identify what is important to the client. The lawyer can then translate what he or she has heard into contract terms. A party's objectives may include:

- To create a separate property regime so that all property acquired at any time from any source will be deemed the property of the party with title;
- To protect a party's nonmarital property (*i.e.*, premarital, inherited, and gifted property) from spousal claims at divorce or death;
- To protect a party's interest in a business or professional services practice from a spousal claim at death or divorce;
- To predetermine the parties' property rights in the event of divorce so as to reduce the transactional costs associated with divorce;
- To put a prospective spouse or partner on notice of preexisting legal or moral obligations to a prior spouse, to children, or to others;
- To secure consent to payment of preexisting obligations with marital or community funds;
- To protect a party's right to dispose of his or her separately titled property at death, or through lifetime transfers, for the benefit of children or other family members;
- To eliminate a claim for spousal support in the event of divorce, or to predetermine an amount and duration so as to reduce the transactional costs of resolving a spousal support claim;
- To provide for compensation for a spouse upon dissolution or death who may give up income, such as support from a prior spouse, make career sacrifices, make nonmonetary contributions, or forgo other opportunities for the benefit of the other party;

- To insulate the party's earnings and acquisitions from debts of the other spouse, especially in a community property state;
- When spouses are estranged, especially if the estrangement is the result of marital misconduct, a party may want an agreement to predetermine disposition of property and spousal support as a condition of attempting reconciliation; and
- A couple in a blended family who intends to stay married may wish to do estate planning to provide for children and grandchildren of each party and may need a postmarital agreement to enable them to carry out their estate planning wishes.

Often a potential client asked to identify objectives is motivated primarily by one end-of-marriage scenario and has not thought much about the other. Older couples tend to be concerned about death, especially if there are children or grandchildren. Younger couples tend to focus more on the possibility of divorce, especially if they have experienced it themselves or within their family or peer group. The lawyer will need to educate the client about both scenarios in order to get a more expansive understanding of his or her objectives. An understanding of the client's objectives will enable the lawyer to suggest a variety of options that the client may consider to develop the terms of agreement.

(e) Premarital Agreement Versus Other Methods of Protecting Assets

Some clients considering a premarital agreement may not be sure that an agreement is what they want or may not be willing to insist on one if the fiancé(e) objects. They may want to consider other options to protect their assets. Parties who live in a state where courts have no authority to award nonmarital property of one spouse to the other at divorce can protect these assets to some degree by keeping them segregated from assets acquired with money earned during the marriage. However, if the parties live in or move to an all-property state, these protective measures will be inadequate. Moreover, under a variety of circumstances, nonmarital property can become the subject of a dispute. Disputes about whether a party commingled separate and marital assets, whether appreciation of a nonmarital asset was the result of active efforts or market forces, or whether an intraspousal transfer was a gift to the marital estate are common and can be costly to resolve.[4]

A party who expects to inherit substantial assets may be able to work with his or her parents or other family members, and their estate planning lawyer, to provide for assets to be held in a third-party trust. In some cases a client's inherited wealth may already be held in a third-party trust. The extent to which the trust vehicle will protect the assets in it from a spousal claim at divorce will vary according to the type of trust and state law.[5] In some states, an interest in a third-party trust can be included in the marital estate at divorce,[6] and in most can be considered in the determination of division of marital or community property and the amount and duration of spousal support.

A premarital or postmarital agreement can offer greater financial protection in several ways:

---

4. *See generally* BRETT TURNER, EQUITABLE DISTRIBUTION OF PROPERTY (4th ed. 2021–22).
5. *See* Marc A. Chorney, *Interests in Trusts as Property in Dissolution of Marriage: Identification and Valuation*, 40 REAL PROP. PROB. & TR. J. 1 (2005).
6. *Id.*

- An agreement can reduce substantially the transactional costs of divorce in the event the marriage does not work out by predetermining disposition of property and, in appropriate cases, fixing spousal support. An agreement can afford greater protection for a party's nonmarital assets while providing for parties who wish to do so to share the fruits of their labor. An agreement is largely portable and, therefore, can provide predictability of result in the event of divorce, regardless of where the parties may be living at the time.
- An agreement can also provide predictability of result even though there may be changes in law after the marriage relating to property rights at death or divorce.
- An agreement can allow parties in a blended family to provide for children and a surviving spouse without having their estate plans upset.
- An agreement can reduce or eliminate some of the more contentious and expensive issues from divorce by, for example, providing that (1) both active and passive appreciation of separate property is separate property; (2) all joint financial institution accounts are marital (or community) property; and (3) a party's business or professional practice, is separate property.

A party who wants to achieve maximum protection for his or her assets should combine a premarital agreement with appropriate estate planning and segregation of assets.

(f) Assessing the Client's Bottom Line

One of the most important questions the lawyer will need to ask the client is whether he or she is prepared to call off the marriage if the other party insists on terms for a premarital agreement that he or she considers unreasonable. This is especially important when the client is the economically weaker party who has been offered terms that may leave him or her vulnerable to becoming impoverished. However, it is appropriate to ask the question of a stronger party as well. It is also sometimes the case that a party will say he or she is prepared to call off the wedding, but, as the negotiations unfold, it becomes quite clear that he or she is not prepared to do so and will make the concessions necessary to get an agreement, even when it means accepting harsh terms. Some weaker parties are willing to take a chance that the marriage will be successful and that a wealthier party will make provisions for him or her at death, despite a waiver. This is a personal choice and one the client will have to live with. Similarly, some wealthier parties are willing to make more financial concessions than the lawyer may feel is appropriate in order to achieve the goal of marrying the person they have chosen. The lawyer needs to understand the client's values and priorities and conduct the negotiations accordingly.

§10.04 CONDUCT OF NEGOTIATIONS

(a) Presentation of the Terms

Once the lawyer has gathered the facts, answered questions, and evaluated the client's objectives, the lawyer for the proponent will need to produce a draft document. When one party has initiated the process, that party's lawyer will generally produce the first draft of either a comprehensive agreement or a term sheet outlining the key substantive terms. When the wedding date is close at hand, the only viable option may be a fully drafted agreement to be presented to the other party, sometimes without input from him or her. When parties have enough time, a term sheet is a viable option with the full draft to be done only after the parties have agreed in principle to the key terms. Some parties will prefer the term sheet; it may be received better as it looks more like a proposal and less like a set of predetermined terms dictated by the proponent. When parties have adequate time, or if the agreement is to be a postmarital agreement and there is no unusual time pressure, they can consider the options discussed below.

(b) Process Options for Conduct of Negotiations

One of the early decisions the lawyer and client will need to make is the best way to conduct the negotiations. It is appropriate to explore the options with the client at an early point. Some options are discussed below.

Direct Party-to-Party Negotiations

Many couples are capable of discussing between them the terms of agreement and exchanging ideas about what would be acceptable to each of them. It is generally a good sign for the ultimate success of the marriage if they are able to do so. Parties will often discuss the terms of agreement whether the lawyer thinks it is a good idea or not. When each party is financially independent and has sufficient resources to meet his or her needs, direct negotiations can often work quite well. Even when there is a disparity in resources, if the weaker party is able to communicate well and to articulate his or her needs and interests, he or she may accomplish more by dealing directly with the fiancé(e) than the lawyer will be able to accomplish by dealing with the other lawyer. The lawyer for that party will need to discuss this option with the client and assess his or her ability to conduct negotiations directly. Similarly, the lawyer for a stronger party will need to explore this option. When there is a significant disparity in resources, and the stronger party intends to drive a hard bargain, it may be better for that party if his or her lawyer takes primary responsibility for delivering the agreement and discussing the terms with the other party's lawyer.

Assuming the client wishes to attempt direct negotiations, the lawyer can add value by playing a coaching role and remaining in the background until it is time to incorporate the result into a draft. The lawyer can suggest some options to address a particular issue the parties are wrestling with and can counsel the client about positions that may be too extreme for the circumstances. The lawyer can also help the client with ideas about how to express his or her needs and interests rather than using a positional or demanding approach that may risk alienating the other party. When the lawyer is representing the stronger party, it is appropriate to counsel the client about the benefits of making some concessions in the negotiations. When the lawyer is representing the weaker party, he or she can counsel the client about how to express a need for financial security in terms that acknowledge the other party's legitimate desire to protect his or her assets. The lawyer can encourage the client to report in between discussions, so that the lawyer can provide additional input to help move the process along.

Direct party-to-party discussions about the terms of agreement can be appropriate whether both parties are represented or not. In fact, many parties, especially when they are already living together, will discuss the terms of agreement with or without the lawyer's approval. MRPC Rule 4.2 prohibits a lawyer from communicating with an adverse party whom the lawyer knows to be represented. However, a comment to Rule 4.2 points out: "Parties to a matter may communicate directly with each other, and a lawyer is not prohibited from advising a client concerning a communication that the client is legally entitled to make."[7] Thus there is no ethical prohibition on the lawyer—or both lawyers, if each is represented—coaching his or her client through direct negotiations in order to assist them to arrive at terms that are acceptable to both.

Lawyer-to-Lawyer Negotiations

Some parties will not want to conduct face-to-face negotiations with the other party. A party may not feel capable of doing so, or may want the lawyer to absorb the blame for proposals that may make the other party unhappy. In some cases the lawyer for the other party may insist on conducting the negotiations. Once the lawyer for the proponent has produced a draft, the other lawyer may initiate a discussion of the terms, by phone or in person, directly with the proponent's lawyer, or suggest one of the methods discussed below. Direct voice contact will give the lawyer an opportunity to discuss his or her client's need for terms that create a reasonable degree of financial security, float some ideas for how to achieve that while respecting the proponent's desire to protect his or her assets, and assess whether he or she is open to making changes or will insist on the terms as proposed.

Four-Way Meetings with Counsel

One or more face-to-face meetings with counsel and parties in attendance to discuss terms can be a helpful way to explore options for terms and discuss parties' objectives. If parties are able to communicate with each other about their wishes regarding terms, but prefer to have their lawyers present to assist, the four-way meeting can be productive. Parties may need to have several meetings. If they elect to conduct most of the negotiations in that manner, the first meeting will likely need to focus on financial disclosure and parties' objectives. Often parties at this stage will say they want to be fair to each other, and this can help set the stage for a negotiation that considers each party's needs and objectives. In one or more subsequent meetings they may consider various options to address specific issues, such as treatment of a marital home, spousal support, and property in the event of divorce, and disposition of property after the death of a spouse.

Mediation

Mediation allows parties to work with a neutral (or more than one) to assist them to reach terms that are acceptable to both of them. A neutral can facilitate a discussion wherein the parties contemplate the inevitable end of the marriage—by death or dissolution—and talk about their goals and objectives for an agreement governing their rights and obligations at the end. The mediation option is suitable for parties who have the time to devote to discussion

7. MRPC r. 4.2 cmt. (4).

and negotiations before the drafting begins, either because they have started the process well in advance of the wedding or because they are already married. It may not be realistic when the wedding is close at hand. Working with a neutral can further a shared goal, assuming parties actually have a shared goal, of getting an agreement that each can live with and by a process that feels more equal, in contrast to the common situation where one party more or less dictates the terms.[8]

As with other options available to the parties, their lawyers will need to evaluate whether mediation is a suitable process for them. It may be especially appropriate when parties are already married and they are estranged and are considering entering into a postmarital agreement as a condition of an attempted reconciliation. However, it can be appropriate for an unmarried couple if both are interested in an outcome over which they can jointly exercise a high degree of control. If one party intends to dictate the terms of agreement, mediation is likely to be a waste of time.

Parties may choose to participate in the mediation with just themselves and the mediator present, or they may choose the mediation model in which their attorneys attend and participate in the discussions. If they choose the former model, the process will need to allow for bringing the parties' separate lawyers into the discussion before an agreement is actually signed. They may choose to go to a single session, sometimes with the understanding that they will stay until they reach agreement; in such event, their lawyers should be present so that they can advise before the signing. A more appropriate plan—under either model—is likely to be a series of shorter sessions with the idea that in the initial session they can begin to exchange information and ideas about the terms, but that each will need time thereafter to reflect on proposed terms and consult separately with counsel, before coming to one or more subsequent sessions.

Collaborative Process

The collaborative process was developed to provide an alternative means to settle divorces outside of the court setting. However, it can also be used by parties who intend to enter into a premarital or postmarital agreement. The key features of a collaborative process are that each party is represented by a lawyer trained in interest-based negotiations and most of the communications take place in face-to-face meetings with parties and lawyers together. In some cases, parties may elect to use a mental health professional to play the role of coach to help manage the emotions that can sometimes interfere with creative problem-solving. For example, a party who was recently divorced may have difficulty making concessions when he or she may feel bitter about the concessions he or she had to make in the divorce. A party may feel extremely unhappy about being told he or she must sign a premarital agreement that violates his or her beliefs about marriage. A mental health professional acting as coach can help the parties have the difficult conversation around the possibility of divorce, or the inevitable death of a spouse, that can sometimes be an obstacle to a resolution that is acceptable to both parties. In the meetings with counsel—and the coach, if the parties elect to use a coach—the parties are encouraged to focus on their needs and interests, rather than taking

8. *See* FORREST S. MOSTEN, THE COMPLETE GUIDE TO MEDIATION (2d ed. ABA 2015).

positions, to brainstorm options, and to come up with solutions that each can live with.[9] Parties in a collaborative process also have the option of bringing in a financial planner who is trained in the collaborative process and who will function as a neutral. A financial neutral can assist in the meetings by contributing to the discussion of ideas for terms that address each party's financial objectives. He or she can also assist with tax projections and with projections of future growth of assets as part of helping parties think about the future and the impact of the agreement on their financial security going forward.

§10.05 COMMUNICATIONS

Communications about the terms for a premarital or postmarital agreement require a delicacy that is somewhat different from the approach parties and lawyers often take in divorce negotiations. In divorce negotiations, parties may take extreme positions. If they cannot agree on acceptable terms, a judge will decide; a party who is dissatisfied with a settlement offer has a viable alternative. If parties to a planned marriage cannot agree on terms, one of them may call off the wedding; for many, this is not a viable alternative. Taking an extreme position in premarital agreement negotiations rarely is the best approach. Even if a party succeeds in getting the other party to accept unreasonable terms, the harshness of the terms may leave a residue of bitterness that will undermine the stability of the marriage. When parties are already married, taking an extreme position is even more inappropriate.

The lawyer can contribute to the success of the negotiation by the words he or she chooses to articulate the client's needs and objectives and by counseling the client about how to talk about them. Terms such as "fair," "entitled," and "rights" rarely have a place in the discussion of a premarital agreement. A discussion framed in terms of the parties' true interests is generally more likely to lead to a successful outcome. The following are some examples of how a lawyer might present the concerns of a client seeking revisions to improve the terms of a premarital or postmarital agreement:

- Jack is concerned about what will happen in a few years when Harry retires. Harry wants Jack to stop working when Harry retires so they can travel, but Jack can't afford to do that. Would he agree to some transfers during the marriage to help Jack build a nest egg? We were thinking that he could give Jack an annual cash gift of $__________ and Jack would invest that money for his future financial security. Would you ask him to consider this?
- Mike knows Elizabeth wants to hold on to the house that she got when she was divorced from her former husband. However, he would not feel good about living there for many years, doing all the repairs and maintenance, contributing to the mortgage, and not having an interest in the property if the marriage doesn't work out or if she dies first. We would like her to consider a trust to hold the home for his benefit if she is the first to die. When he dies, the property can go to her children. He

9. *See* PAULINE TESSLER, COLLABORATIVE LAW: ACHIEVING EFFECTIVE RESOLUTION IN DIVORCE WITHOUT LITIGATION (3d ed., ABA 2016).

would also like her to consider letting him accrue an equity interest over time, say 5 percentage points a year beginning on the fifth anniversary up through the fifteenth anniversary. Would you recommend that to her?

- Sarah tells me she and Jeff have agreed that she will leave her job when they start a family. She could be out of the workforce for many years. We would like to talk about some options for addressing her financial needs if the marriage breaks down. We could agree that she not waive her right to ask for alimony, or we could talk about a fixed amount with a cost-of-living adjustment or a formula tied to the length of the marriage and his income. Those are some ideas we've come up with. We are open to discussing other options. What are your thoughts?
- The proposal we got from you is worrisome. Anne respects Steve's wish to protect his assets for his children. She understands how he feels after having come through a bitter divorce. But she could become impoverished if she outlives Steve, or if the marriage lasts for a long time and then they divorce. We're hoping we can come up with some terms that will strike a reasonable balance between her needs and his objectives. For example, would he consider transferring ownership of his house to joint names so that she will have a house to live in after his death? Also, Steve has a defined benefit pension plan. If Anne got the survivor benefit, whether the marriage ends by death or divorce, it would give her meaningful financial security. Is that something he could live with?

When the client will be conducting some of the negotiations on his or her own behalf, the examples above are equally applicable.

Drafting the Agreement: Overview 11

§11.01 Basic Models

A premarital or postmarital agreement generally starts out as one of two basic models on which parties may build variations according to their needs and wishes:

- *Title Controls.* For parties who wish to have an agreement that is relatively simple and inexpensive to draft and administer and that will produce a well-defined, predictable result, the agreement can define the parties' property rights at death or dissolution almost exclusively by title. In client-friendly terms, this type of agreement can be described as a his-is-his-and-hers-is-hers agreement.
- *Shared Property.* Under a shared property regime, each party maintains exclusive rights at death or dissolution to his or her nonmarital property, however that is defined in the agreement, but property acquired during the marriage through either party's labor or industry is defined as marital or community property. This approach to classification most resembles, but need not be identical to, the treatment of property at divorce in dual classification states.[1]

1. Under the dual classification system, in operation in 31 equitable distribution states (including the U.S. Virgin Islands and the District of Columbia) and seven community property states, property is classified as either marital (or community) property or as the separate (or nonmarital) property of one of the spouses; Brett Turner, Equitable Distribution of Property § 2.9, n.3 (4th ed. 2021–22) (hereafter, Turner). Separate property is generally defined as property acquired before marriage, property acquired through inheritance or gift from a source other than the spouse, and property acquired in exchange for, or that is directly traceable to, any of these sources. Turner §§ 5:2, *et seq.* Generally, all other property acquired during the marriage, regardless of how that property is titled, and regardless of which spouse's efforts produced the property, is marital/community property. Turner § 5:4. In the dual classification system, the court is permitted to make a property award only with respect to marital/ community property. Turner § 2:10. Under the all-property system, a court may divide all property of the parties in a fair and equitable manner, regardless of whether the property was acquired before or during the marriage and regardless of whether the property was acquired through labor or industry during marriage or from a nonmarital source, such as inheritance or gift from a third party. Thus,

Under either model, the agreement can provide for a wealthy party to transfer cash or other assets to an economically disadvantaged party during the marriage, or upon death or dissolution, or make other provisions for his or her economic security.

§11.02 TITLE-CONTROLS MODEL

In a title controls agreement, all separately titled property will belong to the owner, even if acquired through marital labor, and will remain the property of the owner at dissolution (except to the extent the agreement carves out a share for the nonowner). Each party will also control disposition of the assets owned by him or her at death, except as provided by the contract. All jointly titled property will be equally owned and will therefore be equally divided at dissolution, even though the parties may have contributed disproportionately to acquisition costs, and will go to the survivor at death in accordance with title. The material in Chapter 12 consists of the terms for a title-controls agreement with comments about the provisions to aid the lawyer in tailoring the agreement to the needs and wishes of the client. It also includes a number of optional add-in provisions designed to provide for an economically weaker party.

§11.03 SHARED-PROPERTY MODEL

Chapter 13 provides model paragraphs for a shared property agreement. When the parties wish to have an agreement that provides for sharing the fruits of their labor, counsel may start with the title controls agreement and substitute the appropriate paragraphs from Chapter 13. A shared property premarital or postmarital agreement typically provides for each party to have exclusive rights to nonmarital property, usually defined as premarital, inherited, and gifted assets, and to share property acquired from employment during the marriage.

Younger couples often prefer this approach because it comports with their ideas about marriage as an economic partnership. A major benefit of such an agreement is that it can allow parties to protect premarital, gifted, and inherited assets from a spousal claim without violating their feelings about what marriage is supposed to be. A proposal for such an agreement will often be readily accepted by an economically weaker party, thus making the negotiation process relatively easy.

Such an agreement can reduce the cost of divorce by providing certainty and eliminating some issues from contention that can be quite costly to litigate. Several recurring issues in divorce litigation are especially expensive to resolve. Parties who wish to do so can have a shared property agreement that mitigates the risk of these issues becoming the subject of future litigation as long as the terms of the agreement are clear and unambiguous and as long

---

in the absence of an agreement limiting parties' rights, all property owned by either spouse at divorce may be subject to discretionary division. There are 14 all-property states: Alabama, Connecticut, Indiana, Iowa, Kansas, Massachusetts, Montana, New Hampshire, North Dakota, Oregon, South Dakota, Vermont, Washington, and Wyoming. TURNER § 2.8, n.7.

as the party entitled to benefit takes the appropriate steps during the marriage to protect the property rights he or she bargained for.[2]

- The agreement can provide that a party's interest in a business or professional services practice is excluded from the marital property pool of assets but leave the owner's compensation for personal services in the marital property pool along with assets acquired from such compensation.[3] The potentially high cost of a business valuation, with competing expert witnesses, can thus be eliminated, as can the cost of litigating the extent to which appreciation of a premarital business was the result of active efforts or market forces. Taking the business out of the marital estate may also insulate the business from intrusion into its financial affairs through formal discovery.[4]
- The agreement can specifically exclude from the marital estate the appreciation in value of a party's separate property assets resulting from the application of labor, skill, industry, or creativity. In the absence of a premarital or postmarital agreement, active appreciation, as distinguished from passive market forces, can create a marital interest.[5] Active efforts that can serve as the basis for a claim include nonmonetary contributions of either party directly to appreciation of an asset, one party's contributions to the home and family that allow the other to concentrate on making money, and general nonmonetary contributions to build up marital assets in the aggregate. A properly drafted agreement can remove this issue from the determination of parties' property rights at divorce.
- A premarital or postmarital agreement can eliminate litigation over jointly titled fungible hybrid property. In the absence of an agreement, a jointly titled bank or securities account may be classified as marital property even if one party contributed all the funds from a nonmarital source, but the contributing party may be able to argue for a disproportionate division; or, the account may be classified as partly marital and partly nonmarital to the extent a party can clearly trace out his or her separate property contributions.[6] Litigation over a party's attempts to trace his or her separate property contributions into a jointly titled asset can be quite costly, and, like business valuation and arguments over passive versus active appreciation, results are unpredictable. An agreement that provides that a jointly titled financial institution account is marital property, without regard to the source of funds, can eliminate such litigation. A party who signs an agreement with such a provision is on notice and can govern the management of his or her separate and marital funds accordingly.

---

2. See Chapter 8, Postmarriage Issues.
3. *See Vanheusden v. Vanheusden*, 2005 Mich. App. LEXIS 643 (unpub.) (portion of sale price paid for non-compete was part of proceeds and not marital income under premarital agreement based on consideration of particular facts and competing expert opinions); *In re Marriage of Conner*, 713 N.E.2d 883 (Ind. Ct. App. 1999) (enterprise good will in husband's medical practice properly included in marital estate under premarital agreement classifying all property acquired during marriage as marital).
4. However, when child support is at issue, the support claimant may be able to get discovery of the books and records of the business as parties cannot, by contract, oust a court from jurisdiction to decide support for a minor child. See Section 7.03 of this book.
5. TURNER §§ 5:54 *et seq.*
6. *Id.* §§ 5:58 *et seq.*

An agreement that predetermines a division of the marital assets at a time when each party is motivated to be fair can greatly reduce the transactional costs of divorce if the marriage does not work out. A shared property agreement can work well if parties are starting out in comparable circumstances and neither has an incentive to stop contributing other than as a result of shared decisions, for example, a shared decision that a parent will stay home to raise children.

As appealing as a shared property agreement may be for many couples, there are some issues the drafter should consider:

- When one party has substantial wealth going into the marriage, or stands to inherit substantial wealth, he or she may be able to afford to quit working and contributing earnings into the marital property pool of assets. This could leave an economically disadvantaged spouse as the sole contributor to an asset pool that the other spouse will get part of in the event of dissolution.
- One spouse may work hard and save while the other spouse is lazy, wastes money, gambles, makes bad investments, or spends money on outside romantic interests.[7] The model shared property agreement leaves no room for a court to take such factors into account.
- Parties may consume marital income for normal living expenses while a wealthy party holds on to his or her separate property.

More record keeping is required in a shared property regime to maintain a party's exclusive rights to his or her separate property. Some may find it burdensome to maintain separate financial institution accounts for separate and marital funds and securities, and to keep track of and record the source of funds for acquisition of property so as to get accurate attribution. However, in the absence of a marital agreement, a party who wants to segregate his or her premarital and inherited assets will have the same burden.

Some parties may prefer to define and provide for each to retain exclusive rights to separate property but to leave the determination of what is a fair division of marital property to resolution upon dissolution. That approach would allow for consideration of future circumstances, including the factors discussed above.

§11.04 DRAFTING TO AVOID LITIGATION

An agreement can provide a clear roadmap to disposition of property at death or dissolution or it can invite litigation. General principles of contract law govern how a court interprets a premarital or postmarital agreement. These include that the agreement speaks for itself, all parts of the agreement must be given effect, the court will not read into it terms that are not

7. *See K. v. B.*, 12 A.D.3d 12 (N.Y. App. Div. 2004), where, but for the fact that he forgot to mention the premarital agreement until he testified at the divorce trial, the husband would have gotten half the marital assets, although he contributed almost nothing to the accumulation of assets, and the wife raised the parties' children virtually alone while also working very hard.

there, and the general inadmissibility of parol evidence to vary unambiguous terms.[8] As is the case with contracts generally, a court must look to the four corners of the agreement for its meaning. It cannot apply some unexpressed purpose or claimed intent of the parties, nor a vague promise, such as a promise or intent to take care of a weaker party, to interpret its terms.[9]

Much of the litigation about construction of premarital and postmarital agreements arises from a failure to define clearly and unambiguously the key terms of the agreement and the parties' intentions about application of the agreement under the various circumstances that may arise in the future.[10] A poorly drafted agreement will nevertheless be valid as a contract.[11] An agreement that insufficiently delineates the parties' property rights at death or dissolution, or that is ambiguous, contradictory, or incomplete, will serve the parties poorly.[12]

When parties enter into an agreement that purports to completely define their rights regarding property or support, they substitute their contract for the rules that would otherwise apply at death or dissolution in the absence of agreement. As a result, they generally forgo whatever right they might have to ask a court to apply principles of equity to achieve a fair result with very limited exceptions.[13] Changed circumstances will not warrant a reformation of the agreement except in very limited circumstances.[14] Discovery of enforcement problems will not justify a court changing how property is divided at divorce or allocated at death to more effectively carry out the terms of the agreement.[15] Rather, the terms of the parties' contract will determine their rights and obligations. There is little opportunity to alter those contractual terms to take into account intervening events.[16]

---

8. *Levin v. Carlton*, 213 P.3d 884 (Utah 2009); *In re Marriage of Best*, 228 Ill. 2d 107, 886 N.E.2d 939 (2008); *Plunkett v. Plunkett*, 271 Va. 162, 624 S.E.2d 39 (2006); *Seherr-Thoss v. Seherr-Thoss*, 141 P.3d 703 (Wyo. 2006); *Cannon v. Cannon*, 384 Md. 537, 865 A.2d 563 (2005); *Schmidt v. Schmidt*, 812 N.E.2d 1074 (Ind. Ct. App. 2004); *Badger v. Badger*, 2002 Ohio 448 (Ct. App. 2002); *In re Marriage of Conner*, 713 N.E.2d 883 (Ind. Ct. App. 1999); *Wilkes v. O'Bryan*, 98 Wash. App. 411, 989 P.2d 594 (1999); *Stichter v. Zuidema*, 269 Ill. App. 3d 455, 646 N.E.2d 296 (1995); *In re Estate of Barilla*, 535 A.2d 125 (Pa. Super. Ct. 1987).

9. *See Ayers v. Ayers*, 2022 Ala. Civ. App. LEXIS 106, (unpub.).

10. But some of the litigation over construction appears motivated by a party's dissatisfaction with the terms, rather than with any realistic expectation that a court will invalidate the agreement as a whole.

11. *Newman v. Newman*, 291 Ga. 635, 732 S.E.2d 77 (2012).

12. *See, e.g.*, *Montoya v. Montoya*, 280 Conn. 605, 909 A.2d 947 (2006), where one provision of the agreement said marital property included appreciation of certain separate property and another provision said appreciation on separate property was not marital property. The trial court was forced to reconcile a seemingly irreconcilable conflict in the definitions. The ultimate resolution is unreported.

13. *See Wilkes*, 98 Wash. App. 411; *Stichter*, 269 Ill. App. 3d 455 (unambiguous contract must be enforced as written).

14. *See Snedaker v. Snedaker*, 660 So. 2d 1070 (Fla. Dist. Ct. App. 1995) (court may not rewrite otherwise valid premarital agreement to provide more generous support); *In re Marriage of Stout*, 261 Mont. 10, 861 P.2d 856 (1993) (court had no authority to change disposition of property under valid premarital agreement because wife gave up favorable grazing lease at husband's insistence).

15. *See In re Marriage of Applegate*, 567 N.W.2d 671 (Iowa Ct. App. 1997) (court may not award wife different property than that to which she was entitled under premarital agreement due to inability to enforce her right to Cayman Islands property); *De Liedekerke v. De Liedekerke*, 635 A.2d 339 (D.C. 1993) (trial court not required to order immediate offset for division of pensions because of difficulty of enforcing spousal pension rights where premarital agreement did not require this method of division).

16. *D'Arc v. D'Arc*, 164 N.J. Super. 226, 395 A.2d 1270 (Ch. Div. 1978), *rev'd in part, aff'd in part*, 175 N.J. Super. 598, 421 A.2d 602 (App. Div. 1980), is a rare example of extreme intervening events where a court found a way to void an agreement. The wife was a wealthy heiress and the husband a nonworking psychiatrist. At the husband's request, the wife voluntarily signed a postmarital agreement providing extremely generous monthly support for the husband and his children by a prior marriage. The agreement stated it was to be incorporated into

It is worth noting here one of the benefits of each party having independent counsel. Where parties share a common goal of defining their rights clearly and avoiding future litigation, two lawyers working toward the same goal are more likely to catch ambiguities, inconsistencies, and other potential drafting errors and omissions than one lawyer working alone.

a decree of divorce. Subsequently, the husband arranged to have the wife murdered. His plan failed but that did not stop him from seeking alimony under the agreement. Less egregious intervening events would not necessarily afford a basis for relieving a party of his or her obligations under a contract.

12 MODEL TITLE-CONTROLS AGREEMENT WITH PROVISIONS FOR WEAKER PARTY

The material in this chapter consists of model text for a complete agreement coupled with comments about the various provisions. The model terms that follow can be used for a premarital or a postmarital agreement. The model in this chapter is structured such that each party's rights at death or dissolution are determined solely by title; all separately titled property belongs to the owner to dispose of at death as he or she sees fit, and all jointly titled survivorship property will be divided equally in the event of dissolution or become the property of the surviving spouse in the event of death. When there is a big wealth disparity, the lawyers for the parties should consider terms to provide for him or her. The following model terms include options for doing so.

PREMARITAL [POSTMARITAL] AGREEMENT

This Agreement is made this day ____ of ____________, 20__, by and between SPOUSE ONE, [prospective husband/wife], (hereafter referred to as "_____"), and SPOUSE TWO, [prospective husband/wife], (hereafter referred to as "_____").

RECITALS: COMMENT

Recitals are not operative provisions of a contract unless the contract expressly incorporates them as such.[1] They do not create rights, expand rights, or withdraw rights.[2] Recitals deserve attention because they can create mischief when poorly drafted. References in the recitals to parties' intentions should conform to the operative terms

1. The model agreement herein expressly incorporates the recitals as operative terms. See paragraph 57.
2. *Dornemann v. Dornemann*, 48 Conn. Supp. 502, 850 A.2d 273 (2004); *Johnson v. Johnson*, 725 So. 2d 1209 (Fla. Dist. Ct. App. 1999); *Foster v. Foster*, 609 A.2d 1171 (Me. 1992).

of the agreement. For example, in *Cameron v. Cameron*,[3] a recital stated the wife intended to waive her rights to property then owned or to be acquired by the husband. However, the operative provisions of the agreement only waived any rights she might have had to his premarital property. The court held she did not waive her right to make a claim at divorce to a share of property acquired during the marriage.

A recital can provide evidence of the parties' intent but is not dispositive.[4] The language chosen to express the parties' rights and obligations should be words of promise or words of waiver, rather than merely statements of general intent. For example, in *Uhrig v. Pulliam*,[5] the premarital agreement had a recital stating the husband contemplated making a will leaving some or all of his estate to the wife. However, the agreement waived all claims the wife would have had as a surviving spouse. The court held the husband was not obligated to make a will or precluded from revoking one; there was no promise.[6] Similarly, in *Barrows v. Barrows*,[7] a recital said the parties intended the premarital agreement to apply at divorce or death. The text of the agreement did not include an express waiver of each party's rights as a surviving spouse. Rather, it stated all property of a party would remain his or her "personal estate and constitute non-marital property."[8] The court refused to hold that the recitals established the parties' intent to waive the elective share as a matter of law, and it sent the case back to the trial court for an evidentiary hearing on intent. Of course, the deceased husband was unavailable to testify to his intent.

The recitals should state clearly whether the agreement is to apply only upon the death of a party, only upon dissolution of the marriage, or in either event. Some parties, or their lawyers, prefer to avoid using the word *divorce*, perhaps because it seems unromantic, but the failure to make clear the parties' intentions has been the cause of avoidable litigation and, as with all litigation, outcomes are unpredictable.[9] The better approach is to use explicit language referring to both divorce, or another term that makes the parties' intent clear, such as dissolution of the marriage or marital separation, and death.

The recitals should be factually accurate. For example, the recitals should not state that both parties are employed and capable of supporting themselves unless the statement is true.[10]

---

3. 591 So. 2d 275 (Fla. Dist. Ct. App. 1991); *see also Vilseck v. Vilseck*, 45 Va. App. 581, 612 S.E.2d 746 (2005).

4. *See Pisano v. Pisano*, 87 Mass. App. Ct. 403, 31 N.E.3d 1132 (2015); *Dowling v. Rowan*, 270 Va. 510, 621 S.E.2d 397 (2005).

5. 713 S.W.2d 649 (Tenn. 1986).

6. *See also Cameron v. Cameron*, 591 So. 2d 275 (Fla. Dist. Ct. App. 1991); *but see Badger v. Badger*, 2002 Ohio 448 (Ct. App. 2002) (provision that parties contemplated sharing household expenses obligated each to contribute).

7. 913 A.2d 608 (Me. 2006).

8. *Id.* at 613.

9. See *Roth v. Roth*, 565 N.W.2d 782 (S.D. 1997), and *Gentry v. Gentry*, 798 S.W.2d 928 (Ky. 1990), where the courts came to the opposite conclusion about whether the parties intended a premarital agreement to apply at divorce, or only at death. The waiver language in the two agreements was almost identical. *See also Pysell v. Keck*, 263 Va. 457, 559 S.E.2d 677 (2002) (premarital agreement that waived rights acquired by operation of law waived property rights only at divorce; wife entitled to elective share at death); *In re Marriage of Bridge*, 166 Or. App. 458, 998 P.2d 780 (2000) (premarital agreement that waived all spousal rights, but did not mention divorce, applied at divorce); *Stokes v. Stokes*, 98 Ohio App. 3d 238, 648 N.E.2d 83 (1994) (premarital agreement silent on subject of divorce, which waived all spousal claims, followed by listing of rights at death, did not apply at divorce).

10. *See Knutson v. Knutson*, 246 Wis. 2d 988, 632 N.W.2d 123 (2001) (no change in circumstances shown where recital stated wife was unemployed).

Similarly, the recitals should not say the parties made full disclosure or that each party consulted independent counsel unless true.[11]

A premarital agreement typically recites that the parties intend to get married after execution of the agreement. The agreement may recite a planned wedding date. However, when a premarital agreement specifies a planned wedding date, a postponement of the wedding after execution, or a breakup followed by reconciliation and a new wedding date, can create a basis for litigation over whether the parties intended to abrogate the agreement.[12]

The recitals should support the law chosen to govern the agreement by showing a nexus between at least one party and the state of governing law.[13]

The recitals in the model include a statement in boldface that each party has read the agreement. This is intended to highlight for each party the importance of reading the agreement before signing it.

Counsel in a second-look state should pay particular attention to statements in the recitals that can help to create a basis for a court to decide an agreement has become unfair at divorce as a result of changed circumstances.

RECITALS: MODEL TEXT

RECITALS

1. The parties plan to marry after execution of this Agreement. [***Alternative:*** The parties plan to marry on ______ [DATE] and after execution of this Agreement.] [***If parties are already married:*** The parties were married on ______ [DATE] and are now husband and wife/spouses. The parties have ___children together: ______.]

2. Each party currently owns separate property, all of which has been acquired independently of and without the assistance of the other.

3. SPOUSE ONE is employed with ________________________________ as ________________. [***Optional:*** He/She is in good health to the best of his/her knowledge.] SPOUSE TWO is employed with ____________________ as __________________. [***Optional:*** He/She is in good health to the best of his/her knowledge.]

4. The parties are residents of ________. [***Or:*** SPOUSE ONE is currently a resident of ___________________ and SPOUSE TWO is a resident of ______________.]

5. SPOUSE ONE has [never] been married [previously] and has _____/[no] children. SPOUSE TWO has [never] been married [previously] and has _____/[no] children. [***Add, if appropriate:*** _____ has financial obligations for _____ his/her child/ren and for a previous spouse.]

11. *See Remillard v. Remillard*, 2022 Va. App. LEXIS 417 (unpub.); *In re Estate of Eichstadt*, 983 N.W.2d 572 (S.D. 2022); *Moore v. Moore*, 383 S.W.3d 190 (Tex. Ct. App. 5th Dist., 2012); *Cassidy v. Cassidy*, 356 S.W.3d 339 (Mo. Ct. App. So. Dist., 2011).

12. See Section 8.03 for further discussion of this problem.

13. See further discussion of choice-of-law in Comment to paragraph 56.

6. **Each party read this Agreement in its entirety before signing it.**

7. [***If a postmarital agreement, state reason for agreement, e.g.:*** (i) The parties intended to enter into a premarital agreement, but did not have enough time to conclude the negotiations and drafting prior to the date of marriage. (ii) The parties are living apart and are estranged, but intend to pursue reconciliation and believe that entering into this Agreement will promote that goal. In furtherance of their goal, they wish to settle and determine their property rights and any potential claims for spousal support in the event they fail to reconcile. (iii) The parties intend to make certain property transfers to further their estate planning objectives and they intend this Agreement to determine their property rights upon the death of a party or a marital separation.]

8. The parties intend, by this Agreement, to establish their rights in all property currently owned or hereafter acquired by each of them upon the death of a party or in the event of a marital separation or divorce. The parties intend that each of them shall have the right to retain his/her separate property and to share marital property as defined in this Agreement.

9. [***Include following text if agreement provides for waiver of spousal support:*** Each party further desires to waive any right or claim he or she has or may ever have to support from the other in the event of a marital separation or divorce [***add if agreement provides for contractual spousal support:***, except as specifically provided herein]. [***Optional:*** Each party is capable of providing for his or her own support through employment and through other means. Neither party intends to be dependent on the other for support in the future.]

10. The parties to this Agreement do not intend to facilitate or encourage a separation or divorce. Each party believes that the resolution of the issues covered by this Agreement in the manner set forth will promote their married life together, since the interests and values embodied in this Agreement are shared by and important to each party. The parties enter into this Agreement after thoughtful discussions between themselves, consultations with and advice from independent counsel, or the opportunity for such advice, and with love and respect for each other. Both parties intend for this Agreement to eliminate any issues between them in the event this marriage is unsuccessful or between one of them and the other's family upon the death of a spouse.

11. The parties acknowledge that this Agreement is a premarital [***or:*** postmarital] agreement as defined by law. Each party understands and intends that the provisions of this Agreement shall prevail over any statute or law of ____________________, or any other jurisdiction, including any foreign jurisdiction, which may be applicable in the absence of this Agreement, and that this Agreement shall govern their rights and obligations upon death, separation, or divorce regardless of where they may be living at the time.

12. The parties acknowledge that a party may experience changed circumstances during the marriage [***if a postmarital agreement:*** after execution of this Agreement], such as a substantial increase or decrease in property values, or a decline in actual earnings, or earning potential, due to illness, disability, loss of employment, or market conditions, and that such changes may be unanticipated. The parties nevertheless agree that no change in circumstances shall affect the fairness and mutual consideration given at the time this Agreement is entered into nor shall it affect the validity of this Agreement or any provision thereof.

IN CONSIDERATION of the mutual promises and exchanges made by each party to this Agreement, the parties agree as follows:

DEFINITIONS, PROPERTY AND INCOME: COMMENT

The definitions of property, retirement benefits, earnings, and income in the model paragraphs below describe comprehensively the forms of wealth on which the agreement operates.

- The definition of property includes an option to include virtual currency, such as bitcoin, and other digital assets, such as nonfungible tokens (NFTs).
- The definition of property also includes animal companions.[14]
- The definition of property does not include stored embryos.[15]
- The definition of earnings includes contributions to a retirement plan as well as deferred compensation and other cash benefits. It also includes an optional provision for noncash employee benefits, such as paid leave.

If the agreement includes a provision for spousal support as a percentage of earnings, the drafting attorney should consider this text, and make adjustments as necessary; for example, it may not be appropriate to include the value of paid leave for purposes of calculation of support.

Retirement benefits include an individual retirement account, but only if derived from earnings, in order to distinguish such an account from an inherited IRA.

Among the reasons to include these definitions, they can serve to make clear to the other party, especially if unrepresented, the property rights he or she is waiving by entering into the agreement.

There may be some situations where these definitions can be deleted. When the agreement will need to be translated for a weaker party who is not fluent in English, the cost of translation, time constraints, or a desire to reduce the length of the agreement may suggest eliminating all terms that are not absolutely essential. As long as the definitions of separate

14. See BARBARA JOAN GISLASON, PET LAW AND CUSTODY: ESTABLISHING A WORTHY AND EQUITABLE JURISPRUDENCE FOR THE EVOLVING FAMILY (ABA 2017); *see also L.B. v. C.C.B.*, 175 N.Y.S.3d 705 (Sup. Ct., Kings Cnty. 2022) (resolving dispute over dogs as part of property division at divorce).

15. See Section 7.02(d) of this book.

and marital property remain intact, the meaning of the agreement will not be damaged. When both parties have counsel, counsel may make a judgment that these definitions are not necessary since each party will have access to independent advice and will be able to get an explanation of the agreement and its effect on his or her rights. If the drafting attorney elects to delete these definitions, he or she should consider the optional text in model paragraph 6(ii).

DEFINITIONS, PROPERTY AND INCOME: MODEL TEXT

DEFINITIONS

1. **Property**. "Property" means any interest, present or future, legal or equitable, vested or contingent, in any property, including real property, personal property, both tangible and intangible, whenever and wherever acquired or located. "Real property" means land, together with improvements and fixtures thereon. "Tangible personal property" means movable tangible assets, such as, but not limited to, furniture, furnishings, clothing, jewelry, art, automobiles, and equipment, and further includes animal companions. "Intangible personal property" means incorporeal assets, such as, but not limited to, cash, virtual currency, such as bitcoin, nonfungible tokens (NFTs), and other digital assets, certificates of deposit, negotiable instruments such as checks, notes, and mortgages, accounts receivable, insurance, annuities, interest in a trust (whether vested or contingent interest, or current or remainder interest), retirement benefits, an inherited IRA, ownership interest in a business or professional services practice, including, but not limited to, a limited liability company, partnership or "S" corporation, a copyright, patent, software license, or other form of intellectual property, and securities such as stock, bonds, units and options, and where any such property is held in a bank, brokerage, or other financial institution account, the account itself. "Untitled property" shall mean property that lacks a formal document, such as a deed, motor vehicle title, or stock certificate, evidencing ownership.

2. **Retirement Benefits and Plans and Other Forms of Deferred Compensation.** "Retirement benefit" or "retirement plan" means any individual retirement account or annuity funded with or derived from a party's earnings, and any pension plan, profit-sharing plan, employee savings plan, 401(k) plan, and any other deferred compensation benefit or plan, qualified or non-qualified, including, but not limited to, a stock award, stock purchase, restricted share, stock unit, or stock option plan, provided through employment or self-employment.

3. **Earnings**. "Earnings" means monies and other compensation derived from a party's personal services, labor, or employment, including, but not limited to, salary, wages, bonuses, origination fees, and commissions; in the case of an active business owner who reports profit or loss on a Form 1040, Schedule C or E, or who operates as an "S" corporation, partnership, or limited liability company, the active business owner's share of the business profits (defined as gross receipts in the ordinary course of business from the sale of goods or services less reasonable and necessary

business expenses and a reasonable allowance for deferred costs, such as depreciation and amortization); net royalty income (defined as gross royalties less reasonable and necessary expenses, including amortization or depreciation, of producing the income) from intellectual property of which a party is the author, creator, or inventor, or otherwise derived from a party's personal services, labor, or employment; employer and employee contributions to a retirement benefit or plan, or other deferred compensation plan; accrued but unpaid compensation; severance pay; and all other cash compensation derived from personal efforts or employment. [***Optional:*** "Earnings" also includes noncash employee benefits, such as, but not limited to, paid leave, health, life and disability insurance, company-provided vehicle or transportation allowance, expense accounts and allowances, the right to retain for personal use points or other awards from participation in an affiliation program, such as a credit card, hotel, or airline awards program, and all other noncash remuneration derived from personal efforts or employment.] The definition of "earnings" in this Agreement is without regard to whether any such earnings are reportable on an income tax return or are subject to income taxes.

4. **Income**. "Income" means monies derived from sources other than earnings and includes, but is not limited to, dividends, interest, rents, royalties not defined as earnings (including royalties from oil, mineral, or other rights in real property), proceeds from the sale of property, distributions from an estate or trust, and distributions (other than distributions of nonpassive income defined as earnings, as provided in Paragraph 3) from a pass-through entity, such as a limited liability company, partnership or "S" corporation, distributions from a retirement plan or other deferred compensation plan, and other property in which a party has an interest.

DEFINITIONS, SEPARATE AND MARITAL PROPERTY: COMMENT

Model paragraphs 5 and 6 provide comprehensive definitions of separate property and marital property. For an agreement to be effective to determine disposition of property, it must clearly delineate:

- The definition (or classification) of property as separate property, shared property (marital, community), or hybrid property (a mixture); and
- How each category of property will be allocated upon dissolution or death.

Provisions for classification and for disposition of property are both important. Definition without disposition is insufficient. In a Washington case, *In re Marriage of Dewberry and George*,[16] the parties had a premarital agreement that classified each party's earnings and separately titled assets as separate property, but the agreement did not include a waiver of the right to equitable distribution. As a result, the husband got an equitable award. Had the parties

16. 115 Wn. App. 351, 62 P.3d 525 (2003).

intended for classification of property as separate to dictate disposition of such property at divorce, the agreement should have expressly stated that intent.[17]

Similarly, disposition without classification is insufficient. It is insufficient to state that separate property will belong to the owner and marital property will be divided without defining the terms *separate* and *marital*. For example, in *Irwin v. Irwin*,[18] a Florida case, the premarital agreement stated each party would retain property owned by him or her but did not define what was included in and what was excluded from the asset pool to which each party would have exclusive rights at divorce. The appellate court ruled that the wife did not waive the right to property acquired with marital earnings because the agreement did not specifically reserve the husband's exclusive right to these assets.[19] A comprehensive definition of separate property could have averted this result.[20]

In defining each party's separate property, the agreement should be clear about whether separate property consists solely of premarital, inherited, and gifted property, or whether it includes property acquired during the marriage as a result of working, earning money, and acquiring property with earnings.[21] Merely identifying the source and amount of earnings in a pre-execution financial disclosure is not tantamount to making earnings acquired during the marriage separate property.[22] A provision that a party desires to retain exclusive rights to property "now owned or hereafter acquired" is insufficient, standing alone, to make property acquired by one party during the marriage his or her separate property. In *In re Marriage of Irons*,[23] for example, the court rejected the "hereafter acquired" language as including newly acquired assets in the pool of each party's separate property; rather, the court interpreted that phrase to include in separate property only any accretions to premarital property. If parties intend that a party's income and retirement benefits earned from employment during marriage be separate property, the agreement should clearly say so.[24]

The definitions that follow make compensation from employment separate property, consistent with the general approach in this model that property rights are determined exclusively by title.

17. *See also Hankins v. Hankins*, 2018 N.C. App. LEXIS 22, 808 S.E. 2d 621 (unpub.) (premarital agreement gave each party exclusive rights to his/her property, but did not include express waiver of equitable distribution at divorce; agreement did not waive equitable distribution of property acquired during marriage).

18. 857 So. 2d 247 (Fla. App. 2003).

19. The *Irwin* agreement also did not define the husband's property to include appreciation in the value of the husband's separate property during the marriage. Thus the wife did not waive her right to share in the appreciation. This aspect of *Irwin* was overruled in *Hahamovich v. Hahamovich*, 173 So. 3d 983 (Fla. 2015), where the court held that a comprehensive waiver was adequate to waive an interest in appreciation of separate property.

20. *See also Johnson v. Johnson*, 725 So. 2d 1209 (Fla. Ct. App., 3d Dist., 1999) (premarital agreement silent as to disposition of separately titled property acquired during marriage; wife entitled to equitable interest in real estate acquired during marriage); *Brown v. Brown*, 100 Wash. 2d 729, 675 P.2d 1207 (1984) (postmarital agreement providing for sharing of community property, without defining community property, required court to determine whether personal injury settlement was separate or community).

21. *Hankins*, 2018 N.C. App. LEXIS 22, 808 S.E. 2d 621.

22. *Steis v. Steis*, 297 Ga. 483, 775. S.E.2d 139 (2015); *Allard v. Allard*, 308 Mich. App. 536, 867 N.W.2d 866 (2014).

23. 2016 Kan. App. Unpub. LEXIS 574.

24. *Fletcher v. Fletcher*, 2020 Ind. App. Unpub. LEXIS 168 (premarital agreement did not define separate property; income during marriage was therefore marital property); *Dow v. Billing*, 224 N.E.3d 244 (Me. 2020) (premarital agreement providing all property owned at marriage, plus additions and increases, was separate property; contributions to retirement plan during marriage are marital property, subject to division at divorce); *see also In re Marriage of Touhy-Silverman*, 2020 Ill. App. Unpub. LEXIS 964.

The model agreement provides for all joint financial institution accounts to be marital property without regard to the source of funds, consistent with the title-controls approach. Making a joint financial institution account always marital property should eliminate burdensome record-keeping and potential litigation over tracing the source of monies a party may claim is their separate property that went in the account and the disposition of such monies that went out of the account.[25] In this model, all property acquired with funds from a jointly-titled financial institution account is marital property even if titled in one spouse's name (with certain exceptions).

Under this model, all real estate titled in a survivorship form, and any other property titled in survivorship, is marital property without regard to the source of funds for acquisition. The purpose is to eliminate disputes about whether a party intended to make a gift when he or she titled property jointly that would otherwise have been his or her separate property.[26] Moreover, this outcome is consistent with the general approach of the model agreement under which title is dispositive. There is no room for a claim that a spouse did not intend to create marital property when he or she transferred separate real estate into survivorship title. A party who wants to transfer real estate into survivorship, so that a surviving spouse will get it, but who wants the right to reclaim it if the marriage fails, must take steps to carry out that intention and may need to enter into an amendment or a supplemental agreement. He or she could also transfer real estate or other assets into a revocable trust of which the spouse is beneficiary so that the spouse will receive it upon the settlor's death, but which the settlor can revoke upon separation.

The model includes optional text providing that the primary marital home is marital property without regard to the source of funds for acquisition; it does not mandate that title be held in survivorship. Counsel for the disadvantaged party may want to propose a requirement for survivorship title. Such a provision can be appropriate when a wealthy party wants to carve out some benefits for a disadvantaged party.[27]

The definition of separate property expressly includes a party's interest in a closely held business or professional services practice. Protection for a business owner's exclusive rights to the business is often a key motivator for him or her to seek a premarital or postmarital agreement.[28] The definition of separate property does not leave room for a party to claim that a business, or any of its assets, has become marital property other than by a transfer of title. Nevertheless, the owner will be better served by segregating the business and its assets from assets defined as marital property. For example, in *Snyder v. Snyder*,[29] the parties loaned community property funds to the wife's separate property business and used community funds

25. *Steis*, 297 Ga. 483 (resolving dispute about whether joint titling intended as gift to marital estate under premarital agreement); *Parsons v. Parsons*, 2012 Va. App. LEXIS 79 (unpub.) (resolving dispute over jointly titled securities account funded entirely with husband's premarital assets); *see also Bowman v. Bowman*, 332 So. 3d 317 (Miss. 2021); *Hankins*, 2018 N.C. App. LEXIS 22, 808 S.E. 2d 621.

26. *See Est. of Eagle v. Eagle*, 2022 Va. App. LEXIS 474 (unpub.) (husband's transfer of bank account to joint names with right of survivorship caused account to become marital property under parties' premarital agreement; husband could not cause the account to revert to him as his separate property by transferring title back to his sole name); *Zaccardelli v. Zaccardelli*, 2013 Ohio App. LEXIS 1765 (unpub.) (resolving dispute under premarital agreement about whether deed transferring husband's premarital real estate into joint names was an amendment, causing real estate to become marital property).

27. See the following model paragraphs 28–32, and accompanying Comment for terms that enable parties to get back separate property contributions to a home.

28. *See, e.g., Snyder v. Snyder*, 2022 Nev. App. Unpub. LEXIS 475.

29. *Id.*

to pay legal expenses of one of her businesses. The court rejected the husband's attempt to claim a community interest in her businesses, but only after expensive litigation with no guarantee as to the outcome. The owner of a business should not make false representations to the spouse or others that the spouse is a co-owner. Doing so could cause a court to deem the business a joint asset.[30]

Because many types of tangible personal property do not have formal documents of title, the model addresses this type of property in several ways.[31] As discussed below, each party's clothing, jewelry, sports equipment, and personal effects are defined as separate property without regard to the source of funds for acquisition. Similarly, each party's animal companions are defined as separate property without regard to the source of funds for acquisition. Tangible personal property purchased from a joint financial institute account is defined as marital property (except a party's clothing, jewelry, sports equipment, and personal effects). Other tangible personal property without formal title is defined as marital property unless it fits specifically in one of the separate property categories. A party who may acquire expensive items of tangible personal property should keep good records of the source of funds for acquisition.

As a practical matter, it will generally make the most sense for the agreement to provide that each party will own and retain as separate property his or her clothing, jewelry, and personal effects, including any such items that were given as gifts from the other party, without regard to the source of funds for acquisition. However, such a provision could have unintended consequences if a party purchases very expensive items that are used by the other party but that he or she intends as an investment, or purchases expensive items for his or her own use from a joint account. In *Hrudka v. Hrudka*,[32] for example, the parties spent over $1 million on jewelry during the marriage. The wife claimed the purchases were intended as gifts to her as evidenced by the fact that she had possession and that she wore the jewelry. The husband claimed the purchases were intended as investments to benefit them jointly. The courts upheld the husband's position, but there was sufficient evidence to support a contrary result. A similar problem can occur if parties opt to include in the definition of marital property high value tangibles that will be used in a marital home without regard to the source of funds for acquisition. For example, if one party is an art collector who displays some of his or her collection at home, the agreement should make clear whether these items are separate or marital property. The optional text in paragraphs 5(vii), (viii), and 6(xiii) addresses this.

Defining property rights by title, and providing waivers at both death and divorce of each party's claim to property titled in the name of the other, should be sufficient to protect a party's exclusive rights to these assets.[33] However, the model text below fleshes out this principle by identifying specific categories of property, for example, proceeds of a personal

30. *See Simons v. Simons*, 312 Neb. 136, 978 N.W.2d 121 (2022).

31. *See Morabito v. Morabito*, 2013 Pa. Dist. & Cnty. Dec. LEXIS 139 (unpub.) (resolving dispute over construction of premarital agreement where husband claimed marital property limited to property with formal documents of title).

32. 186 Ariz. 86, 919 P.2d 179 (Ct. App. 1995); *see also Connell v. Connell*, 93 So. 3d 1140 (Fla. Ct. App. 2d Dist. 2012).

33. *See Hahamoritch v. Hahamovitch*, 173 So. 3d 983 (Fla. 2015) (premarital agreement waiving each party's rights to property titled in other spouse's name included earnings, assets acquired with earnings and appreciation, even though not specifically mentioned).

injury claim,[34] that are to be treated as separate property. When the definition of separate property is insufficient, a court may fall back on state law to fill in the gap. For example, in *Short v. Short*,[35] the premarital agreement defined property owned prior to marriage as separate property but did not expressly define income from premarital property as separate property. Because Missouri law defined such income as marital property, the trial court used the statutory definition to treat it as marital property. To be effective to protect the separate property interests of a party, the contractual definitions must be sufficiently comprehensive as to preclude any claim under a statutory or case law definition of marital or community property.

The definition of separate property is comprehensive. It may be tempting to include a catchall—all property defined as separate property under the law that would otherwise apply in the absence of agreement—but such a provision will likely add nothing and can introduce an opportunity for litigation.[36] Premarital agreements typically opt out of the statutory scheme with express waivers of rights parties would otherwise acquire by virtue of marriage. An agreement that appears to both opt out of and incorporate the statutory scheme is potentially ambiguous.

The model definitions here resolve a potential conflict when an asset might appear to be classifiable as either marital or separate. Key to this is the opening text of paragraph 6, which provides that separate property is property "not defined as marital property under paragraph 5." Thus, a solely titled securities account funded with money from a joint bank account is marital property, despite paragraph 6(v), because it cannot meet the requirement that it be "not defined as marital property." Similarly, a jointly titled home (which is marital property under paragraph 5(ii)) cannot be one party's separate property, even if purchased entirely with his or her separate property funds, because it fails the "not defined as marital property" test.[37]

DEFINITIONS, MARITAL AND SEPARATE PROPERTY: MODEL TEXT

5. **Marital Property**. "Marital property" of the parties shall be, and is limited to:

(i) funds or securities held in an account of the parties at a financial institution (such as a bank, credit union, or securities brokerage) and titled as tenants by the entirety, joint tenants with right of survivorship, or tenants in common, without regard to the source of funds except as provided in Paragraph 7(G);

34. *See Richman v. Richman*, 2013 Tenn. App. LEXIS 683 (unpub.) (resolving surviving spouse's claim to wrongful death proceeds where premarital agreement waived all marital rights); *see also Roseman v. Glanz*, 2010 Ohio App. LEXIS 556 (unpub.)

35. 356 S.W.3d 235 (Mo. Ct. App., E.D. 2011).

36. *See, e.g.*, *Wolfe v. Wolfe*, 254 N.C. App. 853, 803 S.E.2d 662 (2017).

37. *See, e.g.*, *Bowman v. Bowman*, 332 So. 3d 317 (Miss. App. 2021) (premarital agreement was ambiguous as to classification of real estate titled jointly and acquired solely with husband's separate property funds where provided separate property could not be unintentionally transmuted to marital property by commingling and that jointly titled property was marital property); *Johnson v. Johnson*, 2011 Ohio App. LEXIS 440 (unpub.) (agreement did not clearly answer question whether jointly titled asset acquired solely with one party's separate property was marital or separate; court correctly treated agreement as ambiguous).

(ii) all other jointly titled property owned by the parties as tenants by the entirety or joint tenants with right of survivorship without regard to the source of funds for acquisition, maintenance, or improvement of such property[***add, if appropriate:*** , except as provided in Paragraph __ [***regarding allocation of separate and marital shares of marital home***];

(iii) [***Optional:*** the parties' primary marital home without regard to the source of funds for acquisition costs of the home];

(iv) any appreciation in the value of, all income from, and all proceeds of a loan secured by a lien on marital property;

(v) all property acquired with marital property, including, but not limited to, property acquired with funds from a jointly titled financial institution account, with the proceeds from the sale of, or in exchange for, marital property or with the proceeds of a loan secured by a lien on marital property, including a party's ownership interest as a passive investor or shareholder in a business or professional services practice entity;

(vi) the wedding gifts from third parties, whether received before or after the wedding;

(vii) other gifts that are made to both parties, such as, but not limited to, anniversary gifts, holiday and other special occasion gifts to both parties, and gifts of furniture, equipment, or household effects for the parties' common use [***Optional:*** , with the exception of gifts of family-owned art, antiques, collectibles, or family heirlooms, which shall remain the separate property of the party from whose family of origin such items came];

(viii) [***Optional:***] the furniture, equipment, household effects, and other such items of common use purchased by the parties, or either of them, during the marriage for the parties' marital home(s) without regard to the source of funds for acquisition [***Optional:*** , with the exception of works of art, antiques, and collectibles acquired by a party with his or her separate property which shall remain that party's separate property];

(ix) all other untitled tangible personal property acquired during the marriage, except as specifically provided in Paragraph 6.

6. **Separate Property**. A party's "separate property" shall be any and all property not defined as marital property under Paragraph 5, including, but not limited to:

(i) all property acquired by a party prior to the parties' marriage, including, specifically, the property set forth in SPOUSE ONE's Schedule A, attached, and SPOUSE TWO's Schedule B, attached, and further including, also without limitation, all property acquired by a party from the date of this Agreement to the date of marriage;

(ii) the party's earnings [***add, if appropriate:*** and all other compensation from personal services, labor, or employment];

(iii) the party's retirement benefits and all other deferred compensation plans and benefits;

(iv) any property acquired by the party before or after the date of this Agreement by gift (including a gift from one party to the other regardless of the source of funds) or by inheritance, including an inherited IRA, survivorship, operation of law, under the laws of intestate succession, a will, trust, or similar instrument, or beneficiary designation;

(v) all property titled in the party's name alone or in his or her revocable living trust;

(vi) the party's ownership share of any property titled as joint tenants with right of survivorship with a third party;

(vii) the party's ownership share of any property titled as tenants in common, whether with a third party or with the other party to this agreement, in accordance with such title or other instrument;

(viii) all interests of the party, whether vested or contingent, in any trust created and funded by a third party and any trust created by the party and funded with his or her separate property (whether such trust currently exists or is hereafter created), including, but not limited to, any income, property, benefit, or interest held in or received from any such trust and all the contributions to such trust from a third party, or from a party hereto and made with his or her separate property;

(ix) [***Optional*:** a party's ownership interest as an active owner in a closely held business or in a professional services practice regardless of when such interest was acquired, the form of organization of the business, or the source of funds for acquisition of the interest];

(x) any appreciation in the value of, all income from, and all proceeds of a loan secured by a lien on the party's separate property;

(xi) all money or other property received by a party as compensation for injury to his or her person, whether as a result of a judgment, under an agreement for the settlement or compromise of a claim, as an award under workers' compensation laws or other applicable law, or under any contractual or other arrangement for compensation for such an injury;

(xii) all property, other than jointly titled property defined as marital property under Paragraph 5(i) or 5(ii), acquired with separate property, including, but not limited to, property acquired with funds from a party's separate property financial institution account, the proceeds from the sale of, or in exchange for, a party's separate property or with the proceeds of a loan secured by a lien on the party's separate property, including a party's ownership interest as a passive investor or shareholder in a business or professional services practice entity;

(xiii) all untitled tangible personal property acquired with a party's separate property;

(xiv) the party's clothing, jewelry, sports equipment, and personal effects without regard to the source of funds for acquisition;

(xv) the party's *pro rata* share of any overpayment of income taxes as provided in Paragraph 15 (notwithstanding that a refund may be jointly titled);

(xvi) the party's animal companions without regard to the source of funds for acquisition.

Other Terms Relating to Determination of Separate and Marital Property: Comment

The material in model paragraph 7 fleshes out the classification of separate and marital property and addresses a number of issues that have arisen in litigation over construction of premarital and postmarital agreements. For example, paragraph 6 provides that appreciation of separate property is itself separate property. However, because of the frequency of litigation over appreciation,[38] paragraph 7(A) reiterates this point; appreciation, whether active or passive, and whether attributable to monetary or nonmonetary contributions of either party, is separate property. The text is comprehensive enough to encompass all forms of appreciation in value of separate property.[39]

The better reasoned decisions hold that a comprehensive waiver of rights to solely owned property is adequate to protect these assets, even when the agreement does not specifically mention appreciation,[40] or when it does not specifically distinguish passive from active appreciation.[41] Nevertheless, a specific definition of separate property, including both active and passive appreciation, coupled with comprehensive waivers is the better practice.[42] Similarly,

38. *See, e.g., In re Marriage of Touhy-Silverman*, 2020 Ill. App. LEXIS 964 (unpub.); *Sitz v. Sitz*, 275 Neb. 832, 749 N.W.2d 470 (2008); *Worley v. Worley*, 855 So. 2d 632 (Fla. Ct. App. 2003).

39. *See Berg v. Young*, 175 So. 3d 863 (Fla. App. 2015) (premarital agreement defined business as separate property but was silent about active appreciation; active appreciation was marital property).

40. *Hahamonvitch v. Hahamovitch*, 173 So. 3d 983 (Fla. 2015) (husband entitled to retain all assets titled in his name, including appreciation during marriage, earnings and assets derived from earnings, where agreement specifically waived claims to solely owned property, but did not mention earnings or appreciation).

41. *See Wolf-Sabatino v. Sabatino*, 2011 Ohio App. LEXIS 5626, subsequent appeal on other issues, 2012 Ohio App. LEXIS 5399 (unpub.); *Brummond v. Brummond*, 785 N.W.2d 182 (N.D. 2010).

42. *See Dwoskin v. Dwoskin*, 2020 Va. Cir. LEXIS 129 (Cir. Ct. Fairfax Cnty.) (unpub.) (premarital agreement that identified separately titled property as separate property but did not say appreciation on separate property was separate property and did not waive equitable distribution was ambiguous; but, after trial, court accepted as true husband's testimony about intent); *Thompson v. Wolfram*, 162 N.W.3d 498 (Ind. Ct. App. 2020), *reh. denied*, 2021 Ind. App. LEXIS 60 (unpub.) (premarital agreement that provided all property titled solely in one party's name was separate property, and was silent about appreciation, did not waive spousal rights to share appreciation during marriage); *Sass v. Sass*, 988 So. 2d 1135 (Fla. Ct. App. 2008) (premarital agreement clearly defined

while a court may well hold that a provision defining separate property as any property "hereafter acquired" means income from separate property is separate property, as it did in *Knaus v. Knaus*;[43] a definition of separate property that expressly includes income from separate property is preferable.

The default rules in many states that define marital or community property allow for appreciation resulting from active efforts of either party to be included in the pool of marital/community property.[44] A waiver of the right to claim an interest in appreciation (both active and passive) of a nonmarital asset should be stated expressly.[45] For example, when one party owns a business or other property that may appreciate as a result of marital efforts or that requires active management, counsel for the owner will want to have the agreement state expressly that such appreciation will remain the separate property of the titled spouse.[46] The optional language in paragraph 7(A) can be used for that purpose. When a business owner employs the spouse, he or she should consider paying a salary or other form of compensation.[47] In all events, the owner should not misrepresent to the spouse his or her status, for example, by saying he or she is an owner if the statement is not true. Doing so can put characterization of the business as separate property at risk.[48]

Some states' laws define marital or community property to include property and income from property that the parties used for their common benefit.[49] Paragraph 7(B) makes clear that such common use does not alter a party's separate property rights. There is no support in the case law of premarital and postmarital agreements for the idea that reporting income on a joint tax return or reporting property interests on a joint asset statement converts separate property assets or income to marital property.[50] Nevertheless, the model text includes an express disclaimer that such an action changes the character of property or income.

Paragraphs 7(B) and 7(D) should be sufficient to block a claim that a solely titled asset, such as a home, has become marital property as a result of a course of conduct. Nevertheless,

---

premarital home as separate property, specifically including appreciation, proceeds of sale, and assets acquired with such proceeds); *Fazakerly v. Fazakerly*, 996 S.W.2d 260 (Tex. Ct. App. 1999) (wife's premarital companies remained her separate property upon husband's death notwithstanding community contributions of labor and effort to appreciation where premarital agreement clearly so provided); *Pardieck v. Pardieck*, 676 N.E.2d 359 (Ind. Ct. App. 1997) (specific provision of premarital agreement identifying business and all appreciation as husband's separate property, controlled over general provisions for creation of community assets).

43. 260 A.3d 133 (Pa. Super. Ct. 2021).

44. *See, e.g.*, VA. CODE ANN. § 20-107.3.A.3.a (increase in value of separate property during marriage is marital property only to extent marital property or personal efforts of either party contributed to such increase).

45. *See Deschamps v. Deschamps*, 223 P.3d 324 (Mont. 2009) (premarital agreement lacking express waiver of right to share enhancement in value of nonmarital property did not waive claim); *Nixon v. Nixon*, 1997 Tenn. App. LEXIS 236 (unpub.) (premarital agreement gave each party exclusive rights to premarital assets, but did not expressly waive right to share appreciation resulting from marital contributions; trial court did not err in giving wife share of appreciation).

46. *See Timble v. Timble*, 616 So. 2d 1188 (Fla. Dist. Ct. App. 1993) (specific reference to husband's company coupled with comprehensive waiver of property rights effected waiver of wife's claim to postmarital appreciation).

47. Under a sharing model, see Chapter 13, where compensation is defined as marital property, the spouse who works without a salary will benefit from the owner's compensation.

48. *See Simons v. Simons*, 312 Neb. 136, 978 N.W.2d 121 (2022).

49. *See McMillan v. McMillan*, 51 So. 3d 367 (Ala. Civ. App. 2010) (where postmarital agreement did not expressly identify husband's acreage with home as his separate property and parties used it between date of marriage and execution of agreement one week after marriage, property was marital by virtue of common use).

50. *See Cook v. Cook*, 26 Neb. App. 137, 918 N.W.2d (2018); *Holston v. Holston*, 128 So. 3d 736 (Ala. Ct. Civ. App. 2013); *Estate of Hunt v. Hunt*, 289 S.W.3d 755 (Tenn. Ct. App. 2012).

a party who wants to retain exclusive rights to a home that the parties will use as a family residence should avoid the kind of actions that the Florida court in *Hooker v. Hooker*[51] characterized as evidencing donative intent or that gave the wife reason to believe she had an interest. These included the wife becoming a joint obligor on the mortgage and the husband sending her an anniversary card with a photo of the newly acquired vacation home.

Even when the agreement provides for all property rights to be determined by title, in some circumstances it may be necessary to hold funds jointly for a period of time. For example, parties could sell real estate that is partly separate property and receive a single payment by check or electronic transfer, or they could receive a tax refund that is partly separate property and could deposit it in a joint account.[52] Paragraph 7(H) addresses this contingency.

Paragraphs 7(I) and 7(J) create default rules. Property a party transfers to sole ownership of the other party is the recipient's separate property. There is no requirement that the recipient prove intent to make a gift; the act of creating sole title is sufficient. Similarly, when a party creates joint ownership with survivorship, the resulting joint property is marital property. These terms better protect a weaker party. Some drafting lawyers like to provide that a transfer does not alter the character of the transferred property unless the transfer is documented in an agreement or other signed writing of the parties.[53] When an agreement requires that any such transfer, to be classified as the separate property of the recipient or as marital property, be documented in a signed writing, it permits a stronger party to make such a transfer but to attempt to reclaim the transferred property in the event of dissolution, and may permit heirs of a deceased spouse to make such an attempt.[54] This places the burden on the weaker party to seek an agreement or other writing, something that may not be practical for him or her. The model terms place the burden on the transferor; if he or she wants to transfer property to the spouse, and to have the right to take it back if the marriage fails, he or she must take the initiative to make that known to the recipient and get the necessary understanding in writing.

Other Terms Relating to Determination of Separate and Marital Property: Model Text

7. **Other Terms Relating to Determination of Separate and Marital Property.**

A. The appreciation in value of and the income and profits derived from separate property, whether by way of sale, exchange, investment, reinvestment, forgiveness of debt, or otherwise, including, without limitation, the acquisition

51. 220 So. 3d 397 (Fla. 2017).

52. *See Estate of Hunt*, 389 S.W.3d 755 (resolving disputed claim of refund on joint return); *King v. King*, 40 Va. App. 200, 578 S.E.2d 806 (2003) (where premarital agreement defined jointly titled property as marital, refund check from joint tax return was marital although husband contributed more to create refund).

53. *See In re Marriage of Touhy-Silverman*, 2020 Ill. App. Unpub. LEXIS 964.

54. *See, e.g., Spencer v. Est. of Spencer*, 313 S.W.3d 534 (Ky. 2010) (where premarital agreement required intra-spousal gift to be in separate signed writing, in duplicate, and attached to the original agreement, surviving wife nevertheless entitled to rights in joint securities account created by husband; but, court had to resolve factual dispute about whether husband intended survivorship or tenants in common).

of property with separate property or with the proceeds from the sale or other disposition of separate property, shall be and remain separate property regardless of the "active" or "passive" nature of a party's contributions to such separate property and regardless of any direct or indirect contribution of labor, effort, inventiveness, physical or intellectual skill, creativity, or managerial activity of either party to the acquisition, care, maintenance, or appreciation of such separate property as well as any separate property monetary contribution of either party to such property. A party who devotes labor, effort, inventiveness, physical or intellectual skill, creativity, or managerial activity, or who makes a monetary contribution of his or her separate property to the other party's separate property, shall be deemed to have made a gift to the party who owns such separate property. [***Optional:*** With respect to a separate property business or professional services practice of a party, the party's efforts or contributions as an owner, employee, officer, director, stockholder, consultant, or otherwise, shall not convert such business or practice, or any appreciation thereof, into marital property.]

B. Joint or common use of separate property shall not convert separate property to marital property. Further, a party's expenditure of separate property funds for common or family purposes or to benefit the other party shall not convert the property from which such funds were derived to marital property.

C. The fact that the parties may file a joint state or federal income tax return or that one or both parties may pay taxes due in connection with such joint return shall not be interpreted to mean that the income or property reported in such return is marital income or marital property nor convert separate property to marital property. Further, a party's reporting of property holdings, debts, earnings, or income on a joint loan application, financial statement, or net worth statement shall not be interpreted to mean that any item of property, or earnings or income identified therein, is marital property nor shall it convert separate property to marital property.

D. The parties acknowledge that they may occasionally use such expressions as "our property," "our house," and so on, when referring to property that is, by the terms of this Agreement, a party's separate property. They agree and acknowledge that they do not intend by such casual references to convert separate property to marital property.

E. A party claiming that an item of untitled tangible personal property acquired during the parties' marriage is his or her separate property may establish his or her claim by:

(i) a written acknowledgment by one party that an asset is wholly or partly the separate property of the other party

(ii) a bill of sale, invoice, or similar document, coupled with proof of the source of funds used for payment;

(iii) a will, probate accounting, or other writing of a donor or a donor's legal representative.

Nothing herein shall make these the exclusive means of establishing such a claim.

F. This Agreement contains rules defining property as a party's separate property or as marital property. The parties at any time may expressly otherwise characterize any real or personal property as separate property or as marital property by a writing that clearly identifies the item of property and states how the property or interest in property is to be defined for purposes of this Agreement. The writing may also address to what extent, if any, future contributions to acquisition, maintenance, or improvement of the property will affect the definition of the property. Any such writing must be signed by each party. An exchange of electronic messages shall satisfy the requirement for a signed writing for purposes of this paragraph 7(F).

G. The parties agree and acknowledge that they may from time to time receive a payment of funds (such as an income tax refund [***add if appropriate***: or the proceeds of sale of a marital home]) that is partly separate property of each of them, or is partly separate and partly marital property, and that a party may, for convenience, deposit such funds in a joint financial institution account. They agree that such deposit, in and of itself, will not cause the separate property portion of such funds to become marital property provided that the party who is entitled to the separate portion of such funds promptly transfers his or her separate property share out of the joint account.

H. A party's transfer of title to an existing item of property to, or his or her titling newly acquired property in, the sole name of the other party to this Agreement shall be a gift to the recipient thereof and shall, accordingly, be the recipient's separate property, except as the parties may otherwise agree in writing.

I. If a dispute arises concerning the "separate" or "marital" nature of an item of property, the term "separate property" shall be construed broadly, the term "marital property" shall be construed narrowly, and the party claiming that property titled in the other party's name is "marital property" shall bear the burden of proof. Property titled in the names of the parties as tenants by the entirety or joint tenants with right of survivorship shall conclusively meet the burden of proof that such property is marital property [***add if appropriate***: , except as provided in paragraph ___].

J. Nothing herein is intended to make compliance with paragraph 7(E) through 7(I) the exclusive means by which a party may establish his or her claim that an item of property is his or her separate property or is marital property.

DEFINITIONS, SEPARATE AND MARITAL DEBT: COMMENT

A premarital agreement should define separate debt and marital/community debt. These definitions may govern parties' rights and obligations during marriage and will determine allocation upon death or dissolution. The definitions will need to address both secured and unsecured debt, and both debt acquired in the name of one party and debt on which both parties are obligors.

Generally, unsecured debt used to acquire property defined by the agreement as one party's separate property should be defined as separate debt and the sole responsibility of the obligor (although a stronger party may voluntarily pay such debt on the other party's behalf during the marriage). The model text provides that all joint unsecured debt is marital debt. The model also addresses unsecured debt incurred for living expenses. Options for separately incurred unsecured debt include:

- Unsecured debt in one party's name is always his/her separate debt regardless of what it is used for, and only debt in joint names is marital debt; or
- Separately incurred unsecured debt is treated as marital debt if and to the extent incurred for the parties' usual and customary household and family expenses, and may also include each party's personal expenses.

Where unsecured marital debt is limited to debt acquired in joint names, one party may fund a common expense, such as a family vacation, with his or her separate credit card, simply for convenience, and not be able to recoup if the marriage ends with the debt outstanding. Parties who choose this option will need to decide whether to obtain joint credit cards and agree on what they will use them for. On the other hand, if certain types of separately titled debt can be a shared obligation upon dissolution, one party will have the ability to incur debt that he or she can claim is marital debt, with or without justification, and with or without the knowledge of the other. Parties who can maintain a regime of paying off all credit card bills as received will be at less risk of a dispute. If parties opt to include a provision mandating that one party assume primary or exclusive responsibility for living expenses of the parties,[55] the choice as to definition of separate and marital debt should take account of that obligation.

The model defines marital debt to include debt secured by marital property without regard to what use is made of the borrowed funds. Parties should be mindful of the consequences of encumbering a marital asset and using the borrowed funds for a purpose other than improvement of that asset or refinancing the asset. One obvious situation is the use of an equity loan on real estate that is used to pay off premarital credit cards or student loans. The model also defines marital debt to include debt incurred by either party to acquire marital property; thus, an asset securing the debt could be separate property, but the debt would be marital debt if used to acquire property defined as marital property.[56]

55. See paragraph 13.A, which follows.

56. *See Robbins v. Robbins*, 39 Misc. 3d 1216, 975 N.Y.S.2d 369 (Sup. Ct. N.Y. Cnty. 2013) (husband not entitled to credit for margin loan against his separate property securities account and used to acquire jointly titled marital home defined in the parties' premarital agreement as marital property where agreement did not define such debt as marital debt).

Parties also need to be mindful of the consequences of acquiring property in joint names when only one spouse is the obligor on debt secured by the property. For example, in *Liptrap v. Coyne*,[57] the parties acquired a motel and titled it as tenants by the entirety. However, the husband signed the note as sole obligor and the wife signed only as a guarantor. After his death, the probate court ruled that his estate was obligated to pay off the balance of the note in its entirety and reimburse her for payments she made under the guaranty. A properly drafted agreement could have addressed the issue, for example, by providing that the surviving spouse would take the property subject to the secured debt.[58]

When one spouse owns a business, or may in the future, a spouse may be asked or pressured to co-sign debt for the benefit of the business even when the business is defined as the owner's separate property.[59] The agreement can provide that neither party will be obligated to take on such debt,[60] though that would not prevent him or her from doing so under pressure or voluntarily.

The model text that follows includes an option under which each party is solely responsible for his or her health-care expenses. There may be circumstances under which such a provision will be unenforceable while the parties remain married or in a suit by a third-party provider.[61] Nevertheless, it can be appropriate to include as it should allow the other spouse to argue that the spouse who incurred these expenses must spend down his or her assets first.

DEFINITIONS, SEPARATE AND MARITAL DEBT: MODEL TEXT

8. **Separate and Marital Debt.**

A. "Marital debt" shall be debt incurred by either party to acquire, improve, or maintain marital property and debt secured by marital property, as defined herein. Marital debt shall also include debt incurred during the marriage in the joint names of the parties [***Add, if appropriate:*** and debt incurred by either party for the parties' usual and customary household [***Optional:*** , personal,] and family expenses].

B. "Separate debt" shall be debt incurred by a party to acquire, improve, or maintain his or her separate property, debt secured by separate property, and all other debt incurred by a party in his or her name alone [***Add, if appropriate:*** , except as provided in Paragraph 8(A)]. A party's separate debt also includes his or her income tax liability on his or her earnings and separate property income, as described in paragraph 15, whether on a separate or a joint return. [***Add, if appropriate:*** Further, a party's separate debt shall include all his or her medical and health-care expenses not covered by insurance notwithstanding that the other spouse may be or become liable to a provider of such medical or health-care services.]

57. 675 S.E.2d 693 (N.C. App. 2009).
58. See model paragraph 21 for such a provision.
59. *See Cook v. Cook*, 26 Neb. App. 137, 918 N.W. 2d 1 (2018).
60. See paragraph 10 and accompanying Comment.
61. See Section 5.08 in this book.

DEFINITIONS, MARITAL SEPARATION; DURING THE MARRIAGE: COMMENT

It is common for a premarital or postmarital agreement to give greater rights to a surviving spouse than to a former or estranged spouse. Often a party will want survivor rights under a retirement plan to be contingent on the parties not being separated upon the first spouse's death. It is also common for certain rights to accrue at death or dissolution under a formula measured by the length of marriage. The agreement should therefore specify the termination point (or operative event) that will be used to determine what rights accrue to the estranged or surviving spouse. The operative event in the model agreement is defined as a marital separation with an option to define the operative event as the passage of a specified number of days after the actual date of separation. The model herein provides that the dissolution provisions, not the death provisions, apply if a spouse dies after a marital separation (as defined).

The agreement could provide that separation is the operative event, leaving the definition of separation to local law, but the better practice is to define the term in the agreement.[62] In some circumstances, whether parties are separated, as defined by local law, may be ambiguous. In some jurisdictions, for example, parties may reside under the same roof and yet be considered separated for purposes of a statutory waiting period to file for divorce.[63] Where parties may maintain more than one home, or live apart due to circumstances other than estrangement, such as the demands of employment or a party's residence in a health-care facility, whether they are separated may not be clear.

The following are other possible termination points:

- Filing of a complaint for legal separation, separate maintenance, or divorce;
- Filing, as described above, coupled with service of process;
- Entry of an order regarding the substantive rights of a party, such as a temporary order to pay spousal or child support; and
- Entry of a judgment of legal separation, separate maintenance, or absolute divorce.

The selection of a termination point, and the method of identifying it, can significantly affect the parties' rights.[64] The model text allows for either party to initiate a separation by delivery of written separation notice.[65] This method of termination cuts off the surviving spouse from whatever rights he or she would have under the death provisions of the agreement without requiring the initiator to move out. As the earliest possible date, date of separation will generally be more favorable to the stronger party, or the stronger party's estate, and

62. *See Elias v. Elias*, 152 So. 3d 749 (Fla. Ct. App. 4th Dist. 2014) (resolving question whether agreement was ambiguous where operative event was legal separation "pursuant to judicial proceedings" and where no such cause of action exists in Florida); *In re Marriage of Best*, 228 Ill. 2d 107, 886 N.E.2d 939 (2008) (resolving dispute about whether "separation" as used in premarital agreement meant entry of an order of legal separation, or mere physical separation, in favor of former); *In re Murdock's Estate*, 213 Kan. 837, 519 P.2d 108 (1974) (provision in premarital agreement providing for spousal rights if parties living together as husband and wife requires that there have been a decree of legal separation or separate maintenance to cut off survivor's rights).

63. *See* D.C. CODE ANN. § 16-904(c) (parties deemed separated who live apart under the same roof, sharing neither bed nor board).

64. *See, e.g., In re Estate of Boyd*, 340 Ga. App. 744, 798 S.E.2d 330 (2017) (postmarital agreement defined operative event as filing for divorce; husband died hours after filing; wife not entitled to death provisions).

65. Whether a notice issued by a fiduciary is sufficient to begin a statutory waiting period for divorce, or whether a fiduciary can file a suit for divorce, is a separate question that must be determined under applicable law.

therefore less favorable to an economically weaker spouse. When coupled with the right to terminate the marriage by a separation notice, an early cutoff would give the economically dominant party significant leverage to limit the financial rights of an innocent party. For example, where one party will have the right to exclusive use of a marital home in the event of a separation, a termination effected by written notice could give that party the right to simultaneously initiate a separation and evict the other spouse. Similarly, an agreement that uses separation as the termination point, and that permits separation through written notice, would permit an ailing spouse to issue a deathbed separation notice and cut off more generous benefits that would be due a surviving, unseparated spouse.

On the other hand, a termination point tied to entry of a judgment of divorce carries the risk for the stronger party that the court process will be extended through manipulation and delay to his or her detriment. In jurisdictions where courts are not permitted to bifurcate the divorce from the trial on financial issues, where there is a long wait to get a case to trial, or where a divorce and property determination is not final until an appeal has been decided, there will be abundant opportunities for delay. Provisions for the stronger party to pay moving and resettlement expenses, or that penalize a party who initiates a separation, may balance the incentives. Extending the termination point to a date, such as 90 or 180 days, after a written termination notice can offer some protection for the weaker party against a deathbed separation notice. Counsel should also consider proposing an adequate move-out period—30 days at a minimum, but 60 to 90 might be appropriate in some cases—for a client who will be forced to move. Counsel should also consider the timing of any cash payments that may be due in relation to when that spouse may be required to move and his or her need for funds to acquire a new residence.

Where the agreement provides for a separation by written notice, counsel should consider including the model text that requires that any notice be made by the spouse acting for him- or herself, and precluding a notice by an agent, attorney-in-fact, or other fiduciary.[66] Counsel should also consider language that makes clear that a spouse's residence in a hospice, nursing home, or other health-care facility does not constitute a separation. The model agreement includes these provisions. The former should preclude an adult child, or other interested party with a power of attorney, from issuing a separation notice after a spouse has become ill or incapacitated by age and can provide some protection for a surviving spouse whose interests upon a spouse's death may conflict with those of other family members. The latter is intended to eliminate a potential dispute when spouses live apart due to health-care needs.

Parties could separate and then resume living together. The agreement should acknowledge this. The rights of a weaker spouse may depend upon the duration of the marriage, for example, where the amount of spousal support is tied to duration of the marriage.[67] The following text provides that a separation followed by reconciliation is treated as if it never occurred. Some agreements provide that a reconciliation must be evidenced by a written

66. *See, e.g.*, *Andrews v. Creacey*, 56 Va. App. 606, 696 S.E.2d 218 (2010), where a guardian (an adult child of the parties) prosecuted the divorce on behalf of the incapacitated husband. At the time of trial, the husband was 93, the wife 88, and the parties had been married for 64 years.

67. *See Famiglio v. Famiglio*, 279 So. 3d 736 (Fla. Dist. Ct. App. 2019).

instrument. Such a provision will be disadvantageous to a weaker party, as it could have the result that parties resume living together as spouses, even for an extended period prior to death, with the survivor having to litigate his or her property rights against other surviving family members of the deceased spouse.

DEFINITIONS, MARITAL SEPARATION; DURING THE MARRIAGE: MODEL TEXT

9. **Marital Separation; During the Marriage.**

A. The parties shall be considered separated, and a marital separation shall be deemed to be in effect for purposes of this Agreement, upon the first of the following dates:

(i) [***Optional:*** ____ days after] the date that one party informs the other party in writing that he or she intends to be separated or to terminate the marital relationship, and such marital separation, in fact, commences, including a period of living separate and apart under the same roof after such notice (and without regard to whether living separate and apart under the same roof constitutes grounds of divorce) [***optional***; and provided further that any such notice may only be made by a party in his or her individual capacity and no such notice may be made by an attorney-in-fact, guardian, trustee, or other legal representative];

(ii) the date on which either party serves the other party with a suit for divorce, legal separation, annulment, custody, spousal or child support [***Optional:*** ; and provided that any such suit may only be filed by a party acting in his or her individual capacity and no such suit may be filed by an attorney-in-fact, guardian, trustee, or other legal representative].

B. The phrase "during the marriage" as used in this Agreement shall mean the period from the date of marriage to the date of marital separation; provided, that in the event the parties reconcile after a marital separation and resume living together as spouses, the marital separation shall be treated as if it never occurred [***Add when agreement requires cash payments or transfers of property upon separation:*** , and provided further that, in such event, SPOUSE ONE, or SPOUSE ONE'S estate, as the case may be, shall be entitled to a credit for any monies paid or property transferred to SPOUSE TWO under the terms of this Agreement and retained by ______ [him/her] after a reconciliation against any monies or property that SPOUSE ONE or _____ [his/her] estate may subsequently owe _____ [him/her] hereunder.] Reconciliation shall require either a written confirmation signed by each party or the resumption of a normal marital relationship. Occasional dating or other social relations during a period of living apart shall not, of themselves, constitute reconciliation.

RIGHTS AND OBLIGATIONS DURING THE MARRIAGE: COMMENT

The model paragraphs below address various rights and obligations during the ongoing marriage. They include a provision requiring each party to pay his or her separate debt (as defined by the agreement). This is standard language. However, counsel for a disadvantaged party should consider whether the agreement should make specific provisions when he or she may be unable to pay separate debt, for example, when he or she expects to quit outside employment to care for a child but has education loans that must be repaid.

The model obligates each party to pay separate debt during the marriage from his/her separate property, but is silent as to responsibility for paying whatever debt is defined as marital debt. A party who voluntarily uses his/her separate property to pay marital debt is, therefore, not entitled under the agreement to reimbursement.[68]

The model text gives each party the right of access to documents and information bearing on marital assets and debts, but does not otherwise attempt to dictate how parties conduct themselves with respect to them during the ongoing marriage.

The model text includes standard language giving each party the right to control his or her separate property, however defined, including the right to sell, encumber, transfer, consume, and make a gift of such property, without consent of the other spouse. When the agreement provides for a complete separation of each party's property according to title, with no spousal rights, such a provision will generally pose no risk for the other party's property interests. However, when the agreement provides for transfers or creates other contractual rights for a spouse upon death or dissolution, the lawyer for that party needs to consider how the right to control property during marriage may affect the party's rights. In some cases, the right of a spouse to control his or her property during marriage should be limited in some way. Paragraph 10(D) is an optional paragraph that restricts the wealthier party's right to give away assets so as to defeat the rights of a surviving spouse.

The right to make gifts includes gifts to the other spouse.[69] Unless the agreement provides otherwise, a gift that enhances the value of the recipient's separate property does not alter its status. For example, under this model, a spouse's payment of the mortgage on the other spouse's separate property real estate does not convert it to marital property.[70]

A weaker party who will be marrying a business owner may be asked to co-sign loans during the marriage. Counsel for that party should consider including the following text, which acknowledges that a party has no obligation to co-sign such debt, although it will not prevent him or her from agreeing to do so, whether voluntarily or under pressure.

Paragraph 12 acknowledges that a party may become a fiduciary for the other. A spouse who uses such a position to make transfers in derogation of the other spouse's rights may be found to have breached his or her fiduciary duty.[71] Paragraph 12 expressly makes that obligation a matter of contract.

---

68. *See Reddy v. Adler*, 2020 Va. App. LEXIS 75 (unpub.).

69. *See, e.g., State Farm Life Ins. Co. v. Rogers*, 2022 U.S. App. LEXIS 31635 (4th Cir.) (unpub.) (premarital agreement defining life insurance policy as separate property did not preclude owner-wife from changing beneficiary designation from sons to new husband).

70. *See Bennett v. Bennett*, 103 A.D.3d 825, 960 N.Y.S.2d 179 (2013).

71. *See Kolf v. Authement (In re Estate of Kolf)*, 2019 Miss. App. LEXIS 506 (unpub.).

RIGHTS AND OBLIGATIONS DURING THE MARRIAGE: MODEL TEXT

RIGHTS AND OBLIGATIONS DURING THE MARRIAGE

10. **Separate Property and Separate Debt.**

A. During the marriage, each party shall retain exclusive rights to their separate property and shall be free to sell, use, transfer, exchange, abandon, lease, consume, assign, create a security interest in, encumber, dispose of, pledge, gift or otherwise manage and control his or her separate property [***Add, if appropriate:*** , except as specifically set forth herein]. Nothing herein shall preclude a spouse from making, and the other spouse from accepting, gifts of real or personal property from the other party.

B. During the marriage, each party shall be solely responsible for paying his or her separate debt from his or her separate property. Neither party shall have any obligation to co-sign, become a guarantor, or otherwise to assume any liability to a third party, for any debt incurred, or to be incurred, by the other party for the acquisition or maintenance of his or her separate property or in connection with the property owner's investment or business activities.

C. Each party shall use his or her separate property, and not marital property, to maintain separate property; provided, however, the parties acknowledge that a party may use marital property funds, or his or her separate property funds, for routine expenses of a shared home (such as, but not limited to, property taxes, casualty and liability insurance, utilities, lawn care, repairs and maintenance) notwithstanding that such home may be a party's separate property and they further acknowledge their understanding that the use of marital or separate property funds for this purpose shall not alter the definition of a separate property home as a party's separate property, nor shall it alter the allocation of the separate property and marital property shares of a home acquired during the marriage as provided in paragraph __.

D. [***Add, if appropriate:***] During the marriage, SPOUSE ONE shall not make any gifts or other donative transfers to any person, other than SPOUSE TWO, in excess of the annual gift tax exclusion amount under Section 2503(b) of the Internal Revenue Code of 1986, as adjusted for inflation from time to time, without the prior written consent of SPOUSE TWO; provided, however, SPOUSE ONE shall have the right to pay tuition and to pay for health care for a child or grandchild of his/hers without SPOUSE TWO'S consent and without regard to the exclusion amount. Further, SPOUSE ONE shall not make any donative transfers to any organization without SPOUSE TWO's written consent, provided, however, that SPOUSE ONE shall have the right to make charitable contributions aggregating not more than $ ____ annually without SPOUSE TWO'S consent. If in any year there is no annual gift tax exclusion under the Internal Revenue Code, then the annual exclusion amount most recently in effect prior to the gift will apply for purposes of this paragraph. If SPOUSE ONE makes any gift or donative transfer in excess of the amount permitted under this paragraph, such excess amount shall be added to his/her gross estate as defined herein for purposes of paragraph 19.C of this Agreement.

11. **Marital Property and Marital Debt.**

A. During the marriage, each party agrees to fully disclose all material facts and information regarding the existence, title, and value of all marital property and the existence and amount of all marital debt, and to provide the other party upon his or her request with access to all information, records, and books that pertain to the nature and value of such property and debt. Each party shall have equal access to their marital property financial institution account records, documents evidencing the source of deposits into and the disposition of payments made from such accounts, and to all bills, invoices, credit card statements and other documents evidencing joint obligations paid or to be paid from such marital property accounts. The parties acknowledge their understanding that each will have access to funds they elect to deposit in a joint financial institution account. [***Add, if appropriate:*** The parties agree to share financial decision-making during the marriage and to consult one another with regard to significant expenditures of marital funds.]

B. If a judgment lien, tax lien, or other encumbrance of one party that is his or her separate debt, as defined herein, is placed upon a party's interest in jointly titled real or personal property, the party who incurred the lien or encumbrance shall indemnify and hold the other party harmless from any financial losses incurred by such other party as a result thereof.

12. **Fiduciary Duties.** In the event a party is appointed as a personal representative, executor, agent under a power of attorney, or other fiduciary of the other party's estate, or in the event of the disability of a party, and in the further event the other party is appointed and serves as an attorney-in-fact, conservator, or guardian of the disabled party, the party so appointed shall nevertheless be bound by, and shall comply with, the terms of this Agreement.

PAYMENT OF EXPENSES DURING THE MARRIAGE: COMMENT

There are a variety of approaches to how an agreement may treat living expenses during marriage. These include:

- The agreement is silent concerning responsibility for living expenses;
- One spouse agrees to be solely responsible for all the parties' living expenses;
- One spouse is solely responsible for certain specified expenses, such as the mortgage and maintenance on the shared home(s), and responsibility for other living expenses is left to be worked out informally;

- The parties agree to pool some or all income, or other resources, and to pay some or all expenses from their common funds;
- Each party agrees to contribute to common expenses without a specific formula;
- Each party is to be responsible for his or her own personal expenses and one party is to pay all common expenses;
- Each party is to pay his or her own personal expenses and common expenses are to be shared according to a formula, such as in proportion to income; or
- The parties will share all expenses (household and personal) according to a formula, such as *pro rata.*

A provision regarding parties' obligations for payment of their own personal and the parties' common expenses during marriage is not an essential part of a premarital or postmarital agreement. When there is a large wealth disparity, both parties often assume the stronger party will pay all or most expenses. Many couples prefer to deal with such matters informally in much the way they would if they had no agreement. For parties who wish to state this obligation expressly, paragraph 13 provides one example, requiring a stronger party to pay living expenses during the marriage.

The agreement should be clear about when an obligor's contractual obligation to pay living expenses of the other spouse comes to an end. Similarly, when the parties will both be obligated to contribute to a common account or share certain expenses, the agreement should be clear about whether that obligation continues after a marital separation. In the absence of a clear cutoff, a court may decide the obligation continues after separation.[72] The model text below provides for payment of expenses only during the marriage. "During the marriage" is defined in paragraph 9(B) as the period from date of marriage to date of separation. Therefore, the obligation will end when parties separate, not at some later point. When the agreement provides for spousal support, counsel for the recipient will need to consider language that requires that the start of payments be timed to coordinate with the end of an obligation to pay living expenses or for a lump-sum payment for transitional expenses. In states where a premarital agreement cannot waive temporary spousal support payable during the pendency of a suit for divorce,[73] it will be especially important to take account of the weaker spouse's support needs during this period.

When one party will be contractually obligated to pay the common expenses, or the other spouse's personal expenses, the agreement should allow the obligor to exercise some discretion about the level of expenditure he or she must fund.[74] The agreement should anticipate the various changes in circumstances that may occur over time that may permit or require the payor to reduce the level of expenditure, including retirement, a change in his or her fortunes, children leaving home, and a marital breakup.[75]

72. *See Roberts v. Roberts*, 173 N.C. App. 354, 618 S.E.2d 761 (2005).

73. See Chapter 5 for discussion of spousal support and enforceability of waivers.

74. *See, e.g., Ex Parte Hall*, 854 S.W.2d 656 (Tex. 1993) (agreement requiring husband to pay wife's living expenses interpreted to require husband to pay all of wife's living expenses, whether reasonable or not).

75. *See Badger v. Badger*, 2002 Ohio App. LEXIS 414 (unpub.) (wife fulfilled obligation to contribute to household expenses when she paid her own living expenses after separation).

Courts have enforced sharing provisions, if sufficiently defined.[76] Where the agreement provides for certain expenses to be shared but for parties to pay their own personal expenses, the agreement should define what is included in each category even though it may not be possible to anticipate every type of expense. For example, the agreement should be clear about whether expenses of one party's child will be a shared expense or solely the responsibility of the parent. Model paragraph 13 below provides for each party to pay for gifts for his or her own children and family members and is an option for a couple who will have no children in common and where there will not be a child of one party living in the home. If the parties elect to include specific provisions for sharing certain expenses, the definition of shared and personal expenses should also address support for an elderly parent or other family member, holiday and special occasion gifts to third parties, charitable contributions, country club membership fees, auto expenses, and a variety of other expenses that could fall into either category.

As a practical matter, a party's breach of provision for sharing expenses during marriage, such as a provision requiring each party to contribute to a joint account, may not be enforceable at divorce through money damages if parties simply fail to carry out the obligations and a party who is disadvantaged acquiesces.[77] In some states, a strong public policy mandating that spouses support each other during the marriage may preclude recoupment of past expenses.[78]

It is especially important that an agreement that imposes an obligation on one party to pay personal expenses of the other clearly define the limits on that obligation and that counsel consider whether and what extraordinary expenses should be included. For example, in *Homra v. Nelson*,[79] the premarital agreement required the husband to pay for "daily necessities." The appellate court concluded that, because the wife needed nursing home care, her nursing home care was a daily necessity and the husband had to pay for it. The dissenting judge argued that the term applied only to routine expenses (*e.g.*, toiletries), but not to extraordinary expenses. The agreement was ambiguous; it could have clearly distinguished extraordinary necessities from routine necessities.

Homra also illustrates the importance of thinking of the future, perhaps to a time when a working payor may be retired and when one or both parties may have extraordinary health-care needs. Here, the agreement imposed a burden on the husband that neither party may have intended. The suit was brought by the wife's children from a prior marriage. The opinion does not describe what other resources were available to the wife nor what resources the husband would have left to pay for his care at the assisted living facility where he was living. An agreement can require that each party separately bear his or her own extraordinary health-care expenses, or that each be primarily responsible for his or her own to the extent of his or her resources. When the

---

76. *See, e.g., Soloman v. Murrey*, 103 S.W.3d 431 (Tenn. Ct. App. 2002).

77. *See Tsoucalas v. Tsoucalas*, 2013 Va. App. LEXIS 144 (unpub.) (husband not entitled to reimbursement for living expenses under premarital agreement that did not provide remedy for failure to contribute); *In re Marriage of Byrne*, 179 Ill. App. 3d 944, 535 N.E.2d 14 (1989) (husband did not breach premarital agreement that said it did not eliminate legal duty of support where wife acquiesced in her payment of disproportionate share of expenses during marriage).

78. *See In re Marriage of Mathiasen and Naughton*, 219 Cal. App. 3d 1428, 268 Cal. Rptr. 895 (1990) (wife not entitled to recoup excess contributions to common expenses under agreement to equally share where agreement violated public policy mandating mutual obligation of support).

79. 2008 Tenn. App. LEXIS 148 (2008).

agreement provides for sharing living expenses, such a provision can protect a spouse with fewer resources from a financial burden he or she may not be able to afford.[80]

The agreement could also require one or both parties to maintain a policy of long-term care insurance (LTCI) to pay for nursing home or home care expenses. Such a policy can benefit both parties and may be the only viable resource if both parties need nursing home care. For example, in *Marriage of Tillman*,[81] the premarital agreement required the husband to provide reasonable support to the wife. Both parties became incapacitated. The husband's guardian *ad litem* filed for divorce on his behalf in order to free him from his obligation so that he could conserve his resources for his nursing home expenses. The suit was dismissed because Indiana law does not authorize a guardian to prosecute a divorce. An LTCI policy might have solved the problem of paying for care without dissolving the marriage.

PAYMENT OF EXPENSES DURING THE MARRIAGE: MODEL TEXT

13. **Payment of Expenses During the Marriage.**

A. During the marriage, SPOUSE ONE shall pay the usual and reasonable living expenses of the parties and SPOUSE TWO'S reasonable personal expenses. SPOUSE TWO shall pay for any gifts for her/his children, grandchildren, and other family members, for any luxury items she/he may wish to purchase on her/his own behalf, and for his/her extraordinary health-care expenses, such as home nursing care or the cost of residence in an assisted living facility, nursing home, or other long-term care facility. The parties intend to establish a reasonable and mutually agreed upon budget for their shared living and each party's personal expenses contemporaneous with their marriage, and at least annually, that will take into account projected expenses and each party's income. The parties acknowledge that neither of them expects the other to use assets or capital to fund living expenses and that they intend to live within their means.

B. The parties agree to acquire and maintain a policy of long-term care insurance for SPOUSE TWO. SPOUSE ONE shall pay the premiums in accordance with Paragraph 13(A); provided, however, SPOUSE ONE'S obligation shall not exceed $___ per month. SPOUSE TWO shall be responsible for that portion of the premium, if any, that exceeds $___ per month. SPOUSE ONE'S obligation to pay these premiums shall terminate upon entry of a judgment of divorce or SPOUSE ONE'S death.

80. The doctrine of necessaries may trump a premarital contract in some jurisdictions. See Section 5.04(c). The rules governing Medicaid eligibility will preempt a contract. See Section 5.04(d). However, a contract can offer some protection by requiring a spouse to spend his or her resources first, before looking to the other spouse.

81. 70 N.E.3d 349 (Ind. Ct. App. 2013).

GIFTS OF CASH AND SECURITIES TO SPOUSE: COMMENT

The model text below provides for a wealthier spouse to make gifts to an economically weaker party during the marriage. Such a provision can help create some financial security for a weaker spouse. It can be combined with other provisions for that party, such as transfer of title to a primary residence to survivorship title, spousal support in the event of dissolution, and provisions for the spouse after death. In the alternative, or in addition to, cash gifts, the wealthy spouse might prefer to transfer marketable securities. A spouse who receives appreciated stock during the marriage, or as part of a settlement incident to divorce, will receive the transferor's basis.[82] Because spousal support is no longer deductible to the payor and includible in the income of the payee,[83] a transfer of appreciated securities may be one of the few ways that a wealthier party can do some tax planning in connection with divorce to shift income taxes to a spouse who may become a former spouse and who may be in a lower tax bracket.

An individual can make gifts to a spouse, such as gifts of cash and securities, in any amount during the marriage without incurring any gift tax liability upon transfer. The spouse must be a U.S. citizen for the gift to receive this treatment.[84]

GIFTS OF CASH AND SECURITIES TO SPOUSE: MODEL TEXT

14. **Gifts to SPOUSE TWO During the Marriage.**

A. *Cash Gifts.* Beginning on the ___ anniversary of the parties' marriage and continuing on each anniversary thereafter, SPOUSE ONE shall make a cash gift to SPOUSE TWO to enable him/her to maintain savings and investments as follows: (a) for the first five years, the sum shall be $______ each year; (b) for the second five years, the sum shall be $_____ each year; (c) thereafter, the sum shall be $_____ each year. The parties agree and understand that the purpose of these transfers is to provide SPOUSE TWO with some financial security for his/her future well-being, and they intend and agree that he/she shall not be expected to use these funds for his/her living expenses or any other expenses of his/hers during the marriage except as provided in Paragraph 13. SPOUSE ONE'S obligation hereunder shall terminate on the first to occur of the following events: (i) the parties' ____th wedding anniversary; (ii) the parties' separation as defined in Paragraph 9(A); provided that in the event the parties reconcile and resume living together as husband and wife/spouses, SPOUSE ONE shall resume the cash gift as provided herein; (iii) death of a party.

---

82. I.R.C. §§ 1041, 2503.
83. Tax Cuts and Jobs Act (TCJA), 115 Pub. L. No. 97, 131 Stat. 2054, 2017 Enacted H.R. 1, 115 Enacted H.R. 1.
84. I.R.C. §§ 2056, 2523.

B. *Gifts of Securities*. Upon marriage [***or other date chosen by the parties***] SPOUSE ONE shall transfer to SPOUSE TWO as a gift marketable securities having a value of not less than $__________, valued as of __________. [***Alternative, particularly if the agreement is to be a postmarital agreement***: Upon execution of this Agreement, SPOUSE ONE shall transfer the __________ securities account to the parties as tenants by the entirety and such account shall become marital property.]

INCOME TAXES: COMMENT

Paragraph 15 provides for allocation of income taxes such that each party is responsible for that portion attributable to his or her separate property income and the parties equally bear the tax on marital property income. Parties who elect to follow this paragraph during the marriage may need to have an accountant provide the allocation each year or use a tax preparation program to determine the allocation. The model text does not require joint returns. It will usually not be in a party's interest to mandate that he or she file joint income tax returns. In *Haigh v. Comm'r, I.R.S.*,[85] for example, the premarital agreement required joint returns and the husband was disadvantaged when the wife did not pay taxes and penalties on a premature IRA distribution. There are a variety of circumstances that could cause a party not to want to file a joint return, such as a concern about the other party's underreporting of income, a party's inadequate withholding or failure to pay estimated taxes, or other facts that may put him or her at risk. A party may also want to shield his or her income from discovery in future litigation between a spouse with a support obligation to a previous spouse that is modifiable or that could be the subject of an enforcement action. The model provision allows parties to decide filing status year to year.

The agreement can and should specify the allocation of prepayments of tax. This can become especially important if parties separate or divorce and one spouse has made substantial estimated payments or will be entitled to a big refund.[86] When parties file jointly, and are entitled to a refund, the refund will be payable to both parties. Paragraph 7(H) allows for the refund to be deposited into a joint account without a party's separate share becoming marital property, but only if he or she promptly takes out his or her separate property share.

INCOME TAXES: MODEL TEXT

15. **Income Taxes and Income Tax Returns**. Each party shall be separately and solely liable for any income taxes payable with respect to his or her earnings and separate property income (as defined herein) and shall be entitled to the deductions, credits and adjustments allocable to such earnings and separate property income.

85. 2009 Tax Court Memo LEXIS 140 (unpub.).

86. *See Richlin v. Comm'r*, 2020 Tax Ct. Memo LEXIS 59 (unpub.) (terms of parties' premarital agreement entitled husband to have all his estimated payments allocated to his tax liability).

> Each party shall pay any taxes due on his or her earnings and separate property income from his or her separate property and not from marital property. The parties agree that any income taxes payable with respect to marital property income, after attributing the deductions, credits, and adjustments allocable to such marital property income, are marital debt and shall pay such taxes from marital property, including, as applicable, estimated tax payments and application of overpayments, and they acknowledge their understanding that, as between them, they shall equally bear the tax liability on marital property income [***Optional:*** The parties acknowledge that neither is obligated to file a joint income tax return, and they agree that they shall decide from year to year whether to file joint income tax returns.] In the event the parties file a joint income tax return, they shall each be responsible for their *pro rata* share of the tax, determined as if each filed as [***select:*** a single taxpayer/married, filing separately] taking into account each party's reportable earnings and separate property income, allowable deductions, credits, and other adjustments to income, his or her equal interest in marital property income and allowable deductions, credits, and other adjustments to marital property income, and his or her prepayments of tax (*e.g.*, withholding, refunds applied from prior tax years, and estimated payments), and shall pay his or her *pro rata* share of any underpayment or receive his or her *pro rata* share of any refund, as the case may be. The parties acknowledge that it is not practical to further define the proper allocation of each party's responsibility for the tax on a joint return, and they agree to act in good faith in the spirit of fairness to resolve any issues regarding such responsibility.

GIFT TAXES FOR GIFTS TO THIRD PARTIES: COMMENT

A party may want to start or continue a gifting program for the benefit of existing children, grandchildren, or other family members, or may want to be able to start such a program for future children of the parties. I.R.C. § 2503 permits an individual to make gifts of cash and securities, as well as other forms of property, to anyone without incurring any gift tax so long as the value of the gift does not exceed the annual gift tax exclusion amount.[87] In 2023, the exclusion amount is $17,000. The exclusion amount is adjusted annually for inflation. A married donor can double the annual gifts to each donee so long as the spouse consents. Paragraph 16 is a standard clause to enable each party to double the amount of annual gifts he or she is able to give without exceeding the amount of the annual gift tax exclusion. The text obligates the spouse to consent. The consenting spouse is not obligated to gift his or her own property, merely to consent to the other spouse's gifting, in order to maximize his or her ability to make tax-free transfers.

87. I.R.C. § 2503(b).

GIFT TAXES FOR GIFTS TO THIRD PARTIES: MODEL TEXT

16. **Joining in Gifts and Gift Tax Returns**. Each party shall, upon request of the other, timely join in the execution of gift tax returns consenting to the treatment of gifts made by one of the parties as gifts made one-half by each of the parties in accordance with Section 2513 of the Internal Revenue Code and any applicable state or local gift tax statute, provided, however, that neither party shall be required to do so with respect to any gift in excess of the allowable annual exclusion under Section 2503 of the Internal Revenue Code available to such party with respect to such gift.

PROPERTY RIGHTS UPON DEATH OF A PARTY AND WAIVERS: COMMENT

The material below consists of a standard comprehensive waiver of spousal rights at death, coupled with one approach to specific provisions for an economically weaker party under which the surviving spouse is entitled to a specified percentage of the decedent's estate, with several alternative clauses. There are other options. For example, a payor may prefer to postpone the other party's entitlement to some or all property for a specified duration, such as until the marriage has lasted five or ten years, or may provide for a smaller percentage that increases based on the duration of the marriage; however, when the parties may have children together, the lawyer for the weaker party should consider eliminating such a waiting period if a child is born. The argument for this approach is that a weaker party should have the resources to provide a home and to pay other expenses to raise the parties' child and should not have to rely exclusively on the decisions of a trustee.

The provisions for the weaker party allow, but do not require, the stronger party to provide for his or her assets to go into a trust for the survivor. This will permit the stronger party to direct the ultimate disposition of these assets. The provisions for a trust describe a Qualified Terminable Interest Property (QTIP) trust. The requirements for a QTIP trust are:

- The surviving spouse must be entitled to all of the income from the trust;
- The surviving spouse must be entitled to require the trustee to make the trust assets productive of income; and
- The surviving spouse must be entitled to income for life, whether he or she remarries or not, and there can be no other beneficiary during his or her life.[88]

The trust settlor has a number of other decisions he or she can make, except to the extent limited by the agreement, including choice of trustee and whether the beneficiary will be permitted to invade the principal. The lawyer for the spouse-beneficiary may consider proposing that his/her client be a co-trustee or that the trustee be independent and not a member of the settlor's family.

The pool of assets from which the weaker party's share is determined is defined as the gross estate for federal estate tax purposes. This is an all-inclusive definition. It provides for optional inclusion in the gross estate of adjusted taxable gifts. It also provides for assets

88. I.R.C. § 2056.

the weaker party may receive outside of probate to be counted against his or her share. For example, the decedent's retirement benefits will be included in the gross estate and, if the weaker party receives these benefits, their value will be counted as part of the spouse's share.

There are a variety of other options to provide for a surviving spouse, including:

- A cash bequest. However, unless the bequest is subject to a cost of living adjustment, its value will erode over time.
- The right to receive a specific asset, such as a home. However, such a right may prove illusory if the decedent could sell or encumber the property.
- The right to be beneficiary of a specified amount of life insurance or a specific policy currently in force. Such a right may prove illusory unless the policy can be kept in force solely by payment of premiums. The lawyer for the spouse should consider proposing that the spouse become the owner of an existing policy, or have the right to acquire a new policy of which he/she will be the owner.
- The right to survivor benefits under an employer-sponsored defined contribution retirement plan. The lawyer for the weaker spouse should take account of the employee-spouse retiring or changing jobs and rolling over the plan benefits to an IRA.

The model text states that the surviving spouse is only entitled to the rights provided at death if the parties are married, and not separated, upon the death of the obligor-spouse. If the parties intend any of the death provisions to survive dissolution of the marriage, the agreement should say so expressly.[89] Paragraph 9 defines separation. If parties separate and a spouse dies before entry of a judgment of divorce, the provisions of the agreement for disposition of property at separation apply, and not the death provisions. It is a good idea for the agreement to be explicit that this is what the parties intend. This should eliminate a dispute in the event a spouse dies after a separation. It should also eliminate a dispute about whether provisions for a spouse after death survive entry of a judgment of divorce.[90] The drafting lawyer should also consider whether the waiver should be broad enough to include a wrongful death claim. The following waiver is sufficiently broad.[91]

The agreement should include a comprehensive and express waiver of each of the rights each party would otherwise have as a surviving spouse in the absence of agreement, including the right to an elective share. Other formulations of the waiver of spousal rights that do not mention the elective share expressly have been held to constitute a waiver of the elective share, but it is better to make the waiver express and avoid the risk of a court making the

89. *See Worsham v. Worsham,* 74 Va. App. 151, 867 S.E.2d 63 (2022) (termination of wife's right to QTIP trust upon divorce could not be inferred from text of postmarital agreement).

90. *See Johnson v. Johnson,* 725 So. 2d 1209 (Fla. Ct. App., 3d Dist. 1999), where the court held that a premarital agreement was ambiguous about whether the husband's obligation to create a trust for the wife survived their divorce, although it ultimately ruled in his favor.

91. *See Estate of McConnell v. Rajendran,* 28 Neb. App. 303, 943 N.W.2d 722 (2020) (premarital agreement did not bar estranged wife from wrongful death settlement proceeds where waiver applied only to decedent's separate property); *Rickman v. Rickman,* 2013 Tenn. App. LEXIS 683 (unpub.) (postmarital agreement waiver was comprehensive enough, including all rights parties may have acquired by reason of marriage, to deny wife's claim to wrongful death proceeds).

wrong decision.[92] When the instrument to be executed is a postmarital agreement, the text of the waiver should be clear about whether it includes rights under a pre-existing will,[93] or beneficiary designation.[94]

Paragraph 19(D) says that the share of the surviving spouse will not be reduced by any death taxes. I.R.C. § 2056 permits a U.S. citizen surviving spouse to receive, through the decedent's estate planning documents, assets of unlimited value (known as the unlimited marital deduction) without the estate or the spouse incurring any federal estate tax upon the death of the first spouse. Therefore, any federal estate taxes imposed at the death of the first spouse will be borne by the other heirs.

PROPERTY RIGHTS UPON DEATH OF A PARTY: MODEL TEXT

PROPERTY RIGHTS UPON DEATH OF A PARTY

17. **Waiver of Rights**. Except as otherwise provided in this Agreement, each party shall have the right to dispose of his or her property by will, trust, beneficiary designation, transfer during his or her lifetime, gift, or by any other means. Accordingly, except as otherwise provided in this Agreement, each party waives all of his or her property rights, claims, and interests as a surviving spouse to the other party's property, including, but not limited to, the right of election regarding the estate of the other or to renounce and take against the will of the other, interest in augmented estate, right to inheritance in the event of intestacy, family allowance, homestead rights, exempt property, and all other similar or related rights under applicable law, including the law of any state or foreign jurisdiction where the deceased spouse may be domiciled or own property at death, and further including any rights resulting from changes in law which may take effect after execution of this Agreement.

18. **Surviving Spouse Rights to Marital Property**. Provided the parties are married and are not separated upon the death of a party, the surviving spouse shall be entitled to receive all marital property, outright and free of trust. Each party shall maintain a will, beneficiary designations, pay-on-death and transfer-on-death titles, or other estate planning documents, to carry out his or her obligations under this paragraph. In the event of a marital separation (as defined in paragraph 9), the provisions of this paragraph 18 shall not apply, and the provisions of this Agreement for determining the parties' rights upon a marital separation shall apply instead.

---

92. *See, e.g., In re Estate of Sharpe*, 814 S.E.2d 595 (N.C. App. 2018) (premarital agreement without express waiver of elective share waived elective share where it said each party had sole right to control his or her separate property as if unmarried and waived rights under state law); *see also In re Estate of Stacy*, 96 Mass. App. Ct. 447, 136 N.E.3d 1233 (2019) (premarital agreement under which parties waived rights to separate property as if no marriage took place, but did not mention death or intestacy, waived surviving spouse's intestate share).

93. *See Steffens v. Evans*, 70 So. 3d 758 (Fla. Ct. App., 4th Dist. 2011).

94. *See Kowalski v. Upchurch*, 2015 Ala. Civ. App. LEXIS 162 (unpub.).

19. **Additional Provisions for SPOUSE TWO Upon SPOUSE ONE's Death.** In the event that upon SPOUSE ONE's death the parties are married and are not separated, as defined in Paragraph 9:

A. SPOUSE ONE shall provide for SPOUSE TWO to receive property having a value calculated in accordance with paragraph 19(B). Such property shall be distributed outright to SPOUSE TWO or into a trust for the benefit of SPOUSE TWO, as described below. SPOUSE ONE shall execute, and shall keep in force, a will, beneficiary designation, or other estate planning documents, to carry out his/her obligation hereunder. In the event the parties are separated upon SPOUSE ONE'S death, the provisions of this Agreement for determining their property rights at separation or divorce shall apply instead.

B. The amount SPOUSE ONE shall cause to be distributed outright or in trust for SPOUSE TWO under this paragraph shall be not less than ____ percent of SPOUSE ONE's net estate as defined below. [*Alternative:* The amount SPOUSE ONE shall cause to be distributed outright or in trust for SPOUSE TWO under this Paragraph shall be not less than ___ percent of SPOUSE ONE's net estate if the parties have been married for less than ___ years upon SPOUSE ONE's death and __ percent thereof if the parties have been married __ or more years on the date of SPOUSE ONE's death.] SPOUSE TWO's __ percent of SPOUSE ONE's net estate shall be reduced, but not below zero, by: (1) the amount of any assets includible in SPOUSE ONE's gross estate which pass to SPOUSE TWO, or a trust for SPOUSE TWO, by beneficiary designation, including under a pay-on-death or transfer-on-death designation; (2) one-half of the value of any property includible in SPOUSE ONE's gross estate which passes to SPOUSE TWO, or a trust for SPOUSE TWO, by right of survivorship; (3) the amount of death benefits under SPOUSE ONE's qualified retirement plan payable to SPOUSE TWO; (4) any life insurance proceeds that are payable to, or in trust for, SPOUSE TWO as a result of SPOUSE ONE's death; (5) the value of any other property that passes to SPOUSE TWO, or a trust for SPOUSE TWO, as a result of SPOUSE ONE's death.

C. For purposes of this paragraph:

(i) "Gross estate" shall mean the gross estate for federal estate tax purposes (whether or not a federal estate tax return is filed and whether or not the federal estate tax is in effect at SPOUSE ONE's death) [*Optional:* plus the amount of adjusted taxable gifts shown on the return which were made within three years of death]. If the federal estate tax is not in effect at SPOUSE ONE's death, then the gross estate shall be determined with reference to the definition of gross estate most recently in effect prior to SPOUSE ONE's death.

(ii) "Net estate" shall mean SPOUSE ONE's gross estate, as defined in subparagraph 19(B)(i), less SPOUSE ONE's enforceable debts, funeral expenses, and the reasonable expenses of administering and distributing SPOUSE ONE's probate estate or and/or revocable trust.

D. The gift to SPOUSE TWO shall not be reduced by any federal or state death taxes.

E. If the amount calculated above is left in trust for SPOUSE TWO, the terms of the trust shall in all respects qualify as a Qualified Terminable Interest Property (QTIP) trust as provided in I.R.C. § 2056 and shall include the following provisions: (i) all of the income of the trust shall be distributed to SPOUSE TWO at least quarter-annually; (ii) SPOUSE TWO shall have the power to require that the trust assets be converted to income-producing assets; and (iii) no distributions shall be made to any beneficiary other than SPOUSE TWO during SPOUSE TWO's life. If the trust provides SPOUSE TWO the foregoing rights as a beneficiary, the trust agreement may include such other terms as SPOUSE ONE in his/her sole discretion may determine so long as such terms comply with the requirements of I.R.C. 2056 (b)(7) and the regulations thereunder.

F. The trustee may distribute to SPOUSE TWO from the principal of the trust as the trustee deems necessary for SPOUSE TWO's health and support after taking into account other assets available to SPOUSE TWO. [***Alternative provisions***: (1) The trustee shall not make any distributions of principal to SPOUSE TWO. (2) In the event of the remarriage of SPOUSE TWO, the Trustee shall not make any distributions of principal to SPOUSE TWO.]

G. SPOUSE ONE shall have the right to select the trustee(s) [***Optional provisions:*** (1); provided, however, any trustee shall be an independent trustee. (2); provided, however, SPOUSE TWO shall have the right to serve as co-trustee of the trust. (3); provided, however, SPOUSE TWO shall have the right to appoint a corporate trustee to serve as trustee of the trust and to remove any corporate trustee then serving so long as SPOUSE TWO replaces such trustee with another corporate trustee].

20. **Voluntary Bequests and Transfers.**

A. Nothing in this Agreement shall constitute a waiver or disclaimer of any right or property interest passing to a party under the other party's will or a trust established by the other party, or passing to a party under a beneficiary designation, including a beneficiary designation under his or her retirement plan. Neither party waives any bequest under the will of the other party or the right to serve (and receive compensation for serving) as personal representative, agent under a power of attorney, or trustee if appointed as such under any valid instrument.

B. Each party confirms his or her intention that any funds or securities in any joint financial institution account of the parties held as tenants by the entirety or joint tenants with right of survivorship, and any other property held as tenants by the entirety or joint tenants with right of survivorship, shall become the sole property of the survivor of them, provided the parties are married and are not separated as defined in Paragraph 9. In the event the parties are separated upon the death of a party, the provisions of this Agreement for determining the parties' rights upon a marital separation shall determine the rights of the surviving spouse and the estate of the deceased spouse to such property.

C. This paragraph is not, and shall not be construed as, a promise or representation that either party intends to transfer any real or personal property to the other.

21. **Debts.**

A. In the event property passes to a surviving spouse by operation of law upon the death of a party, the property shall pass to him or her subject to any secured debt on such property and shall be paid by the surviving spouse without any contribution from the estate of the deceased spouse [***add, if appropriate:*** , except as provided in Paragraph 21(C)].

B. [***Add, if appropriate:*** The estate of the deceased party shall pay one-half of the unsecured debt incurred in the joint names of the parties.]

C. Notwithstanding Paragraph 21(A), in the event that the debt secured by property that passes by operation of law to a surviving spouse exceeds the fair market value of the property (determined as provided in Paragraph 34(C)), the estate of the deceased party shall be responsible for one-half of the amount by which the debt exceeds the value of such property.

PORTABILITY ELECTION AND THE DECEASED SPOUSE UNUSED EXCLUSION (DSUE): COMMENT

For federal estate tax and gift purposes, each individual is entitled to an exclusion amount—that is, the amount he or she can pass to his or her heirs free of federal estate taxes (and exclusive of the value of assets that go to a spouse or charity).[95] The 2017 tax act,[96] increased the exclusion amount for decedents dying before January 1, 2026, such that, with cost of living adjustments, the amount is $12.9 million in 2023.[97] I.R.C. § 2010(c)(5) permits a deceased spouse who has not used all of his or her exclusion amount to transfer (or port over) the unused exclusion amount to the surviving spouse, which the surviving spouse could then add to his/her exclusion amount. The deceased spouse unused exclusion (DSUE) is the difference between the amount of the deceased spouse's taxable estate and the applicable exclusion amount. For example, a spouse who died in 2023 with $6 million in taxable assets at death would have a DSUE of $6.9 million, which he or she could transfer to his or her surviving spouse. To obtain this benefit, the deceased spouse's personal representative must file an estate tax return even if such a return would otherwise not be required. Portability allows for

95. 26 U.S.C.A. § 2010. The discussion here does not address any applicable state estate or inheritance taxes.
96. Tax Cuts and Jobs Act (TCJA), 115 Pub. L. No. 97, 131 Stat. 2054, 2017 Enacted H.R. 1, 115 Enacted H.R. 1.
97. I.R.C. § 2010.

estate tax planning that maximizes the opportunity of a married couple to pass assets to their children or other heirs, free of any federal estate tax. The model text below permits a surviving spouse to use this portability election and lays out the specifics of the obligations of each party, including that the surviving spouse must make the appropriate request and must pay the costs of preparation of the estate tax return if a return is not otherwise required.

At least one court has ordered the executor of a deceased spouse's estate to file an estate tax return and make the election where the parties had a premarital agreement that was silent (because the agreement and marriage predated portability).[98] With the advent of portability, the lawyer for a party who could benefit from this tax-planning opportunity can include the following text.

PORTABILITY ELECTION AND THE DSUE: MODEL TEXT

22. **Portability Election**. The parties agree that upon the death of either spouse, the personal representative of the deceased spouse's estate shall at the surviving spouse's written request [***Optional:*** , which shall be made no later than 120 days after the death of the deceased spouse], which request may be made on behalf of the surviving spouse by an attorney-in-fact, guardian, trustee, personal representative, or other agent, timely file any and all documents necessary to make the election provided in § 2010(c)(5) of the Internal Revenue Code of 1986, as amended by § 303(a) of the Tax Relief, Unemployment Insurance Reauthorization, and Job Creation Act of 2010, or any similar or corresponding law (*i.e.*, the "Portability Election"), for the deceased spouse's unused exclusion amount to be available to be used by the surviving spouse and his or her estate. These documents may include, but are not necessarily limited to, an estate tax return for the deceased spouse's estate even if his or her estate does not owe any federal estate tax at his or her death. If the surviving spouse makes this request and the deceased spouse's estate would otherwise not be required to file an estate tax return, or other necessary documents, in order to make the election, the surviving spouse's estate shall make the arrangements for the preparation of the estate tax return (or necessary documents in connection with the election) and pay the cost of preparing the estate tax return, or other documentation, and all other costs incurred in connection with the election. The deceased spouse's personal representative shall fully cooperate with the preparation, execution, and filing of the necessary documents (including the estate tax return) and shall promptly furnish all documents and information as shall be reasonably requested for that purpose.

98. *Vose v. Lee* (In re Estate of Vose) 390 P.3d 238 (Okla. 2017).

DISPOSITION OF RETIREMENT AND SURVIVOR BENEFITS AT DEATH OR DISSOLUTION: COMMENT

The model text below (Paragraphs 23 through 27) provides for waiver of spousal rights to share in retirement benefits at divorce as well as the right to a survivor annuity or lump sum death benefit that may be payable to a surviving spouse.[99] These provisions are important for a party who is still working and who will be entitled to a pension or who has a defined contribution plan.[100]

These are distinct components of the spousal right to retirement benefits, and they implicate both federal law and state law of contracts. In most states, a general waiver in a premarital or postmarital agreement of spousal property rights at divorce will suffice to constitute a waiver of the right to share retirement benefits earned by a participant and payable during the life of the participant.[101] A specific waiver of the right to share in retirement benefits accrued during marriage is the better practice.[102] The model text below provides an express waiver.

The Employee Retirement Income Security Act (ERISA) governs most private sector employee benefit plans.[103] Employee benefit plans comprise two types of benefits, pension benefit plans and welfare benefit plans.[104] Pension plans governed by ERISA are defined as plans that provide for retirement income for employees or that provide for a deferral of income.[105] ERISA pension benefit plans include both "qualified" plans, that is, plans subject to the contribution limits of I.R.C. § 415, and funded "excess benefit" plans.[106]

---

99. See Chapter 13 for a provision for sharing retirement benefits earned during marriage.

100. When a party is already retired, will not return to employment, and is in pay status with respect to a pension, or had a defined contribution plan, such as a 401(k), that he or she rolled over to an IRA, these paragraphs will not be necessary. A new spouse will have no right to a survivor annuity under a defined benefit pension in pay status. Paragraphs 23–27 will not be needed. When a spouse has rolled over a defined contribution plan to an IRA, paragraph 17 will give him or her the power to decide whether to make a surviving spouse the beneficiary, and paragraph 33(B) can be used for the dissolution scenario.

101. *In re Marriage of Smith*, 115 S.W.3d 126 (Tex. Ct. App. 2003) (general waiver clause of postmarital agreement referring to "all property" without mentioning retirement benefits was broad enough to include them); *Moor-Jankowski v. Moor-Jankowski*, 222 A.D.2d 422, 634 N.Y.S.2d 728 (1995) (premarital agreement providing that each party is to retain all separate property, including increments resulting from personal efforts, skills, or services, effected waiver of marital claim to retirement benefits earned during marriage); *but see Thompson v. Wolfram*, 162 N.E.3d 498 (Ind. Ct. App. 2020) *reh. denied* 2021 Ind. App. LEXIS 60 (unpub.) (premarital agreement defining all property titled in one party's name as separate property, property acquired during marriage as marital property to be equally divided at divorce, agreement silent as to new 401(k) contributions during marriage, appreciation on premarital contributions, or pension benefits; all appreciation, new contributions and pension were marital property).

102. *See Robinson v. Robinson*, 746 So. 2d 65 (La. Ct. App. 1999), *rev'd in part and rem'd*, 778 So. 2d 1105 (La. 2001) (postmarital agreement with general waiver of marital property rights did not constitute waiver of wife's vested interest in community share of husband's retirement benefits); *see also Wilson v. Moore*, 929 S.W.2d 367 (Tenn. Ct. App. 1996).

103. 29 U.S.C. §§ 1001, *et seq*. Governmental plans, church plans, and unfunded excess benefit plans are exempt from coverage under ERISA unless they elect to be covered. 29 U.S.C. § 1003(b). A retirement plan of a single-owner business whose only participants are the owner and the owner's spouse can be an ERISA plan. *See Raymond B. Yates, M.D., P.C. Profit Sharing Plan v. Hendon*, 541 U.S. 1, 124 S. Ct. 1330, 158 L. Ed. 2d 40 (2004).

104. 29 U.S.C. § 1002(1), (2).

105. 29 U.S.C. § 1002(2)(A). Welfare plans comprise a variety of other benefits, including employer-sponsored life insurance and health insurance.

106. Excess benefit plans are defined in 29 U.S.C. § 1002(36).

ERISA mandates benefits for a surviving spouse in the absence of an effective waiver:

- A qualified retirement plan must provide for payment of a survivor annuity to a spouse of a participant who dies before the annuity starting date, the qualified preretirement survivor annuity (QPSA).[107]
- A participant in a defined benefit (DB) pension plan who is married on the date of his or her retirement must elect a qualified joint and survivor annuity (QJSA) form of benefit.[108] A plan may limit its obligation to pay a survivor annuity so as to require that a surviving spouse have been married to the participant for at least one year before the participant's death.[109]
- Certain plans, typically defined contribution plans, such as 401(k)s, need not provide a QPSA or QJSA, but such plans must provide for payment in full of a married participant's nonforfeitable accrued benefit to the surviving spouse upon the participant's death and, if the participant is not married, or the spouse consents to the participant's waiver of these benefits, to the participant's designated beneficiary.[110]

Surviving spouse rights are not a function of when the pension benefits accrued. Thus, a spouse who was married to the participant for a short period may nevertheless be entitled to a survivor annuity or lump-sum death benefit based on the accrued benefit over the entire period of participation in the plan except to the extent a portion of the survivor benefits is payable to a former spouse under a qualified domestic relations order (QDRO).[111]

In the absence of an effective waiver of a spouse's rights regarding the participant's ERISA-governed retirement benefits, the spouse will have certain rights upon divorce:

- A state divorce court may award all or a portion of the participant's plan benefits to the spouse (in the terminology of ERISA, the Alternate Payee [AP]) to carry out a division of property. ERISA permits, but does not require, such a division. A court order may be directed to the plan administrator to require such a division. The order can direct the plan administrator to make direct payment to the AP provided the order meets the requirements of ERISA for a QDRO.[112]
- A state divorce court may award a survivor annuity to a divorcing spouse pursuant to a QDRO with respect to a plan that is required to pay a QPSA or a QJSA. The QDRO may order that the former spouse be treated as a surviving spouse for purposes of these benefits.[113] ERISA permits, but does not require, such an award.[114]

---

107. I.R.C. §§ 401(a)(11)(A)(ii), 417(c); 29 U.S.C. § 1055(a)(2).

108. I.R.C. §§ 401(a)(11)(A)(i), 417(b); 29 U.S.C. § 1055(a)(1).

109. 29 U.S.C. § 1055(b)(4).

110. 29 U.S.C. § 1055(b).

111. *See Boggs v. Boggs*, 520 U.S. 833, 117 S. Ct. 1754, 138 L. Ed. 2d 45 (1997) (surviving wife of nine years entitled to surviving spouse benefit accrued over husband's 36-year employment).

112. A QDRO is a domestic relations order that provides for all or a portion of a participant's benefits to be paid to a spouse or former spouse as a division of property. I.R.C. § 414(p)(1). A QDRO can also order the plan to pay benefits to fulfill an alimony or child support obligation. *Id.* For an in-depth treatment of retirement benefits and divorce, see P. SHEWMAKER & J.R. LEWIS, THE COMPLETE QDRO HANDBOOK (4th ed., ABA 2019).

113. 29 U.S.C. § 1056(d)(3)(F).

114. I.R.C. § 414(p)(5); 29 U.S.C. § 1056(d)(3).

ERISA permits a participant to waive his or her spouse's right to survivor or death benefits.[115] Only the participant may waive these rights, and he or she may do so only with the consent of the spouse.[116] ERISA creates certain obstacles to an effective contractual waiver of these spousal rights. A consent to waiver of spousal rights to survivor or lump-sum death benefits in a premarital agreement is not effective. The term *spouse* in U.S.C. § 29-1055(c) has been interpreted literally to exclude a prospective spouse; thus only a spouse, not a prospective spouse, may consent to a participant's waiver.[117] The Treasury Department, which—along with the Department of Labor—is charged with enforcement of ERISA, has interpreted the tax counterpart of the statute to preclude an effective premarital spousal consent to waiver of survivor rights.[118] The Treasury Regulation provides:

> Question 28: Does consent contained in an ante-nuptial agreement or similar contract entered into prior to marriage satisfy the consent requirements of Section § 401(a)(11) and 417?
>
> Answer 28: No. An agreement entered into prior to marriage does not satisfy the applicable consent requirements. . . . [119]

Once parties are married, they can effectively waive their rights to qualified plan death benefits in a contract.[120] A contractual waiver in a premarital or postmarital agreement of survivor or death benefits is effective only if the participant takes the additional steps required by ERISA. Specifically, after the date of marriage or the execution of a postmarital agreement, as the case may be, the participant must obtain the spouse's consent on a form that must be signed by the spouse before a notary or plan representative and the participant must file the consent with the plan administrator along with a beneficiary designation naming the beneficiary of his or her choice. If the participant fails to request the spouse to sign a consent, the spouse does not sign the consent after being asked to do so, or the participant fails to file the consent and beneficiary designation with the plan administrator, the surviving spouse will be entitled to receive the benefits from the plan, notwithstanding a premarital or postmarital agreement under which the spouse waived his or her rights.[121]

When parties agree to waive survivor rights in a premarital or postmarital agreement, counsel should make provisions in the agreement for additional steps to implement the waiver. The agreement should include the following:

---

115. 29 U.S.C. § 1055(c).

116. 29 U.S.C. § 1055(c); I.R.C. § 417; Treas. Reg. § 1.401(a)-20.

117. *Hagwood v. Newton*, 282 F.3d 285 (4th Cir. 2002); *National Auto Dealers & Assoc. Retirement Trust v. Arbeitman*, 89 F.3d 496 (8th Cir. 1996); *Hurwitz v. Sher*, 982 F.2d 778 (2d Cir. 1992), *cert. denied*, 508 U.S. 912 (1993); *Robins v. Geisel*, 666 F. Supp. 2d 463 (D.N.J. 2009); *Ford Motor Co. v. Ross*, 129 F. Supp. 2d 1070 (E.D. Mich. 2001); *Zinn v. Donaldson Company, Inc.*, 799 F. Supp. 69 (D. Minn. 1992).

118. I.R.C. § 417(a) is identical to 29 U.S.C. § 1055(c)(2)(B).

119. Treas. Reg. § 1.401(a)-20.

120. *Appleton v. Alcorn*, 291 Ga. 107, 728 S.E.2d 549 (2012).

121. *Kennedy v. Plan Administrator for Dupont Savings & Investment Plan*, 555 U.S. 285, 129 S. Ct. 865 (2009); *Greenebaum Doll & McDonald PLLC v. Sandler*, 256 Fed. Appx. 765, 2007 U.S. App. LEXIS 28823 (6th Cir. Dec. 3, 2007).

- An express waiver of the right to the survivor annuity or lump-sum death benefits that conforms to the requirements of the statute and the plan and that specifically identifies the plan;[122]
- An express provision requiring the spouse to execute a postmarital consent to the waiver as necessary and upon request of the participant; and
- A provision mandating that a spouse who receives benefits contrary to the contractual waiver turn them over to the deceased spouse's estate, net of taxes paid by the surviving spouse. Whether such a provision is enforceable is an open question, discussed further below.

Content of the Consent

ERISA mandates that the spousal consent to the participant's waiver of survivor benefits designate "a beneficiary (or a form of benefits) which may not be changed without spousal consent (or the consent of the spouse expressly permits a designation by the participant without any requirement of further consent by the spouse) and . . . the spouse's consent acknowledges the effect of such election. . . ."[123] A general waiver of survivor benefits is insufficient; the waiver must either name a beneficiary or expressly give the participant the right to name and change the beneficiary without further spousal consent.[124] Further, the consent must acknowledge the effect of the participant's election not to provide a survivor benefit.[125] The participant's plan should have consent forms that are acceptable to the plan. The plan's form should be used whenever possible.

Formalities

The spousal consent to the waiver must be in writing, and it must be either notarized or witnessed by a plan representative.[126] A marital agreement that is merely signed, but not notarized, can never constitute an effective waiver of the spousal right to a survivor benefit under ERISA, even if the content of the waiver is otherwise adequate.[127]

Timing

A spousal consent to the participant's waiver of the QPSA is not effective until after the participant reaches age 35.[128] A consent to waiver of the QJSA is effective only if made within 90 days of the annuity starting date.[129] A participant may change jobs several times during a career. Therefore, a participant who wishes to retain a contractual waiver of survivor benefits over time may need to obtain a consent to waiver multiple times during the marriage.

---

122. The plan can be identified in a financial disclosure attached to the agreement.
123. I.R.C. § 417(a); 29 U.S.C. § 1055(c)(2)(B).
124. *Hagwood v. Newton*, 282 F.3d 285 (4th Cir. 2002).
125. I.R.C. § 417(a)(2); 29 U.S.C. § 1055(c)(2).
126. I.R.C. § 417(a)(2); 29 U.S.C. § 1055(c)(2).
127. *Lasche v. George W. Lasche Basic Profit Sharing Plan*, 111 F.3d 863 (11th Cir. 1997); *Hurwitz v. Sher*, 982 F.2d 778 (2d Cir. 1992), *cert. denied*, 508 U.S. 912 (1993).
128. 29 U.S.C. § 1055(c)(7)(B).
129. 29 U.S.C. § 1055(c)(7)(A).

Participant's Responsibility

It is the participant's responsibility to request the spouse to sign the necessary consent and to file it, and a new beneficiary designation, with the plan. The model text contains a statement to this effect. Such a provision may aid a weaker surviving spouse who was never asked to sign a postmarital consent.[130]

Advice to Client

The participant should be advised about steps he or she must take after the date of marriage, or after execution of a postmarital agreement, in regard to survivor or death benefits, to the extent the agreement provides for a spousal waiver, including the following:[131]

- The participant should obtain a consent form from the plan administrator for waiver of the QPSA or other death benefits and have the spouse execute it as soon as possible after the marriage, or after the participant reaches his or her 35th birthday;
- The spouse must execute the consent before a notary or plan representative;
- The participant must file the consent with the plan administrator;
- The participant must repeat this process every time he or she takes a new job and participates in a new plan; and
- The participant must obtain a new spousal consent, and must file it with the plan within 90 days of the annuity starting date, in order to effect a waiver of the QJSA.

In addition, the client should be advised of the uncertainties surrounding the intersection of state law governing parties' rights to enforce a contractual waiver of spousal rights under a premarital or postmarital agreement and federal law governing spousal rights to qualified retirement benefits. ERISA's plan documents rule mandates that the plan administrator pay benefits in accordance with the documents governing the plan.[132] These documents include the plan itself and the beneficiary designation. As a result, if there is no effective beneficiary designation on file, the plan must pay the spouse because ERISA mandates that the plan so provide. When a spouse refuses to sign a consent, is never asked to do so, or the participant does not file a signed consent and beneficiary designation, and the participant dies, the plan *must pay* the surviving spouse despite the contractual waiver. Similarly, when a participant voluntarily names a spouse as beneficiary, the parties divorce with a contractual waiver of survivor rights, but the participant fails to change the beneficiary, the plan must pay the former spouse pursuant to the beneficiary designation.[133] ERISA's plan documents mandate preempts the contractual waiver.[134]

In *Kennedy v. Plan Administrator*, the Supreme Court left open the question whether the heirs of a deceased participant can pursue a state law contract or quasi-contract remedy, such as specific performance, money damages, or a constructive trust on the proceeds of

130. *See Greenbaum Doll & McDonald, P.L.L.C. v. Sandler*, 256 Fed. Appx. 765, 2007 U.S. App. LEXIS 2 8823 (6th Cir. Dec. 3, 2007).

131. See Appendix F for model post-execution letter.

132. 29 U.S.C. § 1104(a)(1)(D).

133. *Kennedy v. Plan Administrator*, 555 U.S. 285.

134. 29 U.S.C. § 1144(a); *Egelhoff v. Egelhoff*, 532 U.S. 141, 121 S. Ct. 1322, 149 L. Ed. 2d 264 (2001).

an ERISA plan in the hands of a spouse or former spouse who received them contrary to a contractual waiver. Federal and state courts that have ruled on this issue to date have held that ERISA's preemption rule, coupled with the plan documents rule, is intended merely to allow for efficient administration of plans. Once benefits are paid out according to the plan documents, ERISA has nothing to say about the resolution of a dispute among competing family members.[135] The model text includes an obligation to pay over any funds received contrary to a waiver.

When a premarital or postmarital agreement provides for a cash bequest to a surviving spouse, ERISA does not preclude a contract provision that requires the spouse to make an election between the bequest and the retirement plan benefits. When the agreement provides for the spouse to receive a percentage share of the plan participant's estate, the retirement benefits can be counted against his or her share.[136]

ERISA creates vested rights for surviving spouses to receive survivor or death benefits, as discussed above. By contrast, ERISA creates no substantive spousal right to share retirement benefits at divorce; rather, it defers to state marital property law to determine spousal rights to retirement benefits at divorce.[137] Thus, insofar as state law permits spouses and prospective spouses to waive division of retirement benefits at divorce, ERISA does not stand in the way. That ERISA permits a premarital waiver of spousal rights in a contract to seek a share of retirement benefits at divorce seems clear enough from the plain language of the statute. However, this interpretation has been challenged by spouses seeking a division of retirement benefits at divorce notwithstanding a premarital waiver. Courts in Colorado, Illinois, New Jersey, North Carolina, Pennsylvania, New York, and the District of Columbia have rejected the argument that ERISA precludes such a waiver.[138]

Paragraph 24 includes optional text under which the parties acknowledge that each has the right to name a beneficiary of his or her IRA. This language may be useful in dispelling any claim to the contrary but is not necessary text. IRAs are not governed by ERISA and surviving spouses have no protected rights in them.[139] When the account owner intends for someone other than the spouse to receive an IRA, he or she must file a beneficiary designation

---

135. *Gelschus v. Hogen*, 47 F.4th 679 (8th Cir. 2022); In re Estate of Petelle, 515 P.3d 548 (Wash. Ct. App. 2022); *Andochick v. Byrd*, 709 F.3d 296 (4th Cir. 2013); *In re Estate of Kensinger v. URL Pharma, Inc.*, 674 F.3d 131 (3d Cir. 2012); *Appleton v. Alcorn*, 291 Ga. 107, 728 S.E.2d 549 (2012); *Pardee v. Personal Representative for the Estate of Pardee*, 112 P.3d 308 (Ok. Civ. App. 2004); *Guidry v. Sheet Metal Workers Nat'l Pension Fund*, 39 F. 3d 1078 (10th Cir. 1994): *see also Hoult v. Hoult*, 373 F.3d 47 (1st Cir. 2004); *Wright v. Richmond*, 219 F.3d 905 (9th Cir. 2000); *Alpert v. Taylor*, 2009 U.S. Dist. LEXIS 137782 (D.M.D. Fla. 2009) (widower not entitled to injunction in federal court to preclude personal representative of wife from suing him for funds distributed from her ERISA retirement plan where husband waived in premarital agreement); *Ladov v. Mendelson*, 2008 U.S. Dist. LEXIS 22557 (D.W.D. Pa. 2008) (once husband's survivor benefits paid to wife, breach of contract and constructive trust claims under premarital agreement presented no federal question; case remanded to state court).

136. See model paragraph 19(B).

137. 29 U.S.C. § 1056(d).

138. *Strong v. Dubin*, 75 A.D.3d 66, 901 N.Y.S.2d 214 (2010); *Savage-Keough v. Keough*, 373 N.J. Super. 198, 861 A.2d 131 (2004); *Sabad v. Fessenden*, 825 A.2d 682 (Pa. Super. Ct. 2003); *Stewart v. Stewart*, 141 N.C. App. 236, 541 S.E.2d 209 (2000); *Critchell v. Critchell*, 746 A.2d 282 (D.C. 2000); *In re Marriage of DiFatta*, 306 Ill. App. 3d 656, 714 N.E.2d 1092 (1999); *In re Marriage of Rahn*, 914 P.2d 463 (Colo. Ct. App. 1995); *see also Diller v. Diller*, 6 MFLM Supp. 139 (Md. Ct. Spec. App. 2008) (unpub.).

139. 29 U.S.C. § 1051(6); I.R.C. § 414(p); *Charles Schwab & Co., Inc. v. Debickero*, 593 F.3d 916 (9th Cir. 2012) (surviving spouse not entitled to IRA although originated in 401(k) rollover, surviving spouse has no protected rights in IRA).

and keep it current. A general waiver of rights in a contract is insufficient to waive a spouse's or divorced spouse's rights as a named beneficiary of an IRA.[140]

The provisions in paragraphs 23–27 can also be used for federal government retirement plans. The statutes governing federal statutory retirement plans generally permit a waiver of spousal rights. Neither the governing statutes, nor implementing regulations, expressly address whether a waiver of spousal survivor rights in a premarital agreement is effective. However, it appears that premarital waivers, as well as postmarital waivers, are possible. For example, the U.S. Code provides with respect to Civil Service Retirement System (CSRS) annuities:[141]

> An individual entitled to an annuity from the Fund may decline to accept all or any part of the annuity by a waiver signed and filed with the Office of Personnel Management. The waiver may be revoked in writing at any time. . . .[142]

An annuity may be waived by a participant,[143] by a surviving spouse,[144] and by a surviving former spouse who was awarded a survivor annuity in a court order at divorce.[145] Significantly, the Merit Systems Protection Board (MSPB) has held that the above-quoted language does not prohibit an irrevocable waiver.[146] In addition, the Code provides that a married employee shall receive a joint and survivor annuity upon retirement unless the employee and spouse jointly waive the spouse's survivor rights "in a written election filed with the Office [of Personnel Management] at the time that the employee . . . retires."[147] This provision requires that the waiver be filed with the Office of Personnel Management at the time of retirement; it does not specify a period during which the waiver must be executed. Implementing regulations similarly do not limit the execution of the waiver, or election, to the period immediately prior to retirement.[148]

In *Mackey v. Office of Personnel Mgmt.*,[149] there was a premarital agreement waiving each party's property rights. The parties later divorced but the participant did not remove the former wife as beneficiary for receipt of the lump sum credit. The MSPB ruled that the former wife's statutory right as named beneficiary superseded the pre-existing waiver in the premarital agreement.[150] The MSPB did not address whether a premarital waiver would have been effective to waive the wife's statutory rights to a surviving spouse annuity had the parties still been married at the husband's death. But nothing in 5 U.S.C. § 8345, when read with 5 U.S.C. § 8339(j)(1) and other MSPB decisions, suggests such a waiver is impermissible. The

---

140. *East v. Paine Webber, Inc.*, 131 Md. App. 302, 748 A.2d 1082 (2000).

141. The discussion here is illustrative, using CSRS as an example. No attempt is made to discuss the statutes and regulations governing possible waivers under other federal plans, such as FERS, military retirement, or the two plans covering Foreign Service employees.

142. 5 U.S.C. § 8345(d).

143. *Vesser v. Office of Personnel Mgmt.*, 29 F.3d 600 (Fed. Cir. 1994).

144. *Worley v. Office of Personnel Mgmt.*, 86 M.S.P.R. 237 (Merit Systems Protection Board 2000).

145. *Shelley v. Office of Personnel Mgmt.*, 88 M.S.P.R. 224 (Merit Systems Protection Board 2001).

146. *Id.*

147. 5 U.S.C. § 8339(j)(1).

148. 5 C.F.R. § 831.611(a).

149. 54 M.S.P.R. 158 (Merit Systems Protection Board 1992).

150. 5 U.S.C. § 8342(b) permits an employee to name a beneficiary of the lump sum credit. 5 U.S.C. § 8342(c) mandates payment in an order of precedence beginning with the named beneficiary.

approach taken by MSPB in other cases has been that an action is permissible if not prohibited. For example, it held that a statute permitting a revocable waiver permits the same waiver to be made irrevocable.[151] The same principle should apply to permit waiver of spousal survivor rights at any time, even before marriage, so long as the waiver is filed with the Office of Personnel Management before death or retirement, whichever comes first.[152]

DISPOSITION OF RETIREMENT BENEFITS AT DEATH OR DISSOLUTION: MODEL TEXT

DISPOSITION OF RETIREMENT AND SURVIVOR BENEFITS IN THE EVENT OF MARITAL SEPARATION OR DEATH

23. **Waiver of Interests in Retirement Benefits in the Event of Separation.** In the event of the parties' marital separation, each party shall have the right to retain his or her retirement benefits, whenever accrued, free from any claim or demand of the other party, including any claim for an equitable distribution or other division of these benefits, and each party expressly waives any and all claims he or she may have to any retirement benefits held by the other party. In the event of a marital separation, each party shall, upon request of the other, execute such consent or waiver as may be required to effectuate the participant party's right to retain exclusive rights to his or her retirement benefits, including any consent or waiver that may be required to carry out the terms of this Agreement.

24. **Waiver of Spousal Interest in and Right to Survivor and Death Benefits.** Each party expressly waives any legal right he or she may have under any federal or state law as spouse to participate as a payee or beneficiary of any interest the other party may have now or in the future in any retirement benefits, including, but not limited to, the right to receive any lump sum death benefit, pre-retirement survivor annuity, or post-retirement annuity (also known as the "joint and survivor annuity" or "surviving spouse annuity"). Each party consents to any election previously or hereafter made by the other party with respect to the payee and the form of payment of any benefit upon retirement or death under any such plan. The parties acknowledge that the effect of this waiver is to permit each party, without notice to or consent of the other party, to elect a single life annuity, self-only annuity, lump sum withdrawal benefit, commuted lump sum, or refund of employee contributions, take a distribution or rollover, name a beneficiary of that party's choosing as beneficiary of his or her survivor or death benefits, or elect any other form of payment available under the terms of his or her retirement plan. [***Optional:*** The parties acknowledge

151. *Shelley v. Office of Personnel Mgmt.*, 88 M.S.P.R. 224 (Merit Systems Protection Board 2001); *see also Worley v. Office of Personnel Mgmt.*, 86 M.S.P.R. 237 (Merit Systems Protection Board 2000).

152. The waiver must be signed and filed with the Office of Personnel Management. 5 U.S.C. § 8345(d). To be effective, it should state expressly that it is irrevocable.

their understanding that each party has the right to name a beneficiary of his or her choice under his or her Individual Retirement Account.]

25. **Obligation to Execute Consent to Waiver of Retirement Plan Benefits**. The parties agree that after the date of their marriage each will, upon request of the other, or his or her personal representative, as the case may be, execute any waiver or consent to waiver as may be required by the terms of the other party's plan, or applicable statute or regulation, so as to permit the plan participant to elect any form of payment available under his or her retirement plan and to waive completely any spousal rights the nonparticipant-spouse may otherwise have under such plan. [***Optional:*** Each party acknowledges that it is his or her responsibility to request that the other party execute the necessary consent form after the marriage and to file the executed form with his or her plan administrator.]

26. **Default**. In order to carry out the terms hereof: (i) if a party is unable for any reason to change the beneficiary of the death or survivor benefits of his or her retirement plan or, (ii) if a party fails to designate a beneficiary and the plan provides for payment to the "spouse" or "former spouse," or (iii) if such waiver under this Agreement is for any reason ineffective and the benefits are, in fact, paid to the surviving party contrary to the terms of paragraph 25, then in any of such events the surviving party shall, at the direction of and at the sole discretion of the decedent's personal representative: (A) disclaim any entitlement to any benefits received or receivable; or (B) assign all rights to receive such benefits to the estate of the deceased party or the person designated by the decedent or the decedent's personal representative to receive such benefits, net of all income taxes payable by the surviving party with respect to such benefits; or (C) pay the net after-tax benefits over to the estate of the deceased party or to the person designated by the decedent or by the decedent's personal representative. [***Add if appropriate***: In the event the surviving spouse fails to carry out the terms of this paragraph, the provisions for ____ [him/her] under Paragraphs ___ and ____ of this Agreement [making specific provisions for surviving spouse at death of retirement plan participant] shall be null and void.]

27. **Voluntary Beneficiary Designations**. Nothing in this Agreement shall prevent a party from expressly designating the other party as beneficiary of his or her survivor benefits, pre-retirement survivor benefits, or death benefits under his or her retirement plan. Neither party waives any right to proceeds vesting in him or her by reason of being expressly designated a beneficiary of any retirement benefits of the other party.

SPECIAL PROVISIONS FOR PRIMARY MARITAL HOME: COMMENT

Model paragraphs 28 through 32 provide an example of special treatment for a primary marital home. They can be used with a title controls agreement or with a shared property agreement.[153] These provisions would allow a party who may contribute a disproportionate amount of nonmarital money to acquisition of a marital home to recover his or her contribution and a *pro rata* share of appreciation if the marriage fails. The model agreement (paragraph 5(ii)) provides, as a default, that all real estate titled in a survivorship form is marital property regardless of the source of funds for acquisition; use of the forms below will create an exception to this default definition. These provisions can allow a spouse to recover his or her disproportionate investment if a marriage fails, but to title the home in a survivorship form so as to provide for a surviving spouse to receive the home if the marriage ends at death. These paragraphs are written to provide for a primary marital residence; however, they could be used for a second home as well.

Model paragraph 29(B) is a definition of acquisition costs. At a minimum, acquisition costs will consist of a cash down payment, cash paid for improvements, and payment of the principal of acquisition debt. The definition of acquisition costs gives the drafter the option to include or exclude settlement closing costs, interest on acquisition debt, property taxes, and homeowner's insurance. The choice can significantly affect the outcome for both parties. The model text provides an example that illustrates the different results where parties sell a home at the end of ten years, comparing the outcome when interest and property taxes are excluded and when they are included in the definition of acquisition costs.

Paragraph 30 allows for the possibility the parties may sell a primary home during the marriage and for the classification of proceeds of sale to follow into the next home, if there is one, and to the extent not reinvested, for each party to receive his or her separate property share and to retain an equal interest in the marital property share.

Paragraph 28 does not allocate responsibility for payment of acquisition debt during the marriage. Parties are free to decide how to pay these costs. Paragraph 32 requires a surviving spouse who receives sole title to survivorship property to take subject to secured debt. If parties intend that the estate of the decedent pay off the mortgage, the agreement must say so expressly.

Acquisition debt is defined, and limited to, debt directly attributable to purchase the property, to improve the property, or to refinance acquisition debt. It does not include debt used for another purpose, for example, a home equity loan used to pay off credit cards or a party's premarital debt.

When a premarital or postmarital agreement predetermines that one spouse will have the right to buy out the other's interest, counsel will need to consider some contingencies. For example, if a couple may have children, a buyout provision could give a spouse the right to evict the other spouse and could therefore affect a custody dispute. If one party has a minor child who will be living in the home, a forced move on short notice could be quite disruptive for that child. On the other hand, an owner may not want a court that otherwise has authority to do so to grant exclusive use and possession to the other parent and force the owner-spouse to vacate.[154] Whether a child is involved or not, a weaker spouse may need time to make

153. See Chapter 13 for discussion of and model text for a shared property agreement.

154. *See Woods v. Woods*, 611 S.W.3d 676 (Ark. Ct. App. 2020) (trial court erred in award of exclusive use and possession to custodial parent contrary to terms of premarital agreement).

moving arrangements and may need immediate cash to do so.[155] Similarly, when a couple is older, an elderly or incapacitated spouse may not be able to move on short notice.

The model text requires a purchasing party to remove the selling party as an obligor on the mortgage or other encumbrance on the property. Mortgage instruments typically include a due-on-sale clause that permits a lender to require payoff upon sale to a third party. However, the Garn-St. Germain Act permits an intra-spousal transfer of title without invocation of the due-on-sale clause.[156] Consequently, if the agreement is silent, the buying spouse will have no obligation to refinance, potentially to the detriment of the selling spouse's ability to qualify for a mortgage to acquire a replacement home.

SPECIAL PROVISIONS FOR PRIMARY HOME: MODEL TEXT

SPECIAL PROVISIONS FOR PRIMARY MARITAL HOME

28. **Acquisition and Title of Primary Marital Home.** The parties agree and acknowledge that they may jointly purchase a home during their marriage for use as their primary residence, and they further acknowledge that their contributions to acquisition costs of such property may be disproportionate. They agree that they shall take title to any such property as tenants by the entirety or as joint tenants with right of survivorship [***Add, if appropriate:*** , and they agree to be joint obligors on any loan required to finance the purchase of such property].

29. **Allocation of Parties' Interests in Primary Marital Home.**

A. Notwithstanding the form of title and any other terms of this Agreement, the parties agree that each party's interest in the property in the event of a marital separation, shall be a *pro rata* share determined in accordance with each party's monetary contributions of separate property and the marital monetary contributions, if any, to the acquisition costs of such property as set forth more specifically hereafter. Accordingly, each party's separate share of such property shall be equal to the sum of that party's separate property monetary contributions to acquisition costs, as defined in Paragraph 29(B) of this Agreement, divided by the sum of all monetary contributions to acquisition costs. The marital share of such property shall be equal to the sum of all marital property monetary contributions to acquisition costs divided by the sum of all monetary contributions to acquisition costs. [***Option #1, applicable if acquisition costs exclude interest, property taxes and insurance:*** By way of example, and not by way of limitation, assume the parties purchase a home for $600,000, SPOUSE ONE pays the down payment of $120,000 and settlement closing costs of $12,000, and the parties take a mortgage of $480,000. Assume the parties sell the home at

155. Appendix E includes model text that can be used to address these concerns.
156. 12 U.S.C. § 1701j-3.

the end of ten years for $810,000, and that they paid down the mortgage to $380,000 from a joint bank account (*i.e.*, $100,000 paid on principal) for a total of $232,000 paid for acquisition costs. In that event, SPOUSE ONE's separate property share will be 57 percent ($132,000/$232,000 = 0.57) and the marital share will be 43 percent ($100,000/$232,000 = 0.43). The value of SPOUSE ONE's separate property share (without taking into account costs of sale) will be $242,820 ($810,000 – $380,000 = $426,000; $426,000 × 0.57 = $242,820) and the marital share will be $183,180. ($426,000 × 0.43 = $183,180).] [***Option #2, applicable if acquisition costs include interest and property taxes but not insurance:*** By way of example, and not by way of limitation, assume the parties purchase a home for $600,000, SPOUSE ONE pays the down payment of $120,000 and settlement closing costs of $12,000, and the parties take a mortgage of $480,000. Assume the parties sell the home at the end of ten years for $810,000, that they made principal and interest payments of $2,500 per month from a joint bank account (*i.e.*, a total of $300,000) and paid the mortgage down to $380,000, and that they paid $48,000 in property taxes for a total of $348,000 paid from marital funds and a total of $480,000 paid for acquisition costs. In that event, 27.5 percent will be SPOUSE ONE's separate property share ($132,000/$480,000 = 0.275) and 72.5 percent will be the marital share ($348,000/$480,000 = 0.725). The value of SPOUSE ONE's separate share (without taking into account costs of sale) will be $117,150 ($426,000 × 0.275 = $117,150) and the value of the marital share will be $308,850 ($426,000 × 0.725 = $308,850).]

B. The term "acquisition costs" shall mean the consideration paid for the property and payment for capital improvements, whether paid in cash, by an in-kind exchange, or through payment of debt incurred for acquisition of the specific property, and further including, and limited to, a down payment, settlement closing costs for acquisition and for financing the property, payment of the principal [and interest] of debt used for payoff of a prior loan for acquisition costs [***Add, if appropriate:*** , and payment of property taxes]. [***Add, if appropriate:*** The term "acquisition costs" does not include interest payments, casualty and liability insurance, property taxes, or the expenses of routine repairs and maintenance of the property.]

30. **Sale of the Property**. The parties acknowledge and agree that each party shall retain his or her separate property share of the proceeds of sale of a primary marital home. Therefore, each party shall be entitled to receive and retain his or her separate property share of the net proceeds of sale. The parties shall retain their equal interest in the marital property share of such net proceeds. Further, to the extent the parties use some or all of the proceeds to acquire a subsequent residence, the marital property interest and each party's separate property interest shall be determined in accordance with the same allocation formula set forth above.

31. **Disposition Upon Separation.**

A. In the event of the parties' separation, SPOUSE ONE shall have the right to purchase SPOUSE TWO'S interest in the primary marital home (defined as his/her share of net equity) as set forth more particularly hereafter. SPOUSE ONE shall notify SPOUSE TWO, in writing, within __ days of separation of his/her intent to exercise this right. If SPOUSE ONE declines the first option to purchase, then SPOUSE TWO shall have an option to purchase SPOUSE ONE'S interest in the property and shall notify SPOUSE ONE in writing within __ days of the expiration of SPOUSE ONE'S option. Net equity shall mean the fair market value of the property, determined as provided herein, less the balance of the debt secured by the property [***Add, if appropriate:*** and __ percent of fair market value, representing the broker's commission and the costs for transfer and recordation that would otherwise be incurred upon sale to a third party].

B. In the event the parties do not agree on the fair market value of the property, they shall have the property appraised in accordance with Paragraph 34.C.

C. The purchasing party shall have ____days from the date of his or her notice, or, if later, from the date fair market value is determined, to obtain financing and conclude the buyout. The purchasing spouse shall pay the full amount due the selling spouse in a single lump sum, except as the parties may otherwise agree, and the selling spouse shall simultaneously execute a deed conveying all his or her right, title, and interest in such property to the purchasing spouse. Thereafter, he or she shall have no further interest in such property. Upon such conveyance, the purchasing spouse shall cause the selling spouse to be removed as an obligor on the mortgage/deed of trust note and on any other obligations secured by the property.

D. The selling spouse shall have ___ days from the date of the buyout to move from the home; provided, however, he or she shall have no obligation to move if the home is the home of a minor child of the parties until the parties have entered into an agreement regarding physical custody and access time with respect to such child or a court has entered an order, temporary or final, for custody and access. [***Add/revise, if appropriate:*** provided, however, if the home is the home, whether fulltime or parttime, of a minor child of the selling spouse, he or she shall have an additional ___ days to move.]

E. If neither party elects to purchase the other's interest in the property, or, in the event the purchasing party is unable to obtain financing necessary to remove the other party as an obligor on the mortgage, or any other obligation secured by the property, the property shall be sold and the net proceeds of sale shall be divided as provided in Paragraphs 29 and 30. In such event, the property shall be placed on the market for sale with a licensed real estate broker and sold for the best price obtainable under then-current market conditions. The parties shall cooperate to sell the property as expeditiously as circumstances permit.

32. **Disposition Upon Death.** If upon the death of one party the parties' primary marital residence is a home owned by them in a survivorship form, and if upon such spouse's death they are married and are not separated, as defined herein, then, in that event, the surviving spouse shall become the sole owner of such property by operation of law, subject to any debt secured by the property. In the event the parties are separated at the death of a party, their interests in such property shall be determined in accordance with Paragraphs 29 and 30.

PROPERTY RIGHTS UPON DISSOLUTION: COMMENT

The model text below provides for a comprehensive waiver of all spousal rights to property at dissolution except as specifically provided by the agreement. The text waives any claim either may have to the other spouse's separate property, however defined in the agreement. It provides for an equal division of property defined in the agreement as marital/community property, waiving any claim either party might have for more than half based on equitable principles or other statutory criteria that would govern a trial judge's decision in the absence of contract.

Waivers serve several important functions in an agreement:

- They conclusively determine parties' property rights at divorce;
- To the extent waivers identify specific categories of property rights being waived, they reduce the potential for conflicting claims about parties' true intent and for a court to misinterpret the terms; and
- They identify the property interests on which the agreement operates so as to alert each party to the nature of rights each is waiving.[157]

A general waiver of the right to share in property that the agreement classifies as the separate property of the other spouse at divorce will generally suffice to protect parties' separate property interests. However, it is often useful to include more detailed, specific waivers along with the general comprehensive waivers. Particularly when one party is unrepresented, specific waivers of major categories of property can inform him or her of the marital rights that would exist in the absence of agreement. Doing so enhances validity and reduces the opportunity for a dispute over the scope of the waiver. This model agreement creates specific waivers by identifying the various forms of wealth that a party may have at marriage or acquire thereafter (model paragraphs 1–4), specifically describing the types of assets classified as each party's separate property (model paragraphs 5–7), and expressly waiving claims to such assets (model paragraphs 23–27,[158] 30, 33, and 34(E)).

In the common law title states, spousal rights to property at death and at divorce are derived from different statutes and common law sources and serve different functions.

157. *See Eyster v. Pechenik*, 71 Mass. App. Ct. 773, 887 N.E.2d 272 (2008).

158. If a party with a defined benefit pension is already in pay status, or has rolled over a defined contribution account to an IRA, and does not expect to return to employment, so that a new spouse will not acquire any survivor rights, paragraphs 24–27 can be deleted and paragraph 23 can be moved over and made a subparagraph of paragraph 33.

Therefore, a waiver of one type of spousal right does not necessarily include a waiver of other spousal rights.[159] The agreement should clearly identify what rights are waived. If the parties intend to waive rights accruing at divorce, but not at death, or vice versa, the agreement should say so clearly. While a waiver need not refer expressly to equitable distribution to be effective,[160] it is the better practice to do so.

The agreement should be clear about whether parties are waiving all marital rights or only some. An agreement that has an express waiver of claims to all or specified premarital property, but that fails to expressly waive a claim to property acquired during marriage through marital labor, may not constitute such a waiver.[161] Indeed, "courts construe [marital] agreements narrowly in favor of the community estate."[162] Thus, silence regarding parties' rights to the fruits of marital labor may be tantamount to no waiver,[163] or may create an ambiguity that a court must resolve,[164] sometimes only after competing testimony with the risk that a credibility determination will go the wrong way.

McIntyre v. McIntyre[165] is an example of an inadequate waiver. The waiver consisted only of the following: "[Each party] hereby releases, renounces and forever quitclaims to [the other] all right, title, interest, claim and demand whatsoever including all marital rights in real estate and personal property of [the other] and [each party] may at all times hereafter purchase, acquire, own, hold, possess, encumber, dispose of and convey any and all . . . property . . . as though unmarried."[166] The wife asserted that the quoted text merely permitted each party to deal freely in his/her own property and did not preclude equitable distribution in the event of divorce. The husband argued that the text, especially its reference to "all marital rights" was a complete waiver. The appellate court concluded either interpretation was reasonable; therefore, it upheld the trial court interpretation favoring the wife's position. Key to the result was the fact that the waiver made no reference to equitable distribution, nor

---

159. *See Ventimiglia v. Ventimiglia*, 307 A.D.2d 993, 763 N.Y.S.2d 486 (2003) (premarital agreement waiving interest in "estate" did not waive equitable distribution of property at divorce); *Devault v. Devault*, 80 Ohio App. 3d 341, 609 N.E.2d 214 (1992) (agreement that mentions death but not divorce does not apply at divorce); *In re Estate of Berzinis*, 505 A.2d 86 (Me. 1986) (waiver of rights to separate property referred to property rights at divorce, but not to spousal rights at death where death not mentioned in agreement).

160. *White v. White*, 238 N.C. App. 201, 768 S.E.2d 65 (2014).

161. *Williams v. Williams*, 246 S.W.3d 207 (Tex. Ct. App. 2007) (premarital agreement that did not mention wages and salaries did not waive community property interest); *Worley v. Worley*, 855 So. 2d 632 (Fla. Ct. App. 2003) (premarital agreement that waived claim to property acquired before or after marriage did not waive wife's right to seek share of assets acquired through marital labor or salary or enhanced value of separate assets); *see also Miller v. Miller*, 2007 Va. App. LEXIS 340 (unpub.) (premarital agreement that provided each party would keep and retain sole ownership of property owned at execution or acquired "hereafter" was ambiguous as to whether parties intended to waive property acquired during marriage from wages); *Tolar v. Tolar*, 639 So. 2d 399 (La. Ct. App. 1994) (premarital agreement that listed parties' premarital assets and renounced community property regime "with respect thereto" was not a general renunciation of community property rights).

162. *McClary v. Thompson*, 65 S.W.3d 829, 837 (Tex. App. 2002).

163. *Id.*; *see also Dewey v. Dewey*, 745 S.W.2d 514 (Tex. App. 1988) (premarital agreement that was silent regarding husband's salary from his premarital professional corporation, but that identified professional corporation and all profits, dividends, interests, and proceeds as separate property, did not convert salary from community to separate property).

164. *Dwoskin v. Dwoskin*, 2020 Va. Cir. LEXIS 129 (unpub.) (agreement defining separate property, but lacking express waiver of equitable distribution, was ambiguous; after trial, based on testimony, appreciation on separate property held the separate property of the owner).

165. 654 S.E.2d 798 (N.C. Ct. App. 2008).

166. *Id.* at 799–800.

did it make reference to property acquired after the date of marriage. Similarly, in *Garcia v. Mayer*,[167] the general release paragraph provided: "Each party relinquishes any right, title or interest in or to any earnings, accumulations, future investments, money or property of the other party except as contained herein."[168] The agreement was silent concerning the husband's unvested stock options but provided for division of vested options. The court deemed the agreement ambiguous because the general waiver failed to clarify whether "property of the other party" applied only to each party's separate property or whether it was intended as a waiver of each party's interest in community property held by the other. The appellate court upheld the trial court's finding that the wife did not waive her community interest in the unvested options.

A property interest may be separately titled but be classified as marital/community property in the absence of a contract. The contract should therefore express a party's separate property rights in terms of both separate title and separate property classification. The cases cited earlier illustrate the importance of the agreement making clear that a party's separate property includes not only property titled in his or her name, but also everything that flows from a party's separate property, including appreciation, active or passive (so long as he or she retains sole ownership).

Statutes generally operate prospectively.[169] Nevertheless, it is a good idea to make explicit the parties' intent to waive rights not yet created to the extent they may do so. A marital agreement could be in effect for many years, during which time legislative changes and case law development may affect the property rights parties would otherwise have had in the absence of agreement. Waiver provisions should generally encompass property rights that may be created as a result of such changes.[170]

The model text provides for an equal division of property the agreement defines as marital without regard to the source of funds for acquisition or any other considerations. Parties are free to negotiate for a different percentage allocation of all such property; or, as illustrated in the provisions for disposition of a primary residence,[171] they could make an exception for a specific asset. As written, there may be little or no marital property because the parties may not have any jointly titled assets. When the agreement predetermines division of marital assets, or a methodology for division, in the majority of states, a court at divorce must adhere to the agreement; it is not free to devise a different method of allocation than that specified in the agreement.[172] Some parties may prefer to define what is included in the marital estate,

---

167. 122 N.M. 57, 920 P.2d 522 (Ct. App. 1996).

168. *Id.* at 59, 524.

169. *See DeGarcia's Estate v. Garcia*, 399 So. 2d 486 (Fla. Dist. Ct. App. 1981) (waiver of rights in premarital agreement included right to elective share not created by statute until 20 years after marriage).

170. *See, e.g.*, *Herget v. Herget*, 319 Md. 466, 573 A.2d 798 (1990) (broadly worded waiver of rights to property precluded a monetary award under Maryland's subsequently enacted equitable distribution statute); *see also Ryan v. Ryan*, 659 N.E.2d 1088 (Ind. Ct. App. 1995); *Roos v. Roos*, 206 A.D.2d 293, 614 N.Y.S.2d 522 (1994); *Prevatte v. Prevatte*, 104 N.C. App. 777, 411 S.E.2d 386 (1991).

171. Model paragraphs 28–32.

172. *Simon v. Simon*, 91 So. 3d 214 (Fla. Ct. App. 4th Dist. 2012); but see Section 4.09(d) for discussion of the second-look at divorce.

but leave disposition of these assets for court determination in the event of dissolution.[173] The model here opts for a predetermination of disposition of marital property.

The agreement should have a choice-of-law provision that will govern a dispute about validity, breach, or construction. What law governs an issue not determined in the agreement is a separate question, for example, where the agreement defines marital/community property but leaves the decision as to allocation to a judge at divorce. If parties prefer to leave the decision as to division of property for determination at dissolution, the agreement should specify what law will apply.[174] If the agreement is silent, the court may apply the law of the forum, whether or not the parties were living in that jurisdiction when they signed the agreement.

A premarital or postmarital agreement should generally address responsibility for payment of secured debt in the event of divorce. Often, it will be appropriate for a party who is to receive an asset to assume responsibility for debt secured by the asset. If that is the intent of the parties, the agreement should say so expressly. Similarly, if parties intend that a transferor pay off debt secured by property to be transferred to the other spouse, the agreement should say so clearly. For example, in *In re Marriage of Marnach*,[175] the premarital agreement required the husband to transfer a house to the wife "free and clear." *Free and clear* could mean either free and clear of the husband's interest or free and clear of all encumbrances. The court held the latter interpretation was correct. The agreement could have foreclosed this dispute.

A spouse who is obligated to transfer ownership of an asset may need the transferee to refinance to remove the transferor as an obligor on the debt secured by the property. The agreement should expressly address that obligation and provide a timeline as well as a default obligation to sell the encumbered property.

Model paragraph 35 is an optional paragraph that can be used to provide for a cash property settlement for a disadvantaged spouse in the event of a separation.

PROPERTY RIGHTS UPON DISSOLUTION: MODEL TEXT

PROPERTY RIGHTS AND SUPPORT IN THE EVENT OF MARITAL DISSOLUTION

33. **Separate Property**. In the event of the parties' separation, as defined in Paragraph 9, each party shall retain his or her separate property free from any claim or demand of the other party, and each party shall be solely responsible for paying his or her separate debt. Each party waives the right to make a claim with respect to the separate property of the other party for transfer, monetary award, equitable distribution award, equitable lien, or community property award under __________

173. *See, e.g., Hooker v. Hooker*, 220 So. 3d 397 (Fla. 2017).

174. *See In re Marriage of Proctor*, 203 Ore. App. 499, 125 P.3d 801 (2005), *modified by, adhered to*, 204 Ore. App. 250, 129 P.3d 186, *rev. denied*, 340 Ore. App. 672, 136 P.3d 742, *subs. appeal*, 234 Ore. App. 722, 229 P.3d 635, *remanded*, 235 Ore. App. 641, 234 P.3d 133 (2010) (premarital agreement providing California law governed construction and silent on law governing substantive rights not otherwise determined; Oregon law applies).

175. 2009 Minn. App. LEXIS 1281 (Dec. 8, 2009).

Code § ________, or division of any kind under any applicable statute or law of ____________________, or any other jurisdiction that may govern the disposition of marital or community property upon separation or divorce, including a foreign jurisdiction, as such laws now exist or may hereafter be enacted or amended.

34. **Marital Property**. In the event of the parties' separation as defined in Paragraph 9:

A. Each party shall be entitled to receive one-half of the marital property and shall be charged with one-half of the marital debt, secured or unsecured. In the event a party receives property as part of a division of property upon marital separation or divorce, the property shall be transferred to the recipient subject to any secured debt on such property and shall be paid by the recipient of the property. Further, the parties shall each be responsible for paying one-half of their unsecured marital debt as part of the equal division of marital property, except as they may otherwise agree.

B. In order to carry out the division of marital property and the payoff of marital debt, the parties shall take such steps as they shall agree upon to divide and allocate their marital property and marital debt in accordance with the terms of this Agreement. They agree to negotiate in good faith to allocate their property interests in accordance with the terms of this Agreement. In negotiating the allocation of their property, they shall each give due consideration to the other party's preferences, difficulties of valuation, marketability of assets, and other relevant factors. The parties have not provided specific terms to carry out this division because the nature of the assets and debts and the pertinent circumstances cannot be ascertained at this time. Nevertheless, if an item of marital property lends itself to a distribution in kind, to the extent possible the property shall be distributed equally in kind. If the property does not lend itself to a distribution in kind, or the parties cannot agree on an in-kind division, they shall proceed in accordance with Paragraph 34(D).

C. In the event the parties do not agree as to the fair market value of any specific item of marital property, the parties shall obtain an appraisal of the property subject to division from a qualified, independent appraiser with experience in valuing the type of property in dispute. Such appraisal shall control as to fair market value. If the parties are unable to agree on an appraiser, each party shall select such an appraiser having an office in or reasonably near the community where the property is located, and the average of the two appraisals shall control as to value. A party's failure to respond within 30 days to a written request for selection of an appraiser shall be deemed a waiver of the right to participate in the selection, and the other party's choice of appraiser shall control. The parties shall share the cost of appraisal equally.

D. In the event the parties do not agree as to the appropriate disposition of any item of marital property, they shall offer such item for sale to the general public using a method calculated to achieve the highest price and shall divide the proceeds of sale in accordance with paragraph 34(A). [***Alternative if agreement provides for binding arbitration:*** In the event the parties do not agree as to the appropriate disposition of any item of marital property or marital debt, they shall resolve the dispute in binding arbitration as set forth in Paragraph 61.]

E. This Agreement is a full and complete settlement of all marital property rights of the parties. Accordingly, each party waives the right to make a claim with respect to any marital property for contribution, transfer, monetary award, equitable distribution award, equitable lien, or community property award under __________ Code § _________, or division of any kind under any applicable statute or law of ___________, or any other jurisdiction that may govern the disposition of marital or community property upon separation or divorce, including a foreign jurisdiction, as such laws now exist or may hereafter be enacted or amended.

F. If at any time during the marriage, the parties, or either of them, become residents of a state or country under the laws of which a spouse acquires property interests commonly known as community property or quasi-community property, or any other property interests different from the property interests of spouses under the laws of ___________ their property interests shall nevertheless remain the same as they would have been under the terms of this Agreement construed in accordance with the laws of ______________. Each party hereby agrees, at any time during the marriage, after a marital separation or divorce, or the death a party, to execute, acknowledge and deliver to the other, or his or her representative, any deed and other instrument that may be necessary to waive any interest in any property or estate of the other which he or she may acquire by virtue of any community property, quasi-community property, or equivalent laws.

G. In the event a party predeceases the other after a marital separation, but prior to the full implementation of the provisions of this Agreement for disposition of property, unless otherwise agreed by the surviving party and the deceased party's estate, the surviving party shall, within nine months of the death of the deceased party, execute an irrevocable qualified disclaimer within the meaning of § 2518 of the Internal Revenue Code of 1986, or any similar corresponding law, to disclaim all or any portion of such property passing to the surviving party by right of survivorship, operation of law, under the laws of intestate succession, will, trust, or similar instrument or beneficiary designation, including retirement benefits, which exceeds in value the property to which the surviving party is entitled under this Agreement in the event of marital separation.

35. **Cash Property Settlement.** In the event of the parties' separation, as defined in Paragraph 9, SPOUSE ONE shall make a cash payment to SPOUSE TWO as a property settlement, and not as alimony, in accordance with the following schedule:

(i) in the event the parties have been married for at least ___ years on the date of separation, the cash payment shall be $_______, which sum shall be due in full no later than ___ days after the separation;

(ii) in the event the parties have been married for more than ___ years on the date of separation, in addition to the cash payment under Paragraph 35(i), SPOUSE TWO shall pay SPOUSE ONE the sum of $______ multiplied by the number of full years of marriage over ____ years, which sum shall be due in full not later than ___ days after the separation, and provided further that in no event shall the sum due exceed $______.

SPOUSAL SUPPORT UPON DISSOLUTION: COMMENT

Parties to a premarital or postmarital agreement have a variety of options for treatment of spousal support, including:

- A complete waiver of all support rights;
- An unqualified reservation of rights, leaving the decision to a court or arbitrator to be determined by the law of the forum;
- A conditional reservation of rights, for example a reservation that terminates upon the birth of a child;
- A reservation of rights with specified limitations, such as a durational limit;
- Specific provisions fixing the amount and duration of periodic support, or providing a formula for determining the amount and duration;
- Specific provisions for a lump sum payment, in lieu of periodic payments, that can be based on a formula that includes duration of the marriage or other factors the parties choose.

The model paragraphs that follow consist of a complete waiver of spousal support coupled with a provision for term-limited support. Spousal support is neither deductible from the income of the payor nor includible in the income of the payee, as it was before the 2017 tax act eliminated the alimony deduction.[176]

A waiver of spousal support must be express to be effective. It may not be implied from a general waiver of marital rights or from a provision that permits each party to dispose of his or her separate property during marriage,[177] or from a provision that waives a party's claim to

176. The previously existing provisions for deductibility, Sections 71 and 215, were repealed in the 2017 tax act. Tax Cuts and Jobs Act (TCJA), 115 Pub. L. No. 97, 131 Stat. 2054, 2017 Enacted H.R. 1, 115 Enacted H.R. 1.

177. *Davis v. Davis*, 239 Va. 657, 391 S.E.2d 255 (1990); *see also Beverly v. Parilla*, 165 Ohio App. 3d 802, 848 N.E.2d 881 (2006); *Sabad v. Fessenden*, 825 A.2d 682 (Pa. Super. Ct. 2003); *White v. White*, 617 So. 2d 732 (Fla. Dist. Ct. App. 1993); *Hawley v. Hawley*, 904 S.W.2d 584 (Mo. Ct. App. 1995); *D'Onofrio v. D'Onofrio*, 200 N.J. Super. 361, 491 A.2d 752 (1985).

property held by the other party,[178] or to income derived from separate property.[179] Moreover, because post-divorce support and pre-divorce support serve different purposes, a general waiver of support or alimony is not a waiver of support rights while parties remain married. Rather, a waiver of the right to temporary support during the pendency of a suit for divorce, to the extent state law permits such a waiver, must be express to be effective.[180] When the agreement provides for a specific support payment, the agreement should include an express waiver of all support other than that provided in the agreement. Failure to couple a provision fixing support with a waiver of all other support rights may create sufficient ambiguity about whether parties intended a complete waiver to leave open an opportunity for litigation.[181]

The model text presents one example of a provision for spousal support, a predetermined amount (coupled with a cost of living adjustment) and a duration tied to length of marriage. Many other options are available. In situations where spousal support is appropriate, counsel will need to consider the wealth and age disparity at the outset; each party's resources, including reasonable expectations of a future inheritance; work and earnings history; other provisions made for the support payee; and the likelihood the parties will have children.

States' laws around spousal support generally provide for termination upon the death of either party. However, nothing prevents parties to an agreement from providing for the obligation to extend after the death of the payor. If the agreement does not provide expressly for a support obligation to survive the death of the payor, it will not survive.[182] Counsel for an economically weaker party should consider a provision that continues a fixed, periodic obligation, or an obligation to pay a lump sum in lieu of periodic payments, after the death of the payor. Alternatively, the agreement could provide for the payor to provide life insurance.

If parties intend that support terminate automatically upon the payee's remarriage, the agreement should say so expressly.[183] If parties intend that support terminate on cohabitation, the agreement should say so expressly and should define cohabitation.[184]

When the agreement provides for a reservation of a spousal support claim, counsel should consider whether to specify the law that will govern the determination of a disputed claim. When the agreement reserves a claim, there may be some limitations that are appropriate or that a party may want to negotiate for. For example, the payor may want the court to ignore the income he or she will receive from separate property and limit consideration of income

---

178. *In re Marriage of Cobb*, 2007 Iowa App. LEXIS 930 (unpub.); *Ackerman v. Yates*, 847 A.2d 418 (Me. 2004); *Bloomfield v. Bloomfield*, 97 N.Y.2d 188, 738 N.Y.S.2d 650, 764 N.E.2d 950 (2001).

179. *In re Marriage of Harris*, 828 P.2d 1365 (Mont. 1992); *but see Pisano v. Pisano*, 87 Mass. App. Ct. 403, 31 N.E.3d 1132 (2015) (parties' intent to waive spousal support is evident from waiver of claims to separate property, including income from separate property).

180. *J.S. v. P.S.*, 59 Misc. 3d 560, 23 N.Y.S.3d 355 (Sup. Ct. 2018); *Forgey-Lewis v. Lewis*; 2011 Tenn. App. LEXIS 29 (unpub.); *Bamberger v. Hines*, 2009 LEXIS 32 (unpub.); *Beal v. Beal*, 88 P.3d 104 (Alaska 2004); *Musko v. Musko*, 447 Pa. Super. 150, 668 A.2d 561 (1995); *Scherer v. Scherer*, 249 Ga. 635, 292 S.E.2d 662 (1982).

181. *See deMontluzin v. deMontluzin*, 464 So. 2d 948 (La. Ct. App. 1985) (case remanded to trial court for determination of parties' intent where consent order provided specified support for defined period but was silent on wife's right to return to court to extend support beyond that expressly provided).

182. *See Stigutz v. Stigutz*, 319 So. 3d 39 (Fla. Ct. App. 2021).

183. *Oman v. Oman*, 702 N.W.2d 11 (S.D. 2005) (where state law provides that remarriage is merely *prima facie* evidence supporting termination, silence in settlement as to remarriage requires evidentiary hearing).

184. *See Lee v. Lee*, 228 W.Va. 483, 721 S.E.2d 53 (2011) (premarital agreement providing for termination of support upon wife entering into "another relationship" was ambiguous).

only to income from his or her share of marital property.[185] When the agreement is silent as to whether the court can consider income from separate property, the court may consider it.[186]

SPOUSAL SUPPORT UPON DISSOLUTION: MODEL TEXT

36. **Waiver of Spousal Support**. E[xcept as otherwise provided herein, e]ach party expressly waives any right he or she may ever have to receive alimony, maintenance, or spousal support from the other—including temporary, rehabilitative, indefinite, and permanent, both periodic and lump sum—whether such right or claim results from common law, statutory law, or by way of equitable rights. Each party shall indemnify and hold the other harmless from any such claim made by him or her. Each party waives his or her right to have any court assume jurisdiction for the purpose of modifying this Agreement, and no provision in this Agreement concerning alimony or spousal support shall be subject to modification by any court under any statute or law of any jurisdiction, including a foreign jurisdiction, that may be applicable in the absence of this Premarital [***or:*** Postmarital] Agreement. Each party recognizes the implications of waiving a future right to support from the other party given the uncertainty of each party's future needs and resources, but makes such waiver freely and voluntarily. Each party acknowledges that it is not his or her intent to derive any right of support from the other party in the event of a marital separation or divorce, notwithstanding the law of any state, the passage of time, or any change in the circumstances of the parties. [***Add, if appropriate:*** The parties expressly acknowledge that they may have a child or children together and that the birth of a child constitutes a change of circumstances and may result in further changes in circumstances, such as a parent leaving employment to care for a child. Nevertheless, the parties intend and agree that neither the birth of a child, nor any further attendant change in circumstances, shall have any effect on their waiver of spousal support herein.]

37. **Spousal Support for SPOUSE TWO Upon Separation/Divorce.**

A. *Acknowledgment.* The parties believe it to be in their mutual best interests to enter into a binding agreement relating to the provision of support by SPOUSE ONE to SPOUSE TWO in the event of a marital separation. In this regard, the parties each confirm and acknowledge that the economic circumstances and earning capacities of the parties are such as to make the arrangements herein fair and reasonable. Each of the parties is aware of the possibility of unforeseen events that could affect his or her earning capacity and/or financial situation. Nevertheless, each party is willing to accept such risks.

185. *See Fercho v. Fercho,* 982 N.W.2d 540 (N.D. 2022) (premarital agreement was not substantively unconscionable where reserved claim for spousal support, but provided court could not consider either party's income from nonmarital property in determining amount).

186. *See Folberth v. Folberth,* 2022 Ohio App. LEXIS 3173 (unpub.)

B. *Duration.* In the event of a marital separation, SPOUSE ONE shall pay to SPOUSE TWO spousal support for the number of months equal to [***Alternative:*** one-half of] the months of marriage from the date of the parties' marriage to the date of a marital separation as defined in Paragraph 9 of this Agreement.

C. *Amount.* In the event of a marital separation, SPOUSE ONE shall pay to SPOUSE TWO as spousal support $______ per month for the duration set forth above. The amount of spousal support that may be payable hereunder shall be adjusted annually, effective July 1 of each year, in accordance with the Consumer Price Index for All Urban Consumers (CPI-U), based on changes in the CPI-U for the prior 12 months (but not in excess of __ percent in any year), with the first such adjustment to be effective for any payments that may be due on or after July 1, _____, based upon the increase from July, ____ to July, ____.

D. *Commencement.* Monthly spousal support payments shall commence on the first day of the month following a marital separation; provided, however, that SPOUSE ONE shall have no obligation to make payments hereunder until such time as the parties are living separate and apart under separate roofs.

E. *Termination of Obligation.* All spousal support shall terminate and SPOUSE ONE shall be released from the obligation of payment upon the first to occur of the following: (i) SPOUSE TWO's death, (ii) SPOUSE TWO's remarriage as defined herein; (iii) SPOUSE ONE's completing the number of spousal support payments set forth in this Agreement. "Remarriage" for purposes of this Agreement shall mean and include (i) entry into a marriage, as defined by the law of the jurisdiction where the marriage took place; (ii) entry into a formal civil union or domestic partnership under the law of a state (including the District of Columbia), a territory of the United States, or a foreign nation that provides by law for a formal procedure for recognition and registration of such a legal status; (iii) cohabitation in a marriage-like relationship for a period of __ days or more.

F. *Obligation to Continue After Death of SPOUSE ONE.* In the event of SPOUSE ONE's death, the remaining payments shall be an obligation of SPOUSE ONE's estate, provided, however, his/her personal representative or trustee shall have the option, at any time prior to the completion of all spousal support payments due hereunder, to make a lump sum payment, as hereinafter defined, to SPOUSE TWO in satisfaction of the aggregate unpaid future payments, in full and complete satisfaction of any remaining obligations for spousal support. The lump sum payment shall be equal to the present value, discounted at an annual rate of ___ percent per year, of each unpaid monthly alimony and spousal support payment, without giving effect to any future CPI-U adjustment provided for in Paragraph 37(C) not already in effect at the time of such lump sum payment, and without giving any effect to the risk of death of SPOUSE TWO or the possibility of SPOUSE TWO's remarriage.

LAWYERS' FEES AND COSTS: COMMENT

The model text below addresses three different aspects of lawyers' fees and costs incurred in connection with a premarital or postmarital agreement:

- Fees and costs incurred at the drafting and negotiation stage;
- Fees and costs incurred to implement the agreement upon dissolution of the marriage by death or divorce, including a disagreement as to the proper interpretation of the terms; and
- Fees and costs incurred to resolve a claim of invalidity or breach.

Paragraph 38 is an optional provision for a stronger party to pay the fees incurred by the weaker party to negotiate the agreement. Some proponents may intend to pay some or all such fees but prefer for the agreement itself to be silent on the subject.

The American Rule provides that each party in a legal matter is responsible for his or her own legal fees.[187] However, in domestic litigation (but not in probate matters) trial courts have broad authority to shift fees and costs of one party over to the other party. Model paragraphs 39 and 40 restrict or modify that authority. Paragraph 39 states the general principle that each party will be responsible for his or her own fees incurred to carry out the terms of agreement. Even when there is no dispute about validity, and when parties are in general agreement about their rights under it, often each will wish to be represented to implement the terms. Thus, each will likely incur fees at this stage. This paragraph is intended as a comprehensive waiver of any rights a spouse would otherwise have upon separation or divorce to seek a fee award from a court for these services.

Generally, any waiver of counsel fees for future domestic litigation must be express to be effective.[188] Because courts in many states have specific statutory authority to award fees in domestic litigation, and because the viability of the fee claim may not depend entirely upon the merits of the underlying claim, the waiver, in order to be comprehensive, should encompass all statutory and common law fee-shifting authority that would otherwise exist under applicable state law absent an agreement, including both interim fees

187. See Chapter 6.

188. *See Arizin v. Covello*, 175 Misc. 2d 453, 669 N.Y.S.2d 189 (Sup. Ct. 1998) (attorneys' fees for litigation over validity of premarital agreement, including claim for spousal support contrary to waiver, can be waived if waiver express); *In re Marriage of Cullman*, 185 Ill. App. 3d 1029, 541 N.E.2d 1274 (1989) (comprehensive waiver of property and support that did not expressly mention counsel fees did not waive right to seek fee award from court); *Klyce v. Klyce*, 429 So. 2d 1081 (Ala. Civ. App. 1983) (waiver of alimony does not constitute waiver of attorneys' fees though obligation stems from same source); *Posner v. Posner*, 237 So. 2d 186, 188 (Fla. Dist. Ct. App. 1970) (agreement silent on issue of counsel fees did not waive fee claim for litigation over validity of agreement, disposition of property, and spousal support); *but see Reizfeld v. Reizfeld*, 125 Conn. App. 782, 40 A.3d 320 (2011) (term of premarital agreement that made each party responsible for own liabilities at divorce included legal fees; therefore, fee award was improper).

and fees that could be awarded as part of a final order.[189] Divorce judges generally have authority to make an award of litigation costs in addition to an award of lawyers' fees. Therefore, a waiver should be broad and specific enough to encompass these costs.[190] A fee waiver should be broad enough to preclude a fee and cost award to a party to enable that party to challenge the validity of the agreement itself.

Paragraph 39 includes optional text that makes an exception to the fee waiver for fees incurred in connection with determination of custody or child support. As discussed in Chapter 6, several courts have held that a waiver of fees in a premarital agreement applies only to issues governed by the agreement.[191] Other courts have held such a waiver generally unenforceable or unenforceable when the particular circumstances of the case make the waiver inequitable or unjust.[192] However, the law is still developing. Some courts may strictly construe an unqualified waiver of fees that may be incurred at separation or divorce to encompass all fees incurred in divorce litigation except those expressly allowed by the terms of the agreement. When there is a significant disparity in resources, and the parties may have a child, a comprehensive waiver of all fees at divorce could seriously disadvantage the weaker party in a dispute about custody or child support. Therefore, counsel for the weaker party in such circumstances should consider including the exception for custody and child support. Similarly, when the agreement does not waive spousal support, counsel for a party who may need to seek spousal support should consider including an exception to the fee waiver to allow that party to seek fees for prosecuting the support claim.

A proponent of an agreement may wish to discourage future litigation over validity by forcing the other party to weigh the uncertain outcome against the potential for being required to pay the fees incurred by both parties. Paragraph 41 is a prevailing- party (or, loser-pays) provision; it specifically encompasses fees to defend against a meritless claim that the agreement is invalid. A prevailing-party provision can also be quite useful to the weaker party when he or she is the one who is forced to litigate the agreement to obtain compliance, or in the rare case when the stronger party seeks to be relieved of obligations he or she has come to regret.[193] As discussed in Chapter 6, a court may decide not to enforce a prevailing-party provision against an economically weaker party. However, such a provision may still deter some litigants from challenging validity. Paragraph 40 also includes optional text that makes it clear that a request for an interpretation of the agreement is neither a challenge to validity nor a breach. This text should afford some protection for a weaker party who may need a court to determine his or her rights under a concededly valid agreement, but can also

189. *See In re Marriage of Purcell*, 99 Or. App. 668, 783 P.2d 1038 (1989) (premarital agreement provision for prevailing party fees for enforcement did not constitute waiver of right to seek statutory attorneys' fees; therefore, trial court had authority to award fees under statute).

190. *See Vinik v. Lee*, 96 A.D.3d 522, 947 N.Y.S.2d 424 (2012) (court had authority to award interim fees where not expressly waived); *In re Marriage of Taylor*, 193 Ore. App. 694, 92 P.3d 124 (2004) (waiver of attorneys' fees and costs in premarital agreement was enforceable; but waiver of costs did not encompass expert witness fees, as statutory definition of costs did not include fee for expert).

191. See Section 6.04.

192. *See Kelly v. Kelly*, 518 P.3d 326 (Idaho 2022); .J.A.S. v. S.W.S., 2021 Ala. Civ. App. LEXIS 73 (unpub.).

193. *See Roberts v. Roberts*, 173 N.C. App. 354, 618 S.E.2d 761 (2005); *see also* Section 4.09(d).

protect a stronger party from a fee claim when the court adopts the other spouse's preferred construction.[194]

LAWYERS' FEES AND COSTS: MODEL TEXT

ATTORNEYS' FEES AND COSTS

38. **Fees Incurred for Preparation of this Agreement**. SPOUSE ONE shall be responsible for paying, from his/her separate funds, the attorneys' fees incurred by him/her and the attorneys' fees incurred by SPOUSE TWO in the negotiation and drafting of this Agreement.

39. **Fees and Costs Relating to Separation, Divorce, or in Connection with the Administration of the Estate of a Deceased Party**. The parties acknowledge that, in the event of a marital separation, or upon the death of a party, they may each incur attorneys' fees to represent their interests in carrying out the terms of this Agreement. Each party shall be solely responsible for any such attorneys' fees or costs incurred by him or her and any fees and costs incurred in connection with any suit for divorce, or fees that a party (or his or her estate) may incur in connection with the administration of the estate of a deceased party, except as provided in Paragraph 40. Except as otherwise provided in Paragraph 40, each party waives and releases the other from any claim for any such attorneys' fees and costs associated with any future separation or divorce action, including, but not limited to, fees and costs awarded during the pendency of such action and fees and costs that may be awarded at or after the conclusion of such action [***Add, if appropriate:*** ; provided, however, this waiver does not apply to fees and costs to determine custody or support of a minor child of the parties, and each party expressly reserves the right to make an application for such fees in accordance with the law of the state with jurisdiction to resolve such issues].

40. **Enforcement Costs for Breach or Default.** In the event a party breaches this Agreement, he or she shall pay the other party the reasonable legal fees and costs incurred by that party in the successful enforcement of this Agreement, whether through litigation, negotiations, alternative dispute resolution, or other actions necessary to compel compliance herewith [***Add, if appropriate:*** , including any court action to compel arbitration or to compel compliance with the decision of an arbitrator under Paragraph 61]. Any such reasonable legal fees and costs incurred by a party in the successful defense of a claim of breach shall be paid by the party who made and failed to establish such claim. If a party seeks to have this Agreement, or any provision of this Agreement, declared invalid and fails to establish such

194. *See Berg v. Young*, 175 So. 3d 863 (Fla. Ct. App. 4th Dist. 2015) (husband was entitled to fee award where premarital agreement provided for fee-shifting to party who sought to void agreement; wife who prevailed on dispute over interpretation not entitled to fees where agreement only permitted fee-shifting for disputes over validity).

invalidity, the party who makes the claim of invalidity shall pay the reasonable legal fees and costs incurred by the other party to defend against such claim. [***Optional:*** A request by either party for a court to interpret the terms of this Agreement or declare the rights of the parties under this Agreement shall not be considered a challenge to the validity of this Agreement nor shall it be considered a breach of this Agreement.]

VOLUNTARY EXECUTION AND UNDERSTANDING OF RIGHTS: COMMENT

The model text below consists of standard provisions acknowledging the parties executed the agreement voluntarily, with independent legal advice, or the opportunity for legal advice, and that they have a basic understanding of the rights they are waiving. When one party elects not to be represented, the alternative text of paragraph 41 can be used and adapted as appropriate to accurately state, for example, whether the represented party's lawyer advised the other party to get legal advice, whether he or she did so in writing, and whether the represented party offered to pay the other party's legal fees.[195] The boldface text is intended to highlight for an unrepresented party the importance of such advice and of the significance of the waivers. It is appropriate to have parties initial every page of the agreement as part of the execution; therefore, a party who elects not to have counsel will necessarily be alerted to this text. The agreement should not say both parties got legal advice unless the statement is true; an untrue statement puts validity at risk.[196] Paragraph 42 acknowledges that each party understands that the agreement alters the default rights of a spouse at death or divorce. In jurisdictions where case law requires that a spouse's waiver of rights have been made knowledgeably, and in cases where a weaker party does not have counsel, this text can be especially useful.[197]

VOLUNTARY EXECUTION AND UNDERSTANDING OF RIGHTS: MODEL TEXT

VOLUNTARY EXECUTION AND DISCLOSURES

41. **Voluntary Execution**. Each party acknowledges that he or she is entering into this Agreement freely and voluntarily. Each has been represented by independent counsel of his or her choice. SPOUSE ONE is represented by ___________ of the firm of ______________________. SPOUSE TWO is represented by ____________ of the firm of ______________________. [***If one party is not represented, substitute:*** **SPOUSE TWO had an opportunity to obtain advice from an independent lawyer but has opted not to be represented by counsel in connection with this Agreement.**] Each party had the opportunity to consult his or her counsel concerning the terms of this Agreement and the effect of this Agreement on his or her rights to the extent

195. See Appendix G for model letters to an unrepresented party.

196. *See Knapp v. Ginsberg,* 67 Cal. App. 5th 504, 282 Cal. Rptr. 3d 403 (2021); *Weidel v. Weidel,* 2021 N.J. Super. Unpub. LEXIS 2829 (App. Div.).

197. *See. e.g., In re Estate of Boyd,* 340 Ga. App. 744, 798 S.E.2d 330 (2017) (year's allowance can be waived in postmarital agreement if done with knowledge of specific rights).

each party deemed necessary to decide whether to sign this Agreement. Each party acknowledges that he or she has not received any legal advice from counsel for the other party and that neither is relying on any statement of counsel for the other party. [***If one party is not represented, add and revise as appropriate:*** SPOUSE TWO acknowledges that SPOUSE ONE advised ___ him/her to obtain legal advice before signing this Agreement and that SPOUSE ONE offered to pay SPOUSE TWO's legal fees to enable ___ him/her to retain counsel. SPOUSE TWO further acknowledges that SPOUSE ONE's lawyer, __________, advised him/her in writing to obtain legal advice before signing this Agreement. SPOUSE TWO states that __ he/she considered the advice of SPOUSE ONE and ___his/her lawyer that SPOUSE TWO obtain independent legal advice, but, after having done so, he/she decided to sign this Agreement without such advice.] Each party has fully considered the implications of entering into this Agreement, and each understands that it will govern the property and support rights of each of them upon the death of a spouse or in the event of a separation or divorce regardless of any future change in circumstances. Each party further acknowledges that this Agreement is fair.

42. **Understanding of Rights**. Each party acknowledges that this Agreement alters the rights each would have if they married without a premarital agreement [***if a postmarital agreement:*** if they remained married without a postmarital agreement].

A. Each party has been informed of, or has had the opportunity to be informed of, his or her legal rights as a surviving spouse in the event of the death of the other spouse if the parties married without a premarital agreement [***if a postmarital agreement:*** decided to remain married without entering into a postmarital agreement], including:

(i) the right to renounce and take against the will of the other (also known as the elective share);

(ii) the right to inheritance in the event of intestacy;

(iii) dower and curtesy;

(iv) family allowance and any other allowances provided by law for a surviving spouse;

(v) homestead rights;

(vi) exempt property;

(vii) augmented estate rights; and

(viii) the right to surviving spouse benefits under a retirement plan.

B. Each party has further been informed of, or had the opportunity to be informed of, the legal rights he or she would have in the event of separation and/or divorce if the parties married without a premarital agreement [***if a postmarital agreement:*** decided to remain married without entering into a postmarital agreement], including his or her right to seek:

(i) a court award of spousal support (also known as alimony);

(ii) equitable distribution of marital property and marital debt;

(iii) the right in some jurisdictions to seek an award of exclusive use and possession of a family home or family use personal property; and

(iv) a court award of attorneys' fees and costs of litigation.

FINANCIAL DISCLOSURE: COMMENT

How the agreement will address financial disclosure depends to some extent on what disclosures the parties have made, or will make, and the manner in which they have or will make them. The model text assumes each party will provide a written comprehensive financial disclosure statement that identifies and provides values of all major assets, as well as amounts and sources of income, and that the disclosure will be attached to the agreement. It is nevertheless appropriate to include a waiver of further disclosure and a statement that each party is satisfied with the disclosure he or she received. The waiver can cover any omitted items or inadvertent nondisclosures, the lack of further detail, more comprehensive asset valuations, or the lack of production of supporting documents. The model text will be adequate for many agreements, especially those where each party provided a comprehensive list of assets with reasonable statements of value. When a party expects a future inheritance, especially if its value is large in relation to the party's current assets, counsel should consider the optional text. When a party is an owner of a closely held business for which he or she is unable to provide an appraisal, the disclosure may need to include additional statements about the business to make the disclosure adequate under the circumstances.[198] The model provides an example of such a statement.

FINANCIAL DISCLOSURE: MODEL TEXT

43. **Financial Disclosures**. Prior to executing this Agreement, each party provided the other party with a fair disclosure of his or her property and financial obligations and his or her amounts and sources of income. SPOUSE ONE's financial disclosure is set forth on attached Schedule A. SPOUSE TWO's financial disclosure is set forth on attached Schedule B. Each party is satisfied with the disclosures made by the other party. The parties each acknowledge that some of the values shown on Schedules A and B are estimates, that some property interests are difficult to value, and that a party may be unable to obtain a more accurate value without a formal appraisal conducted by an expert in valuation. Further, the parties acknowledge that some items of property may have been omitted. [***Add and adapt, as appropriate:*** Each party further acknowledges such party's understanding that the other party

198. See Section 4.09 for further discussion of financial disclosure.

expects an inheritance from the other party's parents or other members of the party's family, that such inheritance is difficult to value, and that the other party's family members may not have disclosed the full extent, nature, or value of the holdings in his or her estate, nor whether the party can expect to inherit outright or in trust.] [***Add and adapt, as appropriate:*** SPOUSE TWO acknowledges his/her understanding that SPOUSE ONE is the majority shareholder in a family business, ABC Corp., a subchapter "S" corporation, that ABC Corp. has not been appraised in connection with this Agreement, and that SPOUSE ONE is unable to state the fair market value of the company. SPOUSE TWO further acknowledges that the fair market value may be much higher than book value. SPOUSE TWO acknowledges reviewing with his/her lawyer ABC Corp.'s income tax returns for the three years prior to execution of this Agreement. SPOUSE TWO states that he/she is satisfied with the information and documents provided by SPOUSE ONE regarding ABC Corp.] The parties each waive any right to claim that this Agreement, or any part of this Agreement, is invalid because of a failure of a party to disclose an item of property or income or because of an erroneous estimate of the value of an item of property or the amount of an item of income. The parties further state that they are each familiar with the financial affairs of the other, and with each other's business interests, assets, income, and standard of living. Each party is completely satisfied with the financial disclosures made by the other and each states that, coupled with their preexisting knowledge of each other's financial affairs, he or she has sufficient information on which to base a decision to enter into this Agreement. The parties acknowledge that they each had an opportunity to request additional financial information or documents prior to signing this Agreement, and they each waive the right to make any such further requests. They each acknowledge that the terms of this Agreement would not be different even if an asset was omitted or asset values were different. Each further affirmatively states that it is his and her express intent that this Agreement shall be valid and enforceable based on such disclosures as each has made.

GENERAL PROVISIONS: COMMENT

The provisions below are standard contract provisions.

GENERAL PROVISIONS

PROCEEDING TO SET ASIDE AGREEMENT (NO CONTEST CLAUSE): COMMENT

A party who will make substantial provisions for a spouse through a premarital or postmarital agreement may wish to discourage a future attempt to better his or her circumstances through a challenge to validity. Similarly, when parties resolve a dispute arising under a premarital agreement, or a dispute during an ongoing marriage, that results in a postmarital agreement or an amendment to a premarital agreement, a party who made concessions to achieve peace may wish to discourage an effort to undo the terms. A penalty clause can create an economic disincentive for a spouse to pursue such an effort. Such provisions are generally enforceable under the UPAA.[199] The law elsewhere is undeveloped.

Proceeding to Set Aside Agreement (No Contest Clause): Model Text

44. **Proceeding to Set Aside Agreement or Obtain Different Relief.** In the event SPOUSE TWO challenges the validity or enforceability of this Agreement, or any provision thereof, in any court action (other than for fraud if such allegation is sustained), any obligation by SPOUSE ONE to make any payments to SPOUSE TWO under the terms of this Agreement, including without limitation, the payments payable by SPOUSE ONE to SPOUSE TWO under Paragraphs ___, ____, and ___ of this Agreement, shall be reduced by 50 percent. A request by either party for a court to interpret the terms of this Agreement or declare the rights of the parties under this Agreement shall not be considered a challenge to the validity or enforceability of this Agreement under this Paragraph.

Complete Agreement: Model Text

45. **Complete Agreement.** This Agreement sets forth the parties' present understanding in its entirety. There are no written or oral promises between them that they wish to exchange but have excluded from the text of this contract. The parties are not relying upon any promises other than those expressly set forth herein.

Furnishing Other Instruments: Comment

A provision requiring each party to sign additional documents necessary to carry out the agreement is standard for premarital and postmarital contracts. The burden is generally on the party who needs the instrument to request the other party to execute it or he or she may forfeit rights otherwise created.[200] For example, a party who wants to name someone other than the spouse as beneficiary of qualified retirement benefits must take the initiative to request a waiver.

199. *See Jones v. Jones,* 2016 Nev. Unpub. LEXIS 551.
200. *See Haas v. Hatz*, 2008 Mich. App. LEXIS 2252 (unpub.).

FURNISHING OTHER INSTRUMENTS: MODEL TEXT

46. **Furnishing Other Instruments to Effect Agreement.** Each party shall take any and all steps necessary to timely execute, acknowledge, and deliver any and all further instruments and assurances to the other party that the other party reasonably requires to implement the provisions of this Agreement. Without limitation of the foregoing, if either party should desire to sell or mortgage any real or personal property that constitutes that party's separate property, the other party shall sign and join in such deed or mortgage if to do so is required in order to make the same good, legal, and effectual, and the execution of such document shall not affect the separate nature of the property so transferred or the proceeds or other benefits derived therefrom; provided, however, a party shall have no obligation to become an obligor or guarantor on any liability of the other party.

47. **Prior Agreements and Claims.** The parties acknowledge and agree that they have not previously entered into any other contract, understanding, or agreement, express or implied, with respect to each other's property or earnings or with respect to the support or maintenance of each other. [***Delete if a postmarital agreement:*** Neither party now has or claims any legal right in the present or future property, income, or estate of the other, or a right to support and maintenance or rehabilitation payments of any kind from the other, by reason of the parties' nonmarital relationship.]

THIRD-PARTY BENEFICIARY RIGHTS: COMMENT

The doctrine of third-party beneficiary contracts holds that a person who is not a party to a contract may enforce the contract when it was made for his or her benefit.[201] The lawyer should take care not to create contractual rights in third parties unless the contracting parties intend to do so.[202] For example, where an agreement expressly requires a party to transfer property to a child, or for a surviving spouse to maintain a will leaving his or her assets to a specified person upon his or her death, or to pay expenses of a child the party otherwise has no obligation to pay, the agreement may create third-party rights.[203] An agreement to pay college expenses for a child, for example, may be enforceable by the child as a third-party beneficiary.[204] The text below states the parties' intent to preclude third-party beneficiary

201. WILLISTON, CONTRACTS § 37.1 (4th ed. 2000); *Kester v. Kester*, 108 S.W.3d 213 (Mo. Ct. App. 2003).

202. *See Stichter v. Zuidema*, 269 Ill. App. 3d 455, 646 N.E.2d 296 (1995).

203. *See In re Estate of Draper v. Bank of America*, 205 P.3d 698 (Kan. 2009); *In re Estate of Blumenthal*, 812 A.2d 1279 (Pa. Sup. Ct. 2002); *Labayog v. Labayog*, 927 P.2d 420 (Haw. Ct. App. 1996); *In re Marriage of Smith & Maescher*, 21 Cal. App. 4th 100, 26 Cal. Rptr. 2d 133 (1993); *Morelli v. Morelli*, 102 Nev. 326, 720 P.2d 704 (1986); *see also Drake v. Drake*, 89 A.D.2d 207, 455 N.Y.S.2d 420 (1982) (child has no standing to enforce provisions of parents' separation agreement for basic minority child support, as this obligation runs to custodial parent; but has standing to enforce promise to pay college tuition and make child beneficiary of life insurance).

204. *See Matter of L.M.H. v. D.S.H.*, 2005 Del. Fam. Ct. LEXIS 135 (unpub.) (child is third-party beneficiary of parents' separation agreement to share college expenses); *see also In re Marriage of Smith & Maescher*, 21 Cal. App. 4th 100; *Morelli*, 720 P.2d 704 (Nev. 1986); *Drake*, 455 N.Y.S.2d 420.

status for nonparties. Counsel should consider whether to revise or drop this provision from an agreement that creates an obligation to a third party.

If the parties merely intend the agreement to preserve their rights to give away assets during their lives or leave them to whomever each chooses at death, the agreement should not use text that suggests third-party beneficiary rights. Doing so opens a door to avoidable litigation. For example, in *Stichter v. Zuidema*,[205] the premarital agreement required the husband to leave one-fifth of his estate to the wife and stated parenthetically that his four children would receive the balance in equal shares. The recitals stated the husband had an obligation to preserve his estate for his children. The court held the children were not third-party beneficiaries of the contact and that the statements regarding them were mere statements of intent rather than of promise. The agreement could have made it clear that the husband was preserving his right to provide for his children without suggesting that the agreement created vested rights in them.[206] In *Spencer v. Estate of Spencer*,[207] the premarital agreement required an interspousal gift to be documented in a memorandum executed by the parties in duplicate and attached to the duplicate originals of the agreement. The husband registered his brokerage account in joint names through a letter of authorization but did not comply with the agreement's requirements to create a gift. After his death, his heirs claimed he was prohibited from transferring the securities account except in compliance with the agreement. The wording of the agreement seemed to limit the husband's right to give his own assets to the wife and thus opened the door to this litigation, although the appellate court rejected the estate's argument. An agreement should be worded to enable each party to conduct his or her financial affairs without being answerable to others, such as his or her adult children, or a personal representative after his or her death, except as to provisions the parties expressly intend for their benefit. An agreement that waives spousal rights at death, so as to free each party to leave assets to other family members, does not preclude a party from making lifetime or testamentary gifts.[208] Such an agreement does not create third party beneficiaries.

THIRD-PARTY BENEFICIARY RIGHTS: MODEL TEXT

48. **No Third-Party Beneficiary Rights**. Nothing in this Agreement shall be construed to create any contractual or equitable rights in favor of third parties who are not signatories hereto [***Add, if appropriate:*** , except as expressly set forth herein].

49. **No Waiver of Breach of Contract Provisions**. The failure of a party to insist upon the strict performance of any provision of this Agreement shall not waive the party's right to insist upon strict performance of the same or any other provision at a later time.

205. 646 N.E.2d 296 (Ill. Ct. App. 1995).
206. *See also Wilkes v. O'Bryan*, 98 Wash. App. 411, 989 P.2d 594 (1999).
207. 313 S.W.3d 534 (Ky. 2010).
208. *Berger v. Estate of Levine*, 145 Ariz. 185, 700 P.2d 883 (Ariz. Ct. App., Div. 2, 1985).

SEVERABILITY: COMMENT

Premarital and postmarital agreements should generally include a severability clause. Where the contract contains a clause stating the parties' intent that an invalid provision be severable, a court will generally give effect to their expressed intent.[209] Courts have generally treated spousal support and waivers of lawyers' fees as severable, so that a finding of invalidity of such a provision will not affect the enforceability of the remaining otherwise valid provisions of the agreement.[210] Thus, if the court determines the agreement is valid as a whole under the standards for validity in that jurisdiction, the property disposition provisions will be given effect at death or dissolution.[211] Similarly, an invalid provision regarding custody of or support for a minor child will generally be severable.[212] An invalid arbitration clause will also be severable.[213]

A wealthy party whose primary objective is protection for his or her nonmarital property will generally benefit from a severability provision, even when governing law does not permit a spousal support waiver, or allows a judge at divorce some discretion to make an award over waiver, or when a court at divorce can make an award of lawyers' fees over a waiver. When the agreement provides for a lump-sum payment in lieu of spousal support, or for a disposition of property more generous than the less wealthy party would otherwise be entitled to receive in the event of divorce, it may not be fair for transfers of property from one party's separate estate to the marital estate, or to the other party's separate estate, to stand, thus allowing that party to receive the benefit of the bargain,

209. *Larsen v. Giannakoulias*, 2018 Tenn. App. LEXIS 627 (unpub.) (invalid spousal support waiver in premarital agreement governed by New Mexico law was severable); *Rogers v. Yourshaw*, 18 Va. App. 816, 448 S.E.2d 884 (1994) (where premarital agreement contained severability clause, court could enforce property disposition provision while declining to enforce child support provision, rejecting wife's argument that court could not enforce agreement selectively); *see also Grabe v. Hokin*, 341 Conn. 360, 267 A.3d 145 (2021) (fee-shifting for failed challenged to premarital agreement was unconscionable, but severable); *In re Marriage of Heinrich*, 7 N.E.3d 889 (Ill. Ct. App., 2d Dist. 2014) (contractual ban on fee-shifting was invalid, but remainder of premarital agreement with severability clause is enforceable); *Newman v. Newman*, 291 Ga. 635, 732 S.E.2d 77 (2012) (provision of premarital agreement that cannot be enforced due to vagueness is severable); *Sailer v. Sailer*, 764 N.W.2d 445 (N.D. 2009) (invalid provision of premarital agreement would not render agreement unenforceable in its entirety); *P.B. v. L.B.*, 19 Misc. 3d 186, 855 N.Y.S.2d 836 (Sup. Ct. 2008) (invalid provision of agreement is severable); and *see Rivera v. Rivera*, 149 N.M. 66, 243 P.3d 1148 (2010) (premarital agreement that lacked severability clause was invalid in its entirety due to unconscionability of support waiver).

210. *In re Marriage of Facter*, 212 Cal. App. 4th 967, 152 Cal. Rprt. 3d 79 (2013); *Rogers v. Gordon*, 404 N.J. Super. 213, 961 A.2d 11 (2008); *Edwards v. Edwards*, 16 Neb. App. 297, 744 N.W.2d 243 (2008); *Mason v. Gutierrez-Mason*, 2007 Mich. App. LEXIS 1273 (unpub.); *Lane v. Lane*, 202 S.W.3d 577 (Ky. 2006); *Sanford v. Sanford*, 694 N.W.2d 283 (S.D. 2005); *Werther v. Werther*, 9 Misc. 3d 1114A, 808 N.Y.S.2d 921 (Sup. Ct. 2005); *Hardee v. Hardee*, 348 S.C. 84, 558 S.E.2d 264 n.3 (Ct. App. 2001); *In re Marriage of Pond*, 676 N.E.2d 401 (Ind. Ct. App. 1997); *Cary v. Cary*, 937 S.W.2d 777 (Tenn. 1996); *Rosenblatt v. Kazlow-Rosenblatt*, 39 Mass. App. Ct. 297, 655 N.E.2d 640 (1995); *Clermont v. Clermont*, 198 A.D.2d 631, 603 N.Y.S.2d 923 (1993); *Howell v. Landry*, 96 N.C. App. 516, 531–32, 386 S.E.2d 610, 619 (1989); *Hill v. Hill*, 356 N.W.2d 49 (Minn. Ct. App. 1984); *In re Marriage of Dawley*, 17 Cal. 3d 342, 551 P.2d 323 (1976); *Potter v. Collin*, 321 So. 2d 128 (Fla. Dist. Ct. App. 1975); *In re Murdock's Estate*, 213 Kan. 837, 519 P.2d 108 (1974).

211. *Osborne v. Osborne*, 604 So. 2d 858 (Fla. Dist. Ct. App. 1992) (court may not make property award contrary to valid premarital waiver of property rights in order to correct inadequate spousal support provision).

212. *Ventimiglia v. Ventimiglia*, 307 A.D.2d 993, 763 N.Y.S.2d 486 (2003); *Reese v. Reese*, 984 P.2d 987 (Utah 1999); *Rogers*, 404 N.J. Super. 213; *Masters v. Masters*, 201 Conn. 50, 513 A.2d 104 (1986); *but see Marriage of Iqbal and Khan*, 11 N.E.3d 1 (Ill. Ct. App. 2014) (postmarital agreement was invalid in its entirety where unenforceable terms regarding custody were central to agreement, rejecting severability).

213. *See Buckeye Check Cashing, Inc. v. Cardegna*, 546 U.S. 440, 126 S. Ct. 1204, 163 L. Ed. 2d 1038 (2006).

yet permitting the support claimant to reject the detrimental aspects of the agreement. The lawyer for the wealthy party may therefore need to consider other options, such as a penalty.[214] The agreement could also include a provision that makes a lump sum payment severable in the event a spousal support waiver is held unenforceable without voiding the agreement in its entirety.

SEVERABILITY: MODEL TEXT

> 50. **Severability**. If any provision of this Agreement shall for any reason become invalid or otherwise cannot be enforced, the remainder of this Agreement shall remain in full force and effect, unless an injustice would otherwise result].

EFFECT OF AGREEMENT ON SEPARATION OR DIVORCE: COMMENT

Some premarital and postmarital agreements may be self-executing such that the parties are able to implement the dissolution provisions without entering into a marital settlement agreement (MSA). More often, they will need an MSA to carry out their obligations and to obtain an acknowledgement they have done so. Certain obligations, such as a transfer of retirement benefits, will require a court order incident to divorce; parties will therefore likely need to enter into an MSA after separation to confirm the terms of division. The premarital or postmarital agreement may provide for other transfers that will or may occur after divorce.

A post-divorce transfer required by the agreement may constitute a gift that is subject to the federal gift tax. I.R.C. § 2516 provides:

> Where a husband and wife enter into a written agreement relative to their marital and property rights and divorce occurs within the 3-year period beginning on the date 1 year before such agreement is entered into (whether or not such agreement is approved by the divorce decree), any transfers of property or interests in property made pursuant to such agreement—
>
> (1) to either spouse in settlement of his or her marital or property rights, or
>
> (2) to provide a reasonable allowance for the support of issue of the marriage during minority,
>
> shall be deemed to be transfers made for a full and adequate consideration in money or money's worth.

Unless the parties divorce within the two-year period following execution of a premarital agreement, or during the period beginning one year prior to and ending two years after execution of a postmarital agreement, the agreement will not suffice to avoid gift tax consequences. When the premarital or postmarital agreement requires a postdivorce transfer that could constitute a gift subject to gift tax, and it is in the transferor-spouse's interest that it not be treated

214. See paragraph 44 and accompanying Comment.

as such, the transferor will need for the parties to enter into a new agreement. In some cases, the MSA may only need to state that it confirms the terms of the premarital or postmarital agreement.[215] The model text includes a provision to address this scenario.

Section 2516 is concerned only with transfers incident to divorce. While the parties are still married, including after a marital separation, either spouse can freely transfer cash, securities, real estate, or other property to the other spouse as a nontaxable gift and without the necessity for a court order to implement the transfer (with the exception of the transfer of an interest in a retirement plan or account). The unlimited marital deduction allows such transfers during marriage or upon a spouse's death free of any gift taxes upon transfer.[216] The transferee-spouse will receive a carryover basis; that is, the recipient's basis in the property will be that of the transferor-spouse.[217]

EFFECT OF AGREEMENT ON SEPARATION OR DIVORCE: MODEL TEXT

51. **Effect of Agreement on Separation or Divorce.**

A. This Agreement may, upon advice of counsel, be presented to the appropriate court to be affirmed, ratified, and incorporated, but not merged, in any judgment of legal separation or divorce, limited or final, between the parties. The parties understand that they may need to enter into an additional agreement or seek a court order [***add, if appropriate:*** to enforce an arbitration award under Paragraph 61] addressing disposition of property to carry out the terms of this Agreement; however, the parties' rights to such property shall be determined only in accordance with the terms of this Agreement.

B. [***Include if appropriate:***]The parties intend the transfers from SPOUSE ONE to SPOUSE TWO under this Agreement to be in resolution of the parties' marital rights and do not intend that any of the transfers constitute gifts by either party. Accordingly, SPOUSE ONE shall have no obligation to make the transfers required under Paragraph ___ of this Agreement until after (i) the parties have signed an agreement regarding their marital rights which complies with the provisions of I.R.C. § 2516 and incorporates the provisions thereof; and (ii) their judgment of divorce has become final.

CONSIDERATION: COMMENT

No consideration beyond the marriage itself is necessary to form a valid premarital agreement.[218] Nevertheless, it is customary for the agreement to recite the consideration for the agreement, including the marriage itself, as well as the mutual waivers and other provisions

215. They must also divorce within the statutory period prescribed in Section 2516.
216. I.R.C. § 2056.
217. I.R.C. § 1041(b). However, the carryover basis rule does not apply to a transferee-spouse who is a nonresident alien. Section 1041(d).
218. See Section 2.02(a).

in the agreement. In those jurisdictions that require consideration, beyond the marriage itself, for a valid postmarital agreement, a statement of consideration is necessary. As is the case with a premarital agreement, often mutual waivers are sufficient. In some cases, it will be necessary to identify other consideration. The text that follows includes optional language for the situation where parties have already acquired property, such as a home, did not enter into a joint ownership agreement, and where it is appropriate to have some contractual provisions governing their rights in the event they do not marry.

CONSIDERATION: MODEL TEXT

52. **Consideration and Effective Date of Agreement.** The consideration for this Agreement is the marriage of the parties. This Agreement shall become effective upon the parties' marriage. If the parties do not marry, this Agreement shall be void and of no further effect [***If parties have acquired jointly titled property together prior to execution, add:*** , except that the terms of Paragraph ___ shall govern the disposition of their jointly titled real estate and the terms of Paragraph[s] ___ and ___ shall govern disposition of their joint bank accounts, joint credit card debt, and the furniture and household effects acquired with joint funds and/or joint debt]. [***If postmarital agreement:*** The consideration for this Agreement includes, but is not limited to, the mutual waivers and all the other terms set forth herein.]

REVOCATION AND AMENDMENT; OTHER AGREEMENTS: COMMENT

Every agreement should provide that it cannot be amended except by a signed writing. Similarly, every agreement should provide that it cannot be revoked except by a signed writing. The optional text requires that an amendment or revocation be executed with the same formality as the agreement. Counsel should give some thought to whether this is appropriate in a given case. Many lawyers elect to have a premarital or postmarital agreement notarized and/or witnessed. But it may not be in the interest of the parties to create such an obstacle to freely amending their agreement as their circumstances require. On the other hand, more demanding requirements may offer some protection against a party who may seek to exploit a spouse's diminished capacity to obtain an amendment or revocation.

The model terms require parties' intent with respect to some property transactions during the marriage that affect their rights to be evidenced in a signed writing, for example, paragraph 7(F), but do not require that such a writing be notarized or witnessed. For example, parties might agree to acquire an investment property, to title it in survivorship, and to a *pro rata* allocation based on each party's separate property contribution in the event they separate. Such an understanding is not an amendment or revocation. Paragraph 54 permits such a transaction to be evidenced by a writing less than formal than required for an amendment or revocation.

REVOCATION AND AMENDMENT; OTHER AGREEMENTS: MODEL TEXT

53. **Revocation and Modification.** This Agreement shall remain in full force and effect unless expressly revoked or modified in a writing signed by the parties [***Optional:*** with the same formality as this Agreement]. [***Optional:*** Any such revocation or amendment must refer expressly to this Agreement.] Further, this Agreement shall remain in effect in the event of a marital separation followed by reconciliation.

54. **Other Agreements and Writings.** Except provided in Paragraph 53 or as this Agreement otherwise expressly requires, wherever the terms of this Agreement permit the parties to make a decision as to an issue governed by this Agreement that requires agreement in writing, the parties may agree to an exchange of electronic messages, such as through electronic mail or text message, and such shall suffice for that purpose. Further, except as expressly required herein, where this Agreement requires a signed writing, the parties may agree to utilize an electronic message from his or her account or device and such shall suffice for that purpose.

GOVERNING LAW: COMMENT

Every agreement should include a choice-of-law provision identifying the law that will govern a dispute about the validity or interpretation of the agreement as well as a claim of breach. A choice-of-law clause offers predictability regarding the enforceability and interpretation of the contract if a party, or the couple together, moves to another state and a dispute about the agreement must be resolved in the courts of that state.[219] Where the circumstances afford a choice of more than one state for the law governing validity of the agreement, for example, where parties live in different states, the lawyer should make an informed decision about governing law. It will generally be in the proponent's best interests to choose the state whose law of validity is less demanding, if there is a difference. Nevertheless, the lawyer should conduct the process to meet the highest standards of validity.

The choice of governing law can affect resolution of a future dispute about validity. For example, in *DeLorean v. DeLorean*,[220] the husband's disclosure was inadequate and would have doomed the premarital agreement had its validity been determined under New Jersey law. However, the New Jersey court gave effect to the parties' choice of California law and upheld it as adequate under the California disclosure standards then in effect.[221] When parties

---

219. *See Moeckly v. Hanson*, 947 N.W.2d 630 (S.D. 2020); *Estate of Santos*, 648 So. 2d 277 (Fla. Ct. App. 4th Dist., 1995).

220. 211 N.J. Super. 432, 511 A.2d 1257 (1986).

221. *See also Elgar v. Elgar*, 238 Conn. 839, 679 A.2d 937 (1996) (New York choice-of-law provision upheld, permitting validity to be determined under less strict law of New York).

move from the state of execution to a state with stricter validity standards, silence on choice-of-law may produce an unexpected result for the proponent.[222]

Failure to select governing law can also create an opportunity for litigation over what law a court should apply. For example, in *Black v. Powers*,[223] two Virginia residents traveled to the Virgin Islands, where they signed a premarital agreement with no choice-of-law clause and got married. The appeal resolved the dispute about applicable law in favor of Virgin Islands law although it apparently made no difference to the outcome of the dispute about validity. An express choice-of-law clause could have eliminated one facet of the litigation.

The Uniform Premarital Agreement Act (UPAA) permits parties to contract as to the choice of law governing interpretation of their premarital agreement.[224] The UPAA does not expressly address choice of law to govern a dispute about validity.[225] However, general choice-of-law principles permit parties to contract with respect to the law governing their agreement, including the law that will govern a future dispute about whether the agreement is valid.[226] Some courts treat a choice-of-law provision referring to a dispute about interpretation as including a dispute about validity.[227] The better practice is to provide expressly that the chosen law will govern a dispute about validity.

The governing law should be that of a state with a substantial connection to at least one of the parties or the contract. When the chosen law has some nexus with a party or the contract, a court will generally apply that law.[228] When parties live in different states, the drafting lawyer may be able to choose between them. There can be circumstances where a third state may be a suitable choice. The following will generally be appropriate for governing law:

- The state of residence of either party;
- The state where the marriage is to take place;
- The state where a party owns a second home;
- The state where the parties have bought a home and intend to live upon marriage;
- The state where a party owns and operates a business.

---

222. *See, e.g., Rivers v. Rivers*, 21 S.W.3d 117 (Mo. Ct. App. 2000) (premarital agreement with no choice-of-law provision executed in Louisiana while parties' residence was there was invalid at divorce under Missouri law for lack of required disclosure).

223. 48 Va. App. 113, 628 S.E.2d 546 (2006); *see also Larsen v. Giannakoulias*, 2018 Tenn. App. LEXIS 627 (unpub.).

224. UPAA § 3(a)(7) (1983); *Franzen v. Franzen*, 135 N.C. App. 369, 520 S.E.2d 74 (1999) (court must give effect to valid choice-of-law provision in premarital agreement); *see also Doucettperry v. Doucettperry*, 2020 Nev. App. Unpub. LEXIS 849 (Virginia law, chosen by parties in agreement, applies to determine validity of postmarital agreement, and not somewhat more demanding criteria of Nevada law).

225. The UPMAA would have brought some needed clarity to the right of parties to choose governing law for either type of agreement. Section 4 permits parties to contract as to the choice of law governing "validity, enforceability, interpretation, and construction" of their agreement. The UPMAA, however, has only been enacted in two states, Colorado and North Dakota.

226. *See Restatement Second of Conflict of Laws* § 187; *McNamara v. McNamara*, 40 So. 3d 78 (Fla. Ct. App. 2010); *In re Estate of Davis*, 1999 Ohio App. LEXIS 5751 (unpub.); *In re Estate of Massello*, 1997 Del. Ch. LEXIS 23 (unpub.).

227. *See Hutchins v. Hutchins*, 393 Mont. 283, 430 P.3d 502 (2018) (parties married in Nevada with premarital agreement providing for Nevada law to govern interpretation and enforcement; trial court should have applied Nevada law to resolve dispute about validity).

228. *See Nanini v. Nanini*, 166 Ariz. 287, 802 P.2d 438 (Ct. App. 1990); *DeLorean v. DeLorean*, 211 N.J. Super. 432, 511 A.2d 1257 (1986); *Norris v. Norris*, 419 A.2d 982 (D.C. 1980); *Elgar*, 238 Conn. 839.

Courts generally honor a choice-of-law clause in a premarital or postmarital agreement so long as it comports with general choice-of-law rules.[229] For example, in *Stalb v. Stalb*,[230] the Vermont court upheld application of New York law to determine validity although New York law did not require a finding of conscionability of property disposition provisions at divorce and Vermont law did.

The cases in which courts have considered a choice-of-law clause in a premarital agreement in a challenge to validity have generally involved differences in the procedural requirements.[231] Whether a court in a second-look state will consider substantive fairness as a matter of public policy and, therefore, apply its own law to judge fairness at divorce, is an open question.[232] Moreover, in most states there is little or no authority on the question of whether courts will honor a choice-of-law clause in a premarital or postmarital agreement when the chosen law differs materially on the procedural criteria for validity. Courts in these states may conclude that their public policy mandates application of more stringent procedural requirements. For example, in *In re Estate of J.D. Davis*,[233] the court held that Tennessee law's requirement for full financial disclosure reflected a strong public policy. As a result, the premarital agreement executed in Florida during the parties' residence there, which would have been valid under Florida law even though there was no financial disclosure, was unenforceable under Tennessee law.[234]

Notwithstanding the parties' express selection of governing law, if a party seeks enforcement in a state other than the state of the chosen law, the agreement may prove unenforceable in its entirety or a severable provision, such as a waiver of spousal support, may not be enforceable. Indeed, *Restatement Second of Conflict of Laws* provides that a forum court may decide not to enforce an agreement when application of the law of the chosen state "would be contrary to a fundamental policy" of the forum state and where the law of the forum would be the applicable law in the absence of the parties' choice.[235] In those states that limit parties' rights to fix or waive spousal support, the issue tends to be viewed as a public policy matter in which the state has a significant stake. Thus, a waiver of spousal support may not be given

229. *See McNamara*, 40 So. 3d 78 (Florida trial court correctly applied Georgia law to determination of validity, honoring contractual choice-of-law clause, although Georgia law did not recognize confidential relationship of persons engaged to be married and Florida law did [at that time; Florida has since enacted the UPAA]; mere difference in validity standards does not violate public policy); *Montoya v. Montoya*, 280 Conn. 605, 909 A.2d 947 (2006) (premarital agreement valid under New York law where no fraud underlying choice-of-law provision); *Marcovitz v. Rogers*, 267 Neb. 456, 675 N.W.2d 132 (2004) (postmarital agreement with Michigan choice-of-law clause was valid although may have been invalid under Nebraska law); *In re Marriage of Connet*, 804 P.2d 1036 (Kan. Ct. App. 1991) (Missouri law governs validity where premarital agreement expressly selected); *Hill v. Hill*, 262 A.2d 661 (Del. Ch. 1970), *aff'd*, 269 A.2d 212 (Del. 1970) (agreement that complied with Maryland law as to formalities enforceable in Delaware although not in compliance with Delaware formalities).

230. 168 Vt. 235, 719 A.2d 421 (1998).

231. *See, e.g., Reynolds v. Reynolds*, 175 N.E.3d 611 (Ohio Ct. App. 2021) (chosen law, New Hampshire, properly applied to dispute about validity of premarital agreement where New Hampshire law presumes validity; application does not violate fundamental public policy of Ohio where only difference is lack of presumption of validity).

232. See Sections 2.08 and 4.08 for discussion of substantive fairness and the second look at divorce.

233. 184 S.W.3d 231 (Tenn. App. 2004).

234. This ruling points up the benefits of a premarital agreement that complies with the highest standards for procedural fairness. Moreover, there will be less risk for a wealthier party in the event he or she must enforce in a state other than that of the chosen law if the substantive terms do not create the likelihood that the other party will become impoverished; see Chapter 4, especially the discussion of best practices in Section 4.10.

235. RESTATEMENT SECOND OF CONFLICT OF LAWS § 187(2)(b) (1989).

effect in a forum state that does not permit a premarital waiver, or that otherwise limits parties' contractual rights in this area, even though valid under the law selected by the parties.[236] Similarly, in some states, a contractual ban on fee-shifting at divorce may be deemed a matter of public policy when it applies to fees relating to child custody or support.[237] At the drafting stage it is reasonable to assume, and therefore to advise the client, that in states that limit parties' rights to contract before marriage as to spousal support, a claim of a resident of that state, where the courts of that state otherwise have jurisdiction over the subject matter and the parties, will be deemed sufficiently fundamental that the forum court will apply its own law concerning enforceability of a fee waiver.

Because almost every state permits parties to a premarital or postmarital agreement to effect a full and complete disposition of property, it seems likely that, with rare exceptions, a state will not reject the parties' choice of law governing their agreement, insofar as it disposes of property rights at death or divorce, on fundamental policy grounds.[238] A few states' laws put greater limits on parties' freedom to contract in a postmarital agreement. For example, Iowa law prohibits enforcement of a postmarital agreement that waives the elective share. In *Hussemann v. Husseman*,[239] the court had to decide whether to apply Florida law, the law chosen by the parties, which permits such a waiver. The parties were residents of Florida when they signed their postmarital agreement. In deciding in favor of application of the chosen law, the court recognized the importance of protecting the justified expectations of contracting parties and that a mere difference in policy choices is insufficient to reject the parties' choice.

Where the line will be drawn between mere policy differences and those a forum deems of greater importance is an open question as there are so few appellate cases. The following issues are amenable to a substantial public policy argument:

236. *See McNamara v. McNamara*, 988 So. 2d 1255 (Fla. Dis. Ct. App. 2008) (Florida trial court properly refused to enforce Georgia choice-of-law provision insofar as it would have required enforcement of premarital agreement waiver of attorneys' fees incurred to challenge validity as attorneys' fees are a form of spousal support; public policy of Florida precludes waiver of support payable before divorce); *In re Gudenkauf's Marriage*, 204 N.W.2d 586 (Iowa 1973) (public interest in enforcement of legal obligation to support spouse overrides premarital support waiver); *Padova v. Padova*, 123 Vt. 125, 183 A.2d 227 (1962) (Vermont court will enforce premarital agreement according to law of chosen state except to extent it seeks to avoid duties imposed by law); *Bassler v. Bassler*, 156 Vt. 353, 593 A.2d 82 (1991) (premarital agreement unenforceable as against public policy where property disposition provisions leave one spouse a public charge).

237. *See Marriage of Heinrich*, 7 N.E.3d 889 (Ill. Ct. App., 2d Dist. 2014) (provision of premarital agreement with Missouri choice-of-law that bans fee-shifting is unenforceable as to child issues as it violates Illinois public policy).

238. *See Stalb v. Stalb*, 168 Vt. 235, 719 A.2d 421 (1998) (application of New York law did not contravene public policy of Vermont, although under New York law property disposition did not have to be conscionable at divorce); *Chaudry v. Chaudry*, 159 N.J. Super. 566 (App. Div. 1978) (public policy of New Jersey not offended by enforcement of premarital agreement under law of Pakistan, although it gave wife only small cash payment and no support).

239. 847 N.W.2d 219 (Iowa 2014). In *Marcovitz v. Rogers*, 267 Neb. 456, 675 N.W.2d 132 (2004), the Nebraska court honored a Michigan choice-of-law clause and upheld a postmarital agreement at divorce that was not executed incident to a marital separation. The husband argued that such an agreement was prohibited by Nebraska law, but the Nebraska court did not need to decide that question. A later Nebraska case, *Devney v. Devney*, 295 Neb. 15, 886 N.W.2d 61 (2016), settled the issue, holding that such an agreement was void under Nebraska's common law and public policy and that the Nebraska statutes authorizing such agreements were limited to agreements contemplating death or an immediate or existing marital separation.

- Fairness (or conscionability) at execution in states that reject enforcement of an agreement that was either unfair or unconscionable at execution;
- Fairness (or conscionability) of the agreement as a whole at divorce in the second-look states;
- Enforcement of a waiver of post-divorce support;
- Enforcement of a waiver of support payable during the marriage, which can include a waiver of temporary support payable while a suit for divorce is pending and the right to support while the parties are married and living together, and
- Enforceability of a waiver of the right to seek an award of legal fees and costs.

A provision stating the law that will govern a dispute about validity or construction does not determine the law that will govern issues the agreement does not address. If, for example, the agreement does not determine disposition of property defined as marital or community property, the court can apply the law of the forum to resolve the issue.[240] If the agreement leaves some issues for resolution by a court, such as allocation of shared property or a claim for spousal support, counsel should consider whether the agreement should specify the law that will govern the court's decision on these issues.[241] When an agreement chooses the law that will govern the parties' property rights at divorce, the court must apply the chosen law even when it leads to a result at variance from the result under the law of forum.[242]

GOVERNING LAW: MODEL TEXT

55. **Governing Law.** The validity, enforceability, and interpretation of this Agreement shall be determined and governed by the law of ______, without regard to its choice-of-law rules, regardless of the location of any property that either party may own and regardless of where the parties may live.

PROVISIONS BINDING ON SUCCESSORS: COMMENT

The benefits and obligations of a contract extend to the parties' successors in interest.[243] These can include the right to a fee award under a prevailing party provision after an unsuccessful challenge to validity after the death of a party.[244]

240. *See Hutchins,* 393 Mont. 283, 430 P.3d 502; *see also Blondeau v. Baltierra,* 337 Conn. 127, 252 A.3d 317 (2020).

241. *See Wolfe v. Wolfe,* 254 N.C. App. 853, 803 S.E.2d 662 (2017); *O'Conner v. Miroslaw*, 388 S.W.3d 541 (Mo. Ct. App. 2012) (premarital agreement with Kansas choice of law governing validity; Missouri law governs questions of tracing and commingling and determination of marital share).

242. *Moquin v. Bergeron,* 338 So. 3d 918 (Fla. Dist. Ct. App. 2022) (husband entitled to retain sole rights at divorce to solely titled property under terms of Quebec marriage contract).

243. *AXA Equitable Life Ins. Co. v. Grissom*, 2012 U.S. Dist. LEXIS 166613 (M.D. Tenn. 11/21/12).

244. *Id.*

PROVISIONS BINDING ON SUCCESSORS: MODEL TEXT

56. **Provisions Binding**. All of the provisions of this Agreement shall be binding upon and inure to the benefit of the parties, their agents, attorneys in fact, legal representatives, and successors-in-interest.

MULTIPLE ORIGINALS: COMMENT

It is common and customary for parties to execute multiple originals of a premarital or post-marital agreement so that each party can have one for his or her records and an original can be kept by counsel. The following text acknowledges this but also allows for a complete scanned copy to be treated as an original. As many lawyers, and their clients, may prefer to store important documents only in an electronic form, it is appropriate for such electronic copies to be treated as originals.

MULTIPLE ORIGINALS: MODEL TEXT

57. **Multiple Originals**. This Agreement may be executed in any number of counterparts, any one of which shall be deemed to be the original. A scanned copy of this Agreement, with all signatures and initials visible, shall be treated as an original.

CONSTRUCTION AGAINST DRAFTER: COMMENT

When an agreement is ambiguous, a court may construe it against the drafter.[245] However, when the agreement provides expressly that neither party may be deemed the draftsperson, the court should honor that provision.[246] When both parties have lawyers who participated in drafting, there should be no occasion for a court to construe the agreement against one party passed on general principles of construction.

CONSTRUCTION AGAINST DRAFTER: MODEL TEXT

58. **No Construction against Drafter**. Each party had, or had the opportunity to have, input into the drafting of this Agreement, personally or through counsel. Therefore,

245. *In re Estate of Taris*, 2005 Ohio App. LEXIS 1497 (unpub.); *Sanford v. Sanford*, 355 Ark. 274, 137 S.W.3d 391 (2003); *Sabad v. Fessenden*, 825 A.2d 682 (Pa. Super. Ct. 2003); *Ventimiglia v. Ventimiglia*, 307 A.D.2d 993, 763 N.Y.S.2d 486 (2003).

246. *See Johnson v. Johnson*, 725 So. 2d 1209 (Fla. Dist. Ct. App. 1999) (where both parties had counsel, no reason to construe ambiguity against drafter where agreement expressly prohibited); *Montoya v. Montoya*, 91 Conn. App. 407, 909 A.2d 947 (2006) (trial court erred in resolving ambiguity in premarital agreement against husband where agreement provided both parties negotiated and neither could be deemed the drafter); *but see In re Marriage of Weiss*, 357 Mont. 320, 239 P.3d 123 (2010) (refusing to enforce such a clause where it is contrary to state statute mandating construction against party who caused uncertainty in meaning of contract).

this Agreement shall be construed without regard to any presumption or other rule requiring construction against the party who caused it to have been drafted.

RECITALS INCORPORATED: COMMENT

Recitals are not operative provisions of the agreement unless they are expressly incorporated into the agreement. Whether they are, or are not, they should be consistent with the operative terms.

RECITALS INCORPORATED: MODEL TEXT

59. **Recitals Incorporated.** The Recitals set forth above are hereby incorporated by reference as part of this Agreement.

NONDISCLOSURE AND CONFIDENTIALITY: COMMENT

A voluntarily executed confidentiality agreement is generally enforceable.[247] There are several separate and distinct concerns that parties may wish to address in a confidentiality provision of a marital agreement:

- Each party's financial disclosure, including information about his or her family's wealth, provided in connection with the agreement;
- Information about a party's financial affairs, or the financial affairs of his or her family members, that may be acquired during the marriage;
- The existence and terms of the agreement and the negotiations that led to it;
- Information about a party's business learned prior to execution, or that a party may subsequently learn, that could be of interest to a competitor, regulatory authorities, or the press; and
- Information of a personal nature, facts about a party's conduct before or during the marriage, that a party may not want to be made public.

The model below prohibits disclosure of financial information, as well as disparaging information, but does not include a liquidated damages provision. The agreement could include a penalty consisting of the breaching party's loss of some benefits under the agreement to which he or she may otherwise be entitled.[248] In the absence of such a provision, the injured party may have to prove actual damages,[249] or seek an injunction.[250] Whether a court can grant an injunction against future disparaging statements to enforce a contractual

247. *See Perricone v. Perricone*, 292 Conn. 187, 972 A.2d 666 (2009); *Trump v. Trump*, 179 A.D.2d 201, 582 N.Y.S.2d 1008 (App. Div. 1992); *Irden*, 80 N.Y.2d 760, 605 N.E.2d 874, 591 N.Y.S.2d 138 (1990).

248. *See, e.g.*, *Anonymous v. Anonymous*, 233 A.D.2d 162, 649 N.Y.S.2d 665 (App. Div. 1st Dept. 1996).

249. See *Bias v. Bias*, 132 A.D.3d 502, 19 N.Y.S.3d 21 (App. Div. 1st Dept. 2015).

250. *See Perricone*, 292 Conn. 187.

prohibition is an open question. A Massachusetts court said such a prior restraint on speech violated parties' constitutional rights, but the decision did not involve an agreement to restrict speech.[251]

NONDISCLOSURE AND CONFIDENTIALITY: MODEL TEXT

60. **Nondisclosure and Confidentiality.**

A. Each party recognizes the other party's right to privacy regarding their financial information disclosed in connection with this Agreement, or otherwise, including during their marriage. Each agrees to keep such information in confidence. Neither party shall hereafter purposely disseminate or disclose the other party's financial information [***Optional:*** , the terms of this Agreement, or the negotiations leading to it] to any person or entity without the prior written consent of the other party, except as required by law and, as necessary, on a confidential basis, to a party's accountants, financial advisors, and attorneys. Each party agrees that in the event of any dispute resulting in litigation between the parties, the parties shall jointly request that the court or arbitrator hearing such dispute enter a protective order prohibiting dissemination of such financial information, permitting a party to designate financial records as confidential and, therefore, to be submitted to the court under seal, and otherwise protecting the confidentiality of his or her financial records and information to the maximum extent permitted by law. The parties have agreed to this provision in recognition of the fact that disclosure to the public or to a third party of a party's financial information could harm a party's career and/or business interests.

B. Neither party shall publicize or disseminate information of any kind about the other party that is or may be detrimental to the other party's personal image, employment, business interests, reputation or career.

C. The obligations of each party under this Paragraph shall survive a separation of the parties.

ALTERNATIVE DISPUTE RESOLUTION: COMMENT

Parties to a premarital or postmarital agreement may want the agreement to include a provision for resolving a future dispute that will keep the parties out of court, if possible. Forms of alternative dispute resolution include mediation, with or without lawyers present, a collaborative process, and binding arbitration.

Arbitration may be appealing to some parties to a premarital or postmarital agreement.

In arbitration, the parties, usually spouses, agree to submit one or more issues arising from the dissolution of their relationship to an arbitrator, who is a neutral third party,

251. *See Shak v. Shak,* 484 Mass. 658, 144 N.E.3d 274 (2020).

> for resolution. The arbitrator makes a decision, called an award, based on the facts presented. Unlike litigation, parties choose the arbitrator or the method of selecting the arbitrator and pay the arbitrator's fee. Arbitration awards typically are subject to limited judicial review. In exchange, arbitration offers an alternative for those who want an experienced decision-maker in a proceeding that is potentially faster, more confidential, and less adversarial.

Uniform Family Law Arbitration Act, Prefatory Note.

There are several types of disputes for which an arbitration clause in a premarital or postmarital agreement may be useful:

- Valuation of an asset;
- A disagreement about the meaning of the agreement and the parties' rights under it;
- A dispute about how to implement the allocation of property;
- A claim that a party breached the agreement;
- Resolution of an issue the agreement deliberately left for later determination, such as the amount and duration of spousal support or division of shared property;
- Enforceability of a specific severable provision of an otherwise valid agreement (*e.g.*, a dispute about whether a spousal support waiver has become unenforceable due to a change of circumstances, such as when a putative payee claims to be disabled); and
- Modification of spousal support (*e.g.*, a dispute about whether a payor has become disabled under a clause that allows for reduction under that circumstance);
- A dispute about whether the agreement is valid and binding.

The model paragraph that follows provides for binding arbitration of a dispute arising under the agreement. Optional text allows for the lawyer to include in the list of arbitrable disputes a dispute about the validity of the agreement itself.

The lawyer will need to discuss with the client the pros and cons of a binding arbitration clause. Among other things, it can provide a speedier resolution and will afford privacy. However, the opportunity for appeal of an adverse result is strictly limited; even a mistake of fact or law is not ground for appeal of an arbitrator's decision.[252] Therefore, a party who is dissatisfied may have no ability to have an erroneous ruling corrected on appeal. Parties must pay the arbitrator's fees, usually at an hourly rate comparable to the rates of lawyers in that community. For an extended proceeding with multiple hearing days, the cost could prove quite burdensome for an economically disadvantaged party. An arbitration clause may not be useful for a younger couple who are likely to have children. Some issues in a divorce—custody and child support—may have to be resolved in court in any event; proceedings in two different forums may not be in their best interests. Arbitration may not be appropriate when there is a history of domestic violence, although at the drafting stage, the lawyer may not become aware of any such prior conduct. The Uniform Family Law Arbitration Act (UFLAA), discussed further below, would permit a party to opt out of a binding arbitration

252. *Preston v. Dyer*, 2012 Tex. App. LEXIS 9753 (unpub.); *see also* Blondeau v. Baltierra, 337 Conn. 127, 252 A.3d 317 (2020).

provision if he or she has received an order of protection or if the arbitrator determines his or her safety is at risk.[253]

The model text specifies qualifications for the arbitrator. In a jurisdiction with certified specialists, counsel may wish to specify certification as an additional requirement. To the extent the UFLAA is enacted, it will require an arbitrator to be a lawyer who is trained in identifying domestic violence and child abuse unless the parties waive that requirement.[254]

Certain words in the model text are in bold type in order to call attention to them inasmuch as binding arbitration waives some rights, including, especially, appellate review, that a party would otherwise have.

A substantial majority of jurisdictions have adopted an arbitration act, the Uniform Arbitration Act, the Revised Uniform Arbitration Act (RUAA), or substantially similar legislation. The RUAA provides:

> An agreement contained in a record to submit to arbitration any existing or subsequent controversy arising between the parties to the agreement is valid, enforceable, and irrevocable except upon a ground that exists at law or in equity for the revocation of a contract.[255]

In 2005 the American Academy of Matrimonial Lawyers (AAML) published a Model Family Law Arbitration Act.[256] The AAML Model Arbitration Act would expressly permit arbitration at divorce of a dispute arising out of a premarital agreement.[257] The Uniform Law Commission adopted the UFLAA at its 2016 Annual Conference.[258] The UFLAA permits enforcement of a provision in a premarital or postmarital agreement for binding arbitration of a future dispute.[259] Neither the AAML Model Act nor the UFLAA addresses the enforceability of such a provision after the death of a spouse.

A premarital or postmarital agreement to submit to binding arbitration a future controversy about parties' contractual rights under it should be enforceable. Courts have upheld and enforced agreements for binding arbitration of the issues that may arise in a domestic relations matter, including issues arising out of a premarital agreement.[260] Parties may settle marital claims, such as a claim for spousal support or property, by contract. It is a logical

253. UFLAA § 12 (2016).

254. UFLAA § 8 (2016).

255. Revised Uniform Arbitration Act § 6(a) (2000).

256. Available at www.aaml.org; *see also* George K. Walker, *Family Law Arbitration: Legislation and Trends*, 21 J.A.A.M.L. 521 (2008).

257. AAML Model Arbitration Act § 106(a); Walker, *supra* note 270, at 543.

258. Available at www.uniformlaws.org. As of September 2022, the UFLAA had been enacted in Arizona, Hawaii, Montana, and North Dakota.

259. UFLAA § 3, 6(b) (2016).

260. *Roman v. Herrera*, 2021 Tex. App. LEXIS 2665 (unpub.) (premarital agreement provision for arbitration of dispute about validity of agreement is enforceable); *Kelm v. Kelm*, 92 Ohio St. 3d 223, 749 N.E.2d 299 (2001) (premarital agreement provision to arbitrate was enforceable as to spousal and child support but not as to custody); *Marks v. Marks*, 36 Va. App. 216, 548 S.E.2d 919 (2001) (arbitration award regarding property division and other financial obligations under premarital agreement upheld); *DeLorean v. DeLorean*, 211 N.J. Super. 433, 511 A.2d 1257 (1986) (parties are bound by decision of arbitrator regarding validity of premarital agreement); *Swentor v. Swentor*, 336 S.C. 472, 520 S.E.2d 330 (Ct. App. 1999) (court has no jurisdiction to rule on fairness of property division decision of arbitrator); *see also Dick v. Dick*, 210 Mich. App. 576, 534 N.W.2d 185 (1995); *Miller v. Miller*, 423 Pa. Super. 162, 620 A.2d 1161 (1993); *Kovacs v. Kovacs*, 98 Md. App. 289, 633 A.2d 425 (1993); *Masters v. Masters*, 201 Conn. 50, 513 A.2d 104 (1986); *Faherty v. Faherty*, 97 N.J. 99, 477 A.2d 1257 (1984);

extension of this principle that they can contract in advance to resolve such a claim through binding arbitration.[261]

The RUAA provides that an agreement to arbitrate is enforceable and irrevocable except upon the same grounds as are recognized for revocation of any other contract.[262] A contract may be set aside only on a showing that it was not entered into freely and voluntarily or that there was fraud, duress, or some other contractual defense to enforceability. The RUAA does not permit an inquiry into the substantive fairness of the agreement to arbitrate.[263]

An agreement to hire one or more appraisers to value property and stating that the value so determined is conclusive is tantamount to an agreement for binding arbitration even when the term *arbitration* is not used.[264] An agreement to submit a dispute to a religious tribunal for resolution is an agreement to arbitrate.[265]

A marital agreement may not divest a court of jurisdiction to determine custody or support of a minor child. Parties may nevertheless wish to agree that a future dispute about custody will be submitted to arbitration. The few courts that have ruled on permissibility of arbitration of custody are divided.[266]

The model text below provides for arbitration of a dispute about interpretation, application, or enforcement of the agreement. It includes alternative text that will either provide for arbitration of a dispute about validity of the agreement as a whole or will expressly provide that the arbitration provision does not apply to such a dispute. The rationale for excluding a dispute about validity is that a proponent seeking to defend the agreement who loses at trial will be better served by having a right to appeal than by an unappealable decision of an arbitrator.

Some courts hold that a provision in an agreement to arbitrate a future controversy is enforceable only if the agreement containing the arbitration provision is valid;[267] thus, a

---

Crutchley v. Crutchley, 306 N.C. 518, 293 S.E.2d 793 (1982); *Hirsch v. Hirsch*, 37 N.Y.2d 312, 372 N.Y.S.2d 71, 333 N.E.2d 371 (1975).

261. *Lang v. Levi*, 198 Md. App. 154, 16 A.3d 980 (2011); *Spencer v. Spencer*, 494 A.2d 1279 (D.C. 1985).

262. *Swentor*, 520 S.E.2d at 373.

263. *Id.* at 482–83, 336. But some states' statutes impose a higher standard for judging enforceability of an arbitration clause. *See LaFrance v. Lodmell*, 322 Conn. 828, 144 A.3d 373 (2016) (arbitration clause in premarital agreement is generally enforceable; trial judge must determine agreement to arbitrate was entered into voluntarily, without coercion, and is fair and equitable).

264. *Wash. Auto. Co. v. 1828 L St. Assocs.*, 906 A.2d 869 (D.C. 2006).

265. *Meshel v. Ohev Sholom Talmud Torah*, 869 A.2d 343 (D.C. 2005).

266. *LaFrance*, 322 Conn. 828, 144 A.3d 373; *Wieder v. Wieder*, 105 A.D.3d 948, 963 N.Y.S.2d 372 (2013) (settlement agreement to submit future dispute to arbitration is enforceable, subject to court review of child support for compliance with child support guideline); *Johnson v. Johnson*, 204 N.J. 529, 9 A.3d 1003 (2010) (arbitration of child custody is permissible but must have adequate record to permit judicial review); *Tuetken v. Tuetken*, 320 S.W.3d 262 (Tenn. 2010) (parenting issue cannot be submitted to binding arbitration); *Campbell v. Campbell*, 2010 Ky. LEXIS 27 (unpub.) (domestic relations proceeding not arbitrable under Kentucky Uniform Arbitration Act); *Fawzy v. Fawzy*, 199 N.J. 456, 973 A.2d 347 (2009) (award subject to review if party establishes it threatens the child); *Toiberman v. Tisera*, 998 So. 2d 4 (Fla. Ct. App. 2008) (divorcing parties may not arbitrate alimony if there are non-arbitrable issues, such as custody and child support, in the same case); *Kelm v. Kelm*, 920 Ohio St. 3d 223, 749 N.E.2d 299 (2001) (premarital agreement provision for arbitration of custody unenforceable); *In re Marriage of Popack*, 998 P.2d 464 (Colo. App. 2000); *Miller v. Miller*, 423 Pa. Super. 162, 620 A.2d 1161 (1993) (arbitration clause enforceable but resulting custody award subject to *de novo* review); *Kovacs v. Kovacs*, 98 Md. App. 289, 633 A.2d 425 (1993).

267. *In re Miriam Ayad*, 655 S.W.3d 285 (Tex. 2022); *Bandas v. Bandas*, 16 Va. App. 427, 430 S.E.2d 706 (1993); *see also* 4 AM. JUR. 2D *Alternative Dispute Resolution* § 56 ("Where grounds exist to revoke the entire

dispute about validity of the agreement would have to be resolved by a court preliminarily before the matter goes to arbitration for resolution of other issues under the agreement. Other courts hold that a provision of a premarital agreement requiring arbitration of a dispute about validity of the agreement is enforceable; the arbitrator will therefore determine whether the agreement is valid as a contract.[268] The standards for determining validity of the arbitration clause of an agreement are the same as for the determination of the validity of any other contract; such a contract is unenforceable only if it resulted from fraud or duress or was unconscionable or violated public policy.[269]

An arbitration provision can determine how the arbitrator will be selected and may specify the arbitrator's qualifications. In jurisdictions that have board certification, parties may wish to require that the arbitrator have that credential. The model language that follows provides that a judge will select the arbitrator if the parties are unable to agree. An alternative is to provide for the parties to each select a candidate for arbitrator and, if they cannot agree on one of them, the two chosen candidates will select a third to serve as arbitrator.

BINDING ARBITRATION: MODEL TEXT

61. **Dispute Resolution Through Binding Arbitration.** The parties agree to resolve any dispute about the [***optional:*** validity,] application, interpretation, breach or enforcement [***optional:*** , but not the validity,] of this Agreement through **binding arbitration** in accordance with the _________ [*state*] **Arbitration Act**, Code of _________, with a single arbitrator who shall be a member in good standing of the Bar of _________. However, in the event neither party is a resident of _________ at the time such dispute arises, the arbitrator shall be a member in good standing of the bar of the state of the last marital domicile if the dispute arises after a marital separation, or, in the event the dispute arises after the death of a party, of the state of domicile of the deceased party. The arbitrator shall have at least 15 years of experience as a domestic relations lawyer in the event the dispute arises after a marital separation, or as an estates and trusts lawyer in the event the dispute arises after the death of a party. Service as a circuit court [***Alternative:*** family court or probate court] or appellate judge of the applicable jurisdiction shall count toward the required 15 years of experience. The parties shall jointly select the arbitrator. If they are unable to agree on the selection of an arbitrator within a reasonable period of time, either party may apply to a court with jurisdiction to enforce this Agreement for selection of an arbitrator with the qualifications set forth above. The parties shall initially be responsible for sharing the arbitrator's fees and costs, if any, equally;

---

contract, such grounds will also vitiate the arbitration agreement contained in that contract"); *Jones v. Humanscale Corp.*, 130 Cal. App. 4th 401, 29 Cal. Rptr. 3d 881 (2005) (accord); *R.B.F. Mgmt. Co. v. Sunshine Towers*, 352 So. 2d 561 (Fla. Ct. App. 1977) (accord).

268. *Roman v. Herrera,* 2021 Tex. App. LEXIS 2665 (unpub.) (premarital agreement provision for arbitration of dispute about validity of agreement is enforceable).

269. *Swentor v. Swentor*, 336 S.C. 472, 520 S.E.2d 330 (Ct. App. 1999); *Bandas*, 16 Va. App. at 431, 430 S.E.2d at 708.

however, the arbitrator shall have the power to make an award of arbitrator's fees and costs as well as an award of attorneys' fees and costs under Paragraph 40 of this Agreement.

WAIVER OF STATUTE OF LIMITATIONS DURING MARRIAGE: COMMENT

Both the UPAA and the UPMAA provide that any statute of limitations that may apply to a claim of breach is tolled during the marriage.[270] The model text below is consistent with these uniform acts and may be appropriate for jurisdictions that do not have a tolling statute. It can offer some protection for a spouse who otherwise may have to choose between suing a breaching spouse during the marriage or acquiescing in a breach. However, equitable defenses, such as laches and estoppel may still be available.[271]

WAIVER OF STATUTE OF LIMITATIONS DURING THE MARRIAGE: MODEL TEXT

62. **Waiver of Statute of Limitations.** The parties intend and agree that any statute of limitations that may be applicable to a claim that a party breached this Agreement during the marriage shall not begin to run until [the death of a party, or] a marital separation, as defined herein [whichever occurs first].

EXECUTION FORMALITIES: COMMENT

The UPAA requires only that a premarital agreement be in writing and signed by the parties.[272] The UPMAA similarly requires only that the agreement be in writing and signed.[273] No other formalities are required. Similarly, unless a statute requires more formalities for a postmarital agreement, there is no requirement for witnesses or notarization.[274] Some states' laws require witnesses and/or notarization.[275] Whether required by law or not, many attorneys take the added precaution of having witnesses and/or a notary and having parties sign or initial every page. Having an agreement notarized or witnessed or both, and having the parties sign or initial every page, should make authentication easier should the agreement ever be challenged. It may also encourage parties considering an amendment or revocation to get legal advice.

---

270. UPAA § 8; UPMAA § 11.
271. UPAA § 8; UPMAA § 11.
272. UPAA § 2.
273. UPMAA §§ 2(8), 6.
274. *Marriage of Hall*, 27 N.E.3d 281 (Ind. Ct. App. 2015) (no requirement for notarization); *Rush v. Rush*, 115 So. 3d 508 (La. Ct. App., 1st Dist. 2013) (postmarital agreement modifying or terminating matrimonial regime requires joint petition and court approval).
275. See Appendices B(1) and B(2), State Law Summaries.

EXECUTION FORMALITIES: MODEL TEXT

______________________________ [Seal]
SPOUSE ONE

WITNESS

____

NAME ______________________________ Date: ______________________________

ADDRESS ____

WITNESS

____

NAME ______________________________ Date: ______________________________

ADDRESS ____

______________________________ [Seal]
SPOUSE TWO

WITNESS

____

NAME ______________________________ Date: ______________________________

ADDRESS ____

WITNESS

____

NAME ______________________________ Date: ______________________________

ADDRESS ____

City/County of ______________________
State of ____________________________:

I hereby certify that on this _____ day of ____________, 20__, before me, the subscriber, a notary public in and for the aforesaid jurisdiction, personally appeared SPOUSE ONE, known to me, and he or she acknowledged the foregoing agreement to be his/her act and he/she made oath in due form of law that the facts stated therein are true to the best of his/her knowledge.

Witness my hand and notarial seal.

NOTARY PUBLIC
My commission expires: __________________

City/County of __________________________
State of ______________________________:

I hereby certify that on this _____ day of ____________, 20 __, before me, the subscriber, a notary public in and for the aforesaid jurisdiction, personally appeared SPOUSE TWO, known to me, and he/she acknowledged the foregoing agreement to be his/her act and he/she made oath in due form of law that the facts stated therein are true to the best of his/her knowledge.

Witness my hand and notarial seal.

NOTARY PUBLIC
My commission expires: __________________

Terms for Sharing Agreement 13

The model paragraphs below can be substituted for paragraphs of the title-controls agreement to create a sharing agreement under which parties retain their exclusive rights to premarital, gifted, and inherited property but share the fruits of their labor.

The recitals, definitions of property, earnings, and income in the title-controls model are equally applicable in the sharing model. The definitions of earnings and income, and the delineation between them, is especially important in a sharing agreement where a party is a business owner who earns both compensation for his or her personal services and profits from the sale of goods or services.[1]

Definitions, Separate and Marital Property: Comment

When parties opt for an agreement that provides for sharing assets acquired through their common labor, the agreement should clearly define what is included in the shared pool of assets. The definitions can be aligned with the law that would govern at divorce in a dual property state but need not be identical. Such an agreement can allow each party to retain his or her exclusive right to premarital, inherited, and gifted property, as well as the income from, appreciation in the value of, and property acquired with such separate property,[2] but to share property acquired during the marriage through employment of either party.

Generally, separate property will include:

- Property owned prior to marriage, including property disclosed on the parties' asset disclosure schedules;
- Gifts and inherited assets; and
- Property acquired in exchange for separate property.

Generally, marital property will be defined as all property acquired during the marriage, including through employment, regardless of title, except property

1. *See Kelly v. Kelly,* 518 P.3d 326 (Idaho 2022).
2. Brett Turner, Equitable Distribution of Property § 2.9 (4th ed. 2021–22) (hereafter, Turner).

specifically classified as separate. In defining separate and marital property, counsel should consider a number of issues:

- Will income from separate property be separate property or marital property?
- Will appreciation in the value of separate property be separate or marital property?
- Will intra-spousal gifts be the separate property of the recipient, or marital property?
- What effect will commingling of separate property and marital property have on classification? Will a small amount of commingling, such as a deposit of a small sum of marital property cash into a separately titled bank account that is otherwise separate property, cause the account to become marital property?
- Will jointly titled real estate be treated as marital property, regardless of the source of funds for acquisition, or will it be part separate and part marital property in proportion to each party's monetary contributions to acquisition costs?
- Will a jointly titled financial institution account be entirely marital property, or will the agreement allow for a party to trace out separate property contributions?
- What effect will a monetary contribution of marital property funds to acquisition, improvement, or appreciation of one party's separate property have on classification of that property?
- What effect will one party's monetary contributions of his or her separate property funds to acquisition, improvement, or appreciation of the other party's separate property have on classification of that property?

The agreement should make clear the circumstances under which contractual separate property will become marital property. Some spouses will elect to deposit what would otherwise be separate property into a joint financial institution account. The definitions in the agreement should clearly answer the question whether joint title causes the funds, and assets acquired therefrom, to become marital property. For example, in *Jangula v. Jangula*,[3] a home acquired with funds from a joint account was marital property under the terms of a premarital agreement although the funds were originally the husband's separate property. By contrast, in *Seherr-Thoss v. Seherr-Thoss*,[4] the husband used separate funds to purchase a home in his name and later transferred title into joint names. The premarital agreement provided for separate property to retain its character even if held in joint names unless the parties executed a separate agreement stating a different intent. The husband was therefore entitled to the full proceeds of sale. The model text provides that marital property includes a joint financial institution account without regard to the source of funds. This is intended to eliminate litigation over tracing money in and out of a joint account in which there may be multiple transactions. Such litigation can be expensive. Eliminating it can further the goal of reducing the transactional costs of divorce or the settling of the estate of a deceased spouse.

The model text below provides optional text for a business or professional services practice to be the separate property of the owner-spouse but for compensation from working in the business to be marital property. A party who comes to the marriage with a business or professional practice and seeks a premarital agreement is often motivated by a desire to

3. 706 N.W.2d 85 (N.D. 2005).
4. 141 P.3d 705 (Wyo. 2006).

protect his or her exclusive rights and to avoid a valuation of the business as part of a divorce. This provision can serve that client's objective.

DEFINITIONS, SEPARATE AND MARITAL PROPERTY: MODEL TEXT

5. **"Marital property"** of the parties shall be all property acquired during the marriage, and not defined as separate property, including:

(i) each party's earnings [***Add, if appropriate:*** , including earnings from a party's employment in a business or professional services practice that is defined herein as his or her separate property];

(ii) that portion of a party's retirement benefits and plans acquired during the marriage, as set forth more particularly in paragraph 8(C);

(iii) funds or securities held in an account of the parties at a financial institution (such as a bank, credit union, or securities brokerage) and titled as tenants by the entirety, joint tenants with right of survivorship, or tenants in common, without regard to the source of the funds, except as provided in paragraph 8(J);

(iv) all income from, any appreciation in the value of, and all proceeds of a loan secured by a lien on, marital property;

(v) all property acquired with marital property, including, but not limited to, property acquired with earnings, with funds from a joint financial institution account, with the proceeds from the sale of, or in exchange for, marital property, or with the proceeds of a loan secured by a lien on marital property;

(vi) the marital property share of hybrid property as defined in paragraph 7;

(vii) [***Optional:*** the parties' primary marital home without regard to the source of funds for acquisition costs of the home;]

(viii) [***Optional:*** the furniture, equipment, household effects, and other such items of common use purchased by the parties, or either of them, during the marriage for the marital home(s), without regard to the source of funds for acquisition] [***Optional:*** , with the exception of works of art, antiques, and collectibles as provided in paragraph 6(viii)];

(ix) the wedding gifts from third parties, whether received before or after the wedding;

(x) other gifts that are made to both parties, such as, but not limited to anniversary gifts, holiday and other special occasion gifts to both parties, and gifts of furniture, equipment or household effects for the parties' common use [***Optional:*** , with the exception of gifts of family-owned art, antiques, collectibles, or family heirlooms, which shall remain the separate property of the party from whose family of origin such items came];

(xi) all other untitled property acquired during the marriage, except as specifically provided in paragraph 6.

6. **Separate Property.** A party's "separate property" shall be, but is not limited to:

(i) all property acquired by a party prior to the parties' marriage, including, specifically, the property set forth in SPOUSE ONE's Schedule A, attached, and SPOUSE TWO's Schedule B, attached, and further including, also without limitation, all property acquired by a party during any time they may cohabit prior to marriage;

(ii) any property acquired by the party, before or after the date of marriage, by gift (including a gift from one spouse to the other regardless of the source of funds for acquisition), or by inheritance, including an inherited IRA, survivorship, operation of law, under the laws of intestate succession, a will, trust, or similar instrument, or beneficiary designation;

(iii) all interests of the party, whether vested or contingent, in any trust created and funded by a third party and any trust created by the party and funded with his or her separate property (whether such trust currently exists or is hereafter created), including, but not limited to, any income, property, benefit, or interest held in or received from any such trust and all the contributions to such trust from a third party, or from a party hereto and made with his or her separate property;

(iv) [***Optional:*** a party's ownership interest as an active owner in a closely held business, or in a professional services practice, regardless of when such interest was acquired, the form of organization of the business, or the source of funds for acquisition of the interest (a party's ownership interest as a passive investor or shareholder in a business or professional services practice entity will be marital, separate, or hybrid property based upon the source of the funds for such investment)];

(v) any appreciation in the value of, all income from, and all proceeds of a loan secured by a lien on the party's separate property;

(vi) all property acquired with the proceeds from the sale of, in exchange for, or with the proceeds of a loan secured by a lien on the party's separate property;

(vii) the party's clothing [, jewelry,] [sports equipment,] and personal effects without regard to the source of funds for acquisition of such property;

(viii) any works of art, antiques, or collectibles acquired by a party with his or her separate property notwithstanding such property may be in the parties' home(s) and used by them jointly;

(ix) all other untitled property acquired by a party with his or her separate property;

(x) the separate property share of hybrid property, as defined in paragraph 7;

(xi) any retirement benefits and other deferred compensation acquired before the date of marriage or after the date of marital separation, as provided in paragraph 8(C);

(xii) the party's *pro rata* share of any overpayment of income taxes as provided in paragraph __ (notwithstanding that a refund may be jointly titled).

DEFINITION, HYBRID PROPERTY AND OTHER TERMS DEFINING SEPARATE AND MARITAL PROPERTY: COMMENT

The model text below adds a third category, hybrid property, to the classification scheme of the sharing agreement. In the absence of a marital agreement, in most states, property that receives monetary contributions of both separate and marital funds may be treated as part marital property and part separate property (hybrid property).[5] Parties can, by agreement, similarly provide for property to be allocated between the marital share and each party's separate share *pro rata*. When parties agree to share the fruits of their labor but to preserve their separate property, either or both may want to be able to use inherited or premarital assets to enhance the family's standard of living and to provide for the other party at death, but may want to get back the nonmarital contribution to an asset if the marriage fails. This provision would permit that. The ratio is generally the value of monetary contributions to acquisition costs from each source (*i.e.*, each party's separate property contributions and the marital property contributions) divided by the sum of all such monetary contributions.

Note that the model definition in paragraph 5 makes all joint financial institution accounts marital property regardless of the source of funds; therefore, such an account can never be hybrid property. However, a separately titled account can be hybrid property, as can real estate, tangible personalty, and retirement benefits.

If parties opt to define a primary marital home as marital property (paragraph 5 (vii)), the hybrid property definition will not apply to it. Paragraph 8(B) defines acquisition costs. In addition to any cash paid directly to purchase the property, the drafter should consider the following in defining acquisition costs:

- Acquisition transaction costs, such as transfer taxes and other closing costs in the case of real estate and broker's commissions in the case of securities;
- Interest on acquisition debt (whether secured or unsecured);
- Additional cash paid for improvements;
- Property taxes;
- Insurance;
- Major repairs and maintenance;
- Routine repairs and maintenance;
- Transaction costs for a refinance;

5. TURNER § 5:20.

- Payments on a home equity loan used for purposes other than improvements, such as to purchase furniture or a car, or to pay off credit card debt; and
- Income taxes attributed to property, such as taxes on rental income and taxes on dividends and interest income.

Paragraph 8(C) provides an elaboration of paragraphs 5(ii) and 6(xii) as to the marital and separate shares of retirement benefits and other forms of deferred compensation. A party who is in a retirement plan upon marriage, and will continue to participate during the marriage, will likely have hybrid retirement benefits. An agreement should also take account of the prospect that a participant will receive or make post-dissolution contributions to his or her plan. The terms of the agreement should clearly define the nonmarital share so as to take account of a rollover to an IRA or to a new employer's plan, as well as appreciation and reinvested income, and should distinguish between new contributions during the marriage and the increase in value of the nonmarital share.[6]

DEFINITION, HYBRID PROPERTY AND OTHER TERMS DEFINING SEPARATE AND MARITAL PROPERTY: MODEL TEXT

7. **Hybrid Property.** Except as the parties may otherwise later agree in writing, and except as provided in paragraph 5(iii), "hybrid property" shall be all property, regardless of title, acquired during the marriage with a combination of marital and separate property or a combination of separate property from each party. A party's separate property share of such hybrid property shall be and remain his or her separate property. Hybrid property shall be allocated between a party's separate property share and the marital share in the same ratio as the party's separate property monetary contributions to acquisition costs, as defined herein, and the marital property monetary contributions to acquisition costs bear to the sum of the monetary contributions to acquisition costs of such property.

8. **Other Terms Relating to Determination of Separate and Marital Property**

A. The appreciation in value of and the income and profits derived from separate property, whether by way of sale, exchange, investment, reinvestment, forgiveness of debt, or otherwise, including, without limitation, the acquisition of property with separate property or with the proceeds from the sale or other disposition of separate property, shall be and remain separate property regardless of the "active" or "passive" nature of a party's contributions to such separate property and regardless of any direct or indirect contribution of labor, effort, inventiveness, physical or intellectual skill, creativity or managerial

6. *See Sembower v. Sembower*, 2021 Ariz. App. Unpub. LEXIS 257 (contributions to retirement plan during marriage were marital property under parties' premarital agreement, rejecting husband's argument that new contributions to existing account defined as his separate property were separate property); *Dow v. Billing*, 224 A.3d 244 (Me. 2020) (premarital agreement defined separate property as property "now owned . . . and all increases and additions thereto"; retirement benefits earned during marriage were marital property).

activity of either or both parties to the acquisition, care, maintenance, or appreciation of such separate property. A party who devotes labor, effort, inventiveness, physical or intellectual skill, creativity, or managerial activity to the other party's separate property shall be deemed to have made a gift to the other party. With respect to a separate property business of a party, the party's efforts or contributions to the business as an owner, employee, officer, director, stockholder, consultant, or otherwise shall not convert such business, or any appreciation thereof, into marital property.

B. "Acquisition costs" shall be the consideration paid for the property and payment for capital improvements, whether paid in cash, by an in-kind exchange, or through payment of the principal [***add, if appropriate:*** and interest] of debt incurred for acquisition of the specific property, and further including, but not limited to, a down payment and transaction costs, for example, settlement closing costs for acquisition and for financing in the case of real property, or broker's commission in the case of securities, and payment of the principal [***add, if appropriate:*** and interest] of debt used for payoff of a prior loan for acquisition costs. [***Add and revise, if appropriate:*** The term "acquisition costs" does not include interest payments, casualty and liability insurance, property taxes, or the expenses of routine repairs and maintenance of the property.] [***Add if appropriate, e.g., if agreement does not have section on special provisions for marital home:*** Hybrid property includes, but is not limited to, real estate, such as a marital home, regardless of title, that the parties acquire in part through contributions to acquisition costs from one or both parties of his or her separate property (including gifts from a parent or other family member without regard to how such gifts may be reported on the donor's gift or estate tax return) and contributions from marital property to such costs, such as mortgage payments made from a joint financial institution account.]

C. For purposes of determining a party's separate property share and the marital property share of a party's retirement benefits and plans and other forms of deferred compensation, the following shall apply:

(i) With respect to a defined contribution retirement account, such as a 401(k), 403(b), or Thrift Savings Plan (TSP), including a nonqualified plan account and an IRA, the party's separate property share shall be the account balance as of the day prior to the marriage of the parties, adjusted for all gains, losses, interest and dividends applicable to such premarital account balance from that date to the date of any division thereof, plus any contributions to such account made at any time from separate property, or after the date of marital separation with separate property, including post-separation earnings, adjusted for gains, losses, interest, and dividends applicable to such separate property contributions from the date of contribution to the date of division. The marital property share shall, accordingly, be all contributions of earnings or other marital property to such an account during the marriage, adjusted for all gains, losses, interest, and dividends applicable to such marital property contributions through the date of division or other distribution thereof. Any withdrawals from such an account shall be allocated *pro rata*, determined as of the date of withdrawal, to the owner's separate property share and to the marital property share, subject to paragraph 8(J).

(ii) With respect to a party's stock options, stock units, restricted shares, stock awards, and other similar forms of deferred compensation, the separate property share shall be any and all such grants received prior to the date of marriage, regardless of when such grants vest, and any and all such grants received after the date of marital separation. The marital property share of any such grants shall be those granted and fully vested during the marriage and prior to marital separation and a *pro rata* share of any such grants received during the marriage that vest after the date of marital separation, the *pro rata* share defined as the fraction of which the numerator is the total number of full months of marriage from date of grant to date of marital separation and the denominator is total number of full months from date of grant to date of vesting.

(iii) In the event a party is or becomes a participant in a defined benefit pension plan, the marital portion thereof shall be a fraction of which the numerator is the total number of full months of participation in the plan during the marriage, and prior to marital separation, and the denominator is the total number of full months of participation in the plan.

D. Joint or common use of separate or hybrid property shall not convert separate property to marital property. Further, a party's expenditure of separate property funds for common or family purposes or to benefit the other party shall not convert the property from which such funds were derived to marital property.

E. The fact that the parties may file a joint state or federal income tax return, or that one or both parties may pay taxes due in connection with such joint return, shall not be interpreted to mean that the income or property reported in such return is marital income or marital property nor convert separate property to marital property. Further, a party's reporting of property holdings, debts, earnings, or income on a joint loan application, financial statement, or net worth statement shall not be interpreted to mean that any item of property or income identified therein is marital property, nor shall it convert separate property to marital property.

F. The parties acknowledge that they may occasionally use such expressions as "our property," "our house," and so on, when referring to property that is, by the terms of this Agreement, separate property. They agree and acknowledge that they do not intend by such casual references to convert separate property to marital property.

G. A party claiming that an item of untitled tangible personal property acquired during the parties' marriage is his or her separate property may establish his or her claim by:

(i) A written acknowledgment the other party;

(ii) A bill of sale, invoice, or similar document, coupled with proof of the source of funds used for payment;

(iii) A will, probate accounting, or other writing of a donor or a donor's legal representative.

Nothing herein shall make these the exclusive means of establishing such a claim.

H. This Agreement contains rules defining property as a party's separate property or as marital property. The parties at any time may expressly otherwise characterize any real or personal property as separate property or as marital property by a writing that clearly identifies the property and states how the property or interest in property is to be defined for purposes of this Agreement. The writing may also address to what extent, if any, future contributions to acquisition costs will affect the definition of the property. Any such writing must be signed by each party. Electronic mail shall satisfy the requirement for a signed writing for purposes of this paragraph 8(H).

I. Nothing herein is intended to make compliance with paragraph 8(F), (G), or (H) the exclusive means by which a party may establish his or her claim that an item of property is his or her separate property or is marital property.

J. The parties agree and acknowledge that a party, or the parties, may from time to time receive a payment of funds (such as an income tax refund, the proceeds of a sale of hybrid property, or a distribution from a retirement plan) that is partly the separate property of one or each of them, or is partly separate and partly marital property, and that a party may, for convenience, deposit such funds in a joint financial institution account. They agree that such deposit, in and of itself, will not cause the separate property portion of such funds to become marital property, provided that the party who is entitled to the separate portion of such funds promptly transfers his or her separate property share out of the joint account.

DEFINITIONS, SEPARATE AND MARITAL DEBT: COMMENT

The paragraphs below define separate and marital debt. The definitions track the definitions in the title controls agreement in Chapter 12 but include additional text to take account of debt incurred to acquire, or secured by, property defined as hybrid property.

When a party has other preexisting obligations, such as an obligation to pay spousal support to a former spouse, to pay basic child support on behalf of a minor child, or to pay post-majority expenses of a child, such as college tuition, counsel should consider whether to include restrictions on the source for such payments. When one party is wealthy, the other is of modest means, and the agreement will provide for sharing the fruits of their labor, the less wealthy party may be disadvantaged if the wealthy party is able to use marital funds for these obligations while preserving his or her separate property.

DEFINITIONS, SEPARATE AND MARITAL DEBT: MODEL TEXT

9. **Separate and Marital Debt.**

A. "Marital debt" shall be debt incurred to acquire, improve, or maintain marital property, as defined herein. Marital debt includes a *pro rata* share of such debt incurred for hybrid property in the same ratio as the marital share portion of such hybrid property bears to the property as a whole. Marital debt shall also include debt incurred in the joint names of the parties [***Add, if appropriate:*** and debt incurred by either party for the parties' usual household, personal, and family expenses].

B. "Separate debt" shall be debt incurred by a party to acquire, improve, or maintain his or her separate property and the *pro rata* share of such debt incurred for hybrid property in the same ratio as the separate portion of such property bears to the property as a whole. Separate debt includes all other debt incurred by a party in his or her name alone [***Add, if appropriate:*** except as provided in paragraph 9(A)]. A party's separate debt also includes his or her separate income tax liability, as described in paragraph__. [***Add, if appropriate:*** Further, a party's separate debt shall include all his or her medical and health-care expenses not covered by insurance notwithstanding that the other spouse may be or become liable to a provider of such medical or health-care services.]

DISPOSITION OF PROPERTY AT DEATH: COMMENT

The paragraphs below provide for a surviving spouse to have the right to death benefits under a retirement plan, without regard to when these benefits were accrued, and for the surviving spouse to receive all marital property. Each party would have the right to determine disposition of his or her separate property as defined in the agreement. However, the separate property component of hybrid property that is titled in a survivorship form would go to the survivor by operation of law. Some terms in Chapter 12 and in Appendix E can be used to make additional specific provisions for a surviving spouse. For example, where one spouse has a large separate estate, the parties may want to agree that he or she will leave a portion of these assets to the other spouse, outright or in a trust, make a cash bequest, or maintain life insurance for the other spouse.

DISPOSITION OF PROPERTY AT DEATH: MODEL TEXT

Survivor and Death Benefits Under Parties' Retirement Plans. Neither party waives any legal rights he or she may have to a surviving spouse annuity, lump sum death benefit, or other benefits payable on the death of a spouse under the terms of the other party's retirement plan, provided they are living together and are not separated. The parties agree and acknowledge that if one of them dies while they are married and not separated, the surviving spouse shall have the same rights to survivor and death benefits under the other party's retirement plan as he or she would have in the absence of this Premarital/Postmarital Agreement, without regard to whether such plan is marital property, separate property, or hybrid property. [***Optional:*** The parties acknowledge their understanding that each of them has the right to name a beneficiary of his or her choice under his or her Individual Retirement Account.]

Disposition of Marital Property at Death. Provided the parties are married, and are not separated, upon the death of a spouse, the surviving spouse shall be entitled to all of the marital property, as defined herein, outright and free of trust. Each party shall maintain a will, beneficiary designations, pay-on-death and transfer-on-death titles, and other estate planning documents as may be necessary to carry out his or her obligations under this Paragraph. In the event of a marital separation as defined herein, the provisions of this Paragraph shall not apply and the provisions of this Agreement for determining the parties' rights upon a marital separation shall apply instead.

Disposition of Separate Property at Death. E[xcept as set forth herein, e]ach party shall have the right to dispose of his or her separate property, as defined herein, by will, trust, beneficiary designation, transfer during his or her lifetime, gift, or by any other means. Accordingly, and only with respect to each party's separate property, each party waives all of his or her property rights, claims, and interests as a surviving spouse, including, but not limited to, dower, curtesy, right of election regarding the estate of the other or to renounce and take against the will of the other, interest in augmented estate, right to inheritance in the event of intestacy, family allowance, homestead rights, exempt property, and all other similar or related rights under applicable law, including the law of any state or foreign jurisdiction where the deceased spouse may be domiciled or own property at death, and further including any rights resulting from changes in law that may take effect after the execution of this Agreement.

DISPOSITION OF PROPERTY IN THE EVENT OF MARITAL SEPARATION: COMMENT

This model provides for each party to retain exclusive rights to his or her separate property and for parties to share marital property equally. The cutoff date after which newly acquired property is defined as separate property is the date of separation, not the date of divorce, but parties are free to negotiate for a different cutoff date. Most provisions for disposition of property can be implemented without a court order or a judgment of divorce. Division of marital retirement benefits and other deferred compensation, however, requires a court order incident to divorce for implementation. The text also provides for the possibility that a party may have a plan that does not permit a direct-pay order for division of retirement benefits, such as a non-qualified plan. This text would require the parties to come up with another method of dividing benefits but does not attempt to specify the method.

Disposition of Property in the Event of Marital Separation: Model Text

Separate Property.

A. In the event of the parties' marital separation, as defined in paragraph __, each party shall retain his or her separate property and his or her separate property share of hybrid property, free from any claim or demand of the other party, and each party shall be solely responsible for paying his or her separate debt. Each party waives the right to make a claim with respect to the separate property of the other party for transfer, monetary award, equitable distribution award, equitable lien, or property award under ________________ , or division of any kind under any applicable statute or law of ____________, or any other jurisdiction that may govern the disposition of marital or community property upon separation or divorce, including a foreign jurisdiction, as such laws now exist or may hereafter be enacted or amended.

B. The parties agree that in the event of a marital separation, as defined herein, each will, upon request of the other, or his or her legal representatives, execute any waiver as may be required by the terms of the other party's retirement plan, or applicable statute or regulation, with respect to any retirement plan that is entirely such other party's separate property and with respect to the separate property portion of such other party's retirement plan that is hybrid property, so as to permit the plan participant to elect any form of payment available under his or her retirement plan and to waive completely any spousal rights the nonparticipant spouse may otherwise have under such plan with respect to such separate property plan or portion thereof. If, notwithstanding the foregoing, a nonparticipant party fails or refuses to timely execute a waiver or consent to a waiver after being requested to do so, and in the further event that he or she receives a distribution from the other party's retirement plan contrary to the terms of this Agreement, in addition to any other remedies to which the participant may be entitled, the receiving party shall receive such distribution solely as the agent of the participant, or his or her estate or designated beneficiary, and shall thereupon immediately transfer the same to the other party, or his or her estate or designated beneficiary, provided that he or she is indemnified for all tax liability resulting from his or her receipt thereof.

Marital Property. In the event of the parties' separation as defined in paragraph __:

A. Each party shall be entitled to receive one-half of the marital property, including the marital property share of hybrid property, and shall be charged with one-half of the marital debt, secured or unsecured. In the event a party receives property as part of a division of property upon marital separation or divorce, the property shall be transferred to the recipient subject to any secured debt on such property, which shall be paid by the recipient without any contribution from the other spouse. Further, the parties shall each be responsible for paying one-half of their unsecured marital debt as part of the equal division of marital property except as they may otherwise agree in writing.

B. In order to carry out the division of marital property and payoff of marital debt, the parties shall take such steps as they shall agree upon to divide and allocate their marital property and marital debt in accordance with the terms of this Agreement. They agree to negotiate in good faith to allocate their property interests in accordance with the terms of this Agreement. In negotiating the allocation of their property, they shall each give due consideration to the other party's preferences, difficulties of valuation, marketability of assets, and other relevant factors. The parties have not provided specific terms to carry out this division because the nature of the assets and debts and the pertinent circumstances cannot be ascertained at this time. Nevertheless, if an item of marital property lends itself to a distribution in-kind, to the extent possible the property shall be distributed equally in-kind. If the property does not lend itself to a distribution in-kind, or the parties cannot agree on an in-kind division, they shall sell the property in accordance with following paragraph __(D).

C. In the event the parties do not agree as to the fair market value of any specific item of marital property, the parties shall obtain an appraisal of the property subject to division from a qualified, independent appraiser with experience in valuing the type of property in dispute. Such appraisal shall control as to fair market value. If the parties are unable to agree on an appraiser, each party shall select such an appraiser having an office in or reasonably near the community where the property is located and the average of the two appraisals shall control as to value. A party's failure to respond within 30 days to a written request for selection of an appraiser shall be deemed a waiver of the right to participate in the selection and the other party's choice of appraiser shall control. The parties shall share the cost of appraisal equally.

D. In the event the parties do not agree as to the appropriate disposition of any item of marital or hybrid property, they shall promptly offer such item for sale to the general public using a method calculated to achieve the highest price and shall divide the proceeds of sale in accordance with paragraph __(A).

E. Except as the parties may otherwise agree, the marital portion of a party's retirement benefits or other deferred compensation shall be divided as follows:

(i) To the extent permitted by law and the terms of the plan, such retirement benefits shall be divided equally in accordance with a Qualified Domestic Relations Order (QDRO) in the case a of private qualified retirement plan, or a retirement benefits court order (RBCO) in accordance with governing law and the terms of the plan in the case of governmental or other forms of retirement benefits, including an Individual Retirement Account.

(ii) The marital portion of a party's defined benefit pension shall be divided equally between the parties based on the self-only annuity, also known as the single life annuity. If available under the plan, the parties shall elect a separate interest division. If a separate interest division is not available under the plan, for example in the case of a participant in the FERS pension, the participant shall elect the joint and survivor annuity form of payment and the nonparticipant shall have the right to the [marital property share of the] joint and survivor annuity. The cost of the [nonparticipant's share of the] survivor annuity shall be deducted from [***Select:*** the nonparticipant's share of the annuity/the self-only annuity]. Further, in the event the nonparticipant predeceases the participant under a joint and survivor annuity, the nonparticipant's share of the annuity shall revert to the participant. If the plan is a qualified or governmental plan, the distribution shall be made in accordance with the appropriate QDRO, RBCO, or other appropriate retirement benefits court order and shall prohibit the participant from taking a refund of employee contributions without the consent of the nonparticipant. In the case of any pension or other retirement plan that provides for cost-of-living adjustments (COLAs) after the participant goes into pay status, the order dividing such benefit shall provide for the nonparticipant spouse to receive his or her *pro rata* share of the COLAs.

(iii) In the event governing law or the terms of the plan do not permit entry of a court order enforceable against the plan, for example, in the case of a nonqualified pension plan, or a stock award, stock purchase, or stock option plan, the parties shall determine an alternative method of allocating the marital portion of such benefits to carry out the principle of equal division of the marital share as expressed in this Agreement. Any division of such benefits shall be effected so as to result in each party bearing the income and payroll tax consequences attributable to the benefits received or retained by him or her based on federal and state marginal tax rates applicable to the owner of such benefits in effect on the date of division.

F. This Agreement is a full and complete settlement of all marital property rights of the parties. Accordingly, each party waives the right to make a claim with respect to any marital property for contribution, transfer, monetary award, equitable distribution award, equitable lien, or community property award under ______________ or division of any kind under any applicable statute or law of __________ or any other jurisdiction that may govern the disposition of marital or community property upon separation or divorce, including a foreign jurisdiction, as such laws now exist or may hereafter be enacted or amended.

FINANCIAL DISCLOSURE: COMMENT

Apart from the question of the extent of financial disclosure required to comply with rules about validity, discussed in Chapter 4, the lawyer will need to consider what additional disclosure the client may need to make that relates to the particular terms of the sharing agreement. For example, in *In re Marriage of Irons,*[7] the agreement defined, and appeared to limit, separate property as the property on each party's attached disclosure statement. Thus, it was important that each party disclose all assets he or she intended to preserve as separate property. In the husband's case, he "forgot" some assets. Even when a party does not deliberately fail to include some assets, there are often items of property that a party simply does not think to include. For example, it is rare that a party entering into a premarital agreement will make an inventory of all of his or her tangible personal property, nor should this be necessary in most cases. However, when a party owns high-value tangibles, such as valuable art, antiques, collectibles, jewelry, and the like, he or she may need to provide some data about these items. This can be especially important if the party will continue to add to a collection during the marriage with funds defined as marital property. Moreover, when parties are already married and have accumulated assets that will be defined as marital property in a postmarital agreement, it may be necessary for the parties, or each of them separately, to identify property he or she claims as separate property and to provide full disclosure of marital property titled in his or her name.

7. 2016 Kan. App. Unpub. LEXIS 574 (July 15, 2016).

APPENDIX

A(1)

TEXT OF UNIFORM PREMARITAL AGREEMENT ACT

1. Definitions.

As used in this Act:

(1) "Premarital agreement" means an agreement between prospective spouses made in contemplation of marriage and to be effective upon marriage.

(2) "Property" means an interest, present or future, legal or equitable, vested or contingent, in real or personal property, including income and earnings.

2. Formalities.

A premarital agreement must be in writing and signed by both parties. It is enforceable without consideration.

3. Content.

(a) Parties to a premarital agreement may contract with respect to:

(1) the rights and obligations of each of the parties in any of the property of either or both of them whenever and wherever acquired or located;

(2) the right to buy, sell, use, transfer, exchange, abandon, lease, consume, expend, assign, create a security interest in, mortgage, encumber, dispose of, or otherwise manage and control property;

(3) the disposition of property upon separation, marital dissolution, death, or the occurrence or nonoccurrence of any other event;

(4) the modification or elimination of spousal support;

(5) the making of a will, trust, or other arrangement to carry out the provisions of the agreement;

(6) the ownership rights in and disposition of the death benefit from a life insurance policy;
(7) the choice of law governing the construction of the agreement; and
(8) any other matter, including their personal rights and obligations, not in violation of public policy or a statute imposing a criminal penalty.

(b) The right of a child to support may not be adversely affected by a premarital agreement.

4. Effect of Marriage.
A premarital agreement becomes effective upon marriage.

5. Amendment, Revocation.
After marriage, a premarital agreement may be amended or revoked only by a written agreement signed by the parties. The amended agreement or the revocation is enforceable without consideration.

6. Enforcement.

(a) A premarital agreement is not enforceable if the party against whom enforcement is sought proves that:
  (1) that party did not execute the agreement voluntarily; or
  (2) the agreement was unconscionable when it was executed and, before execution of the agreement, that party:
    (i) was not provided a fair and reasonable disclosure of the property or financial obligations of the other party;
    (ii) did not voluntarily and expressly waive, in writing, any right to disclosure of the property or financial obligations of the other party beyond the disclosure provided; and
    (iii) did not have, or reasonably could not have had, an adequate knowledge of the property or financial obligations of the other party.

(b) If a provision of a premarital agreement modifies or eliminates spousal support and that modification or elimination causes one party to the agreement to be eligible for support under a program of public assistance at the time of separation or marital dissolution, a court, notwithstanding the terms of the agreement, may require the other party to provide support to the extent necessary to avoid that eligibility.

(c) An issue of unconscionability of a premarital agreement shall be decided by the court as a matter of law.

7. Enforcement: Void Marriage.
If a marriage is determined to be void, an agreement that would otherwise have been a premarital agreement is enforceable only to the extent necessary to avoid an inequitable result.

8. Limitation of Actions.
Any statute of limitations applicable to an action asserting a claim for relief under a premarital agreement is tolled during the marriage of the parties to the agreement. However, equitable defenses limiting the time for enforcement, including laches and estoppel, are available to either party.

9. Application and Construction.
This [Act] shall be applied and construed to effectuate its general purpose to make uniform the law with respect to the subject of this [Act] among states enacting it.

10. Short Title.
This [Act] may be cited as the Uniform Premarital Agreement Act.

11. Severability.
If any provision of this [Act] or its application to any person or circumstance is held invalid, the invalidity does not affect other provisions or applications of this [Act] which can be given effect without the invalid provision or application, and to this end the provisions of this [Act] are severable.

12. Time of Taking Effect.
This [Act] takes effect ____________ and applies to any premarital agreement executed on or after that date.

13. Repeal.
The following acts and parts of acts are repealed:

APPENDIX

A(2)

TEXT OF UNIFORM PREMARITAL AND MARITAL AGREEMENTS

SECTION 1. SHORT TITLE. This [Act] may be cited as the Uniform Premarital and Marital Agreements Act.

SECTION 2. DEFINITIONS. In this [Act]:

(1) "Amendment" means a modification or revocation of a premarital agreement or marital agreement.

(2) "Marital agreement" means an agreement between spouses who intend to remain married which affirms, modifies, or waives a marital right or obligation during the marriage or at separation, marital dissolution, death of one of spouses, or the occurrence or nonoccurrence of any other event. The term includes an amendment, signed after the spouses marry, of a premarital agreement or marital agreement.

(3) "Marital dissolution" means the ending of a marriage by court decree. The term includes a divorce, dissolution, and annulment.

(4) "Marital right or obligation" means any of the following rights or obligations arising between spouses because of their marital status:

 (A) spousal support;

 (B) a right to property, including characterization, management, and ownership;

 (C) responsibility for a liability;

 (D) a right to property and responsibility for liabilities at separation, marital dissolution, or death of a spouse; or

 (E) award and allocation of attorney's fees and costs.

(5) "Premarital agreement" means an agreement between individuals who intend to marry which affirms, modifies, or waives a marital right or obligation during the marriage or at separation, marital dissolution, death of one of the spouses, or the occurrence or nonoccurrence of any

other event. The term includes an amendment, signed before the individuals marry, of a premarital agreement.

(6) "Property" means anything that may be the subject of ownership, whether real or personal, tangible or intangible, legal or equitable, or any interest therein.

(7) "Record" means information that is inscribed on a tangible medium or that is stored in an electronic or other medium and is retrievable in perceivable form.

(8) "Sign" means with present intent to authenticate or adopt a record:

 (A) to execute or adopt a tangible symbol; or

 (B) to attach to or logically associate with the record an electronic symbol, sound, or process.

(9) "State" means a state of the United States, the District of Columbia, Puerto Rico, the United States Virgin Islands, or any territory or insular possession subject to the jurisdiction of the United States.

SECTION 3. SCOPE.

(a) This [Act] applies to a premarital agreement or marital agreement signed on or after [the effective date of this [Act]].

(b) This [Act] does not affect any right, obligation, or liability arising under a premarital agreement or marital agreement signed before [the effective date of this [Act]].

(c) This [Act] does not apply to:

 (1) an agreement between spouses which affirms, modifies, or waives a marital right or obligation and requires court approval to become effective; or

 (2) an agreement between spouses who intend to obtain a marital dissolution or court-decreed separation which resolves their marital rights or obligations and is signed when a proceeding for marital dissolution or court-decreed separation is anticipated or pending.

(d) This [Act] does not affect adversely the rights of a bona fide purchaser for value to the extent that this [Act] applies to a waiver of a marital right or obligation in a transfer or conveyance of property by a spouse to a third party.

SECTION 4. GOVERNING LAW. The validity, enforceability, interpretation, and construction of a premarital agreement or marital agreement are determined:

(1) by the law of the jurisdiction designated in the agreement if the jurisdiction has a significant relationship to the agreement or either party and the designated law is not contrary to a fundamental public policy of this state; or

(2) absent an effective designation described in paragraph (1), by the law of this state, including the choice-of-law rules of this state.

SECTION 5. PRINCIPLES OF LAW AND EQUITY. Unless displaced by a provision of this [Act], principles of law and equity supplement this [Act].

SECTION 6. FORMATION REQUIREMENTS. A premarital agreement or marital agreement must be in a record and signed by both parties. The agreement is enforceable without consideration.

SECTION 7. WHEN AGREEMENT EFFECTIVE. A premarital agreement is effective on marriage. A marital agreement is effective on signing by both parties.

SECTION 8. VOID MARRIAGE. If a marriage is determined to be void, a premarital agreement or marital agreement is enforceable to the extent necessary to avoid an inequitable result.

SECTION 9. ENFORCEMENT.

(a) A premarital agreement or marital agreement is unenforceable if a party against whom enforcement is sought proves:

(1) the party's consent to the agreement was involuntary or the result of duress;

(2) the party did not have access to independent legal representation under subsection (b);

(3) unless the party had independent legal representation at the time the agreement was signed, the agreement did not include a notice of waiver of rights under subsection (c) or an explanation in plain language of the marital rights or obligations being modified or waived by the agreement; or

(4) before signing the agreement, the party did not receive adequate financial disclosure under subsection (d).

(b) A party has access to independent legal representation if:

(1) before signing a premarital or marital agreement, the party has a reasonable time to:

(i) decide whether to retain a lawyer to provide independent legal representation; and

(ii) locate a lawyer to provide independent legal representation, obtain the lawyer's advice, and consider the advice provided; and

(2) the other party is represented by a lawyer and the party has the financial ability to retain a lawyer or the other party agrees to pay the reasonable fees and expenses of independent legal representation.

(c) A notice of waiver of rights under this section requires language, conspicuously displayed, substantially similar to the following, as applicable to the premarital agreement or marital agreement:

"If you sign this agreement, you may be:

Giving up your right to be supported by the person you are marrying or to whom you are married.

Giving up your right to ownership or control of money and property.

Agreeing to pay bills and debts of the person you are marrying or to whom you are married.
Giving up your right to money and property if your marriage ends or the person to whom you are married dies.
Giving up your right to have your legal fees paid."

(d) A party has adequate financial disclosure under this section if the party:
   (1) receives a reasonably accurate description and good-faith estimate of value of the property, liabilities, and income of the other party;
   (2) expressly waives, in a separate signed record, the right to financial disclosure beyond the disclosure provided; or
   (3) has adequate knowledge or a reasonable basis for having adequate knowledge of the information described in paragraph (1).

(e) If a premarital agreement or marital agreement modifies or eliminates spousal support and the modification or elimination causes a party to the agreement to be eligible for support under a program of public assistance at the time of separation or marital dissolution, a court, on request of that party, may require the other party to provide support to the extent necessary to avoid that eligibility.

(f) A court may refuse to enforce a term of a premarital agreement or marital agreement if, in the context of the agreement taken as a whole[:]
   (1) the term was unconscionable at the time of signing[; or
   (2) enforcement of the term would result in substantial hardship for a party because of a material change in circumstances arising after the agreement was signed].

(g) The court shall decide a question of unconscionability [or substantial hardship] under subsection (f) as a matter of law.

SECTION 10. UNENFORCEABLE TERMS.

(a) In this section, "custodial responsibility" means physical or legal custody, parenting time, access, visitation, or other custodial right or duty with respect to a child.

(b) A term in a premarital agreement or marital agreement is not enforceable to the extent that it:
   (1) adversely affects a child's right to support;
   (2) limits or restricts a remedy available to a victim of domestic violence under law of this state other than this [Act];
   (3) purports to modify the grounds for a court-decreed separation or marital dissolution available under law of this state other than this [Act]; or
   (4) penalizes a party for initiating a legal proceeding leading to a court-decreed separation or marital dissolution.

(c) A term in a premarital agreement or marital agreement which defines the rights or duties of the parties regarding custodial responsibility is not binding on the court.

SECTION 11. LIMITATION OF ACTION. A statute of limitations applicable to an action asserting a claim for relief under a premarital agreement or marital agreement is tolled during the marriage of the parties to the agreement, but equitable defenses limiting the time for enforcement, including laches and estoppel, are available to either party.

SECTION 12. UNIFORMITY OF APPLICATION AND CONSTRUCTION. In applying and construing this uniform Act, consideration must be given to the need to promote uniformity of the law with respect to its subject matter among states that enact it.

SECTION 13. RELATION TO ELECTRONIC SIGNATURES IN GLOBAL AND NATIONAL COMMERCE ACT. This [Act] modifies, limits, or supersedes the Electronic Signatures in Global and National Commerce Act, 15 U.S.C. Section 7001 et seq., but does not modify, limit, or supersede Section 101(c) of that act, 15 U.S.C. Section 7001(c), or authorize electronic delivery of any of the notices described in Section 103(b) of that act, 15 U.S.C. Section 7003(b).

[SECTION 14. REPEALS. CONFORMING AMENDMENTS.]

(a) [Uniform Premarital Agreement Act] is repealed.

(b) [Uniform Probate Code Section 2-213 (Waiver of Right to Elect and of Other Rights)] is repealed.

SECTION 15. EFFECTIVE DATE. This [Act] takes effect . . . .

Appendix B(1)

State Law Summary—Premarital Agreements

State	UPAA	Post-Divorce Spousal Support Waiver Enforceable	2d Look at Divorce	Key Statutes and Cases
Alabama		Y		Ala. Code § 8-9-2(4) (2022) (Statute of Frauds; agreement on consideration of marriage must be in writing); § 43-8-72 (2022) (right of election of surviving spouse, homestead allowance, exempt property and family allowance can be waived by written contract); *Brown v. Brown*, 26 So. 3d 1222 (Ala. 2009) (premarital agreement must be fair or be entered into voluntarily with competent independent advice and knowledge of financial affairs); *Barnhill v. Barnhill*, 386 So. 2d 749, 751 (Ala. Civ. App.), *cert. denied*, 386 So. 2d 752 (Ala. 1980) (mutual waivers of rights can be adequate consideration even when one party's property is more valuable); *Ex parte Walters*, 580 So. 2d 1352 (Ala. 1991) (alimony waiver enforceable; attorney fees may be waived unless inequitable and unjustified); *Woolwine v. Woolwine*, 549 So. 2d 512 (Ala. Civ. App. 1989) (spousal support waiver upheld; trial court had discretion to award attorney fees); *Klyce v. Klyce*, 429 So. 2d 1081 (Ala. Civ. App. 1983) (waiver of legal fees must be express).
Alaska	Y	Y	Y	Alaska Stat. § 13.12.213 (2022) (rights of surviving spouse can be waived before marriage by written agreement executed voluntarily and, if unconscionable, with fair and reasonable financial disclosure, adequate knowledge, or express waiver of disclosure); § 25.24.160(e) (2022) (at divorce court distributes property not disposed of in community property agreement); § 34.77.030 (2022) (premarital community property agreement may classify property as individual property or as community property); § 34.77.090 (2022) (premarital community property agreement may determine property rights at death or divorce; not enforceable if executed involuntarily, or unconscionable and no financial disclosure, express waiver or constructive knowledge); *Andrew B. v. Abbie B.*, 494 P.3d 522 (Alaska 2021) (confidential relationship requires court to consider recipient's time to consider, access to counsel, and ability to understand terms); *Brooks v. Brooks*, 733 P.2d 1044 (Alaska 1987) (premarital agreement generally enforceable if properly procured; not enforceable at divorce where facts and circumstances changed since execution); *Beal v. Beal*, 88 P.3d 104 (Alaska 2004) (spousal support can be waived in premarital agreement; interim support is waivable; waiver must be express).
Arizona	Y	Y		Ariz. Rev. Stat. §§ 25-201–25-205 (2022) (UPAA, eff. 3.25.91) (criteria for award of spousal support over waiver is welfare eligibility); § 14-2207 (2022) (surviving spouse rights may be waived by written contract before marriage); *Smith v. Tang*, 412 P.2d 697 (Ariz. 1966) (agreement to waive widow's allowance must be clear and explicit to be valid); *Schlaefer v. Financial Mgt. Svc. Inc.*, 196 Ariz. 336, 996 P.2d 745 (2000) (parties can prospectively abrogate community debt in premarital agreement; creditor of one spouse has no claim against other spouse for payment of debt incurred during marriage); *Soldwedel v. Soldwedel*, 2021 Ariz. App. Unpub. LEXIS 688 (contractual fee-shifting to losing party violates public policy; but court can make fee award to prevailing party under statute permitting award in court's discretion).
Arkansas	Y+	Y		Ark. Code Ann. §§ 9-11-401–9-11-413 (2022) (UPAA, eff. 8.20.87) (requires actual advice of counsel to waive financial disclosure; criteria for award of spousal support over waiver is welfare eligibility); § 9-11-301 (2022) (marriage contract must be in writing and acknowledged by parties or witnessed by one or more subscribing witnesses); *Medlock v. Fort Smith Service Finance Corp.*, 803 S.W.2d 930 (Ark. 1991) (W not liable for necessaries under statute).

State	UPAA	Post-Divorce Spousal Support Waiver Enforceable	2d Look at Divorce	Key Statutes and Cases
California	Y+	Y	Y (only as to spousal support)	Cal. Fam. Code §§ 1610–1617 (2022) (UPAA, eff. 1.1.86; amended, eff. 1.1.02, 1.1.20); § 1615(c) (agreement deemed involuntary unless party represented by counsel or advised of right and expressly waived in separate signed writing; no less than 7 days between receipt of final agreement and execution, whether or not party is represented; unrepresented party fully informed in writing of terms and effect and rights and obligations he/she gives up, proficient in language of agreement and explanation of rights; explanation delivered to party prior to signing, and signed acknowledgment of receipt; agreement and separate waivers not signed under duress, fraud, undue influence, or lack of capacity); § 1612 (support provision, including waiver, not enforceable if party against whom enforcement is sought [1] did not have advice of independent counsel or [2] unconscionable at divorce); Prob. Code § 147 (2022) (parties may waive rights at death in premarital agreement); Fam. Code § 720 (2022) (spouses contract obligation of mutual support); Cal. Fam. Code § 4300 (2022) (subject to certain other statutory provisions, person shall support spouse); Cal. Fam. Code § 4301 (2022) (married person shall support spouse while living together); *In re Marriage of Pendleton and Fireman*, 99 Cal. Rptr. 2d 278, 5 P.3d 839 (2000) (spousal support waiver not per se unenforceable).
Colorado		Y	Y (only as to spousal support)	Colo. Rev. Stat. §§ 14-2-301–14-2-313 (2022) (Uniform Premarital and Marital Agreements Act (UPMAA), eff. 7.1.14) (parties may contract re disposition of property at death or divorce; parties may contract re support and attorney's fees provided not unconscionable at enforcement; must be voluntary, with access to counsel, or notice of rights, and after adequate financial disclosure); § 15-11-213 (2022) (affirmation, modification, or waiver of marital right or obligation is only enforceable if contained in premarital or marital agreement compliant with UPMAA); *Newman v. Newman*, 653 P.2d 728 (Colo. 1982) (unconscionability not ground to void premarital agreement as a whole); *In re Marriage of Dechant*, 867 P.2d 193 (Colo. Ct. App. 1993) (support waiver unconscionable if results in spouse having insufficient property to meet reasonable needs; fee waiver may become unconscionable); *In re Marriage of Ikeler*, 161 P.3d 663 (Colo. 2007) (court can review attorney fee waiver for unconscionability at divorce); *In re Marriage of Christen*, 899 P.2d 339 (Colo. Ct. App. 1995) (wealthier spouse sought finding of invalidity; court is obligated to enforce clear term of premarital agreement requiring loser to pay fees).
Connecticut	Y+	Y	Y	Conn. Gen. Stat. §§ 46b-36a to 46b-36j (2022) (UPAA, eff. 10.1.95) (premarital agreement must be voluntary, made after full disclosure, with opportunity to consult independent counsel, and not unconscionable at execution or enforcement; criteria for award of spousal support over waiver is welfare eligibility); § 46b-37 (2022) (spouses have mutual duty of support during marriage; both spouses liable for necessaries including medical); *McHugh v. McHugh*, 181 Conn. 482, 436 A.2d 8 (1980) (provision waiving right to support during ongoing marriage violates public policy) (*dicta*); *Scharer v. Scharer*, 2001 Conn. Super. Lexis 2140 (premarital agreement waiving post-divorce spousal support does not preclude award payable while validity of agreement is litigated); *Montoya v. Montoya*, 91 Conn. App. 407, 881 A.2d 319 (2005), *rev'd in part on other grounds*, 280 Conn. 605, 909 A.2d 947 (2006) (premarital agreement fee waiver and prevailing party provisions were enforceable where agreement valid); *Bevilacqua v. Bevilacqua*, 201 Conn. App. 261, 242 A.3d 542 (2020) (spousal support waiver unenforceable where W injured in auto accident and unable to return to usual profession).

State	UPAA	Post-Divorce Spousal Support Waiver Enforceable	2d Look at Divorce	Key Statutes and Cases
Delaware	Y	Y		13 Del. Code Ann. §§ 321–328 (2022) (UPAA, eff. 9.1.96) (silent on criteria for award of spousal support over waiver); § 12-905 (2022) (spouses can waive right of election by written contract before marriage); § 13-502 (2022) (duty to support spouse rests on other spouse); *Silverman v. Silverman*, 206 A.3d 825 (Del. 2019) (challenging party must prove both nondisclosure and unconscionability).
District of Columbia	Y	Y		D.C. Code Ann. §§ 46-501–46-510 (2022) (UPAA, eff. 2.9.96) (criteria for award of spousal support over waiver is welfare eligibility) § 16-910 (2022) (parties can exclude property from marital estate by valid agreement); § 46-601 (b)(2) (2022) (both spouses liable on debt for necessaries; § 16-916 (2022) (party can be ordered to support needy spouse).
Florida	Y	Y		Fla. Stat. Ann. § 61.079 (2022) (UPAA, eff. 10.1.07) (premarital agreement unenforceable if not signed voluntarily, or was the product of fraud, duress, coercion or overreaching, or unconscionable and no financial disclosure or effective waiver); § 732.702 (2022) (rights of surviving spouse can be waived in contract before marriage signed in presence of two witnesses; no consideration required except execution; no financial disclosure required for premarital waiver); *Posner v. Posner*, 237 So. 2d 186 (Fla. Dist. Ct. App. 1970) (parties can contract re post-divorce support); *Belcher v. Belcher*, 271 So. 2d 7 (Fla. 1972) (parties may not contract re pre-divorce support; premarital agreement provisions for spouse are factor in determining need but not conclusive); *Lashkajani v. Lashkajani*, 911 So. 2d 1154 (Fla. 2005) (prevailing party clause enforceable when challenge to validity lacked merit; distinction between fees incurred to protect agreement itself, and fees incurred while litigation is pending, which is a form of nonwaivable temporary spousal support); *Lord v. Lord*, 993 So. 2d 562 (Fla. Ct. App. 2008) (long-standing policy against enforcement of attorney fee waiver intact); *Blanton v. Blanton*, 654 So. 2d 1240 (Fla. Dist. Ct. App. 1995) (duty of support during marriage includes fees incurred to challenge premarital agreement validity when normal criteria for award met; abuse of discretion not to award where result of premarital agreement validity was harsh).
Georgia		Y	Y	Ga. Code Ann. §§ 19-3-62–19-3-64 (2022) (parties can enter into premarital agreement; must be in writing, signed by parties, attested by two witnesses, including notary, and must be voluntary); § 13-5-30 (2022) (Statute of Frauds; premarital agreement must be in writing); *Sullivan v. Sullivan*, 286 Ga. 53, 684 S.E.2d 861 (2009) (premarital agreement provisions for rights at death not valid without two witnesses; statutory requirement strictly construed); *Scherer v. Scherer*, 249 Ga. 635, 292 S.E.2d 662 (1982) (premarital agreement must be executed voluntarily after adequate disclosure, and result must not be unconscionable; parties can contract re spousal support); *Sieg v. Sieg*, 265 Ga. 384, 455 S.E.2d 830 (1995) (premarital agreement can control disposition of property at death); *Langley v. Langley*, 279 Ga. 374, 613 S.E.2d 614 (2005) (temporary spousal support not waivable).
Hawaii	Y	Y		Haw. Rev. Stat. §§ 572D-1–572D-10 (2022) (UPAA, eff. 7.1.87) (criteria for award of spousal support over waiver is welfare eligibility); *L.R.O. v. N.D.O.*, 148 Haw. 336, 475 P.3d 1167 (2020) (voluntariness is to be judged using factors adopted from California case law: proximity of execution to wedding; surprise in presentation; independent counsel or opportunity for legal advice; inequality of bargaining power; financial disclosure; understanding of rights being waived).

State	UPAA	Post-Divorce Spousal Support Waiver Enforceable	2d Look at Divorce	Key Statutes and Cases
Idaho	Y	Y		Idaho Code §§ 32-921–32-929 (2022) (UPAA, eff. 3.20.95) (criteria for award of spousal support over waiver is welfare eligibility); § 32-917 (2022) (contract for marriage settlement must be in writing and executed as land conveyance); § 32-712 (2022) (factors court must consider in division of community property at divorce include any premarital agreement of parties, but court has no authority to amend or rescind agreement); § 32-901 (2022) (spouses contract toward each other obligations of mutual respect, fidelity and support); *Dunagan v. Dunagan*, 147 Ida. 599, 213 P.3d 384 (2009) (agreement that purports to characterize community property as separate property must meet strict statutory formalities); *State of Idaho v. Suiter*, 138 Idaho 662, 67 P.3d 1274 (2003) (§ 32-901 precludes enforcement of waiver of spousal obligation of support during marriage); *Kelly v. Kelly*, 518 P.3d 326 (Idaho 2022) (waiver of attorney's fees at divorce unenforceable as to fees for custody and child support).
Illinois	Y	Y	Y (only as to spousal support)	750 Ill. Comp. Stat. §§ 10/1–10/11 (2022) (UPAA, eff. 1.1.90); § 10/7(b) (2022) (court may award support over waiver if waiver causes undue hardship not reasonably foreseeable at execution); 750-5/503 (2022) (marital property at divorce does not include property excluded by valid premarital agreement); 750-65/15 (2022) (spouses jointly liable to third-party creditors for expenses of family); *Barnes v. Barnes*, 324 Ill. App. 3d 514, 755 N.E.2d 522 (2001) (wife's hardship at end of marriage was foreseeable where parties had gross disparity in income at execution; hardship not undue where she was employed at divorce); *Eule v. Eule*, 24 Ill. App. 3d 83, 320 N.E.2d 506 (1974) (spouse cannot avoid support obligation during marriage by premarital agreement); *Warren v. Warren*, 169 Ill. App. 3d 226, 523 N.E.2d 680 (1988) (fee waiver unenforceable where support waiver not fair at divorce); *In re Marriage of Cullman*, 185 Ill. App. 3d 1029, 541 N.E.2d 1274 (1989) (fee waiver must be express).
Indiana	Y+	Y	Y (only as to spousal support)	Ind. Code §§ 31-11-3-1 to 31-11-3-10 (2022) (UPAA, eff. 7.1.95) (premarital agreement not enforceable if [1] not executed voluntarily; or [2] unconscionable at execution; agreement can determine disposition of property at death or divorce; agreement can waive spousal support, but court can award if waiver causes one party extreme hardship not reasonably foreseeable); § 29-1-2-13 (2022) (spouse rights at death can be waived before marriage in written agreement; in absence of fraud, promise of marriage is sufficient consideration); *Boetsma v. Boetsma*, 768 N.E.2d 1016 (Ind. Ct. App. 2002); § 35-46-1-6 (2022) (criminal failure to support needy spouse).
Iowa	Y+	N		Iowa Code §§ 596.1–596.12 (2022) (UPAA, eff. 1.1.92) (premarital agreement is unenforceable if challenging party proves [1] executed involuntarily; or [2] unconscionable at execution; or [3] challenger did not receive financial disclosure and did not have actual or constructive knowledge; right to spousal support not waivable); *In re Estate of Spurgeon*, 572 N.W.2d 595 (Iowa 1998) (spouse can waive elective share; court can award spousal support after death for 12 months as part of administration under probate code; award is discretionary); *In re Estate of Thompson*, 812 N.W.2d 726 (Iowa Ct. App. 2012) (probate court can award spousal allowance despite waiver in premarital agreement); *Huegli v. Huegli*, 884 N.W.2d 223 (Iowa Ct. App. 2016) (court cannot consider parties' intent, as stated in premarital agreement, to waive spousal support in making support award over unenforceable waiver).

State	UPAA	Post-Divorce Spousal Support Waiver Enforceable	2d Look at Divorce	Key Statutes and Cases
Kansas	Y	Y		Kan. Stat. Ann. §§ 23-2401–23-2411 (2022) (UPAA, eff. 5.9.88) (criteria for award of spousal support over waiver is welfare eligibility); § 59-6a 213 (2022) (surviving spouse rights can be waived in agreement before marriage; validity criteria same as UPAA; waiver of homestead, homestead allowance, or family allowance must be express and made understandably and knowledgeably); *In re Broadie's Estate*, 493 P.2d 289 (Kan. 1972) (valid premarital agreement controls disposition of surviving spouse's portion of decedent's estate).
Kentucky		Y	Y	Ky. Rev. Stat. Ann. § 403.190 (2022) (no equitable distribution of property excluded by valid agreement); Ky. Rev. Stat. Ann. § 404.040 (2022) (husband liable for necessaries provided to wife during marriage); § 530.050 (2022) (criminal nonsupport of indigent spouse); *Edwardson v. Edwardson*, 798 S.W.2d 941 (Ky. 1990) (premarital agreement must be executed voluntarily following adequate disclosure, and result must not be unconscionable; premarital agreement can waive support after divorce); *Gentry v. Gentry*, 798 S.W.2d 928, 934 (Ky. 1990) (spouses can by agreement define rights in each other's property at divorce); *Lane v. Lane*, 202 S.W.3d 577 (Ky. 2006) (court can modify support waiver to require post-divorce support where waiver unconscionable or unfair and unreasonable at enforcement); *Atkins v. Atkins*, 203 Ky. 291, 262 S.W. 268 (1924) (premarital agreement making each party liable for own necessaries during marriage valid between parties but not binding on third-party creditors).
Louisiana		Y		La. Civ. Code Ann. Art. 2328–2330 (2022) (parties can establish separate property regime; parties may enter into agreement before marriage for any matter not prohibited by law; parties may not renounce or alter marital portion or established order of succession; agreement may not with respect to third party limit right of one spouse to obligate community or alienate, encumber, or lease community property); Art. 2371 (2022) (under separate property regime, each spouse can use own property without consent of other spouse); La. Civ. Code Ann. art. 2372–2373 (2022) (spouses contribute to marital expenses in accordance with marital agreement; each spouse liable with other for necessaries for spouse/family); art. 98 (2022) (married persons owe each other fidelity, support, and assistance); *McAlpine v. McAlpine*, 679 So. 2d 85 (La. 1996) (premarital agreement can waive spousal support); *Vogt v. Vogt*, 831 So. 2d 428 (La. App. 2002) (premarital agreement fixing support at specified percent of husband's income, provided wife not guilty of adultery, is permissible); *Hall v. Hall*, 4 So. 3d 254 (La. App. 2009) (premarital agreement may not relieve spouse of duty to support during marriage).
Maine	Y	Y		19-A Me. Rev. Stat. Ann. §§ 601–611 (2022) (UPAA, eff. 6.15.87) (criteria for award of spousal support over waiver is welfare eligibility); 18-C §2-213 (2022) (spouses can waive right of election in premarital agreement); § 19-A-1652 (2022) (spouses are obligated to support one another if able); § 22-4319 (2022) (liability for support of spouse); *In re Estate of Martin*, 938 A.2d 812 (Me. 2008) (common law presumption of fraud where provisions for surviving spouse are disproportionate abrogated by UPAA); *Riemann v. Toland*, 269 A.3d 229 (Me. 2022) (parties can waive attorney's fees at divorce in PMA; but not as to fees to determine custody).

State	UPAA	Post-Divorce Spousal Support Waiver Enforceable	2d Look at Divorce	Key Statutes and Cases
Maryland		Y		Md. Code Ann., Est. & Trusts § 3-205 (2022) (right of election can be waived before marriage by written agreement); Fam. Law. § 11-101(c) (2022) (court bound by agreement of parties regarding spousal support); Md. Code Ann., Fam. Law § 8-201(c)–(e) (2022) (family home and tangible personalty not awardable to custodial parent if excluded by valid agreement; parties can exclude property from marital estate at divorce by valid agreement); *Stewart v. Stewart,* 214 Md. App. 458, 76 A.3d 1221 (2013) (proponent must prove agreement not the result of overreaching; full, frank and truthful disclosure proves no overreaching); *Cannon v. Cannon*, 384 Md. 537, 865 A.2d 563 (2005) (premarital agreement must either be fair to disadvantaged party or executed voluntarily with fair financial disclosure); *Frey v. Frey*, 298 Md. 552, 471 A.2d 705 (1984) (parties can contract in premarital agreement re property at divorce; parties can contract re post-divorce spousal support; validity of temporary support waiver turns on validity of premarital agreement).
Massachusetts		Y	Y	Mass Laws. Ann., ch. 259, § 1 (2016) (Statute of Frauds; agreement on consideration of marriage must be in signed writing); ch. 209, § 25. (2022), (parties may make written premarital agreement regarding property rights); ch. 209, § 32F (2022) (court may order support to spouse living apart from spouse); *DeMatteo v. DeMatteo*, 436 Mass. 18, 762 N.E.2d 797 (2002) (premarital agreement must be executed voluntarily after adequate disclosure, and result must be fair and reasonable); *Osborne v. Osborne*, 384 Mass. 591, 428 N.E.2d 810 (1981) (premarital agreement settling spousal support at divorce may be modified if spouse will become public charge; left open validity of provision that purports to limit duty of spouse to support other during marriage).
Michigan		Y	Y	Mich. Comp. Laws Serv. § 557.28 (2022) (contract re property between persons in contemplation of marriage is valid after marriage); § 700.2205 (2022) (surviving spouse rights can be waived in written contract before marriage with fair disclosure); §§ 401.1, 401.3 (2022) (spouse must support poor spouse); *In re Estate of Muxlow*, 367 Mich. 133, 116 N.W.2d 43 (1962) (premarital agreement re disposition of property at death is valid); *In re Estate of Benker*, 416 Mich. 681, 331 N.W.2d 193 (1982) (premarital agreement must be executed voluntarily after adequate disclosure and result must be fair); *Woodington v. Shokoohi,* 288 Mich. App. 352, 792 N.W.2d 63 (2010) (premarital agreements providing for division of property at divorce are generally enforceable); *Hutchison v. Hutchison*, 2009 Mich. App. Lexis 1594 (unpub,) (premarital agreement unenforceable due to unforeseeable changed circumstances, husband's physical abuse of wife and harassment to quit work, making her financially dependent; spousal support properly awarded despite waiver); *Mason v. Gutierrez-Mason*, 2007 Mich. App. Lexis 1273 (unpub.) (spousal support waiver in premarital agreement was enforceable); *Rinvelt v. Rinvelt*, 190 Mich. App. 372, 475 N.W.2d 478 (1991) (parties may resolve spousal support in premarital agreement).

State	UPAA	Post-Divorce Spousal Support Waiver Enforceable	2d Look at Divorce	Key Statutes and Cases
Minnesota		Y	Y	Minn. Stat. Ann. § 519.11 (2022) (premarital agreement valid to determine rights to nonmarital property at death or dissolution (a) with full disclosure of earnings and property, (b) parties had opportunity to consult with counsel of their choice); § 518.003 (2022) (at divorce, nonmarital property includes property excluded from marital estate by valid premarital contract); *Kremer v. Kremer*, 912 N.W.2d 617 (Minn. 2018) (§ 519.11 creates procedural safe harbor for provisions re nonmarital property; agreement terms determining disposition of marital property must comply with common law test: (1) full and fair disclosure; (2) adequate consideration; (3) knowledge of terms, how terms impacted rights in the absence of agreement; (4) not procured by abuse of fiduciary relations, undue influence or duress); *In re Marriage of Mazzitelli*, 2005 Minn. App. Lexis 125 (unpub.) (property disposition terms of premarital agreement unfair where wife stayed home with children for 10 years); *McKee-Johnson v. Johnson*, 444 N.W.2d 259 (Minn. 1989) (proponent of agreement has burden of proving procedural and substantive fairness); *Hill v. Hill*, 356 N.W.2d 49 (Minn. Ct. App. 1984) (premarital agreement re support generally enforceable but subject to revision if unconscionable at divorce; trial court may award fees if necessary for substantial justice despite waiver of fees in premarital agreement).
Mississippi		N	Y	Miss. Code Ann. § 15-3-1 (2022) (Statute of Frauds); *Estate of Hensley v. Estate of Hensley*, 524 So. 2d 325 (Miss. 1988) (premarital agreement can dispose of property at death); *Mabus v. Mabus*, 890 So. 2d 806 (Miss. 2003) (criteria for determining spousal support under premarital agreement with waiver is same as applies if agreement has no waiver).
Missouri		Y		Mo. Rev. Stat. § 452.330(2) (2022) (excludes property from division at divorce that is subject of valid agreement); § 451.220 (2022) (marriage contract must be in writing and acknowledged or proved); § 474.220 (2022) (rights at death can be waived before marriage by written contract or signed waiver, with full disclosure and fair consideration); § 568.040 (2022) (criminal nonsupport); *Miles v. Werle*, 977 S.W.2d 297 (Mo. Ct. App. 1998) (premarital agreement must be executed voluntarily after adequate disclosure and not be substantively unconscionable at execution); *Dardick v. Dardick*, 948 S.W.2d 268 (Mo. Ct. App. 1997) (parties may exclude property from marital estate at divorce by valid agreement); *McMullin v. McMullin*, 926 S.W.2d 108 (Mo. Ct. App. 1996) (premarital agreement waiving all interest in marital property is unenforceable); *Gould v. Rafaeli*, 822 S.W.2d 494 (Mo. Ct. App. 1991) (premarital agreement waiving spousal support enforceable); *Darr v. Darr*, 950 S.W.2d 867 (Mo. Ct. App. 1997) (validity of temporary support waiver depends on validity of premarital agreement; attorney fee waiver not per se violation of public policy; court determines if waiver fair based on economic circumstances at divorce); *Hawley v. Hawley*, 904 S.W.2d 584 (Mo. Ct. App. 1995) (questionable whether premarital agreement can waive third-party claim for necessaries).
Montana	Y	Y		Mont. Code Ann. §§ 40-2-601–40-2-610 (2021) (UPAA, eff. 10.1.87) (criteria for award of spousal support over waiver is welfare eligibility); § 72-2-224 (2021) (prospective spouse may waive right of election, homestead allowance, and exempt property in written contract); § 40-2-101 (2021) (marriage is contract for respect, fidelity, and support); §§ 40-2-103, -104, -106 (2021) (spouses liable to third parties for cost of necessities, except if abandoned); § 40-2-301 (2021) (spouses can contract re property rights subject to rules governing confidential relations); § 45-5-621 (2021) (criminal nonsupport).

State	UPAA	Post-Divorce Spousal Support Waiver Enforceable	2d Look at Divorce	Key Statutes and Cases
Nebraska	Y	Y		Neb. Rev. Stat. §§ 42-1001–42-1011 (2022) (UPAA, eff. 3.25.94); (criteria for award of spousal support over waiver is welfare eligibility); § 42-362 (2022) (spouse must provide for mentally ill spouse even after divorce); § 42-201 (2022) (nonexempt property of wife, except 90% of wages, liable for necessaries); *Mamot v. Mamot,* 283 Neb. 659, 813 N.W.2d 440 (2012) (wife signed premarital agreement under duress where husband presented agreement and told her must sign that day); *Edwards v. Edwards*, 16 Neb. App. 297, 744 N.W.2d 243 (2008) (Nebraska UPAA permits limit on temporary spousal support).
Nevada	Y+	Y		Nev. Rev. Stat. Ann. §§ 123A.010–123A.100 (2021) (UPAA, eff. 6.24.89) (premarital agreement invalid if involuntary, or unconscionable, or no financial disclosure or effective waiver; criteria for award of spousal support over waiver is welfare eligibility); § 146.005 (2021) (valid premarital agreement prevails over statutory spousal rights at death); § 201.020 (2021) (criminal nonsupport); *Dimick v. Dimick*, 112 Nev. 402, 915 P.2d 254 (1996) (husband ordered to pay house note to fulfill support obligation during marriage; husband not entitled to set-off against post-divorce support owed wife under premarital agreement; fee shift to loser generally enforceable); *Hutchins v. Hutchins*, 430 P.3d 502 (Mont. 2018) (under Nevada version of UPAA, per parties' choice of law, challenger must prove signed involuntarily, or unconscionable at execution or no financial disclosure or effective waiver).
New Hampshire		Y	Y	N.H. Rev. Stat. Ann. §§ 460:2-a (2022) (man and woman in contemplation of marriage may enter into written interspousal contract); § 458:52 (2022) (right of persons to enter into enforceable premarital agreement concerning property rights); § 458:16-a (2022) (in determining equitable division of marital property, court can consider value of property allocated by premarital agreement); *MacFarlane v. Rich*, 132 N.H. 608, 567 A.2d 585 (1989) (premarital agreement must be voluntary with full disclosure, and result must not be unconscionable); *In re Estate of Hollett*, 150 N.H. 39, 834 A.2d 348 (2003); *Yannalfo v. Yannalfo*, 147 N.H. 597, 794 A.2d 795 (2002) (provisions may become unenforceable if circumstances at divorce so far beyond contemplation of parties that enforcement unconscionable).
New Jersey	Y+	Y		N.J. Stat. Ann. §§ 37:2-31 to 37:2-41 (2022) (UPAA, eff. 11.3.88; amended 2007, 2013) (party challenging enforceability of premarital agreement must prove by clear and convincing evidence that [1] agreement executed involuntarily or [2] agreement was unconscionable because of no financial disclosure, waiver of disclosure, adequate knowledge, counsel, or waiver of counsel; statement of assets must be annexed to agreement; parties can waive spousal support); § 3B:8-10 (2022) (spouse or domestic partner can waive elective share in signed agreement before marriage with fair disclosure); § 2C:24-5 (2022) (criminal nonsupport); N.J. Stat. Ann. § 2C:62-1 (2022) (court can order temporary support after spouse charged with willful nonsupport).

State	UPAA	Post-Divorce Spousal Support Waiver Enforceable	2d Look at Divorce	Key Statutes and Cases
New Mexico	Y	N		N.M. Stat. Ann. §§ 40-3A-1–40-3A-10 (2022) (UPAA, eff. 7.1.95) (premarital agreement may not adversely affect right to spousal support; premarital agreement may be amended or revoked by consistent course of conduct); § 45-2-407 (2022) (spouse may waive statutory surviving spouse rights by agreement); § 30-6-2 (2022) (criminal failure to support); § 40-2-1 (2022) (marriage contract is obligation of support, fidelity, and respect); *Lebeck v. Lebeck*, 118 N.M. 367, 881 P.2d 727 (Ct. App. 1994) (fee waiver in premarital agreement is not enforceable; trial court award of fees for meritorious claims and denial of fees for nonmeritorious claims upheld).
New York		Y	Y (only as to spousal support)	N.Y. CLS Dom. Rel. § 236(B)(1)(d) (2022) (at divorce separate property includes property defined as such by written agreement); § 236(B)(3), (5) (premarital agreement must be in writing subscribed and acknowledged in manner required for recordation of deed; parties can contract re disposition of property at death or divorce; parties can contract re support; support waiver must be fair at execution and not unconscionable at divorce); § 236(B) (5-a) (except where parties entered into agreement for maintenance, court shall order presumptive amount of temporary maintenance under guideline, and may depart upon consideration of factors, including acts of domestic violence that inhibit a party's earning capacity); N.Y. Gen. Oblig. Law § 5-311 (2022) (except as provided in Dom. Rel. Law § 236, spouses cannot contract to relieve each other of liability for support if likely to make spouse a public charge); N.Y. Est. Powers & Trusts Law § 5-1.1(b) (2022) (spouse can waive elective share before or after marriage; in writing, subscribed and acknowledged); N.Y. Gen. Oblig. Law § 3-303 (2022) (contract in contemplation of marriage in full force after marriage); N.Y. Soc. Serv. Law § 101 (2022) (spouse liable to state for support); N.Y. Fam. Ct. Act § 412 (2022) (spouse has duty to support spouse); *Panossian v. Panossian*, 172 A.D.2d 811, 569 N.Y.S.2d 182 (1991) (criteria for spousal support award over waiver); *Medical Business Associates v. Steiner*, 183 A.D.2d 86, 588 N.Y.S.2d 890 (1992) (recipient has primary liability for necessaries); *Tregellas v. Tregellas*, 169 A.D.2d 553, 564 N.Y.S.2d 406 (1991) (temporary support waiver must be express); *Koons v. Koons*, 212 A.D.2d 370, 622 N.Y.S.2d 242 (1995) (temporary fees not barred by premarital agreement waiver of fees in event of divorce); *Kessler v. Kessler*, 33 A.D. 3d 42, 818 N.Y.S. 2d 571 (2006) (court can award fees to litigate property rights under a premarital agreement where waiver was unconscionable due to vast disparity in resources).
North Carolina	Y	Y		N.C. Gen. Stat. §§ 52B-1–52B-11 (2022) (UPAA eff. 7.1.87) (criteria for spousal support award is welfare eligibility); § 30-3.6 (2022) (right of surviving spouse to elective share waivable before marriage, with or without consideration, by written waiver signed by spouse; not enforceable if not executed voluntarily, or no fair financial disclosure and no waiver of disclosure in writing); § 52-10(a) (2022) (parties about to marry may release rights they would otherwise acquire by marriage); § 30-15 (2022) (surviving spouse entitled to one-year allowance unless forfeited by valid agreement); § 14-322 (2022) (criminal nonsupport); *Perkins v. Brinkley*, 45 S.E. 465 (N.C. 1903) (premarital agreement can waive one-year allowance at death); *Motley v. Motley*, 255 N.C. 190, 120 S.E.2d 422 (1961) (premarital agreement unenforceable insofar as waives temporary spousal support; premarital agreement unenforceable insofar as waives attorney's fees incurred before divorce); *Kuder v. Schroeder*, 110 N.C. App. 355, 430 S.E.2d 271 (1993) (spouses have duty to support each other during marriage which cannot be abrogated by agreement).

State	UPAA	Post-Divorce Spousal Support Waiver Enforceable	2d Look at Divorce	Key Statutes and Cases
North Dakota		Y	Y	N.D. Cent. Code §§ 14-03.2-01 to 14-03.2-11 (2021) (UPMAA eff. 8.1.13) (court may refuse enforcement of term to avoid substantial hardship because of material change in circumstances; criteria for award of spousal support over waiver is welfare eligibility); § 14-07-08 (2021) (spouses jointly liable for debts for necessaries incurred while living together); § 14-07-03 (2021) (spouses have duty of support); § 14-07-10 (2021) (spouses mutually liable for necessaries); *Sailer v. Sailer*, 764 N.W.2d 445 (N.D. 2009) (premarital agreement was voluntary where wife had time to review and declined counsel); *Lutz v. Lutz*, 563 N.W.2d 90 (N.D. 1997) (substantive effect of premarital agreement voluntarily and validly obtained may be unconscionable and therefore unenforceable).
Ohio		Y	Y (only as to spousal support)	Ohio Rev. Code Ann. § 1335.05 (2022) (Statute of Frauds); § 3105.171(A)(6)(a)(v) (2022) (separate property at divorce includes all property excluded by valid premarital agreement); § 3103.03 (2022) (duty to support self and spouse; third party may recover reasonable value of necessaries supplied to spouse); *Fletcher v. Fletcher*, 68 Ohio St. 3d 464, 628 N.E.2d 1343 (1994) (premarital agreement must be fair or must be executed voluntarily with opportunity for independent advice and full knowledge); *Gross v. Gross*, 11 Ohio St. 3d 99, 464 N.E.2d 500 (1984) (premarital agreement re disposition of property at divorce and death recognized; must satisfy 3 special conditions beyond basic requirements of any contract: [1] voluntary, without fraud, duress or overreaching; [2] full disclosure or knowledge; [3] terms must not promote divorce or profiteering by divorce; spousal support provision is enforceable unless changed circumstances make unconscionable; attorney fees incurred in attempt to void premarital agreement generally subject to premarital agreement waiver; fees incurred to increase spousal support can be awarded in court's discretion); *Ohio State University Hospital v. Kinkaid*, 48 Ohio St. 3d 78, 549 N.E.2d 517 (1990) (spouses must each support other with property and labor; married person can be sued by third-party creditor if fails to support); *Mulvey v. Mulvey*, 1996 Ohio App. Lexis 5518 (unpub.) (court may award temporary support pending divorce despite premarital agreement).
Oklahoma		Y		84 Okla. Stat. § 44(B) (2022) (will is subject to premarital agreement; however, decedent spouse may not devise away so much that survivor gets less than half of assets acquired through joint industry); § 43-121.B (2022) (at divorce court divides marital property subject to valid premarital agreement, superseding prior case law prohibiting waiver of marital property rights); 43 Okla. Stat. § 201 (2022) (spouses contract towards each other obligations of mutual respect, fidelity, and support); 43 Okla. Stat. § 202 (2022) (spouses have duty to support); *Taylor v. Taylor*, 832 P.2d 429 (Okla. Ct. App. 1991) (premarital agreement must be executed voluntarily and either [1] not unconscionable or [2] with adequate financial disclosure; waiver of attorney's fees is valid if premarital agreement is valid); *Senter v. Senter*, 420 P.2d 879 (Okla. 1966) (premarital agreement governs right to elective share); *Griffin v. Griffin*, 94 P.3d 96 (Okla. Civ. App. 2004) (premarital agreement may waive right to equitable distribution); *Hudson v. Hudson*, 350 P.2d 596 (parties may contract regarding spousal support).

State	UPAA	Post-Divorce Spousal Support Waiver Enforceable	2d Look at Divorce	Key Statutes and Cases
Oregon	Y	Y		Or. Rev. Stat. §§ 108.700–108.740 (2022) (UPAA, eff. 1.1.88); (criteria for award of spousal support over waiver is welfare eligibility); § 114.620 (2022) (agreement before marriage can waive right of election); *In re Marriage of Purcell*, 99 Or. App. 668, 783 P.2d 1038 (1989) (absent express waiver of statutory right to attorney's fees, court may award statutory attorney's fees although premarital agreement had general waiver of fees); *In re Marriage of Bowers*, 143 Or. App. 24, 922 P.2d 722 (1996) (premarital agreement provision to shift legal fees to loser was enforceable; court can award fees to winner per premarital agreement and make statutory award to loser based on need; awards could cancel each other out).
Pennsylvania		Y		20 Pa. Cons. Stat. § 2207 (2022) (right of election of surviving spouse can be waived before marriage); § 23-3501 (2022) (at divorce marital property does not include property excluded by valid agreement entered into before marriage); § 23-4321 (2022) (married persons liable for support of each other); § 23-4102 (2022) (both spouses liable to creditors for debts for necessaries); § 23-4603 (2022) (person must financially assist indigent spouse); *Simeone v. Simeone*, 380 Pa. Super. 37, 551 A.2d 219 (1988), *aff'd*, 525 Pa. 392, 581 A.2d 162 (1990) (premarital agreement must be voluntary and either [1] not unconscionable or [2] with fair financial disclosure); *Karkaria v. Karkaria*, 405 Pa. Super. 176, 592 A.2d 64 (1991) (premarital agreement re property disposition at divorce presumed valid if adequate provisions or full disclosure; court cannot enforce premarital agreement selectively; if valid, provisions re property, spousal support, and attorney fees enforceable; court must enforce valid premarital agreement re temporary spousal support).
Rhode Island	Y	Y		R.I. Gen. Laws §§ 15-17-1 to 15-17-11 (2022) (UPAA, eff. 7.1.87) (premarital agreement not enforceable if [1] involuntary *and* [2] unconscionable coupled with no financial disclosure or effective waiver of disclosure, or knowledge; proof by clear and convincing evidence; criteria for award of spousal support over waiver is welfare eligibility); § 11-2-1 (2022) (criminal nonsupport); *Penhallow v. Penhallow*, 649 A.2d 1016 (R.I. 1994) (party challenging validity must prove both involuntary and unconscionable); *Landmark Medical Center v. Gauthier*, 635 A.2d 1145 (R.I. 1994) (non-recipient spouse has secondary liability for medical care).
South Carolina		Y	Y	S.C. Code Ann. § 20-3-630 (2022) (at divorce property excluded by valid written premarital agreement is nonmarital; agreement is presumptively fair and equitable if voluntarily executed, each party had separate counsel, with full disclosure of income, debts and assets); § 63-5-20 (2022) (criminal nonsupport); *Hardee v. Hardee*, 355 S.C. 382, 585 S.E.2d 501 (2003) (parties can waive spousal support in premarital agreement; test of enforceability is [1] whether agreement was obtained through fraud, duress, mistake, misrepresentation, or nondisclosure of material facts, [2] whether agreement was unconscionable, and [3] whether facts have changed unforeseeably since execution so that agreement is unconscionable at enforcement); *Gilley v. Gilley*, 327 S.C. 8, 488 S.E.2d 310 (1997) (spousal support waiver generally enforceable; attorney fee waiver generally enforceable); *Richland Memorial Hospital v. Burton*, 282 S.C. 159, 318 S.E.2d 12 (1984) (liability for necessaries).

State	UPAA	Post-Divorce Spousal Support Waiver Enforceable	2d Look at Divorce	Key Statutes and Cases
South Dakota	Y	N		S.D. Codified Laws §§ 25-2-16 to 25-2-25 (2022) (UPAA, eff. 3.1.89) (omitted authority for spousal support waiver); § 29A-2-213 (2022) (prospective spouses can waive rights at death by written agreement or waiver); § 25-7-1 (2022) (person shall support self and spouse from property or labor); § 25-7-2 (2022) (spouse liable to third party for necessaries); § 25-7-4 (2022) (criminal nonsupport); § 25-7-5 (2022) (must support spouse from separate property if spouse cannot support self and has not deserted); *Sanford v. Sanford*, 694 N.W.2d 283 (S.D. 2005) (rejecting invitation to modernize law by permitting premarital support waiver); *Walker v. Walker*, 765 N.W. 2d 747 (S.D. 2009) (court can consider terms of premarital agreement spousal support waiver in deciding whether to award spousal support; because spousal support waiver is unenforceable, trial court has discretion to award attorney's fees to spousal support claimant, but only that portion related to spousal support request).
Tennessee		Y		Tenn. Code Ann. §§ 36-3-501 (2022) (premarital agreement must be executed voluntarily and knowledgeably; agreement re premarital property binding on court at divorce); § 36-4-121(g)(2) (2022) (distribution of marital property; nothing herein affects validity of premarital agreement enforceable under Tenn. Code Ann. § 36-3-501); § 39-15-101 (2022) (criminal liability for failure to support disabled spouse or child); *Randolph v. Randolph*, 937 S.W.2d 815 (Tenn. 1996) (requirement that premarital agreement be signed knowledgeably can be met by proof that proponent made full and fair disclosure of nature, extent and value of assets, or that challenger had independent knowledge; burden of proof on party relying on agreement); *Perkinson v. Perkinson*, 802 S.W.2d 600 (Tenn. 1990) (premarital agreement re marital property binding on court at divorce and does not violate public policy; fairness determined as of execution); *Cary v. Cary*, 937 S.W.2d 777 (Tenn. 1996) (premarital agreement support waiver enforceable unless spouse will become public charge); *O'Daniel v. O'Daniel*, 419 S.W. 3d 280 (Tenn. App. 2013) (criteria for support award over waiver are the same as criteria for support award in absence of premarital agreement); *Erickson v. Erickson-Mitchell*, 2007 Tenn. App. Lexis 345 (unpub.) (waiver of spousal support is tantamount to waiver of attorney's fees; waiver enforceable).
Texas	Y	Y		Tex. Fam. Code Ann. §§ 4.001–4.010 (2021) (UPAA, eff. 9.17.97) (criteria for award of spousal support over waiver is welfare eligibility); Tex. Const. Art. XVI, § 15 (2021) (persons about to marry may by written agreement partition and exchange community property and constitute it separate property); Fam. Code Ann. § 2.501 (2021) (duty to support spouse; liable to third party for necessaries); *Jurek v. Couch-Jurek*, 296 S.W.3d 864 (Tex. Ct. App., 8th Dist. 2009) (parties to premarital agreement can partition income from separate property).

State	UPAA	Post-Divorce Spousal Support Waiver Enforceable	2d Look at Divorce	Key Statutes and Cases
Utah	Y	Y		Utah Code Ann. §§ 30-8-1 to 30-8-9 (2022) (UPAA, eff. 6.2.94) (parties may contract for choice of law governing construction, but court may apply law of legal domicile of either party if fair and equitable; premarital agreement not enforceable if involuntary or if fraudulent and no financial disclosure, effective waiver or knowledge; criteria for award of spousal support over waiver is welfare eligibility); § 75-2-213 (2022) (surviving spouse rights can be waived in written agreement before marriage; unenforceable if involuntary or unconscionable and no financial disclosure, waiver or knowledge); § 76-7-201 (criminal nonsupport); *Keyes v. Keyes*, 351, P.3d 90 (Utah Ct. App. 2015) (challenger must prove *both* fraud and nondisclosure); *Levin v. Carlton*, 213 P.3d 884 (Utah 2009) (premarital agreement does not have to be substantively fair at divorce).
Vermont		?	Y	12 Vt. Stat. Ann.§ 181 (2022) (Statute of Frauds; agreement in consideration of marriage must be in signed writing); *Stalb v. Stalb*, 168 Vt. 235, 719 A.2d 421 (1998) (premarital agreement is unconscionable if property disposition terms would leave spouse a public charge); *Bassler v. Bassler*, 156 Vt. 353, 593 A.2d 82 (1991) (premarital agreement must be executed voluntarily after adequate disclosure, and result must be fair or not unconscionable); *Stearns v. Stearns*, 66 Vt. 187, 28 A. 875 (1894) (premarital agreement may not waive spousal support).
Virginia	Y	Y		Va. Code Ann. §§ 20-147 to 20-155 (2022) (UPAA, eff. 7.1.86) (deleted provision of UPAA permitting knowledge of financial affairs in lieu of actual disclosure or waiver; silent on criteria for award of spousal support over waiver); § 20-109.C (2022) (court may not award support, attorney's fees, or suit money contrary to contract); § 64.2-422 (2022) (if spouse omitted from will executed before marriage, spouse takes share of estate to which would be entitled if testator left no will, unless omission intentional based on premarital agreement); § 64.2-314 (2022) (spouse can expressly waive homestead allowance, family allowance, and exempt property by premarital agreement in compliance with Va. Code Ann. § 20-147, et seq.); § 55-37 (2022) (common law necessaries doctrine applies equally to both spouses except if living permanently apart; no liability between spouses); § 20-61 (2022) (criminal nonsupport); § 8.01-220.2 (2022) (spouses jointly liable for emergency medical care furnished spouse, while spouse are living together, by physicians licensed in state or hospital located in state).
Washington		?		Wash. Rev. Code § 19.36.010 (2022) (Statute of Frauds; agreement on consideration of marriage must be in signed writing); § 26.16.250 (2022) (spouses can dispose of quasi-community property at death by premarital agreement); § 26.20.035 (2022) (criminal nonsupport); *In re Marriage of Matson*, 107 Wash. 2d 479, 730 P.2d 668 (1986) (parties can contract regarding disposition of property at divorce; premarital agreement must be either substantively fair or executed voluntarily with financial disclosure, competent advice, and full knowledge of marital rights); *In re Marriage of Burke*, 96 Wash. App. 474, 980 P.2d 265 (1999) (parties can contract re rights affecting themselves and property; parties cannot divest court of jurisdiction to award fees to litigate issues as to which premarital agreement could not bind court, *i.e.*, custody and child support); *In re Marriage of Ressa*, 2001 Wash. App. Lexis 2709 (attorney's fees generally waivable).

State	UPAA	Post-Divorce Spousal Support Waiver Enforceable	2d Look at Divorce	Key Statutes and Cases
West Virginia		Y	Y	W. Va. Code § 42-3-3a (2022) (surviving spouse rights can be waived in agreement before marriage; agreement must be voluntary and, if unconscionable, with financial disclosure, actual or constructive knowledge, or waiver of disclosure); § 48-1-203 (2022) (premarital agreement is agreement before and in consideration of marriage that determines property upon divorce or death); § 55-1-1(e) (2022) (Statute of Frauds; contract upon consideration of marriage must be in writing); *Gant v. Gant*, 329 S.E.2d 106 (W. Va. 1985) (premarital agreement must be executed voluntarily, with knowledge of content and legal effect, free of fraud, duress, or misrepresentation, after adequate disclosure, and result at divorce must not be unconscionable; spousal support waiver presumed valid but subject to modification due to unforeseen circumstances at divorce); *Ware v. Ware*, 687 S.E. 2d 382 (W. Va. 2009) (presumption of validity only when recipient had independent counsel; burden of proof of validity on proponent when challenging party was unrepresented).
Wisconsin		Y	Y	Wis. Stat. Ann. § 766.58 (2022) (premarital agreement enforceable without consideration, must be in writing, voluntary, not unconscionable at execution, and made after fair disclosure; can determine disposition of property at divorce unless inequitable; can determine property rights at death; court presumes equitable; may waive spousal support during marriage unless results in spouse having less than adequate support; court may award post-dissolution support necessary to keep recipient off welfare); § 767.61(3)(L) (2022) (in determining disposition of property at divorce, court must consider any written premarital agreement as binding unless terms are inequitable as to either party; court shall presume agreement is equitable); § 766.55 (2022) (obligations of spouses; necessaries; third party creditor rights); *Warren v. Warren*, 147 Wis. 2d 704, 433 N.W.2d 295 (Ct. App. 1988) (premarital agreement enforceable if equitable at divorce; equitable means circumstance at divorce foreseeable at execution; criteria for spousal support award is whether equitable at divorce); *Button v. Button*, 131 Wis. 2d 84, 91, 388 N.W.2d 546, 551 (1986) (premarital agreement must be executed voluntarily after adequate disclosure and must have fair result); *Jones v. Estate of Jones*, 253 Wis. 2d 158, 646 N.W.2d 280 (2002) (premarital agreement may waive homestead exemption); *Hengel v. Hengel*, 122 Wis. 2d 737, 365 N.W.2d 16 (Ct. App. 1985) (premarital agreement may waive spousal support if equitable at execution); *In re Marriage of Meis*, 316 Wis. 2d 773, 766 N.W.2d 241 (Ct. App. 2009) (temporary spousal support generally waivable); *Marshfield Clinic v. Discher*, 105 Wis. 2d 506, 314 N.W.2d 326 (1982) (both parties liable for necessaries; H primarily liable).
Wyoming		?		Wyo. Stat. Ann. § 1-23-105(a)(iii) (2022) (Statue of Frauds; agreement on consideration of marriage must be in signed writing); § 2-5-102 (2022) (surviving spouse rights can be waived in written agreement before marriage with fair disclosure; waiver of all rights includes elective share, homestead allowance, exempt property and family allowance); § 20-3-101 (2022) (criminal nonsupport); *Laird v. Laird*, 597 P.2d 463 (Wyo. 1979) (premarital agreement must be executed voluntarily and either [1] must not be unconscionable or [2] there must have been adequate disclosure); *Lund v. Lund*, 849 P.2d 731 (Wyo. 1993) (court must enforce property provision of valid premarital agreement); *Dorr v. Newman*, 785 P.2d 1172 (Wyo. 1990) (spousal support may be modified after divorce based on changed circumstances, even if originally determined in contract, in this case, by separation agreement).

APPENDIX B(2)

STATE LAW SUMMARY – POSTMARITAL AGREEMENTS

State	Key Statutes and Cases	Enforceability of Post- Divorce Spousal Support Waiver	Enforceability of Provisions re Waiver of Support during Marriage
Alabama	Ala. Code § 30-4-9 (2022) (spousal contracts subject to rules re contracts between parties in confidential relation); § 43-8-72 (2022) (right of election of surviving spouse, homestead allowance, exempt property and family allowance can be waived by postmarital agreement; waiver of rights must be made in writing after fair disclosure); *Tibbs v. Anderson*, 580 So. 2d 1337 (Ala. 1991) (validity of postmarital agreement governed by same standards as premarital agreement); *Barnhill v. Barnhill*, 386 So. 2d 749, 751 (Ala. Civ. App.), *cert. denied*, 386 So. 2d 752 (Ala. 1980)) (mutual waivers can be adequate consideration); *Ray v. Ray*, 189 So. 895 (Ala. 1939) (spousal contracts subject to rules re confidential relations).	*Tibbs v. Anderson*, 580 So. 2d 1337 (Ala. 1991) (does not address spousal support but treats postmarital agreements same as premarital agreements, citing *Ruzic v. Ruzic*, 549 So. 2d 72 (Ala. 1989))	
Alaska	Alaska Stat. § 34.77.010 (2022) (spouse must act in good faith re community property); § 34.77.030 (2022) (community property agreement may classify property as individual property or as community property); § 34.77.090 (2022) (spouses can enter into a community property agreement regarding disposition of property at death or divorce; agreement is valid if not unconscionable, executed voluntarily, with fair and reasonable disclosure or constructive knowledge); §13.12.213 (2022) (rights of surviving spouse can be waived during marriage by written agreement executed voluntarily and, if unconscionable, with fair and reasonable financial disclosure, adequate knowledge, or express waiver of disclosure); § 25.24.160(e) (2022) (at divorce court distributes community property equitably unless otherwise provided in community property agreement); *Estate of Lampert v. Estate of Lampert*, 896 P.2d 214 (Alas. 1995) (spouses can sign postmarital agreement providing for disposition of property at death).	Alaska Stat. § 34.77.090 (2022) (subjects on which spouses can contract; silent on spousal support)	
Arizona	Ariz. Rev. Stat. § 14-2207 (2022) (surviving spouse rights may be waived by written contract during marriage; same validity standards as UPAA); Ariz. Fam. Law Proc. R. 69 (2022) (agreement between spouses is valid if in writing and signed; not binding on court until approved; presumed valid, challenger has burden to prove defect); *Estate of Harber*, 104 Ariz. 79, 449 P.2d 7 (1969) (spouses may enter into postmarital agreement governing property rights at divorce); *Hanner v. Hanner*, 95 Ariz. 191, 388 P.2d 239 (1964) (agreement to drop divorce can be sufficient consideration for postmarital agreement; spouses can agree to disposition of property at death or divorce); *Austin v. Austin*, 237 Ariz. 201, 348P.3d 897 (Ct. App. 2015) (spouses entering into postmarital agreement regarding property rights at divorce are in confidential and fiduciary relationship); *In re Hutki v. Hutki*, 244 Ariz. 39, 417 P.3d 804 (Ct. App. 2018) (court must determine if postmarital agreement fair; burden on challenger).		

State	Key Statutes and Cases	Enforceability of Post- Divorce Spousal Support Waiver	Enforceability of Provisions re Waiver of Support during Marriage
Arkansas	Ark. Code Ann. § 9-11-301 (2022) (marriage contract must be in writing and acknowledged or witnessed); *Stewart v. Combs,* 368 Ark. 121, 243 S.W. 3d 294 (2006) (postmarital agreement is valid if meets criteria for valid contract; consideration need not be equal); *Simmons v. Simmons,* 98 Ark. App. 12, 249 S.W. 3d 843 (2007) (marriage alone is not sufficient *consideration for postmarital agreement);* Myrick v. Myrick, 339 Ark. 1, 2 S.W.3d 60 (1999) (presumption of undue influence applies to shift burden to donee of interspousal transfer only when evidence shows donee was dominant party who occupied such superior position of dominance as to amount to duress, coercion, or undue influence).		
California	Cal. Fam. Code § 721 (2022) (spouses can contract with each other re property rights at death or divorce; spouses in fiduciary relationship; highest duty of good faith and fair dealing; neither shall take unfair advantage); § 852(a) (2022) (transmutation of community property to separate property invalid unless made in writing by express declaration of spouse affected); Cal. Prob. Code § 142 (2022) (waiver of rights at death must be in writing; no consideration required; enforceable under either Cal. Prob. Code § 143 or § 144); § 143 (2022) (waiver enforceable unless surviving spouse proves either: (1) no disclosure or waiver of disclosure made with advice of independent counsel, or (2) no independent representation); § 144 (2022) (waiver of surviving spouse rights enforceable if fair disposition of spousal rights, or spouse had adequate knowledge and no violation of fiduciary obligation under Fam. Code § 721; court can deny enforcement if unconscionable); *Friedman v. Friedman,* 100 Cal.App. 4th 65, 122 Cal. Rptr. 2d 412 (2002) (postmarital agreement enforceable at divorce re property division unless induced through mistake, undue influence, fraud, misrepresentation, false promise, concealment, non-disclosure, or other breach of confidential relationship); *Gabaig v. Gabaig,* 717 P.2d 835 (Alaska 1986) (interpreting California law; postmarital agreement subject to rules governing confidential relationship; when one spouse gains advantage, transaction presumed result of undue influence and that spouse has burden to prove fair, just and reasonable).	Cal. Fam. Code § 1620 (2022) (spousal agreement cannot alter legal relationship except for property provisions)	Cal. Fam. Code § 720 (2022) (spouses contract obligation of mutual support); § 4300 (2022) (subject to certain other statutory provisions, person shall support spouse); § 4301 (2022) (married person shall support spouse while living together); § 4302 (2022) (person not liable to support spouse living apart by agreement)
Colorado	Colo. Rev. Stat. §§ 14-2-301–14-2-313 (2022) (Uniform Premarital and Marital Agreement Act (UPMAA), eff. 7.1.14); (parties may contract re disposition of property at death or divorce; parties may contract re support and attorney's fees provided not unconscionable at enforcement); § 14-2-309(1) (postmarital agreement must be voluntary, with access to counsel, or notice of rights, and after adequate financial disclosure); § 15-11-213 (2022) (affirmation, modification, or waiver of marital right or obligation is only enforceable if contained in premarital or marital agreement compliant with UPMAA).	*In re Marriage of Ikeler,* 161 P.3d 663 (Colo. 2007) (court can review marital agreement waiver of spousal support and attorney's fees for unconscionability at divorce); *In re Marriage of Christen,* 899 P.2d 339 (Colo. Ct. App. 1995) (spousal support provision which equalizes parties' incomes not unconscionable)	

State	Key Statutes and Cases	Enforceability of Post- Divorce Spousal Support Waiver	Enforceability of Provisions re Waiver of Support during Marriage
Connecticut	Conn. Gen. Stat. § 46b-36 (2022) (spouses have power to make contract with each other); *Bedrick v. Bedrick,* 300 Conn. 691, 17 A.3d 17 (2011) (postmarital agreements are generally enforceable; are subject to special scrutiny; terms must be fair and equitable at execution and not unconscionable at dissolution).		Conn. Gen. Stat. § 46b-37 (2022) (spouses not liable for each other's debts; spouses have mutual duty of support, including for medical expenses; both liable for necessaries)
Delaware	13 Del. Code Ann. §§ 311–314 (2022) (married woman may contract with husband); § 12-905 (2022) (spouses can waive right to election by written contract); § 13-1513 (b) (2022) (spouses can waive division of property at divorce in valid agreement); *Stewart v. Stewart,* 41A.3d 401 (De. 2012) (spouses are presumptively in confidential relationship, therefore, equity subjects their contract to higher degree of scrutiny); *Wolhar v. Wolhar (In re Est. of Wolhar)*, 2018 Del. Ch. LEXIS 43 (unpub.) (suggesting validity determined under same criteria as premarital agreement); *Conigliaro v. Conigliaro*, 1992 Del. Fam. Ct. Lexis 41 (intended premarital agreement signed after marriage was valid postmarital agreement); *Harry M.P. v. Nina M.P.*, 437 A.2d 158 (Supr. Ct. Del. 1981) (validity of contract between spouses governed by contract principles).	13 Del. Code § 1512 (d) (2022) (spouses can waive alimony in valid agreement); *Stewart v. Stewart,* 41 A.3d 401 (De. 2014) (unconscionable spousal support can be modified)	13 Del. Code § 502 (2022) (duty to support spouse rests on other spouse); *Hyland v. Southwell,* 320 A.2d 767 (Del. Super. Ct. 1974) (personal injury case; suggests erosion of historic disabilities of married woman; W may be liable for own necessaries)
District of Columbia	D.C. Code Ann. § 46-601 (2022) (Married Women's Property Act; married person has right to contract with spouse); § 16-910 (2022) (spouses can exclude property from marital estate at divorce by postmarital agreement); § 19-113 (2022) (surviving spouse's rights can be waived in postmarital agreement); *Simon v. Smith*, 273 A.3d 321 (D.C. App. 2022) (spouses are in confidential relationship; spousal agreement during marriage is subject to more careful scrutiny than ordinary contract).		D.C. Code § 46-601 (b)(2) (2022) (both spouses liable on debt for necessaries; § 16-916 (2022) (party can be ordered to support needy spouse)
Florida	Fla. Stat. Ann. § 708.09 (2022) (Married Women's Property Act; spouses can contract); § 732.702 (2022) (spouses can waive rights at death by written contract with two witnesses; spouses must make fair disclosure; no consideration required except execution); *Casto v. Casto*, 508 So. 2d 330 (Fla. 1987) (postmarital agreements generally enforceable; may be set aside only if (1) result of fraud, duress, deceit, coercion, misrepresentation or overreaching; or (2) provisions for challenging spouse disproportionate, shifting burden to other spouse to show adequate knowledge; mere bad bargain or lack of competent counsel not basis for invalidity); *In re Estate of Duggan,* 639 So. 2d 1071 (Fla. Dist. Ct. App. 1994) (agreement re disposition of property incident to separation survives reconciliation unless contrary intent shown).	*Casto v. Casto*, 508 So. 2d 330 (Fla. 1987) (postmarital agreement re spousal support generally enforceable); *Hahn v. Hahn*, 465 So. 2d 1352 (Fla. Dist. Ct. App. 1985) (court may not *sua sponte* modify contractual support provision)	*Khan v. Khan,* 79 So.3d 99 (Fla. Dist. Ct. App. 2012) (spouse may not in postmarital agreement contract away right to temporary support and legal fees)

State	Key Statutes and Cases	Enforceability of Post- Divorce Spousal Support Waiver	Enforceability of Provisions re Waiver of Support during Marriage
Georgia	Ga. Code Ann. § 19-3-10 (2022) (spouses can contract with each other if does not defraud creditors); *Curry v. Curry*, 260 Ga. 302, 392 S.E.2d 879 (1990) (reconciliation agreement enforceable under same validity criteria as premarital agreement); *Scherer v. Scherer*, 249 Ga. 635, 292 S.E.2d 662 (1982) (agreement in contemplation of divorce settling property, support, custody and child support not invalid).	*Scherer v. Scherer*, 249 Ga. 635, 292 S.E.2d 662 (1982) (agreement in contemplation of divorce settling property, support, custody, and child support not invalid); *Sanders v. Colwell*, 283 S.E.2d 461 (Ga. 1981) (distinction between agreement incident to divorce and agreement in contemplation of divorce obliterated)	
Hawaii	Haw. Rev. Stat. § 560:2-213 (2022) (surviving spouse rights can be waived during marriage by written agreement; criteria for validity same as UPAA); § 572-22 (2022) (spouses can contract regarding property rights); *Epp v. Epp,* 80 Haw. 79, 905 P.2d 54 (1995) (postmarital agreements recognized in Hawaii); *Chen v. Hoeflinger*, 127 Haw. 346, 279 P.3d 11 (Haw. Int. Ct. App. 2012) (postmarital agreement is enforceable if not unconscionable, executed voluntarily with knowledge of financial affairs; unconscionability determined as of execution); *Kreytak v. Kreytak*, 82 Haw. 543, 923 P.2d 960 (Ct. App. 1996) (spouses can convert marital property to separate property at divorce by valid postmarital agreement).	Haw. Rev. Stat. § 572-22 (2022) (contract between spouses for support made in contemplation of divorce valid but subject to court approval and modifiable)	
Idaho	Idaho Code § 15-2-208 (2022) (rights of surviving spouse can be waived in written agreement during marriage with fair disclosure); §§ 32-906 (2022) (property can be excluded from marital estate at divorce by written agreement); § 32-916 (2022) (property rights determined by court at divorce unless agreement during marriage contains contrary stipulations); § 32-917 (2022) (contract for marriage settlement must be in writing and executed and acknowledged like land conveyance); § 32-918 (2022) (marriage contract recorded in land records); *Pike v. Pike,* 139 Idaho 406, 80 P.3d 342 (2003) (requirement for signed and acknowledged writing for agreement dividing community property at divorce strictly construed); *Stevens v. Stevens*, 16 P.3d 900 (Idaho 2000) ("marriage settlement" as used in §§ 32-916 and 917 encompasses postmarital agreements); *Bell v. Bell,* 122 Idaho 520, 835 P.2d 1331 (1992) (spouses can enter into postmarital agreement to allocate community debt); *Griffin v. Griffin*, 102 Idaho 858, 642 P.2d 949 (1982) (agreement required to transmute separate property to community property).		Idaho Code § 32-901 (2022) (spouses contract toward each other obligations of mutual respect, fidelity, and support)

State	Key Statutes and Cases	Enforceability of Post- Divorce Spousal Support Waiver	Enforceability of Provisions re Waiver of Support during Marriage
Illinois	750 Ill. Comp. Stat. § 5/503(a)(4) (2022) (at divorce marital property does not include property excluded by valid agreement); *In re Marriage of Vella*, 237 Ill. App. 3d 194, 603 N.E.2d 109 (1992) (postmarital agreement to settle divorce, followed by dismissal of suit for divorce, was valid, did not require court approval for validity at time of making to remain valid after reconciliation, and was not dependent on divorce); *Tabassum v. Younis*, 377 Ill.App.3d 761, 881 N.E.2d 369, reh. den. (2007) (consideration); *Turner v. Black*, 19 Ill. 2d 296, 166 N.E.2d 588 (1960) (parties to premarital agreement may alter or revoke after dissolution of marriage except as to children or third party purchasers).	*In re Marriage of Vella*, 237 Ill. App. 3d 194, 603 N.E.2d 109 (1992) (postmarital agreement settling spousal support rights may be enforceable but is subject to court approval at divorce); *Henderson v. Henderson*, 290 Ill. App. 448, 8 N.E.2d 545 (1937) (postmarital agreement obligating husband to pay spousal support was valid and did not violate public policy)	*Eule v. Eule*, 24 Ill. App. 3d 83, 320 N.E.2d 506 (1974) (clause in postmarital agreement waiving H's legal duty of support during marriage void); *Volid v. Volid*, 6 Ill. App. 3d 386, 286 N.E.2d 42 (1972) (postmarital agreement waiving support during ongoing marriage violates public policy)
Indiana	Ind. Code § 29-1-2-13 (2022) (spouse may waive intestate share, right to elect against will, or other expectancy with full disclosure and fair consideration); § 29-1-3-6 (2022) (waiver of elective share); *Hall v. Hall*, 281 (Ind. Ct. App. 2015) (reconciliation agreement; adequate consideration can include intent to preserve a troubled marriage); *Beaman v. Beaman*, 844 N.E.2d 525 (Ind. Ct. App. 2006) (court may reject postmarital agreement only if result of fraud, duress, other imperfections of consent, or manifest inequity resulting from great disparity in bargaining power); *Estate of Stack v. Venzke*, 485 N.E.2d 907 (Ind. Ct. App. 1985) (criteria for validity of premarital agreement as basis for validity of postmarital agreement); *Womack v. Womack*, 622 N.E.2d 481 (Ind. 1993) (no presumption of undue influence from confidential relationship; burden on party claiming invalidity); *Flansburg v. Flansburg*, 581 N.E.2d 430 (Ind. Ct. App. 1991) (reconciliation agreement determined on same validity criteria as premarital agreement; is enforceable at divorce).		Ind. Code. Am. § 35-46-1-6 (2022) (criminal nonsupport); *Marriage of Pond*, 676 N.E.2d 401 (Ind. Ct. App. 1997) (court has discretion to award *pendente lite* support despite parties' waiver of all support in separation agreement)

State	Key Statutes and Cases	Enforceability of Post- Divorce Spousal Support Waiver	Enforceability of Provisions re Waiver of Support during Marriage
Iowa	Iowa Code § 597.1 (2022) (property rights of married woman same as property rights of husband); Iowa Code § 597.2 (2022) (when property is owned by husband or wife, other spouse has no interest therein which can be subject of contract between them); *Hussemann v. Hussemann,* 847 N.W.2d 219 (Iowa 2014) (postmarital agreement that waives spousal elective share is unenforceable); *Marriage of Cooper*, 769 N.W. 2d 582 (Iowa 2009) (no statute expressly authorizes or prohibits enforcement of reconciliation agreement); *Estate of Shaffer*, 2009 Iowa App. Lexis 184 (unpub.) (postmarital agreement is void as to elective share and surviving spouse allowance; postmarital agreement waiving spousal rights at death not expressly authorized by statute); *Estate of Kennedy*, 154 Iowa 460, 135 N.W. 53 (1912) (postmarital agreement to waive rights in estate is prohibited by statute); *Punelli v. Punelli*, 364 N.W.2d 259 (Iowa. Ct. App. 1984) (reconciliation agreement enforceable at divorce; no presumption of fiduciary relationship solely from fact parties married); *Hansen v. Hansen*, 924 N.W.2d 873 (Iowa Ct. App. 2018) (Iowa law allows PMA to be revoked but not amended during marriage; at divorce court can consider terms of postmarital agreement but is not bound by them).		
Kansas	Kan. Stat. Ann. § 23-2602 (2022) (married persons can contract); § 23-2607 (2022) (marriage settlement or contract is valid); § 59-6a 213 (2022) (surviving spouse rights can be waived in agreement after marriage; validity criteria same as UPAA); § 23-2712 (a) (2022) (separation agreement must be valid, just and equitable); *Traster v. Traster,* 339 P.3d 778 (Kan. 2014) (postmarital agreement executed during marriage, not in contemplation of imminent separation, is a "separation agreement" as defined in Kan. Stat. Ann. § 60-1610 (b)(5) and is governed by same criteria; trial court must review at divorce and determine whether property division is just and equitable); *Davis v. Miller*, 269 Kan. 732, 7 P.3d 1223 (2000) (spouses may contract for application of UPAA to validity of postmarital agreement); *Estate of Loughmiller*, 229 Kan. 584, 629 P.2d 156 (1981) (postmarital agreement fairly and understandingly made settling property rights is binding whether divorce filed or not; court approval not required to establish validity when parties carried out intent by making transfers).	*Davis v. Miller*, 269 Kan. 732, 7 P.3d 1223 (2000) (spouses can contract for application of UPAA to postmarital agreement)	
Kentucky	Ky. Rev. Stat. Ann. § 403.190 (2022) (equitable distribution of marital property at divorce, except property excluded by valid agreement); § 404.020 (2022) (Married Women's Property Act; married woman can transfer or sell real estate and personal property; transfer between spouses not valid as to third party unless in writing and not fraudulent); *Campbell v. Campbell,* 377 S.W. 2d 93 (Ky. Ct. App. 1964) (spouses can enter into postmarital agreement regarding property rights at death); *Smith v. Smith*, 295 Ky. 50, 173 S.W.2d 813 (1943) (postmarital agreement valid with fair consideration).		Ky. Rev. Stat. Ann. § 404.040 (2022) (husband liable for wife's necessaries); § 530.050 (criminal non-support)

State	Key Statutes and Cases	Enforceability of Post- Divorce Spousal Support Waiver	Enforceability of Provisions re Waiver of Support during Marriage
Louisiana	La. Civ. Code Ann. Art. 2328 (2022) (spouses can establish separate property regime by agreement); Art. 2329 (2022) (postmarital agreement that alters matrimonial regime requires joint petition and court approval; court must find in parties' best interests and that both understand governing principles; spouses may subject themselves to legal regime by matrimonial agreement at any time); Art. 2330 (2022) spouses may not by agreement renounce or alter marital portion or established order of succession); La. Rev. Stat. Ann. § 9:384 (2022) (spouses separated under judicial decree who reconcile reestablish community property unless they execute matrimonial agreement prior to reconciliation); Art. 2331 (2022) (matrimonial agreement must be made by authentic act or act under private signature duly acknowledged); Art. 2336 (2022) (spouses may partition community property by agreement); Art. 2370 (2022) (matrimonial agreement can establish regime of separation of property); *McAlpine v. McAlpine*, 679 So. 2d 85 (La. 1996) (spouses can contract during marriage to alter legal regime and convert community property to separate property); *Poirier v. Poirier*, 626 So. 2d 868 (La. Ct. App. 1993) (two types of postmarital agreements: (i) termination of matrimonial regime under La. Civ. Code Ann. art. 2329 requires court approval; (ii) partition of community property under La. Civ. Code Ann. art. 2336, does not require court approval); *Boyer v. Boyer*, 616 So. 2d 730 (La. Ct. App. 1993) (court must find termination of matrimonial regime under La. Civ. Code Ann. art. 2329 was voluntary, that both parties understood principles in change of matrimonial regime and that was in parties' best interests; best interest evaluation does not require perfect symmetry of assets or opportunities; should not be judged in hindsight); *Sharpe v. Sharpe*, 536 So. 2d 434 (La. Ct. App. 1988) (premarital agreement may be amended after marriage by written agreement).	*McAlpine v. McAlpine*, 679 So. 2d 85 (La. 1996) (postmarital agreement can waive spousal support); *Boudreaux v. Boudreaux*, 745 So. 2d 61 (La. Ct. App. 1999) (postmarital agreement to pay spousal support regardless of fault is void as against public policy); *Unkle v. Unkle*, 699 So. 2d 472 (La. Ct. App. 1997) (spouses can contract for any lawful purpose, including waiver of permanent and temporary alimony)	La. Civ. Code Ann. Art. 98 (2022) (married persons owe each other fidelity, support, and assistance); Art. 2372–2373 (2022) (spouses contribute to marital expenses in accord with marital agreement; each spouse liable with other for necessaries for spouse and family); *Hall v. Hall*, 4 So.3d 254 (La. Ct. App. 2009) (spousal right to claim interim support is based on statutorily imposed duty & nonwaivable)
Maine	18-C Me. Rev. Stat. Ann. § 2-213 (2022) (spouses can waive right of election in agreement; standard of validity is UPAA standard).		Me. Rev. Stat. Ann. 22, § 4319 (2022) (spouse shall support his/her spouse in proportion to ability); § 19-A-1652 (2022) (spouses are obligated to support one another if able)
Maryland	Md. Code Ann., Est. & Trusts § 3-406 (2022) (right of election can be waived during marriage by written agreement); Fam. Law § 4-204 (2022) (Married Women's Property Act; married woman can enter into contract with husband); Fam. Law §§ 8-101–8-103 (2022) (spouses can make valid agreement re property rights whether living together or apart); *McGeehan v. McGeehan*, 455 Md. 268, 167 A.3d 579 (2017) (postmarital agreement generally valid when fair and regular, not unconscionable or product of fraud, duress, mistake, or undue influence); *Lloyd v. Niceta*, 284 A.3d 808 (Md. App. 2022), cert. granted, 482 Md. 733, 290 A.3d 603 (2023) (challenger must prove both procedural and substantive unconscionability).	Md. Code Ann., Fam. Law §§ 8-101–8-103 (2022) (spouses can make valid agreement re spousal support whether living together or apart; nonmodifiable if expressly made so in agreement); Fam. Law § 11-101 (2022) (court bound by final agreement re spousal support)	Md. Code Ann., Fam. Law §§ 8-101–8-103 (2022) (court can modify agreement re spousal support unless agreement says not modifiable)

State	Key Statutes and Cases	Enforceability of Post- Divorce Spousal Support Waiver	Enforceability of Provisions re Waiver of Support during Marriage
Massachusetts	*Ansin v. Craven-Ansin*, 457 Mass. 283, 929 N.E.2d 955 (2010) (spouses may enter into postmarital agreement; rejecting application of same validity criteria as premarital agreement; subject to careful scrutiny at divorce to determine whether (1) each party had opportunity for independent lawyer; (2) there was fraud or coercion; (3) all assets fully disclosed; (4) each knowingly and explicitly agreed in writing to waive judicial division of assets and all marital rights at divorce; (5) terms are fair and reasonable at execution and enforcement at divorce; challenging spouse has burden of proof).		Mass. Ann. Laws ch. 209, § 32F (2022) (married person may file petition for support from spouse if living apart)
Michigan	Mich. Comp. Laws § 557.27(7) (2022) (married woman may enter into contract with husband); § 700.2205 (2022) (surviving spouse rights can be waived in written contract after marriage with fair disclosure); *Skaates v. Kayser*, 959 N.W.2d 33 (Mich. Ct. App. 2020) (postmarital agreement signed six weeks after wedding was valid where negotiated for 16 months before marriage, where terms did not incentivize divorce); *Ransford v. Yens*, 132 N.W.2d 150 (Mich. 1965) (postmarital agreement settling property rights at death or divorce not made to effect immediate separation was valid); *Hodge v. Parks*, 303 Mich. App. 552, 844 N.W. 2d 189 (2014) (postmarital agreement not enforceable if encourages divorce by leaving one spouse in a more favorable position to abandon marriage; postmarital reconciliation agreement generally enforceable); *Cheff v. Cheff*, 2012 Mich. App. Lexis 753 (unpub.) (postmarital agreement signed six months after wedding, providing for disposition of property and spousal support at divorce, where couple was not separated, was void as against public policy); *Wright v. Wright*, 279 Mich. App. 291, 761 N.W.2d 443 (2008) (couple maintaining marital relationship may not enter into enforceable contract that provides for disposition of property upon future separation; agreement void as against public policy as calculated to leave husband in more favorable position to abandon marriage); *Dettloff v. Dettloff*, 2006 Mich. App. Lexis 3790 (unpub.) (postmarital reconciliation agreement enforceable as written); *Rockwell v. Rockwell*, 24 Mich. App. 593,180 N.W.2d 498 (1970) (postmarital agreement to settle rights at death is enforceable.		Mich. Comp. Laws §§ 401.1, 401.3 (2022) (spouse must support poor spouse)
Minnesota	Minn. Stat. Ann. § 519.06 (2022) (spouses can contract regarding property); § 519.11 (2022) (parties can contract during marriage re anything they can contract about in premarital agreement; must be procedurally and substantively fair at execution and enforcement; spouses must be represented by separate counsel; presumed unenforceable if divorce suit within two years unless proponent proves is fair and equitable; does not impair validity of waiver of rights at death); § 524.2-213 (2022) (rights at death may be waived after marriage; contract to waive rights must be in writing and signed by waiving party after fair disclosure); § 524.2-514 (2022) (proof of contract to make will).	Minn. Stat. Ann. § 519.11(1a) (2022) (parties can contract after marriage re anything they can contract about in premarital agreement); *Hill v. Hill*, 356 N.W.2d 49 (Minn. Ct. App. 1984) (premarital agreement re support generally enforceable but subject to review if unconscionable at divorce)	

State	Key Statutes and Cases	Enforceability of Post- Divorce Spousal Support Waiver	Enforceability of Provisions re Waiver of Support during Marriage
Mississippi	Miss. Code Ann. § 89-1-29 (2022) (conveyance of real estate or other encumbrance on homestead not valid unless signed by spouse of owner); § 93-3-7 (2022) (spouses shall not contract with each other for compensation for services; husband may not carry on business with wife's property without written agreement); *Grier v. Grier*, 616 So. 2d 337 (Miss. 1993) (postmarital agreement incident to separation which states is for purpose of no-fault divorce is unenforceable if party withdraws from no-fault divorce; but parties may provide that applies regardless of grounds); *Crosby v. Peoples Bank of Indianola*, 472 So. 2d 951 (Miss. 1985) (spouses can contract re property rights at divorce; court approval not required to make agreement binding).		Miss. Code Ann. § 93-3-7 (2022) (not lawful for spouses to contract with each other for compensation for labor or for husband to rent wife's property, but all business done by husband with wife's property is for her account unless contract between spouses changes relation)
Missouri	Mo. Rev. Stat. § 452.330.2(4) (2022) (no equitable distribution at divorce of property excluded by valid agreement); § 474.220 (2022) (rights at death can be waived during marriage by written contract or waiver signed by waiving party after full disclosure and with fair consideration); *Lipic v. Lipic*, 103 S.W.3d 144 (Mo. App. 2003) (criteria for validity of postmarital agreement same as for premarital; must be entered into freely, fairly, knowingly, understandingly, in good faith, with full disclosure); *Estate of Soper*, 598 S.W.2d 528 (Mo. Ct. App. 1980) (spouses may contract to waive rights in estate; contract must have consideration; mutual waivers is consideration); *Hosmer v. Hosmer*, 611 S.W.2d 32 (Mo. Ct. App. 1980) (fairness judged as of date of execution; valid so long as surviving spouse had actual or constructive knowledge of property; not invalid merely because surviving spouse got less than would have in absence of postmarital agreement).		Mo. Rev. Stat. § 568.040 (2022) (criminal nonsupport)
Montana	Mont. Code Ann. § 72-2-224 (2021) (spouse may waive right of election, homestead allowance, and exempt property in written contract; validity criteria same as for premarital agreement under UPAA); § 40-2-101 (2021) (marriage is contract for respect, fidelity, and support); §§ 40-2-103, -104, -106 (2021) (spouses liable to third parties for cost of necessities, except if abandoned); § 40-2-301 (2021) (spouses can contract with each other regarding property as if unmarried subject to rules governing confidential relations); § 40-2-304 (2021) (mutual assent is sufficient consideration); *Marriage of Myers*, 210 Mont. 173, 682 P.2d 718 (1984) (postmarital agreement invalid where husband conditioned continuance of marriage on wife signing agreement giving him share of her separate property).	Mont. Code Ann. § 40-2-303 (2021) (spouses cannot by contract alter legal relation except as to property and except may agree in writing to immediate separation and make provisions for support)	Mont. Code Ann. § 40-2-303 (2021) (spouses cannot by contract alter legal relation except as to property and except that may agree in writing to immediate separation and make provisions for support); § 45-5-621 (2021) (criminal nonsupport)
Nebraska	Neb. Rev. Stat. § 30-2316 (2022) (spousal rights at death can be waived during marriage; agreement must be in writing, voluntary, and either conscionable when executed or executed after fair disclosure or waiver of disclosure); *Blanchard v. White*, 217 Neb. 877, 351 N.W.2d 707 (1984) (contract to make will must have adequate consideration); *Devney v. Devney*, 295 Neb. 15, 886 N.W.2d 61 (2016) (postmarital agreements determining property rights at divorce are not authorized by Nebraska common law or statute unless incident to separation or divorce).	Neb. Rev. Stat. § 42-362 (2022) (must provide for mentally ill spouse even after divorce)	Neb. Rev. Stat. § 42-201 (2022) (wife's liability for necessaries)

State	Key Statutes and Cases	Enforceability of Post- Divorce Spousal Support Waiver	Enforceability of Provisions re Waiver of Support during Marriage
Nevada	Nev. Rev. Stat. Ann. § 123.070 (2021) (spouses can enter into contract as if unmarried; subject to general rules re persons occupying confidential relations); § 123.080 (2021) (spouses cannot contract to alter legal relations except as to property and except may agree to immediate separation and with provision for support); *Williams v. Waldman*, 108 Nev. 466, 836 P.2d 614 (1992) (spouses may be in fiduciary relationship if party purports to act in other party's best interest).	Nev. Rev. Stat. Ann. § 123.080 (2021) (spouses cannot contract to alter legal relations except as to property and except may agree to immediate separation and to provision for support)	Nev. Rev. Stat. Ann. § 123.080 (2021) (spouses cannot contract to alter legal relations except as to property and except for immediate separation and may agree to provision for support); § 201.020 (criminal nonsupport)
New Hampshire	N.H. Rev. Stat. Ann. § 460:5 (2022) (spouses can convey real estate between each other directly); *In re Estate of Wilber,* 165 N.H. 246, 75 A.3d 1096 (2013) (spouses can enter into postmarital agreement; challenging party has burden to prove fraud, duress, nondisclosure of material fact, unfairness; court declined to decide whether enhanced scrutiny required (as required for premarital agreements) or whether fairness standard is unconscionability); *Adams v. Adams*, 113 A. 279 (N.H. 1921) (spouses can contract for sale of property between each other; common law disabilities of married women abrogated).		
New Jersey	N.J. Stat. Ann. § 3B:8-10 (2022) (surviving spouse elective share rights can be waived in contract after marriage with fair disclosure); *Pacelli v. Pacelli*, 319 N.J. Super. 185, 725 A.2d 56 (1999) (postmarital agreement re property and support at divorce must (1) be closely scrutinized; (2) not be product of duress or coercion; and (3) be fair at enforcement; postmarital agreement where husband threatened divorce if wife refused to sign and which provided grossly disproportionate amount for wife was unfair, inequitable, and unconscionable); *Nicholson v. Nicholson*, 199 N.J. Super. 525, 489 A.2d 1247 (App. Div. 1985) (reconciliation agreement enforceable at divorce); *Steele v. Steele*, 467 N.J. Super. 414, 253 A.3d 1190 (App. Div. 2021) (unlike PMAs, postmarital agreement is not entitled to presumption of enforceability).	*Pacelli v. Pacelli*, 319 N.J. Super. 185, 725 A.2d 56 (1999)	§ 2C:24-5 (2022) (criminal nonsupport); N.J. Stat. Ann. § 2C:62-1 (court can order temporary support after spouse charged with willful nonsupport)
New Mexico	N.M. Stat. Ann. § 40-2-2 (2022) (spouses can contract re property rights subject to rules re confidential relations); § 40-2-4 (2022) (contract for marriage settlement must be in writing, executed, and acknowledged or proved as land transfer); § 40-2-8 (2022) (spouses cannot enter into contract to alter legal relations, except as to property, in writing, and except for immediate separation) § 40-2-9 (2022) (mutual consent is sufficient consideration for contract described in § 40-2-8); *Gabriele v. Gabriele*, 421 P.3d 828 (N.M. Ct. App. 2018) (consideration is necessary, but not sufficient, for validity of postmarital agreement; spouses in fiduciary relationship; spouse who received decided advantage must prove adequate disclosure of value of assets and of spouse's rights in assets, competent and independent advice).	N.M. Stat. Ann. § 40-2-1 (2022) (spouses contract toward each other obligations of mutual respect, fidelity and support); § 40-2-8 (spouses cannot by contract alter legal relations, except as to property, and except may agree in writing to immediate separation and for support)	

State	Key Statutes and Cases	Enforceability of Post- Divorce Spousal Support Waiver	Enforceability of Provisions re Waiver of Support during Marriage
New York	N.Y. Dom. Rel. Law § 236(B)(3) (2022) (spouses can contract re disposition of property at death or divorce; agreement must be in writing, subscribed, and acknowledged in manner required for recordation of deed; spouses can contract re support; support waiver must be fair at execution and not unconscionable at divorce); Est. Powers & Trusts Law § 5-1.1(b) (2022) (spouse can waive elective share during marriage in writing, subscribed and acknowledged); *Petracca v. Petracca*, 101 A. D.3d 695, 956 N.Y.S. 2d. 77 (2012) (spouses have fiduciary relationship; postmarital agreement scrutinized for fairness of process and terms); *Zagari v. Zagari*, 191 Misc.2d 733, 746 N.Y.S.2d 235 (Sup.Ct. 2002) (to invalidate postmarital agreement, court must find both procedural and substantive unconsionability); *Arizin v. Covello*, 175 Misc. 2d 453, 669 N.Y.S.2d 189 (Sup. Ct. 1998) (spouses have same right to enter into postmarital agreement as premarital agreement; same requirements for validity).	N.Y. Dom. Rel. Law § 236(B)(3) (2022) (spouses can contract re support; must be fair at execution and conscionable at divorce); Gen. Oblig. Law § 5-311 (2022) (except as provided in N.Y. Dom. Rel. Law § 236(B)(3), spouses cannot contract to relieve liability of support if results in spouse becoming public charge); *Arizin v. Covello*, 175 Misc. 2d 453, 669 N.Y.S.2d 189 (Sup. Ct. 1998) (spouses have same right to enter into postmarital agreement as premarital agreement re support)	N.Y. Fam. Ct. Act § 412 (2022) (spouses have duty to support of spouse); Soc. Serv. Law § 101 (2022) (spouse liable to state for support); Dom. Rel. Law § 236(B) (5-a) (2022) (except where parties entered into agreement for maintenance, court shall order temporary maintenance under guideline, may depart upon consideration of factors, including acts of domestic violence); Gen. Oblig. Law § 5-311 (2022) (except as provided in Dom. Rel. Law § 236, spouses cannot contract to relieve each other of liability for support if likely to make spouse a public charge; *Demis v. Demis*, 168 A.D.2d 840, 564 N.Y.S.2d 515 (1990) (no *pendente lite* attorney fee award where valid postmarital agreement waives)
North Carolina	N.C. Gen. Stat. § 30-3.6 (2022) (right of surviving spouse to elective share waivable during marriage, with or without consideration, by written waiver signed by spouse; not enforceable if not executed voluntarily or not provided fair financial disclosure and did not waive disclosure in writing); § 52-2 (2022) (every married person is authorized to contract and deal with his/her property as if unmarried); § 52-10 (2022) (spouses can contract if not inconsistent with public policy; contract must be in writing if affects rights to real estate for more than three years; no consideration required); § 52-20 (2022) (spouses can enter into written agreement during marriage providing for distribution of marital property at divorce; must be executed and acknowledged); *Dawbarn v. Dawbarn*, 175 N.C. App. 712, 625 S.E.2d 186 (2006) (spouses can enter into agreement re property rights at divorce); *Turner v. Turner*, 89 S.E.2d 245 (N.C. 1955) (premarital agreement may be modified or rescinded after marriage; full and free consent of parties required).	*Stegall v. Stegall*, 100 N.C. App. 398, 397 S.E.2d 306 (1990), *cert. denied*, 328 N.C. 274, 400 S.E.2d 461 (1991) (property settlement agreement survives reconciliation, but support provision abrogated; provision for spousal support enforceable only if executed incident to separation); *Motley v. Motley*, 255 N.C. 150, 120 S.E.2d 422 (1961) (statute authorizing interspousal contracts is limited to property rights, does not permit postmarital agreement to waive spousal support)	N.C. Gen. Stat. § 14-322 (2022) (criminal nonsupport); *Kuder v. Schroeder*, 110 N.C. App. 355, 430 S.E.2d 271 (1993) (spouses have duty to support each other; duty may not be altered by contract)

State	Key Statutes and Cases	Enforceability of Post- Divorce Spousal Support Waiver	Enforceability of Provisions re Waiver of Support during Marriage
North Dakota (UPAA)	N.D. Cent. Code §§ 14-03.2-01 to 14-03.2-11 (2021) (UPMAA eff. 8.1.13) (court may refuse enforcement of term to avoid substantial hardship because of material change in circumstances; criteria for award of alimony over waiver is welfare eligibility); § 14-07-06 (2021) (spouses can contract re property); *Weber v. Weber,* 589 N.W. 2d 358, 362, n.2 (N.D. 1999) (equitable principles determine property division at divorce in absence of postmarital agreement).	*Toni v. Toni*, 636 N.W.2d 396 (N.D. 2001) (divorce agreement regarding spousal support subject to court approval at divorce)	N.D. Cent. Code § 14-07-08 (2021) (spouses jointly liable for debts for necessaries incurred while living together); § 14-07-03 (2021) (spouses have duty of support); § 14-07-10 (2021) (spouses mutually liable for necessaries)
Ohio	Ohio Rev. Code Ann. § 3103.05 (2023) (spouses can enter into agreement subject to rules re confidential relations; agreement that alters legal relations must comply with § 3103.061); § 3103.06 (2023) (spouses can enter into postmarital agreement to alter legal relations, and to modify or terminate a premarital or postmarital agreement; must comply with § 3103.061); § 3103.061 (2023) (agreement under §§ 3103.05 or 3103.06 must be in signed writing, entered freely, without fraud, duress, coercion, or overreaching, with full disclosure or full knowledge and understanding of nature, value and extent of property of both spouses, and terms do not promote divorce or profiteering by divorce).		Ohio Rev. Code Ann. § 3103.03 (2022) (duty to support self, children, and spouse); *Ohio State University Hospital v. Kinkaid*, 48 Ohio St. 3d 78, 549 N.E.2d 517 (1990) (spouses must each support other with property and labor; married person can be sued by third party creditor if fails to support)
Oklahoma	43 Okla. Stat. § 205 (2022) (spouses cannot by contract alter legal relations except as to property and except may agree in writing to immediate separation and for support); § 43-204 (spouses can contract re property subject to general rules re confidential relations); *Manhart v. Manhart*, 725 P.2d 1234 (Okla. 1986) (spouses can contract with each other re property, subject to rules re confidential relations; transfer taking property out of marital estate enforceable at divorce); *Boyer v. Boyer*, 925 P.2d 82 (Okla. Ct. App. 1996) (postmarital amendment to premarital agreement valid as to property rights if meets validity criteria for postmarital agreement); *but see Hendrick v Hendrick*, 976 P.2d 1071 (Okla. Ct. App. 1998) (amendment to premarital agreement is postmarital agreement; postmarital agreements not authorized by Oklahoma law, distinguishing *Manhart* and *Boyer*, without citing § 43-205); *and see Crane v. Howard*, 206 Okla. 278, 243 P.2d 998 (1951) (Okla. law does not authorize postmarital agreement waiving spousal rights at death).	43 Okla. Stat. § 205 (2022) (spouses cannot by contract alter legal relations except as to property and except may agree in writing to immediate separation and for support); *Boyer v. Boyer*, 925 P.2d 82 (Okla. Ct. App. 1996) (postmarital agreement or amendment to premarital agreement cannot affect spousal support obligation).	43 Okla. Stat. § 201 (2022) (spouses contract obligations of mutual respect, fidelity, and support); § 43-202 (2022) (husband must support self and wife out of community property or separate property; if community property insufficient, wife must support husband when husband has not deserted her out of community property or separate property if husband has no community or separate property and is unable to support himself); § 43-205 (2022) (spouses cannot by contract alter legal relations, except as to property and except may agree in writing to immediate separation and non-support)

State	Key Statutes and Cases	Enforceability of Post- Divorce Spousal Support Waiver	Enforceability of Provisions re Waiver of Support during Marriage
Oregon	Or. Rev. Stat. Ann. § 114.620 (2022) (right of election can be waived during marriage by written contract); *Grossman v. Grossman*, 191 Ore. App. 294, 82 P.3d 1039 (2003) (postmarital agreement must be fair and equitable); *Daywalt v. Bertrand*, 10 Or. App 418, 500 P.2d 484 (1972) (postmarital property settlement can abolish surviving spouse's statutory rights if explicit provision in agreement).		
Pennsylvania	20 Pa. Cons. Stat. Ann. § 2207 (2022) (right of election of surviving spouse can be waived during marriage); § 23-3501 (2022) (at divorce marital property does not include property excluded by valid agreement executed during marriage); *Stoner v. Stoner*, 819 A.2d 529 (Pa. 2005) (principles applicable to premarital agreements equally applicable to postmarital agreements); *Vaccarello v. Vaccarello*, 757 A.2d 909 (Pa. 2000) (postmarital agreement enforceable at divorce after reconciliation); *Estate of Kester*, 405 A.2d 1244 (Pa. 1979) (postmarital agreement presumed valid; burden on party seeking to invalidate); *Lugg v. Lugg*, 64 A.3d 1109 (Pa. Super. Ct. 2013) (parties can waive financial disclosure).	*Vaccarello v. Vaccarello*, 757 A.2d 909 (Pa. 2000) (enforceable postmarital agreement governs spousal support claim)	23 Pa. Cons. Stat. § 4321 (2022) (married persons liable for support of each other); § 23-4102 (2022) (both spouses liable to creditors for debts for necessaries); § 23-4603 (2022) (person must financially assist indigent spouse)
Rhode Island (UPAA)	R.I. Gen. Laws §§ 15-4-3, 15-4-4 (2022) (spouse can contract with anyone including other spouse); § 15-4-6 (2022) (married woman can release right to life estate in H's property by deed).		
South Carolina	S.C. Code Ann. § 20-5-50 (2022) (marriage contract, deed, or settlement must specify property to be conveyed or included; contract must be in writing, signed and witnessed); § 20-3-630 (2022) (at divorce property excluded by valid contract is nonmarital and not divisible); *Gilley v. Gilley*, 327 S.C. 8, 488 S.E.2d 310 (1997) (property excluded by valid written agreement is nonmarital at divorce); *Bailey v. Bailey*, 330 S.C. 326, 498 S.E.2d 891 (Ct. App. 1998) (family court has no jurisdiction to apportion property excluded from marital estate by valid postmarital agreement).	*Hardee v. Hardee*, 355 S.C. 382, 388, 585 S.E.2d 501, 504, N.3 (2003) (postmarital reconciliation agreement waiving spousal support does not violate public policy)	S.C. Code Ann. § 63-5-20 (2022) (criminal nonsupport)
South Dakota (UPAA)	S.D. Codified Laws § 25-2-10 (2022) (spouses can contract regarding property subject to rules re confidential relations); § 25-2-13 (2022) (spouses can contract re property); § 29A-2-213 (2022) (spouse may waive rights as surviving spouse; agreement to waive is not enforceable if waiver not executed voluntarily, or unconscionable at execution and spouse was not provided fair financial disclosure, did not expressly waive disclosure, and did not have adequate knowledge of decedent's financial affairs); *Estate of Gab*, 364 N.W.2d 924 (S.D. 1985) (spouses can contract re disposition of property at death and divorce; agreement subject to close scrutiny; relationship of spouses is one of special confidence; less evidence required to establish fraud, oppression, or deception than if arm's length transaction); *Keith v. Keith*, 37 S.D. 132, 156 N.W. 910 (1916) (action to cancel postmarital agreement for fraud; H fraudulently concealed his lack of property and insolvency to get W to commit her separate property to mutual support).	S.D. Codified Laws § 25-2-13 (2022) (spouses cannot contract to alter legal relations, except as to property and except for immediate separation with provision for spousal support); *Connolly v. Connolly*, 270 N.W.2d 44 (S.D. 1978) (postmarital agreement not binding on court re spousal support)	S.D. Codified Laws § 25-7-1 (2022) (person shall support self and spouse from property or labor); § 25-7-2 (2022) (spouse liable to third party for necessaries); § 25-7-4 (2022) (criminal nonsupport); § 25-7-5 (2022) (must support spouse with separate property if spouse cannot support self and has not deserted)

State	Key Statutes and Cases	Enforceability of Post- Divorce Spousal Support Waiver	Enforceability of Provisions re Waiver of Support during Marriage
Tennessee	Tenn. Code Ann. § 36-4-121(g)(1) (2022) (provisions of Code for equitable distribution of property at divorce do not preclude enforcement of property agreement); *Dospil v. Dospil*, 2007 Tenn. App. Lexis 684 (unpub.) (postmarital agreements generally recognized; subject to close scrutiny; generally governed by same principles as premarital agreements); *Bratton v. Bratton*, 136 S.W.3d 595 (Tenn. 2004) (consideration required for postmarital agreement); *Estate of Wiseman*, 889 S.W.2d 215 (Tenn. Ct. App. 1994) (validity determined according to same criteria as premarital agreement); *Gilley v. Gilley*, 778 S.W.2d 862 (Tenn. Ct. App. 1989) (reconciliation agreement re disposition of marital property enforceable at divorce); *Hoyt v. Hoyt*, 213 Tenn. 117, 372 S.W.2d 300 (1963) (spousal contract that contemplates but does not encourage divorce generally valid and enforceable re property and spousal support; must be free of fraud and at least meet requirements for premarital agreement).	Tenn. Code Ann. § 36-5-121 (f)(2)(A) (2022) (future spousal support payments modifiable upon substantial material changed circumstances); *Dospil v. Dospil*, 2007 Tenn. App. Lexis 684 (unpub.) (marital agreement providing for fixed payment at dissolution is not modifiable; marital agreement for future spousal support payments is modifiable if circumstances change; provision for each party to pay his/her own debts after execution precludes award of attorney fees); *Hoyt v. Hoyt*, 213 Tenn. 117, 372 S.W.2d 300 (1963) (bona fide reconciliation agreement enforceable re spousal support)	Tenn. Code Ann. § 39-15-101 (2022) (criminal liability for failure to support disabled spouse or child)
Texas	Tex. Const. Art. XVI, § 15 (2021) (spouses, without intent to defraud creditor, may partition existing or future property or exchange community interest by written instrument); Tex. Fam. Code Ann. § 4.102 (2021) (spouses may partition or exchange between themselves community property in existence or to be acquired; property so transferred is separate property); § 4.105 (2021) (partition and exchange agreement not enforceable if not voluntary or if unconscionable at execution and no financial disclosure, knowledge, or waiver); § 4.203 (2021) (agreement to convert separate property to community property must be in writing, identify property converted, and specify that converted to community property; no consideration required); § 4.205 (2021) (agreement to convert property to community property not enforceable if not voluntary and no disclosure of legal effect of converting separate property to community property); *Izzo v. Izzo*, 2010 Tex. App. Lexis 3623 (unpub.) (spouses have fiduciary duty in entering into postmarital agreement); *Sheshunoff v. Sheshunoff*, 1725.W.3d 686 (Tex. Ct. App. 2005) (parties to post-marital agreement can allocate property and debt in event of divorce).		Tex. Fam. Code Ann. § 2.501 (2021) (duty to support spouse; liable to third party for necessaries)

State	Key Statutes and Cases	Enforceability of Post- Divorce Spousal Support Waiver	Enforceability of Provisions re Waiver of Support during Marriage
Utah	Utah Code Ann. § 30-2-3 (2022) (spouses can transfer property to each other same as if single); § 75-2-208 (2022) (value of separate property excluded from augmented estate at death if designated as separate by written waiver); § 75-2-213 (2022) (surviving spouse rights can be waived in written agreement after marriage; must be voluntary and if unconscionable, financial disclosure, knowledge, or effective waiver); *Beesley v. Harris*, 883 P.2d 1343 (Utah 1994) (postmarital agreement must have consideration); *D'Aston v. D'Aston*, 808 P.2d 111 (Utah. Ct. App. 1990) (postmarital agreement enforceable at divorce).		Utah Code Ann. § 76-7-201 (2022) (criminal nonsupport)
Vermont	15 Vt. Stat. Ann. § 61 (2021) (spouses may enter into contract but only for business partnership); *Griffin v. Griffin*, 217 A.2d 400 (Vt. 1966) (transactions between spouses must be fair and reasonable, voluntary, and understandingly made, and without fraud or undue influence); *Maier v. Maier*, 266 A.3d 778 (Vt. 2021) (postmarital agreement may be enforceable outside of divorce action, *e.g.*, because parties never file for divorce or a spouse dies while divorce is pending); *Allen v. Allen*, 161 Vt. 526, 641 A.2d 1332 (1994) (implicitly approving application of premarital agreement case, *Bassler v. Bassler*, 156 Vt. 353, 593 A.2d 82 (1991), to determine validity of postmarital agreement); *Estate of Ladd v. Estate of Ladd*, 161 Vt. 270, 640 A.2d 29 (1994) (marital settlement agreement enforceable after spouse's death if parties evidenced intent to be effective from date of execution without regard to whether parties divorced).	*Stearns v. Stearns*, 66 Vt. 187, 28 A. 875 (1894) (premarital agreement may not waive spousal support)	15 Vt. Stat. Ann. § 202 (2021) (criminal penalty for nonsupport of family)
Virginia	Va. Code Ann. §§ 20-147–20-155 (2022) (UPAA) (Virginia Marital Agreement Act governing both premarital and postmarital agreements; same validity criteria); § 64.2-314 (2022) (spouse can expressly waive homestead allowance, family allowance, and exempt property by marital agreement in compliance with Va. Code Ann. § 20-147, et seq.); § 20-109.C (2022) (court may not award support, attorney's fees, or suit money contrary to contract).	Va. Code Ann. § 20-151 (2022) (spouses can agree to any terms of postmarital agreement as could agree to in premarital agreement); § 20-109.C (2022) (court may not award support, attorney's fees, or suit money contrary to contract)	Va. Code § 55-37 (2022) (necessaries doctrine as at common law applies equally to both spouses except if living permanently apart; no liability between spouses); § 20-61 (2022) (criminal nonsupport); § 8.01-220.2 (2022) (spouse jointly liable for emergency medical care furnished spouse, while spouses are living together, by physicians licensed in state or hospital located in state)

State	Key Statutes and Cases	Enforceability of Post- Divorce Spousal Support Waiver	Enforceability of Provisions re Waiver of Support during Marriage
Washington	Wash. Rev. Code Ann. § 26.16.050 (2022) (spouse can convey interest in community real estate to other spouse as grantee's separate property; grantor must sign, seal, execute, and acknowledge; does not affect rights of existing creditors of grantor); § 26.16.120 (2022) (spouses can agree re disposition of community property at death; must be witnessed, acknowledged, and certified in same manner as deed to real estate); § 26.16.150 (2022) (every married person has same right to dispose of property as if unmarried); § 26.16.250 (2022) (spouses can agree to disposition of quasi-community property at death by postmarital agreement, community property agreement, or other agreement re property); *Whitney v. Seattle-First Nat'l Bank*, 90 Wash. 2d 105, 579 P.2d 937 (1978) (postmarital agreement must have either fair provision or be voluntary with full disclosure); *Marriage of Schweitzer*, 132 Wash. 2d 318, 937 P.2d 1062 (1997) (three pronged community property agreement under Wash. Rev. Code Ann. § 26.16.120, converting all separate property to community property, applies at divorce as well as at death); *Marriage of Dewberry and George*, 115 Wash. App. 351, 62 P.3d 525 (2003) (spouses can enter into agreement to modify status of property from community to separate); *Getty v. Damson*, 63 Wash. 2d 526, 387 P.2d 964 (1964) (spouses may freely contract to hold property then owned or thereafter acquired as separate estate).		Wash. Rev. Code § 26.20.035 (2022) (criminal nonsupport)
West Virginia	W. Va. § 42-3-3a (2022) (surviving spouse's rights can be waived in agreement during marriage; agreement must be voluntary and, if unconscionable, with financial disclosure, actual or constructive knowledge, or waiver of disclosure); *Marshall v. Marshall*, 166 W. Va. 304, 273 S.E.2d 360 (1980) (reconciliation agreement invalid at divorce where H failed to meet fiduciary duty); *Chambers v. Pierce*, 94 W.Va. 766, 120 S.E. 912 (1929) (contract between spouses is enforceable to determine property rights at death).		
Wisconsin	Wis. Stat. Ann. § 766.58 (2022) (marital contract can determine disposition of property at death; enforceable without consideration; can determine disposition of property at divorce unless inequitable; must be in writing, voluntary, not unconscionable at execution, and made with fair disclosure); § 767.61 (3)(L) (2022) (court divides property at divorce equally, but may consider written agreement during marriage; agreement binding unless inequitable; court presumes equitable); *Button v. Button*, 131 Wis. 2d 84, 388 N.W.2d 546 (1986) (postmarital agreement is enforceable at divorce); *In re Greiling's Will*, 59 N.W.2d 241 (Wis. 1953) (construction of will made subject to terms of postmarital agreement).	Wis. Stat. Ann. § 766.58 (3)(d), (9)(b) (2022) (marital property agreement can determine spousal support at divorce; but spousal support waiver not enforceable at divorce if spouse eligible for public assistance; award must be sufficient to keep spouse off public assistance); *Button v. Button*, 131 Wis. 2d 84, 388 N.W.2d 546 (1986)	Wis. Stat. Ann. § 766.55 (2022) (obligations of spouses; necessaries; third party creditor rights); §766.58(9)(a) (2022) (marital agreement that modifies spousal support during marriage may not result in spouse having less than necessary support during marriage)

State	Key Statutes and Cases	Enforceability of Post- Divorce Spousal Support Waiver	Enforceability of Provisions re Waiver of Support during Marriage
Wyoming	Wyo. Stat. § 2-5-102 (2022) (surviving spouse rights can be waived in written agreement during marriage with fair disclosure; waiver of "all rights" includes elective share, homestead allowance, exempt property and family allowance); *Combs v. Sherry-Combs*, 865 P.2d 50 (Wyo. 1993) (postmarital agreement is different from separation agreement; must have consideration for postmarital agreement); *Campbell v. Prater*, 64 Wyo. 293, 191 P.2d 160 (1948) (consideration for postmarital reconciliation agreement must be bona fide; separation rendered postmarital agreement for reconciliation with favorable property provision invalid for lack of consideration); *Lund v. Lund*, 849 P.2d 731 (Wyo. 1993) (parties may amend premarital agreement during marriage so long as usual requirements for validity are present).	*Lipps v. Loyd*, 967 P.2d 558 (Wyo. 1998) (postmarital agreement regarding spousal support is enforceable as a contract but is modifiable by court); *Dorr v. Newman*, 785 P.2d 1172 (Wyo. 1990) (spousal support may be modified after divorce based on changed circumstances, even if originally determined in contract, in this case, separation agreement)	Wyo. Stat. Ann. § 20-3-101 (2022) (criminal nonsupport)

Note: Except where indicated, UPAA adopted without change to the substantive requirements for validity. States that adopted the UPAA with enhancements to the criteria for validity are indicated with a "+."

APPENDIX

C

PERSONAL INFORMATION WORKSHEET AND QUESTIONNAIRE

PERSONAL INFORMATION WORKSHEET FOR PREMARITAL (OR POSTMARITAL) AGREEMENT

Please provide the information requested below. This questionnaire is divided into two parts. The first part asks for personal information about you and your fiancé(e)/spouse. The second part asks for information about your financial affairs. Your responses will help us understand your objectives and evaluate your needs. The information you provide us, including the answers to the questions below, is confidential, meaning we will not share it with your fiancé(e)/spouse, or with his or her attorney, unless you authorize us to do so.

Today's Date:
Expected date of marriage:
Marriage will take place at:
If married, date of marriage:
Who referred you:
ABOUT MYSELF
1. Name:
2. Social security number:

3.	Phone Numbers	O.K. to phone here?	
		Yes	No
Home		☐	☐
Do you have caller ID on home phone?		☐	☐
Work		☐	☐
Mobile		☐	☐
Other		☐	☐
		Call before sending fax?	
		Yes	No
Work Fax		☐	☐
Home Fax		☐	☐

4. Sex	Age:	Place of Birth:	
Date of Birth:			
Country(ies) of citizenship:			
5. Addresses		Is this e-mail address password protected?	
		Yes	No
Work e-mail:		☐	☐
Home e-mail:		☐	☐
Other e-mail:		☐	☐
Mailing address:			
Should this be marked Personal & Confidential? ☐ No ☐ Yes			
Residential address (if different):			
County/state of residence:			
How long resident of state (years/months):			

6. Former name(s):	
7.	
Employer:	
Address:	
Position/occupation:	
Length of this employment:	
Approximate monthly gross pay:	
8. Health problems for which special attention or care is necessary:	

9. Education:

Level	Graduate? Yes	No	Degree type/subject	Date	School
High School	☐	☐			
Undergraduate	☐	☐			
Graduate/Prof.	☐	☐			
Doctorate	☐	☐			
Post Doc	☐	☐			

	Yes	No	Type of degree seeking	Expected date of graduation
Are you currently in school?	☐	☐		

10. I was married ___ times before this marriage.[1]

	Former Spouse Name	Date marriage terminated	How terminated (death, divorce)
i.			
ii.			
iii.			
iv.			
v.			

11. For each child born to or adopted by you:

Name	Age	Birth date	With whom does child reside?	School	Grade

12. Financial obligations to former spouse(s)/children:

13. Names and ages of any children of this marriage/relationship:

Name	Age	Birth date	With whom does child reside?	School	Grade

14. Major (nonroutine) financial obligations to children of current relationship (*e.g.*, college expenses):

15. Do you have any stored embryos or other stored genetic material? If yes, please provide particulars.

16. Wills and estate planning:	
	I do not have a will.
	I have a will executed on (date):
	I have the following estate planning arrangements in place (*e.g.*, annual cash gifts, revocable or irrevocable trust; life insurance trust, etc.):
	I have an estate planning attorney (Name):
	I do not have an estate planning attorney.

ABOUT MY FIANCÉ(E)/SPOUSE
17. Name:
18. Social security number:

19.	Phone Numbers	Note: We will not contact your fiancé(e)/spouse if he/she is represented by counsel.	
Home			
Does your fiancé(e)/spouse have caller ID on home phone? ☐ Yes ☐ No			
Work			
Mobile			
Other			
		Call before sending fax?	
		Yes	No
Work Fax		☐	☐
Home Fax		☐	☐

20. Sex	Age:	Date of Birth:	Place of Birth:
21. Country(ies) of citizenship:			
If not U.S. citizen, what is immigration status?			
Did you sign an I-864 Form (Affidavit of Support) on behalf of your fiancé(e)/spouse?			

22. Addresses	
Work e-mail:	
Home e-mail:	
Other e-mail:	
Mailing address:	Residential address:
Should this be marked personal & confidential? ☐ No ☐ Yes	
23. County/state of residence:	
How long resident of state:	

24. Former name(s):
25. Health problems for which special attention or care is necessary:

26. Education:					
Level	Graduate? Yes	No	Degree type/subject	Date	School
High School	☐	☐			
Undergraduate	☐	☐			
Graduate/Prof.	☐	☐			
Doctorate	☐	☐			
Post Doc	☐	☐			
Is fiancé(e)/spouse currently in school? Yes ☐ No ☐				Type of degree seeking	Expected date of graduation
27. Fiancé(e)/spouse currently has an attorney? ☐ Yes ☐ No					
28. If yes, list contact information for opposing counsel if known:					
Attorney's name:					
Firm:					
Address:					
Phone:					

29. My fiancé(e)/spouse was married ___ times before the marriage.[2]			
	Former Spouse Name	Date marriage terminated	How terminated (death, divorce)

30. For each child born or adopted into previous marriage(s)/relationships, list the following:					
Name	Age	Birth date	With whom does child reside?	School	Grade
31. Financial obligations to former spouse(s), children:					

32. Does fiancé(e)/spouse have any stored embryos or other stored genetic material? If yes, please provide particulars.

ABOUT THE MARRIAGE			
33. Date:		Place:	
What plans have already been made and/or carried out:			
ABOUT THE PREMARITAL/POSTMARITAL AGREEMENT			
34. Agreement is desired by:			
Me	Fiancé(e)/Spouse	Both	Other
If other, please explain:			
35. My objectives in seeking a premarital/postmarital agreement are:			

36. My fiancé(e)'s/spouse's objectives in seeking a premarital/postmarital agreement are:
37. I foresee the following problems in dealing with my fiancé(e)/spouse regarding a premarital/postmarital agreement:
38. I have some questions and issues I would like to explore as follows:

39. I have already made some decisions about the terms I want included in the agreement, as follows:

FINANCIAL DISCLOSURE

Parties entering into a premarital/postmarital agreement should make disclosure of all assets, liabilities, and sources and amounts of income. A failure to do so may render the agreement unenforceable. You will have an opportunity to discuss with us any concerns you may have about the extent of the disclosure required to create an enforceable agreement in your particular case.

Please provide us with full and complete information about your financial circumstances. You may use the worksheet that begins below if you wish. Also, please provide us with your fiancé(e)'s/spouse's financial disclosure, if possible. He/she may use the attached worksheet as well.

ASSETS AND DEBTS WORKSHEET	
Name:	Date:

1. Amounts and Sources of Income:

Source	Type*	Expected amt. this calendar year	Amt. last calendar year	Amt. 2 calendar years ago	Significant changes expected

* S = salary; P = pension; D = dividends; I = interest; C = capital gains; T = trust; R = rent; O = other

2. Real Estate:

Type**	Address	Date purchased	Price	Current value	Balance owed on mortgage	How titled?

** R = residence; I = investment/rental; U = unimproved land; F = farm or ranch; C = commercial property; V = vacation property (non-rental)

3. Automobiles and other motor vehicles (including motorcycles, RVs, motorboats):

How titled?	Year	Make & model	Amount owed	Current value

4. Personal property: Identify items of special monetary or sentimental value and then aggregate remaining items into general categories, such as furniture, books, sports and hobby equipment, etc.

Description	Date of acquisition	Purchase price	Amount of lien, if any	Fair market value

5. Cash (checking, savings credit union, money market, treasury bills, CDs, etc.)

How titled? Joint owners/% of interest?	Name of financial institution	Type of account	Balance as of ______ [date]	Held in pay-on-death or other survivorship form?

6. Defined contribution retirement plans (*e.g.*, IRA, SEP-IRA, 401(k), profit sharing, ESOP, federal TSP, 403(b), other)

Participation date	Financial institution/ Name of plan administrator	Type of plan or account	Current value	Valuation date	Name of current beneficiary

7. Defined benefit pension plans (*e.g.*, private sector pension plan, CSRS, FERS, military, Foreign Service, state or other government, international organization)

Participation date	Sponsoring entity (*e.g.*, company, union, government, or organization)	Name of plan	Accrued benefit	Date eligible for retirement	Name of current beneficiary

8. Other deferred compensation plans or benefits (*e.g.*, stock options, stock bonus, stock awards, supplemental retirement plans, restricted shares)

Sponsoring entity (*e.g.*, company, union, government, or organization)	Type of benefit	Number of shares or units	Present value	Valuation date	Name of current beneficiary

9. Are any of your retirement benefits or deferred compensation subject to the rights of a former spouse? If yes, please provide particulars and a copy of the court order:

10. Securities (mutual funds, bonds, limited partnerships, stocks) or attach account statement.

Name of other owners; % of interest	Broker/Name of fund/Name of company	Description (# of shares, % interest)	Current value	Valuation date

11. Life insurance policies:

Name of insurance company	Policy no.	Type (whole life, term)	Death benefit	Annual premium	Cash value	Name of current beneficiary

12. Business interests. Describe any interest in a business or professional practice, giving approximate value of interest, where possible:

13. Intellectual property. Describe any interest you have in any patents, copyrights, software licenses, or other intellectual property.

14. Other. Identify any other assets if substantial value, such as digital assets (*e.g.*, bitcoin).

15. Are you the beneficiary of any trusts or estates? If yes, please provide detail.

16. Do you regularly receive substantial gifts from, or make substantial gifts to, a family member (*e.g.*, an annual gift of cash or property valued at $17,000 or more)? If so, please provide details:

17. Do you expect any significant change in your assets over the next three years (*e.g.*, an inheritance, distribution from a trust, sale of a business)? If so, please explain:

18. Unsecured debts (*e.g.*, credit cards, lines of credit, personal loans, student loans)

Creditor	Co-obligor	Type of debt (*e.g.*, credit card, personal loan)	Purpose/how used	Current balance	Monthly payment

19. Appraisals and statements of net worth:
Have you prepared a loan application, life insurance application, statement identifying your assets and liabilities, or other statement of a similar nature in the past three years? If so, please provide a copy.

20. In the past three years, has any third party prepared a valuation or appraisal of an asset, such as a business, real estate, or nonmarketable securities, in which you have an interest? If so, please provide a copy.

1. Include state-recognized civil unions, registered domestic partnerships, or other legal relationships requiring formal registration under the law of a state or foreign country.
2. Include state-recognized civil unions, registered domestic partnerships, or other legal relationships requiring formal registration under the law of a state or foreign country.

APPENDIX

D

BASIC TITLE CONTROLS AGREEMENT

The model below is a plain title controls agreement under which parties waive all claims at death or dissolution. Chapter 12 consists of the same model paragraphs coupled with comments as well as additional model terms. Appendix E (Additional and Optional Terms) has a number of other optional terms.

PREMARITAL [POSTMARITAL] AGREEMENT

This Agreement is made this day ____ of ____________, 20__, by and between SPOUSE ONE, [prospective husband/wife] (hereafter referred to as "_____"), and SPOUSE TWO, [prospective husband/wife] (hereafter referred to as "_____").

Recitals

1. The parties plan to marry after execution of this Agreement. [***Alternative:*** The parties plan to marry on ______ [DATE] and after execution of this Agreement.] [***If parties are already married:*** The parties were married on ______ [DATE] and are now husband and wife/spouses. The parties have ___children together: ______.]

2. Each party currently owns separate property, all of which has been acquired independently of and without the assistance of the other.

3. SPOUSE ONE is employed with ______________________________ as _________________________. [***Optional:*** He/She is in good health to the best of his/her knowledge.] SPOUSE TWO is employed with ____________________ as ___________________. [***Optional:*** He/She is in good health to the best of his/ her knowledge.]

4. The parties are residents of ____________________ [*Or:* SPOUSE ONE is currently a resident of ______________________ and SPOUSE TWO is a resident of ______________.]

5. SPOUSE ONE has [never] been married [previously] and has _____ / [no] children. SPOUSE TWO has [never] been married [previously] and has _____ / [no] children. [***Add, if appropriate:*** _____ has financial obligations for _____ his/her child/ren and for a previous spouse.]

6. Each party read this Agreement in its entirety before signing it.

[7. ***If a postmarital agreement, state reason for agreement, e.g.:*** (i) The parties intended to enter into a premarital agreement, but did not have enough time to conclude the negotiations and drafting prior to the date of marriage. (ii) The parties are living apart and are estranged but intend to pursue reconciliation and believe that entering into this Agreement will promote that goal. In furtherance of their goal, they wish to settle and determine their property rights and any potential claims for spousal support in the event they fail to reconcile. (iii) The parties intend to make certain property transfers to further their estate planning objectives and they intend this Agreement to determine their property rights upon the death of a party or a marital separation.]

8. The parties intend, by this Agreement, to establish their rights in all property currently owned or hereafter acquired by each of them upon the death of a party or in the event of a marital separation or divorce. The parties intend that each of them shall have the right to retain his/her separate property and to share marital property as defined in this Agreement.

9. [***Include following text if agreement provides for waiver of spousal support:***] Each party further desires to waive any right or claim he or she has or may ever have to support from the other in the event of a marital separation or divorce [***Add if agreement provides for contractual spousal support:*** , except as specifically provided herein]. [***Optional:*** Each party is capable of providing for his or her own support through employment and through other means. Neither party intends to be dependent on the other for support in the future.]

10. The parties to this Agreement do not intend to facilitate or encourage a separation or divorce. Each party believes that the resolution of the issues covered by this Agreement in the manner set forth will promote their married life together, since the interests and values embodied in this Agreement are shared by and important to each party. The parties enter into this Agreement after thoughtful discussions between themselves, consultations with and advice from independent counsel, or the opportunity for such advice, and with love and respect for each other. Both parties intend for this Agreement to eliminate any issues between them in the event this marriage is unsuccessful or between one of them and the other's family upon the death of a spouse.

11. The parties acknowledge that this Agreement is a premarital [***or:*** postmarital] agreement as defined by law. Each party understands and intends that the provisions of this Agreement shall prevail over any statute or law of ____________________, or any other jurisdiction, including any foreign jurisdiction, which may be applicable in the absence of this Agreement, and that this Agreement shall govern their rights and obligations upon death, separation, or divorce regardless of where they may be living at the time.

12. The parties acknowledge that a party may experience changed circumstances during the marriage [***If a postmarital agreement:*** after execution of this Agreement], such as a substantial increase or decrease in property values, or a decline in actual earnings, or earning potential, due to illness, disability, loss of employment, or market conditions, and that such changes may be unanticipated. The parties nevertheless agree that no change in circumstances shall affect the fairness and mutual consideration given at the time this Agreement is entered into nor shall it affect the validity of this Agreement or any provision thereof.

IN CONSIDERATION of the mutual promises and exchanges made by each party to this Agreement, the parties agree as follows:

Definitions

1. Property. "Property" means any interest, present or future, legal or equitable, vested or contingent, in any property, including real property; personal property, both tangible and intangible, whenever and wherever acquired or located. "Real property" means land, together with improvements and fixtures thereon. "Tangible personal property" means movable tangible assets, such as, but not limited to, furniture, furnishings, clothing, jewelry, art, automobiles, and equipment, and further includes animal companions. "Intangible personal property" means incorporeal assets, such as, but not limited to, cash, virtual currency, such as bitcoin, nonfungible tokens (NFTs) and other digital assets, certificates of deposit, negotiable instruments, such as checks, notes and mortgages, accounts receivable, insurance, annuities, interest in a trust (whether vested or contingent interest, or current or remainder interest), retirement benefits, an inherited IRA, ownership interest in a business or professional services practice, including, but not limited to, a limited liability company, partnership or "S" corporation, a copyright, patent, software license, or other form of intellectual property, and securities such as stock, bonds, units and options, and where any such property is held in a bank, brokerage, or other financial institution account, the account itself. "Untitled property" shall mean property that lacks a formal document, such as a deed, motor vehicle title, or stock certificate, evidencing ownership.

2. Retirement Benefits and Plans and Other Forms of Deferred Compensation. "Retirement benefit" or "retirement plan" means any individual retirement account or annuity funded with or derived from a party's earnings, and any pension plan, profit-sharing plan, employee savings plan, 401(k) plan, and any other deferred compensation benefit or plan, qualified or non-qualified, including, but not limited to, a stock award, stock purchase, restricted share, stock unit, or stock option plan, provided through employment or self-employment or plan.

3. Earnings. "Earnings" means monies and other compensation derived from a party's personal services, labor or employment, including, but not limited to, salary, wages, bonuses, origination fees, and commissions; in the case of an active business owner who reports business income on a Form 1040, Schedule C or E, or who operates as an "S" corporation, partnership, or limited liability company, the active business owner's share of the business profits (defined as gross receipts in the ordinary course of business from the sale of goods or services less reasonable and necessary business expenses and a reasonable allowance for deferred costs, such as depreciation and amortization); net royalty income (defined as gross royalties less reasonable and necessary expenses, including amortization or depreciation, of producing the income) from intellectual property of which a party is the author, creator or inventor, or otherwise derived from a party's personal services, labor, or employment; employer and employee contributions to a retirement benefit or plan or other deferred compensation plan; accrued but unpaid compensation; severance pay; and all other cash compensation derived from personal efforts or employment. [***Optional:*** "Earnings" also includes noncash employee benefits, such as, but not limited to, paid leave, health, life and disability insurance, company-provided vehicle or transportation allowance, expense accounts and allowances, the right to retain for personal use points or other awards from participation in an affiliation program, such as a credit card, hotel or airline awards program, and all other noncash remuneration derived from personal efforts or employment.] The definition of "earnings" in this Agreement is without regard to whether any such earnings are reportable on an income tax return or are subject to income taxes.

4. Income. "Income" means monies derived from sources other than earnings and includes, but is not limited to, dividends, interest, rents, royalties not defined as earnings (including royalties from oil, mineral, or other rights in real property), proceeds from the sale of property, distributions from an estate or trust, and distributions (other than distributions of nonpassive income defined as earnings, as provided in Paragraph 3) from a pass-through entity, such as a limited liability company, partnership, or "S" corporation; distributions from a retirement plan or other deferred compensation plan; and other property in which a party has an interest.

5. Marital Property. "Marital property" of the parties shall be, and is limited to:

(i) funds or securities held in an account of the parties at a financial institution (such as a bank, credit union, or securities brokerage) and titled as tenants by the entirety, joint tenants with right of survivorship, or tenants in common, without regard to the source of funds except as provided in Paragraph 7(G);

(ii) all other jointly titled property owned by the parties as tenants by the entirety or joint tenants with right of survivorship without regard to the source of funds for acquisition, maintenance, or improvement of such property [***add if appropriate:*** , except as provided in Paragraph ___ [***regarding allocation of separate and marital shares of marital home***]];

(iii) [***Optional:*** the parties' primary marital home without regard to the source of funds for acquisition costs of the home;]

(iv) any appreciation in the value of, all income from, and all proceeds of a loan secured by a lien on marital property;

(v) all property acquired with marital property, including, but not limited to, property acquired with funds from a jointly titled financial institution account, with the proceeds from the sale of, or in exchange for, marital property or with the proceeds of a loan secured by a lien on marital property, including a party's ownership interest as a passive investor or shareholder in a business or professional services practice entity;

(vi) the wedding gifts from third parties, whether received before or after the wedding;

(vii) other gifts that are made to both parties, such as, but not limited to, anniversary gifts, holiday and other special occasion gifts to both parties, and gifts of furniture, equipment, or household effects for the parties' common use [***Optional:*** , with the exception of gifts of family-owned art, antiques, collectibles, or family heirlooms, which shall remain the separate property of the party from whose family of origin such items came];

(viii) [***Optional:*** the furniture, equipment, household effects, and other such items of common use purchased by the parties, or either of them, during the marriage for the parties' marital home(s) without regard to the source of funds for acquisition [***Optional:*** , with the exception of works of art, antiques and collectibles acquired by a party with his or her separate property, which shall remain that party's separate property];

(ix) all other untitled tangible personal property acquired during the marriage, except as specifically provided in Paragraph 6.

6. Separate Property. A party's "separate property" shall be any and all property not defined as marital property under Paragraph 5, including, but not limited to:

(i) all property acquired by a party prior to the parties' marriage, including, specifically, the property set forth in SPOUSE ONE's Schedule A, attached, and SPOUSE TWO's Schedule B, attached, and further including, also without limitation, all property acquired by a party from the date of this Agreement to the date of marriage;

(ii) the party's earnings [***add, if appropriate:*** and all other compensation from personal services, labor, or employment];

(iii) the party's retirement benefits and all other deferred compensation plans and benefits;

(iv) any property acquired by the party before or after the date of this Agreement by gift (including a gift from one party to the other regardless of the source of funds), or by inheritance, including an inherited IRA, survivorship, operation of law, under the laws of intestate succession, a will, trust, or similar instrument, or beneficiary designation;

(v) all property titled in the party's name alone or in his or her revocable living trust;

(vi) the party's ownership share of any property titled as joint tenants with right of survivorship with a third party;

(vii) the party's ownership share of any property titled as tenants in common, whether with a third party or with the other party to this Agreement, in accordance with such title or other instrument;

(viii) all interests of the party, whether vested or contingent, in any trust created and funded by a third party and any trust created by the party and funded with his or her separate property (whether such trust currently exists or is hereafter created), including, but not limited to, any income, property, benefit, or interest held in or received from any such trust and all the contributions to such trust from a third party, or from a party hereto and made with his or her separate property;

(ix) [***Optional:*** a party's ownership interest as an active owner in a closely held business or in a professional services practice regardless of when such interest was acquired, the form of organization of the business, or the source of funds for acquisition of the interest];

(x) any appreciation in the value of, all income from, and all proceeds of a loan secured by a lien on the party's separate property;

(xi) all money or other property received by a party as compensation for injury to his or her person, whether as a result of a judgment, under an agreement for the settlement or compromise of a claim, as an award under workers' compensation laws or other applicable law, or under any contractual or other arrangement for compensation for such injury;

(xii) all property, other than jointly titled property defined as marital property under Paragraph 5(i) or 5(ii), acquired with separate property, including, but not limited to, property acquired with funds from a party's separate property financial institution account, the proceeds from the sale of, or in exchange for, a party's separate property or with the proceeds of a loan secured by a lien on the party's separate property, including a party's ownership interest as a passive investor or shareholder in a business or professional services practice entity;

(xiii) all untitled tangible personal property acquired with a party's separate property;

(xiv) the party's clothing, jewelry, sports equipment, and personal effects without regard to the source of funds for acquisition;

(xv) the party's *pro rata* share of any overpayment of income taxes as provided in Paragraph 13 (notwithstanding that a refund may be jointly titled);

(xvi) the party's animal companions without regard to the source of funds for acquisition.

7. Other Terms Relating to Determination of Separate and Marital Property.

A. The appreciation in value of and the income and profits derived from separate property, whether by way of sale, exchange, investment, reinvestment, forgiveness of debt or otherwise, including, without limitation, the acquisition of property with separate property or with the proceeds from the sale or other disposition of separate property, shall be and remain separate property regardless of the "active" or "passive" nature of a party's contributions to such separate property and regardless of any direct or indirect contribution of labor, effort, inventiveness, physical or intellectual skill, creativity, or managerial activity of either party to the acquisition, care, maintenance, or appreciation of such separate property as well as any separate property monetary contribution of either party to such property. A party who devotes labor, effort, inventiveness, physical or intellectual skill, creativity, managerial activity, or who makes a monetary contribution of his or her separate property to the other party's separate property shall be deemed to have made a gift to the party who owns such separate property. [***Optional:*** With respect to a separate property business of a party, the party's efforts or contributions as an owner, employee, officer, director, stockholder, consultant, or otherwise, shall not convert such business or practice, or any appreciation thereof, into marital property.]

B. Joint or common use of separate property shall not convert separate property to marital property. Further, a party's expenditure of separate property funds for common or family purposes or to benefit the other party shall not convert the property from which such funds were derived to marital property.

C. The fact that the parties may file a joint state or federal income tax return or that one or both parties may pay taxes due in connection with such joint return shall not be interpreted to mean that the income or property reported in such return is marital income or marital property nor convert separate property to marital property. Further, a party's reporting of property holdings, debts, earnings, or income on a joint loan application, financial statement, or net worth statement shall not be interpreted to mean that any item of property, or earnings or income identified therein, is marital property nor shall it convert separate property to marital property.

D. The parties acknowledge that they may occasionally use such expressions as "our property," "our house," etc., when referring to property that is, by the terms of this Agreement, a party's separate property. They agree and acknowledge that they do not intend by such casual references to convert separate property to marital property.

E. A party claiming that an item of untitled tangible personal property acquired during the parties' marriage is his or her separate property may establish his or her claim by:

(i) a written acknowledgment by one party that an asset is wholly or partly the separate property of the other party;

(ii) a bill of sale, invoice, or similar document, coupled with proof of the source of funds used for payment;

(iii) a will, probate accounting, or other writing of a donor or a donor's legal representative.

Nothing herein shall make these the exclusive means of establishing such a claim.

F. This Agreement contains rules defining property as a party's separate property or as marital property. The parties at any time may expressly otherwise characterize any real or personal property as separate property or as marital property by a writing which clearly identifies the item of property and states how the property or interest in property is to be defined for purposes of this Agreement. The writing may also address to what extent, if any, future contributions to acquisition, maintenance, or improvement of the property will affect the definition of the property. Any such writing must be signed by each party. An exchange of electronic messages shall satisfy the requirement for a signed writing for purposes of this Paragraph 7(F).

G. The parties agree and acknowledge that they may from time to time receive a payment of funds (such as an income tax refund [add, if appropriate: or the proceeds of sale of a marital home]) that is partly separate property of each of them, or is partly separate and partly marital property, and that a party may, for convenience, deposit such funds in a joint financial institution account. They agree that such deposit, in and of itself, will not cause the separate property portion of such funds to become marital property provided that the party who is entitled to the separate portion of such funds promptly transfers his or her separate property share out of the joint account.

H. A party's transfer of title to an existing item of property to, or his or her titling newly acquired property in, the sole name of the other party to this Agreement shall be a gift to the recipient thereof and shall, accordingly, be the recipient's separate property, except as the parties may otherwise agree in writing.

I. If a dispute arises concerning the "separate" or "marital" nature of an item of property, the term "separate property" shall be construed broadly, the term "marital property" shall be construed narrowly, and the party claiming that property titled in the other party's name is "marital property" shall bear the burden of proof. Property titled in the names of the parties as tenants by the entirety or joint tenants with right of survivorship shall be conclusively deemed to meet the burden of proof that such property is marital property [***add if appropriate:*** , except as provided in Paragraph ____].

J. Nothing herein is intended to make compliance with Paragraphs 7(E) through 7(I) the exclusive means by which a party may establish his or her claim that an item of property is his or her separate property or is marital property.

8. Separate and Marital Debt.

A. "Marital debt" shall be debt incurred by either party to acquire, improve, or maintain marital property and debt secured by marital property, as defined herein. Marital debt shall also include debt incurred during the marriage in the joint names of the parties [***Add, if appropriate:*** and debt incurred by either party for the parties' usual and customary household [***Optional:*** , personal,] and family expenses].

B. "Separate debt" shall be debt incurred by a party to acquire, improve, or maintain his or her separate property, debt secured by separate property, and all other debt incurred by a party in his or her name alone [***Add, if appropriate:*** , except as provided in Paragraph 8(A)]. A party's separate debt also includes his or her income tax liability on his or her earnings and separate property income, as described in

Paragraph 13, whether on a separate or a joint return. [Add, if appropriate: Further, a party's separate debt shall include all his or her medical and health-care expenses not covered by insurance notwithstanding that the other spouse may be or become liable to a provider of such medical or health-care services.]

9. Marital Separation; During the Marriage.

A. The parties shall be considered separated, and a marital separation shall be deemed to be in effect for purposes of this Agreement, upon the first of the following events:

(i) [***Optional:*** ____ days after] the date that one party informs the other party in writing that he or she intends to be separated or to terminate the marital relationship, and such marital separation, in fact, commences, including a period of living separate and apart under the same roof after such notice (and without regard to whether living separate and apart under the same roof constitutes grounds of divorce) [***optional;*** and provided further that any such notice may only be made by a party in his or her individual capacity and no such notice may be made by an attorney-in-fact, guardian, trustee, or other legal representative];

(ii) the date on which either party serves the other party with a suit for divorce, legal separation, annulment, custody, spousal or child support [***Optional:*** ; and provided that any such suit may only be filed by a party acting in his or her individual capacity and no such suit may be filed by an attorney-in-fact, guardian, trustee, or other legal representative].

B. The phrase "during the marriage" as used in this Agreement shall mean the period from the date of marriage to the date of marital separation; provided, that in the event the parties reconcile after a period of marital separation and resume living together as spouses, the separation shall be treated as if it never occurred [***Add when agreement requires cash payments or transfers of property upon separation:*** , and provided further that, in such event, SPOUSE ONE, or SPOUSE ONE's estate, as the case may be, shall be entitled to a credit for any monies paid or property transferred to SPOUSE TWO under the terms of this Agreement and retained by ____ [him/her] after a reconciliation against any monies or property that SPOUSE ONE or _____ [his/her] estate may subsequently owe _____ [him/her] hereunder]. Reconciliation shall require either a written confirmation signed by both parties or the resumption of a normal marital relationship. Occasional dating or other social relations during a period of living apart shall not, of themselves, constitute a reconciliation.

Rights and Obligations During Marriage

10. Separate Property and Separate Debt.

A. During the marriage, each party shall retain exclusive rights to his or her separate property and shall be free to sell, use, transfer, exchange, abandon, lease, consume, assign, create a security interest in, encumber, dispose of, pledge, gift, or otherwise manage and control his or her separate property [***Add, if appropriate:*** , except as specifically set forth herein]. Nothing herein shall prelude a spouse from making, and the other spouse from accepting, gifts of real or personal property.

B. Each party shall be solely responsible for paying his or her separate debt from his or her separate property. Neither party shall have any obligation to co-sign, become a guarantor, or otherwise to assume any liability to a third party, for any debt incurred, or to be incurred, by the other party for the acquisition or maintenance of his or her separate property or in connection with the property owner's investment or business activities.

C. Each party shall use his or her separate property, and not marital property, to maintain separate property; provided, however, the parties acknowledge that a party may use marital property funds, or his or her separate property funds, for routine expenses of a shared home (such as, but not limited to, property taxes, casualty and liability insurance, utilities, lawn care, repairs, and maintenance) notwithstanding that such home may be a party's separate property and they further acknowledge their understanding that the use of marital or separate property funds for this purpose shall not alter the definition of a separate property home as a party's separate property, nor shall it alter the allocation of the separate property and marital property shares of a home acquired during the marriage as provided in Paragraph __.

D. [***Add, if appropriate:***] During the marriage, SPOUSE ONE shall not make any gifts or other donative transfers to any person, other than SPOUSE TWO, in excess of the annual gift tax exclusion amount under section 2503(b) of the Internal Revenue Code of 1986, as adjusted for inflation from time to time, without the prior written consent of SPOUSE TWO; provided, however, SPOUSE ONE shall have the right to pay tuition and to pay for health care for a child or grandchild of ____ [his/hers] without SPOUSE TWO's consent and without regard to the exclusion amount. Further, SPOUSE ONE shall not make any donative transfers to any organization without SPOUSE TWO's written consent, provided, however, that SPOUSE ONE shall have the right to make charitable contributions aggregating not more than $ ____ annually without SPOUSE TWO's consent. If in any year there is no annual gift tax exclusion under the Internal Revenue Code, then the annual exclusion amount most recently in effect prior to the gift will apply for purposes of this paragraph.

11. Marital Property and Marital Debt.

A. During the marriage, each party agrees to fully disclose all material facts and information regarding the existence, title, and value of all marital property and the existence and amount of all marital debt and to provide the other party, upon his or her request, with access to all information, records, and books that pertain to the nature and value of such property and debt. Each party shall have equal access to their joint financial institution account records, documents evidencing the source of deposits into and the disposition of payments made from such accounts, and to all bills, invoices, credit card statements, and other documents evidencing marital debt or other marital obligations paid or to be paid from such marital property accounts. The parties acknowledge their understanding that each will have access to funds they elect to deposit in a joint financial institution account. [***Add, if appropriate:*** The parties agree to share financial decision-making during the marriage and to consult one another with regard to significant expenditures of marital funds.]

B. If a judgment lien, tax lien, or other encumbrance of one party that is his or her separate debt, as defined herein, is placed upon a party's interest in jointly titled real or personal property, the party who incurred the lien or encumbrance shall indemnify and hold the other party harmless from any financial losses incurred by such other party as a result thereof.

12. Fiduciary Duties. In the event a party is appointed as a personal representative, executor, agent under a power of attorney, or other fiduciary of the other party's estate, or in the event of the disability of a party, and in the further event the other party is appointed and serves as an attorney-in-fact, conservator, or guardian of the disabled party, the party so appointed shall nevertheless be bound by, and shall comply with, the terms of this Agreement.

13. Income Taxes and Income Tax Returns. Each party shall be separately and solely liable for any income taxes payable with respect to his or her earnings and separate property income (as defined herein) and shall be entitled to the deductions, credits, and adjustments allocable to such earnings and separate property income. Each party shall pay any taxes due on his or her earnings and separate property income from his or her separate property and not from marital property. The parties agree that any income taxes payable with respect to marital property income, after attributing the deductions, credits, and adjustments allocable to such marital property income, are marital debt and shall pay such taxes from marital property, including, as applicable, estimated tax payments and application of overpayments, and they acknowledge their understanding that, as between them, they shall equally bear the tax liability on marital property income. [***Optional:*** The parties acknowledge that neither is obligated to file a joint income tax return, and they agree that they shall decide from year to year whether to file joint income tax returns]. In the event the parties file a joint income tax return, they shall each be responsible for their *pro rata* share of the tax, determined as if each filed as [***select:*** a single taxpayer/married, filing separately], taking into account each party's reportable earnings and separate property income, allowable deductions, credits, and other adjustments to income, his or her equal interest in marital property income and allowable deductions, credits, and other adjustments to marital property income, and his or her prepayments of tax (*e.g.*, withholding, refunds applied from prior tax years, and estimated payments), and shall pay his or her *pro rata* share of any underpayment or receive his or her *pro rata* share of any refund, as the case may be. The parties acknowledge that it is not practical to further define the proper allocation of each party's responsibility for the tax on a joint return, and they agree to act in good faith in the spirit of fairness to resolve any issues regarding such responsibility.

14. Joining in Gifts and Gift Tax Returns. Each party shall, upon request of the other, timely join in the execution of gift tax returns consenting to the treatment of gifts made by one of the parties as gifts made one-half by each of the parties in accordance with Section 2513 of the Internal Revenue Code and any applicable state or local gift tax statute, provided, however, that neither party shall be required to do so with respect to any gift in excess of the allowable annual exclusion under Section 2503 of the Internal Revenue Code available to such party with respect to such gift.

PROPERTY RIGHTS UPON DEATH OF A PARTY

15. Waiver of Rights. Except as otherwise provided in this Agreement, each party shall have the right to dispose of his or her property by will, trust, beneficiary designation, transfer during his or her lifetime, gift, or by any other means. Accordingly, each party waives all of his or her property rights, claims, and interests as a surviving spouse to the other party's property, including but not limited to the right of election regarding the estate of the other or to renounce and take against the will of the other, interest in augmented estate, right to inheritance in the event of intestacy, family allowance, homestead rights, exempt property, and all other similar or related rights under applicable law, including the law of any state or foreign jurisdiction where the deceased spouse may be domiciled or own property at death, and further including any rights resulting from changes in law which may take effect after execution of this Agreement.

16. Surviving Spouse Rights to Marital Property. Provided the parties are married and are not separated upon the death of a party, the surviving spouse shall be entitled to receive all marital property, outright and free of trust. Each party shall maintain a will, revocable living trust, beneficiary designations, pay-on-death and transfer-on-death titles, or other estate planning documents, to carry out his or her obligations under this Paragraph. In the event of a marital separation (as defined in Paragraph 9), the provisions of this Paragraph 16 shall not apply and the provisions of this Agreement for determining the parties' rights upon a marital separation shall apply instead.

17. Voluntary Bequests and Transfers.

A. Nothing in this Agreement shall constitute a waiver or disclaimer of any right or property interest passing to a party under the other party's will or a trust established by the other party, or passing to a party under a beneficiary designation, including a beneficiary designation under his or her retirement plan. Neither party waives any bequest under the will of the other party or the right to serve (and receive compensation for serving) as personal representative, agent under a power of attorney, or trustee if appointed as such under any valid instrument.

B. Each party confirms his or her intention that any funds or securities in any joint financial institution account of the parties held as tenants by the entirety or joint tenants with right of survivorship, and any other property held as tenants by the entirety or joint tenants with right of survivorship, shall become the sole property of the survivor of them, provided the parties are married and are not separated as defined in Paragraph 9. In the event the parties are separated upon the death of a party, the provisions of this Agreement for determining the parties' rights upon a marital separation shall determine the rights of the surviving spouse and the estate of the deceased spouse to such property.

C. This Paragraph is not, and shall not be construed as, a promise or representation that either party intends to transfer any real or personal property to the other.

18. Debts.

A. In the event property passes to a surviving spouse by operation of law upon the death of a party, the property shall pass to him or her subject to any secured debt on such property and shall be paid by the surviving spouse without any contribution from the estate of the deceased spouse, except as provided in Paragraph 18(C).

B. [***Add, if appropriate:*** The estate of the deceased party shall pay one-half of the unsecured debt incurred in the joint names of the parties].

C. Notwithstanding Paragraph 18(A), in the event that the debt secured by property that passes by operation of law to a surviving spouse exceeds the fair market value of the property (determined as provided in Paragraph 26(C)), the estate of the deceased party shall be responsible for one-half of the amount by which the debt exceeds the value of such property.

19. Portability Election. The parties agree that upon the death of either spouse, the personal representative of the deceased spouse's estate shall at the surviving spouse's written request [***Optional:***, which shall be made no later than 120 days after the death of the deceased spouse], which request may be made on behalf of the surviving spouse by an attorney-in-fact, guardian, trustee, personal representative, or other agent, timely file any and all documents necessary to make the election provided in §2010(c)(5) of the Internal Revenue Code of 1986, as amended by §303(a) of the Tax Relief, Unemployment Insurance Reauthorization, and Job Creation Act of 2010, or any similar or corresponding law (*i.e.*, the "Portability Election"), for the deceased spouse's unused exclusion amount to be available to be used by the surviving spouse and his or her estate. These documents may include, but are not necessarily limited to, an estate tax return for the deceased spouse's estate even if his or her estate does not owe any federal estate tax at his or her death. If the surviving spouse makes this request and the deceased spouse's estate would otherwise not be required to file an estate tax return, or other necessary documents, in order to make the election, the surviving spouse's estate shall make the arrangements for the preparation of the estate tax return (or necessary documents in connection with the election) and pay the cost of preparing the estate tax return, or other documentation, and all other costs incurred in connection with the election. The deceased spouse's personal representative shall fully cooperate with the preparation, execution and filing of the necessary documents (including the estate tax return) and shall promptly furnish all documents and information as shall be reasonably requested for that purpose.

Disposition of Retirement and Survivor Benefits in the Event of Marital Separation or Death

20. Waiver of Interests in Retirement Benefits in the Event of Separation. In the event of the parties' marital separation, each party shall have the right to retain his or her retirement benefits, whenever accrued, free from any claim or demand of the other party, including any claim for an equitable distribution or other division of these benefits, and each party expressly waives any and all claims he or she may have to any retirement benefits held by the other party. In the event of a marital separation, each party shall, upon request of the other, execute such consent or waiver as may be required to effectuate the participant party's right to retain exclusive rights to his or her retirement benefits, including any consent or waiver that may be required to carry out the terms of this Agreement.

21. Waiver of Spousal Interest in and Right to Survivor and Death Benefits. Each party expressly waives any legal right he or she may have under any federal or state law as spouse to participate as a payee or beneficiary of any interest the other party may have now or in the future in any retirement benefits, including, but not limited to, the right to receive any lump sum death benefit, pre-retirement survivor annuity, or post-retirement annuity (also known as the "joint and survivor annuity" or "surviving spouse annuity"). Each party consents to any election previously or hereafter made by the other party with respect to the payee and the form of payment of any benefit upon retirement or death under any such plan. The parties acknowledge that the effect of this waiver is to permit each party, without notice to or consent of the other party, to elect a single life annuity, self-only annuity, lump sum withdrawal benefit, commuted lump sum, or refund of employee contributions, take a distribution or rollover, name a beneficiary of that party's choosing as beneficiary of his or her survivor or death benefits, or elect any other form of payment available under the terms of his or her retirement plan. [***Optional:*** The parties acknowledge their understanding that each party has the right to name a beneficiary of his or her choice under his or her Individual Retirement Account.]

22. Obligation to Execute Consent to Waiver of Retirement Plan Benefits. The parties agree that after the date of their marriage each will, upon request of the other, or his or her personal representative, as the case may be, execute any waiver or consent to waiver as may be required by the terms of the other party's plan, or applicable statute or regulation, so as to permit the plan participant to elect any form of payment available under his or her retirement plan and to waive completely any spousal rights the nonparticipant-spouse may otherwise have under such plan. [***Optional:*** Each party acknowledges that it is his or her responsibility to request that the other party execute the necessary consent form after the marriage and to file the executed form with his or her plan administrator.]

23. Default. In order to carry out the terms hereof: (i) if a party is unable for any reason to change the beneficiary of the death or survivor benefits of his or her retirement plan or, (ii) if a party fails to designate a beneficiary and the plan provides for payment to the "spouse" or "former spouse," or, (iii) if such waiver under this Agreement is for any reason ineffective and the benefits are, in fact, paid to the surviving party contrary to the terms of Paragraph

22, then in any of such events the surviving party shall, at the direction of and at the sole discretion of the decedent's personal representative: (A) disclaim any entitlement to any benefits received or receivable; or (B) assign all rights to receive such benefits to the estate of the deceased party or the person designated by the decedent or the decedent's personal representative to receive such benefits, net of all income taxes payable by the surviving party with respect to such benefits; or (C) pay the net after-tax benefits over to the estate of the deceased party or to the person designated by the decedent or by the decedent's personal representative. [***Add if appropriate:*** In the event the surviving spouse fails to carry out the terms of this paragraph, the provisions for ____ [him/her] under Paragraphs ___ and ____ of this Agreement [***making specific provisions for surviving spouse at death of retirement plan participant***] shall be null and void.]

24. Voluntary Beneficiary Designations. Nothing in this Agreement shall prevent a party from expressly designating the other party as beneficiary of his or her survivor benefits, pre-retirement survivor benefits, or death benefits under his or her retirement plan. Neither party waives any right to proceeds vesting in him or her by reason of being expressly designated a beneficiary of any retirement benefits of the other party.

Property Rights and Support in the Event of Marital Dissolution

25. Separate Property. In the event of the parties' separation, as defined in Paragraph 9, each party shall retain his or her separate property free from any claim or demand of the other party, and each party shall be solely responsible for paying his or her separate debt. Each party waives the right to make a claim with respect to the separate property of the other party for transfer, monetary award, equitable distribution award, equitable lien, or community property award under __________ Code § _________, or division of any kind under any applicable statute or law of ____________________, or any other jurisdiction that may govern the disposition of marital or community property upon separation or divorce, including a foreign jurisdiction, as such laws now exist or may hereafter be enacted or amended.

26. Marital Property. In the event of the parties' separation as defined in Paragraph 9:

A. Each party shall be entitled to receive one-half of the marital property and shall be charged with one-half of the marital debt, secured or unsecured. In the event a party receives property as part of a division of property upon marital separation or divorce, the property shall be transferred to the recipient subject to any secured debt on such property and shall be paid by the recipient of the property. Further, the parties shall each be responsible for paying one-half of their unsecured marital debt as part of the equal division of marital property, except as they may otherwise agree.

B. In order to carry out the division of marital property and the payoff of marital debt, the parties shall take such steps as they shall agree upon to divide and allocate their marital property and marital debt in accordance with the terms of this Agreement. They agree to negotiate in good faith to allocate their property interests in accordance with the terms of this Agreement. In negotiating the allocation of their property, they shall each give due consideration to the other party's preferences, difficulties of valuation, marketability of assets, and other relevant factors. The parties have not provided specific terms to carry out this division because the nature of the assets and debts and the pertinent circumstances cannot be ascertained at this time. Nevertheless, if an item of marital property lends itself to a distribution in kind, to the extent possible the property shall be distributed equally in kind. If the property does not lend itself to a distribution in kind, or the parties cannot agree on an in-kind division, they shall proceed in accordance with Paragraph 26(D).

C. In the event the parties do not agree as to the fair market value of any specific item of marital property, the parties shall obtain an appraisal of the property subject to division from a qualified, independent appraiser with experience in valuing the type of property in dispute. Such appraisal shall control as to fair market value. If the parties are unable to agree on an appraiser, each party shall select such an appraiser having an office in or reasonably near the community where the property is located, and the average of the two appraisals shall control as to value. A party's failure to respond within 30 days to a written request for selection of an appraiser shall be deemed a waiver of the right to participate in the selection, and the other party's choice of appraiser shall control. The parties shall share the cost of appraisal equally.

D. In the event the parties do not agree as to the appropriate disposition of any item of marital property, they shall offer such item for sale to the general public using a method calculated to achieve the highest price and shall divide the proceeds of sale in accordance with Paragraph 26(A). [***Alternative if agreement provides for binding arbitration:*** In the event the parties do not agree as to the appropriate disposition of any item of marital property or marital debt, they shall resolve the dispute in binding arbitration as set forth in Paragraph 51.]

E. This Agreement is a full and complete settlement of all marital property rights of the parties. Accordingly, each party waives the right to make a claim with respect to any marital property for contribution, transfer, monetary award, equitable distribution award, equitable lien, or community property award under __________ Code § __________, or division of any kind under any applicable statute or law of __________, or any other jurisdiction that may govern the disposition of marital or community property upon separation or divorce, including a foreign jurisdiction, as such laws now exist or may hereafter be enacted or amended.

F. If at any time during the marriage, the parties, or either of them, become residents of a state or country under the laws of which a spouse acquires property interests commonly known as community property or quasi-community property, or any other property interests different from the property interests of spouses under the laws of __________ their property interests shall nevertheless remain the same as they would have been under the terms of this Agreement construed in accordance with the laws of __________. Each party hereby agrees, at any time during the marriage, after a marital separation or divorce, or the death a party, to execute, acknowledge, and deliver to the other, or his or her representative, any deed and other instrument that may be necessary to waive any interest in any property or estate of the other which he or she may acquire by virtue of any community property, quasi-community property, or equivalent laws.

G. In the event a party predeceases the other after a marital separation, but prior to the full implementation of the provisions of this Agreement for disposition of property, unless otherwise agreed by the surviving party and the deceased party's estate, the surviving party shall, within nine months of the death of the deceased party, execute an irrevocable qualified disclaimer within the meaning of § 2518 of the Internal Revenue Code of 1986, or any similar corresponding law, to disclaim all or any portion of such property passing to the surviving party by right of survivorship, operation of law, under the laws of intestate succession, will, trust, or similar instrument or beneficiary designation, including retirement benefits, which exceeds in value the property to which the surviving party is entitled under this Agreement in the event of marital separation.

28. Waiver of Spousal Support. Each party expressly waives any right he or she may ever have to receive alimony, maintenance, or spousal support from the other—including temporary, rehabilitative, indefinite, and permanent, both periodic and lump sum—whether such right or claim results from common law, statutory law, or by way of equitable rights. Each party shall indemnify and hold the other harmless from any such claim made by him or her. Each party waives his or her right to have any court assume jurisdiction for the purpose of modifying this Agreement, and no provision in this Agreement concerning alimony or spousal support shall be subject to modification by any court under any statute or law of any jurisdiction, including a foreign jurisdiction, that may be applicable in the absence of this Premarital [***or:*** Postmarital] Agreement. Each party recognizes the implications of waiving a future right to support from the other party given the uncertainty of each party's future needs and resources, but makes such waiver freely and voluntarily. Each party acknowledges that it is not his or her intent to derive any right of support from the other party in the event of a marital separation or divorce, notwithstanding the law of any state, the passage of time, or any change in the circumstances of the parties. [***Add, if appropriate:*** The parties expressly acknowledge that they may have a child or children together and that the birth of a child constitutes a change of circumstances and may result in further changes in circumstances, such as a parent leaving employment to care for a child. Nevertheless, the parties intend and agree that neither the birth of a child, nor any further attendant change in circumstances, shall have any effect on their waiver of spousal support herein.]

Attorneys' Fees and Costs

29. Fees Incurred for Preparation of this Agreement. SPOUSE ONE shall be responsible for paying, from his/her separate funds, the attorneys' fees incurred by him/her and the attorneys' fees incurred by SPOUSE TWO in the negotiation and drafting of this Agreement.

30. Fees and Costs Relating to Separation or Divorce or in Connection with the Administration of the Estate of a Deceased Party. The parties acknowledge that, in the event of a marital separation, or upon the death of a party, they may each incur attorneys' fees to represent their interests in carrying out the terms of this Agreement. Each party shall be solely responsible for any such attorneys' fees or costs incurred by him or her and any fees and costs incurred in connection with any suit for divorce, or fees that a party (or his or her estate) may incur in connection with the administration of the estate of a deceased party, except as provided in Paragraph 31. Except as otherwise provided in Paragraph 31, each party waives and releases the other from any claim for any such attorneys' fees and costs associated with any future separation or divorce action, including, but not limited to, fees and costs awarded during the pendency of such action and fees and costs that may be awarded at or after the conclusion of such action [***Add, if appropriate:*** ; provided, however, this waiver does not apply to fees and costs to determine custody or support of a minor child of the parties, and each party expressly reserves the right to make an application for such fees in accordance with the law of the state with jurisdiction to resolve such issues].

31. Enforcement Costs for Breach or Default. In the event a party breaches this Agreement, he or she shall pay the other party the reasonable legal fees and costs incurred by that party in the successful enforcement of this Agreement, whether through litigation, negotiations, alternative dispute resolution, or other actions necessary to compel compliance herewith [***Add, if appropriate:*** , including any court action to compel arbitration or to compel compliance with the decision of an arbitrator under Paragraph 51]. Any such reasonable legal fees and costs incurred by a party in the successful defense of a claim of breach shall be paid by the party who made and failed to establish such claim. If a party seeks to have this Agreement, or any provision of this Agreement, declared invalid and fails to establish such invalidity, the party who makes the claim of invalidity shall pay the reasonable legal fees and costs incurred by the other party to defend against such claim. [***Optional:*** A request by either party for a court to interpret the terms of this Agreement or declare the rights of the parties under this Agreement shall not be considered a challenge to the validity of this Agreement nor shall it be considered a breach of this Agreement.]

Voluntary Execution and Disclosures

32. Voluntary Execution. Each party acknowledges that he or she is entering into this Agreement freely and voluntarily. Each has been represented by independent counsel of his or her choice. SPOUSE ONE is represented by ____________ of the firm of ______________________. SPOUSE TWO is represented by ____________ of the firm of ______________________. [***If one party is not represented, substitute***: **SPOUSE TWO had an opportunity to obtain advice from an independent lawyer but has opted not to be represented by counsel in connection with this Agreement.**] Each party had the opportunity to consult his or her counsel concerning the terms of this Agreement and the effect of this Agreement on his or her rights to the extent each party deemed necessary to decide whether to sign this Agreement. Each party acknowledges that he or she has not received any legal advice from counsel for the other party and that neither is relying on any statement of counsel for the other party. [***If one party is not represented, add and revise as appropriate:*** SPOUSE TWO acknowledges that SPOUSE ONE advised him/her to obtain legal advice before signing this Agreement and that SPOUSE ONE offered to pay SPOUSE TWO's legal fees to enable ___him/her to retain counsel. SPOUSE TWO further acknowledges that SPOUSE ONE's lawyer, __________, advised ___ him/her in writing to obtain legal advice before signing this Agreement. SPOUSE TWO states that he/she considered the advice of SPOUSE ONE and ___ his/her lawyer that SPOUSE TWO obtain independent legal advice, but, after having done so, he/she decided to sign this Agreement without such advice.] Each party has fully considered the implications of entering into this Agreement, and each understands that it will govern the property and support rights of each of them upon the death of a spouse or in the event of a separation or divorce regardless of any future change in circumstances. Each party further acknowledges that this Agreement is fair.

33. Understanding of Rights. Each party acknowledges that this Agreement alters the rights each would have if they married without a premarital agreement. [***If a postmarital agreement:*** if they remained married without a postmarital agreement.]

A. Each party has been informed of, or has had the opportunity to be informed of, his or her legal rights as a surviving spouse in the event of the death of the other spouse if the parties married without a premarital agreement [if a postmarital agreement: decided to remain married without entering into a postmarital agreement], including:
   (i) the right to renounce and take against the will of the other (also known as the elective share);
   (ii) the right to inheritance in the event of intestacy;
   (iii) dower and curtesy;
   (iv) family allowance;
   (v) homestead rights;
   (vi) exempt property;
   (vii) augmented estate rights; and
   (viii) the right to surviving spouse benefits under a retirement plan.

B. Each party has further been informed of, or had the opportunity to be informed of, the legal rights he or she would have in the event of separation and/or divorce if the parties married without a premarital agreement [if a postmarital agreement: decided to remain married without entering into a postmarital agreement], including his or her right to seek:
   (i) a court award of spousal support (also known as alimony);
   (ii) equitable distribution of marital property and marital debt;
   (iii) the right in some jurisdictions to seek an award of exclusive use and possession of a family home or family use personal property;
   (iv) a court award of attorneys' fees and costs of litigation.

34. Financial Disclosures. Prior to executing this Agreement, each party provided the other party with a fair disclosure of his or her property and financial obligations and his or her amounts and sources of income. SPOUSE ONE's financial disclosure is set forth on attached Schedule A. SPOUSE TWO's financial disclosure is set forth on attached Schedule B. Each party is satisfied with the disclosures made by the other party. The parties each acknowledge that some of the values shown on Schedules A and B are estimates, that some property interests are difficult to value, and that a party may be unable to obtain a more accurate value without a formal appraisal conducted by an expert in valuation. Further, the parties acknowledge that some items of property may have been omitted. [***Add and adapt, as appropriate:*** Each party further acknowledges such party's understanding that the other party expects an inheritance from the other party's parents or other members of the party's family, that such inheritance is difficult to value, and that the other party's family members may not have disclosed the full extent, nature, or value of the holdings in his or her estate, nor whether the party can expect to inherit outright or in trust.] [***Add and adapt, as appropriate:*** SPOUSE TWO acknowledges his/her understanding that SPOUSE ONE is the majority shareholder in a family business, ABC Corp., a subchapter "S" corporation, that ABC Corp. has not been appraised in connection with this Agreement, and that SPOUSE ONE is unable to state the fair market value of the company. SPOUSE TWO further acknowledges that the fair market value may be much higher than book value. SPOUSE TWO acknowledges reviewing with his/her lawyer ABC Corp.'s income tax returns for the three years prior to execution of this Agreement. SPOUSE TWO states that he/she is satisfied with the information and documents provided by SPOUSE ONE regarding ABC Corp.] The parties each waive any right to claim that this Agreement, or any part of this Agreement, is invalid because of a failure of a party to disclose an item of property or income or because of an erroneous estimate of the value of an item of property or the amount of an item of income. The parties further state that they are each familiar with the financial affairs of the other, and with each other's business interests, assets, income, and standard of living. Each party is completely satisfied with the financial disclosures made by the other and each states that, coupled with their preexisting knowledge of each other's financial affairs, he or she has sufficient information on which to base a decision to enter into this Agreement. The parties acknowledge that they each had an opportunity to request additional financial information or documents prior to signing this Agreement, and they each waive the right to make any such further requests. They each acknowledge that the terms of this Agreement would not be different even if an asset was omitted or asset values were different. Each further affirmatively states that it is his and her express intent that this Agreement shall be valid and enforceable based on such disclosures as each has made.

General Provisions

35. Complete Agreement. This Agreement sets forth the parties' present understanding in its entirety. There are no written or oral promises between them that they wish to exchange but have excluded from the text of this contract. The parties are not relying upon any promises other than those expressly set forth herein.

36. Furnishing Other Instruments to Effect Agreement. Each party shall take any and all steps necessary to timely execute, acknowledge, and deliver any and all further instruments and assurances to the other party that the other party reasonably requires to implement the provisions of this Agreement. Without limitation of the foregoing, if either party should desire to sell or mortgage any real or personal property that constitutes that party's separate property, the other party shall sign and join in such deed or mortgage if to do so is required in order to make the same good, legal and effectual, and the execution of such document shall not affect the separate nature of the property so transferred or the proceeds or other benefits derived therefrom; provided, however, a party shall have no obligation to become an obligor or guarantor on any liability of the other party.

37. Prior Agreements and Claims. The parties acknowledge and agree that they have not previously entered into any other contract, understanding, or agreement, express or implied, with respect to each other's property or earnings or with respect to the support or maintenance of each other. [Delete if a postmarital Agreement: Neither party now has or claims any legal right in the present or future property, income, or estate of the other, or a right to support and maintenance or rehabilitation payments of any kind from the other, by reason of the parties' nonmarital relationship.]

38. No Third-Party Beneficiary Rights. Nothing in this Agreement shall be construed to create any contractual or equitable rights in favor of third parties who are not signatories hereto [Add, if appropriate: , except as expressly set forth herein].

39. No Waiver of Breach of Contract Provisions. The failure of a party to insist upon the strict performance of any provision of this Agreement shall not waive the party's right to insist upon strict performance of the same or any other provision at a later time.

40. Severability. If any provision of this Agreement shall for any reason become invalid or otherwise cannot be enforced, the remainder of this Agreement shall remain in full force and effect, unless an injustice would otherwise result.

41. Effect of Agreement on Separation or Divorce. This Agreement may, upon advice of counsel, be presented to the appropriate court to be affirmed, ratified, and incorporated, but not merged, in any judgment of legal separation or divorce, limited or final, between the parties. The parties understand that they may need to enter into an additional agreement or seek a court order [***Add, if appropriate:*** to enforce an arbitration award under Paragraph 51] addressing disposition of property to carry out the terms of this Agreement; however, the parties' rights to such property shall be determined only in accordance with the terms of this Agreement.

42. Consideration and Effective Date of Agreement. The consideration for this Agreement is the marriage of the parties. This Agreement shall become effective upon the parties' marriage. If the parties do not marry, this Agreement shall be void and of no further effect [***If parties have acquired jointly titled property together prior to execution, add***: , except that the terms of Paragraph ___ shall govern the disposition of their jointly titled real estate and the terms of Paragraph[s] ___ shall govern disposition of their joint bank accounts and joint credit card debt and the furniture and household effects acquired with joint funds and/or joint debt]. [***If postmarital agreement:*** The consideration for this Agreement includes, but is not limited to, the mutual waivers and all the other terms set forth herein.]

43. Revocation and Modification. This Agreement shall remain in full force and effect unless expressly revoked or modified in a writing signed by the parties [***Optional:*** with the same formality as this Agreement]. [***Optional:*** Any such revocation or amendment must refer expressly to this Agreement.] Further, this Agreement shall remain in effect in the event of a marital separation followed by reconciliation.

44. Other Agreements and Writings. Except provided in Paragraph 43 or as this Agreement otherwise expressly requires, wherever the terms of this Agreement permit the parties to make a decision as to an issue governed by this Agreement that requires agreement in writing, the parties may agree to an exchange of electronic messages, such as through electronic mail or text message, and such shall suffice for that purpose. Further, except as expressly required herein, where this Agreement requires a signed writing, a party may utilize an electronic message from his or her account or device and such shall suffice for that purpose.

45. Governing Law. The validity, enforceability, and interpretation of this Agreement shall be determined and governed by the law of ______, without regard to its choice-of-law rules, regardless of the location of any property that either party may own and regardless of where the parties may live.

46. Provisions Binding. All of the provisions of this Agreement shall be binding upon and inure to the benefit of the parties, their agents, attorneys in fact, legal representatives, and successors-in-interest.

47. Multiple Originals. This Agreement may be executed in any number of counterparts, any one of which shall be deemed to be the original. A scanned copy of this Agreement, with all signatures and initials visible, shall be treated as an original.

48. No Construction against Drafter. Each party had, or had the opportunity to have, input into the drafting of this Agreement, personally or through counsel. Therefore, this Agreement shall be construed without regard to any presumption or other rule requiring construction against the party who caused it to have been drafted.

49. Recitals Incorporated. The Recitals set forth above are hereby incorporated by reference as part of this Agreement.

50. Nondisclosure and Confidentiality.

A. Each party recognizes the other party's right to privacy regarding their financial information disclosed in connection with this Agreement, or otherwise, including during their marriage. Each agrees to keep such information in confidence. Neither party shall hereafter purposely disseminate or disclose the other party's financial information [***Optional:*** , the terms of this Agreement, or the negotiations leading to it] to any person or entity without the prior written consent of the other party, except as required by law and, as necessary, on a confidential basis, to a party's accountants, financial advisors and attorneys. Each party agrees that in the event of any dispute resulting in litigation between the parties, the parties shall jointly request that the court or arbitrator hearing such dispute enter a protective order prohibiting dissemination of such financial information, permitting a party to designate financial records as confidential and, therefore, to be submitted to the court under seal, and otherwise protecting the confidentiality of his or her financial records and information to the maximum extent permitted by law. The parties have agreed to this provision in recognition of the fact that disclosure to the public or to a third party of a party's financial information could harm a party's career and/or business interests.

B. Neither party shall publicize or disseminate information of any kind about the other party that is or may be detrimental to the other party's personal image, employment, business interests, reputation or career.

C. The obligations of each party under this Paragraph shall survive a separation of the parties.

51. Dispute Resolution through Binding Arbitration. The parties agree to resolve any dispute about the [optional: validity,] application, interpretation, breach or enforcement, [optional: but not the validity,] of this Agreement through binding arbitration in accordance with the __________ [***state***] Arbitration Act, Code of ______ § ______, et seq., with a single neutral arbitrator who shall be a member in good standing of the Bar of __________. However, in the event neither party is a resident of __________ at the time such dispute arises, the arbitrator shall be a member in good standing of the bar of the state of the last marital domicile in the event the dispute arises after a marital separation, or, in the event the dispute arises after the death of a party, of the state of domicile of the deceased party. The arbitrator shall have at least 15 years of experience as a domestic relations lawyer in the event the dispute arises after a marital separation, or as an estates and trusts lawyer in the event the dispute arises after the death of a party. Service as a circuit court [***Alternative:*** family court or probate court] or appellate judge of the applicable jurisdiction shall count toward the required 15 years of experience. The parties shall jointly select the arbitrator. If they are unable to agree on the selection of an arbitrator within a reasonable period of time, either party may apply to a court with jurisdiction to enforce this Agreement for selection of an arbitrator with the qualifications set forth above. The parties shall initially be responsible for sharing the arbitrator's fees and costs, if any, equally; however, the arbitrator shall have the power to make an award of arbitrator's fees and costs as well as an award of attorneys' fees and costs under Paragraph 31 of this Agreement.

52. Waiver of Statute of Limitations. The parties intend and agree that any statute of limitations that may be applicable to a claim that a party breached this Agreement during the marriage shall not begin to run until [the death of a party, or] a marital separation, as defined herein [whichever occurs first].

________________________________ [Seal]
SPOUSE ONE

WITNESS

____

NAME ______________________________ Date: ______________

ADDRESS

____

WITNESS

____

NAME ______________________________ Date: ______________

ADDRESS

____

________________________________ [Seal]
SPOUSE TWO

WITNESS

____

NAME ______________________________ Date: ______________

ADDRESS

____

WITNESS

____

NAME ______________________________ Date: ______________

ADDRESS

____

City/County of ______________________

State of ________________________:

I hereby certify that on this _____ day of ____________, 20__, before me, the subscriber, a notary public in and for the aforesaid jurisdiction, personally appeared SPOUSE ONE, known to me, and he/she acknowledged the foregoing agreement to be his/her act and he/she made oath in due form of law that the facts stated therein are true to the best of his/her knowledge.

Witness my hand and notarial seal.

____

NOTARY PUBLIC

My commission expires: _________________

City/County of ________________________

State of ______________________________:

I hereby certify that on this _____ day of ____________, 20 __, before me, the subscriber, a notary public in and for the aforesaid jurisdiction, personally appeared SPOUSE TWO, known to me, and he/she acknowledged the foregoing agreement to be his/her act and he/she made oath in due form of law that the facts stated therein are true to the best of his/her knowledge.

Witness my hand and notarial seal.

____

NOTARY PUBLIC

My commission expires: _________________

APPENDIX

E

ADDITIONAL AND OPTIONAL TERMS

Transfers During Marriage

One-Time Cash Gift

In order to provide financial security for SPOUSE TWO, and as additional consideration for the execution of this Agreement, on or before __________, SPOUSE ONE shall transfer to SPOUSE TWO the sum of $__________ in cash. Upon receipt, these funds shall become SPOUSE TWO's separate property. The parties agree that SPOUSE TWO shall have the right to invest these funds to provide for his/her future security and that he/she shall not be expected to use the principal or income for his/her or the parties' routine living expenses during the marriage.

Periodic Cash Gift.

A. Beginning on the ___ anniversary of the parties' marriage and continuing on each anniversary thereafter, _____ SPOUSE ONE shall make a cash gift to SPOUSE TWO to enable ___[him/her] to maintain savings and investments as follows: (a) for the first five years, the sum shall be $______ each year; (b) for the second five years, the sum shall be $_____ each year; (c) thereafter, the sum shall be $_____ each year.

B. The parties agree and understand that the purpose of these transfers is to enable SPOUSE TWO to save and invest for ___ [his/her] future financial security and they intend and agree that ___ [he/she] shall not be expected to use these funds for ____ [his/her] living expenses or any other expenses of ___ [his/hers] during the marriage.

C. SPOUSE ONE's obligation hereunder shall terminate on the first to occur of the following events: (a) the parties' ____th wedding anniversary; (b) the parties' marital separation; provided that in the event the parties reconcile and resume living together as spouses, SPOUSE ONE shall resume the cash gift as provided herein;

(c) death of a party; (d) the later of SPOUSE ONE's retirement from full-time employment or __ [his/her] 67th birthday.

D. SPOUSE ONE shall have no obligation to make a cash gift to SPOUSE TWO in any year in which SPOUSE ONE's earnings for the previous calendar year were less than $XX.

Nonowner Spouse Accrues Ownership Interest in Specified Real Estate Over Time

Beginning on the ___th anniversary of the parties' marriage and continuing annually thereafter on each subsequent anniversary of the parties' marriage, SPOUSE TWO shall accrue a ___percent interest in the _______ property until such time as SPOUSE TWO has a ___ percent interest in the property; provided, however, that SPOUSE TWO shall not accrue any additional interest after a marital separation as defined in Paragraph ___. SPOUSE ONE shall execute and record the appropriate transfer documents to transfer such interest to SPOUSE TWO as a tenant in common within 30 days after each such anniversary.

Contribution to IRA

Annually, not later than _____ of each year during the parties' marriage, SPOUSE ONE shall make a contribution to SPOUSE TWO's Individual Retirement Account in the amount of $ ________ [***Alternative:*** in the maximum amount permitted by law for that year].

Payment of Expenses During the Marriage

Share Family Expenses Pro Rata; Each Party Pays Personal Expenses

1. The parties agree that upon marriage they will establish one or more joint bank or financial institution accounts for the purpose of paying their shared marital and household expenses, including any marital debt incurred for such expenses as defined in Paragraph ___. The parties shall contribute *pro rata* to the account in accordance with the ratio that each party's gross income bears to the sum of the parties' gross incomes. Initially SPOUSE ONE's *pro rata* share shall be ___ percent and SPOUSE TWO's share shall be ___ percent. The parties' *pro rata* monthly shares shall be redetermined annually effective on _______ using their gross incomes for the prior calendar year. Gross income, for purposes of this Paragraph, shall mean each party's earnings and income from all sources as defined herein.

2. The joint account shall be used to pay the following types of debts and expenses:
   (i) the expenses of any children they may have together;
   (ii) if the parties jointly own a home, the payments on any note secured by the property to the extent proceeds of the loan were used for acquisition costs, as defined herein;
   (iii) the usual and ordinary household expenses of the parties' home, whether or not jointly owned, including homeowner's insurance, utilities, cable and Internet services, telephone service, lawn maintenance, routine repairs and maintenance of the property, cleaning services, and other necessary household services;
   (iv) the purchase of household equipment, small appliances, furniture, linens, and items of a similar nature;

(v) food and groceries for the household;
(vi) family health insurance premiums;
(vii) family entertainment and vacations;
(viii) all other expenses of a family or household nature;
(ix) payments of principal and interest, and other charges, such as loan fees and penalties, for debts incurred by the parties on credit cards, lines of credit, or otherwise, for shared or marital expenses as defined herein;
(x) charitable contributions not exceeding $ ________ per donee per year and any additional amounts as the parties may agree;
(xi) routine holiday, birthday, and special occasion gifts to others, including each party's children and grandchildren, not exceeding $ ______ per year per donee and any additional amounts as the parties may agree;
(xii) all other expenses that the parties jointly agree to share.

3. Each party shall maintain separate bank and credit card accounts for the purpose of paying his or her own personal expenses. Each party shall be separately and solely responsible for paying for his or her personal expenses, such as clothing, transportation, including costs for acquisition, insurance premiums for and maintenance of his or her own auto, meals at work, personal care, such as haircuts and nail treatments, uninsured medical expenses, any debts incurred by him or her for such personal expenses, and all other expenses of a personal nature; contributions to savings and investments, retirement plans, and IRA accounts; life and disability insurance; acquisition of property for investment purposes, and the costs and expenses of maintaining his or her separate property investments; the costs of any real estate owned by the party, including payments on the note secured by the property, and any other liens on the property, property taxes, major repairs and improvements, and the cost of major appliances, fixtures, except as set forth in Paragraph 2, and other items of a similar nature; personal property taxes, if any, on his or her separate property; political contributions; charitable contributions exceeding $ ______ per donee per year and for any gifts to the extent such contributions or gifts exceed $ _____ per donee per year.

Nursing Home and Other Expenses of Long-Term Care

The parties agree that each shall be solely responsible for the cost of his or her long-term care, such as home nursing and other home care necessary to assist with the activities of daily living, nursing home care, assisted living facility, hospice care, and the like. Each party has a policy of long-term care insurance. Each party shall continue to maintain such insurance and pay all premiums thereon. Neither party shall be responsible for paying the other's long-term care insurance premiums.

Health Insurance—Spouse Obligated to Provide

In the event SPOUSE TWO does not have health insurance available to him/her through his/her employment, SPOUSE ONE agrees to provide health insurance coverage for him/her and to pay the premiums for such insurance during the marriage until _____________ [*e.g.*, SPOUSE TWO becomes eligible for Medicare].

Health Insurance—Paid from Marital Funds

During the marriage, the parties agree to maintain comprehensive medical, hospitalization, and health insurance for each of them and for any children they may have, and shall pay the premiums from marital property, but in the event that there is no available marital property from which to pay, each party shall pay for one-half of such coverage from ______[his/her] separate property. In the event a party is employed during the marriage with an employer that offers an employer-sponsored group plan, they shall obtain coverage through such plan except as they may otherwise agree. In the event neither party has an employer-sponsored group health insurance plan available to him or her, or in the event comparable or better coverage is available elsewhere, they shall obtain such coverage as is available and shall maintain it as provided herein. In the event of separation, they shall maintain, without interruption, their then-current health insurance coverage for them and their children until the first of the following to occur: (a) entry of a judgment of absolute divorce; (b) entry of an interim court order otherwise providing for health insurance coverage; or (c) execution of a settlement agreement between the parties providing for such coverage or waiving such coverage.

Provisions for Spouse at Death

Life Insurance for Spouse and/or Child

Each party shall purchase and maintain a life insurance policy with a death benefit of not less than $ ______________ and shall name the other party as the beneficiary thereof. Each party shall maintain his or her life insurance policy in full force and effect until the obligation terminates as provided hereafter. The parties shall pay the premiums on such policies with marital property. [***Alternative:*** SPOUSE ONE shall pay the premiums on such policies with ___his/her separate property.] Each party shall provide proof to the other upon reasonable request that such premiums have been paid and that the beneficiary designation complies with the party's obligation hereunder. Each party's obligation to maintain life insurance for the benefit of the other shall terminate upon [***or:*** ____ days after] a marital separation; provided, however, that in the event the parties have a child, each party's obligation shall only terminate upon the first of the following events: (a) the youngest surviving child of the parties attains the age of __; (b) death of the spouse-beneficiary; (c) remarriage of the spouse-beneficiary.

In the event the parties become the parents of a child, the parties shall jointly purchase an additional life insurance policy on [SPOUSE ONE/each party]'s life that provides a death benefit of at least $ ____________ per child and shall name the surviving parent as beneficiary thereof. The parties shall pay the premiums on such policy from marital property so long as the parties are living together and are not separated. In the event of a marital separation, [SPOUSE ONE/SPOUSE TWO] shall be solely responsible for paying the premiums. The obligation pursuant to this paragraph for each child shall terminate upon the child attaining the age of ___ or upon such child's death prior to attaining such age.

Fixed Cash Payment Tied to Length of Marriage

SPOUSE ONE agrees that in the event of his/her death while the parties are married, and are not separated, as defined in Paragraph __, SPOUSE TWO shall receive [***Optional:*** , outright and free of trust,] property in the minimum amount shown on the following schedule based on the years of marriage and valued as of the date of SPOUSE ONE's death:

Completed Years of Marriage Prior to SPOUSE ONE's Death	Amount Due to SPOUSE TWO
Less than 1 year	$__________
2 through 5 years	$__________
6 through 10 years	$__________
More than 10 years	$__________

Any property received by SPOUSE TWO as a result of SPOUSE ONE's death, whether by operation of law, by will or trust established by SPOUSE ONE, by intestacy, or as proceeds of a life insurance policy, annuity contract, or a retirement plan, shall be credited against the minimum amount due to SPOUSE TWO hereunder. The obligation to pay this amount shall be a claim on SPOUSE ONE's estate until satisfied.

Household Furniture and Furnishings to Pass With Home

The parties agree that all of the furniture, furnishings, and household effects in the primary marital home (including any works of art that furnish the home) shall pass to the surviving spouse [***Alternative:*** a trust for the surviving spouse] except for the following items that are owned by and are the separate property of SPOUSE ONE and that he/she may dispose of as he/she in his/her sole discretion determines: ______________________________. ____________________.

Provisions for Primary Marital Home

Transfer of Solely Owned Premarital Home to Survivorship Title

SPOUSE ONE owns a home located at ______________ that is titled in his/her name. Upon marriage the home shall become marital property. Further, no later than ______, SPOUSE ONE shall transfer title to such property into the names of both parties as tenants by the entirety.

Acquisition of Jointly Titled Marital Home; One Party Pays All

The parties agree that upon marriage they shall jointly acquire a primary marital home and shall take title to such property as tenants by the entirety. SPOUSE ONE shall provide the funds for the down payment, improvements, payment of the mortgage, and all other costs of acquisition and of maintaining such property. The property shall be marital property regardless of the source of funds for acquisition costs.

Allocation of Interest Equally Without Regard to Title or Source of Funds.

Notwithstanding any other provisions of this Agreement, in the event the parties, or either of them, purchase real estate that becomes the primary home of the parties, the property shall be marital property and each party shall have an equal interest in such property [***add, if appropriate:*** , and shall be equally responsible for payment of the debt secured by the property] regardless of how such property is titled or the source of funds for acquisition of the property.

Owner Retains Premarital Equity in Existing Home; Appreciation and All Mortgage Paydown During Marriage Is Marital Property.

A. The parties acknowledge that SPOUSE ONE owns a home at ______ titled in ___ [his/her] name alone. In the event of a marital separation, and in the further event that SPOUSE ONE alone, or the parties jointly, own the _________ property, the parties intend and agree that SPOUSE ONE shall retain as ____ [his/her] separate property the first $_________ of the equity in such property (calculated based on the agreed current market value of $_________ less the current balance of the mortgage), and that any additional equity in the property resulting from appreciation, or paydown of the mortgage, or payment for improvements, shall be marital property. In the event of a marital separation, SPOUSE TWO shall execute a deed and any other transfer documents or other waivers as may be required to transfer any ownership or other interest __ [he/she] may have in and to such property back to SPOUSE ONE or ___ [his/her] estate. Simultaneously, SPOUSE ONE shall pay SPOUSE TWO a cash sum equal to one-half of the value, if any, of the marital property portion [add, if appropriate: , such sum to be further reduced by ___ per cent (representing the *pro rata* share of assumed costs of sale)].

B. In the event of a sale of the _____ property during the marriage, SPOUSE ONE shall be entitled to receive as ___ [his/her] separate property the first $________ of the net proceeds of sale (gross proceeds of sale, less the balance of any liens or encumbrances and less a *pro rata* share of the broker's commission and other costs of sale). The remaining net proceeds shall be marital property.

Trust for Surviving Spouse's Life Intended to Qualify for the Unlimited Marital Deduction

In the event that the parties are married and are not separated at the death of a spouse and that one party is the sole owner of the parties' primary marital home upon his or her death, or that each party owns a share of the home as tenant in common, each party agrees to provide in his or her will, trust, or other testamentary document that his or her interest in the marital home [***add, if appropriate:*** , as well as the furniture and furnishings in that home,] shall be held in a trust for the surviving spouse. The trust shall provide at a minimum that during the surviving spouse's life, the surviving spouse shall have the right to all the income from the trust, if any, and the rent-free use of any home held by the trust. The surviving spouse shall have the right to direct that the trustee sell the home and invest the proceeds, or a portion thereof, in another home selected by the surviving spouse, or to hold the sale proceeds and pay the income from those proceeds to the surviving spouse for life. The trust shall have such other terms as may be required so that the trust qualifies for the unlimited marital deduction from estate taxes and shall not have any provisions that are inconsistent with the requirements of the unlimited marital deduction. Each party shall execute the estate planning documents necessary to carry out the provisions of this paragraph within ___ days of marriage. The trustee shall be entitled to inspect the premises at least once annually upon reasonable notice to the surviving spouse.

Surviving Spouse Receives Primary Home Free of Liens

The parties intend and agree that, in the event SPOUSE ONE predeceases SPOUSE TWO, and in the further event they are married and are not separated upon SPOUSE ONE's death, SPOUSE TWO shall have the right to sole ownership of the _____________ property, or to such successor primary marital home as SPOUSE ONE, or the parties jointly, owns and as the parties may then occupy, free and clear of any mortgages, liens, or other encumbrances all of which shall be paid by SPOUSE ONE's estate.

Surviving Spouse Has Limited Right to Occupy Deceased Spouse's Solely Owned Home

SPOUSE ONE currently owns a home located at __________. In the event SPOUSE ONE owns the ___________ home at ___his/her death, and in the further event that at ___his/her death the parties are married and are not separated and that the _______ home is their sole or primary home, SPOUSE TWO shall have the right to continue to occupy the property for a period not to exceed ___ months after SPOUSE ONE's death. [***Options for allocating responsibility for payment of expenses after death of owner-spouse include:*** (1) During such period the legal representative of SPOUSE ONE's estate shall pay for any major repairs or maintenance of the property, defined as a repair or maintenance expense of more than $______ for any single condition, and SPOUSE TWO shall pay the mortgage, property taxes, liability, and homeowner's insurance, and for the usual and necessary costs of living in the home, including, but not limited to, utilities, water, Internet, telephone, cleaning services, yard work, and routine repairs and maintenance. SPOUSE ONE's legal representative may, at his or her option, make the mortgage payments and payments of property taxes and insurance directly, in which case SPOUSE TWO agrees to reimburse SPOUSE ONE's legal representative within 30 days of ___ his/her receipt of a request for reimbursement with supporting documentation. (2) SPOUSE ONE's estate shall pay all of the expenses of maintaining the home during this period, including mortgage, property taxes, liability, and homeowner's insurance, and the usual and necessary costs of living in the home, including, but not limited to, utilities, water, Internet, telephone, cleaning services, yard work, and repairs and maintenance.] SPOUSE TWO's right to occupy the property is personal to ___him/her; SPOUSE TWO may not assign ___his/her right to occupy the property to any other person nor shall SPOUSE TWO permit any other person to occupy the property with the exception of a person providing health-care or personal care services to SPOUSE TWO necessary to assist ___ him/her with the activities of daily living. SPOUSE TWO's right to occupy the _________ home shall terminate, and ___ he/she agrees to vacate the property, upon the first to occur of the following events:

(i) _____months after SPOUSE ONE's death;

(ii) SPOUSE TWO no longer occupies the property as ___ his/her primary home (including if ___ he/she becomes a permanent resident of a nursing home, assisted living facility, or similar health-care facility);

(iii) [***Include, if appropriate:*** SPOUSE TWO fails to pay a mortgage payment, property taxes, or insurance on the property, or to reimburse SPOUSE ONE's legal representative for such payments as provided herein;]

(iv) SPOUSE TWO remarries;

(v) any third person occupies the property except as set forth above.

Exclusive Use; Eviction

In the event of a marital separation, SPOUSE ONE shall have exclusive use of the marital home, and SPOUSE TWO shall vacate the property as set forth herein [***Add, if appropriate:*** , but only provided SPOUSE ONE first exercises ___ his/her first right to purchase SPOUSE TWO's interest in the property. In the event he/she opts not to purchase SPOUSE TWO's interest, the parties' rights to occupy such property pending a sale shall be determined as the parties may agree at that time or as determined by a court of competent jurisdiction in accordance with governing law]. Further, in the event SPOUSE ONE initiates a marital separation, ___ his/her right to exclusive use of the marital home shall only commence after reasonable notice to SPOUSE TWO, which in no event shall be less than ___ days; provided, however, that in no event shall SPOUSE TWO be obligated by the terms of this Agreement to vacate the marital home if such home is, at the time he/she receives notice, or was immediately prior to receiving such notice, the home of a minor child of the parties.

Moving and Resettlement Expenses

SPOUSE ONE shall provide SPOUSE TWO with a lump sum in cash to enable ___ [him/her] to pay ___ [his/her] moving and transition expenses, specifically (a) if the parties have been married for less than ____ years upon separation, the cash sum shall be $_____; (b) if the parties have been married more than ____ years upon separation, the cash sum shall be $______. Such sum shall be due and payable no later than 30 days from a party's written notice of to the other of his or her intent to separateion, a party's moving out of the marital residence with intent to separate, whichever occurs first as provided in Paragraph __.

Definition and Treatment of Business

A. Waiver of Formal Appraisal of SPOUSE ONE's Interest in Family Business. SPOUSE ONE currently owns certain interests in Family Business as identified on Schedule A attached. Further, SPOUSE ONE may inherit additional interests in Family Business during the marriage. The parties agree that SPOUSE TWO has been provided with the following: a balance sheet for Family Business for the year ending _______; a copy of the tax return for Family Business for the year ending ______; a statement of the shareholders' equity in Family Business for the year ending _____; and a statement of income and expenses of Family Business for the year ending ______. SPOUSE TWO understands that there has been no independent appraisal of SPOUSE ONE's interests in the Family Business and that such a valuation would be expensive and time-consuming to obtain. SPOUSE TWO acknowledges that the value of SPOUSE ONE's interests in Family Business may be substantially in excess of the value shown on the statements and tax returns provided. Nevertheless, SPOUSE TWO accepts the information provided as full disclosure and waives the necessity of obtaining a fair market value appraisal of Family Business or of obtaining any further information concerning any of the Family Business interests that SPOUSE ONE may inherit in the future.

B. Waiver of Interest in Family Business. SPOUSE TWO agrees that SPOUSE ONE's interest in any Family Business shall be SPOUSE ONE's separate property, including any increase in value of Family Business during the marriage, whether or not attributable to SPOUSE ONE's efforts during the marriage, and except as otherwise provided in this Agreement, hereby waives any rights in such property in the event of separation, divorce, or SPOUSE ONE's death.

C. Definition of Family Business. "Family Business" shall mean any interest, outright or in trust, direct or indirect, in the following business entities: Family Corporation, a _______ [state] corporation; Family LLC, a _______ [state] limited liability corporation; and Family Partners Ltd., a _________ [state] limited partnership; including any interests that SPOUSE ONE may now own or that SPOUSE ONE may receive in such business entities in the future from members of ____ [his/her] family and/or trusts created for SPOUSE ONE by members of _____ [his/her] family; any additional interest in such business entities that SPOUSE ONE receives in the future as a result of a stock dividend, stock split, recapitalization, or any similar transaction; any interest in any successors-in-interest to such business entities that SPOUSE ONE receives, outright or in trust, as a result of a sale, merger, reorganization, spin-off, conversion, or other business combination and shall include any cash proceeds that SPOUSE ONE receives from any sale or exchange of any of the foregoing interests, the cash proceeds received from the sale of the assets of any such business entities, or any cash distributions of principal or income received by SPOUSE ONE from these entities. "Family Business" _______ [shall/shall not] include any amounts received as compensation for services rendered by SPOUSE ONE to any of the Family Business entities during the marriage. "Member of family" shall mean SPOUSE ONE's grandparents ________ and _______, and any descendants of _______ and ________.

Implementation of Property Division; Nontransferable Assets

A party shall not be required to transfer an item of marital property titled in his or her sole name to the other party in order to effect a division of marital property if a transfer is restricted by the terms of an agreement with a third party or if the property is subject to a lien or a funding obligation (for example, a limited partnership interest for which the owner-spouse is subject to a cash call) that is not assumable by the transferee-spouse. If an asset cannot be transferred, the parties may agree, nevertheless, that in lieu of offsetting the value by transferring some other asset, or cash, the titled owner may continue to hold the other party's fractional interest in trust for that other party. In such event, the titled owner shall cause the beneficial owner to timely receive all information and distributions (net of taxes) relating to the beneficial interest. Upon notice, the beneficial owner shall timely pay any obligations, such as cash calls required, relating to the fractional interest. If the beneficial owner shall fail to pay a required expense or call, and ownership of the asset would be forfeited for failure to pay, the beneficial owner's interest shall terminate, and the titled owner may pay the required amount and retain the asset free of any claim of the beneficial owner.

Provisions for Spouse and Child Upon Separation

Provisions for Home for SPOUSE TWO and Child of the Marriage

In the event of a marital separation, and that upon separation the parties are the parents of a minor child, including a child in gestation who is born alive, SPOUSE ONE shall provide funds for a home for SPOUSE TWO suitable for ___him/herself and such child in accordance with the terms set forth herein.

A. SPOUSE ONE shall provide not less than $ ______ for the purchase of a home for the use of SPOUSE TWO and any child of the parties. SPOUSE ONE shall have the right to pay some or all of the cost of acquisition of the property using borrowed funds secured by the property; provided, however, in such event __ he/she shall be solely responsible to pay the mortgage on the property.

B. For purposes of this paragraph, a minor child is defined as a child who is under the age of 18, except that a child who is over the age of 18 and is a high school student shall be deemed a minor child.

C. SPOUSE TWO shall be entitled to select the home for purchase, in consultation with SPOUSE ONE [***Add if appropriate:*** ; provided, however, the home shall be located in the same general geographic area as the primary marital home. Nothing herein shall require SPOUSE TWO to live in the general geographic area of the primary marital home, subject to any court order that may be entered regarding custody of a minor child of the parties; however, SPOUSE ONE shall have no obligation hereunder unless he/she does so.].

D. At SPOUSE ONE's option the home may be owned by ___him/her, or by an entity, such as a trust or a limited liability company owned by ___ him/her. Except as otherwise provided herein, SPOUSE ONE shall have the right to determine all terms governing such trust or other entity.

E. During ___ his/her occupancy, SPOUSE TWO shall be responsible for utilities, cleaning services, routine maintenance expenses, and other usual and customary expenses of living in the home. SPOUSE ONE shall be responsible for the mortgage payments, property taxes, homeowner's insurance, and major repairs and maintenance.

F. SPOUSE TWO shall be entitled to occupy the home until 90 days after the last child of the parties reaches age 23. At such time ___ he/she shall surrender the property to SPOUSE ONE, or the trust or other entity, as the case may be.

G. Notwithstanding the foregoing, in the event that upon separation the youngest child of the parties is not a minor child, as defined herein, but has not reached his or her 23rd birthday, SPOUSE ONE shall have no obligation to make funds available to purchase a home. In lieu thereof, SPOUSE ONE shall establish a trust for SPOUSE TWO's benefit funded with not less than $ _____________. SPOUSE TWO shall be entitled to all of the income from the trust and shall be taxable on all of such income. SPOUSE TWO shall have the right to require the trustee to make assets of the trust productive of income. SPOUSE TWO's rights hereunder shall terminate when the last living child of the parties reaches age 23 or upon SPOUSE TWO's death, whichever first occurs. It is the parties' express intent that SPOUSE TWO, and not the trust or SPOUSE ONE, shall be taxable on the income from the trust. Accordingly, in the event that federal tax law applicable at the time this obligation comes into being does not permit the income of the trust to be taxed to SPOUSE TWO, the parties shall reform the terms of this paragraph so as to permit the trust terms to take account of the then-applicable law and to carry out their intent that SPOUSE TWO bear the income tax cost of receiving these payments.

Education Expenses for Child of the Marriage

A. In the event of a marital separation, SPOUSE ONE shall be responsible for the cost of education for any children of the parties through completion of an undergraduate degree or the child's attainment of age 23, whichever occurs first. SPOUSE ONE's obligation hereunder to pay private school tuition for a minor child of the parties is expressly contingent on ____ his/her agreement that such child attend private school and ___ his/her approval of the school. ___ He/She shall not unreasonably withhold ___ his/her consent to private school or to the selection of a particular school. SPOUSE ONE's obligation to pay college expenses hereunder is expressly contingent on ___ his/her approval of the school chosen by the child and the child's course of study. ___ He/She shall further have the right to impose reasonable conditions on the child for ___ his/her payment of such expenses, such as, but not limited to, that the child maintain an adequate grade-point average, attend school full time, make reasonable progress toward completion of a degree, refrain from abuse of alcohol, drugs, or other substances, maintain good behavior, or that the child make a reasonable contribution to his or her own education through savings from gifts or employment.

B. The parties acknowledge that, except as provided above, this Agreement does not purport to establish support for a minor child and they acknowledge that a marital contract does not limit the authority of a court to determine support for a minor child in the event of a marital separation. They nevertheless agree that the provisions for SPOUSE TWO set forth above, including provisions for a cash property settlement, a home for SPOUSE TWO, spousal support, and provisions for payment of children's education expenses, are intended to provide for ___ his/her economic security and that of any child of the parties, and that SPOUSE ONE shall be entitled to have all such provisions taken into account in determining the amount of support that SPOUSE ONE may be ordered to pay for such minor child.

SPOUSAL SUPPORT

Reservation of Right to Seek Support and Maintenance and Attorneys' Fees

In the event of a marital separation, each party reserves the right to make a claim for alimony, support and maintenance, including temporary support and support payable upon entry of a final judgment of divorce, and further including both term-limited and indefinite spousal support, and an award attorneys' fees and suit money, to the full extent provided by the laws of the forum court.

Compensation for Lost Wages Resulting From Unpaid Parental Leave.

In the event of a marital separation within five years of the birth of a child of the parties, and in the further event that either or both parties took unpaid leave from full-time employment to recover from childbirth in the case of the wife, or to care for their child at any time during such five-year period in the case of either party, one party shall be entitled to a single lump sum payment of spousal support from the other party, which sum shall be due and payable no later than ______ days from the date of separation. The amount due shall be: The total amount of lost wages, computed daily for each day of unpaid leave, which would have been earned by the spouse who took more days of unpaid leave, multiplied by 50 per cent, less the total amount of lost wages, computed daily for each day of unpaid leave, which would have been earned by the spouse who took fewer days of unpaid leave, multiplied by 50 per cent; provided, however, that in the event the spouse who took fewer days of unpaid leave lost a larger amount of wages, the amount due shall be zero. Further, the maximum amount of unpaid leave that may be counted for this formula shall be 13 weeks or 65 workdays. By way of example, and not by way of limitation: If SPOUSE TWO took 65 days of unpaid leave and ____ [his/her] rate of pay were $500 per day (or the approximate equivalent of $120,000 per year) and SPOUSE ONE took 15 days of unpaid leave and ____[his/her] rate of pay were also $500 per day, SPOUSE ONE would owe SPOUSE TWO $12,500 (65 "x" $500 = $32,500 "x" .50 = $16,250; 15 "x" $500 = $7,500 "x" .50 = $3,750; $16,250 – $3,750 = $12,500).

Claims Resulting From Permanent Residence Sponsorship.

SPOUSE ONE, a United States citizen, and SPOUSE TWO , a citizen of ______ , may agree that SPOUSE ONE will sponsor SPOUSE TWO for permanent resident status in the United States. The parties acknowledge that sponsorship requires the filing of INS Form I-864, Affidavit of Support, under which SPOUSE ONE must assume responsibility for all public assistance which may be provided to SPOUSE TWO until _____[he/she] is either granted U.S. citizenship or has completed 40 quarters of covered employment under the Social Security system. They further acknowledge that divorce will not terminate SPOUSE TWO's obligations under Form I-864. Nevertheless, the parties intend to be bound by their spousal support waiver as set forth in Paragraph ___ to the fullest extent permitted by law. SPOUSE TWO agrees to indemnify and hold SPOUSE ONE harmless from any costs or expenses incurred by _______ [him/her], or any monies paid by ____ [him/her], to comply with ___ [his/her] obligations under Form I-864, or other law or regulation, in consideration of such sponsorship.

Modification of Spousal Support; Changed Circumstances of Payor.

The parties acknowledge and agree that SPOUSE ONE's obligations under Paragraph ____ could become unduly burdensome in the event ____ [he/she] experiences a substantial loss in ___ [his/her] net worth before ____ [he/she] satisfies ____ [his/her] obligations hereunder. They therefore agree that, in such event, SPOUSE ONE shall have the right to seek a downward modification of ___ [his/her] obligations under Paragraph ____. The parties further acknowledge that it is not practical to specify a formula for such a modification because all of the relevant circumstances cannot be known at this time. Accordingly, SPOUSE ONE shall notify SPOUSE TWO in writing of ___ [his/her] contention that ____ [he/she] is entitled to a downward modification of ___ [his/her] obligations under Paragraph ___ and shall state the pertinent facts supporting ____ [his/her] contention. In the event the parties are unable to negotiate a resolution of the matter within ____days of SPOUSE ONE's written notice, they shall resolve the dispute in binding arbitration in accordance with Paragraph ___ of this Agreement. In resolving ____ SPOUSE ONE's claim for downward modification, the arbitrator shall have the right to consider all then-current circumstances, including each party's income from all sources and each party's property interests.

PRE-EXECUTION WAIVER OF FINANCIAL DISCLOSURE

SPOUSE ONE and SPOUSE TWO intend to marry after execution of a premarital agreement. [***If postmarital agreement:*** The parties intend to enter into a postmarital agreement.]

The parties acknowledge that each has the right to receive a fair and adequate disclosure of the financial affairs of the other party, including his/her amounts and sources of income and his/her assets and liabilities, with a reasonable statement of the value thereof, before signing a premarital/postmarital agreement.

The parties agree to waive their right to financial disclosure. Each party is satisfied with the information he or she has about the other party's financial affairs, and each agrees that the other party need not provide any additional information or make a formal, written statement of financial disclosure. Each party believes he or she has sufficient information about the financial affairs of the other party to make a decision about the terms of their premarital/postmarital agreement and to decide whether to sign the agreement.

Each party consulted with independent counsel before deciding to sign this waiver. SPOUSE ONE received legal advice from ______________, and SPOUSE TWO received legal advice from ____________. Each party had sufficient time to discuss with his/her lawyer whether to waive financial disclosure and to get answers to any questions he/she may have had about the benefits of receiving financial disclosure before signing a premarital/postmarital agreement.

_______________________________ _______________________________

SPOUSE ONE SPOUSE TWO

Bonus for Executing Ratification of Agreement

In the event of the parties' marital separation, in addition to any other transfers or other property rights SPOUSE TWO may have hereunder, SPOUSE ONE shall pay SPOUSE TWO the sum of $________ within ___ days after such separation, provided that before such payment SPOUSE TWO executes a statement acknowledging the validity of this Agreement and stating that SPOUSE TWO waives irrevocably any claim he/she may have that this Agreement, or any term thereof, is invalid or unenforceable.

Execution Formalities

The parties acknowledge the execution of this Agreement by their electronic signatures below with the intent that their electronic signatures constitute their voluntary adoption of this Agreement as their act. Each party consents to the use of electronic signatures in the execution of this Agreement. Each party acknowledges his/her understanding that the use of electronic signatures has the same effect as inked signatures on paper to create a valid and enforceable Agreement.

Postmarital Ratification of Premarital Agreement

Ratification of Premarital Agreement

This Ratification of Premarital Agreement is made this ____ day of ____________________, 202__, by and between SPOUSE ONE, husband/wife (hereafter referred to as "______"), and SPOUSE TWO, wife/husband (hereafter referred to as "______").

1. SPOUSE ONE and SPOUSE TWO married on __________________________, 202__.

2. On ______________________, 202__, prior to their marriage, the parties entered into a Premarital Agreement.

3. By their signatures below, the parties do hereby ratify their Premarital Agreement.

4. Each party signs this Ratification voluntarily.

____

SPOUSE ONE

____

SPOUSE TWO

[INSERT NOTARY BLOCKS]

APPENDIX

F

LETTERS TO CLIENT

Client Letter—Instructions for Execution

[Date]

____
____
____

RE: Premarital Agreement

Dear _______:

Enclosed are _____[1] originals of [***or:*** Attached to this email is] your Premarital/Postmarital Agreement for execution. This document includes a financial disclosure schedule for you and the financial disclosure that _______ provided. I understand you will arrange directly with _________ to go to a notary and execute the Agreement.

Therefore, please:

- [***Include if appropriate:*** Print out ___complete sets, including financial disclosures.]

1. One for each party plus the number needed for counsel including, as appropriate, a party's estate planning lawyer. Some lawyers may prefer to receive only a scan of a signed original and may not want to be responsible to retain a paper original.

- Read the Agreement through from beginning to end. Do not sign it unless it sets forth the terms as you intend.
- Make sure a set of financial disclosures is attached by staple to each original of the agreement before it is signed.
- Initial each page of each original as indicated. Initial each page of the financial disclosures.
- Take all _____ originals to a notary, and sign each original of the Agreement in the space provided in the presence of the notary.
- _________ should do the same, including reading the Agreement through before signing, initialing every page, and signing before a notary.
- [***If agreement is to be witnessed as well as notarized:*** In addition to notarization, you must sign the agreement in the presence of two disinterested witnesses, neither of whom can be the notary, and the witnesses must sign where indicated and include their printed names and addresses.]

You and ______ may go together to sign the Agreement before one notary on the same day, or you may each go separately. You need not use the same notary or sign on the same day. If you sign on different days, the second to sign should fill in the execution date on page 1. If you sign on the same day, either one of you, or the notary, can fill in the execution date.

Once you and ________ have signed all ____ originals before a notary [***add, if appropriate:*** and witnesses], and initialed all the pages and the financial disclosures, please [***select:*** scan one original and email it to me/return one original to me to maintain in my files.] _________ should keep one for _____self and give one to his/her lawyer. You should keep your original in a safe place.

Please let me know if there is anything else I can do for you.

Very truly yours,

____

Enclosure: Premarital/Postmarital Agreement

Client Letter—Post-Execution Checklist to Carry Out Terms of Agreement

[Date]

____

____

____

Dear __________________________________:

You must take the following steps to carry out your obligations and to secure your rights under your Premarital/Postmarital Agreement:

- No later than ______, transfer title to the home at ______ to yourself and ______ as tenants by the entirety/joint tenants with right of survivorship/tenants in common with ___ % titled to you and ___ % to ______.
- Retain your records regarding your premarital initial investment in the ______ home, the mortgage balance on the date of marriage, and any records of the source of funds for future payment of the mortgage and for improvements to the property.
- No later than ______, obtain a new life insurance policy on your life in the amount of at least $______ [and place ownership of the policy in ___________'s name]. You must pay the premium during the marriage from your separate funds. [***Alternative:*** You may pay the premium from marital property funds.]
- No later than _________, create an irrevocable life insurance trust with ________ as the primary beneficiary and arrange for the trust to acquire a life insurance policy on your life with a death benefit of at least $________.
- No later than ______, change the beneficiary designation on your existing _______ [individual life insurance policy/group life insurance policy provided through your employer] with ________ Insurance Company to name ______ as beneficiary and file the new beneficiary designation with the ______ Insurance Company/your employer's human resources department.
- [***For a party who will use employer-sponsored group insurance to fulfill a contractual obligation for life insurance***] If you change employers and transfer into a new group life insurance plan, repeat the above steps.
- Keep the ___________ insurance policy in force until _____, and pay the premiums from your separate property funds/marital property funds.
- No later than ______, sign a new will/trust providing for ______ at your death in accordance with Paragraph ____ of the Agreement.
- Each year on ______, transfer the sum of $______ to ______ in accordance with Paragraph ______ of the Agreement.
- Each year on _____, give ____ $_____, or the maximum amount allowed by law for that year, for _____'s IRA contribution, or you may make the deposit yourself into _____'s IRA.
- As soon as possible after the marriage, [***or for a party who is not yet 35:*** but not until you reach your 35th birthday,] have ______ sign a consent and waiver of pre-retirement survivor and death benefits under your current employer's qualified retirement plan and file the consent with the Plan Administrator.
- If you change jobs and enter a new qualified retirement plan, repeat the step above.
- Within the period that is 90 days before your retirement date, have ______ sign a new consent and waiver of the post-retirement (Qualified Joint and Survivor Annuity or QJSA) survivor benefits under your employer's qualified retirement plan;
- No later than ____, transfer the sum of $____ to ____ as his/her separate property in accordance with Paragraph ___ of the Agreement.
- No later than _____, establish a joint financial institution account in which you and ________ will deposit your paychecks.In the event you decide to separate or ___________ decides to do so:

- Notify ______ in writing of your intent to be separated as of the date of the notice under Paragraph ____ of the Agreement.
- Within ___ days of separation, pay _______ the cash sum of $_________ as a property settlement under Paragraph ___ of the Agreement.
- Within ___ days of separation, pay ________ a cash sum for his/her interest in the marital home in accordance with Paragraph ___ of the Agreement.

In the event you and _____ decide to change a term of the Agreement, you should put your amendment in writing and both of you should sign it; otherwise, it will not be enforceable. [***For an agreement that requires amendments be executed with the same formally as the agreement:*** The amendment must be signed in front of a notary [***add, if appropriate:*** and two witnesses]]. It is in your best interest to get legal advice before agreeing to amend and before signing an amendment.

In addition to carrying out your estate planning obligations under the Agreement, you should review your entire estate plan to determine whether any other changes are in order. If you and ___________ have a child together, or if you adopt ___________'s child, you should review your estate planning again.

Very truly yours,

____

Client Letter—Advice Not to Sign

[Date]

Dear __________:

Based on my discussions with your fiancé(e)'s/spouse's lawyer, I do not believe __________ will agree to make any further revisions to your premarital/postmarital agreement. [***Add, if appropriate***: He/she has made it clear that you must sign the premarital agreement in its present form or he/she will call off the wedding.]

In my opinion, **it is not in your economic interest to sign the agreement** [***add, if appropriate:*** even though that would mean ___________ will cancel the wedding.] There is a huge disparity between your assets and __________'s. Yet, the agreement makes no [***or:*** inadequate] provisions for your financial security after ___________'s death or in the event the marriage does not work out and you and ___________ separate. In my opinion, this is not reasonable.

Given your present resources, you are at risk of becoming impoverished at the end of the marriage if you sign the agreement. Accordingly, **I advise you not to sign it**.

If you do decide to sign the agreement against my advice, I advise you of the following:

- After the passage of several years you could ask ________ to consider transferring title to the marital home into joint names. Keep in mind, however, that he/she will have the absolute right to refuse to do so.
- ____________ may make a will to benefit you. However, he/she can change his/her will at any time. Therefore, this is not something you can count on.
- You should not quit your job to travel with ____________ or to care for him/her during an extended illness. As the agreement is currently written, if you quit your job, you would be giving up your only source of financial security in order to benefit ___________ but would not be able to count on substitute provisions to make up for that loss.
- You should not agree to work for ______'s company unless he/she gives you an employment contract that provides for a market rate salary and the same employee benefits he/she provides the other employees of the company, including a retirement plan, as well as severance pay in the event he/she decides to terminate your employment.
- You should contribute the maximum amount allowed by law to your retirement plan and should save as much of your employment earnings as you can. Under the current terms of agreement, the only opportunity you will have to create savings for your retirement and your future security is through your own savings and investment.
- If you receive an inheritance from your parents or other family members, you should preserve and invest it to meet your future needs. You should not deposit inherited money or securities into a joint account, and you should not use it for common expenses, to pay down the mortgage on _________'s solely titled home, or for any purpose other than savings and investment for yourself.
- You should not contribute any of your earnings to the mortgage on the marital home because you do not have an ownership interest in it.
- You should not use your earnings or income to support the household, pay for common expenses, or to help support _________'s children. For example, if you and ____________ were to allocate financial responsibility so that he/she pays the mortgage and you pay for groceries and utilities, he/she would be able to build equity in his/her home, in which you have no interest, while your earnings would go toward consumption and not to build savings. This is not in your best interests.
- You and ________ could agree during the marriage to amend the premarital/postmarital agreement to provide some financial security for you at the end of the marriage. You could ask ________ to consider such an amendment after the passage of several years. Keep in mind, however, that he/she will have the absolute right to refuse to do so. To be valid and enforceable, an amendment must be in writing and

both of you must sign it. [***Add if agreement requires amendments to be executed with the same formality as the agreement***: You and ______ must sign the amendment in front of a notary [***add, if appropriate:*** and two witnesses, neither of whom can be the notary].] You should call me for legal advice if you and _______ start to discuss an amendment.

- An oral promise that ________ may make during the marriage to provide for you by will, or by another means, such as a life insurance beneficiary designation, is not enforceable. ________ can change his/her mind and write a new will or revoke a beneficiary designation. Therefore, you should not make a change in your circumstances, such as leaving your job, on the basis of such a promise. Rather, you and ________ should amend the agreement in writing so that the promise becomes an enforceable contract.

Please let me know if you have any questions about the advice in this letter.

Very truly yours,

____

APPENDIX

G

LETTERS TO UNREPRESENTED PARTY

Letter to Unrepresented Party—Providing Referrals

[Date]

____
____
____

Dear __________________________:

As you know I am representing your fiancé(e) for the premarital/postmarital agreement you and he/she will be signing before your wedding date. _________ tells me you would like a referral for your own representation. Below is a list of lawyers who do work of this type with their contact information:

____

____

____

____

You are free to choose one of these lawyers, but you are not obligated to do so. You are entitled to have the lawyer of your choice. You may want to ask others among your friends and colleagues for referrals. If you have an estate planning lawyer, you could also ask him or her for recommendations.

When you have engaged a lawyer, please ask him or her to contact me so that we can move forward with the negotiations and drafting of the agreement.

[*Add if appropriate:* _________ will pay the fees for your representation.]

Very truly yours,

____

First Letter to Unrepresented Party Forwarding Proposed Draft

[Date]

____

____

____

Dear ________________________________:

Enclosed is a proposed Premarital/Postmarital Agreement I drafted on behalf of ____________. Please take this draft to your lawyer and ask him or her to advise you about the terms and answer any questions you may have about it.

The agreement has _________'s financial disclosure attached. _________ believes the financial disclosure presents a fair and accurate picture of his/her financial affairs [and the family financial affairs]. However, if you would like any additional information, or if you would like to receive documents, such as tax returns or account statements, verifying the financial disclosure, please have your lawyer contact me, and I will arrange to have _________ provide what you need.

It is in your best interests to receive legal advice before you decide whether to sign the agreement. Therefore, I urge you to set up an appointment with a lawyer as soon as possible.

Very truly yours,

____

Second Letter to Unrepresented Party Forwarding Final Draft

[Date]

____

____

____

Dear ________________________________:

I understand you are ready to sign the proposed Premarital/Postmarital Agreement I drafted on behalf of ____________ and that you do not plan to get independent legal advice before doing so. I urge you to reconsider your decision and to get legal advice before you sign the agreement.

The Premarital/Postmarital Agreement addresses important matters relating to your legal rights. You should get advice from a lawyer who can explain what your rights would be if you and _______ were to marry without a premarital agreement [if you and _____ were to remain married without entering into a postmarital agreement] and how the agreement affects those rights. There may be features of the existing draft that affect you in ways that are not obvious. If you get legal advice, your lawyer will be able to answer any questions you may have and to make sure you understand the terms of the agreement and how they affect you. **I urge you to get independent legal advice before you sign the agreement.**

The proposed agreement provides that you give up any right to a share of property owned by ________ in the event he/she dies before you. He/she gives up the same rights in the event you die first. This agreement would permit each of you to make a will to benefit the other, but neither of you is required to do so. It permits each of you to decide who will be beneficiary of your life insurance, retirement benefits, and other assets. It does not require either of you to provide for the other party at death, although you may each choose to do so. In other words, the surviving spouse will not have any automatic rights upon the death of the first to die. If you and _________were to marry without a premarital agreement [If you and _____ were to remain married without entering into a postmarital agreement], and _________ died first, you would have certain automatic property rights under the law as the surviving spouse. **Under this proposed agreement, you are each giving up all of your rights as a surviving spouse.**

Further, the Premarital/Postmarital Agreement provides that, in the event the marriage does not work out and you and _________ separate, neither of you will have a right to a share of property acquired by the other during the marriage unless the property is titled in both of your names. Each of you will have the right to keep any money earned during marriage and any assets acquired with money earned during marriage. For example, you will each have the right to keep your retirement benefits; neither of you will have the right to a share of the retirement benefits of the other. If you and _________ were to marry without a premarital agreement [remain married without a postmarital agreement], retirement benefits earned during marriage would be considered marital property and a court could divide them between you. As another example, _________ owns a home. __________ will have the right to pay the mortgage on the home from his/her earnings during the marriage; however, under this agreement, the home will remain his/her separate property and you will have no right to claim a share of the equity. If you and __________ were to marry without a premarital agreement [remain married without a postmarital agreement], you would have the right to ask a court to make an award to you based on the value of the home and __________'s contribution of earnings to pay down the mortgage. You are giving up that right under this proposed agreement.

Neither of you will have a right to ask a court to award spousal support (also known as alimony) in the event of separation or divorce. If you and ___________ were to marry without a premarital agreement [remain married without a postmarital agreement], in the event of divorce, you would each have the right to ask a court to award you spousal support. You are each giving up that right under this proposed agreement.

The above is just a brief summary of the key features of the proposed agreement. It is not legal advice. It does not address whether the agreement is fair or whether it is in your best interests to sign it.

You should obtain legal advice from an independent lawyer about whether the agreement is in your best interests before you make a final decision to sign it. [*Add, if appropriate:* ____________ is willing to pay your legal fees to enable you to get legal advice.] If you need assistance to find a lawyer with expertise in premarital/postmarital agreements, please let me know in writing, such as by electronic mail, and I will give you in writing a list of lawyers I know to be competent and experienced in this area of the law.

Please have your lawyer contact me at his or her earliest convenience to discuss the proposed agreement and any questions or concerns you may have about it.

Very truly yours,

____

INDEX